CANADA YEAR BOOK 2008

Statistics Canada

Published by authority of the Minister responsible for Statistics Canada

Available in Canada through authorized bookstore agents and other bookstores or from:
Statistics Canada
Finance Division
R.H. Coats Bldg., 6th Floor
150 Tunney's Pasture Driveway
Ottawa (Ontario) K1A 0T6
Phone (Canada and United States): 1-800-267-6677
Fax (Canada and United States): 1-877-287-4369
E-mail: Infostats@statcan.gc.ca

October 2008
Catalogue no. 11-402-XPE
ISSN 0068-8142
ISBN 978-0-660-19840-8
Frequency: Annual
Ottawa
Cette publication est disponible en français sur demande (n° 11-402-XPF au catalogue).

Note of appreciation

Canada owes the success of its statistical system to a long-standing partnership between Statistics Canada, the citizens of Canada, its businesses, governments and other institutions. Accurate and timely statistical information could not be produced without their continued cooperation and goodwill.

The paper used in this publication meets the minimum requirements of American national Standard for Information Sciences – Permanence of Paper for Printed Library Materials, ANSI Z39.48 – 1984.
∞

Printed in Canada

Library and Archives Canada Cataloguing in Publication Data
Canada year book
Issued also in French under title: Annuaire du Canada.
ISBN 978-0-660-19840-8 (paper)
ISBN 978-1-100-10296-2 (PDF)
CS11-402-XPE
CS11-402-XIE
1. Canada – Statistics. I. Statistics Canada. Communications and Library Services Division.
HA744 S8114 2008 317.1

Statistics Canada

Canada Year Book
2008 Edition

A compact almanac for reference about Canada, with a focus on tables, charts, maps and succinct analytical articles that cover 31 subject areas, plus a list of sources and a glossary of technical terms.

Please visit www.statcan.gc.ca/canadayearbook to discover the *Canada Year Book* online collection, which presents digitized archival material from previous *Canada Year Books* going back to the first one published in 1867. Turn to www.statcan.gc.ca to explore all of Statistics Canada's online resources.

Acknowledgements

This *Canada Year Book* is the result of the work of dozens of people over many months. In addition to the production team, we would like to thank the many Statistics Canada employees who helped to make this volume possible.

Production
- Catherine Pelletier

Writers
- Edelweiss D'Andrea, Andrew Bisson, Thérèse Brown, Alan Chaffe, Susan Dewar, Jennifer Etter, Peter Hammerschmidt, Kathryn Harley Haynes, Laurel Hyatt, Jennifer Kerr, Wili Lieberman, Suzanne Lucier, Nacia Miller, Catherine Pelletier, Patricia Presti, Tim Prichard, Tom Vradenburg

Senior editors
- Julie Morin (French), Tim Prichard (English)

Fact-checking
- Brian Drysdale, Hugh Jarrett, Craig Pratt

Analyst
- Peter Tarassoff

Tables editor
- Brodie Fraser

Charts editor
- Brian Drysdale

Table and chart production
- Danielle Baum, Diane Leblanc, Christian Massicotte, Paul McDermott, Monica Nuyens, Vanessa Savage, Juli-Ann Rowsell

Mapping
- Allan Rowell

Editorial assistant
- Vanessa Savage

Editing and proofreading
- Edelweiss D'Andrea, David Blouin, Christine Duchesne, Brodie Fraser, Geneviève Corbin Geoffroy, Paula Gherasim, Jennifer Kerr, Elizabeth Irving, Luc Moquin, Robin Redmond

Translators
- Official Languages and Translation Division, Statistics Canada

Cover designers
- Rachel Penkar, Jennifer Pfitzer

Composition and graphics
- Cécile Bourque, Louise Demers, Lynne Durocher, Juli-Ann Rowsell, Kelly Stockall

Indexing
- Patricia Buchanan (English), Monique Dumont (French)

Printing procurement
- Johanne Beauseigle, Perry Doris

Marketing
- Marc Bazinet, Jeff Jodoin

Management
- Bernie Gloyn, Martine Grenier, Leila Ronkainen, Eric St. John

Penny Stuart and Tom Vradenburg
Editors-in-chief

Abbrevations and symbols

Provinces and territories	
Newfoundland and Labrador	N.L.
Prince Edward Island	P.E.I.
Nova Scotia	N.S.
New Brunswick	N.B.
Quebec	Que.
Ontario	Ont.
Manitoba	Man.
Saskatchewan	Sask.
Alberta	Alta.
British Columbia	B.C.
Yukon	Y.T.
Northwest Territories	N.W.T.
Nunavut	Nvt.

Measurements	
centimetre	cm
metre	m
kilometre	km
gram	g
kilogram	kg
litre	L
millilitre	mL
hour	h
watt	W
kilowatt	kW
degrees Celsius	°C

The symbols described in this document apply to all data published by Statistics Canada from all origins, including surveys, censuses and administrative sources, as well as straight tabulations and all estimations.

.	not available for any reference period
..	not available for a specific reference period
...	not applicable
0	true zero or a value rounded to zero
0^{s}	value rounded to zero where there is a meaningful distinction between true zero and the value that was rounded
^{p}	preliminary
^{r}	revised
x	suppressed to meet the confidentiality requirements of the *Statistics Act*
^{E}	use with caution
F	too unreliable to be published

When the figure is not accompanied by a data quality symbol, it means that the quality of the data was assessed to be 'acceptable or better' according to the policies and standards of Statistics Canada.

In some tables, figures may not add to totals because of rounding.

Contents

Aboriginal peoples

1

Overview

The number of Aboriginal people surpassed the one million mark in the 2006 Census, when 1,172,790 people identified themselves as an Aboriginal person, either North American Indian (or First Nations person), Métis or Inuit.

Aboriginal people make up a growing share of Canada's total population—3.8% of people enumerated in the recent census, up from 3.3% in 2001 and 2.8% in 1996.

In 2006, First Nations people accounted for 60% of the total Aboriginal population, Métis 33%, and Inuit, 4%. Most First Nations people are Status Indians, meaning they are registered under the *Indian Act*. In 2006, 564,870 First Nations people reported they were Registered Indians; they made up 81% of the total First Nations population.

The Aboriginal population has been growing faster than the non-Aboriginal population: it increased 45% from 1996 to 2006, nearly six times faster than the 8% growth rate of the non-Aboriginal population in the same period. (Only the Indian reserves and settlements that participated in both these censuses are included in this comparison.)

Of the three Aboriginal groups, the fastest population gain is among the Métis. Their numbers almost doubled (up 91%) to 389,785 people from 1996 to 2006. This growth rate is nearly three times as fast as the 29% increase for First Nations people, whose numbers reached 698,025. The number who identified themselves as Inuit increased 26% to 50,485 people.

Demographic trends, such as high birth rates, are one factor. As well, more people are identifying themselves as an Aboriginal person, and more Indian reserves participated in the 2006 Census than in previous censuses.

The Aboriginal population is also younger: in 2006, its median age was 27 years, compared with 40 years for non-Aboriginal peoples. (Median age is the point where half of the population is older, and half is younger.)

Chart 1.1
Population growth, by Aboriginal identity, 1996 and 2006

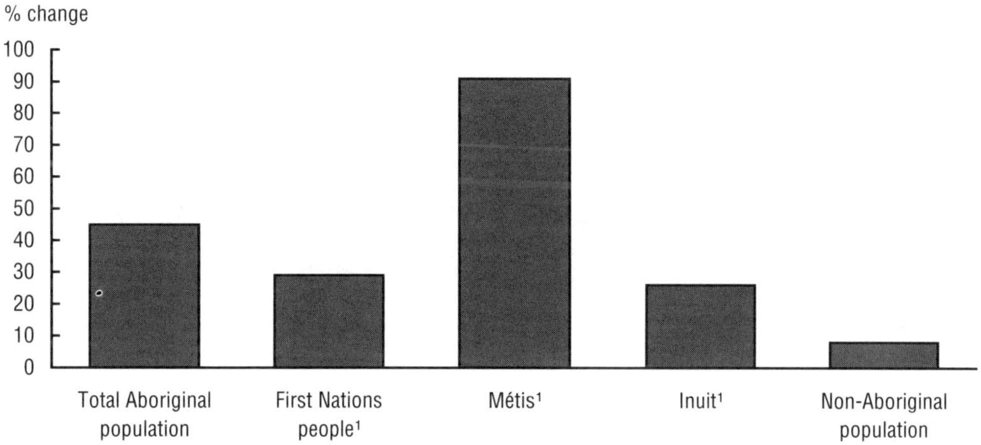

Note: Only the Indian reserves and settlements that participated in both censuses are included when comparing data from 1996 and 2006.
1. Includes people who reported a North American Indian, Métis or Inuit identity only.
Source: Statistics Canada, Census of Population, 1996 and 2006.

Housing conditions only modestly improved

While the housing conditions of some Aboriginal people have improved in the past decade, others are living in poorer conditions—overcrowded and in homes needing major repair—than those enjoyed by non-Aboriginal people. This is particularly true of First Nations people on reserves and Inuit in the North.

Inuit live in some of the most crowded living conditions in Canada. (Crowding is defined as more than one person per room in the dwelling.) Most Inuit live in Inuit Nunaat, the northern region spanning the Northwest Territories, Nunavut, Quebec, and Labrador. In that region, more than 15,000 Inuit—38% of the total Inuit Nunaat population—lived in crowded conditions in 2006, down from 43% in 1996.

Crowding, combined with extreme weather, can cause much wear and tear on homes in Inuit Nunaat. In 2006, 31% of Inuit lived in houses that, in the judgment of the respondent, needed major repairs, up from 19% in 1996. Crowding and the need for major repairs are also more prevalent on reserves. In 2006, 26% of First Nations people living on reserves lived in crowded conditions, down from 33% in 1996. However, 44% of First Nations people on reserves lived in a home in need of major repairs, up from 36% in 1996. Crowding and the need for major repairs are especially common for First Nations people on reserves in the Prairie provinces.

Chart 1.2
Aboriginal and non-Aboriginal people living in dwellings in need of major repairs, 2006

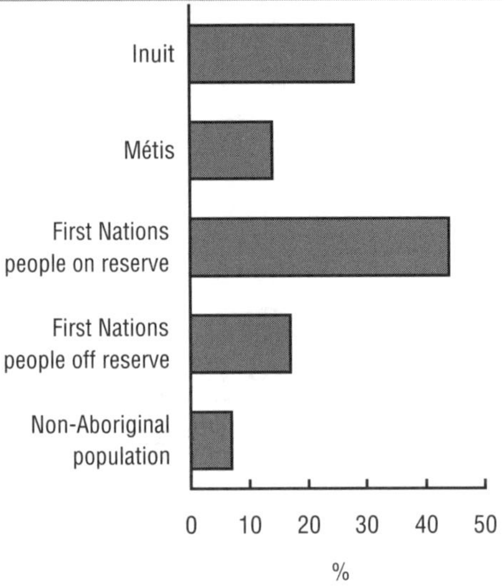

Source: Statistics Canada, 2006 Census of Population.

Table 1.a
Aboriginal population in Canada, the territories and selected provinces, 2006

	% of population
Canada	**3.8**
Nunavut	85.0
Northwest Territories	50.3
Yukon	25.1
Saskatchewan	14.9
Manitoba	15.5

Source: Statistics Canada, Census of population, 2006.

More Métis living in rural areas are in crowded housing conditions than those living in urban areas—5% versus 3% in 2006. These figures were down from 1996, when the rates were 11% for rural and 5% for urban areas. The same pattern is evident for those living in dwellings in need of major repairs: 18% of Métis in rural areas lived in homes in need of major repairs in 2006, compared with 12% of Métis in urban areas.

Inadequate housing may be associated with myriad health problems. Crowded living conditions can lead to the transmission of infectious diseases, and can add to the risk of injuries, mental health problems, tensions within the family, and violence.

Sports participation just as strong among Aboriginal children

Aboriginal children are just as likely to take part in sports as their non-Aboriginal counterparts, according to the 2001 Aboriginal Peoples Survey (APS).

Approximately 65% of Aboriginal children aged 14 and younger participated in sports at least once a week outside school hours, a rate comparable to that of non-Aboriginal children. Twenty-three percent of children reported never having participated, 12% took part less than once a week, 39% participated one to three times a week, and 26% took part in some type of sport four or more times per week. Aboriginal boys were more likely to take part in sports than girls. Children aged 5 to 11 were more active in sports than younger or older children.

Métis and Inuit children were more likely to participate than were First Nations children. First Nations children living off reserves were also more active than those living on reserves. Otherwise, the children's region of residence was not relevant; the results showed no differences in sports participation between Aboriginal children who lived in urban, rural, and Arctic regions. (These data were gathered from a select number of reserves that participated in the 2001 APS: they are not representative of the entire on-reserve population.)

Chart 1.3
Aboriginal and non-Aboriginal people living in a crowded dwelling, 2006

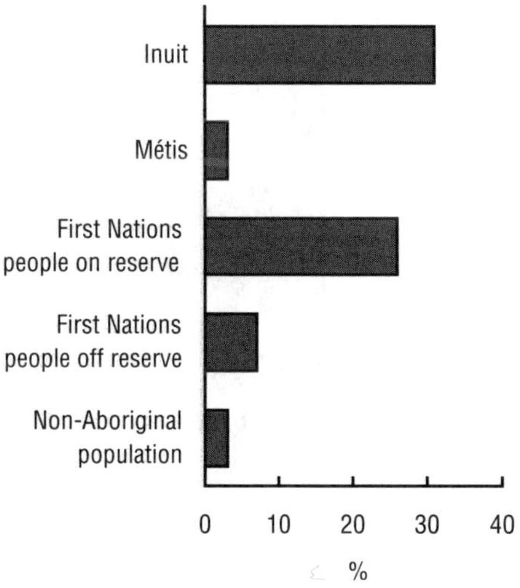

Source: Statistics Canada, 2006 Census of Population.

Aboriginal children who take part in sports are more likely to come from higher-income families and to have parents with higher levels of education, according to the APS. Sports participants are also more likely to take part if they have fewer siblings and live with both parents.

Obesity a serious health problem

A 2008 study of Aboriginal people aged 19 to 50 living in Ontario and the western provinces, excluding reserves, found that they were 2.5 times more likely to be obese or overweight in 2004 as their non-Aboriginal contemporaries. The differences in rates were sharpest among Aboriginal women, particularly those aged 19 to 30, compared with non-Aboriginal women.

Aboriginal people in the study are more likely than other Canadians to report chronic health problems, notably conditions such as diabetes, hypertension and arthritis, which have been linked to obesity. Besides eating habits, the differences in obesity and overweight rates may also reflect differences in income, education and leisure-time physical activity.

For example, inactive leisure time is associated with excess weight for both Aboriginal and non-Aboriginal people. Both groups in the study were equally likely to be inactive; however, among the inactive, 50% of Aboriginal people were obese, compared with 23% of non-Aboriginal people.

Overweight and obesity rates among Aboriginal and non-Aboriginal men are similar. Among Aboriginal women, the higher rates compared with non-Aboriginal women are associated, in part, with higher calorie intake by those aged 19 to 30: these Aboriginal women's average daily intake exceeds that of non-Aboriginal women by 359 calories.

Inuktitut still strong but in slight decline

In much of the North, Inuktitut, the Inuit language, continues to be one of the most widely spoken Aboriginal tongues, though its use is declining. Some Inuit are learning it as a second language.

In the 2006 Census, 32,200 Inuit, or 64% of the Inuit population, reported Inuktitut as their mother tongue, a decline of four percentage points since 1996. Mother tongue is the first language a person learns at home in childhood and still understands today.

The proportion of Inuit who speak Inuktitut most often at home is also decreasing. In 2006, about 25,500 Inuit, or 50% of the population, reported it as their 'home language'—the language they speak most often at home—down eight percentage points from 1996.

Some Inuit learn Inuktitut as a second language. About 11,100 Inuit youth aged 14 and younger, 63% of the Inuit youth population, know it as their mother tongue. About 12,200 Inuit, or 69%, can speak Inuktitut well enough to carry on a conversation, down from 72% in 1996.

Inuit living in the North are much more likely than those in Canada's southern urban areas to speak Inuktitut.

In 2006, just 15% of Inuit in urban areas could converse in Inuktitut, compared with 84% in Inuit Nunaat—the Inuit homeland in northern Canada.

However, fluency with Inuktitut varies greatly across Inuit Nunaat. In Nunavik, 99% of Inuit could speak it well enough to converse; in Nunavut, 91% could.

By contrast, just 27% of Inuit in Nunatsiavut could converse in the language and only 20% in the Inuvialuit region could do so.

Chart 1.4
Inuit population, by use of Inuktitut

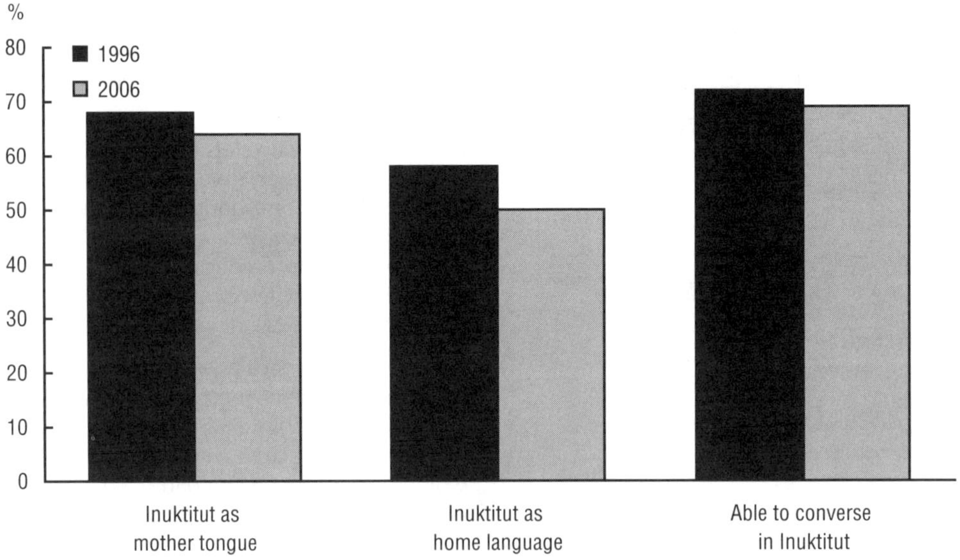

Source: Statistics Canada, Census of Population, 1996 and 2006.

The urban Aboriginal population

The 2006 Census counted 623,470 Aboriginal people living in urban centres. An estimated 50% of the urban Aboriginal population were First Nations people and 43% were Métis. Few Inuit live in urban centres in the South. An estimated 68% of the urban First Nations population reported that they were registered under the *Indian Act*.

About 291,000 Aboriginal people, or 25% of the total Aboriginal population, lived in 9 of Canada's 33 census metropolitan areas in 2006. Even so, Aboriginal people comprise a small share of the population in Canada's biggest cities.

Winnipeg is home to the largest number of Aboriginal people: 68,380 people in 2006, or 10% of Winnipeg's population. Métis comprise the majority of Winnipeg's Aboriginal population, at 40,980 people, followed by First Nations, at 25,900, and Inuit, at 350.

Edmonton has the second largest Aboriginal population: 52,100 people or 5% of the city's population. The Métis also make up the largest segment of the Aboriginal population in Edmonton, with 27,740 people. Also, 22,435 First Nations people and 595 Inuit lived there in 2006.

Vancouver is home to 40,310 Aboriginal people, or 2% of its population. First Nations people make up the Aboriginal majority there, with a count of 23,515. The Métis population is next with 15,070 people, followed by the Inuit, at 210 people.

The 26,575 Aboriginal people in Toronto in 2006 made up 0.5% of its population; 26,575 Aboriginal people lived in Calgary (2% of its population). Saskatoon had 21,535 Aboriginal inhabitants or 9% of its population, and Regina had 17,105, about 9% of its population.

Chart 1.5
Urban Aboriginal population, selected census metropolitan areas, 2006

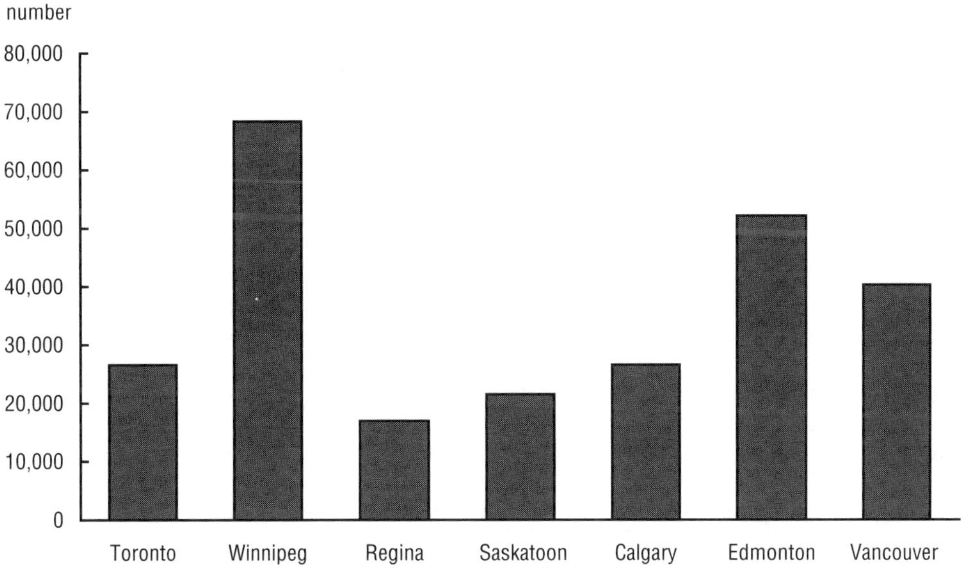

Source: Statistics Canada, 2006 Census of Population.

Table 1.1 Aboriginal identity population, by sex and by province and territory, 2006

	Canada	Newfoundland and Labrador	Prince Edward Island	Nova Scotia	New Brunswick	Quebec	Ontario
	number						
Both sexes							
Total Aboriginal identity population[1]	**1,172,790**	**23,450**	**1,730**	**24,175**	**17,655**	**108,430**	**242,490**
North American Indian	**698,025**	7,765	1,230	15,240	12,385	65,085	158,400
Métis	**389,785**	6,470	385	7,680	4,270	27,980	73,605
Inuit	**50,480**	4,715	30	320	185	10,950	2,040
Non-Aboriginal identity population	**30,068,240**	477,155	132,475	878,915	701,995	7,327,475	11,786,405
Males							
Total Aboriginal identity population[1]	**572,090**	11,525	760	11,770	8,645	53,525	117,590
North American Indian	**338,050**	3,820	565	7,320	5,810	31,690	75,955
Métis	**193,500**	3,170	145	3,940	2,450	14,305	37,030
Inuit	**25,025**	2,365	10	140	70	5,475	940
Non-Aboriginal identity population	**14,754,175**	232,445	64,230	423,800	342,505	3,592,455	5,760,285
Females							
Total Aboriginal identity population[1]	**600,695**	11,925	970	12,405	9,010	54,905	124,905
North American Indian	**359,975**	3,950	660	7,915	6,575	33,395	82,440
Métis	**196,280**	3,310	245	3,740	1,815	13,680	36,580
Inuit	**25,455**	2,345	20	180	110	5,480	1,095
Non-Aboriginal identity population	**15,314,065**	244,715	68,245	455,115	359,495	3,735,020	6,026,115

	Manitoba	Saskatchewan	Alberta	British Columbia	Yukon	Northwest Territories	Nunavut
	number						
Both sexes							
Total Aboriginal identity population[1]	**175,395**	**142,045**	**188,215**	**196,075**	**7,580**	**20,665**	**24,890**
North American Indian	100,645	91,550	97,130	129,575	6,275	12,640	105
Métis	71,810	48,120	85,500	59,445	805	3,580	130
Inuit	565	220	1,610	795	255	4,190	24,610
Non-Aboriginal identity population	958,115	811,960	3,067,990	3,878,310	22,610	20,445	4,380
Males							
Total Aboriginal identity population[1]	85,720	69,640	91,670	94,855	3,665	10,180	12,545
North American Indian	48,715	44,530	47,155	63,190	3,035	6,210	55
Métis	35,615	23,945	41,985	28,595	400	1,860	60
Inuit	280	110	790	335	100	1,990	12,405
Non-Aboriginal identity population	471,200	399,840	1,539,125	1,903,530	11,545	10,790	2,425
Females							
Total Aboriginal identity population[1]	89,675	72,400	96,545	101,215	3,915	10,480	12,345
North American Indian	51,935	47,020	49,970	66,390	3,245	6,430	50
Métis	36,185	24,175	43,515	30,855	400	1,715	65
Inuit	280	105	820	455	150	2,200	12,205
Non-Aboriginal identity population	486,915	412,120	1,528,860	1,974,780	11,070	9,655	1,960

1. The total Aboriginal identity population includes the Aboriginal groups (North American Indian, Métis and Inuit), multiple Aboriginal responses and Aboriginal responses not included elsewhere.

Source: Statistics Canada, 2006 Census of Population.

Table 1.2 Population, by Aboriginal identity, highest level of schooling and sex, 2006

	All levels	Less than high school	High school only	Trade school[1]	College[1]	University[2]	University[3]
	number						
Both sexes	**25,664,220**	**6,098,330**	**6,553,425**	**2,785,420**	**4,435,135**	**1,136,150**	**4,162,225**
Aboriginal identity population	**823,890**	359,780	179,585	93,885	119,680	22,950	42,280
North American Indian	**473,235**	228,985	94,380	49,240	62,340	13,685	21,440
Métis	**291,330**	100,770	74,575	38,220	49,210	8,035	18,265
Inuit	**32,775**	19,885	4,435	3,135	3,935	505	790
Multiple Aboriginal identities	**5,590**	2,010	1,435	755	835	165	355
Other Aboriginal identity	**20,960**	8,125	4,760	2,535	3,350	555	1,410
Non-Aboriginal population	**24,840,335**	5,738,550	6,373,835	2,691,535	4,315,455	1,113,195	4,119,950
Males	**12,470,785**	**3,004,625**	**3,032,870**	**1,778,080**	**1,906,335**	**479,095**	**2,045,725**
Aboriginal identity population	**393,680**	182,410	81,210	58,525	45,755	8,190	15,610
North American Indian	**223,370**	115,165	41,725	30,705	22,870	4,790	7,065
Métis	**142,840**	52,845	34,745	24,020	19,760	2,975	7,670
Inuit	**15,965**	9,795	2,005	2,020	1,660	170	260
Multiple Aboriginal identities	**2,610**	1,020	650	450	310	55	100
Other Aboriginal identity	**8,895**	3,585	2,075	1,325	1,145	190	505
Non-Aboriginal population	**12,077,100**	2,822,210	2,951,660	1,719,555	1,860,580	470,905	2,030,105
Females	**13,193,435**	**3,093,700**	**3,520,555**	**1,007,335**	**2,528,800**	**657,055**	**2,116,505**
Aboriginal identity population	**430,205**	177,365	98,380	35,360	73,925	14,760	26,665
North American Indian	**249,865**	113,825	52,660	18,530	39,465	8,895	14,370
Métis	**148,490**	47,925	39,825	14,205	29,455	5,050	10,600
Inuit	**16,810**	10,090	2,430	1,110	2,270	335	540
Multiple Aboriginal identities	**2,975**	990	785	300	525	110	240
Other Aboriginal identity	**12,065**	4,540	2,680	1,210	2,210	370	910
Non-Aboriginal population	**12,763,230**	2,916,335	3,422,175	971,980	2,454,875	642,295	2,089,840

Note: Population aged 15 years and older.

1. Certificate or diploma.
2. Certificate or diploma below bachelor's degree.
3. Degree at the bachelor's level or higher.

Source: Statistics Canada, 2006 Census of Population.

Table 1.3 Aboriginal identity population, by age group, sex and province and territory, 2006

	Canada	Newfoundland and Labrador	Prince Edward Island	Nova Scotia	New Brunswick	Quebec	Ontario
	number						
Both sexes, all ages	**1,172,790**	**23,450**	**1,730**	**24,175**	**17,655**	**108,430**	**242,490**
0 to 4	**108,895**	1,445	230	1,745	1,350	8,680	19,815
5 to 9	**114,765**	1,805	210	2,080	1,605	9,185	21,075
10 to 14	**125,235**	2,145	160	2,480	1,490	9,650	23,435
15 to 19	**118,105**	2,300	170	2,430	1,695	9,590	22,335
20 to 24	**93,905**	1,920	100	1,905	1,240	8,200	18,540
25 to 34	**161,570**	3,035	235	3,220	2,195	14,440	33,680
35 to 44	**169,465**	3,675	230	3,630	2,870	16,005	37,935
45 to 54	**143,285**	3,395	215	3,515	2,645	14,775	33,720
55 to 64	**81,090**	2,175	100	1,930	1,445	9,910	19,340
65 and older	**56,465**	1,545	75	1,230	1,105	7,995	12,615
Males, all ages	**572,090**	**11,525**	**760**	**11,770**	**8,645**	**53,525**	**117,590**
0 to 4	**55,380**	700	120	880	690	4,460	10,150
5 to 9	**58,910**	920	95	1,060	815	4,560	10,685
10 to 14	**64,120**	1,135	75	1,240	715	5,015	11,840
15 to 19	**60,250**	1,150	65	1,170	885	4,840	11,600
20 to 24	**45,390**	940	70	945	615	3,975	8,925
25 to 34	**76,220**	1,375	120	1,455	1,040	7,015	15,440
35 to 44	**79,205**	1,735	70	1,690	1,390	7,865	17,945
45 to 54	**67,540**	1,735	85	1,715	1,310	7,225	15,895
55 to 64	**39,420**	1,140	30	1,020	720	5,005	9,475
65 and older	**25,650**	695	30	595	460	3,565	5,620
Females, all ages	**600,695**	**11,925**	**970**	**12,405**	**9,010**	**54,905**	**124,905**
0 to 4	**53,515**	745	110	870	660	4,215	9,660
5 to 9	**55,860**	885	110	1,015	795	4,625	10,390
10 to 14	**61,110**	1,005	80	1,240	780	4,640	11,595
15 to 19	**57,855**	1,150	105	1,260	810	4,750	10,740
20 to 24	**48,510**	980	35	960	625	4,220	9,610
25 to 34	**85,350**	1,660	115	1,770	1,155	7,420	18,240
35 to 44	**90,260**	1,940	160	1,940	1,480	8,140	19,985
45 to 54	**75,745**	1,660	125	1,805	1,335	7,550	17,825
55 to 64	**41,670**	1,040	70	910	720	4,910	9,865
65 and older	**30,810**	855	50	635	645	4,425	7,000

See source at end of table.

Table 1.3 Aboriginal identity population, by age group, sex and province and territory, 2006 (continued)

	Manitoba	Saskatchewan	Alberta	British Columbia	Yukon	Northwest Territories	Nunavut
	number						
Both sexes, all ages	**175,395**	**142,045**	**188,215**	**196,075**	**7,580**	**20,665**	**24,890**
0 to 4	18,810	16,600	18,315	16,195	640	1,875	3,195
5 to 9	19,180	16,540	19,300	18,005	690	1,950	3,135
10 to 14	20,200	17,510	20,945	21,045	735	2,355	3,070
15 to 19	17,910	16,130	19,630	19,945	700	2,290	2,980
20 to 24	14,250	11,990	16,535	14,875	550	1,590	2,200
25 to 34	23,830	19,365	28,730	25,605	990	2,770	3,475
35 to 44	23,720	17,845	26,510	29,615	1,230	3,020	3,175
45 to 54	19,215	13,705	20,420	26,425	1,045	2,350	1,850
55 to 64	10,940	7,115	10,695	14,420	580	1,330	1,100
65 and older	7,340	5,240	7,125	9,930	420	1,125	705
Males, all ages	**85,720**	**69,640**	**91,670**	**94,855**	**3,665**	**10,180**	**12,545**
0 to 4	9,585	8,395	9,405	8,130	315	920	1,630
5 to 9	10,100	8,655	9,930	9,155	345	990	1,590
10 to 14	10,475	8,925	10,625	10,960	370	1,190	1,550
15 to 19	8,805	8,275	9,940	10,400	395	1,170	1,550
20 to 24	6,630	5,770	8,105	7,180	280	850	1,105
25 to 34	11,375	8,775	14,010	12,175	445	1,270	1,725
35 to 44	10,895	8,415	12,005	13,525	635	1,470	1,550
45 to 54	9,050	6,620	9,385	12,085	460	1,080	890
55 to 64	5,390	3,345	4,985	6,790	240	700	575
65 and older	3,405	2,455	3,280	4,460	180	540	370
Females, all ages	**89,675**	**72,400**	**96,545**	**101,215**	**3,915**	**10,480**	**12,345**
0 to 4	9,230	8,200	8,910	8,065	325	955	1,565
5 to 9	9,080	7,885	9,375	8,850	340	965	1,540
10 to 14	9,725	8,585	10,320	10,090	370	1,160	1,520
15 to 19	9,105	7,855	9,690	9,545	300	1,120	1,430
20 to 24	7,620	6,220	8,430	7,695	275	740	1,095
25 to 34	12,450	10,590	14,720	13,430	540	1,500	1,750
35 to 44	12,820	9,425	14,505	16,095	595	1,550	1,625
45 to 54	10,165	7,080	11,035	14,345	585	1,270	960
55 to 64	5,550	3,775	5,710	7,635	335	635	520
65 and older	3,935	2,780	3,845	5,470	240	585	330

Source: Statistics Canada, 2006 Census of Population.

Table 1.4 Population, by Aboriginal identity, labour force characteristics and sex, 2006

	All labour force status	In the labour force	Employed	Unemployed	Not in the labour force
			number		
Both sexes	**25,664,220**	**17,146,135**	**16,021,180**	**1,124,960**	**8,518,085**
Aboriginal identity population	**823,890**	519,250	442,395	76,860	304,635
North American Indian	**473,235**	278,455	228,285	50,175	194,780
Métis	**291,325**	204,165	183,785	20,375	87,165
Inuit	**32,775**	20,100	16,020	4,080	12,675
Multiple Aboriginal identities	**5,590**	3,595	3,290	310	1,990
Other Aboriginal identity	**20,960**	12,935	11,015	1,920	8,025
Non-Aboriginal population	**24,840,335**	16,626,880	15,578,780	1,048,100	8,213,450
Males	**12,470,785**	**9,020,595**	**8,431,530**	**589,065**	**3,450,190**
Aboriginal identity population	**393,680**	264,980	222,350	42,625	128,700
North American Indian	**223,370**	141,100	113,150	27,950	82,275
Métis	**142,840**	105,790	94,720	11,070	37,050
Inuit	**15,965**	10,195	7,770	2,430	5,770
Multiple Aboriginal identities	**2,610**	1,810	1,615	195	800
Other Aboriginal identity	**8,890**	6,085	5,100	985	2,805
Non-Aboriginal population	**12,077,100**	8,755,615	8,209,180	546,435	3,321,485
Females	**13,193,435**	**8,125,540**	**7,589,650**	**535,890**	**5,067,895**
Aboriginal identity population	**430,205**	254,270	220,040	34,230	175,935
North American Indian	**249,860**	137,360	115,135	22,220	112,505
Métis	**148,490**	98,370	89,060	9,310	50,120
Inuit	**16,810**	9,905	8,255	1,645	6,905
Multiple Aboriginal identities	**2,975**	1,785	1,670	115	1,190
Other Aboriginal identity	**12,065**	6,850	5,920	935	5,215
Non-Aboriginal population	**12,763,230**	7,871,265	7,369,605	501,660	4,891,960

	Participation rate	Employment rate	Unemployment rate
		%	
Both sexes	**66.8**	**62.4**	**6.6**
Aboriginal identity population	63.0	53.7	14.8
North American Indian	58.8	48.2	18.0
Métis	70.1	63.1	10.0
Inuit	61.3	48.9	20.3
Multiple Aboriginal identities	64.3	58.9	8.6
Other Aboriginal identity	61.7	52.6	14.8
Non-Aboriginal population	66.9	62.7	6.3
Males	**72.3**	**67.6**	**6.5**
Aboriginal identity population	67.3	56.5	16.1
North American Indian	63.2	50.7	19.8
Métis	74.1	66.3	10.5
Inuit	63.9	48.7	23.8
Multiple Aboriginal identities	69.3	61.9	10.8
Other Aboriginal identity	68.4	57.4	16.2
Non-Aboriginal population	72.5	68.0	6.2
Females	**61.6**	**57.5**	**6.6**
Aboriginal identity population	59.1	51.1	13.5
North American Indian	55.0	46.1	16.2
Métis	66.2	60.0	9.5
Inuit	58.9	49.1	16.6
Multiple Aboriginal identities	60.0	56.1	6.4
Other Aboriginal identity	56.8	49.1	13.6
Non-Aboriginal population	61.7	57.7	6.4

Note: Population aged 15 and older.

Source: Statistics Canada, 2006 Census of Population.

Agriculture

2

Overview

The landscape on a Canadian farm might seem appealingly idyllic and unchanging, but agriculture as a business sees as much risk, change and disruption as any other.

Recent disruptions in Canadian agriculture have affected only certain commodities: the BSE (bovine spongiform encephalopathy) crisis, for example, was devastating but mainly confined to the cattle industry.

Now, three major changes are pressing agriculture in Canada, and worldwide. Rising middle classes in other parts of the world can now afford to eat more food, especially animal protein. The global food supply has been further squeezed by recent droughts and other bad weather in key crop-growing areas. In North America, the push to grow corn, wheat and other feedstocks for the expanding ethanol fuel industry is having an effect.

Canada's farmland is vast—about 167 million acres according to the 2006 Census of Agriculture—but ultimately a limited resource. A sudden rush to plant more of one crop displaces others, pushing up prices of those other commodities as well.

More acres planted in corn

In late 2006, corn demand and prices started to rise, pushed in part by the expanding corn-based ethanol industry, particularly in the United States. Responding to rising prices, farmers planted 3.4 million acres of grain corn in 2007, compared with 2.7 million acres in 2006. In 2008, farmers planted 3.0 million acres.

Canada's biggest corn provinces are Ontario, with 58% of Canada's corn acreage, and Quebec, with 35% in 2006.

Chart 2.1
Farm Product Price Index, selected commodities

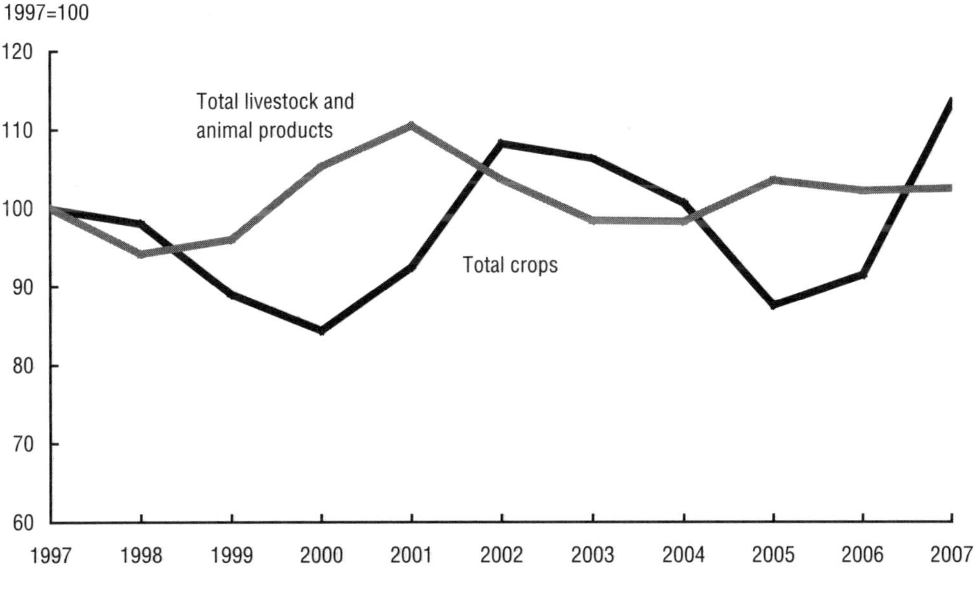

Source: Statistics Canada, CANSIM table 002-0022.

Other grain crops valuable too

In the spring of 2008, prairie farmers were busy taking advantage of rising canola and wheat prices by planting record acreages of those crops. To make room for 14% more wheat acreage and 0.9% more canola acreage, they planted 19% less area in oats and 18% less in barley, which are lower-value crops that are often fed to livestock, as well as 5% less in grain corn, and left 21% fewer acres fallow for the season.

Rising prices, however, are just a recent development. In the first half of this decade, low commodity prices and rising costs for inputs, such as fertilizer, seed and pesticides, pushed farmers in many provinces to shift from annual crops, such as wheat and barley, to lower-cost perennial forages, such as alfalfa, tame hay and improved pasture. Grain prices dropped about 11% from 2000 to 2005, and years of either drought or flood presented other challenges. However, oilseed prices rose about 15% in that period: canola, in particular, has been gaining popularity among producers since the 1980s.

Chart 2.2
Exports of live cattle and calves

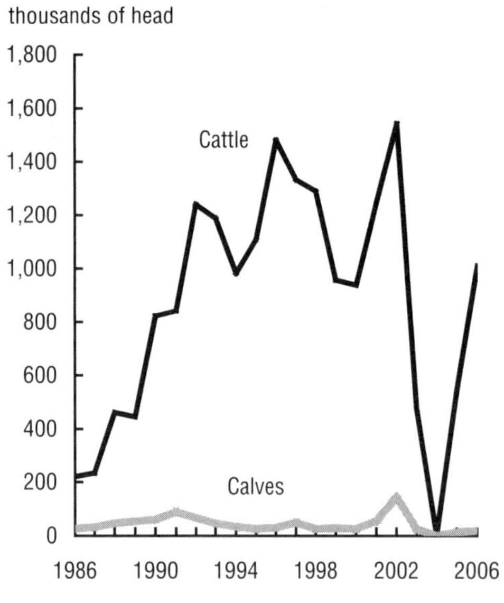

Source: Statistics Canada, CANSIM table 003-0026.

Table 2.a
Number and area of farms, 2006

Number of farms	229,373
Average size of farms (acres)	728
Area of farms as a percentage of country's total land area	7.3

Sources: Food and Agriculture Organization of the United Nations; Statistics Canada, Census of Agriculture, 2006.

Prices received by dairy farms for their milk rose 19% from 2000 to 2005. Cattle prices, however, dropped over 11% from 2000 to 2005 because of the BSE crisis, bottoming out in 2004 with a 26% drop from 2000. When the borders were partly re-opened to Canadian cattle in 2005—and by the time the census was taken in May 2006—cattle prices rebounded somewhat from their lows.

That was then, this is now

Much has changed since then: farmers' cash receipts from marketing their products totalled $40.6 billion in 2007, up 10% from 2006, and 15% above the 2002-to-2006 average, a period marked by the BSE crisis and low commodity prices.

But in agriculture, like in other diverse sectors, the aggregate numbers can conceal gainers and losers. The farm cash receipts' rise was primarily driven by grain and oilseed prices. So, grain and oilseed farmers took advantage of strong prices by selling more product out of long-term storage. The value of crop sales, including grains and oilseeds, was up 25% from 2006 and 29% higher than the previous five-year average.

Livestock producers did not fare so well. In 2007, livestock receipts rose 2% from 2006 to $18.2 billion. Dairy, poultry and egg producers received more because of higher prices, although they faced higher feed costs. For cattle and hog producers, those feed costs were compounded by lower livestock prices in Canada and the higher Canadian dollar, which clouded their export prospects.

Farming near CMAs

Farming isn't just a rural phenomenon: more than 35,000 farms, or 16% of the 229,373 counted in the 2006 Census of Agriculture, had their headquarters in one of Canada's 33 census metropolitan areas (CMAs).

Farming in a CMA might evoke images of cornfields planted next to big-box malls, but in fact CMAs extend far out from the limits of the urban core, sometimes dozens of kilometres into the countryside. Being near a city poses some challenges for farming, but offers benefits too.

Urban areas offer a ready market for many farm products, a supply of labour (and some competition for it), and opportunities for farmers to diversify their income with off-farm revenue.

Chart 2.3
Organic production by province

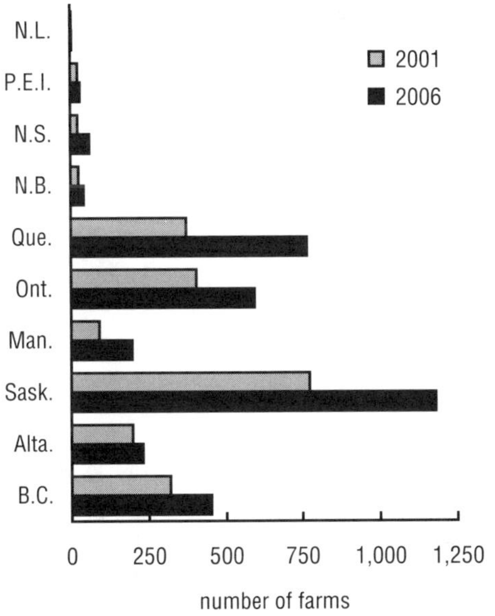

Source: Statistics Canada, Catalogue no. 96-325-XIE.

Farmland in a CMA is likely more valuable than that in regions farther away from the city, making it more expensive to own land for farming: taxes may be higher, for example. Agriculture competes with other economic interests for land: farmland often becomes segmented into smaller tracts, making it more difficult to work. Neighbours' complaints over farming practices create friction.

High land values and proximity to markets make CMAs a good fit for greenhouse, nursery, and floriculture operations. Fruit and vegetable operations are also more common in CMAs. Livestock and field crop farms are less common in CMAs than in rural areas.

Organics we don't see

Canadians regularly see organically grown fruits and vegetables in stores, but they do not see the majority of what is produced on the nation's organic farms.

The most common type of certified-organic product grown on Canadian farms was hay and field crops, such as wheat and other grains, oilseeds, and pulses, such as lentils and chick peas. Some of those products are transformed into processed goods; others are fed to livestock. (Organically raised livestock of course must be given organic feed.) According to a study based on data from the 2006 Census of Agriculture, 2,462 farms reported growing organic hay and field crops, most of it for export.

In 2006, 916 of Canada's 3,555 certified organic farms reported growing fruits and vegetables. 'Organic farms' are classified in the Census of Agriculture in three groups: certified organic by a certifying agency; organic but not certified; or in transition to becoming certified. Nearly 12,000 farms reported producing organic but non-certified products; another 640 farms were in the process of becoming certified.

Organic farms make up 2% of Canada's 229,373 agricultural operations.

Ups and downs in the fruit business

Blueberries and wine grapes are leading the way in the ever-changing fruit business. In 2006, nearly 272,000 acres were planted with fruit, up 5% from 2001.

Blueberries, with their reputation as a healthy food rich in cancer-fighting antioxidants, are finding their way into all sorts of processed foods. They are also finding their way onto more and more land: the acreage devoted to blueberries was up 17% in 2006 from 2001 to 127,000 acres.

Quebec's blueberry acreage rose 25% between the censuses to nearly 42,000 acres. Quebec's growth pushed Nova Scotia, whose area rose 3%, into second place, followed by New Brunswick and British Columbia.

The success of Canadian wines has led to more and more vineyards, principally in Ontario and British Columbia, but on a smaller scale in Quebec and the Maritimes as well. In 2006, grapes grew on 30,000 acres across the country, 15% more acreage than in 2001. Wine grapes, often varieties suited to cooler climates, are taking root in regions such as Montérégie, in Quebec; Ontario's Prince Edward County; Nova Scotia's Annapolis Valley; and on Vancouver Island.

These areas were traditionally known for apples and other tree fruits, but apple producers across Canada had a difficult time in the first half of this decade. Canada's apple area dropped 14% from 2001 to 2006, to less than 55,000 acres: foreign competition and changing consumer tastes were a factor in the decline.

Growers of other fruits have felt the same pressures: strawberry acreage fell 13% between censuses, and raspberry acreage, 5%. However, cranberries are enjoying the same health-driven wave of popularity as blueberries: their acreage rose 13% from 2001 to 2006.

Chart 2.4
Planted area of major fruits

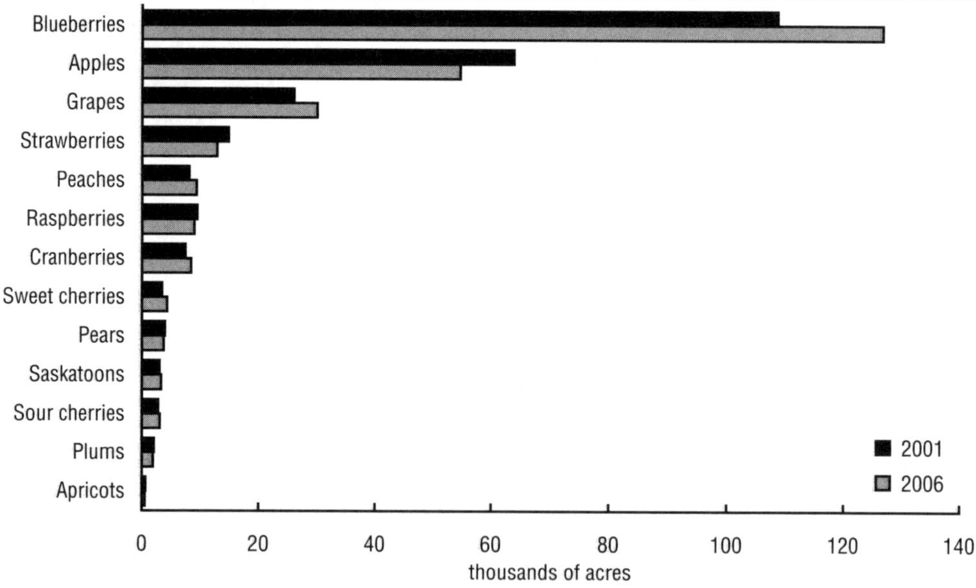

Source: Statistics Canada, 2006 Census of Agriculture.

Livestock's leading edge

Sometimes farmers explore the leading edge of their business in search of profits. In the 1970s, grain farmers first tried canola; in the 1980s, livestock producers began to explore alternative species. It was a way for them to diversify, which can insulate them from risk, and to make use of marginal farmland.

Some of the species have found growing market niches, such as bison, llamas and alpacas and, to a lesser degree, goats. Other species have burst onto the scene, peaked and retreated.

About 195,700 bison were roaming on Canadian farms in 2006, 35% more than in 2001. The average herd on a farm has grown from 77 animals in 2001 to 103 in 2006.

Llamas and alpacas have seen similar growth: 31,700 were counted in 2006, 23% more than in 2001. The average farm with these animals keeps a herd of about seven.

Canada's goat herd peaked in 2001, at 182,900 animals, and slipped 3% by 2006. The number of farms reporting goats dropped 13% between the censuses, and the average herd size rose 11% to a herd of 26 animals suggesting consolidation in the industry.

While goat milk and meat, bison meat, and llama and alpaca textiles and clothing have found market niches, other alternative products have been less successful.

Ostrich, emu and rhea numbers grew substantially in the 1990s, but the bubble burst in this decade. Farmers reported 58,900 emus and rheas in 1996, but just 4,000 in 2006. In the same period, ostrich numbers declined from 14,900 in 1996 to 2,700 a decade later. Duck and wild boar followed a similar trajectory: duck numbers crested at 1.26 million in 2001, but dropped 14% by 2006; wild boars peaked at 37,700 in 1996, but declined to 20,900 in 2006.

Chart 2.5
Livestock other than cattle

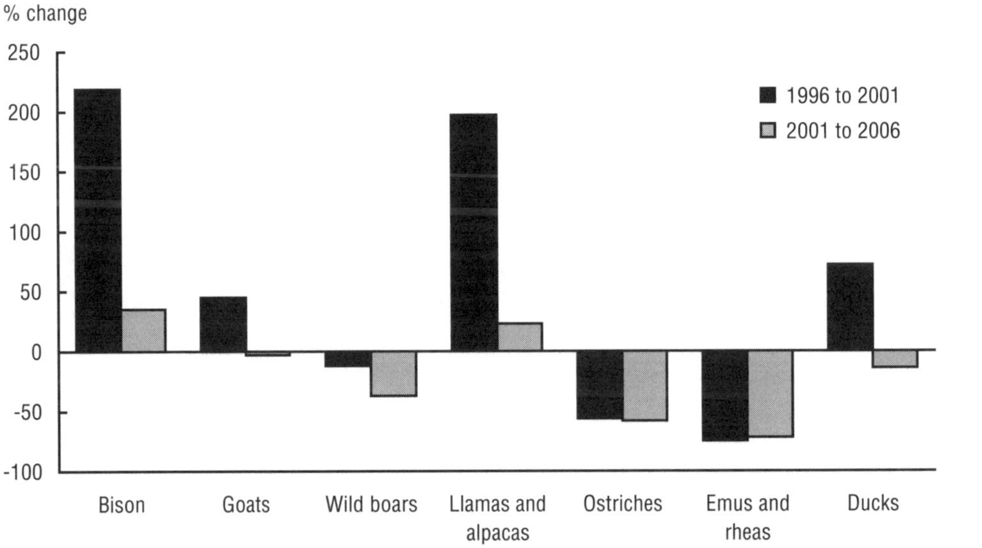

Source: Statistics Canada, Catalogue no. 23-502-XIE.

Table 2.1 Livestock and poultry, 1993 to 2007

	1993	1994	1995	1996	1997	1998	1999	2000
	thousands							
Cattle	11,860	12,012	12,709	13,402	13,412	13,360	13,211	13,201
Bulls[1]	226	233	249	249	246	236	225	230
Milk cows	1,223	1,224	1,245	1,237	1,231	1,184	1,157	1,103
Beef cows	3,912	3,982	4,252	4,381	4,387	4,361	4,386	4,452
Dairy heifers[2]	537	532	528	524	531	511	494	487
Beef heifers[2]	1,226	1,182	1,290	1,418	1,388	1,433	1,309	1,347
For breeding	647	699	778	814	724	687	605	645
For market	579	484	512	604	664	746	704	703
Steers[3]	768	806	775	864	981	1,004	1,197	1,267
Calves	3,969	4,053	4,370	4,728	4,648	4,631	4,443	4,315
Pigs	10,566	10,888	11,522	11,490	11,740	12,363	12,721	13,377
Breeding stock	1,138	1,173	1,179	1,192	1,239	1,307	1,326	1,374
Boars,[4] six months and older	63	65	63	60	58	56	50	47
Sows[5] and gilts,[6] six months and older	1,075	1,108	1,115	1,132	1,181	1,251	1,276	1,327
All other pigs	9,427	9,715	10,344	10,299	10,501	11,056	11,395	12,003
Under 20 kilograms	3,137	3,233	3,339	3,349	3,433	3,686	3,851	4,026
20 to 60 kilograms	3,288	3,371	3,531	3,538	3,630	3,781	3,884	4,104
Over 60 kilograms	3,002	3,110	3,473	3,412	3,437	3,589	3,660	3,873
Sheep	469	466	441	456	447	465	490	543
Rams[7]	22	24	23	22	23	24	25	28
Ewes[8]	447	443	418	434	425	441	465	515
Lambs	164	173	176	187	180	197	227	251
Chickens	430,258	486,338	486,218	501,289	516,952	541,278	570,468	590,623
Turkeys	19,448	19,811	21,255	21,475	20,999	20,070	20,087	21,268

See notes and source at the end of the table.

Table 2.1 Livestock and poultry, 1993 to 2007 (continued)

	2001	2002	2003	2004	2005	2006	2007
	thousands						
Cattle	13,608	13,752	13,466	14,555	14,925	14,655	14,155
Bulls[1]	239	237	239	270	273	264	245
Milk cows	1,091	1,084	1,066	1,055	1,041	1,019	1,005
Beef cows	4,602	4,636	4,752	5,019	5,284	5,247	5,010
Dairy heifers[2]	498	508	512	504	518	495	480
Beef heifers[2]	1,475	1,518	1,453	1,558	1,583	1,615	1,551
For breeding	674	654	648	688	638	628	587
For market	801	865	805	871	945	987	964
Steers[3]	1,222	1,195	1,174	1,203	1,160	1,147	1,145
Calves	4,482	4,574	4,270	4,945	5,067	4,868	4,720
Pigs	14,107	14,724	14,703	14,828	15,118	14,976	14,397
Breeding stock	1,467	1,549	1,598	1,628	1,619	1,586	1,552
Boars,[4] six months and older	45	43	40	38	36	34	32
Sows[5] and gilts,[6] six months and older	1,423	1,506	1,558	1,590	1,584	1,552	1,519
All other pigs	12,640	13,175	13,105	13,200	13,498	13,389	12,846
Under 20 kilograms	4,195	4,387	4,488	4,500	4,561	4,531	4,657
20 to 60 kilograms	4,338	4,509	4,397	4,470	4,627	4,578	4,109
Over 60 kilograms	4,107	4,279	4,220	4,229	4,311	4,280	4,079
Sheep	606	644	641	641	633	589	584
Rams[7]	30	29	29	27	27	26	26
Ewes[8]	576	615	613	613	606	563	558
Lambs	342	349	334	354	345	305	295
Chickens	624,792	625,692	615,939	613,527	626,251	622,261	640,342
Turkeys	20,191	19,672	19,834	19,526	20,492	21,172	21,756

Note: Data reflect the annual average number of animals.

1. Uncastrated male bovines.
2. Female bovines that have never borne young.
3. Castrated male bovines.
4. Uncastrated male pigs.
5. Female pigs that have borne young.
6. Female pigs that have never borne young.
7. Male sheep.
8. Female sheep that have borne young.

Source: Statistics Canada, CANSIM tables 003-0004, 003-0018, 003-0019, 003-0031 and 003-0032.

Table 2.2 Principal field crops, seeded areas, 1992 to 2007

	1992	1993	1994	1995	1996	1997	1998	1999
	hectares							
All wheat	14,391,200	12,982,500	10,997,400	11,365,800	12,488,361	11,576,100	10,870,600	10,469,000
Spring wheat	12,532,300	11,240,300	8,298,100	8,822,500	9,983,447	9,016,600	7,533,200	8,288,900
Winter wheat	347,400	279,300	352,100	358,000	441,114	327,600	403,500	395,400
Durum wheat	1,511,500	1,462,900	2,347,200	2,185,300	2,063,800	2,231,900	2,933,900	1,784,700
Oats	1,663,400	1,728,800	1,840,400	1,579,400	2,060,342	1,876,300	2,062,600	1,885,700
Barley	4,086,700	4,559,200	4,329,600	4,654,300	5,238,025	5,021,500	4,632,300	4,409,100
All rye	226,900	241,400	239,200	215,300	218,265	208,000	267,300	225,000
Fall rye	192,500	217,100	204,800	197,100	202,065	191,800	249,100	208,800
Spring rye	34,400	24,300	34,400	18,200	16,200	16,200	18,200	16,200
Mixed grains	287,300	311,800	306,800	321,000	291,619	317,800	275,200	278,700
Corn for grain	1,081,300	1,035,900	987,900	1,006,500	1,130,775	1,052,500	1,126,500	1,166,200
Buckwheat	24,600	11,800	11,300	17,100	17,775	15,800	14,700	13,900
Dry field peas	273,100	505,800	696,100	819,400	544,300	848,500	1,084,500	851,300
Dry white beans	53,200	49,200	45,000	61,700	42,560	47,900	39,800	79,200
Coloured beans	19,800	37,200	38,600	43,200	43,144	43,900	54,100	70,700
Flaxseed	297,400	528,100	732,400	876,100	592,900	736,600	878,200	809,400
Soybeans	642,600	751,900	821,100	826,100	875,993	1,061,700	980,600	1,004,000
Mustard seed	119,400	190,200	323,600	267,000	239,100	292,200	283,200	279,900
Canola (rapeseed)	3,235,500	4,172,300	5,797,100	5,344,000	3,540,311	4,905,900	5,477,400	5,598,700
Sunflower seed	74,400	85,000	83,000	48,600	36,400	50,600	68,800	85,000
Sugar beets	22,600	22,200	25,500	24,900	23,800	14,200	18,200	18,200
Tame hay	6,414,200	6,514,700	6,738,800	6,577,600	6,395,660	6,349,500	6,578,600	6,937,100
Fodder corn	205,800	179,600	165,800	170,700	190,523	204,600	200,200	188,600
Lentils	279,200	372,300	398,600	333,800	303,500	329,000	378,400	506,300
Canary seed	94,300	126,300	204,300	147,600	248,800	113,300	210,400	149,800
Fababeans	5,600	3,600	2,800	4,000	1,840	2,400	5,600	2,800
Triticale	1,200	15,400	25,900	23,000	25,100	23,000	56,600	74,800
Safflower	..	4,000	2,000	2,000	800	0	1,200	4,000
Caraway seed	..	..	..	..	..	..	..	..
Coriander seed	..	..	..	..	..	..	..	..
Borage seed	..	..	..	..	..	..	..	..
Chick peas	..	..	..	..	..	10,500	38,800	141,600

See source at the end of the table.

Table 2.2 Principal field crops, seeded areas, 1992 to 2007 (continued)

	2000	2001	2002	2003	2004	2005	2006	2007
	hectares							
All wheat	11,072,200	10,950,500	10,370,400	10,413,300	9,885,100	9,653,900	9,852,200	8,849,500
Spring wheat	8,001,100	8,325,400	7,454,800	7,353,900	7,116,200	6,827,300	7,585,000	6,157,200
Winter wheat	428,500	460,100	436,900	647,400	630,200	519,900	731,200	743,700
Durum wheat	2,642,600	2,165,000	2,478,700	2,412,000	2,138,700	2,306,700	1,536,000	1,948,600
Oats	1,825,700	1,907,400	2,345,900	2,033,200	1,924,100	1,767,900	2,063,500	2,188,400
Barley	5,101,300	4,700,200	5,070,200	4,989,400	4,432,100	4,142,600	3,689,900	4,396,800
All rye	188,200	181,400	159,900	246,400	258,200	207,600	276,200	171,900
Fall rye	167,900	163,200	143,700	228,200	242,000	207,600	276,200	171,900
Spring rye	20,300	18,200	16,200	18,200	16,200	0	0	0
Mixed grains	290,200	364,200	284,000	240,700	222,400	213,700	335,700	170,700
Corn for grain	1,206,000	1,294,200	1,299,300	1,264,600	1,184,800	1,113,100	1,093,100	1,391,500
Buckwheat	15,900	15,900	12,100	9,300	6,100	4,000	7,200	2,000
Dry field peas	1,240,200	1,348,500	1,213,900	1,169,300	1,282,900	1,303,000	1,260,500	1,469,000
Dry white beans	80,600	84,400	115,300	72,900	68,800	76,900	76,900	60,700
Coloured beans	84,400	94,900	109,700	88,800	88,900	114,800	101,300	92,500
Flaxseed	594,900	671,800	692,000	744,600	700,000	760,800	804,800	528,000
Soybeans	1,068,700	1,081,500	1,030,300	1,052,800	1,223,000	1,172,400	1,213,500	1,180,100
Mustard seed	212,300	165,800	289,300	339,800	298,600	194,100	133,800	176,000
Canola (rapeseed)	4,937,000	3,826,800	3,876,800	4,735,700	5,218,200	5,369,900	5,283,300	6,321,600
Sunflower seed	74,800	72,800	99,500	108,400	80,900	87,000	77,000	80,900
Sugar beets	17,000	12,100	12,100	12,100	14,200	13,800	15,700	13,800
Tame hay	7,270,700	7,663,400	7,806,500	7,879,000	8,024,500	8,169,900	8,237,000	8,239,200
Fodder corn	211,500	233,800	226,000	233,900	234,800	222,800	270,700	246,400
Lentils	698,900	708,200	540,200	513,400	738,400	802,800	516,300	540,200
Canary seed	165,900	170,000	279,200	259,000	347,900	184,200	135,600	178,100
Fababeans	6,100	5,200	5,200	4,800	6,000	4,800	8,400	6,100
Triticale	70,800	47,300	87,000	78,100	72,900	53,800	57,300	48,600
Safflower	5,200	2,400	2,000	..	..	..	..	..
Caraway seed	..	7,300	8,100	8,100	4,000	0	5,800	8,100
Coriander seed	..	..	8,100	8,100	10,100	10,100	..	..
Borage seed	..	..	2,000	2,000	4,000	0	0	2,000
Chick peas	295,400	485,700	192,200	62,700	46,600	78,800	129,100	174,000

Source: Statistics Canada, CANSIM table 001-0010.

Table 2.3 Principal field crop production, 1992 to 2007

	1992	1993	1994	1995	1996	1997	1998	1999
	tonnes							
All wheat	29,877,200	27,225,900	22,919,500	24,989,400	29,801,400	24,299,400	24,082,300	26,959,900
Spring wheat	25,360,400	23,100,000	16,944,400	18,847,100	24,146,900	19,032,400	16,564,600	20,900,800
Winter wheat	1,378,900	767,500	1,340,300	1,493,900	1,027,900	915,300	1,475,800	1,718,200
Durum wheat	3,137,900	3,358,400	4,634,800	4,648,400	4,626,600	4,351,700	6,041,900	4,340,900
Oats	2,828,500	3,556,800	3,640,500	2,872,800	4,361,100	3,489,300	3,957,500	3,641,300
Barley	11,031,500	12,972,100	11,692,000	13,032,500	15,562,000	13,533,900	12,708,700	13,196,000
All rye	281,100	318,600	399,700	309,600	309,400	320,000	408,200	386,600
Fall rye	243,000	280,500	348,900	291,800	291,100	303,400	391,700	366,800
Spring rye	38,100	38,100	50,800	17,800	18,300	16,600	16,500	19,800
Mixed grains	604,100	712,100	630,900	653,300	581,900	626,400	540,000	462,800
Corn for grain	4,882,600	6,755,200	7,189,900	7,280,900	7,541,700	7,179,800	8,952,400	9,161,300
Buckwheat	10,750	7,500	12,400	21,200	22,200	16,500	14,800	12,500
Dry field peas	504,800	970,200	1,441,000	1,454,700	1,173,000	1,762,300	2,336,800	2,251,900
Dry white beans	53,100	77,800	84,800	116,200	61,200	82,600	73,900	149,100
Coloured beans	20,100	53,000	85,900	86,900	71,800	85,400	111,200	135,400
Flaxseed	336,600	627,400	967,700	1,104,900	851,000	895,400	1,080,900	1,022,400
Soybeans	1,453,300	1,944,900	2,253,700	2,297,500	2,169,500	2,737,700	2,736,600	2,780,900
Mustard seed	133,300	215,900	319,300	244,300	230,800	243,400	238,600	306,400
Canola (rapeseed)	3,872,400	5,524,900	7,232,500	6,434,200	5,062,300	6,393,100	7,643,300	8,798,300
Sunflower seed	64,800	78,500	117,000	66,200	54,900	65,100	111,800	121,900
Sugar beets	775,700	782,900	1,091,300	1,026,900	1,034,200	635,000	880,000	743,900
Tame hay	27,694,600	29,703,700	31,141,300	26,851,400	28,025,000	21,137,500	21,825,000	25,032,900
Fodder corn	5,273,800	5,248,800	4,743,800	4,995,700	5,375,400	5,466,600	6,425,600	6,611,500
Lentils	349,000	348,700	450,400	431,900	402,500	378,800	479,800	723,800
Canary seed	124,100	127,800	240,400	154,600	284,600	115,000	235,300	166,000
Fababeans	11,200	5,200	6,800	5,800	5,520	4,300	13,700	6,500
Triticale	2,800	31,100	40,700	39,900	35,200	31,000	85,300	126,200
Safflower	..	500	1,100	2,000	700	0	1,400	3,800
Caraway seed	..	..	..	..	..	..	..	..
Coriander seed	..	..	..	..	..	..	..	..
Borage seed	..	..	..	..	..	..	..	..
Chick peas	..	..	..	..	..	14,500	50,900	187,200

See source at the end of the table.

Table 2.3 Principal field crop production, 1992 to 2007 (continued)

	2000	2001	2002	2003	2004	2005	2006	2007
	tonnes							
All wheat	26,535,500	20,630,200	15,961,300	23,048,600	24,795,500	25,748,100	25,265,400	20,054,000
Spring wheat	19,027,000	16,010,200	10,531,200	16,124,700	17,530,300	17,803,300	18,617,300	13,873,400
Winter wheat	1,800,000	1,570,500	1,553,200	2,712,300	2,463,800	2,030,200	3,301,900	2,499,200
Durum wheat	5,708,500	3,049,500	3,876,900	4,211,600	4,801,400	5,914,600	3,346,200	3,681,400
Oats	3,403,300	2,690,700	2,910,700	3,376,700	3,467,200	3,282,700	3,852,200	4,696,300
Barley	13,228,600	10,845,600	7,467,700	12,164,200	12,556,700	11,677,600	9,573,100	10,983,900
All rye	260,300	227,800	133,800	327,100	397,500	330,400	382,900	233,000
Fall rye	247,000	215,600	129,400	307,800	383,500	330,400	382,900	233,000
Spring rye	13,300	12,200	4,400	19,300	14,000	..	..	..
Mixed grains	434,900	446,500	358,900	384,400	342,500	316,400	346,500	262,600
Corn for grain	6,953,700	8,389,200	8,998,800	9,587,300	8,836,800	9,332,200	8,989,800	11,648,700
Buckwheat	13,600	16,300	12,200	9,900	1,500	4,600	7,400	2,300
Dry field peas	2,864,300	2,044,800	1,283,800	1,930,900	3,097,200	2,993,600	2,519,900	2,934,800
Dry white beans	119,300	136,200	209,700	151,000	80,700	117,900	159,700	105,200
Coloured beans	142,100	153,000	197,100	193,300	137,400	199,600	212,900	171,600
Flaxseed	693,400	715,000	679,400	754,400	516,900	990,600	988,800	633,500
Soybeans	2,703,000	1,635,200	2,335,700	2,273,300	3,043,900	3,155,600	3,465,500	2,695,700
Mustard seed	202,200	107,100	154,300	226,100	286,700	183,800	108,200	114,300
Canola (rapeseed)	7,205,300	5,017,100	4,520,500	6,771,200	7,673,600	9,483,300	9,000,300	9,528,500
Sunflower seed	119,300	103,800	157,400	142,300	52,200	84,400	157,300	124,800
Sugar beets	821,000	544,300	344,700	680,400	743,900	607,800	870,900	762,000
Tame hay	23,921,600	20,373,500	18,396,700	23,265,800	27,329,200	29,576,000	29,999,800	30,244,600
Fodder corn	5,890,300	6,079,000	6,355,800	7,213,000	7,795,400	7,380,900	9,680,600	8,136,600
Lentils	914,100	566,300	328,000	484,600	915,800	1,164,300	629,500	673,900
Canary seed	170,800	113,900	177,500	234,600	300,500	227,200	133,100	162,000
Fababeans	15,400	10,200	9,100	8,400	15,300	9,800	16,000	10,900
Triticale	89,700	31,200	26,000	64,400	80,000	43,200	26,900	47,000
Safflower	6,700	2,900	1,100	..	..	..	..	..
Caraway seed	..	2,000	2,400	3,200	2,500	..	..	..
Coriander seed	..	..	5,200	4,800	7,900	8,900	..	..
Borage seed	..	..	800	500	700	0	0	200
Chick peas	387,500	455,000	144,500	67,600	51,200	103,900	163,200	224,800

Source: Statistics Canada, CANSIM table 001-0010.

Table 2.4 Principal field crop production, by province, 2007

	Canada	Newfoundland and Labrador	Prince Edward Island	Nova Scotia	New Brunswick	Quebec
	tonnes					
All wheat	**20,054,000**	.	33,000	5,000	5,400	173,700
Spring wheat	**13,873,400**	.	23,200	1,600	4,600	165,000
Winter wheat	**2,499,200**	.	9,800	3,400	800	8,700
Durum wheat	**3,681,400**	.	.	.	.	.
Oats	**4,696,300**	.	12,100	4,500	24,000	280,000
Barley	**10,983,900**	.	93,500	6,900	45,300	308,000
Fall rye	**233,000**	.	..	..	.	..
Mixed grains	**262,600**	.	8,800	..	..	70,000
Corn for grain	**11,648,700**	.	.	27,800	19,200	4,100,000
Buckwheat	**2,300**	.	.	.	.	..
Dry field peas	**2,934,800**	.	.	.	.	.
Dry white beans	**105,200**	.	.	.	.	..
Coloured beans	**171,600**	.	.	.	.	12,600
Flaxseed	**633,500**	.	.	.	.	.
Soybeans	**2,695,700**	.	11,100	.	.	472,000
Mustard seed	**114,300**	.	.	.	.	.
Canola (rapeseed)	**9,528,500**	.	.	.	.	18,500
Sunflower seed	**124,800**	.	.	.	.	.
Sugar beets	**762,000**	.	.	.	.	..
Tame hay	**30,244,600**	27,200	301,200	375,600	381,000	4,039,700
Fodder corn	**8,136,600**	.	70,800	72,600	58,100	1,879,700
Lentils	**673,900**	.	.	.	.	.
Canary seed	**162,000**	.	.	.	.	.
Fababeans	**10,900**	.	.	.	.	.
Triticale	**47,000**	.	.	.	.	.
Chick peas	**224,800**	.	.	.	.	.

See source at the end of the table.

Table 2.4 Principal field crop production, by province, 2007 (continued)

	Ontario	Manitoba	Saskat-chewan	Alberta	British Columbia
	tonnes				
All wheat	1,442,400	3,211,400	9,058,400	6,076,100	48,600
Spring wheat	250,400	2,469,800	5,679,600	5,230,600	48,600
Winter wheat	1,192,000	741,600	367,400	175,500	..
Durum wheat	.	..	3,011,400	670,000	.
Oats	87,900	1,204,500	2,401,200	627,400	54,700
Barley	217,700	1,195,300	3,945,200	5,114,300	57,700
Fall rye	43,200	53,900	99,100	36,800	..
Mixed grains	147,000	4,300	8,400	24,100	..
Corn for grain	6,985,300	493,500	.	22,900	.
Buckwheat	..	2,300	.	.	.
Dry field peas	.	97,700	2,309,600	527,500	..
Dry white beans	62,100	43,100	.	..	.
Coloured beans	45,500	59,000	.	54,500	.
Flaxseed	.	105,400	511,800	16,300	.
Soybeans	2,000,300	212,300	.	.	.
Mustard seed	.	..	87,300	27,000	.
Canola (rapeseed)	27,800	1,950,400	4,082,300	3,401,950	47,600
Sunflower seed	.	119,800	5,000	..	.
Sugar beets	.	..	.	762,000	.
Tame hay	5,216,300	3,538,000	5,511,100	9,276,000	1,578,500
Fodder corn	3,991,600	816,500	.	839,100	408,200
Lentils	.	..	673,900	..	.
Canary seed	.	6,300	155,700	..	.
Fababeans	.	10,900	..	..	.
Triticale	.	.	29,200	17,800	.
Chick peas	.	.	198,100	26,700	.

Source: Statistics Canada, CANSIM table 001-0010.

Table 2.5 Farm cash receipts, 1994 to 2007

	1994	1995	1996	1997	1998	1999	2000
	$ thousands						
Farm cash receipts	**25,881,396**	**27,123,321**	**29,075,327**	**29,838,629**	**29,686,323**	**30,357,110**	**32,960,524**
Receipts from crops	11,542,606	13,114,105	14,016,229	14,102,990	13,822,114	13,217,869	13,062,085
Wheat	2,436,389	2,823,648	3,482,441	3,520,740	2,413,393	2,337,436	2,350,429
Oats	144,883	224,863	305,427	269,170	193,228	174,621	196,413
Barley	517,327	719,800	960,127	727,160	510,285	421,352	477,987
Canada Wheat Board payments[1]	1,367,430	1,432,766	1,123,878	725,720	948,849	948,353	811,564
Rye	24,310	30,776	38,989	34,242	19,743	17,212	15,285
Flaxseed	184,905	230,310	220,875	291,632	262,858	138,965	148,743
Canola (rapeseed)	2,111,164	1,906,362	1,968,956	2,127,750	2,663,207	1,771,010	1,560,025
Soybeans	506,678	661,659	626,673	814,222	800,348	618,194	677,947
Corn	505,789	704,294	808,128	696,106	642,363	742,902	676,073
Sugar beets	40,548	52,043	40,670	34,483	39,838	30,527	32,899
Potatoes	533,104	517,641	533,124	512,581	612,166	700,669	679,916
Vegetables	863,319	923,155	..	..	..	..	..
Greenhouse vegetables	..	..	218,473	270,361	376,949	438,491	504,713
Other vegetables	..	..	749,685	773,255	787,818	779,893	796,238
Tree fruits	207,773	252,265	241,440	234,840	231,839	252,633	260,280
Berries and grapes	219,213	240,738	254,740	251,236	254,377	320,013	286,441
Floriculture and nursery	883,978	941,540	999,335	1,095,216	1,220,579	1,322,114	1,588,698
Tobacco	373,946	296,647	345,332	353,267	358,610	356,706	348,427
Other crops	621,850	1,155,598	1,097,936	1,371,009	1,485,664	1,846,778	1,650,007
Receipts from livestock and their products[2]	12,513,891	12,703,800	13,857,294	14,626,880	14,442,665	15,163,207	17,089,735
Cattle and calves	4,812,930	4,607,189	4,730,759	5,285,317	5,704,605	6,185,002	6,874,942
Hogs	2,031,823	2,252,460	2,884,759	2,989,333	2,201,165	2,395,395	3,355,238
Sheep	2,908	3,206	3,026	3,494	4,034	4,013	5,214
Lambs	60,875	66,403	74,812	71,843	67,727	70,464	81,526
Dairy products	3,354,465	3,463,085	3,514,733	3,709,267	3,846,077	3,920,935	4,029,833
Hens and chickens	1,060,948	1,050,960	1,248,291	1,298,789	1,356,008	1,320,852	1,368,143
Turkeys	221,061	237,891	266,906	258,588	248,836	240,235	263,253
Eggs	559,998	590,826	644,956	482,874	466,165	477,591	511,052
Other livestock and products	408,883	431,780	489,052	527,375	548,048	548,720	600,534
Receipts from direct payments	1,824,899	1,305,416	1,201,804	1,108,759	1,421,544	1,976,034	2,808,704
Crop insurance payments	414,825	306,725	256,832	302,721	318,356	239,544	451,382
Private hail Insurance	198,180	174,738	81,613	71,068	55,855	68,628	159,254
Provincial stabilization payments	300,472	308,128	300,359	170,846	507,947	572,776	411,180
Dairy subsidy	222,304	213,553	170,657	146,610	132,113	103,652	72,666
Other payments	648,499	255,976	277,627	264,192	138,549	209,689	836,148
Net Income Stabilization Account payments	40,619	46,296	114,716	153,322	268,724	444,918	456,221
Income disaster assistance programs	..	..	..	..	..	339,321	421,853

See notes and source at the end of the table.

Table 2.5 Farm cash receipts, 1994 to 2007 (continued)

	2001	2002	2003	2004	2005	2006	2007
				$ thousands			
Farm cash receipts	**36,320,804**	**36,075,277**	**34,419,826**	**36,470,624**	**36,683,856**	**36,909,923**	**40,457,714**
Receipts from crops	13,590,638	14,454,970	13,400,716	14,464,290	13,463,667	14,561,516	18,167,638
Wheat	2,548,885	2,474,708	2,246,500	2,158,843	1,760,910	2,183,290	2,899,455
Oats	273,962	307,737	244,503	231,377	256,827	331,701	432,127
Barley	621,288	505,702	379,483	454,885	343,625	353,502	652,099
Canada Wheat Board payments[1]	1,042,085	981,534	337,267	1,007,545	842,575	728,644	1,454,342
Rye	16,210	12,182	12,440	29,457	13,050	15,913	33,270
Flaxseed	162,780	239,835	192,160	198,714	171,004	158,775	236,910
Canola (rapeseed)	1,723,047	1,778,264	1,889,576	2,151,363	1,826,137	2,502,259	3,412,573
Soybeans	534,483	587,657	758,345	630,764	760,350	678,542	1,032,151
Corn	630,884	819,169	786,685	794,416	622,774	746,081	1,027,186
Sugar beets	19,333	20,072	22,732	30,921	32,140	38,180	34,726
Potatoes	722,879	917,617	846,378	821,873	787,452	895,586	846,282
Vegetables	..	..	..	..	..	..	..
Greenhouse vegetables	589,710	593,763	637,136	716,726	722,312	796,372	789,771
Other vegetables	873,847	844,869	876,876	907,683	889,923	919,704	910,100
Tree fruits	258,050	233,864	244,591	222,914	207,056	210,857	223,603
Berries and grapes	280,447	294,783	312,930	375,083	344,320	381,524	359,613
Floriculture and nursery	1,665,576	1,828,717	1,902,346	1,925,250	1,887,211	1,950,492	2,002,329
Tobacco	240,007	274,150	222,256	231,181	194,942	178,683	76,515
Other crops	1,387,160	1,735,689	1,488,513	1,575,298	1,801,061	1,491,416	1,744,581
Receipts from livestock and their products[2]	18,964,226	18,191,366	16,170,994	17,144,069	18,296,767	17,814,733	18,199,616
Cattle and calves	7,891,897	7,654,142	5,119,181	5,073,526	6,286,028	6,379,563	6,292,129
Hogs	3,827,869	3,284,628	3,442,646	4,269,870	3,948,452	3,436,040	3,328,220
Sheep	4,743	3,568	4,395	4,245	6,211	6,692	6,197
Lambs	92,273	99,486	96,459	80,088	104,374	125,663	115,558
Dairy products	4,142,313	4,135,287	4,480,779	4,598,535	4,841,889	4,833,132	5,196,542
Hens and chickens	1,522,306	1,452,936	1,528,417	1,579,731	1,615,170	1,547,233	1,748,631
Turkeys	262,534	258,822	262,642	267,824	271,505	278,481	320,202
Eggs	547,878	574,980	570,337	560,448	540,508	560,564	567,541
Other livestock and products	672,413	727,517	666,138	709,802	682,630	647,365	624,596
Receipts from direct payments	3,765,940	3,428,941	4,848,116	4,862,265	4,923,422	4,533,674	4,090,460
Crop insurance payments	917,589	1,407,047	1,707,485	755,810	820,072	600,268	574,010
Private hail Insurance	123,657	86,071	104,507	108,718	116,304	138,832	188,443
Provincial stabilization payments	516,476	395,673	711,321	626,336	390,763	496,919	837,851
Dairy subsidy	41,885	8,758	..	..	..	..	..
Other payments	1,097,940	528,782	1,161,407	1,423,217	1,376,781	220,282	69,414
Net Income Stabilization Account payments	441,711	615,685	723,065	934,140	442,340	316,946	272,203
Income disaster assistance programs	626,682	386,925	440,331	1,014,044	1,777,161	2,760,427	2,148,539

1. Payments made directly to producers.
2. Data do not add to totals because data for horses and their products are suppressed for confidentiality.

Source: Statistics Canada, CANSIM table 002-0001.

Table 2.6 Farm operators, by farm type and by province, 2006

	Canada	Newfoundland and Labrador	Prince Edward Island	Nova Scotia	New Brunswick	Quebec
	number					
All operators[1,2]	**327,055**	**715**	**2,335**	**5,095**	**3,695**	**45,470**
Farm type[3]						
Dairy cattle and milk production	**25,770**	55	360	495	430	12,545
Beef cattle ranching and farming, including feedlots	**86,000**	60	475	905	670	6,375
Hog and pig farming	**9,245**	10	90	85	65	2,975
Chicken egg production	**2,680**	20	20	75	45	225
Broiler and other meat-type chicken production	**2,935**	5	15	90	15	555
Turkey production	**445**	0	5	15	5	70
Poultry hatcheries	**70**	0	0	5	0	10
Combination poultry and egg production	**240**	0	0	10	0	30
Other poultry production	**390**	0	0	0	0	100
Sheep farming	**4,260**	30	20	80	25	930
Goat farming	**1,525**	5	0	35	20	235
Apiculture	**2,170**	5	10	30	35	215
Horse and other equine production	**22,905**	15	115	260	195	1,200
Fur-bearing animal and rabbit production	**535**	25	15	125	20	95
Livestock combination farming	**10,860**	20	80	220	150	885
All other miscellaneous animal production	**3,770**	0	5	25	30	270
Soybean farming	**8,390**	0	10	0	5	475
Oilseed (except soybean) farming	**13,505**	0	0	0	0	20
Dry pea and bean farming	**1,590**	0	0	0	0	0
Wheat farming	**15,480**	0	15	5	10	100
Corn farming	**4,880**	0	0	10	5	2,535
Other grain farming	**38,145**	5	70	15	35	1,580
Potato farming	**2,405**	30	495	20	340	435
Other vegetables (except potato) and melon farming	**5,315**	95	70	175	100	1,240
Fruit and tree-nut farming	**12,185**	50	205	1,185	485	1,840
Mushroom production	**235**	0	0	5	5	25
Other food crops grown under cover	**1,410**	10	5	40	10	395
Nursery and tree production	**6,895**	60	25	500	215	910
Floriculture production	**4,135**	75	15	145	110	740
Tobacco farming	**910**	0	0	0	0	5
Hay farming	**24,090**	85	110	345	395	2,360
Fruit and vegetable combination farming	**865**	30	10	35	30	160
All other miscellaneous crop farming	**12,815**	20	90	165	245	5,935

See notes and source at the end of the table.

Table 2.6 Farm operators, by farm type and by province, 2006 (continued)

	Ontario	Manitoba	Saskat-chewan	Alberta	British Columbia
			number		
All operators[1,2]	**82,410**	**26,620**	**59,185**	**71,660**	**29,870**
Farm type[3]					
Dairy cattle and milk production	8,540	820	360	1,050	1,115
Beef cattle ranching and farming, including feedlots	15,000	9,240	16,795	30,115	6,365
Hog and pig farming	3,395	1,155	315	950	200
Chicken egg production	935	180	75	220	880
Broiler and other meat-type chicken production	1,260	135	110	295	455
Turkey production	165	35	15	50	85
Poultry hatcheries	20	10	5	10	10
Combination poultry and egg production	70	15	5	25	85
Other poultry production	135	15	10	35	85
Sheep farming	1,515	195	260	615	590
Goat farming	555	105	80	265	225
Apiculture	530	350	350	395	255
Horse and other equine production	6,560	1,265	1,600	7,095	4,600
Fur-bearing animal and rabbit production	170	25	0	10	45
Livestock combination farming	3,665	660	1,285	2,365	1,535
All other miscellaneous animal production	445	180	725	1,605	485
Soybean farming	7,665	225	5	5	0
Oilseed (except soybean) farming	35	1,940	7,130	4,270	115
Dry pea and bean farming	195	170	1,085	130	5
Wheat farming	1,225	1,645	8,730	3,680	70
Corn farming	2,270	35	0	10	15
Other grain farming	6,155	5,050	16,110	8,945	185
Potato farming	345	240	130	250	110
Other vegetables (except potato) and melon farming	2,250	145	60	185	1,000
Fruit and tree-nut farming	2,835	185	230	360	4,815
Mushroom production	105	0	0	10	80
Other food crops grown under cover	510	10	35	135	260
Nursery and tree production	2,080	215	115	820	1,960
Floriculture production	1,525	210	220	415	690
Tobacco farming	900	0	0	0	0
Hay farming	7,965	1,655	2,470	5,855	2,850
Fruit and vegetable combination farming	255	15	20	60	250
All other miscellaneous crop farming	3,115	510	845	1,435	460

Note: Each census farm is classified according to the commodity or group of commodities that accounts for 50% or more of its total potential receipts.

1. Data may not add to totals because of rounding. Minor differences can be expected in figures appearing in other tables.
2. Farm operators are defined as the people responsible for the management decisions made in the operation of a census farm or agricultural operation. Up to three farm operators could be reported per farm.
3. The farm type is based on the North American Industry Classification System (NAICS) farm-typing categories. Although NAICS is revised periodically, the classifications for Canadian agriculture have remained the same and the data for the two census years are comparable.

Source: Statistics Canada, 2006 Census of Agriculture.

Table 2.7 Farm operators, by sex and age group, census years 2001 and 2006

	2001		2006		2001 to 2006
	number	% of total	number	% of total	% change
All operators[1,2]	**346,195**	**100.0**	**327,055**	**100.0**	**-5.5**
Under 35	39,920	11.5	29,925	9.1	-25.0
35 to 54	185,575	53.6	164,160	50.2	-11.5
55 and older	120,705	34.9	132,975	40.7	10.2
Median age	49	...	51	...	4.1
Male operators	255,015	73.7	236,220	72.2	-7.4
Under 35	29,430	8.5	22,170	6.8	-24.7
35 to 54	132,060	38.1	114,695	35.1	-13.1
55 and older	93,530	27.0	99,360	30.4	6.2
Median age	49	...	52	...	6.1
Female operators	91,180	26.3	90,835	27.8	-0.4
Under 35	10,490	3.0	7,755	2.4	-26.1
35 to 54	53,510	15.5	49,465	15.1	-7.6
55 and older	27,175	7.8	33,615	10.3	23.7
Median age	48	...	50	...	4.2

1. Data may not add to totals because of rounding. Minor differences can be expected in figures appearing in other tables.
2. Farm operators are defined as the people responsible for the management decisions made in the operation of a census farm or agricultural operation. Up to three farm operators could be reported per farm.

Source: Statistics Canada, censuses of agriculture, 2001 and 2006.

Table 2.8 Total farm area, land tenure and land in crops, census years from 1986 to 2006

	1986	1991	1996	2001	2006
			number		
Total number of farms	**293,089**	**280,043**	**276,548**	**246,923**	**229,373**
Total farm area					
Area in hectares[1]	67,825,757	67,753,700	68,054,956	67,502,446	67,586,739
Farms reporting	293,089	280,043	276,548	246,923	229,373
Average area in hectares per farm reporting	231	242	246	273	295
Total area owned					
Area in hectares[1]	43,218,905	42,961,352	43,060,963	42,265,706	41,377,673
Farms reporting	273,963	264,837	262,152	235,131	220,513
Average area in hectares per farm reporting	158	162	164	180	188
Total area rented or leased from others[2]					
Area in hectares[1]	24,606,852	24,792,348	24,993,993	25,236,740	26,209,066
Farms reporting	118,735	111,387	111,718	103,484	97,989
Average area in hectares per farm reporting	207	223	224	244	267
Land in crops (excluding Christmas tree area)					
Area in hectares[1]	33,181,235	33,507,780	34,918,733	36,395,150	35,912,247
Farms reporting	264,141	248,147	237,760	215,581	194,717
Average area in hectares per farm reporting	126	135	147	169	184

1. Conversion factor: 1 hectare equals 2.47 acres.
2. Total area rented or leased from others includes land leased from governments, rented or leased from others and crop-shared from others.

Source: Statistics Canada, censuses of agriculture, 1986 to 2006.

Business, consumer and property services

3

Overview

The services sector is the mainstay of the Canadian economy. Besides accounting for more than two-thirds of Canada's gross domestic product (GDP), business, consumer and property service providers help the entire economy function: businesses and families use them to ensure that their operations succeed and to meet household needs.

The boom in commodities prices will not end the dominance of the services sector anytime soon. Canada's services-producing industries have outpaced the goods-producing industries in both size and growth for decades, and in 2007 generated 69% of the country's GDP.

Geography creates some big differences, however. In our resource-rich provinces and territories, such as Newfoundland and Labrador, Saskatchewan, Alberta and the Northwest Territories, services make smaller contributions to the economy, between 50% and 60% of provincial production. In major business and population centres such as Ontario and British Columbia, or in smaller economies such as Prince Edward Island, New Brunswick and Manitoba, services account for up to 75% of GDP. And with all the activity involved in supporting Canadians in the remote corners of the country, service providers comprise up to 85% of the Yukon and Nunavut economies.

Businesses powering business

Running a business is hard work, and most companies cannot perform every business task themselves. Most rely on outside firms to provide services that are essential to the success and health of their operations.

One of the business world's most important groups of service providers are the bankers, traders and insurers that provide companies with money to grow and that protect

Chart 3.1
GDP for goods- and services-producing industries

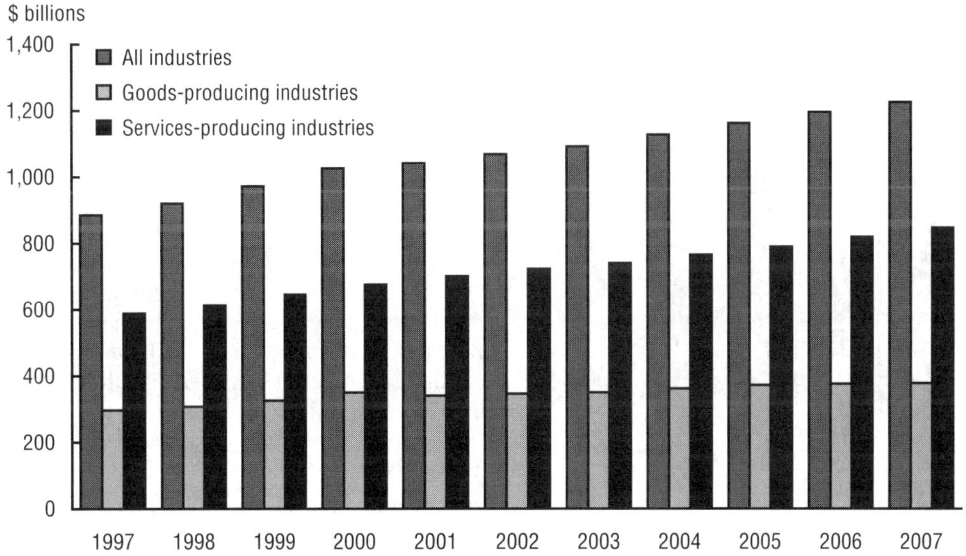

Source: Statistics Canada, CANSIM table 379-0027.

companies' investments. The finance and insurance industries generated $79 billion in economic activity in 2007: banks accounted for most of this output. Riding low interest rates and robust economic growth, the finance and insurance industry has been one of the fastest-growing areas of the economy, expanding 25% since 2001. It's also one of the most profitable, earning nearly 27 cents of profit for every dollar of revenue.

Manufacturers need distribution networks, warehouses, wholesalers and drivers to get their goods on store shelves across the country and around the world. The commodities boom and strong manufacturing growth in recent years has propelled strong growth in many of these industries. The wholesale trade industry in particular—the companies that buy goods directly from manufacturers and resell them to individual stores and companies—gained 36%, from $53.2 billion in 2001 to $72.3 billion in 2007. The transportation and warehousing industry advanced about 14% during the

Chart 3.2
Operating revenues and expenses, personal services industry

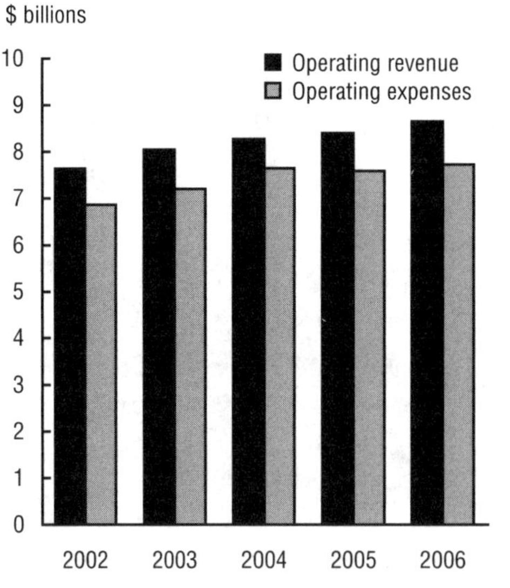

Source: Statistics Canada, CANSIM table 359-0001.

Table 3.a
GDP at basic prices

	1997	2007
	$ millions	
Wholesale trade	41,715	71,950
Retail trade	43,526	73,011
Finance and insurance	54,258	77,856

Source: Statistics Canada, CANSIM table 379-0027.

same period; although air, rail, water and truck transporters all grew, the air industry grew the fastest. Interestingly, the oil industry's spectacular growth had little effect on the oil and gas pipeline transportation industries, which saw only slight expansion during this period.

Companies turn to service providers for specialized skills and advice on a broad range of issues. The management, scientific and technical consulting services industry—which earns almost half its revenues in Ontario—posted 15% growth in 2006, earning nearly $11 billion in revenues. Environmental consulting and scientific and technical consulting providers saw revenues rise almost three times as fast as those of management consulting providers from 2004 to 2005.

Outsourcing for the family

With increasingly busy lives, Canadians often turn to the services sector to take care of regular chores and offer a little leisure and entertainment. Firms providing personal services earned $9.1 billion in 2005, up from $8.5 billion in 2004. Within the personal services industry, laundry and dry cleaning companies earned $2.1 billion in 2005, and personal care providers—such as hairdressers, spas and salons accounted for $4.1 billion in earnings.

Leaving the cooking and dishwashing to others has also become more popular for Canadians. From 2003 to 2006, revenues among full-service restaurants rose 17%

to $17.9 billion. Pubs, clubs and bars saw a slight drop in revenues over that period. However, spending in shopping malls and stores has grown. Record consumer spending helped the retail trade industry generate $72.9 billion in 2007, up 32% since 2001.

Real estate rides the wave

The real estate industry has been quick to cash in on the consumer spending boom by building or renting more retail space throughout the country. Rising demand for real estate space—both commercial and residential—helped the real estate rental and leasing and property management industries grow 6% in 2005: revenues reached $55.6 billion. While two-thirds of this total was generated in heavily-populated Ontario and Quebec, the fastest growth was seen in Western Canada.

About 42% of revenues in the industry came from the residential sector. Revenues of residential real estate lessors jumped 10% in both 2004 and 2005.

Chart 3.3
Operating revenues, real estate rental and leasing industries and property management

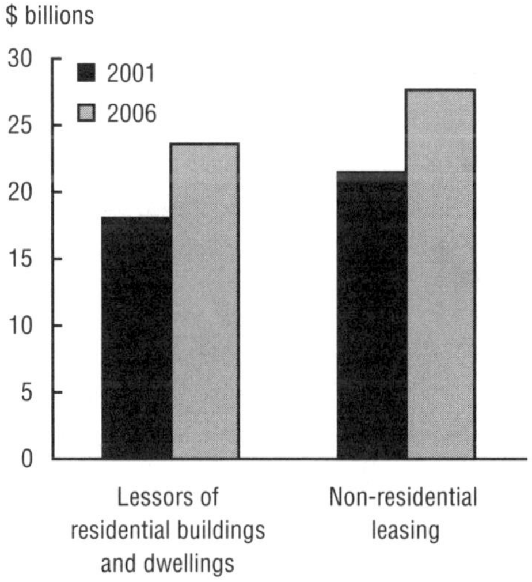

Source: Statistics Canada, CANSIM table 352-0003.

With continued low mortgage rates and steady economic growth, Canadians have remained active home buyers, keeping real estate agents, brokers and appraisers busy buying and selling homes. From 2003 to 2005 their industry's operating revenue has grown by 37%, reflecting both higher sales volumes and higher prices of real estate.

Salaries in services vary greatly

As a sector based on people serving people—from computer technicians to managers to hoteliers and restaurateurs—the service sector is very labour-intensive. More than three out of four of employed Canadians works in a service capacity.

Earnings in the services sector can vary. The hot housing market does not necessarily translate into large paycheques in the real estate industry. Salaried real estate workers earn an average of $709 per week in 2007—below the service sector average of $732.

Workers in food services and drinking places are the lowest paid workers in the service sector, earning about $294 every week. Retail trade workers aren't far ahead, pulling in an average of $486 per week, but this depends greatly on the type of store. Convenience store employees made about $378 per week in 2007, and gas station attendants made around $357 per week, whereas salespeople in furniture, electronics and car dealerships earned much more than the retail trade sector average.

The best salaries in the services sector are found in industries requiring specialized knowledge, such as information and culture, finance and insurance, professional, scientific and technical services, public administration, and management. Average weekly earnings in each of these industries in 2007 ranged from $945 to $998.

Even the best-paying service industries cannot compete with average weekly earnings in the goods sector. Workers in the goods sector pulled in an average of $1,235 a week in 2007.

Servicing Alberta's oil boom

Alberta's boom may be built on the oil patch, but it could not have happened without the services sector. Before even one drop of oil is extracted, a wide range of companies has done preparatory work. Thus, many service industries have seen revenues climb dramatically in Alberta.

With current high oil prices, companies are rushing in to set up new operations or expand existing ones. The impact ripples through the economy: each project brings new construction, more technology and more workers.

Specialized expertise has been in high demand. Building and running technology-intensive refineries and extraction facilities requires engineers, environmental scientists and technicians. In the engineering services industry, revenues in Alberta grew 19% in 2006 from 2005, compared with 6% in Ontario and 7% in Quebec. Measured on revenues by project, the largest revenue sources of the $15.4 billion engineering services industry were petroleum and petrochemicals (19%) and buildings and structures (15%).

The management, scientific and technical consulting services industry—firms that provide expert advice and assistance in areas such as environmental issues, security, and science and technology—saw business in Alberta expand by 16% from 2005 to 2006.

Finding workers was a challenge for the services sector. Recruiting and staffing new workers helped generate a 25% rise in revenues for Alberta's employment services industry in 2006. More workers create more demand for office space and housing: rental agencies and property managers saw higher than average growth, and real estate agents saw revenues climb 37% in 2006, and 20% the year before.

Chart 3.4
Operating revenue, selected service industries, Alberta

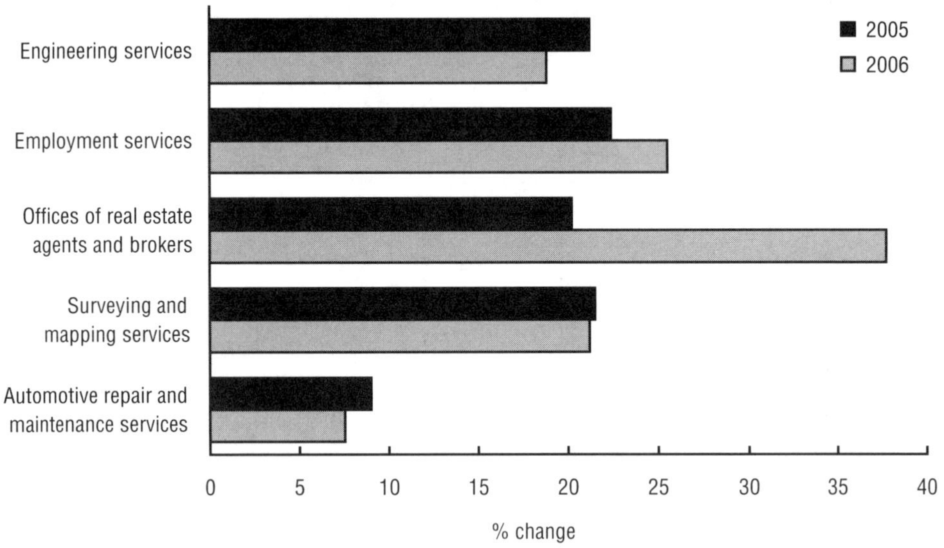

Source: Statistics Canada, CANSIM tables 352-0005, 360-0005, 361-0001 and 361-0006.

The printed word in the Internet age

As the Internet caught on and newspapers, magazines and publishers steadily expanded their web-based operations, many claimed the death of the printed word was approaching fast. In fact, the 'paperless world' boldly predicted with the coming of the Internet has not quite materialized: books, magazines and newspapers are still popular with Canadians.

Despite rising operating expenses, periodical publishers have distributed enough magazines and other regular publications to stay financially stable. Operating revenues—the vast majority coming from print and online advertising, subscriptions and circulation sales—have climbed each year, from $1.85 billion in 2004 to $2.07 billion in 2006. While expenses such as production, printing, marketing and distribution have climbed at a slightly faster pace, the periodicals industry maintained healthy profit margins over the same period. In 2006, periodical publishers earned about 11 cents of profit on every dollar earned.

Periodical publishers in Ontario enjoyed most of the growth, while publishers in Quebec, the Prairies and British Columbia and the Territories saw small increases. Revenues declined slightly in the Atlantic provinces.

Newspaper publishers have also stayed profitable. From 2002 to 2006, their revenues increased 15% to $5.3 billion. With operating expenses rising 14% during the same period, profit margins held steady at 13% in 2006.

Revenue growth in book publishing, however, has been weaker, rising 1.6% in 2005. Overall profits for the $2.4-billion industry increased, from $227 million in 2004 to $285 million in 2005.

Chart 3.5
Operating revenues for the periodical publishing industry, by region

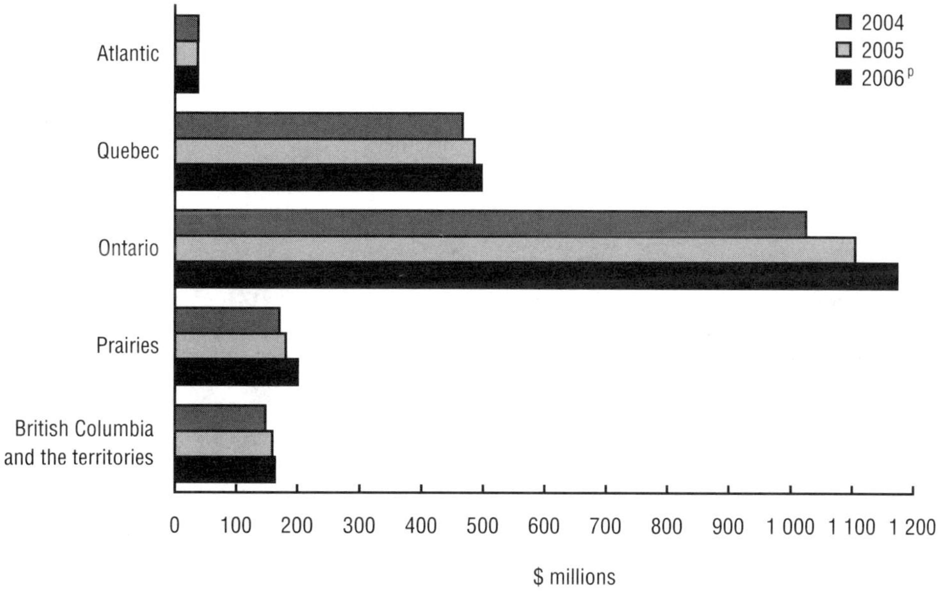

Source: Statistics Canada, Catalogue no. 87F0005XIE.

Table 3.1 Gross domestic product of goods- and services-producing industries, by province and territory, 2002 to 2006

	2002	2003	2004	2005	2006
	chained (1997) $ millions				
Canada					
Goods-producing industries	**311,482.0**	**315,935.0**	**325,202.0**	**331,595.0**	**334,264.0**
Services-producing industries	**672,177.0**	**687,921.0**	**709,800.0**	**732,506.0**	**758,840.0**
Newfoundland and Labrador					
Goods-producing industries	5,227.1	5,905.8	5,635.4	5,634.9	5,889.5
Services-producing industries	7,927.9	8,130.6	8,261.2	8,306.5	8,470.1
Prince Edward Island					
Goods-producing industries	746.4	733.9	787.3	785.0	811.0
Services-producing industries	2,201.3	2,258.1	2,307.1	2,364.4	2,408.6
Nova Scotia					
Goods-producing industries	5,586.0	5,609.2	5,511.4	5,499.8	5,339.8
Services-producing industries	16,899.2	17,274.3	17,542.9	17,927.7	18,424.7
New Brunswick					
Goods-producing industries	5,686.9	5,854.5	5,982.8	5,806.6	6,067.5
Services-producing industries	12,621.9	12,874.6	13,162.4	13,390.3	13,686.9
Quebec					
Goods-producing industries	71,095.8	70,903.6	72,345.6	72,916.1	72,865.6
Services-producing industries	138,578.6	141,548.1	145,585.2	149,345.2	153,300.1
Ontario					
Goods-producing industries	125,226.0	125,040.2	127,656.8	128,467.2	125,823.2
Services-producing industries	286,927.5	292,652.9	302,039.8	312,355.9	323,882.7
Manitoba					
Goods-producing industries	8,386.8	8,461.0	8,646.5	8,893.4	9,442.6
Services-producing industries	22,866.7	23,134.8	23,659.6	24,237.3	24,895.8
Saskatchewan					
Goods-producing industries	9,775.2	10,797.3	11,211.5	11,787.5	11,429.0
Services-producing industries	18,591.1	19,019.2	19,560.3	20,009.3	20,582.9
Alberta					
Goods-producing industries	47,005.6	48,225.3	50,909.0	53,330.5	56,636.5
Services-producing industries	74,393.2	77,440.1	80,764.8	84,734.7	90,744.4
British Columbia					
Goods-producing industries	30,966.9	31,574.8	33,217.2	34,326.9	35,332.1
Services-producing industries	87,937.4	90,218.3	93,612.8	96,851.4	100,747.3
Yukon					
Goods-producing industries	159.8	146.5	183.0	209.5	208.9
Services-producing industries	928.5	940.7	955.0	984.4	1,019.6
Northwest Territories					
Goods-producing industries	1,544.8	2,052.1	2,293.5	2,260.1	2,305.3
Services-producing industries	1,445.0	1,501.6	1,531.7	1,571.8	1,606.8
Nunavut					
Goods-producing industries	244.1	192.2	209.7	188.5	242.8
Services-producing industries	651.4	678.9	681.0	691.5	702.2

Note: North American Industry Classification System (NAICS), 2002.
Source: Statistics Canada, CANSIM table 379-0026.

Table 3.2 Average weekly earnings, by sector, 2003 to 2007

	2003	2004	2005	2006	2007
			$		
All industries (excluding unclassified)	**688.11**	**702.61**	**725.26**	**746.89**	**770.82**
Goods-producing sector	869.31	887.27	915.47	939.24	976.79
Forestry, logging and support	855.94	891.16	916.51	959.30	975.97
Mining and oil and gas extraction	1,185.86	1,251.77	1,314.5	1,350.71	1,409.12
Utilities	1,068.89	1,061.59	1,065.7	1,087.82	1,126.58
Construction	831.48	841.18	872.70	895.09	935.81
Manufacturing	846.09	862.57	886.82	906.09	938.14
Services-producing sector	636.64	650.83	672.89	694.77	716.48
Trade	554.41	563.26	581.08	600.23	613.13
Transportation and warehousing	762.37	757.03	775.95	784.71	800.02
Information and cultural industries	822.71	833.66	881.17	933.13	972.61
Finance and insurance	876.37	897.76	932.91	962.04	998.11
Real estate and rental and leasing	607.83	627.99	651.86	676.11	708.65
Professional, scientific and technical services	914.61	928.10	951.39	962.75	983.78
Management of companies and enterprises	859.07	863.11	907.21	948.43	944.54
Administrative and support, waste management and remediation services	542.33	560.65	578.83	601.91	637.97
Educational services	735.43	761.02	787.81	815.80	833.20
Health care and social assistance	612.15	636.54	654.94	678.91	703.04
Arts, entertainment and recreation	427.29	422.60	429.47	436.62	453.65
Accommodation and food services	270.11	279.59	291.47	304.36	324.34
Public administration	855.15	872.05	899.05	930.85	969.04
Other services	527.67	546.85	565.48	583.34	608.45

Notes: North American Industry Classification System (NAICS), 2002.
Data include overtime.
Source: Statistics Canada, CANSIM table 281-0027.

Table 3.3 Labour force employment, by job permanency, 2002 to 2007

	2002	2003	2004	2005	2006	2007
			thousands			
Permanent employees						
All industries	11,314.8	11,619.1	11,772.4	11,860.6	12,163.1	12,408.8
Goods-producing sector	2,894.1	2,946.9	2,968.7	2,946.5	2,944.1	2,914.4
Services-producing sector	8,420.7	8,672.2	8,803.7	8,914.1	9,219.0	9,494.4
Temporary employees						
All industries	1,681.2	1,651.3	1,721.2	1,797.6	1,823.2	1,842.6
Goods-producing sector	370.5	347.8	358.4	369.9	353.9	363.3
Services-producing sector	1,310.7	1,303.5	1,362.8	1,427.7	1,469.3	1,479.3

Note: North American Industry Classification System (NAICS), 2002.
Source: Statistics Canada, CANSIM table 282-0080.

Table 3.4 Operating statistics, selected services, 2002 to 2006

	2002			2003			2004		
	Revenue	Expenses	Profit margin	Revenue	Expenses	Profit margin	Revenue	Expenses	Profit margin
	$ millions		%	$ millions		%	$ millions		%
Personal and laundry services	7,640.3	6,861.5	10.2	8,044.7	7,199.7	10.5	8,282.7	7,641.3	7.7
Personal care	3,228.9	2,883.0	10.7	3,539.9	3,142.4	11.2	3,748.8	3,503.3	6.5
Funeral	1,313.8	1,178.2	10.3	1,399.6	1,253.0	10.5	1,425.9	1,283.1	10.0
Dry cleaning and laundry	1,885.3	1,707.9	9.4	1,920.8	1,740.8	9.4	1,881.6	1,717.7	8.7
Other personal services	1,212.3	1,092.4	9.9	1,184.4	1,063.5	10.2	1,226.4	1,137.2	7.3
Management consulting	6,710.0	5,410.0	19.4	6,634.4	5,449.6	17.9	6,683.0	5,304.4	20.6
Scientific and technical consulting	1,725.5	1,437.6	16.7	1,908.3	1,614.7	15.4	2,022.3	1,646.1	18.6
Offices of real estate agents and brokers	6,672.5	4,214.0	36.8	7,024.5	4,583.3	34.8	7,834.1	5,132.4	34.5
Offices of real estate appraisers	271.7	251.0	7.6	505.7	412.8	18.4	577.5	477.8	17.3
Automotive equipment rental and leasing	4,963.5	4,253.3	14.3	4,639.8	4,072.2	12.2	4,839.5	4,285.7	11.4
Consumer goods rental	1,940.8	1,820.5	6.2	1,893.4	1,766.4	6.7	1,979.0	1,834.8	7.3
General rental centres	271.8	238.6	12.2	271.0	237.1	12.5	318.3	280.0	12.0
Food services and drinking places	35,538.8	33,850.2	4.8	35,260.0	34,120.7	3.2	37,366.0	35,994.3	3.7
Full-service restaurants	15,993.2	15,283.4	4.4	15,380.0	14,998.6	2.5	16,465.6	16,016.2	2.7
Limited-service eating places	13,809.2	13,142.5	4.8	14,029.5	13,480.3	3.9	14,873.1	14,177.6	4.7
Special food services	2,915.3	2,775.1	4.8	2,973.7	2,840.0	4.5	3,095.7	2,982.2	3.7
Drinking places (alcoholic beverages)	2,821.2	2,649.2	6.1	2,876.8	2,801.7	2.6	2,931.6	2,818.4	3.9
Specialized design services	2,042.4	1,799.2	11.9	2,016.8	1,816.6	9.9	2,229.9	1,975.2	11.4
Interior design	561.2	514.0	8.4	541.6	494.6	8.7	618.1	540.3	12.6
Industrial design	163.4	133.9	18.1	209.3	196.2	6.3	222.5	210.5	5.4
Graphic design	1,195.5	1,043.4	12.7	1,135.1	1,003.8	11.6	1,246.2	1,098.6	11.8
Other specialized design services	122.2	107.9	11.7	130.7	122.0	6.6	143.1	125.7	12.1
Advertising agencies	2,218.7	1,990.3	10.3	2,151.6	1,963.7	8.7	2,231.0	1,988.7	10.9
Other advertising and advertising-related services	2,675.4	2,480.8	7.3	2,583.0	2,432.4	5.8	2,781.8	2,544.4	8.5
Architectural services	1,824.7	1,553.4	14.9	1,873.1	1,573.8	16.0	1,920.3	1,620.3	15.6
Engineering services	10,866.3	9,679.0	10.9	11,044.5	9,941.9	10.0	12,147.8	10,734.8	11.6
Surveying and mapping services	1,833.1	1,676.8	8.5	1,865.4	1,703.8	8.7	1,957.6	1,783.6	8.9
Accounting, tax preparation, bookkeeping and payroll services	7,854.6	5,550.6	29.3	8,244.0	5,837.7	29.2	8,713.3	6,082.3	30.2
Employment services	5,420.7	5,227.4	3.6	5,689.1	5,491.9	3.5	6,268.9	6,033.4	3.8
Lessors of residential buildings and dwellings (except social housing projects)	18,704.0	15,123.3	19.1	18,884.1	14,843.7	21.4	20,815.1	16,471.7	20.9
Non-residential leasing	22,999.3	18,324.0	20.3	24,735.8	18,804.0	24.0	26,347.3	20,812.4	21.0
Real estate property managers	2,278.8	1,951.9	14.3	2,771.6	2,353.7	15.1	3,450.7	2,897.8	16.0

See note and source at the end of table.

Table 3.4 Operating statistics, selected services, 2002 to 2006 (continued)

	2005			2006		
	Revenue	Expenses	Profit margin	Revenue	Expenses	Profit margin
	$ millions		%	$ millions		%
Personal and laundry services	8,402.5	7,584.9	9.7	8,656.4	7,727.7	10.7
Personal care	3,757.0	3,409.8	9.2	3,856.5	3,423.5	11.2
Funeral	1,452.9	1,285.1	11.6	1,484.3	1,330.8	10.3
Dry cleaning and laundry	1,936.7	1,758.0	9.2	2,046.4	1,828.2	10.7
Other personal services	1,256.0	1,132.1	9.9	1,269.2	1,145.2	9.8
Management consulting	7,116.9	5,585.3	21.5	7,836.8	6,228.0	20.5
Scientific and technical consulting	2,374.6	1,973.2	16.9	3,055.9	2,535.2	17.0
Offices of real estate agents and brokers	8,554.1	5,237.0	38.8	9,199.5	5,943.5	35.4
Offices of real estate appraisers	651.2	548.1	15.8	721.0	615.8	14.6
Automotive equipment rental and leasing	5,034.0	4,558.5	9.4	4,967.8	4,525.3	8.9
Consumer goods rental	2,112.1	1,995.9	5.5	2,123.8	2,011.7	5.3
General rental centres	366.5	322.0	12.1	385.5	357.9	7.2
Food services and drinking places	38,826.1	37,367.0	3.8	40,583.6	38,828.8	4.3
Full-service restaurants	17,270.5	16,743.1	3.1	17,961.5	17,407.1	3.1
Limited-service eating places	15,364.5	14,616.9	4.9	16,395.7	15,464.8	5.7
Special food services	3,378.0	3,286.1	2.7	3,587.2	3,437.0	4.2
Drinking places (alcoholic beverages)	2,813.1	2,720.9	3.3	2,639.2	2,519.8	4.5
Specialized design services	2,332.9	2,071.2	11.2	2,538.9	2,230.3	12.2
Interior design	682.2	616.7	9.6	814.9	731.9	10.2
Industrial design	228.6	207.3	9.3	243.1	213.2	12.3
Graphic design	1,265.6	1,106.8	12.6	1,311.3	1,134.7	13.5
Other specialized design services	156.5	140.4	10.3	169.5	150.5	11.2
Advertising agencies	2,388.8	2,186.8	8.5	2,478.1	2,233.3	9.9
Other advertising and advertising-related services	2,967.8	2,741.1	7.6	3,186.0	2,914.5	8.5
Architectural services	2,059.0	1,708.2	17.0	2,373.0	2,017.3	15.0
Engineering services	13,793.5	11,919.7	13.6	15,371.7	13,576.9	11.7
Surveying and mapping services	2,288.8	2,053.6	10.3	2,702.0	2,389.6	11.6
Accounting, tax preparation, bookkeeping and payroll services	9,910.3	6,924.0	30.1	11,108.9	7,817.5	29.6
Employment services	7,402.0	7,130.8	3.7	8,035.7	7,756.3	3.5
Lessors of residential buildings and dwellings (except social housing projects)	22,804.4	17,901.7	21.5	23,598.0	18,942.1	19.7
Non-residential leasing	26,029.4	19,909.1	23.5	27,659.3	21,083.9	23.8
Real estate property managers	3,802.3	3,131.0	17.7	4,381.9	3,673.1	16.2

Note: North American Industry Classification System (NAICS), 2002.
Source: Statistics Canada, CANSIM tables 352-0003, 352-0005, 352-0008, 352-0010, 355-0005, 359-0001, 360-0001, 360-0002, 360-0004, 360-0005, 360-0006, 360-0007 and 361-0001.

Table 3.5 Labour force employment, by sector and by province, 2007

	Canada	Newfoundland and Labrador	Prince Edward Island	Nova Scotia	New Brunswick	Quebec
	thousands					
All industries	**16,866.4**	**217.1**	**69.3**	**447.6**	**362.8**	**3,851.7**
Goods-producing sector	**3,993.0**	48.6	17.9	88.2	83.4	872.1
Agriculture	**337.2**	1.3	3.6	5.6	6.3	65.3
Forestry, fishing, mining, oil and gas	**339.3**	16.2	2.4	12.2	11.1	35.8
Utilities	**138.0**	1.7	0.3	1.9	4.1	32.3
Construction	**1,133.5**	13.5	5.0	27.2	24.0	195.5
Manufacturing	**2,044.9**	15.9	6.7	41.4	37.9	543.2
Services-producing sector	**12,873.5**	168.6	51.4	359.4	279.4	2,979.6
Trade	**2,682.4**	36.8	10.5	77.0	57.2	646.0
Transportation and warehousing	**822.8**	10.2	2.3	18.4	19.1	178.4
Finance, insurance, real estate and leasing	**1,060.4**	7.3	2.7	23.2	16.4	231.6
Professional, scientific and technical services	**1,136.9**	8.2	2.2	17.5	15.5	256.7
Business, building and other support services	**702.1**	8.6	2.8	27.1	20.2	147.4
Educational services	**1,183.2**	17.1	4.7	36.3	26.8	259.3
Health care and social assistance	**1,846.1**	31.5	8.3	61.5	48.0	455.2
Information, culture and recreation	**782.0**	8.3	2.7	19.5	13.4	171.9
Accommodation and food services	**1,069.4**	14.8	5.9	30.2	24.2	236.5
Public administration	**864.6**	16.5	6.6	28.1	21.4	219.8
Other services	**723.5**	9.3	2.8	20.5	17.1	176.7

	Ontario	Manitoba	Saskatchewan	Alberta	British Columbia
	thousands				
All industries	**6,593.8**	**596.5**	**501.8**	**1,959.4**	**2,266.3**
Goods-producing sector	1,552.4	144.8	132.8	557.0	495.7
Agriculture	96.1	28.7	43.8	50.4	36.2
Forestry, fishing, mining, oil and gas	34.8	6.4	22.1	151.0	47.3
Utilities	58.3	5.4	4.2	19.6	10.3
Construction	412.6	33.8	32.1	193.1	196.9
Manufacturing	950.6	70.6	30.7	142.9	205.1
Services-producing sector	5,041.4	451.7	368.9	1,402.4	1,770.6
Trade	1,027.2	89.4	82.6	290.6	365.0
Transportation and warehousing	304.1	34.3	24.6	105.7	125.6
Finance, insurance, real estate and leasing	474.4	34.9	26.6	98.4	145.0
Professional, scientific and technical services	477.8	25.4	21.1	146.3	166.3
Business, building and other support services	294.9	17.1	11.5	73.9	98.5
Educational services	466.1	46.5	40.2	130.0	156.1
Health care and social assistance	671.0	79.8	61.7	189.5	239.7
Information, culture and recreation	328.2	24.1	19.9	76.2	117.8
Accommodation and food services	399.7	38.0	30.8	116.8	172.7
Public administration	331.0	37.4	27.7	80.1	95.9
Other services	267.1	24.8	22.4	94.9	88.0

Note: North American Industry Classification System (NAICS), 2002.
Source: Statistics Canada, CANSIM table 282-0008.

Business performance and ownership

4

Overview

From mom-and-pop shops on Main Street to corporate headquarters on Bay Street, Canadian companies have played a big role in this country's robust economic growth over the last decade. By steadily increasing their operating revenues and profits, Canadian firms—the overwhelming majority of them small businesses with 19 or fewer employees—have helped fuel the economic boom by expanding, creating more jobs, and fostering consumer spending.

Setting new records for revenue

Collectively, these firms generated more than $3 trillion in revenue in 2006, hitting a new all-time high and continuing an unbroken run of revenue growth begun in 1999. Most industries saw their revenues climb in 2006, and operating profits—the amount of revenue left over once pre-tax expenses are accounted for—also pushed upwards. Canadian corporations earned operating profits of $269.1 billion in 2007. Growth in operating profit has been strong in recent years, rising 5.9% in 2007 and in the double digits in each of the preceding four years.

Thanks to trends in the overall economy, banking, retail and petroleum refining companies have been exceptionally strong performers. Low interest rates have helped banks generate more income from business loans, mortgages and other financial programs, and chartered banks saw operating profits rise nearly 19% to $32.5 billion in 2007.

With Canadians continuing to shop at a fast pace, the retail industry generated an all-time high of $16.5 billion in operating profits, up from $13.6 billion in 2006. Clothing, department and other general

Chart 4.1
Operating revenue and operating profit, all industries

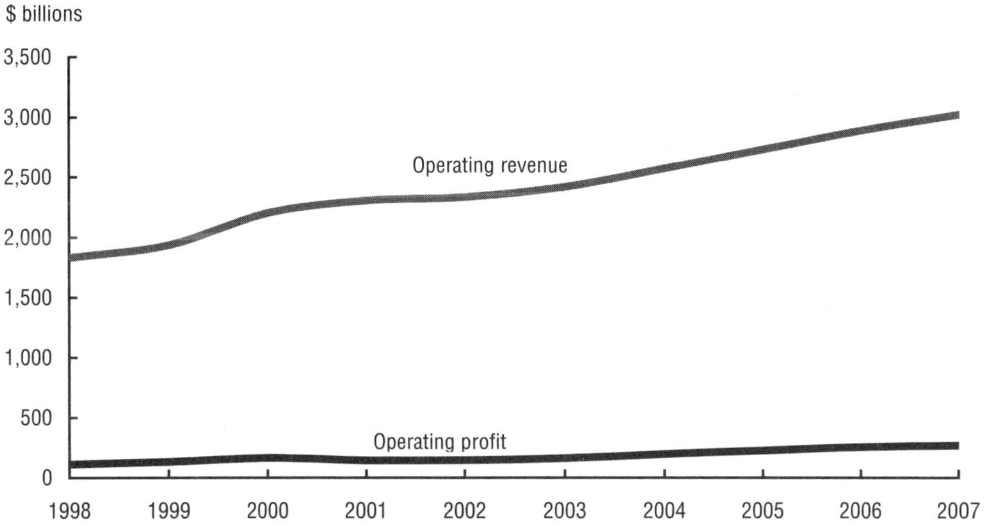

Note: Seasonally adjusted data.
Source: Statistics Canada, CANSIM table 187-0002.

merchandise stores did particularly well. And the steady increase in the price of oil meant that petroleum companies were extracting more revenue from every barrel—earning operating profits of $12.7 billion.

Other industries also saw big growth in operating profits in 2007. Food and soft drink producers' profits rose by one-fifth, and computer and electrical products manufacturers' by one-third. The wholesale trade industry saw widespread profit growth, expanding by one-eighth overall.

However, some industries saw their fortunes decline in 2007. Some manufacturing industries grew, but revenues for the manufacturing sector overall shrank in each quarter of 2007. Wood and paper manufacturers continued to struggle with weak demand and lower prices, and posted a 76% decline in profits. The year was also difficult for primary metal producers, who saw profits drop 34%, and the motor vehicles and parts manufacturing industry, whose profits fell 22%. Manufacturing was particularly hit by the higher value of the Canadian dollar in 2007.

Chart 4.2
Profit margin, all industries

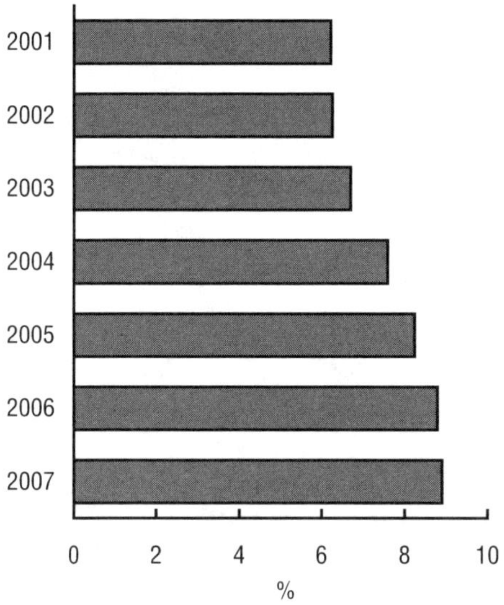

Note: Seasonally adjusted data.
Source: Statistics Canada, CANSIM table 187-0002.

Table 4.a
Business bankruptcies, selected industries

	2006	2007
	number	
All industries	**6,742**	**6,293**
Construction	1,152	1,091
Retail trade	987	895
Finance and insurance	80	87
Accommodation and food services	765	734

Source: Statistics Canada, CANSIM table 177-0007.

Traditional industries such as agriculture, forestry, fishing and hunting, and mining (other than oil and gas) also saw lower revenues over the course of the year.

Some companies are more profitable than others

The average profit margin for all Canadian industries rose for a sixth consecutive year in 2007, to 8.9%. In other words, for every $100 earned by providing goods or services, Canadian companies kept almost $9 as profit on average.

The companies that manage Canadians' money made up the industry with the highest profit margins. Firms in the finance and insurance industries outpaced all other Canadian companies, generating overall profit margins of 26.7% in 2007. The securities and financial investment subsector did particularly well, at 39%.

The real estate, mining, and oil and gas industries were also strong performers, keeping about 20%, 18% and 17% of their revenues as profits, respectively. Profit margins were slimmer than average for the wholesale trade, retail trade, construction and accommodation and food industries, at 4% to 5%. The utilities and manufacturing industries were slightly higher, tracking closer to the average.

More profit, more taxes

Healthy bottom lines for Canadian companies mean more taxes payable to the government, and in 2006 taxes owed by companies increased across the board. Taxable income rose 18.4% to $170.8 billion, generating $55.0 billion in total taxes. Of this total, the federal government claimed $37.3 billion, and the provinces $17.7 billion.

Non-financial companies generated $42.8 billion in taxes payable; the oil and gas industry accounted for $5.3 billion of that total. Of the $12.2 billion owed by the finance and insurance industries, banks accounted for $4.3 billion, or about one-third of the total.

To help maintain a competitive environment for businesses, the government also provides some tax relief. A total of $33.2 billion in tax credits were used in 2006, the largest portion of which was a federal tax abatement in recognition of the fact that provincial governments collect their own income taxes.

Chart 4.3
Foreign control in Canadian non-financial industries

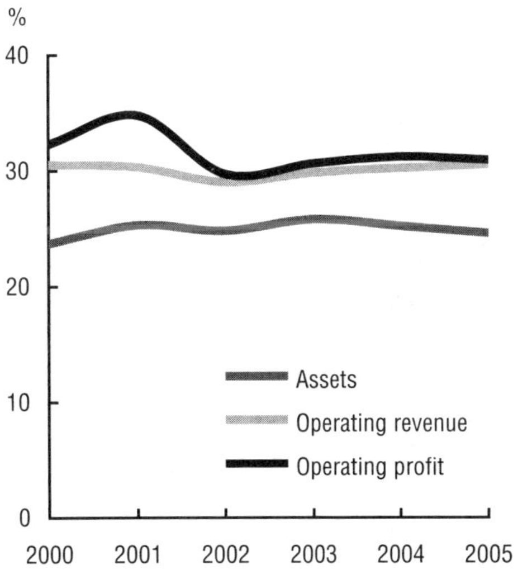

Source: Statistics Canada, CANSIM table 179-0004.

About $6 billion in tax credits were generated by deductions granted to small businesses.

Foreign control in the economy largely unchanged

Of the 1.2 million corporations doing business in Canada in 2005, less than 1% were foreign-controlled—a proportion that has changed very little over time. But despite their small numbers, foreign-controlled corporations are big players in the economy, accounting for about 30% of all operating revenues and 30% of all operating profits.

All told, these corporations generated $76.2 billion in profits in 2005. While profit growth for foreign-controlled companies was strong in 2005, at 12.5%, Canadian-controlled corporations saw their profits rise even faster, by 15.9%.

The large majority of foreign-controlled firms operate in the non-financial sector, as stricter regulations on foreign control in industries such as banking limit foreign investment. Nearly four-fifths of all profits generated by foreign firms came from the non-financial sector. However, profits for the foreign-controlled corporations that do operate in the finance and insurance industries have grown stronger than Canadian ones in recent years.

Since setting up operations in another country requires considerable resources, foreign-controlled corporations are typically larger than Canadian firms. Other differences also set them apart from Canadian companies: foreign-controlled plants are generally larger, have a higher rate of labour productivity, pay more per worker and have a higher percentage of white-collar workers. Foreign firms are also more likely to diversify across different industries.

Foreign-controlled firms create new head-office jobs in Canada: about 60% of new head-office jobs from 1999 to 2005 were in foreign firms. In fact, foreign takeovers during this period have resulted in more being opened than being closed.

Shifting levels of productivity

Productivity is about how efficient a business produces goods or services. The better use a company makes of the materials it uses and the people it employs, the more productive it is. And as labour productivity increases, companies produce more with fewer hours worked—improving their competitiveness and their profitability.

Thus, the productivity of a company, industry or even a country can be a key indicator of economic health. And while productivity of Canadian businesses has grown almost every year over the past decade, the 0.6% increase in 2007 was the slowest growth in the three last years, and significantly lower than the peak of 3.5% seen in 2000.

Labour productivity grew slightly faster in Canada's services sector than in the goods-producing sector in 2007. Wholesale and retail trade accounted for most of the increase among service industries, posting 2.4% and 3.5% jumps, respectively. The financial industry also raised its productivity, by 1.5%.

The utilities industry saw the largest increase in 2007, at 5.3%. Hours worked in manufacturing decreased more than production in 2007, which resulted in a 1.9% gain in manufacturing productivity.

For U.S. businesses, the labour productivity rose 1.9% in 2007. While Canada led the United States in productivity growth in 2005 and 2006, the gap swung back in favour of the United States in 2007, largely because the number of hours worked by Canadians rose faster than those of U.S. workers.

Wages increased at an above-average pace in 2007, and the value of the loonie rose against the U.S. greenback. So, Canada's unit labour cost—measured by the cost of workers' wages and benefits per unit of economic output, in U.S. dollars—jumped 9.5%, compared with 3.1% south of the border.

Chart 4.4
Labour productivity, hours worked and real gross domestic product

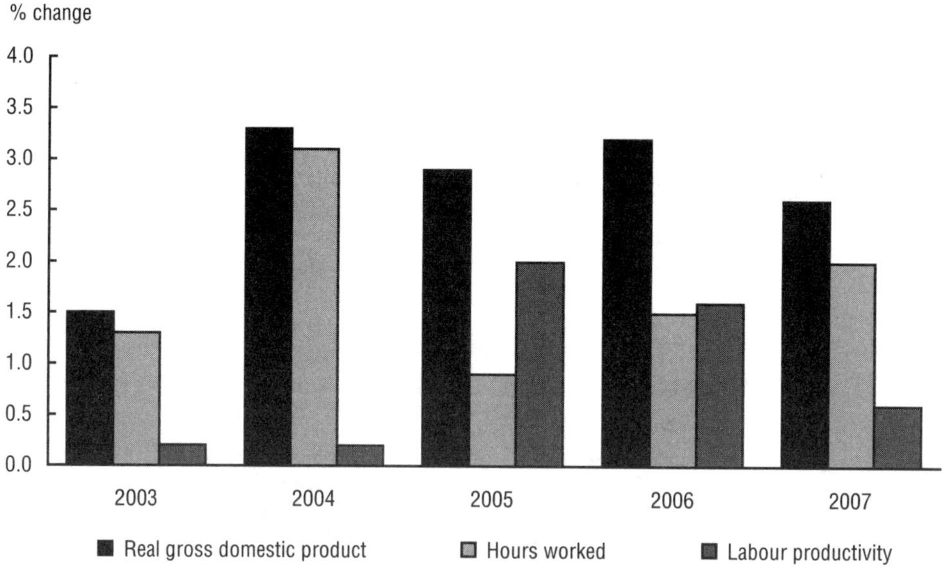

Source: Statistics Canada, CANSIM table 383-0008.

Borrowing to grow

Just as individual Canadians borrow money to purchase a home or car, businesses borrow to invest in plants and machinery, open new stores, or develop new products and services. In recent years, Canadian companies have taken advantage of historically low interest rates and the booming economy, and have steadily increased business debt to expand their operations.

The debt load held by Canadian businesses increased for the third straight year in 2006, growing 10.7% to $444.3 billion. All told, about two million business loans were outstanding at the end of the year. Businesses turned to banks, credit unions and caisse populaires to supply three-quarters of these funds: finance companies, venture capitalists and insurance companies provided the rest.

The largest businesses did the most borrowing in 2006, accounting for 57% of all outstanding debt and for most of the increase in business debt over the previous year. Small and medium-sized enterprises accounted for 21.4% of all outstanding debt.

Not surprisingly, the most capital-intensive industries—those that rely heavily on expensive machinery, assets or property to conduct their operations—have the most debt. Canada's agriculture, manufacturing, and real estate, rental and leasing industries were the three largest borrowers in 2006, each accounting for between 11% and 12% of all outstanding business debt. However, the knowledge-based industries accounted for 6.5% of total debt.

New financing allows businesses to grow, but not all ventures are successful. While the rate of Canadian business bankruptcies hit a 25-year low in 2005, a number of companies fail every year. In 2007, 6,293 businesses went bankrupt: construction companies, retail outlets, transportation firms and manufacturers accounted for half of all business failures.

Chart 4.5
Outstanding business debt, by province and territory

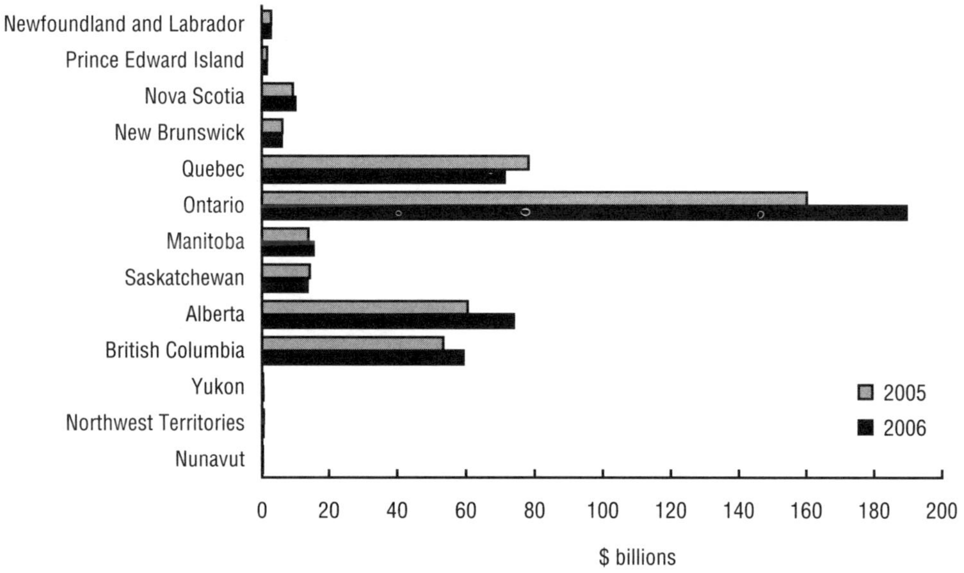

Source: Statistics Canada, Survey of Suppliers of Business Financing.

Table 4.1 Businesses, by province and territory, 1995 to 2005

	Canada	Newfoundland and Labrador	Prince Edward Island	Nova Scotia	New Brunswick	Quebec
	thousands					
1995	**961.4**	21.6	7.6	32.0	27.8	227.5
1996	**963.0**	20.4	7.5	31.4	27.5	227.3
1997	**983.9**	20.4	7.6	32.1	27.6	228.0
1998	**1,004.0**	20.4	7.7	32.4	28.2	231.3
1999	**1,016.1**	20.2	7.7	32.9	28.3	233.3
2000	**1,019.8**	19.8	7.3	32.2	27.8	232.8
2001	**1,031.0**	19.8	7.2	32.2	27.8	232.3
2002	**1,042.2**	19.5	7.2	31.9	27.6	232.6
2003	**1,056.9**	19.8	7.1	31.9	27.3	233.6
2004	**1,090.5**	20.3	7.1	32.4	27.7	237.4
2005	**1,120.8**	20.4	7.0	32.4	28.0	239.9

	Ontario	Manitoba	Saskatchewan	Alberta	British Columbia	Territories[1]
	thousands					
1995	303.5	35.7	40.7	112.4	148.9	3.7
1996	303.5	35.7	40.9	114.4	150.6	3.8
1997	311.0	36.1	41.6	121.1	154.6	3.8
1998	319.7	36.7	41.2	126.6	156.0	3.8
1999	326.7	36.8	40.8	129.5	156.1	3.8
2000	331.6	36.1	40.1	132.4	155.7	4.0
2001	337.2	36.4	40.0	137.1	156.9	4.1
2002	342.7	36.8	39.9	140.6	159.2	4.2
2003	349.7	36.8	39.8	144.2	162.4	4.3
2004	363.3	37.6	40.0	150.0	170.2	4.5
2005	374.4	38.3	40.1	157.8	177.9	4.6

Note: A firm may exist in more than one province and, therefore, firm counts at the provincial and at the national levels may vary.

1. Includes data for Yukon, Northwest Territories and Nunavut.

Source: Statistics Canada, Catalogue no. 61-534-XIE.

Table 4.2 Bankruptcies, by sector and by province and territory, 2007

	Canada	Newfoundland and Labrador	Prince Edward Island	Nova Scotia	New Brunswick	Quebec
	number					
All sectors	**6,307**	52	32	206	151	2,037
Agriculture, forestry, fishing and hunting	**298**	7	7	12	13	88
Mining and oil and gas extraction	**28**	0	0	0	0	5
Utilities	**5**	0	0	0	0	3
Construction	**1,095**	8	3	35	22	235
Manufacturing	**591**	1	1	13	5	240
Wholesale trade	**312**	2	3	3	10	132
Retail trade	**895**	11	5	22	21	288
Transportation and warehousing	**608**	4	0	23	27	166
Information and cultural industries	**92**	0	0	5	2	39
Finance and insurance	**87**	1	0	4	2	47
Real estate and rental and leasing	**159**	0	1	7	7	54
Professional, scientific and technical services	**401**	2	1	18	7	135
Management of companies and enterprises	**36**	0	0	0	1	17
Administrative and support, waste management and remediation services	**270**	1	1	14	8	82
Educational services	**37**	1	0	0	0	11
Health care and social assistance	**74**	0	1	4	1	23
Arts, entertainment and recreation	**146**	2	0	8	5	34
Accommodation and food services	**733**	7	4	20	7	297
Public administration	**8**	1	0	0	0	6
Other services (excluding public administration)	**432**	4	5	18	13	135

	Ontario	Manitoba	Saskatchewan	Alberta	British Columbia	Territories[1]
	number					
All sectors	2,595	102	204	451	470	7
Agriculture, forestry, fishing and hunting	57	15	57	24	18	0
Mining and oil and gas extraction	1	1	1	14	5	1
Utilities	0	0	0	0	2	0
Construction	469	14	40	171	98	0
Manufacturing	241	3	15	28	44	0
Wholesale trade	123	2	2	16	19	0
Retail trade	420	15	17	35	60	1
Transportation and warehousing	259	21	19	46	43	0
Information and cultural industries	37	0	2	1	6	0
Finance and insurance	23	0	1	2	7	0
Real estate and rental and leasing	69	1	3	10	7	0
Professional, scientific and technical services	175	1	6	16	39	1
Management of companies and enterprises	13	0	1	1	3	0
Administrative and support, waste management and remediation services	107	1	5	28	22	1
Educational services	19	0	1	1	4	0
Health care and social assistance	32	0	2	5	6	0
Arts, entertainment and recreation	72	2	4	6	13	0
Accommodation and food services	293	15	21	25	41	3
Public administration	1	0	0	0	0	0
Other services (excluding public administration)	184	11	7	22	33	0

Note: North American Industry Classification System (NAICS), 2002.

1. Includes data for Yukon, Northwest Territories and Nunavut.

Source: Statistics Canada, CANSIM table 177-0006.

Table 4.3 Businesses, by firm size, 1985 to 2005

	All businesses	0 to 19 employees	20 to 99 employees	100 to 499 employees	500 employees and over
			thousands		
1985	**810.2**	759.3	42.7	6.5	1.7
1986	**835.6**	781.5	45.3	7.0	1.8
1987	**866.3**	808.6	48.6	7.3	1.8
1988	**889.8**	829.7	50.8	7.5	1.9
1989	**908.8**	848.7	50.7	7.5	1.9
1990	**918.0**	858.2	50.4	7.5	1.9
1991	**906.7**	842.8	53.4	8.4	2.1
1992	**907.2**	845.5	51.8	7.9	2.0
1993	**909.7**	847.2	52.5	8.0	2.0
1994	**917.3**	853.5	53.3	8.4	2.1
1995	**922.2**	856.5	54.9	8.7	2.1
1996	**924.1**	857.2	56.0	8.8	2.2
1997	**943.5**	874.2	57.9	9.2	2.2
1998	**956.3**	885.3	59.2	9.5	2.3
1999	**968.4**	896.8	59.5	9.8	2.3
2000	**978.8**	904.3	61.8	10.3	2.4
2001	**988.9**	912.1	63.5	10.8	2.5
2002	**999.3**	920.4	65.4	11.0	2.5
2003	**1,013.3**	933.3	66.4	11.1	2.5
2004	**1,045.0**	964.4	66.7	11.3	2.5
2005	**1,074.9**	993.5	67.4	11.5	2.6

Note: Data prior to 1991 were backcasted from a model.

Source: Statistics Canada, Catalogue no. 61-534-XIE.

Table 4.4 Corporations carrying on activities in Canada, major financial statistics, by country of control, 2001 to 2005

	2001	2002	2003	2004	2005
			$ millions		
Canadian- and foreign-controlled corporations					
Assets	4,195,238	4,372,325	4,580,424	4,990,267	5,235,806
Operating revenue	2,401,139	2,430,061	2,514,887	2,671,764	2,848,520
Operating profit	170,466	170,455	188,832	217,529	249,887
			% change		
Assets	5.9	4.2	4.8	8.9	4.9
Operating revenue	4.0	1.2	3.5	6.2	6.6
Operating profit	-11.0	0.0	10.8	15.2	14.9
			$ millions		
Canadian-controlled corporations					
Assets	3,239,003	3,380,500	3,573,855	3,911,392	4,126,848
Operating revenue	1,672,272	1,713,607	1,767,131	1,869,121	1,997,197
Operating profit	119,264	121,675	133,262	149,758	173,643
Private corporations					
Assets	2,896,124	3,028,373	3,221,276	3,550,860	3,767,819
Operating revenue	1,583,575	1,627,343	1,677,966	1,766,939	1,890,670
Operating profit	93,702	95,835	105,873	126,014	148,033
Government business corporations					
Assets	342,879	352,127	352,578	360,531	359,028
Operating revenue	88,697	86,264	89,165	102,182	106,527
Operating profit	25,562	25,839	27,389	23,744	25,610
Foreign-controlled corporations					
Assets	956,235	991,825	1,006,570	1,078,875	1,108,959
Operating revenue	728,867	716,454	747,756	802,643	851,323
Operating profit	51,202	48,780	55,571	67,771	76,244
United States corporations					
Assets	609,557	637,457	622,361	657,637	659,809
Operating revenue	482,955	469,367	472,522	505,923	536,128
Operating profit	34,460	31,207	35,771	44,164	48,448
European Union corporations					
Assets	258,313	261,943	282,095	320,463	344,923
Operating revenue	155,760	155,996	179,360	191,724	207,331
Operating profit	11,850	12,666	14,090	16,739	19,737
Other foreign corporations					
Assets	88,365	92,425	102,114	100,776	104,227
Operating revenue	90,153	91,091	95,874	104,996	107,864
Operating profit	4,892	4,908	5,709	6,867	8,060

Source: Statistics Canada, CANSIM table 179-0004.

Table 4.5 Balance sheet for the banking sector, 2003 to 2007

	2003	2004	2005	2006	2007
			$ millions		
Assets	**1,408,877**	**1,565,617**	**1,649,313**	**1,842,850**	**2,055,589**
Cash and deposits	22,446	44,520	39,599	41,572	46,123
Accounts receivable and accrued revenue	5,137	4,542	5,462	5,800	8,136
Investments and accounts with affiliates	81,370	91,455	85,561	98,899	100,520
Portfolio investments	257,589	277,946	316,657	375,913	415,880
Loans	869,138	970,474	1,041,937	1,153,926	1,269,534
Mortgage	436,101	477,267	515,635	557,206	611,601
Non-mortgage	433,037	493,207	526,302	596,720	657,932
Allowance for losses on investments and loans	-10,765	-8,100	-7,427	-6,443	-6,074
Bank customers' liabilities under acceptances	33,102	33,769	39,434	52,936	60,839
Net capital assets	8,877	8,796	9,222	9,670	10,217
Other assets	141,983	142,216	118,868	110,573	150,412
Liabilities	**1,315,616**	**1,466,510**	**1,536,139**	**1,712,014**	**1,922,333**
Deposits	965,529	1,064,463	1,141,463	1,248,120	1,396,306
Accounts payable and accrued liabilities	12,270	11,090	11,722	15,143	17,539
Loans and accounts with affiliates	17,962	19,115	11,466	11,365	15,611
Borrowings	25,934	29,588	33,446	37,317	45,657
Loans and overdrafts	2,999	5,012	6,897	7,802	8,994
From banks	935	283	608	574	763
From others	2,064	4,729	6,289	7,228	8,232
Bankers' acceptances and paper	0	0	0	0	0
Bonds and debentures	20,692	22,618	25,495	28,060	31,279
Mortgages	231	72	145	251	1,001
Future income tax	600	694	322	336	256
Bank customers' liabilities under acceptances	33,104	33,769	39,310	52,936	60,905
Other liabilities	260,216	307,792	298,410	346,797	386,059
Equity	**93,261**	**99,107**	**113,173**	**130,835**	**133,256**
Share capital	37,176	36,672	42,018	44,145	47,547
Contributed surplus	5,684	6,487	9,410	10,128	7,456
Retained earnings	50,401	55,949	61,745	76,562	78,253

Notes: North American Industry Classification System (NAICS), 2002.
Balance sheet values reflect the fourth-quarter levels.
Includes Canadian-only business of chartered banks, independent trust and mortgage companies, credit unions and other depository credit intermediation.

Source: Statistics Canada, CANSIM table 187-0001.

Table 4.6 Balance sheet for the insurance sector, 2003 to 2007

	2003	2004	2005	2006	2007
			$ millions		
Assets	**325,419**	**345,653**	**361,903**	**391,640**	**426,496**
Cash and deposits	5,351	6,907	5,717	6,223	6,032
Accounts receivable and accrued revenue	21,195	21,613	19,353	19,447	21,795
Investments and accounts with affiliates	32,818	35,600	43,578	54,830	60,026
Portfolio investments	186,503	198,386	208,852	225,414	239,545
Loans	44,269	45,240	45,198	46,938	47,557
Mortgage	39,366	39,947	39,778	40,860	40,843
Non-mortgage	4,903	5,293	5,420	6,078	6,714
Allowance for losses on investments and loans	-93	-126	-52	-54	-60
Bank customers' liabilities under acceptances	0	0	0	0	0
Net capital assets	8,155	7,686	7,933	8,222	9,008
Other assets	27,220	30,346	31,324	30,621	42,593
Liabilities	**250,958**	**261,586**	**273,670**	**289,153**	**310,733**
Deposits	4,962	5,159	5,335	5,549	5,938
Actuarial liabilities of insurers	144,992	149,839	152,698	158,559	176,580
Accounts payable and accrued liabilities	55,533	60,248	60,339	61,940	65,646
Loans and accounts with affiliates	4,221	4,667	8,171	11,868	13,048
Borrowings	8,645	8,088	8,807	9,789	12,929
Loans and overdrafts	4,521	3,458	2,772	3,384	3,104
From banks	3,305	1,489	1,088	1,360	1,296
From others	1,216	1,970	1,684	2,024	1,807
Bankers' acceptances and paper	5	5	6	6	6
Bonds and debentures	4,979	5,104	5,202	6,332	6,788
Mortgages	202	206	236	319	427
Future income tax	-93	-394	-499	-680	66
Other liabilities	32,699	33,978	38,820	42,127	36,526
Equity	**74,461**	**84,068**	**88,233**	**102,487**	**115,762**
Share capital	22,458	26,485	26,514	28,616	29,777
Contributed surplus	2,448	1,831	2,091	2,377	2,372
Retained earnings	49,555	55,752	59,629	71,494	83,613

Notes: North American Industry Classification System (NAICS), 2002.
Balance sheet values reflect the fourth-quarter levels.
Includes Canadian-only business of all insurers including reinsurers.

Source: Statistics Canada, CANSIM table 187-0001.

Table 4.7 Business credit, annual average for selected sources, 2003 to 2007

	2003	2004	2005	2006	2007
			$ millions		
All business credit	**904,791**	**945,556**	**1,005,261**	**1,063,287**	**1,141,016**
Short-term business credit	254,876	252,218	266,636	297,539	338,667
Business loans					
Chartered banks	122,012	125,688	135,757	147,619	166,498
Other institutions	24,816	27,032	29,841	33,082	36,000
Chartered bank foreign currency loans to residents	18,534	18,064	17,870	20,054	23,354
Bankers' acceptances	39,308	35,929	37,878	48,362	60,433
Adjustment to short-term business credit	671	-1,322	-1,634	-1,121	-1,089
Long-term business credit	649,915	693,337	738,624	765,748	802,349
Non-residential mortgages					
Chartered banks	16,965	17,731	18,621	19,629	20,478
Trust and mortgage loan companies	553	668	1,039	1,275	1,764
Credit unions and caisses populaires	11,698	12,263	13,785	15,856	17,624
Life insurance companies	24,800	26,178	27,499	28,242	28,306
Leasing receivables					
Chartered banks	4,807	5,070	5,555	6,384	7,224
Trust and mortgage loan companies	25	15	46	58	59
Other business credit					
Bonds and debentures	241,212	253,049	262,235	258,304	266,457
Equity and other	274,418	286,190	297,206	300,958	310,184

Source: Statistics Canada, CANSIM table 176-0023.

Children and youth

5

Overview

On July 1, 2007, Canada had about 10.1 million people under the age of 25. About 5.6 million of them were under 15 years old, 2.2 million were aged 15 to 19, and 2.3 million were aged 20 to 24. These children and youth made up 31% of the Canadian population.

The number of youth under 25 in the Canadian population increased 1% during the last decade, but changes in different age groups have varied. For example, the number of young children under 5 fell from 2.0 million in 1994 to 1.7 million in 2007. During the same period, the number of youth aged 20 to 24 increased from 2.0 million in 1994 to 2.3 million in 2007.

Although most young people under 25 were born in Canada, many were foreign-born and are immigrants. In 2006, 894,965 youth under 25 were immigrants, which comprises 9% of youth.

Immigrant youth are concentrated in Canada's most populated census metropolitan areas (CMAs). In the Toronto and Vancouver CMAs, slightly more than one-fifth of the population under 25 was foreign-born in 2006. However, 2% of youth were immigrants in Peterborough, Ontario; Saint John, New Brunswick; and Trois-Rivières, Quebec—three of the least populated CMAs in Canada.

More children living with common-law parents

Most children still live with married parents; however, more and more children live with common-law parents. In 1981, 81% of children under 15 lived with married parents, and 5% lived with common-law parents. In 2006, 66% of children in this age group lived with married parents and 15% with common-law parents—the latter share is a

Chart 5.1
Population under 25

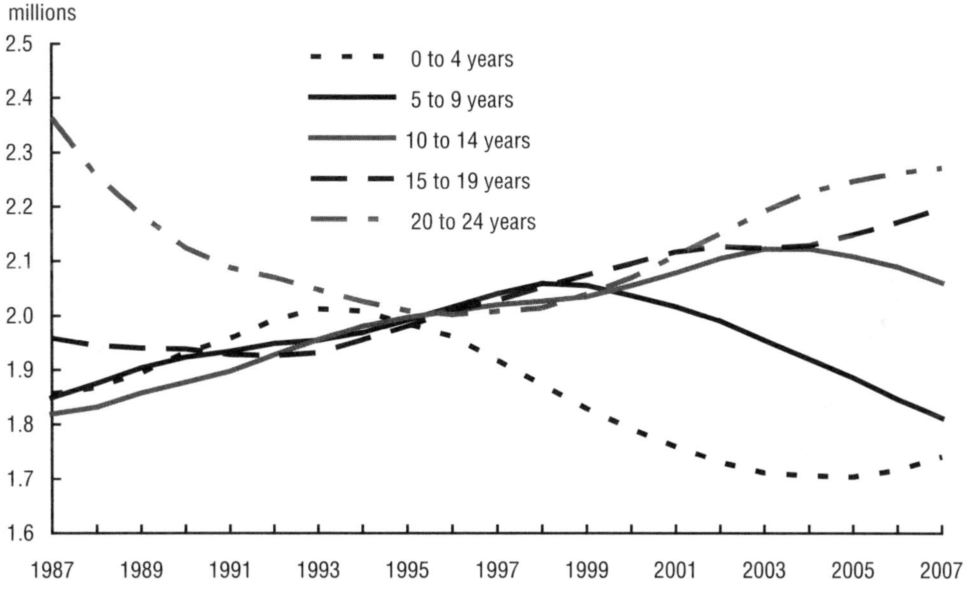

Note: Population as of July 1.
Source: Statistics Canada, CANSIM table 051-0001.

threefold increase from 1981. Common-law couples tend to be less stable and less likely to have children, according to the 2006 General Social Survey (GSS), but they tend to be younger than married couples and their children also tend to be younger.

The proportion of children living with lone parents has also grown since the mid-1980s. About 18.3% of children under 15 lived with lone parents in 2006, a slight increase from 17.8% in 2001.

Although rare, some children live under the same roof with at least one grandparent. Most of these children, 181,700 of them in 2006, lived with parents and grandparents in an extended family arrangement. A smaller number, 28,200, lived only with one or more grandparent: this group made up 0.5% of children under 15. The proportions of children living in either of these arrangements has changed little since 2001.

Most young adults aged 20 to 24 live with their parents, and they are more likely to do so today than 25 years ago. In 2006, 60% of the 2.3 million young adults in this age group lived in the parental home, compared

Chart 5.2
Types of families with children aged 15 and younger

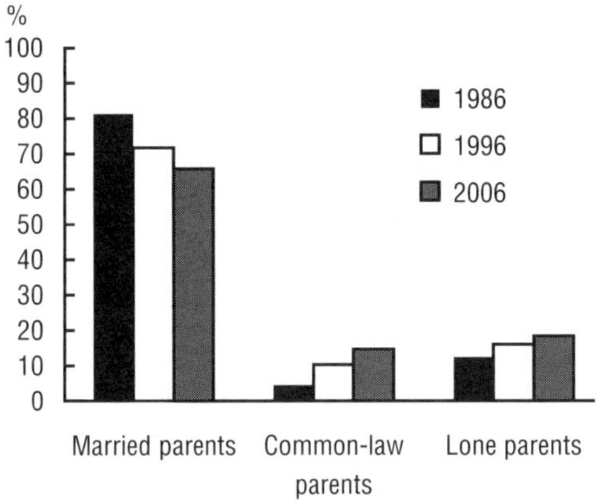

Note: Historical comparisons for census families, particularly lone-parent families, must be interpreted with caution because of conceptual changes in 2001.
Source: Statistics Canada, Catalogue no. 97-553-XIE.

Table 5.a
Population under 25, 2007

	Both sexes	Males	Females
		number	
Total	**10,082,417**	**5,162,913**	**4,919,504**
0 to 4	1,740,197	890,661	849,536
5 to 9	1,812,357	927,173	885,184
10 to 14	2,060,492	1,057,116	1,003,376
15 to 19	2,197,739	1,126,189	1,071,550
20 to 24	2,271,632	1,161,774	1,109,858

Source: Statistics Canada, CANSIM table 051-0001.

with 49% in 1986. Only 18% of young adults aged 20 to 24 were in a couple in 2006, compared with 28% in 1986.

Women having children later

Women are waiting longer to have children, and this creates a wider age gap between mother and child. In 2003, the average age at which women had their first child was 28 years, up from an average age of 24 years during the 1960s.

Married mothers of children aged 4 and under are slightly older: in 2006, the most common age group for married mothers of young children was 30 to 34 years, while it was 25 to 29 years for lone mothers and mothers living common-law.

A growing proportion of children under 5 have a mother in her forties, whereas the proportion of children with a younger mother is decreasing. In 2001, 8% of children under 5 had a mother aged 40 to 49; this proportion reached 9% in 2006. Conversely, in 2001, 12% of children in this age group had a mother who was under 25, compared with 10% in 2006.

Fewer children in low-income families

Fewer children under 18 lived in low-income families in 2005 than in 1996. An estimated 788,000 children under 18 lived in low-income families in 2005, down from

1.3 million in 1996. About 12% of children under 18 lived in a low-income family in 2005, well under the record of 19% in 1996.

In 2005, of 320,000 children living in low-income families, slightly less than half lived in female lone-parent families. The low-income rate of children in female lone-parent families was more than four times that of children living in two-parent families. However, the low-income rate for these children fell in the space of a year from 40% in 2004 to 33% in 2005.

Active and healthy children

Many children aged 4 and 5 participated in regularly scheduled activities outside school hours. In 2004/2005, participation in sports with a coach or instructor was the most common activity: 38% of girls and 46% of boys took part at least once a week. The boys' share was significantly higher than in 2000/2001, when it was 38%.

In 2004/2005, girls (43%) were more likely than boys (21%) to take regular lessons in

Chart 5.3
Children living in low-income families

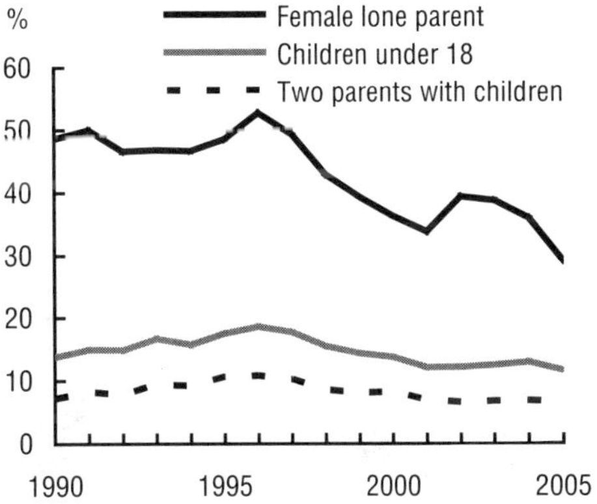

Note: Data for male lone-parent families are not shown because the data are not reliable for certain years.
Source: Statistics Canada CANSIM tables 202-0802 and 202-0804.

dance, gymnastics or martial arts. The share of girls practising these activities was up sharply from 37% in 2000/2001.

A little less popular were music, art and other non-sport activities, which attracted about 11% of boys and 17% of girls in 2004/2005. About 15% of 4- and 5-year-olds participated in clubs, groups or community programs.

According to their parents, the majority of 4-year-olds looked at magazines, comics or books by themselves every day at home, but a gender gap is apparent: 77% of girls spent time with such printed materials every day, compared with 61% of boys.

Young children who are surrounded by reading material, who see adults reading regularly and who are read to at a very early age often develop their own appetite for reading. This seems to have been the environment for most 4- and 5-year-olds in 2004/2005: about 60% had an adult read to them every day.

Canadian parents of 4- and 5-year-olds generally reported that their children were in good health in 2004/2005. Most boys (89%) and girls (92%) were in 'excellent' or 'very good' health, according to their parents.

However, asthma and chronic allergies are prevalent among today's children. In 2004/2005, 18% of boys and 9% of girls had received a diagnosis of asthma at some point in their lives. Sixteen percent of boys and 10% of girls had chronic allergies, according to their parents.

Only small proportions of 4- and 5-year-olds had physical challenges such as difficulty seeing, hearing, walking or being understood when speaking. For example, 8% of boys and 5% of girls aged 4 and 5 had difficulty being understood when speaking.

Busy teenagers

Many teenagers aged 15 to 19 have schedules just as busy as those of some adults. In 2005, these teenagers did an average 9.2 hours of school work, homework, paid work and housework on school days, and 3.5 hours on weekends. This was equal to a 50-hour work week, the same time that adults aged 20 to 64 spent on these activities.

From 1986 to 2005, the number of hours that teenagers devoted to both unpaid and paid work remained relatively stable. However, their hours spent on paid work increased during those years. In 2005, the average amount of time spent at paid work was around 7.6 hours a week, 2.0 hours more than in 1986.

After school attendance, homework was the most time-consuming unpaid activity for teens: 60% averaged 2 hours and 20 minutes of homework every day; as well, 39% of teenagers spent 1 hour per day doing household chores.

Teenagers were much more likely to do homework if their parents had a university education, if they lived in a two-parent family in which the parents have not divorced, or if their parents were foreign-born. Boys did much less homework than girls, and teenagers who devoted 20 or more hours per week to paid work did significantly less homework than those without a job.

Teenagers can feel stressed because of the responsibilities of daily work, paid or unpaid. Teenagers who spend more than 2.5 hours a day doing homework and who have a paid job of 20 or more hours a week have higher stress levels, according to a study based on the Labour Force Survey.

Chart 5.4
Teenagers' daily activities

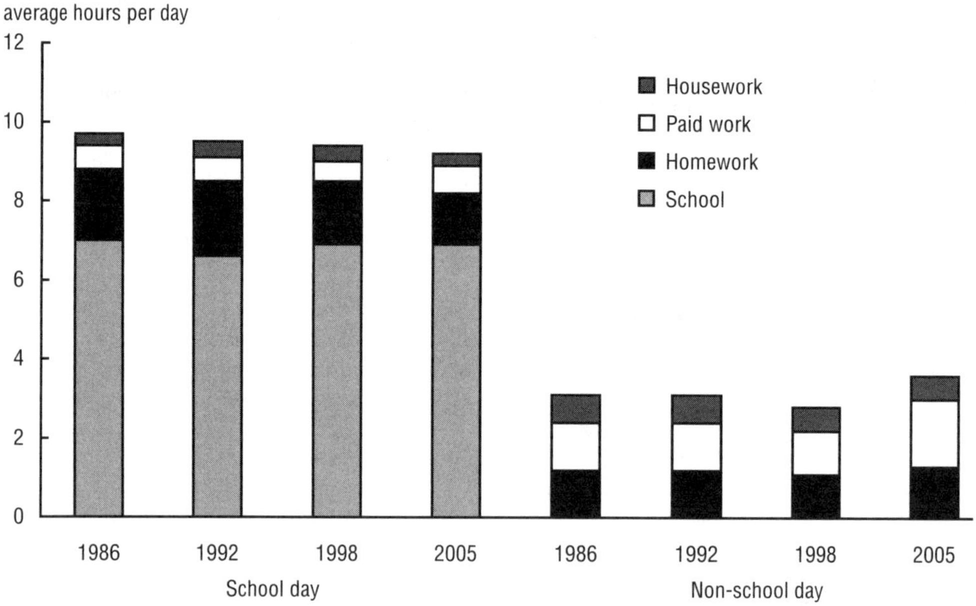

Note: Population aged 15 to 19.
Source: Statisics Canada, Catalogue no. 75-001-XIE.

Violence against children and youth

Violence against children is an important problem. In 2005, 36,895 children and youth in Canada under age 18 reported to police that they had been physically or sexually assaulted. The victimization rate of assaulted youth was 563 per 100,000 population, and for sexual assault it was 206 per 100,000.

Most violent acts against children and youth are committed by people known to them. For every 100,000 population, 348 youth were victims of physical or sexual assault at the hands of a friend or an acquaintance, 200 were victimized by a family member, and 120 were victimized by a stranger, according to 2005 police-reported data.

Physical injuries are one of the most visible consequences of violence against youth. In 2005, 36% of victimized children and youth suffered a minor physical injury and 1% suffered a serious physical injury. Although the rates of physical assault perpetrated within the family were similar for boys and girls, boys were more likely than girls to have suffered serious physical injuries.

The rate of sexual assault was highest among girls—almost four times higher than that for boys. The rate of sexual assault committed by family members was three times higher for girls than for boys.

Sixty children and youth under age 18 were the victims of homicide in 2005: more than one-third of these homicides were committed by a family member, most likely by a parent. Fathers were more likely than mothers to have been the perpetrators.

From 1996 to 2005, 28% of children and youth killed by a family member were infants. Male infants were more likely than female infants to be killed by a family member.

Chart 5.5
Child and youth victims of homicide by a family member, by age group, 1996 to 2005

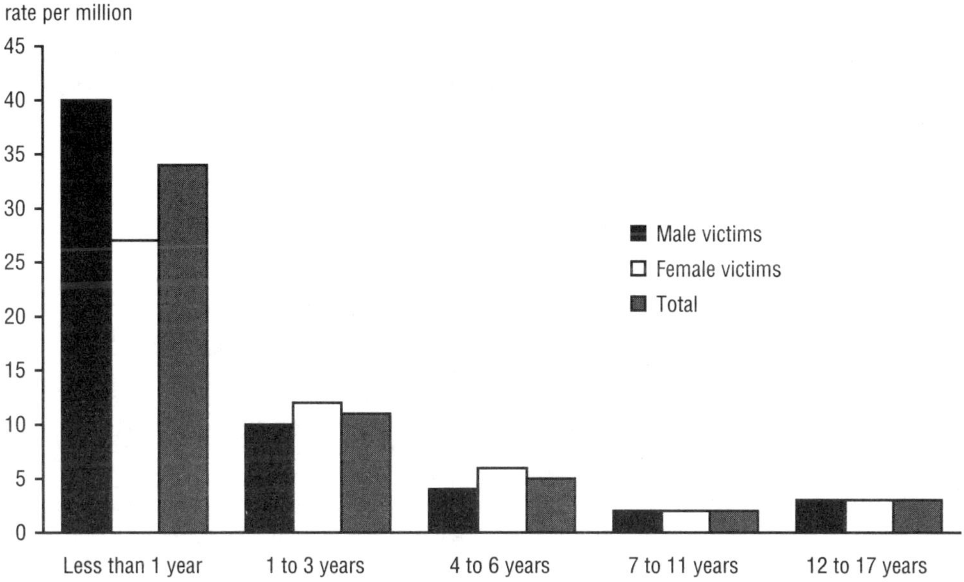

Note: Rates are calculated per million children and youth (under 18) according to the applicable age group and sex category using population estimates.
Source: Statistics Canada, Catalogue no. 85-224-XIE.

Table 5.1 Population of children and youth, by age group, selected years from 1972 to 2007

	1972		1977		1982		1987	
	number	%	number	%	number	%	number	%
Both sexes, less than 25 years	**10,550,315**	**47.5**	**10,573,045**	**44.6**	**10,312,060**	**41.1**	**9,846,717**	**37.2**
Less than 1 year	346,849	1.6	354,182	1.5	368,773	1.5	370,482	1.4
1 to 4 years	1,455,362	6.6	1,406,799	5.9	1,452,201	5.8	1,485,670	5.6
5 to 9 years	2,187,559	9.8	1,879,447	7.9	1,792,998	7.1	1,849,149	7.0
10 to 14 years	2,348,690	10.6	2,224,749	9.4	1,911,354	7.6	1,819,558	6.9
15 to 19 years	2,221,180	10.0	2,406,958	10.1	2,292,376	9.1	1,958,631	7.4
20 to 24 years	1,990,675	9.0	2,300,910	9.7	2,494,358	9.9	2,363,227	8.9
Males, less than 25 years	**5,374,822**	**24.2**	**5,390,431**	**22.7**	**5,270,503**	**21.0**	**5,044,192**	**19.1**
Less than 1 year	178,481	0.8	181,350	0.8	188,904	0.8	189,278	0.7
1 to 4 years	743,776	3.3	721,472	3.0	745,039	3.0	760,861	2.9
5 to 9 years	1,119,194	5.0	964,419	4.1	919,436	3.7	949,621	3.6
10 to 14 years	1,200,973	5.4	1,138,490	4.8	981,251	3.9	930,605	3.5
15 to 19 years	1,129,771	5.1	1,226,793	5.2	1,174,414	4.7	1,005,045	3.8
20 to 24 years	1,002,627	4.5	1,157,907	4.9	1,261,459	5.0	1,208,782	4.6
Females, less than 25 years	**5,175,493**	**23.3**	**5,182,614**	**21.8**	**5,041,557**	**20.1**	**4,802,525**	**18.2**
Less than 1 year	168,368	0.8	172,832	0.7	179,869	0.7	181,204	0.7
1 to 4 years	711,586	3.2	685,327	2.9	707,162	2.8	724,809	2.7
5 to 9 years	1,068,365	4.8	915,028	3.9	873,562	3.5	899,528	3.4
10 to 14 years	1,147,717	5.2	1,086,259	4.6	930,103	3.7	888,953	3.4
15 to 19 years	1,091,409	4.9	1,180,165	5.0	1,117,962	4.5	953,586	3.6
20 to 24 years	988,048	4.4	1,143,003	4.8	1,232,899	4.9	1,154,445	4.4
	1992		**1997**		**2002**		**2007**	
	number	%	number	%	number	%	number	%
Both sexes, less than 25 years	**9,864,705**	**34.8**	**10,013,967**	**33.5**	**10,103,054**	**32.2**	**10,082,417**	**30.6**
Less than 1 year	402,639	1.4	357,097	1.2	327,487	1.0	352,107	1.1
1 to 4 years	1,589,684	5.6	1,560,197	5.2	1,402,986	4.5	1,388,090	4.2
5 to 9 years	1,948,120	6.9	2,040,325	6.8	1,989,704	6.3	1,812,357	5.5
10 to 14 years	1,927,658	6.8	2,019,911	6.8	2,105,261	6.7	2,060,492	6.2
15 to 19 years	1,926,515	6.8	2,028,130	6.8	2,127,246	6.8	2,197,739	6.7
20 to 24 years	2,070,089	7.3	2,008,307	6.7	2,150,370	6.9	2,271,632	6.9
Males, less than 25 years	**5,052,650**	**17.8**	**5,129,785**	**17.2**	**5,175,108**	**16.5**	**5,162,913**	**15.7**
Less than 1 year	206,356	0.7	183,860	0.6	167,710	0.5	180,402	0.5
1 to 4 years	814,196	2.9	799,184	2.7	717,173	2.3	710,259	2.2
5 to 9 years	999,038	3.5	1,044,311	3.5	1,019,639	3.3	927,173	2.8
10 to 14 years	989,880	3.5	1,036,707	3.5	1,077,954	3.4	1,057,116	3.2
15 to 19 years	989,834	3.5	1,042,249	3.5	1,093,259	3.5	1,126,189	3.4
20 to 24 years	1,053,346	3.7	1,023,474	3.4	1,099,373	3.5	1,161,774	3.5
Females, less than 25 years	**4,812,055**	**17.0**	**4,884,182**	**16.3**	**4,927,946**	**15.7**	**4,919,504**	**14.9**
Less than 1 year	196,283	0.7	173,237	0.6	159,777	0.5	171,705	0.5
1 to 4 years	775,488	2.7	761,013	2.5	685,813	2.2	677,831	2.1
5 to 9 years	949,082	3.3	996,014	3.3	970,065	3.1	885,184	2.7
10 to 14 years	937,778	3.3	983,204	3.3	1,027,307	3.3	1,003,376	3.0
15 to 19 years	936,681	3.3	985,881	3.3	1,033,987	3.3	1,071,550	3.2
20 to 24 years	1,016,743	3.6	984,833	3.3	1,050,997	3.4	1,109,858	3.4

Note: Percent of the total population of Canada.

Source: Statistics Canada, CANSIM table 051-001.

Table 5.2 Population of children and youth, by age group and by province and territory, 2007

	Canada	Newfoundland and Labrador	Prince Edward Island	Nova Scotia	New Brunswick	Quebec	Ontario
	%						
Both sexes, less than 25 years	**30.6**	**27.9**	**31.2**	**28.9**	**28.5**	**28.6**	**31.1**
Under 1 year	**1.1**	0.9	1.0	0.9	0.9	1.1	1.0
1 to 4 years	**4.2**	3.7	4.0	3.7	3.7	4.0	4.2
5 to 9 years	**5.5**	4.9	5.5	5.0	5.0	5.0	5.7
10 to 14 years	**6.2**	5.7	6.5	5.9	5.8	5.9	6.5
15 to 19 years	**6.7**	6.4	7.4	6.7	6.5	6.3	6.7
20 to 24 years	**6.9**	6.3	6.9	6.7	6.6	6.3	6.9
Males, less than 25 years	**15.7**	**14.2**	**15.8**	**14.7**	**14.6**	**14.6**	**15.9**
Under 1 year	**0.5**	0.4	0.5	0.5	0.5	0.6	0.5
1 to 4 years	**2.2**	1.9	1.9	1.9	1.9	2.0	2.2
5 to 9 years	**2.8**	2.5	2.8	2.6	2.6	2.6	2.9
10 to 14 years	**3.2**	2.9	3.4	3.0	3.0	3.0	3.3
15 to 19 years	**3.4**	3.3	3.7	3.4	3.3	3.2	3.4
20 to 24 years	**3.5**	3.1	3.4	3.4	3.4	3.2	3.5
Females, less than 25 years	**14.9**	**13.7**	**15.4**	**14.1**	**13.9**	**14.0**	**15.2**
Under 1 year	**0.5**	0.4	0.5	0.4	0.4	0.5	0.5
1 to 4 years	**2.1**	1.8	2.0	1.8	1.8	1.9	2.1
5 to 9 years	**2.7**	2.4	2.7	2.5	2.4	2.4	2.8
10 to 14 years	**3.0**	2.7	3.1	2.9	2.8	2.9	3.2
15 to 19 years	**3.2**	3.2	3.7	3.3	3.1	3.1	3.3
20 to 24 years	**3.4**	3.2	3.5	3.3	3.2	3.1	3.4

	Manitoba	Saskatchewan	Alberta	British Columbia	Yukon	Northwest Territories	Nunavut
	%						
Both sexes, less than 25 years	**33.6**	**34.2**	**33.6**	**29.3**	**32.3**	**39.9**	**52.6**
Under 1 year	1.2	1.2	1.3	1.0	1.0	1.6	2.3
1 to 4 years	4.8	4.8	5.0	3.8	4.1	6.2	9.3
5 to 9 years	6.3	6.1	6.0	5.1	5.5	7.5	11.0
10 to 14 years	7.0	6.9	6.4	5.9	6.7	8.3	10.4
15 to 19 years	7.2	7.6	7.0	6.5	7.5	8.1	10.3
20 to 24 years	7.1	7.5	7.9	7.1	7.5	8.2	9.2
Males, less than 25 years	**17.2**	**17.6**	**17.3**	**15.0**	**16.4**	**20.4**	**26.7**
Under 1 year	0.6	0.6	0.7	0.5	0.5	0.8	1.1
1 to 4 years	2.4	2.5	2.5	2.0	2.1	3.1	4.7
5 to 9 years	3.2	3.2	3.1	2.6	2.6	3.9	5.8
10 to 14 years	3.6	3.5	3.3	3.0	3.3	4.4	5.3
15 to 19 years	3.7	3.9	3.6	3.3	4.1	4.0	5.2
20 to 24 years	3.7	3.9	4.1	3.6	3.8	4.2	4.5
Females, less than 25 years	**16.4**	**16.6**	**16.3**	**14.3**	**15.9**	**19.5**	**25.9**
Under 1 year	0.6	0.6	0.6	0.5	0.5	0.7	1.2
1 to 4 years	2.3	2.4	2.4	1.9	2.0	3.1	4.6
5 to 9 years	3.0	3.0	2.9	2.5	2.9	3.6	5.2
10 to 14 years	3.4	3.3	3.1	2.9	3.5	3.9	5.1
15 to 19 years	3.6	3.7	3.4	3.2	3.4	4.1	5.1
20 to 24 years	3.5	3.6	3.8	3.5	3.6	4.0	4.7

Note: Percent of the total population of Canada, the province or territory.

Source: Statistics Canada, CANSIM table 051-0001.

Table 5.3 Children and youth, by family structure, 2005

	Total children and youth	Family structure		
		Couple families	Lone-parent families	Non-family persons
	number			
Age of child				
0 to 4 years	**1,688,180**	1,375,990	312,080	110
5 to 9 years	**1,824,430**	1,405,370	418,790	270
10 to 14 years[1]	**2,107,930**	1,571,800	534,950	1,180
15 to 19 years[1]	**2,239,220**	1,532,110	534,480	172,630
20 to 24 years[1]	**1,487,090**	885,790	174,640	426,660

1. Excludes those who are parents.

Source: Statistics Canada, CANSIM table 111-0010.

Table 5.4 Young parents, by family structure, 2001 to 2005

	2001	2002	2003	2004	2005
	number				
Parents aged 15 to 19 years					
Couple families	59,690	52,080	55,690	57,720	57,770
Lone-parent families	13,850	13,210	12,680	11,750	10,890
Parents aged 20 to 24 years					
Couple families	421,950	380,840	407,700	409,740	406,680
Lone-parent families	73,840	73,040	73,080	71,340	67,630

Source: Statistics Canada, CANSIM table 111-0010.

Table 5.5 Deaths and death rates of children, by age group, 1995, 2000 and 2005

	1995		2000		2005	
	number	rate	number	rate	number	rate
All ages[1]	**210,733**	**7.2**	**218,062**	**7.1**	**230,132**	**7.1**
Males	111,396	7.7	111,742	7.3	116,006	7.3
Females	99,337	6.7	106,320	6.8	114,126	7.0
Under 1 year	**2,321**	**6.1**	**1,737**	**5.3**	**1,863**	**5.4**
Males	1,303	6.7	986	5.9	1,030	5.9
Females	1,018	5.5	751	4.7	833	5.0
1 to 4 years	**436**	**0.3**	**300**	**0.2**	**282**	**0.2**
Males	243	0.3	170	0.2	170	0.2
Females	193	0.2	130	0.2	112	0.2
5 to 9 years	**318**	**0.2**	**254**	**0.1**	**198**	**0.1**
Males	181	0.2	150	0.1	120	0.1
Females	137	0.1	104	0.1	78	0.1
10 to 14 years	**405**	**0.2**	**329**	**0.2**	**311**	**0.1**
Males	221	0.2	190	0.2	186	0.2
Females	184	0.2	139	0.1	125	0.1

Note: Rate per 1,000 population.

1. Total number of deaths for all Canadians in all age groups

Source: Statistics Canada, CANSIM table 102-0504.

Table 5.6 Causes of death of children, by age group, 2002 to 2004

	2002		2003		2004	
	number	rate	number	rate	number	rate
Under 1 year						
Perinatal conditions	918	279.2	981	292.7	1,019	302.3
Congenital malformations, deformations and chromosomal abnormalities	427	129.9	423	126.2	412	122.2
Sudden infant death syndrome	111	33.9	96	29.1	84	24.9
1 to 4 years						
Accidents (unintentional injuries)	85	6.0	86	6.3	67	4.9
Malignant neoplasms	33	2.3	29	2.1	36	2.6
Congenital conditions	41	2.9	35	2.5	38	2.8
5 to 9 years						
Accidents (unintentional injuries)	83	4.2	69	3.5	72	3.8
Malignant neoplasms	50	2.5	45	2.3	45	2.3
Congenital conditions	17	0.9	12	0.6	15	0.8
10 to 14 years						
Accidents (unintentional injuries)	131	6.2	110	5.2	90	4.2
Malignant neoplasms	42	2.0	40	1.9	52	2.5
Suicide (intentional self-harm)	35	1.7	27	1.3	28	1.3
15 to 19 years						
Accidents (unintentional injuries)	454	21.4	444	20.9	414	19.5
Suicide (intentional self-harm)	215	10.1	216	10.2	210	9.9
Malignant neoplasms	56	2.6	83	3.9	66	3.1

Note: Rate per 100,000 population.

Source: Statistics Canada, CANSIM tables 102-0538 and 102-0551.

Table 5.7 Participation rate and average time spent on household chores, 1986 and 2005

	All housework	Core housework				Non-core housework[1]
		Total	Meal preparation	Meal clean up	Indoor cleaning	
	daily participation rate (%)					
1986						
Both sexes	**43**	39	23	19	13	8[E]
Girls	**53**	52	30	27	18[E]	F
Boys	**33**[2]	28[2]	17[2,E]	12[2,E]	9[2,E]	11[E]
2005						
Both sexes	**39**	35	26	3	9	9
Girls	**43**	39	27	4[E]	13	8[E]
Boys	**36**	30	26	F	F	11[E]
	average minutes per day[3]					
1986						
Both sexes	**28**	21	9	5	7[E]	7[E]
Girls	**34**	30	13	8	9[E]	F
Boys	**24**[E]	13[2,E]	5[2,E]	2[2,E]	F	F
2005						
Both sexes	**23**	17	7	1[E]	8[E]	7[E]
Girls	**27**	22	8[E]	1[E]	12[E]	F
Boys	20	11[2,E]	6	F	F	9[E]

Note: Population aged 15 to 19.

1. Includes such items as outdoor cleaning, mending or sewing, interior or exterior maintenance or repairs, gardening, pet and plant care, or household paperwork.
2. Statistically significant difference with girls at the < 0.05 level.
3. Time averaged over 7 days; numbers may not add because of rounding.

Source: Statistics Canada, Catalogue no. 75-001-XIE.

Table 5.8 Homework participation and time spent on homework, 2005

	Population	Participation rate	Time per day	
			Participants	Population
	thousands	%	hours : minutes	
Total	**1,228**	**57**	**2:17**	**1:19**
Age group				
15 to 17	676	57	1:58	1:07
18 to 19	552	58	2:41	1:33
Sex				
Boys	593	54	2:09	1:09
Girls	635	61	2:24	1:28
Immigrant parents				
Boys	132	71	2:37	1:52
Girls	128	74	1:56	1:25
Canadian-born parents				
Boys	453	50	1:57	0:58
Girls	494	58	2:35	1:30
Family structure				
Two parents (intact family)	862	63	2:22	1:29
Two parents (blended family)	132	49	2:00	0:58
One parent	235	43	2:04	0:53
Education level of parents				
University	213	69	2:48	1:57
Mixed	358	61	2:10	1:19
Both high school or less	384	51	2:15	1:09
Type of day				
School day	773	68	1:57	1:20
Non-school day	456	39	3:16	1:17
Location of home				
Urban	979	59	2:21	1:23
Rural	250	51	1:58	1:01
Employment status				
Not employed	770	57	2:21	1:20
Usual weekly job hours				
1 to 9	106	59	2:50	1:40
10 to 19	173	70	2:17	1:35
20 or more	172	46	1:36	0:45

Source: Statistics Canada, Catalogue no. 75-001-XIE.

Table 5.9 Participation rate and average time spent on paid work, 2005

	Population	Participation rate	Time per day	
			Participants	Population
	thousands	%	hours : minutes	
Total	**1,228**	**21**	**5:04**	**1:05**
Age group				
15 to 17	676	14	4:33	0:39
18 to 19	552	30	5:22	1:36
Sex				
Boys	593	19	5:03	0:59
Girls	635	23	5:04	1:10
Immigrant parents				
Boy	132	F	F	F
Girl	128	F	F	F
Canadian-born parents				
Boy	453	21	4:59	1:01E
Girl	494	25	5:05	1:18
Family structure				
Two parents (intact family)	862	22	5:11	1:08
Two parents (blended family)	132	24E	4:08E	0:59
One parent	235	18E	5:15	0:56E
Education level of parents				
Both university	213	16E	3:45	0:36E
Mixed	358	27	4:24	1:10
Both high school or less	384	22	6:21	1:23
Type of day				
School day	773	17	4:00	0:42
Non-school day	456	28	6:12	1:43
Location of home				
Urban	979	21	5:03	1:05
Rural	250	21E	5:06	1:04E

Source: Statistics Canada, Catalogue no. 75-001-XIE.

Construction

6

Overview

Construction is one of Canada's largest industries, essential to the nation's economic health and prosperity. There are more than 260,000 Canadian construction firms, more than 65,000 in residential construction and 150,000 in trades contracting.

The construction industry remained relatively strong in 2007 despite some market factors exerting significant downward pressure, particularly a sluggish U.S. economy and the higher value of the Canadian dollar.

In 2007, construction added $76.9 billion to Canada's gross domestic product (GDP). Construction generated 20.4% of the GDP of goods-producing industries, and 6.3% of all industries. Evidence of its importance to the overall economy: the construction industry's annual GDP growth rate since 2002 has consistently outpaced goods-producing industries and all industries.

However, the industry is starting to feel the impact of adverse market conditions. Construction's GDP growth rate was 3.8% in 2007 compared with 2006 when it rose 8.1%. Each of the three construction industries—residential building construction, non-residential building construction, and engineering, repair and other construction activities—has seen similar pattern of continuous annual growth since 2003, followed by deceleration from 2006 to 2007.

The value of building permits—governmental permissions for the construction of new buildings or improvements to existing structures—is one important measure of the construction industry's overall health. In 2007, the value of building permits rose 12.2% over 2006 to $74.4 billion. This growth was fuelled by demand in Ontario and Quebec, as well as in the booming urban centres of Western Canada. In Ontario, the

Chart 6.1
Gross domestic product, construction industry

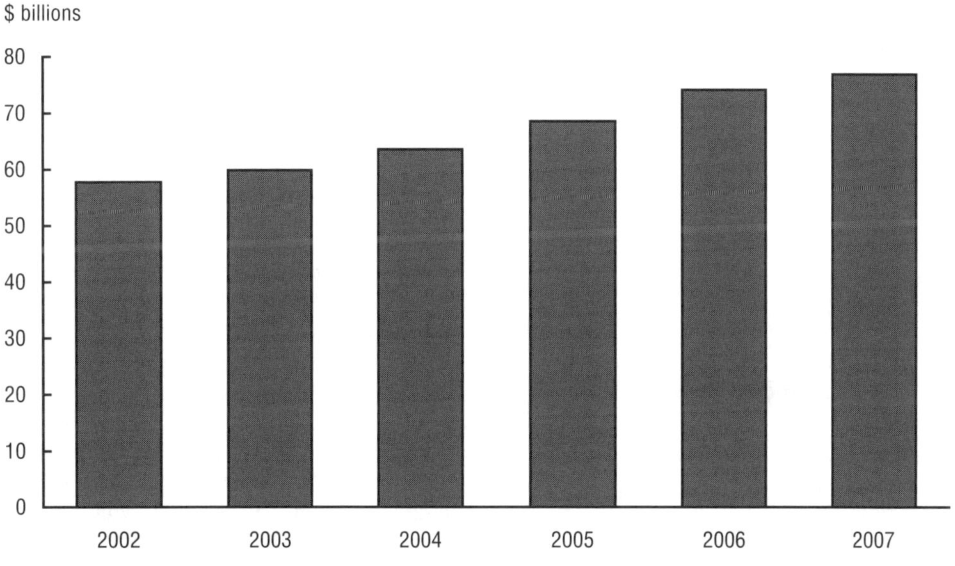

Source: Statistics Canada, CANSIM table 379-0027.

value of building permits gained 14.7% to $26.7 billion; in Quebec it grew 9.2% to $13.0 billion. Saskatchewan's gain of 44.6% was the largest percentage of growth by far among all provinces. Alberta saw a 13.4% increase in the value of building permits, and British Columbia, 8.7%.

Also a leader in employment growth

In 2007, construction recorded 5.9% employment growth, stronger than any other goods-producing industry except utilities. Construction employed 1,133,500 people in 2007. Employment has grown at least 5% each year since 2003.

This growth has put pressure on the supply of qualified construction workers. The workforce has generally managed to adapt to the higher demand, though shortages have sometimes forced contractors to delay or scale back activities. The age profile of the construction labour force remains a concern, as there is a growing need to replace skilled laborers who are nearing retirement age.

Chart 6.2
New Housing Price Index

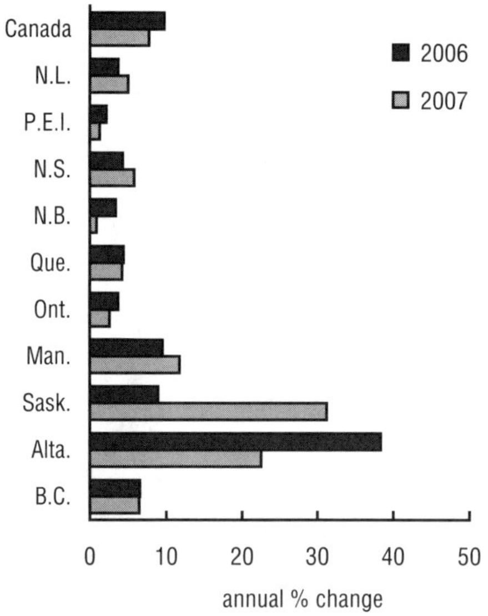

Note: Index base period 1997=100.
Source: Statistics Canada, CANSIM table 327-0005.

Table 6.a
Annual GDP growth of the construction industry, 2002 to 2007

	2002 to 2003	2003 to 2004	2004 to 2005	2005 to 2006	2006 to 2007
			%		
Construction	**3.6%**	**6.2%**	**7.8%**	**8.1%**	**4.2%**
Residential building construction	6.7%	7.7%	3.6%	2.8%	2.3%
Non-residential building construction	-2.5%	2.6%	2.9%	3.6%	1.2%
Engineering, repair and other construction activities	3.9%	6.5%	12.5%	13.0%	6.3%

Note: The GDP data were in chained 2002 dollars, seasonally adjusted at annual rates.
Source: Statistics Canada, CANSIM table 379-0027.

Investment in new homes

The Canadian economy began to slow in the last quarter of 2007, even though the country's housing market remained robust throughout the year. Positive factors such as strong employment, rising incomes and relatively low mortgage rates drove the growth in residential construction.

Spending on new single-family housing increased 10.5%, and on apartment or condominium construction, 14.0% in the fourth quarter of 2007 compared with the fourth quarter of 2006.

Housing starts were brisk in 2007, at 228,343 units, up slightly from 2006. New housing investment advanced 8.7% to $43.3 billion. This increase was mainly due to investments in single-family homes, which rose 7.3% to $27.4 billion, and in apartment and condominium construction, which gained 9.7% to $10.3 billion. Among the provinces, the largest dollar increases came in Alberta and in Quebec.

Rising prices for new homes continued to push up new housing investment. According to the Canada Mortgage and Housing Corporation (CMHC), in December 2007, the average house price in census metropolitan areas increased to $439,860, up 12% from the previous December. In Toronto, the average price in December was $682,551, up slightly from $650,666 in December of 2006. In Calgary and Edmonton, prices rose in December to averages of $467,889 and $426,512 respectively, while the average price in Vancouver increased to $862,780. The lowest average price of a new home in a metropolitan area was in Moncton, $171,064.

Renovations

Canadians undertook $37.0 billion worth of renovations in 2007, accounting for 42% of all residential construction investment. This was a 10% increase from $33.7 billion in 2006.

Chart 6.3
Value of building permits

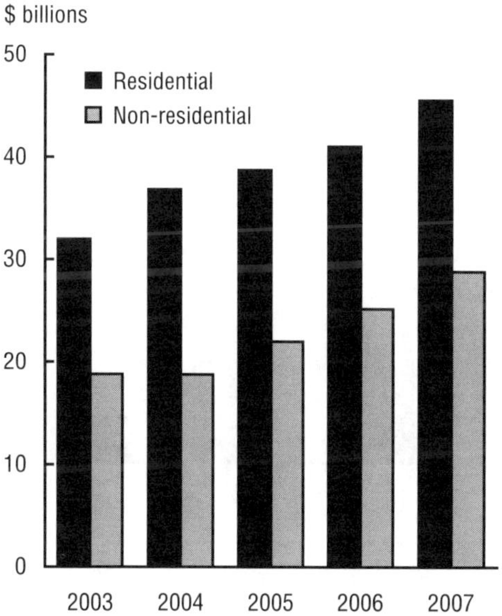

Source: Statistics Canada, CANSIM table 026-0008.

According to CMHC's Renovation and Home Purchase Survey, 37% of homeowner households in 10 of Canada's major centres renovated their primary residence in 2007. This was down from 39% in 2006. The share of households that renovated last year was the largest in Winnipeg (44%), Halifax (43%), St. John's (42%), and Ottawa (40%); Calgary and Québec (35%) had the lowest share of household renovations in 2007.

Non-residential construction

Thanks largely to huge gains in office building construction in Alberta and British Columbia, investment in non-residential building construction set a seventh consecutive annual record in 2007. Investment in commercial, industrial and institutional projects hit $39.5 billion, up 12.3% from 2006.

Western Canada's robust economy continued to play a part. Alberta and British Columbia accounted for more than 75% of the increase in non-residential investment nationally. In both provinces, commercial projects dominated investment. Contributing factors were low vacancy rates for office buildings, strong consumer demand for durable goods and high corporate profits, in particular for banks and the oil and gas industry.

The value of non-residential building permits was $28.8 billion in 2007, up 14.4% from 2006. Ontario and the booming western provinces of Saskatchewan and Alberta showed the highest increases in dollars, and together these three provinces accounted for almost 65% of the total value of non-residential building permits in Canada. Permits for commercial construction rose 17.6% to $17 billion; building permits for industrial construction went from $4.5 billion to $5.0 billion, a 10% jump.

Sales of building material are slowing down

The building materials industry—both wholesale and retail—continued to exhibit signs of erosion in 2007, following a pattern of declining year-to-year growth since 2003. Slower growth is partly the result of poor conditions in the residential construction sector in the United States.

The U.S. construction boom, which peaked in 2005, led to an oversupplied market in 2006. This coincided with a slowdown of the American economy and, as a result, residential housing construction fell. The housing market in Canada has followed a similar but much less severe trend.

The reduction in North American housing starts has resulted in a much lower demand for lumber. Canadian production of sawn lumber dropped 11% in 2007, a fourth consecutive annual decline.

Canadian wholesalers of building supplies, such as paint and hardware, had sales of more than $45 billion in 2007—a modest 5.4% increase over 2006, and down from the moderate 8.3% growth posted from 2005 to 2006. Wholesalers of metal products posted sales of $17.8 billion in 2007, a negligible rise from 2006.

Although sales growth for many commodities reached historic peaks in 2007, retail sales of lumber and other building products advanced 8.4%, the lowest annual increase since 2001. Lumber prices also remained weak, falling about 12% through the year.

Chart 6.4
Wholesale trade sales of building materials

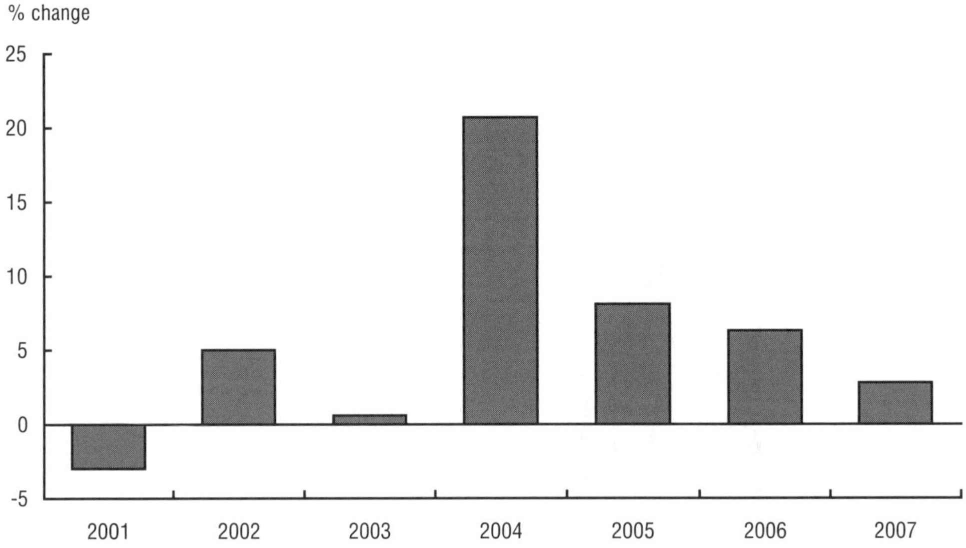

Note: North American Industry Classification System, 2002 special aggregation.
Source: Statistics Canada, Catalogue no. 82-003-XIE.

Condos are rising

In recent years, more Canadians are choosing to live in condominiums, townhouses or other multi-family dwellings. Rising gasoline prices, which are pushing up the cost of suburban commuting, are one possible factor. In larger centres, first-time homebuyers are often choosing small condos and townhouses near their jobs or downtown.

The boom in downtown condominium development is changing the urban landscape. As more people choose to live close to work in high-density city neighbourhoods, services like restaurants, shops and entertainment venues begin to locate in the area, helping to create 24-hour (rather than nine-to-five) neighbourhoods.

In 2006, 74% of homeowners owned detached single-family houses, down from 80% in 1996. Over the 10 years, this trend was most evident in British Columbia (where the proportion of homeowners in single-family houses declined from 74% to 63%) Ontario (from 80% to 74%), and Alberta (from 84% to 78%). From 2001 to 2006, the trend away from detached single-family dwellings was most noticeable in Vancouver (from 61% to 49%) and Toronto (from 66% to 59%). In other urban centres, the slip in proportions was more modest.

In 2007, the number of multi-family projects approved totalled 121,285 units, up 6.2% from 2006 and the highest since 1977. By contrast, the number of single-family projects approved declined 2.1% to 116,525 units. Meanwhile, the share of multi-family dwellings went from 48.9% in 2006 to 51.0% in 2007, the highest since 1982.

As another indication of the condo trend, the value of multi-family building permits rose 16.1% to $16.7 billion in 2007, while the value of single-family permits gained 8.2% to $28.9 billion.

Chart 6.5
Building permits, by type of structure

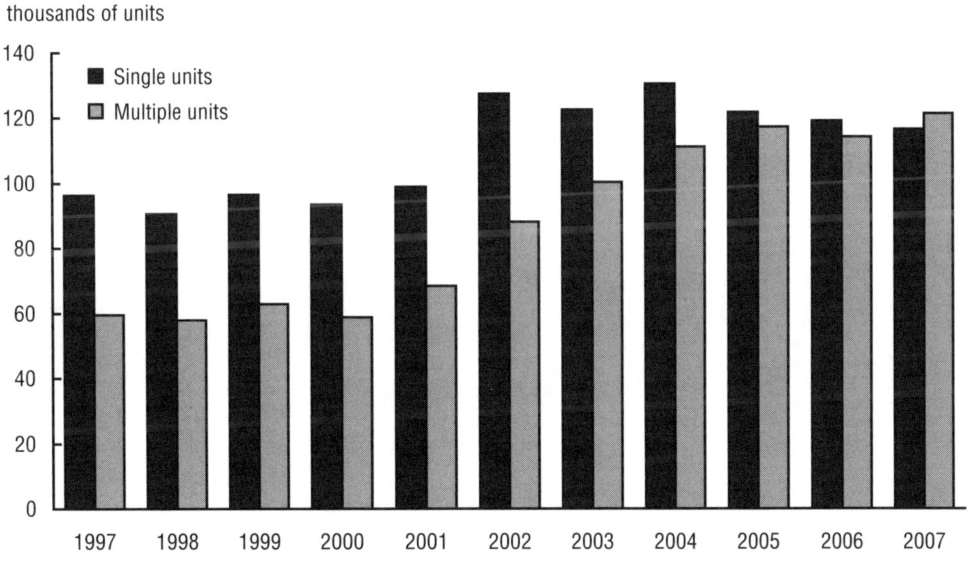

Source: Statistics Canada, CANSIM table 026-0006.

Table 6.1 Housing starts, by province, 1993 to 2007

	1993	1994	1995	1996	1997	1998	1999	2000
	number							
Canada	**155,443**	**154,057**	**110,933**	**124,713**	**147,040**	**137,439**	**149,968**	**151,653**
Newfoundland and Labrador	2,405	2,243	1,712	2,034	1,696	1,450	1,371	1,459
Prince Edward Island	645	669	422	554	470	524	616	710
Nova Scotia	4,282	4,748	4,168	4,059	3,813	3,137	4,250	4,432
New Brunswick	3,693	3,203	2,300	2,722	2,702	2,447	2,776	3,079
Quebec	34,015	34,154	21,885	23,220	25,896	23,138	25,742	24,695
Ontario	45,140	46,645	35,818	43,062	54,072	53,830	67,235	71,521
Manitoba	2,425	3,197	1,963	2,318	2,612	2,895	3,133	2,560
Saskatchewan	1,880	2,098	1,702	2,438	2,757	2,965	3,089	2,513
Alberta	18,151	17,692	13,906	16,665	23,671	27,122	25,447	26,266
British Columbia	42,807	39,408	27,057	27,641	29,351	19,931	16,309	14,418

	2001	2002	2003	2004	2005	2006	2007
	number						
Canada	**162,733**	**205,034**	**218,426**	**233,431**	**225,481**	**227,395**	**228,343**
Newfoundland and Labrador	1,788	2,419	2,692	2,870	2,498	2,234	2,649
Prince Edward Island	675	775	814	919	862	738	750
Nova Scotia	4,092	4,970	5,096	4,717	4,775	4,896	4,750
New Brunswick	3,462	3,862	4,489	3,947	3,959	4,085	4,242
Quebec	27,682	42,452	50,289	58,448	50,910	47,877	48,553
Ontario	73,282	83,597	85,180	85,114	78,795	73,417	68,123
Manitoba	2,963	3,617	4,206	4,440	4,731	5,028	5,738
Saskatchewan	2,381	2,963	3,315	3,781	3,437	3,715	6,007
Alberta	29,174	38,754	36,171	36,270	40,847	48,962	48,336
British Columbia	17,234	21,625	26,174	32,925	34,667	36,443	39,195

Source: Statistics Canada, CANSIM table 027-0009.

Table 6.2 Value of building permits, by province and territory, 1993 to 2007

	1993	1994	1995	1996	1997	1998	1999	2000
	$ millions							
Canada	**25,586.3**	**27,636.7**	**24,589.3**	**26,155.4**	**30,838.2**	**33,340.8**	**35,736.1**	**36,950.1**
Newfoundland and Labrador	255.4	262.7	201.7	224.1	213.6	252.7	296.8	282.9
Prince Edward Island	112.5	112.7	95.2	95.8	110.0	116.1	140.9	98.8
Nova Scotia	594.9	669.2	619.6	689.0	630.7	637.1	907.2	878.5
New Brunswick	427.4	440.5	487.9	441.1	459.0	481.0	481.2	484.6
Quebec	5,375.6	5,898.5	4,947.4	4,938.0	5,133.2	5,897.4	5,939.6	6,272.0
Ontario	8,774.7	10,001.3	9,192.2	9,597.6	12,888.7	13,839.8	16,732.5	17,556.5
Manitoba	528.6	685.3	525.4	592.3	689.6	1,031.8	879.4	853.9
Saskatchewan	326.8	372.3	478.2	543.0	626.8	672.9	721.6	609.0
Alberta	2,713.5	2,740.5	2,506.6	2,883.1	4,446.3	5,552.2	4,801.9	5,296.4
British Columbia	6,389.2	6,317.9	5,401.4	6,053.1	5,543.8	4,739.6	4,695.5	4,492.0
Yukon	42.2	51.0	74.0	51.8	49.6	39.9	48.8	55.5
Northwest Territories (including Nunavut)	45.7	84.9	59.6	46.6	46.9	80.2	90.6.	..
Northwest Territories	..	..	..	..	..	..	..	23.0
Nunavut	..	..	..	..	..	..	..	47.2

	2001	2002	2003	2004	2005	2006	2007
	$ millions						
Canada	**40,856.1**	**47,262.1**	**50,772.0**	**55,578.6**	**60,750.7**	**66,265.8**	**74,379.7**
Newfoundland and Labrador	298.3	383.3	421.0	501.2	494.1	538.4	660.1
Prince Edward Island	217.2	146.2	178.1	223.8	244.0	207.0	163.8
Nova Scotia	699.9	877.3	1,014.1	1,125.8	1,188.0	1,291.4	1,288.9
New Brunswick	535.1	663.8	696.3	797.3	829.0	933.3	965.2
Quebec	7,571.1	8,628.4	10,090.9	11,629.6	11,288.0	11,878.3	12,973.4
Ontario	19,069.3	22,281.4	23,235.2	23,905.3	24,129.6	23,292.2	26,710.4
Manitoba	739.2	888.9	1,065.0	1,150.4	1,128.5	1,378.8	1,480.1
Saskatchewan	703.3	708.6	772.6	770.0	905.7	1,138.6	1,646.4
Alberta	5,911.7	6,846.5	6,667.2	7,327.1	10,201.7	13,875.7	15,729.7
British Columbia	4,954.8	5,659.4	6,394.2	7,938.7	10,182.9	11,541.5	12,544.7
Yukon	49.8	31.3	52.6	75.9	77.3	95.6	79.6
Northwest Territories (including Nunavut)	..	..	..	..	..	..	..
Northwest Territories	76.0	91.6	86.2	105.3	68.7	37.7	74.0
Nunavut	30.4	55.4	98.6	28.1	13.2	57.4	63.5

Source: Statistics Canada, CANSIM table 026-0003.

Table 6.3 Investment in non-residential building construction, by selected census metropolitan area, 2003 to 2007

	2003	2004	2005	2006	2007
	$ millions, not seasonally adjusted				
St. John's	141.2	128.3	191.1	174.6	156.7
Halifax	238.4	254.7	402.9	471.2	333.2
Saint John	71.6	94.3	64.4	96.8	131.3
Saguenay	137.3	108.5	92.9	125.1	150.5
Québec	499.6	585.4	677.9	697.5	770.2
Sherbrooke	129.8	128.6	120.0	165.6	169.7
Trois-Rivières	168.7	158.0	109.8	126.9	198.7
Montréal	2,804.6	3,162.1	3,208.8	2,964.9	3,387.6
Ottawa–Gatineau	1,465.0	1,391.8	1,350.8	1,665.0	1,661.2
Quebec part	229.7	218.4	275.2	206.9	190.3
Ontario part	1,235.2	1,173.4	1,075.6	1,458.1	1,470.9
Kingston	166.5	151.1	161.5	130.2	189.5
Oshawa	419.4	536.3	536.3	417.2	369.2
Toronto	5,013.2	6,547.4	6,818.1	6,417.0	6,667.6
Hamilton	705.8	797.6	613.7	659.1	536.1
St. Catharines–Niagara	414.6	419.4	323.1	316.5	269.4
Kitchener	580.6	565.7	649.9	539.6	534.1
London	591.6	584.0	625.1	487.6	499.7
Windsor	408.0	320.9	309.0	361.4	334.1
Greater Sudbury / Grand Sudbury	170.2	99.7	139.8	131.1	239.2
Thunder Bay	150.3	132.6	111.9	123.2	80.2
Winnipeg	568.0	535.1	566.0	706.8	594.1
Regina	224.6	193.8	188.9	244.2	282.2
Saskatoon	212.6	181.7	245.8	384.6	367.5
Calgary	1,257.1	1,411.4	1,751.4	2,589.3	4,517.1
Edmonton	915.0	1,024.5	1,204.5	1,617.0	1,852.0
Abbotsford	105.8	85.1	153.6	277.4	273.5
Vancouver	1,657.6	1,737.8	2,331.1	2,895.6	3,346.2
Victoria	291.2	379.6	298.3	407.5	379.6

Source: Statistics Canada, CANSIM table 026-0016.

Table 6.4 Capital expenditures for construction, by sector, 2004 to 2008

	Actual			Preliminary	Intentions
	2004	2005	2006	2007[1]	2008[2]
	$ millions				
Canada	**154,125.2**	**171,964.8**	**195,762.9**	**208,146.2**	**218,513.5**
Agriculture, forestry, fishing and hunting	1,476.2	1,359.4	1,228.5	1,231.7	1,173.5
Mining and oil and gas extraction	29,942.4	39,397.4	45,800.8	41,443.8	40,539.9
Utilities	8,843.5	9,861.4	11,687.8	14,709.1	15,672.3
Construction	500.5	531.0	586.6	638.3	671.1
Manufacturing	2,611.6	2,235.7	2,665.9	2,306.7	2,689.4
Wholesale trade	900.8	1,106.7	1,540.7	1,364.4	1,415.8
Retail trade	4,063.5	3,665.8	4,170.7	4,298.7	4,805.0
Transportation and warehousing	3,510.7	3,966.3	5,767.2	7,934.5	12,016.7
Information and cultural industries	2,411.1	2,693.5	2,124.4	2,558.4	2,544.1
Finance and insurance	525.9	809.0	868.2	967.2	1,163.4
Real estate and rental and leasing	3,308.3	3,550.1	4,385.5	5,003.3	6,139.6
Professional, scientific and technical services	358.2	330.8	481.7	422.3	324.3
Management of companies and enterprises	43.4	26.5	44.1	23.9	21.8
Administrative and support, waste management and remediation services	214.2	248.8	384.6	429.9	379.2
Educational services	4,355.1	4,707.7	5,192.1	5,846.0	5,467.9
Health care and social assistance	3,061.0	3,708.7	4,506.8	4,176.4	4,271.0
Arts, entertainment and recreation	901.7	692.6	837.5	1,064.9	661.8
Accommodation and food services	1,231.5	1,508.6	1,786.2	1,983.5	1,919.4
Housing	70,060.2	73,574.9	81,708.8	88,459.0	89,331.9
Public administration	15,316.1	17,511.6	19,504.9	22,775.7	26,766.4
Other services (excluding public administration)	489.1	478.4	489.7	508.6	539.0

Notes: The Capital Expenditures Survey collects data on the intentions for capital investment and the expenditures for the previous two years.
North American Industry Classification System (NAICS), 2002.

1. Data reflect the preliminary actuals for capital expenditures for 2007.
2. Data reflect the intentions for capital expenditures for 2008.

Source: Statistics Canada, CANSIM table 029-0005.

Table 6.5 Labour force employed in construction, by province, 2002 to 2007

	2002	2003	2004	2005	2006	2007
	thousands					
Canada	**865.2**	**906.0**	**951.7**	**1,019.5**	**1,069.7**	**1,133.5**
Newfoundland and Labrador	9.3	9.5	11.7	12.4	12.9	13.5
Prince Edward Island	4.3	4.2	4.1	4.7	5.7	5.0
Nova Scotia	24.0	24.5	28.2	27.7	27.3	27.2
New Brunswick	19.7	19.2	19.4	18.6	21.1	24.0
Quebec	153.4	162.9	164.5	179.2	186.1	195.5
Ontario	344.5	369.1	367.6	394.8	405.2	412.6
Manitoba	26.0	26.9	27.7	28.2	29.9	33.8
Saskatchewan	24.8	23.3	24.0	26.3	29.6	32.1
Alberta	141.4	146.6	160.5	159.7	172.6	193.1
British Columbia	118.1	119.8	144.0	168.0	179.3	196.9

Note: Annual data.

Source: Statistics Canada, CANSIM table 282-0008.

Table 6.6 Production of building materials, 2003 to 2007

	2003	2004	2005	2006	2007
	thousands of cubic metres				
Dry sawn lumber	79,319.3	84,589.6	82,888.9	80,870.4	72,042.6
	thousands of bundles				
Asphalt shingles, all sizes	39,747.0	43,639.0	40,284.7	44,590.3	41,143.2
	thousands of metric tonnes				
Cement	13,418.0	13,862.9	14,179.4	14,335.5	15,077.6
Steel pipe and tubing	2,431.6	2,647.2	2,837.1	2,948.5	2,614.7

Note: Standard Classification of Goods (SCG).

Source: Statistics Canada, CANSIM tables 303-0001, 303-0003, 303-0006, 303-0009, 303-0046, 303-0052 and 303-0060.

Crime and justice

Overview

Led by a decline in non-violent incidents, Canada's crime rate fell to a 25-year low in 2006, with every province and territory reporting a drop. However, youth crime rates were up 3%, the first increase since 2003.

In 2006, the national crime rate was 7.5 incidents per 100 people, the lowest since 1978 and 27% below its 1991 peak of 10.3 crimes per 100 people.

Non-violent crime accounted for approximately 9 in 10 of the 2.5 million *Criminal Code* incidents reported in 2006. About 60,000 fewer non-violent crimes were reported than in 2005: counterfeiting incidents fell 29%, break-ins, 5%, and thefts under $5,000, 4%.

Violent crimes made up 13% of the *Criminal Code* incidents in 2006. While the rate remained steady from 2005, Canada's homicide rate dropped by 10%, whereas incidents of kidnapping and forcible confinement rose 12% in 2006.

Crime prevention

There may be many reasons for the drop in crime: changes in legislation, shifts in police enforcement or changes in the willingness of victims to report crime. As well, our population is aging and older people are less likely to engage in crime.

Canadians may also have taken action to protect themselves and their property. According to the 2004 General Social Survey on victimization, people who perceive crime as higher in their neighbourhood are most likely to use crime prevention measures, as are those who believe crime has increased in their community.

Chart 7.1
Crimes, by province, 2006

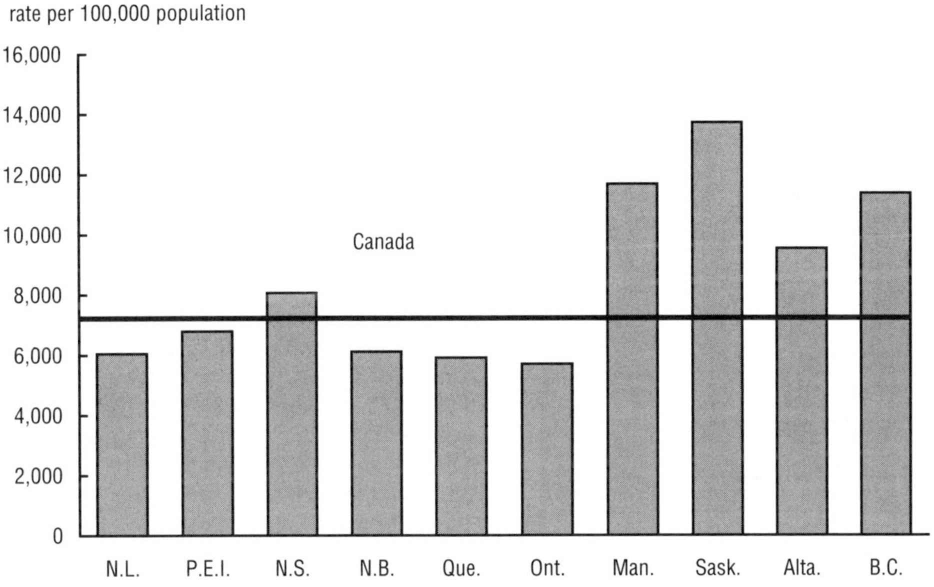

Note: All *Criminal Code* offences, excluding traffic.
Source: Statistics Canada, CANSIM table 252-0013.

During their lifetime, some Canadians have taken preventive steps such as: changing their routine or avoiding certain places, 35%; installing burglar alarms or motion detectors, 34%; or installing new locks or security bars, 31%.

Many Canadians routinely use precautionary measures. For example, when alone in a car, almost 60% of us routinely lock car doors; 43% report planning the route of a trip on the basis of safety.

Crime rates vary

Crime rates declined in every province and territory from 2005 to 2006. Prince Edward Island and Nunavut had the largest declines, 11%.

Saskatchewan's rate fell 4% but, at 13.7 incidents per 100 people, was still the highest provincial crime rate for a ninth consecutive year. The lowest crime rate was in Ontario at 5.7 crimes per 100 people.

In cities, the most sizable declines were in Western Canada. Saskatoon led with a 9% drop; Abbotsford and Regina both reported 8% declines. Even with declines, crime rates in large Western cities remained high relative to other large cities. For instance, Regina had the highest homicide rate of all Canadian cities at 4.5 per 100,000 people, followed by Edmonton at 3.7 per 100,000 people.

Chart 7.2
Homicides, by province, 2006

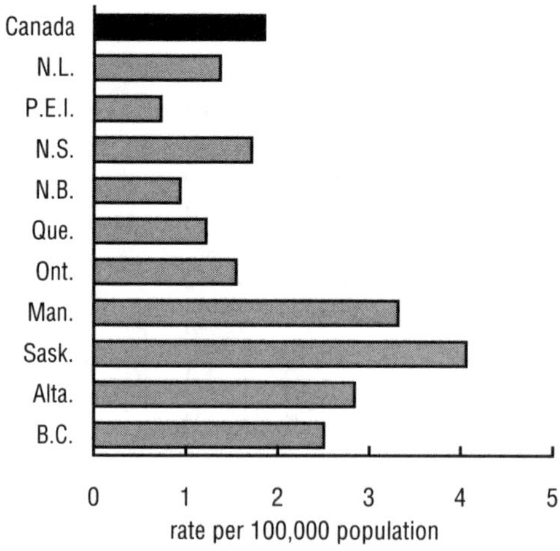

Source: Statistics Canada, CANSIM table 252-0013.

Table 7.a
Violent crimes

	2005	2006
	%	
Total	**100.0**	**100.0**
Homicide	0.2	0.2
Attempted murder	0.3	0.3
Assaults (level 1 to 3)[1]	77.1	77.2
Sexual assault	7.7	7.1
Other sexual offences	0.9	0.9
Robbery	9.4	9.9
Other violent crimes[2]	4.4	4.4

1. Constitutes the intentional application of force without consent, the attempt or threat to apply force to another person or openly wearing a weapon (or an imitation) while accosting or impeding another person.
2. Includes unlawfully causing bodily harm, discharging firearms with intent, abductions, assaults against police officers, assaults against other peace or public officers and other assaults.

Source: Statistics Canada, CANSIM table 252-0013.

Homicide rate falls

In 2006, police reported 605 homicides in Canada—a rate of 1.9 per 100,000 people. Of these deaths, 210 people were fatally stabbed and 190 people were shot. Handguns remain the most commonly used firearm, accounting for over half of all firearm-related homicides that year.

Seventy-eight spousal homicides were reported in 2006. The rate of spousal homicide has declined by more than half since 1975, possibly related to heightened awareness of spousal violence, changes in police procedures, and increased services for family violence victims . The annual rate of spousal homicide against women is three to five times higher than against men.

Gang-related homicides accounted for one in six homicides in 2006. In Quebec, just over one in four murders were gang-related, the highest proportion in the country. Also, in 2006, police solved 45% of gang-related killings, compared with 80% of other types of homicides.

Youth crime increases

Among young Canadians aged 12 to 17, the crime rate rose 3% from 2005 to 2006, the first increase since 2003. All provinces except Quebec (-4%) reported rising youth crime rates in 2006.

In 2006, the youth homicide rate reached its highest level since 1961. Eighty-four youths—72 males and 12 females—were charged with homicides involving 54 different victims in 2006. Youth homicide accounts for 15% of all persons accused of homicides in Canada.

Among Canada's 2.6 million young people, only a small proportion is involved in crime. Approximately 74,000 youths were charged with a criminal offence in 2006. Another 104,000 came into contact with the police—for committing non-violent and minor crimes—and were cleared by other non-court measures, such as informal police warnings, referrals to community programs, formal police cautions, Crown cautions, and extrajudicial sanction programs.

Of 31,700 young persons admitted to correctional services in 2004/2005, half were placed in custody and the other half were placed under community supervision, in most cases probation.

Chart 7.3
Elapsed time to complete a case in adult criminal court, 2006/2007

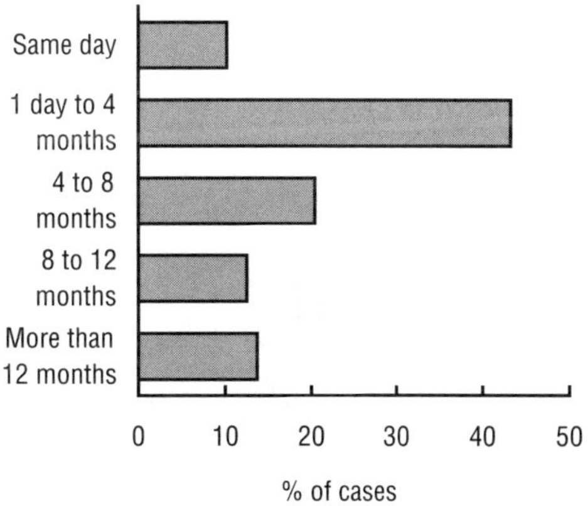

Note: Elapsed time from first to last court appearance.
Source: Statistics Canada, Catalogue no. 85-002-XIE.

Longer delays in court cases

Recently, cases appearing in adult criminal court have become more complex and they have taken longer to get through the system. In 2006/2007, 61% of cases involved multiple charges, compared with 53% in 1996/1997. The average time required to complete cases in adult court increased to eight months from an average of six months five years earlier.

Canada's courts completed 372,000 cases, down 7% from five years earlier. Of those cases, 25% involved crimes against the person, 24% involved crimes against property, 17% were administration of justice offences and 14% were *Criminal Code* traffic offences. The remaining 20% involved other *Criminal Code* and federal statute offences.

The proportion of impaired driving cases has declined over the years. Property crimes, such as fraud or breaking and entering, have also declined. However, administration of justice offences, including breach of probation and failure to comply with a court order, doubled as a proportion of cases.

Two out of three adult cases received a guilty disposition in 2006/2007. In those cases, 89% of the accused had pleaded guilty. *Criminal Code* traffic violations were most likely to lead to a guilty finding (79%). Crimes against the person had the lowest percentage of guilty findings (53%).

After a finding of guilt, probation was imposed in 43% of cases, prison terms in 34% and fines in 30%.

Smaller centres see their share of crime

Crime is not just a fact in large urban centres, though it might sometimes look that way in popular television programs. People living in Canada's smaller urban areas face higher overall crime rates than their big-city neighbours, according to 2005 police-reported data. And, although rural residents live in areas with the lowest overall crime rates, they also had the highest homicide rates in 2005.

These findings apply to all provinces and territories except Quebec and Alberta. Quebec's overall crime rate is highest in its large urban areas; in Alberta, the rate is lowest in large urban areas.

In small urban areas—those with a minimum population of 1,000 persons and a population density of at least 400 persons per square kilometre—the crime rate is about 43% higher than in census metropolitan areas (CMAs) and about 58% higher than in rural areas. Nationally, these small urban areas have the highest rates of both total violent crimes (murder, assault, sexual assault and robbery) and total property crime.

Rural areas also reported higher overall rates of violent crime than did CMAs. In 2005, the highest homicide rates were in rural areas. Although weapons in general are used more often in violent crimes in CMAs, homicides committed with a firearm are more frequent in rural areas (39%) than in either CMAs (35%) or small urban areas (23%).

Despite differences in crime rates, residents of the large urban, small urban and rural areas were equally likely to report feeling satisfied about their safety from crime, according to the 2004 General Social Survey. Over 90% of respondents, living in all three types of areas, reported such satisfaction.

Chart 7.4
Crimes in Canada, 2005

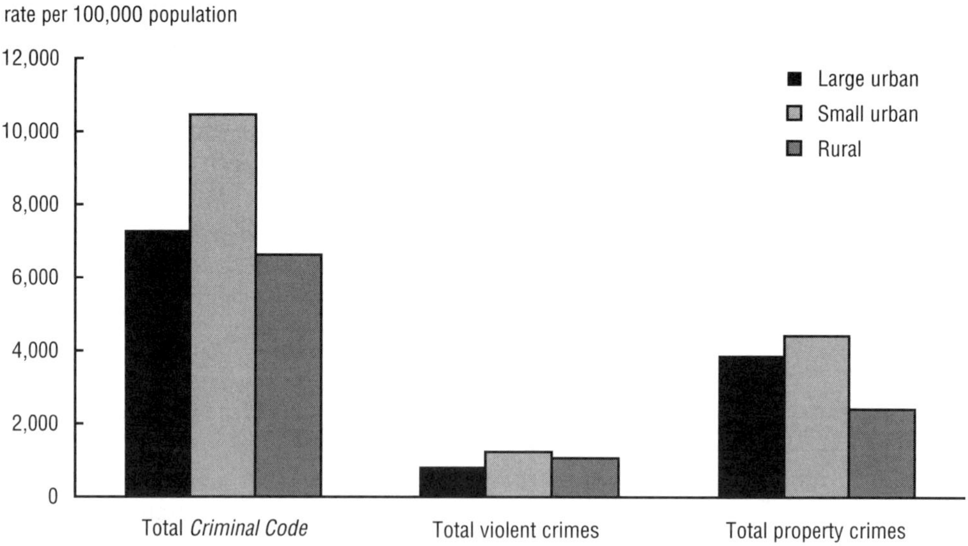

Source: Statistics Canada, Catalogue no. 85-002-XIE.

Violence in the workplace

For some Canadians, work is a dangerous place.

According to the 2004 General Social Survey on victimization, 17% of self-reported incidents of violent victimization occurred in the workplace. These incidents—including sexual assault, robbery and physical assault—added up to 356,000 violent workplace incidents in the 10 provinces in 2004.

In Newfoundland and Labrador, the victim's workplace was the location of 40% of all violent incidents—a proportion two times higher than in any other province. Among the other provinces, in 2004 the rate ranged from 11% in Nova Scotia to 20% in both Saskatchewan and Alberta.

Certain workers are more likely to be affected: in the survey, 33% of the victims worked in social assistance or health care, 14% in accommodation or food services, and 11% in education.

Someone known to the victim committed two out of three of the workplace incidents, whereas one in three incidents was committed by a stranger. In 18% of incidents where the victim knew the accused, the victim was a coworker of the perpetrator; in 11%, the victim knew the perpetrator.

In 38% of the reported incidents, the accused was either someone else known by the victim or had an 'other' type of relationship with the victim. The accused may, for example, have been a patient, a client, a customer or a former coworker. In 46% of incidents, the victim believed the incident was related to the perpetrator's use of drugs or alcohol.

One in five victims reported suffering injuries. For some, the consequence was emotional. The most commonly reported emotional impacts for victims were being angry (21%), being upset, confused or frustrated (20%) and feeling fearful (15%).

Chart 7.5
Violent incidents in the workplace, 2004

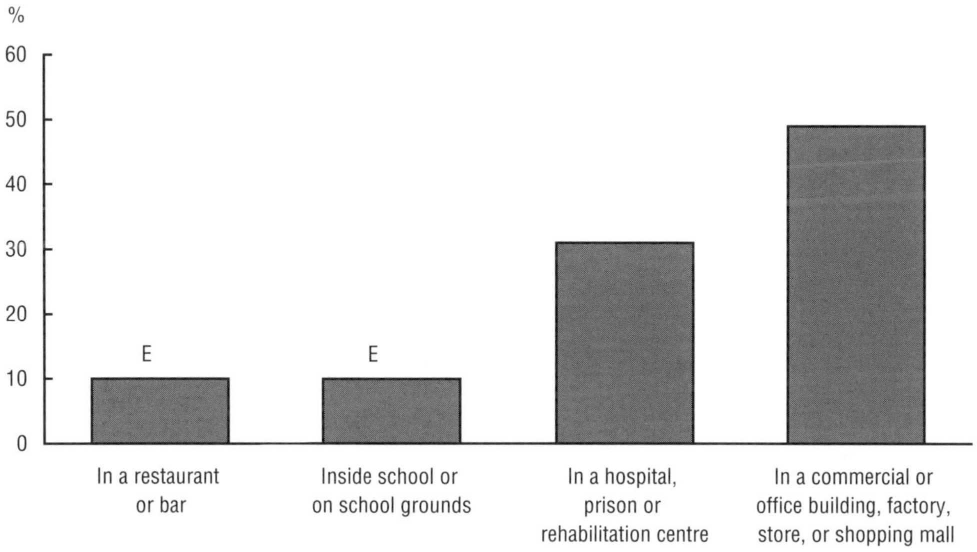

Source: Statistics Canada, General Social Survey, 2004.

Table 7.1 Crimes, by type of offence and by province and territory, 2006

	Canada	Newfoundland and Labrador	Prince Edward Island	Nova Scotia	New Brunswick	Quebec	Ontario
	rate per 100,000 population						
All offences	**8,269.0**	**6,571.0**	**7,485.6**	**8,697.8**	**6,780.5**	**6,625.7**	**6,251.4**
Criminal Code offences (excluding traffic offences)	**7,518.5**	6,054.8	6,792.6	8,068.6	6,110.5	5,909.0	5,689.2
Crimes against the person	**951.2**	850.7	714.0	1,134.8	848.8	755.9	755.7
Homicide	**1.9**	1.4	0.7	1.7	0.9	1.2	1.5
Attempted murder	**2.6**	1.0	0.7	3.0	1.2	3.3	2.5
Assault (level 1 to 3)[1]	**734.8**	733.8	624.5	918.8	706.0	540.4	563.3
Sexual assault	**67.9**	67.1	47.7	86.0	66.6	66.8	55.6
Other sexual offences	**8.6**	4.5	10.8	6.7	17.8	12.6	4.9
Robbery	**94.1**	23.4	17.3	84.6	29.5	91.3	86.6
Other crimes against the person[2]	**41.4**	19.6	12.3	34.0	26.8	40.3	41.4
Property crimes	**3,587.6**	2,362.9	2,999.6	3,514.2	2,562.2	3,113.8	2,811.4
Break and enter	**767.8**	736.5	537.1	734.7	598.8	866.9	541.3
Motor vehicle theft	**487.2**	130.7	114.8	263.3	186.9	507.4	302.7
Theft over $5,000	**52.3**	14.7	31.0	44.4	38.2	64.7	43.6
Theft $5,000 and under	**1,888.8**	1,251.8	2,001.9	1,939.7	1,445.6	1,398.5	1,530.8
Possession of stolen goods	**107.7**	34.1	52.0	232.9	53.7	42.8	110.0
Fraud	**283.8**	195.0	262.8	299.2	239.1	233.6	283.1
Other *Criminal Code* offences	**2,979.7**	2,841.2	3,079.0	3,419.5	2,699.5	2,039.3	2,122.1
Criminal Code traffic offences	**367.7**	279.4	507.5	328.3	320.6	415.1	245.0
Impaired driving	**227.9**	220.7	395.6	254.6	241.6	214.3	139.1
Other *Criminal Code* traffic offences[3]	**139.9**	58.7	111.9	73.7	79.0	200.8	105.9
Federal statute offences	**382.8**	236.8	185.5	300.9	349.3	301.6	317.3
Drugs[4]	**294.8**	128.3	127.1	218.3	247.9	265.8	238.5
Other federal statute offences	**88.1**	108.5	58.5	82.6	101.5	35.7	78.7

See notes and source at the end of the table.

Table 7.1 Crimes, by type of offence and by province and territory, 2006 (continued)

	Manitoba	Saskatchewan	Alberta	British Columbia	Yukon	Northwest Territories	Nunavut
	rate per 100,000 population						
All offences	**12,324.6**	**15,276.2**	**10,336.0**	**12,563.7**	**22,197.3**	**44,074.4**	**32,830.9**
Criminal Code offences (excluding traffic offences)	11,678.5	13,710.8	9,523.4	11,365.1	20,593.0	41,468.2	31,265.0
Crimes against the person	1,597.5	2,038.8	1,101.0	1,218.3	3,006.8	6,447.5	6,763.7
Homicide	3.3	4.1	2.8	2.5	0.0	0.0	6.5
Attempted murder	2.2	4.7	2.3	2.1	0.0	0.0	13.0
Assault (level 1 to 3)[1]	1,243.0	1,670.5	888.1	979.9	2,654.6	5,833.6	5,893.1
Sexual assault	108.1	124.7	63.5	74.7	195.3	372.7	597.8
Other sexual offences	10.5	14.6	6.5	10.2	51.2	54.9	45.5
Robbery	182.4	149.6	93.4	110.3	57.6	35.8	39.0
Other crimes against the person[2]	48.0	70.6	44.3	38.6	48.0	150.5	168.9
Property crimes	4,951.2	4,775.8	4,480.0	5,685.3	5,107.4	6,356.8	4,255.7
Break and enter	1,074.1	1,227.7	767.9	1,088.3	1,466.6	2,331.5	1,965.4
Motor vehicle theft	1,375.7	633.3	725.1	682.2	445.1	926.9	620.5
Theft over $5,000	48.5	42.1	65.9	57.7	60.8	64.5	35.7
Theft $5,000 and under	2,151.8	2,392.1	2,383.1	3,366.9	2,779.5	2,654.0	1,315.7
Possession of stolen goods	87.5	160.4	187.8	139.4	76.9	136.2	139.7
Fraud	213.7	320.2	350.3	350.8	278.6	243.7	178.7
Other *Criminal Code* offences	5,129.7	6,896.2	3,942.4	4,461.5	12,478.8	28,663.9	20,245.6
Criminal Code traffic offences	284.0	963.0	490.4	440.9	973.5	1,392.7	808.9
Impaired driving	212.8	473.8	346.5	339.6	701.3	1,168.2	685.5
Other *Criminal Code* traffic offences[3]	71.2	489.2	143.9	101.3	272.2	224.6	123.5
Federal statute offences	362.1	602.4	322.3	757.7	630.8	1,213.5	756.9
Drugs[4]	182.8	275.2	257.9	616.8	467.5	769.2	672.5
Other federal statute offences	179.3	327.2	64.4	141.0	163.3	444.3	84.5

1. Constitutes the intentional application of force without consent, the attempt or threat to apply force to another person or openly wearing a weapon (or an imitation) while accosting or impeding another person.
2. Includes unlawfully causing bodily harm, discharging firearms with intent, abductions, assaults against police officers, assaults against other peace or public officers and other assaults.
3. Includes dangerous operation of a motor vehicle, boat, vessel or aircraft; dangerous operation of a motor vehicle, boat, vessel or aircraft causing bodily harm or death; driving a motor vehicle while prohibited; and failure to stop or remain.
4. Includes possession, trafficking, importation and production.

Source: Statistics Canada, CANSIM table 252-0013.

Table 7.2 Crimes, by type of offence, 2001 to 2006

	2001	2002	2003	2004	2005	2006
	rate per 100,000 population					
All offences	**8,453.7**	**8,504.0**	**8,900.6**	**8,950.6**	**8,535.4**	**8,269.0**
Criminal Code offences (excluding traffic offences)	7,655.4	7,705.6	8,142.3	8,162.0	7,772.5	7,518.5
Crimes against the person	983.8	968.8	965.0	944.5	949.5	951.2
Homicide	1.8	1.9	1.7	2.0	2.1	1.9
Attempted murder	2.3	2.2	2.2	2.1	2.5	2.6
Assault (level 1 to 3)[1]	763.9	751.3	747.6	732.3	732.8	734.8
Sexual assault	77.5	78.1	74.2	72.0	72.8	67.9
Other sexual offences	8.7	8.8	8.1	8.2	8.6	8.6
Robbery	88.0	85.0	89.8	86.0	89.2	94.1
Other crimes against the person[2]	41.7	41.6	41.3	42.0	41.6	41.4
Property crimes	4,003.5	3,973.2	4,120.6	3,970.1	3,737.2	3,587.6
Break and enter	900.9	878.4	899.5	862.4	809.2	767.8
Motor vehicle theft	543.5	516.1	550.0	531.4	495.4	487.2
Theft over $5,000	67.2	63.2	61.3	53.0	53.3	52.3
Theft $5,000 and under	2,126.3	2,127.1	2,211.8	2,106.9	1,977.4	1,888.8
Possession of stolen goods	86.9	95.8	104.7	111.7	106.7	107.7
Fraud	278.8	292.7	293.4	304.6	295.3	283.8
Other *Criminal Code* offences	2,668.1	2,763.6	3,056.8	3,247.4	3,085.7	2,979.7
Criminal Code traffic offences	387.6	374.8	369.7	377.1	376.4	367.7
Impaired driving	266.7	255.1	245.1	251.1	242.6	227.9
Other traffic offences[3]	120.9	119.6	124.6	126.0	133.8	139.9
Federal statute offences	410.7	423.6	388.5	411.5	386.5	382.8
Drugs[4]	288.2	295.7	274.0	305.2	290.0	294.8
Other federal statute offences	122.5	127.9	114.5	106.3	96.5	88.1

1. Constitutes the intentional application of force without consent, the attempt or threat to apply force to another person or openly wearing a weapon (or an imitation) while accosting or impeding another person.
2. Includes unlawfully causing bodily harm, discharging firearms with intent, abductions, assaults against police officers, assaults against other peace or public officers and other assaults.
3. Includes dangerous operation of a motor vehicle, boat, vessel or aircraft; dangerous operation of a motor vehicle, boat, vessel or aircraft causing bodily harm or death; driving a motor vehicle while prohibited; and failure to stop or remain.
4. Includes possession, trafficking, importation and production.

Source: Statistics Canada, CANSIM table 252-0013.

Table 7.3 Persons charged, by type of offence, 1996 and 2006

	1996			2006		
	Youth and adults charged	Youths charged	Adults charged	Youth and adults charged	Youths charged	Adults charged
	rate per 100,000 population					
All offences	**2,723.4**	**5,320.8**	**2,443.4**	**2,228.5**	**3,327.0**	**2,117.9**
Criminal Code offences (excluding traffic offences)	2,131.8	4,942.8	1,828.9	1,717.4	2,862.2	1,602.2
Crimes against the person	562.9	932.2	523.1	500.7	793.5	471.2
Homicide	2.0	2.0	2.0	1.8	3.2	1.7
Attempted murder	3.1	3.8	3.0	2.1	2.7	2.1
Assault (level 1 to 3)[1]	433.9	660.0	409.5	391.8	548.1	376.1
Sexual assault	41.3	65.4	38.7	27.8	46.0	26.0
Other sexual offences	4.8	7.4	4.6	2.8	5.4	2.6
Robbery	43.6	154.9	31.6	40.5	143.4	30.1
Other crimes against the person[2]	34.3	38.7	33.9	33.9	44.8	32.8
Property crimes	924.9	2,761.0	727.0	515.7	997.9	467.2
Break and enter	188.5	767.1	126.2	87.1	287.8	66.9
Motor vehicle theft	65.3	290.2	41.0	33.6	116.6	25.3
Theft over $5,000	13.2	26.8	11.7	6.1	5.9	6.1
Theft $5,000 and under	439.5	1,317.4	344.9	219.2	354.7	205.6
Possession of stolen goods	92.5	263.9	74.0	91.1	189.6	81.2
Fraud	126.0	95.7	129.2	78.5	43.3	82.0
Other *Criminal Code* offences	644.0	1,249.6	578.7	701.0	1,070.7	663.8
Criminal Code traffic offences	373.2	0.0	413.4	268.1	0.0	295.1
Impaired driving	319.6	0.0	354.0	213.8	0.0	235.4
Other *Criminal Code* traffic offences[3]	53.6	0.0	59.4	54.3	0.0	59.8
Federal statute offences	218.3	378.0	201.1	242.9	464.8	220.6
Drugs[4]	176.9	224.8	171.8	199.4	247.0	194.6
Other federal statute offences	41.4	153.2	29.4	43.5	217.7	26.0

1. Constitutes the intentional application of force without consent, the attempt or threat to apply force to another person or openly wearing a weapon (or an imitation) while accosting or impeding another person.
2. Includes unlawfully causing bodily harm, discharging firearms with intent, abductions, assaults against police officers, assaults against other peace or public officers and other assaults.
3. Includes dangerous operation of a motor vehicle, boat, vessel or aircraft; dangerous operation of a motor vehicle, boat, vessel or aircraft causing bodily harm or death; driving a motor vehicle while prohibited; and failure to stop or remain.
4. Includes possession, trafficking, importation and production.

Source: Statistics Canada, CANSIM table 252-0014.

Table 7.4 Homicides, by province and territory, 2004 to 2006

	2004		2005		2006	
	number	rate per 100,000 people	number	rate per 100,000 people	number	rate per 100,000 people
Canada	**624**	**2.0**	**663**	**2.1**	**605**	**1.9**
Newfoundland and Labrador	2	0.4	11	2.1	7	1.4
Prince Edward Island	0	0.0	0	0.0	1	0.7
Nova Scotia	14	1.5	20	2.1	16	1.7
New Brunswick	7	0.9	9	1.2	7	0.9
Quebec	111	1.5	100	1.3	93	1.2
Ontario	187	1.5	219	1.7	196	1.5
Manitoba	50	4.3	49	4.2	39	3.3
Saskatchewan	39	3.9	43	4.3	40	4.1
Alberta	86	2.7	108	3.3	96	2.8
British Columbia	113	2.7	101	2.4	108	2.5
Yukon	7	22.7	1	3.2	0	0.0
Northwest Territories	4	9.4	0	0.0	0	0.0
Nunavut	4	13.5	2	6.7	2	6.5

Note: Homicide includes murder, manslaughter and infanticide.
Source: Statistics Canada, CANSIM table 253-0001.

Table 7.5 Homicides, by method, 2004 to 2006

	2004		2005		2006	
	number	%	number	%	number	%
All methods	**624**	**100.0**	**663**	**100.0**	**605**	**100.0**
Shooting	173	27.7	223	33.6	190	31.4
Stabbing	205	32.9	197	29.7	210	34.7
Beating	136	21.8	144	21.7	117	19.3
Strangulation	63	10.1	47	7.1	48	7.9
Fire (burns/suffocation)	13	2.1	10	1.5	12	2.0
Other methods	21	3.4	26	3.9	14	2.3
Not known	13	2.1	16	2.4	14	2.3

Note: Homicide includes murder, manslaughter and infanticide.
Source: Statistics Canada, CANSIM table 253-0002.

Table 7.6 Solved homicides by type of accused–victim relationship, 2001 to 2006

	2001	2002	2003	2004	2005	2006
	number					
Total accused–victim relationship	**453**	**469**	**432**	**478**	**493**	**452**
Total family relationships	187	184	142	163	158	165
Spouse	89	84	78	75	74	78
Parent	43	36	31	36	22	31
Other family relationship	55	64	33	52	62	56
Other intimate relationship	13	17	11	24	17	15
Acquaintance	155	133	161	173	162	140
Stranger	62	72	61	73	89	75
Accused–victim relationship unknown	6	7	9	2	3	3

Source: Statistics Canada, CANSIM table 253-0006.

Table 7.7 Homicides, by selected census metropolitan area, 1995 to 2005

	Average from 1995 to 2004		2005[1]		
	Victims		Population of census[2] metropolitan area	Victims	
	number	rate per 100,000 population		number	rate per 100,000 population
Population of 500,000 or more					
Toronto	81	1.7	5,306,912	104	2.0
Montréal[3]	70	2.0	3,675,155	48	1.3
Vancouver[4]	53	2.6	2,156,509	62	2.9
Calgary	15	1.6	1,061,524	26	2.5
Edmonton[3]	24	2.5	1,024,946	44	4.3
Ottawa[5]	10	1.2	876,798	11	1.3
Québec	8	1.2	720,787	5	0.7
Winnipeg	21	3.1	698,791	26	3.7
Hamilton[6]	11	1.7	697,239	11	1.6
Population from 100,000 to 499,999					
Kitchener	5	1.0	485,248	7	1.4
London	5	1.0	471,033	14	3.0
St. Catharines–Niagara	6	1.4	434,347	14	3.2
Halifax	7	2.0	380,844	10	2.6
Victoria	6	1.9	336,030	2	0.6
Oshawa	2	0.8	333,617	1	0.3
Windsor	6	2.0	333,163	5	1.5
Gatineau[7]	4	1.3	284,963	3	1.1
Saskatoon	6	2.5	244,826	9	3.7
Regina	6	3.2	201,435	8	4.0
St. John's	2	1.1	181,527	2	1.1
Abbotsford[8]	5	3.0	162,907	4	2.5
Greater Sudbury / Grand Sudbury	3	1.6	160,912	2	1.2
Kingston[8,9]	3	1.6	154,389	5	3.2
Sherbrooke	2	1.1	148,225	0	0.0
Saguenay	1	0.8	147,071	1	0.7
Trois-Rivières	2	1.0	145,567	0	0.0
Saint John	1	0.9	145,363	0	0.0
Thunder Bay	2	1.8	124,262	3	2.4

1. Thirteen homicides included in the 2005 totals occurred in previous years: two in Montréal, one in Toronto, one in Kitchener, one in Edmonton, three in Vancouver and five in areas with a population less than 100,000.
2. Estimates have been revised and adjusted by the Canadian Centre for Justice Statistics to correspond with police boundaries.
3. Includes one homicide that occurred in a correctional institution in 2005.
4. As a result of ongoing investigations in Port Coquitlam, British Columbia, there were five homicides reported in the Vancouver total for 2004 that occurred in previous years, since homicides are counted according to the year in which police file the report.
5. Ottawa refers to the Ontario part of Ottawa–Gatineau.
6. Includes one homicide that occurred in a correctional institution in 2004.
7. Gatineau refers to the Quebec part of Ottawa–Gatineau.
8. Abbotsford and Kingston became census metropolitan areas in 2001. Average number and rate are calculated from 2001 to 2004.
9. Includes one homicide that occurred in a correctional institution and one that occurred in a halfway house in 2005.

Source: Statistics Canada, Catalogue no. 85-002-XIE.

Table 7.8 Composition of the adult correctional population, 2003 to 2006

	2003	2004	2005	2006
	number			
All correctional services	**157,834**	**153,225**	**151,442**	**152,331**
Custodial supervision	31,896	31,359	31,725	33,120
All provincial/territorial custody	19,294	18,979	19,424	20,538
Provincial/territorial custody, sentenced	10,304	9,557	9,529	9,569
Remand	8,658	9,086	9,556	10,668
Other temporary detention, provincial/territorial	332	336	339	301
Federal custody, sentenced	12,602	12,380	12,301	12,582
Community supervision	125,938	121,866	119,717	119,211
All provincial community supervision	118,714	114,771	112,762	112,416
Probation	104,516	100,276	98,061	97,454
Provincial parole	1,014	885	810	927
Conditional sentences	13,184	13,610	13,891	14,035
Community releases[1]	7,224	7,095	6,955	6,795

Notes: Data refer to the average daily midnight count of offenders who are legally required to be at a facility and are present at the time a head count is taken.

Excludes Prince Edward Island, Northwest Territories and Nunavut due to missing data.

1. Movement from custody to federal conditional release and includes provincial/territorial and federal offenders on day parole and full parole, and federal offenders on statutory release. Offenders released on warrant expiry and other release types are excluded.

Source: Statistics Canada, Catalogue no. 85-002-XIE.

Table 7.9 Adult correctional services, incarceration and probation rates in federal, provincial and territorial programs, selected years from 1996 to 2006

	1996	1998	2000	2002	2004	2006
	rate per 100,000 adults					
Incarceration rates[1]						
Canada[2]	152	143	135	133	128	132
Provinces and territories[3]	88	82	79	80	78	82
Federal jurisdiction[4]	64	61	56	53	51	50
Probation rates						
Canada[2]	455	468	442	435	410	387
Provinces and territories[3]	455	468	442	435	410	387
Federal jurisdiction[4]	.	.	.	.	.	.

Notes: Not all variables are applicable to or available for all jurisdictions. Interjurisdictional comparisons of the data should be made with caution.

Excludes Prince Edward Island, Northwest Territories and Nunavut due to missing data.

1. Based on total actual-in counts.
2. Represents the total or weighted average of provincial, territorial and federal jurisdiction figures.
3. Represents the total for all reporting jurisdictions and therefore does not represent a complete provincial and territorial total where data for some jurisdictions are incomplete or not available. The sentenced and other actual-in counts for 1999/2000 and 2000/2001 were revised in 2003/2004.
4. Federal values represent the total of the five Correctional Service Canada regions.

Source: Statistics Canada, CANSIM table 251-0004.

Culture and leisure

8

Overview

Every day Canadians enjoy theatres, concerts, movies, sporting events, radio programs, television shows, books and magazines. We also take part in a wide variety of sports and recreational activities.

Canada's heritage institutions—including historic sites, art galleries and museums, zoos, planetariums and observatories as well as botanical gardens—attract millions of visitors from home and around the world. Visitors to such sites numbered 35 million in 2004, up from 32 million in 2002.

Radio listening in decline

Canadians devoted less time to radio listening in 2006: an average 18.6 hours per week in 2006, down from 19.1 hours in 2005 and 20.5 hours in 1999. The most avid listeners are seniors: senior women tuned in 22.7 hours per week in 2006, and senior men, 19.5 hours. Seniors favour the Canadian Broadcasting Corporation, but the CBC is the least popular choice among young adults who listen to the radio.

Radio listening by young people has declined over the years. Listening by teenagers dropped from 11.3 hours per week in 1999 to 8.6 hours in 2005, and to 7.6 hours in 2006. Digital music players and online music services appear to have had a large impact on the listening habits of teens and young adults.

Movie theatres regain some glitter

Motion picture theatres—including indoor theatres, drive-ins and film festivals— sold 102.9 million tickets in 2006, up 2% from $101.0 million in 2005. On a per capita basis, each Canadian made 3.3 visits to theatres, drive-ins, and film festivals in 2006, based on population projections for the year

Chart 8.1
Average household spending on selected recreational activities

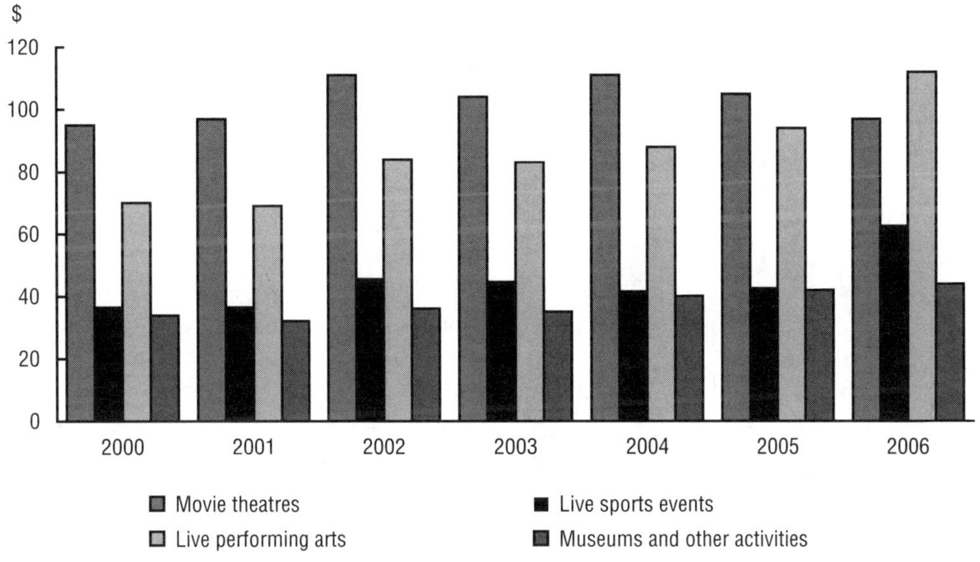

Source: Statistics Canada, CANSIM table 203-0010.

and the number of paid admissions from the 2006 Survey of Service Industries: Motion Picture Theatres. Only residents of Alberta (4.4 visits) and Ontario (3.5) surpassed the national average.

Attendance rebounded from weak years in 2004 and 2005. Box office receipts totaled $744.8 million in 2006, up 3% from $729.3 million in 2005.

Total operating revenues reached $1.2 billion in 2006, up 2% from 2005. Operating expenses dropped in 2006. With attendance up and expenses down, operating profits totalled $111.5 million, up sharply from $21.6 million in 2005. The industry posted an operating profit margin of 9% in 2006 compared with 2% in 2005.

The top chain-operated theatres accounted for the lion's share of revenues and profits. These companies accounted for 84% of national operating revenues in 2006, as they did the year before. Profit margins for the top chain-operated theatres increased to 10% in 2006 from 1% in 2005. Smaller theatres saw more modest profit margins: 5% in 2006, up from 3% in 2005.

Chart 8.2
Radio listening

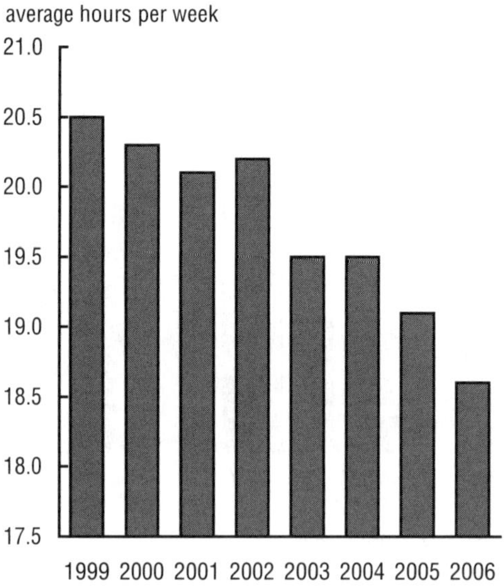

Source: Statistics Canada, CANSIM table 503-0001.

Table 8.a
Financial statistics for performing arts, 2006

	Operating revenue	Operating expenses	Operating profit margin
	$ millions		%
Performing arts companies	**1,207.6**	**1,139.4**	**5.7**
Theatre (except musical) companies	341.6	334.7	2.0
Musical theatre and opera companies	170.8	169.2	1.0
Dance companies	x	x	x
Musical groups and artists	335.5	283.3	15.5
Other performing arts companies	x	x	x

Note: All establishments, by North American Industry Classification system (NAICS).
Source: Statistics Canada, CANSIM table 361-0009.

Performing arts are pulling them in

The performing arts industry—which includes theatre, musical theatre and opera, musical groups and artists, dance companies and other performing arts companies—earned $1.2 billion in total operating revenues in 2006, nearly unchanged from 2005. These revenues were split almost equally between the for-profit and not-for-profit sectors.

The industry's operating profit margin was 6% in 2006, up from 4% in 2005. For-profit companies' margin reached 10%, up from 9% in 2005; not-for-profit companies' margin was 1%, up from a loss of 0.4% the year before.

Not-for-profit performing arts companies attracted an estimated 12.9 million spectators in 2006, down 1% from 2004.

Public sector grants are an important source of revenue for the companies surveyed: in 2006, federal grants totaled $55.5 million for those companies; provincial and territorial, $73.7 million; and municipal, $28.2 million.

Among the not-for-profit companies, ticket sales generated 42% of revenue; merchandising, royalties and rentals, 9%; government grants and subsidies, 26%; and private sector revenue, which includes sponsorships, fundraising events and donations, 23%.

Theatres were the largest part of the not-for-profit sector in 2006, attracting 57% of total attendance and 48% of total revenues. Revenues for these companies were up 2% over 2004; attendance rose 5%.

Virtually all disciplines in the not-for-profit sector posted surpluses in 2006.

Sound recording seeking its groove online

Despite declining record sales and competition from other entertainment, recording industries managed, with difficulty, to turn a profit for a second consecutive year in 2006.

Chart 8.3
Motion picture theatres, paid admissions (attendance)

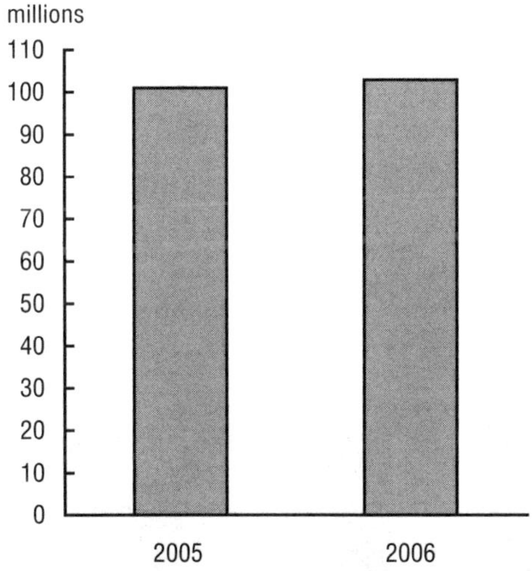

Note: Includes indoor theatres, drive-ins and film festivals.
Source: Statistics Canada, Catalogue no.87F0009XIE.

The music industry comprises three major segments: record production and distribution, music publishing and recording studios. All three recorded profits in 2006 for a second consecutive year, but only recording studios saw a higher profit margin than in 2005.

Record production, the largest segment of the three, took in 77% of the revenues, music publishing, 13%, and recording studios, 10%.

Record production companies realized a profit margin of 10% in 2006, down slightly from 13% in 2005 but up considerably from 0.1% in 2003. Revenues shrank 7% to $712 million. In 2005, firms achieved profitable growth by streamlining and restructuring; the effect of this was less significant in 2006.

One way companies have streamlined operations has been by emphasizing digital products. Digital products make for lower inventory and distribution expenses. Electronic music sales made up 4% of national sales in 2005.

Canadian artists' sales (of both current and older releases) totalled $123 million in 2005, up 3% from 2003. They produced 521 new releases in 2005, up 9% from 2003.

Music publishers represent and publicize songwriters, collecting royalties from performances of their music and promoting the use of their songs in recordings, movies, and on television. The music publishing industry posted $118.6 million in revenues in 2005, with a profit margin of 16%.

Sound recording studios posted revenues of $74.3 million in 2005, for an overall profit margin of 12%. Only 35% of the revenues accrued from music recording: 54% came from commercial audio production and other work.

Sports participation has tumbled

Canadians' participation in organized sports has tumbled, from 45% of those 15 and older in 1992 to 28% in 2005. (Recreational activities such as running, fitness classes and cycling are excluded.)

The aging of the population may be the major factor, as well as family and career responsibilities and other entertainment diversions. For men, lack of time was the main reason given for non-participation; for women, lack of interest was the primary reason. The presence of children in a household increases the liklihood that household members will be involved in sport, either as participants or volunteers.

Among children (aged 5 to 14), soccer is the most popular sport: 44% play it. This enthusiasm for soccer is equal for boys and girls. Soccer's popularity in Canada can be traced to the country's increasingly multicultural population and to the minimal equipment required. Ice hockey, which ranks second in popularity among children, has gained popularity among girls. In 2005, 16% of girls who participated in sports played ice hockey, compared with 6% in 1998.

Parental involvement is a motivator for children. When at least one parent helps out as an administrator, children's participation rate was 80%. Without parental involvement, their rate was just 35%.

Women now outnumber men as coaches. In 2005, 874,000 men and 882,000 women coached amateur sports—four times more women than in 1992. Women have also increased their presence as officials. In 1998, there were five male officials for each female official. By 2005, there were just two males for each female.

For adult men, ice hockey and golf were the most popular sports; among women, swimming and golf were the top two sports.

Chart 8.4
Sport participation, by age and sex, 2005

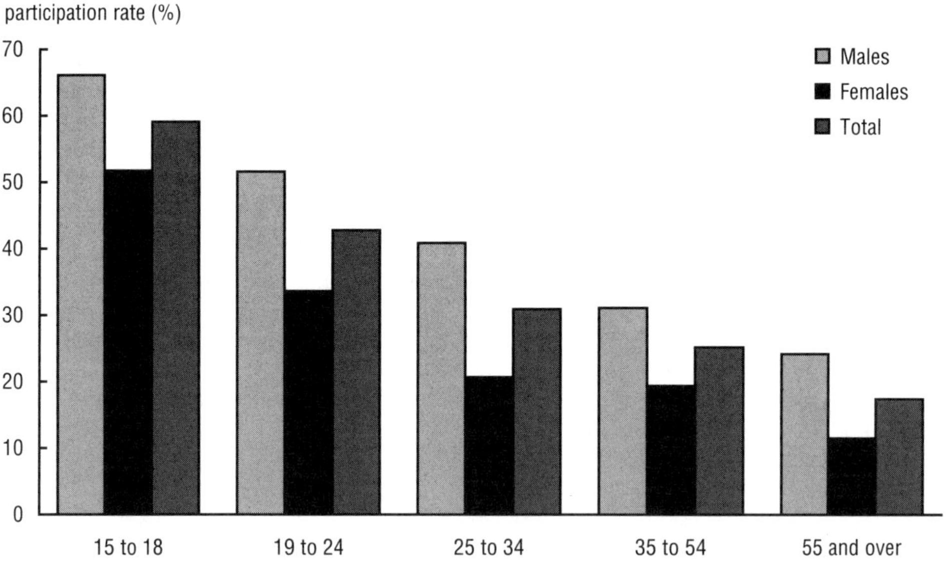

Source: Statistics Canada, Catalogue no. 81-595-MIE.

Culture workers throughout the economy

Culture workers apply their knowledge, creativity and skills in many industries outside the culture sector. Nearly half of all culture workers in the 1991, 1996 and 2001 censuses worked in non-culture industries, particularly in manufacturing, business services, educational services and retail trade sectors.

According to a study released in 2008, Canada had 260,000 'core culture workers' in 2001. About 104,000 of them worked in non-culture industries, comprising 0.8% of the non-culture labour force.

Core culture workers are those directly involved in creative and artistic production or heritage collection or preservation such as writers, architects, graphic and interior designers, actors, producers and directors, musicians, dancers, librarians, conservators and archivists.

An example of a core culture worker in a non-culture sector would be an architect designing a commercial building, or a graphic designer creating a logo for a marketing campaign.

In 2001, about 19,000 core culture workers were employed in manufacturing, 55% more than in 1991. Another 25,000 worked in business services firms in 2001, about double the number a decade earlier. In both sectors, employment growth for core culture workers far outstripped employment growth for the sector as a whole. Another 10,000 core culture workers were employed in retail trade industries, down from nearly 15,000 in 1991.

These numbers suggest that culture-based creativity, as well as scientific and technical expertise, can be a key ingredient for firms that are producing goods and services.

Chart 8.5
Culture worker employment, by selected non-culture industries, 2001

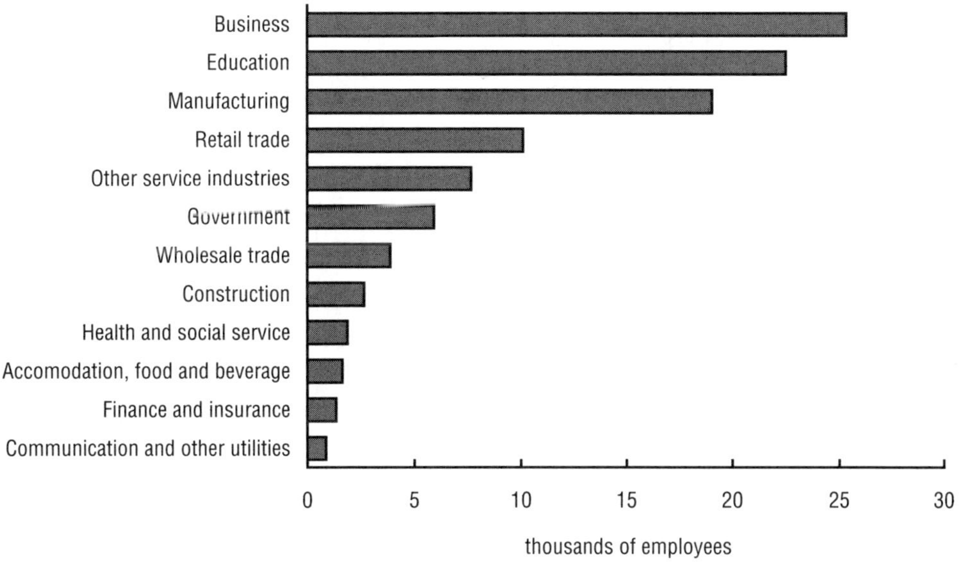

Source: Statistics Canada, Catalogue no. 81-595-MIE.

Table 8.1 Federal government expenditures on culture, by cultural activity and by province and territory, 2003/2004

	Canada[1]	Newfoundland and Labrador	Prince Edward Island	Nova Scotia	New Brunswick	Quebec	Ontario	Manitoba
	$ thousands							
All cultural activities	**3,499,568**	45,048	19,023	117,397	56,009	1,171,180	1,463,715	85,078
Libraries	**43,289**	0	2	15	15	28,165	14,809	28
Heritage resources	**937,218**	20,917	8,809	50,067	14,654	267,773	339,321	34,281
Arts education[2]	**18,263**	0	0	0	2	7,484	8,024	703
Literary arts	**162,144**	555	128	1,653	813	40,004	81,108	1,653
Performing arts	**184,503**	1,896	2,613	5,428	5,711	37,967	90,970	8,256
Visual arts and crafts	**23,226**	261	187	921	435	6,011	7,943	1,581
Film and video	**386,183**	1,032	578	14,307	3,163	173,930	129,526	7,696
Broadcasting[3]	**1,605,488**	17,122	4,625	42,667	27,474	555,195	749,519	28,201
Sound recording	**28,507**	4	78	50	86	18,670	9,216	36
Multiculturalism	**14,317**	234	108	303	304	3,571	2,624	487
Multidisciplinary activities[4]	**81,474**	2,969	1,866	1,842	2,887	28,543	20,613	2,008
Other culture activities	**14,956**	59	30	145	466	3,868	10,041	147

	Saskatchewan	Alberta	British Columbia	Yukon	Northwest Territories	Nunavut	Other national organizations and foreign countries[5]
	$ thousands						
All cultural activities	45,762	152,848	203,084	16,425	30,471	11,125	82,402
Libraries	7	53	66	10	7	7	105
Heritage resources	15,534	74,823	73,414	10,172	15,210	9,055	3,188
Arts education[2]	0	1,562	488	0	0	0	0
Literary arts	1,080	3,718	8,095	108	76	17	23,136
Performing arts	2,942	9,442	14,679	672	754	131	3,042
Visual arts and crafts	980	1,043	3,373	60	33	70	330
Film and video	2,129	13,191	36,712	106	37	230	3,548
Broadcasting[3]	21,108	43,288	58,211	5,059	14,100	1,490	37,428
Sound recording	45	63	238	11	0	0	10
Multiculturalism	642	1,629	903	0	58	0	3,453
Multidisciplinary activities[4]	1,257	3,997	6,837	173	196	124	8,162
Other culture activities	38	38	68	54	0	0	0

Note: Figures may not add to totals because of rounding.

1. Total expenditures at the national level exclude intramural (operating and capital) expenditures by Human Resources Development Canada directly related to training and employment development in the culture sector.
2. Refers to the fine, applied and performing arts rather than to strictly academic fields such as language, history, literature, etc. The term 'arts,' as used here, includes theatre, music, dance, painting, drama, photography and any other area of arts study reported by arts education institutions.
3. The Canadian Broadcasting Corporation distributes its program costs by location of production activities. Station transmission and network distribution costs are related to the geographic location of the transmitter except for landlines and satellite channels, which are paid by Ottawa, but transferred to Toronto and Montréal network centres. Payments to private station affiliates are charged to the responsible network centres and relate also to the province where these centres are located. Administration costs and capital expenditures are distributed according to the province where the administration function is located geographically and the location of capital assets.
4. Includes financial support given to cultural facilities, centres, festivals, municipalities, cultural exchange programs and arts organizations for various cultural activities.
5. Includes national organizations, foreign countries and unallocated expenditures.

Source: Statistics Canada, CANSIM table 505-0001.

Table 8.2 Federal government expenditures on culture, by cultural activity, 1998/1999 to 2003/2004

	1998/1999	1999/2000	2000/2001	2001/2002	2002/2003	2003/2004
	$ thousands					
All cultural activities[1]	**2,817,086**	**2,809,375**	**2,954,793**	**3,216,927**	**3,425,691**	**3,499,568**
Libraries	45,079	36,794	39,896	51,218	45,285	43,289
Heritage resources	654,391	638,856	709,491	739,495	786,199	937,218
Arts education[2]	7,489	11,404	10,881	11,996	14,227	18,263
Literary arts	123,486	129,158	160,038	174,679	183,357	162,144
Performing arts	112,001	126,093	131,787	164,477	207,858	184,503
Visual arts and crafts	17,023	17,520	18,423	21,227	21,351	23,226
Film and video	292,547	294,072	305,945	328,585	397,786	386,183
Broadcasting[3]	1,455,905	1,435,663	1,475,316	1,585,541	1,600,551	1,605,488
Sound recording	9,279	9,777	10,210	18,606	22,977	28,507
Multiculturalism	1,744	3,635	3,520	888	11,720	14,317
Multidisciplinary activities[4]	79,142	97,217	80,453	108,259	102,671	81,474
Other culture activities	19,000	9,185	8,832	11,954	31,709	14,956

Note: Figures may not add to totals because of rounding.

1. Total expenditures at the national level exclude intramural (operating and capital) expenditures by Human Resources Development Canada directly related to training and employment development in the culture sector.
2. Arts education refers to the fine, applied, and performing arts rather than to strictly academic fields such as language, history, literature, etc. The term 'arts' as used here includes theatre, music, dance, painting, drama, photography and any other area of arts study reported by arts education institutions.
3. The Canadian Broadcasting Corporation distributes its program costs by location of production activities. Station transmission and network distribution costs are related to the geographic location of the transmitter except for landlines and satellite channels, which are paid by Ottawa, but transferred to Toronto and Montréal network centres. Payments to private station affiliates are charged to the responsible network centres and relate also to the province where these centres are located. Administration costs and capital expenditures are distributed according to the province where the administration function is located geographically and the location of capital assets.
4. Includes financial support given to cultural facilities, centres, festivals, municipalities, cultural exchange programs and arts organizations for various cultural activities.

Source: Statistics Canada, CANSIM table 505-0001.

Table 8.3 Attendance of not-for-profit cultural performances, by cultural activity, 2004 and 2006

	Total performances		Total attendance		Average attendance per performance	
	2004	2006p	2004	2006p	2004	2006p
	number					
All cultural activities	**41,145**	**37,888**	**13,029,049**	**12,889,186**	**317**	**340**
Theatre	28,326	26,063	7,003,437	7,331,922	247	281
Musical theatre, dinner theatre, opera	3,226	2,099	1,094,678	980,758	339	467
Dance	3,063	2,771	1,429,400	1,442,583	467	521
Musical group or artist	4,534	4,971	3,038,944	2,758,672	670	555
Other performing arts companies	1,996	1,984	462,589	375,251	232	189

Note: Data may not add to totals because of rounding.

Source: Statistics Canada, Catalogue no. 87F0003XIE.

Table 8.4 Performances and attendance of not-for-profit cultural performances, by province, 2004 and 2006

	Total performances		Total attendance		Average attendance per performance	
	2004r	2006p	2004r	2006p	2004r	2006
	number					
Canada	**41,145**	**37,888**	**13,029,049**	**12,889,186**	**317**	**340**
Newfoundland and Labrador	2,171	805	318,519	140,361	147	174
Prince Edward Island	x	..	x	..	x	..
Nova Scotia	877	1,152	377,806	392,553	431	341
New Brunswick	761	x	227,817	x	299	x
Quebec	12,177	12,031	3,768,377	3,501,636	309	291
Ontario	12,208	11,276	4,380,554	4,462,032	359	396
Manitoba	1,306	1,432	496,205	594,761	380	415
Saskatchewan	854	x	293,210	x	343	394
Alberta	3,987	4,251	1,100,458	1,391,396	276	327
British Columbia	6,654	5,786	2,048,902	2,016,356	308	348

Note: Data may not add to totals because of rounding.
Source: Statistics Canada, Catalogue no. 87F0003X.

Table 8.5 Government expenditures on culture, by level of government and by province and territory, 2003/2004

	Total gross expenditures	Federal government	Provincial and territorial governments	Local governments[1]
	$ thousands			
Total expenditures	**7,706,675[2]**	**3,499,568**	**2,200,067**	**2,007,040**
Newfoundland and Labrador	**96,057**	45,048	39,006	12,003
Prince Edward Island	**33,486**	19,023	11,753	2,710
Nova Scotia	**209,243**	117,397	57,007	34,839
New Brunswick	**131,943**	56,009	52,082	23,852
Quebec	**2,317,653**	1,171,180	726,842	419,631
Ontario	**2,969,512**	1,463,715	628,228	877,569
Manitoba	**262,407**	85,078	111,832	65,497
Saskatchewan	**206,349**	45,762	87,733	72,854
Alberta	**537,275**	152,848	198,518	185,909
British Columbia	**777,259**	203,084	264,668	309,507
Yukon	**29,885**	16,425	12,779	681
Northwest Territories	**41,942**	30,471	9,620	1,851
Nunavut	**11,262**	11,125	..	137
Other[3]	**82,403**	82,403	0	0

1. Calculated on a calendar-year basis.
2. Includes intergovernmental transfers of about $365 million.
3. Includes national organizations, foreign countries and unallocated expenditures.

Source: Statistics Canada, Catalogue no. 87F0001XIE.

Table 8.6 Summary statistics for periodical publishing industry, by province or region, 2004 to 2006

	Canada	Atlantic region	Quebec	Ontario	Prairies	British Columbia and the territories
	$ thousands					
Operating revenue[1]						
2004[r]	**1,847,115**	37,754	466,241	1,023,519	171,028	148,573
2005[r]	**1,968,718**	37,490	485,338	1,104,693	181,667	159,530
2006	**2,072,748**	37,425	496,964	1,173,523	200,748	164,088
Operating expenses[2]						
2004[r]	**1,620,153**	35,523	415,625	890,199	150,795	128,011
2005[r]	**1,789,480**	36,311	448,440	993,239	169,089	142,400
2006	**1,846,379**	37,804	435,397	1,050,173	173,189	149,816
Salaries, wages and benefits[3]						
2004[r]	**466,597**	11,586	82,378	277,471	52,140	43,021
2005[r]	**499,817**	12,163	91,385	298,839	51,714	45,715
2006	**512,026**	13,281	88,988	297,331	62,123	50,303
	%					
Operating profit margin[4]						
2004[r]	**12.3**	5.9	10.9	13.0	11.8	13.8
2005[r]	**9.1**	3.1	7.6	10.1	6.9	10.7
2006	**10.9**	-1.0	12.4	10.5	13.7	8.7

Notes: Data may not add to totals because of rounding.
Estimates for the most recent year are preliminary. Preliminary data are subject to revision.

1. Operating revenue excludes investment income, capital gains, extraordinary gains and other non-recurring items.
2. Operating expenses exclude write-offs, capital losses, extraordinary losses, interest on borrowing, and other non-recurring items.
3. Salaries, wages and benefits include vacation pay and commissions for all employees for whom T4 slips were completed. This category also includes the employer portion of employee benefits for items such as Canada/Quebec Pension Plans or Employment Insurance premiums. Salaries and wages do not include working owners' dividends nor do they include the remuneration of owners of unincorporated business. Therefore the relative level of salaries, wages and benefits will be lower in industries where unincorporated businesses are significant contributors.
4. Profit margin is derived as follows: operating revenue minus operating expenses, expressed as a percentage of total revenue. The derived figure excludes corporation income tax paid by incorporated businesses and individual income tax paid by unincorporated businesses. For unincorporated businesses, profit margin includes unpaid remuneration accruing to partners and proprietors, which is not recorded as salaries, wages and benefits. Therefore the profit estimate will be higher in industries where unincorporated proprietorships and partnerships are significant contributors.

Source: Statistics Canada, Catalogue no. 87F0005XIE.

Table 8.7 Not-for-profit heritage institutions, 2004

	Total	Museums	Arts museums and galleries	Historic sites and galleries	Zoos and botanical gardens
			number		
Total heritage institutions	**614**	**299**	**109**	**173**	**33**
			$ thousands		
Total operating revenues	**897,402**	**435,485**	**235,335**	**90,755**	**135,827**
Unearned operating revenues	**581,851**	313,460	172,535	51,360	44,496
Federal government	**202,283**	126,702	x	x	1,146
Provincial government	**192,706**	109,126	60,439	14,270	8,871
Other government	**74,074**	24,863	x	x	21,427
Institutional/private	**112,788**	52,769	x	x	13,052
Earned operating revenues	**329,683**	132,981	64,930	39,915	91,858
Admissions	**134,547**	56,546	12,609	14,610	50,782
Memberships	**14,680**	6,013	4,320	589	3,759
Other earned revenues	**180,456**	70,422	48,001	24,716	37,317
Total operating expenditures	**921,519**	**450,063**	**243,591**	**93,535**	**134,330**
Wages	**431,674**	206,362	105,190	50,717	69,405
Artifacts	**26,081**	6,247	19,027	711	96
Other operating expenses	**463,765**	237,453	119,374	42,108	64,830
Operating profit	**-24,117**	**-14,578**	**-8,256**	**-2,780**	**1,497**
			number		
Employment					
Full time	**6,466**	3,231	1,557	640	1,038
Part time	**9,384**	3,156	1,350	3,053	1,826
Volunteers	**47,856**	15,771	17,033	10,310	4,743

Note: Data may not add to totals because of rounding.
Source: Statistics Canada, Catalogue no. 87F0002XIE.

Table 8.8 Music publishing industry, 2005 and 2006

	Operating revenue[1]		Salaries, wages and benefits[2]		Operating expenses[3]		Operating profit margin[4]	
	2005	2006	2005	2006	2005	2006	2005	2006
	$ thousands						%	
Canada	118,600	124,300	17,200	20,300	100,000	111,800	15.7	10.1

Note: Data may not add to totals because of rounding.
1. Operating revenue excludes investment income (dividends and interest).
2. Salaries, wages and benefits include employer contributions to pension, medical/life insurance plans, employment insurance, etc., for all employees who have been issued a T4 statement.
3. Operating expenses exclude interest on borrowing, write-offs, capital losses, extraordinary losses, and other non-recurring items.
4. Operating profit margin is derived as follows: total operating revenue minus total operating expenses, expressed as a percentage of total operating revenue.

Source: Statistics Canada, Catalogue no. 87F0008X.

Table 8.9 Profile of the music publishing industry, 2005 and 2006

	2005	2006
	$ thousands	
Operating revenue	**107,447**	**116,012**
Revenue from sales of goods and services	7,321	10,900
Revenue from royalties, rights, licensing and franchise fees	95,258	99,123
All other operating revenue[1]	4,869	5,988
Operating expenses	**89,870**	**104,085**
Royalties, rights or franchise fees	49,929	58,569
Salaries, wages and benefits	14,785	18,898
Commissions paid to non-employees	6,013	2,776
Cost of goods sold	3,760	2,623
Amortization of tangible and intangible assets	5,905	5,570
All other operating expenses[2]	9,477	15,648
	%	
Operating profit margin[3]	**16.4**	**10.3**

Note: Data may not add to totals because of rounding.

1. All other operating revenue includes grants and subsidies and other revenue.
2. All other operating expenses include professional and business services fees, payments for services provided by head office, office supplies, rental and leasing, repair and maintenance, insurance, advertising, marketing and promotions, travel, meals and entertainment, utilities, telephone and telecommunications, property and business taxes, licences and permits, delivery, warehousing, postage and courier, financial service fees, charitable donations, bad debts and all other expenses.
3. Operating profit margin is derived as follows: total operating revenue minus total operating expenses, expressed as a percentage of total operating revenue.

Source: Statistics Canada, Catalogue no. 87F0008X.

Table 8.10 Record production and integrated record production and distribution industry, by region, 2005 and 2006

	Operating revenue[1]		Salaries, wages and benefits[2]		Operating expenses[3]		Operating profit margin[4]	
	2005	2006	2005	2006	2005	2006	2005	2006
	$ thousands						%	
Canada	**765,400**	**712,300**	**89,400**	**94,200**	**664,800**	**644,400**	**13.1**	**9.5**
Atlantic Provinces	6,300	4,000	800	600	5,200	3,600	17.7	10.7
Quebec	148,700	90,900	17,600	10,700	141,900	82,500	4.6	9.3
Ontario	479,400	533,400	55,700	73,600	406,000	502,400	15.3	5.8
Prairie Provinces	39,200	20,300	4,900	5,700	31,500	17,700	19.7	12.5
British Columbia and Territories	91,800	63,800	10,500	3,600	80,300	38,300	12.5	40.0

Notes: Data may not add to totals because of rounding.

1. Operating revenue excludes investment income (dividends and interest).
2. Salaries, wages and benefits include employer contributions to pension, medical/life insurance plans, employment insurance, etc., for all employees who have been issued a T4 statement.
3. Operating expenses exclude interest on borrowing, write-offs, capital losses, extraordinary losses, and other non-recurring items.
4. Operating profit margin is derived as follows: total operating revenue minus total operating expenses, expressed as a percentage of total operating revenue.

Source: Statistics Canada, Catalogue no. 87F0008X.

Table 8.11 Summary statistics for the sound recording studio industry, by region, 2005 and 2006

	Operating revenue[1]		Salaries, wages and benefits[2]		Operating expenses[3]		Operating profit margin[4]	
	2005	2006	2005	2006	2005	2006	2005	2006
	$ thousands						%	
Canada	**92,500**	**82,900**	**19,000**	**18,900**	**82,200**	**72,600**	**11.2**	**12.5**
Atlantic Provinces	3,100	2,300	700	700	2,900	2,000	6.7	11.8
Quebec	26,900	21,200	5,800	5,100	24,200	18,400	9.9	13.4
Ontario	36,400	34,500	6,800	7,300	32,100	29,600	11.8	14.3
Prairie Provinces	7,000	5,700	1,400	1,400	5,800	5,200	16.2	9.4
British Columbia and Territories	19,100	19,200	4,200	4,400	17,100	17,500	10.8	9.2

Notes: Data may not add to totals because of rounding.

1. Operating revenue excludes investment income (dividends and interest).
2. Salaries, wages and benefits include employer contributions to pension, medical/life insurance plans, employment insurance, etc., for all employees who have been issued a T4 statement.
3. Operating expenses exclude interest on borrowing, write-offs, capital losses, extraordinary losses, and other non-recurring items.
4. Operating profit margin is derived as follows: total operating revenue minus total operating expenses, expressed as a percentage of total operating revenue.

Source: Statistics Canada, Catalogue no. 87F0008X.

Table 8.12 Distribution revenue for the film and video distribution industry, by Canadian and non-Canadian productions, primary market, 2005 and 2006

	2005[r]	2006
	$ thousands	
Distribution revenue of Canadian productions[1]	**163,810**	**152,438**
Theatrical market	11,123	11,558
Pay TV market	47,607	52,702
Conventional TV market	12,335	38,719
Home video market	x	x
Other markets	x	x
Distribution of Canadian productions to foreign clients	79,504	27,645
Distribution revenue of non-Canadian productions[1]	**963,229**	**995,114**
Theatrical market	314,401	326,750
Pay TV market	71,490	79,659
Conventional TV market	237,808	256,217
Home video market	x	x
Other markets	x	x
Distribution of non-Canadian productions to foreign clients	10,740	5,187

Note: Industry estimates are based on the surveyed portion and are augmented by administrative data for establishments that were too small to be eligible for sampling.

1. By domestic market.

Source: Statistics Canada, Survey of Service Industries, 2006.

Table 8.13 Selected financial statistics for performing arts, all industries, by province, 2005 and 2006

	Operating revenue		Salaries, wages and benefits		Operating expenses		Operating profit margin	
	2005r	2006p	2005r	2006p	2005r	2006p	2005r	2006p
	$ thousands						%	
For-profit establishments								
Canada	**630,750**	**590,618**	**149,633**	**142,732**	**576,313**	**530,011**	**8.6**	**10.3**
Newfoundland and Labrador	5,336	5,706	881	904	5,168	5,024	3.1	12.0
Prince Edward Island	x	x	x	x	x	x	x	x
Nova Scotia	6,875	7,539	1,303	1,069	6,118	6,414	11.0	14.9
New Brunswick	2,372	x	651	x	2,181	x	8.1	x
Quebec	353,870	321,929	94,226	94,550	338,276	303,925	4.4	5.6
Ontario	172,765	161,485	38,623	34,982	150,291	143,601	13.0r	11.1
Manitoba	15,546	11,527	1,961	2,413	13,437	9,232	13.6	19.9
Saskatchewan	3,902	4,293	375	655	3,160	3,402	19.0	20.8
Alberta	27,778	28,981	5,537	4,813	24,243	24,341	12.7	16.0
British Columbia	41,084	46,054	5,789	2,192	32,319	30,800	21.3	33.1
Not-for-profit establishments								
Canada	**584,227**	**617,008**	**193,390**	**213,117**	**586,680**	**609,361**	**-0.4**	**1.2**
Newfoundland and Labrador	3,643	3,662	1,725	1,273	3,815	3,590	-4.7	2.0
Prince Edward Island	x	x	x	x	x	x	x	x
Nova Scotia	9,504	10,252	3,182	3,394	8,868	10,444	6.7	-1.9
New Brunswick	4,627	x	1,623	x	4,604	x	0.5	x
Quebec	160,193	162,471	48,168	48,511	159,441	159,053	0.5	2.1
Ontario	247,700	253,635	81,289	98,457	252,225	253,747	-1.8	0.0
Manitoba	24,325	24,172	11,458	10,562	24,299	23,529	0.1	2.7
Saskatchewan	8,391	8,815	2,890	3,373	8,126	8,244	3.2	6.5
Alberta	62,569	74,705	21,967	23,303	62,794	71,263	-0.4	4.6
British Columbia	62,592	73,681	20,883	22,700	61,854	73,368	1.2	0.4

Note: Data may not add to totals because of rounding.

Source: Statistics Canada, Catalogue no. 87F0003X.

Table 8.14 Motion picture theatre industry, by selected characteristics, 2006

	Canada	Quebec	Ontario	Saskatchewan	Alberta	British Columbia
	$ thousands					
Total operating revenue	**1,189,647**	**210,546**	**508,193**	**31,605**	**171,863**	**163,997**
Total admission receipts	**744,822**	136,426	316,556	17,840	103,426	107,997
Sales of food and beverages	**343,547**	51,665	142,948	11,118	57,389	45,273
All other operating revenue	**101,279**	22,456	48,690	2,647	11,049	10,728
Total operating expenses	**1,079,074**	**201,406**	**474,366**	**26,576**	**137,210**	**147,569**
Salaries, wages and benefits	**170,256**	37,739	70,638	4,456	21,207	21,171
Cost of goods sold	**74,031**	12,079	31,579	2,702	13,178	7,703
Film rental and royalty payments	**374,144**	66,491	160,044	8,782	50,587	55,322
All other operating expenses	**460,643**	85,096	212,105	10,636	52,238	63,372
	number					
Theatre operations						
Paid admissions (attendance)	**102,927,624**	20,700,371	41,955,618	3,130,483	14,418,135	13,326,854
Screens	**2,831**	633	1,056	107	376	380
	%					
Operating profit margin	**9.3**	**4.3**	**6.7**	**15.9**	**20.2**	**10.0**

Note: Data for the Atlantic provinces, Manitoba, Yukon, Northwest Territories and Nunavut are suppressed for confidentiality.

Source: Statistics Canada, Catalogue no. 87F0009X.

Economic accounts

9

Overview

In the last five years, ours has become a different economy. Starting in 2003, rising oil, metal and other commodity prices, among other events, started a transformation. By 2007, finance and insurance, retail and wholesale trade as well as construction were the main sectors contributing to growth. Western Canada had displaced Central Canada as the driver of national economic growth, the Canadian dollar had reached par with the U.S. greenback, the manufacturing sector was in flux, and consumer spending was strong.

Growth slowed gradually during 2007 because of flagging U.S. demand. However, the real gross domestic product (GDP), measured year to year, was 2.7% greater in 2007 than in 2006. Annual GDP rose from \$1.0 trillion in 2003 to \$1.2 trillion in 2007, an increase of 12.1%.

A measure of the value of all goods and services produced, GDP gauges an economy's size and performance. Canada's GDP, which is measured monthly and quarterly as well as annually, recorded 18 consecutive quarter-to-quarter increases after the second quarter of 2003, when the SARS crisis occurred.

The country's GDP growth has been broad-based: since 2003 all but a few industries have seen output rise. The services-producing sector, which accounts for over two-thirds of Canada's GDP, has been particularly strong. Services grew 14% from 2003 to 2007, driven mainly by wholesale trade, with 23% growth in GDP; retail trade, 20%; and finance, insurance and real estate, 16%.

The goods-producing sector grew more slowly, about 8%, from 2003 to 2007. After increasing 3% in 2004, growth in goods-producing industries slowed each year to 0.8% in 2007; some industries posted year-over-year declines. After spectacular growth

Chart 9.1
Real gross domestic product at market prices, by province and territory

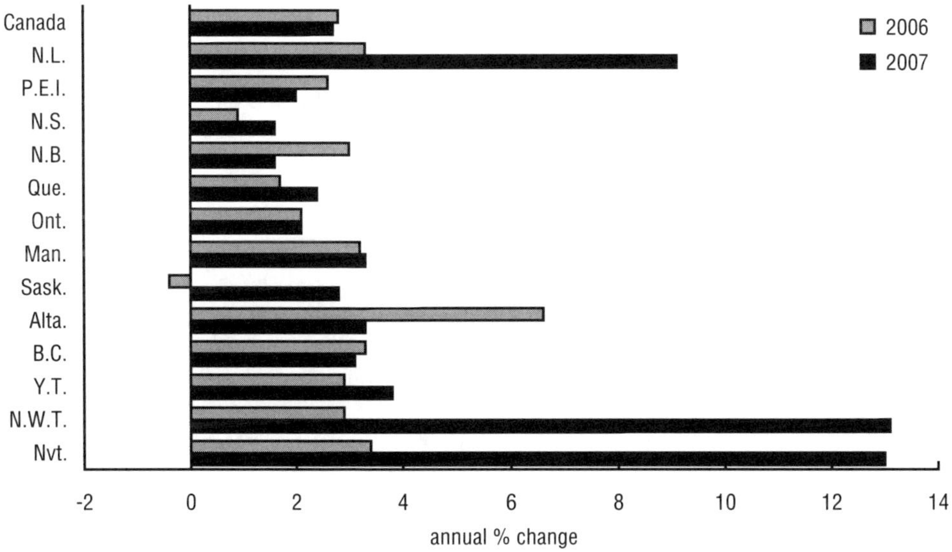

Note: Chained 2002 dollars.
Source: Statistics Canada, CANSIM table 384-0002.

in 2003 and 2004, the agriculture, forestry, fishing and hunting industry shrank in 2006 and 2007. Manufacturing, struggling with stiff competition and the higher loonie, has not seen output grow since 2005.

Construction has been the fastest-growing industry over the last five years. From 2003 to 2007, it expanded output 29%, from $59.9 billion to $76.9 billion. The hot construction sector has been buoyed by Western Canada's growing economy. However, in 2007, both non-residential and residential construction were slowing.

Western Canada is leading

Rising commodity prices have stoked expansion in primary industries with a strong presence in Western Canada, such as agriculture, mining and oil and gas extraction. GDP growth was noticeably stronger among western provinces, except for a decline in Saskatchewan in 2006. Mining caused strong GDP growth in Newfoundland

Chart 9.2
Consumer borrowing

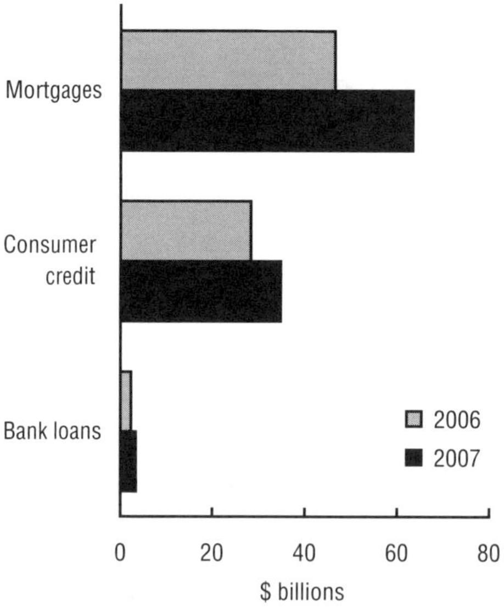

Note: Seasonally adjusted data at annual rates.
Source: Statistics Canada, Catalogue no. 13-010-XWE.

Table 9.a
National balance sheet

	2003	2007
	$ millions	
Assets	12,194,457	16,587,961
Liabilities	8,243,656	11,080,632
Net worth	3,950,801	5,507,329

Source: Statistics Canada, CANSIM table 378-0004.

and Labrador (9.1%), the Northwest Territories (13.1%), and Nunavut (13.0%).

Alberta's economy grew by 3.3% in 2007, half the 2006 rate, but still outpaced all the provinces and territories from 2004 to 2006. Although oil and gas exploration was curtailed in 2006 and 2007, their extraction increased. Canadians kept flocking to Alberta in 2007, drawn by its low unemployment rate, and this spurred residential and non-residential investment.

Although growth slowed to 3.1% in British Columbia, 2007 was the sixth year in a row that the province's growth rate exceeded the national average. A rising population, construction for the 2010 Olympic Games and gains in financial services, wholesale trade and retail trade have been the major drivers of growth.

Ontario, at 2.1%, and Quebec, at 2.4%, grew slower than the national average, as they have each year since 2003. The rising loonie and a slowdown in the U.S. economy hampered both provinces' export-oriented manufacturing industries in 2007.

Although Newfoundland and Labrador led the provinces in GDP growth in 2007, the rest of Atlantic Canada posted growth that lagged behind the national average.

More income, more spending, more borrowing

Wallets and bank accounts have expanded with the economy. Income Canadians earn—from wages, investments, government benefits and their unincorporated businesses—increased 39% from 2000 to 2007. Individual Canadians earned a total $1.17 trillion in 2007.

Canadians have been quicker to spend than to save: while expenditures, including taxes, climbed 43% from 2000 to 2007, savings dropped 20%. In 2007, real consumer spending rose 4.5%, its largest gain since 1997.

Companies are benefitting from a strong economy. Since 2002, consistently rising operating profits have enabled businesses to put money back into their operations. Businesses raised nearly $75 billion in 2007 by borrowing from banks and selling bonds and shares to invest in plants, machinery and equipment, and engineering projects.

But businesses could not keep up with individual Canadians. Collectively, Canadians have been borrowing more each year since 2003—just under $120 billion in 2007. About two-thirds of these funds were for mortgages; most of the other third was borrowed via consumer credit programs such as credit cards.

Chart 9.3
Canadian and foreign direct investment

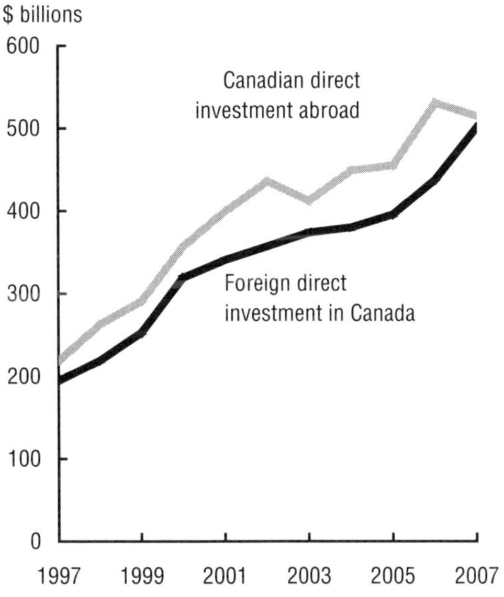

Source: Statistics Canada, CANSIM table 376-0051.

Investing in Canada, investing in the world

The expanding economy, particularly the resource sector, ensured that Canada continued to be attractive for foreign direct investors. Foreign corporate inflows to Canada gained 14.4% in 2007, one of the largest rises in the past 22 years. It was led mainly by acquisitions of Canadian firms.

For a second straight year, the growing foreign corporate investment in Canada was led by investors from countries besides the United States, traditionally the biggest foreign direct investor in Canadian firms. In 2007, the biggest growth came from the United Kingdom, the Netherlands, France, Switzerland and Germany.

Foreign direct investment in Canada reached the half-trillion-dollar mark at the end of 2007. The United States still accounted for nearly 58% of foreign direct investment in Canada, with holdings of $288.6 billion in 2007. Foreign direct investment was concentrated in the manufacturing and oil and gas industries.

Canadian direct investors are similarly active overseas, although the amount they held overseas in 2007 fell by $15.4 billion from 2006. This was only the second annual decline since 1986. Both times, the rise in the value of the Canadian dollar played a significant role.

Financial, insurance and management industries accounted for nearly half of the money Canadian direct investors held overseas in 2007: manufacturing, mining, and oil and gas firms absorbed most of the rest. About 44% of Canada's $514.5 billion in direct investment abroad was in American firms.

The value of Canada's natural resources

Canada's natural resource wealth, the dollar value of selected natural resource reserves, was $1.3 trillion in 2007. It had increased 10% per year, on average, during the preceding decade.

Minerals and timber contribute greatly to Canada's total wealth. Metal prices rose quickly in 2003, and prices for nickel, copper, zinc, iron ore and other metals and metal ores set new records.

Prices of nonmetallic minerals—notably potash, uranium and diamonds—also rose steadily. Metals and minerals accounted for 66% of Canada's exports of industrial goods.

Canada exported $40 billion worth of metal alloys, which are ores refined to a finished or semi-finished state, and $11 billion of ores, which require smelting and refining. Exports of precious metals, particularly diamonds, rose from 2002 to 2004, as did gold prices from 2004 to 2007.

Forestry exports, however, have lost share compared with other exports in recent decades. Forestry products accounted for 17.8% of exports in 1978, 10.8% in 1998 and 6.5% in 2007. The value of exports of forestry products peaked at $42.8 billion in 2000, then fell steadily to $30.9 billion in 2007. Lower prices, the rising value of the Canadian dollar compared with the U.S. dollar, and declining demand for lumber, pulp, and paper pushed down the value of forestry products.

Paper products have shown the most persistent weakness among forestry exports. The demand for paper products has fallen steadily since 2001; newsprint demand from the United States has dropped 47% since early 2001.

Natural resource extraction and processing can be controversial. Harvesting of forestry products impacts wildlife habitat, air and water quality, aesthetics and recreational access.

Chart 9.4
Selected natural resource assets

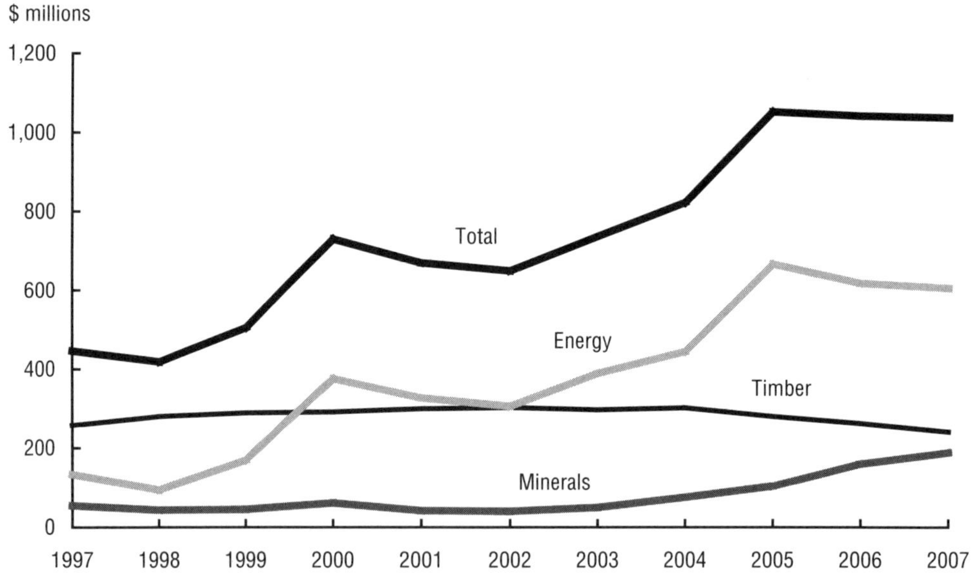

Source: Statistics Canada, CANSIM table 378-0005.

Indicators offer a look at emerging trends

Although predicting the future is difficult, economists and statisticians have devised tools to help provide early warnings of change in the business cycle.

These 'leading indicators' measure the economic decisions people and companies make based on many factors, including what their financial situation might be a few months from now. For example, families are less likely to spend a lot of money on big-ticket household goods if they are unsure about their jobs or the state of the economy.

So, Statistics Canada tracks sales of furniture, appliances and other durable goods as leading indicators of household sentiment—how confident Canadians are about their economic situations. Their confidence affects consumer spending, which is a major contributor to economic health. In June 2008, retail sales of furniture and appliances rose 0.3% and sales of other durable goods, 0.5%, suggesting that the job market was healthy and that families were confident enough to buy big-ticket items.

Similarly, if manufacturers see signs of a spending slowdown, or fewer orders arriving, they may curb their employees' hours of work. After averaging 38.1 hours per week in the first three months of 2008, employees worked slightly less in April and May.

Other popular leading indicators include the housing index (measures new housing starts and existing home sales), the stock market and inventories.

The composite index, which combines 10 leading indicators, uses a five-month moving average to smooth out irregular fluctuations and revisions in the index. This allows users to better judge what it is signaling about the underlying trend of the economy in the months ahead.

Chart 9.5
Composite leading indicator

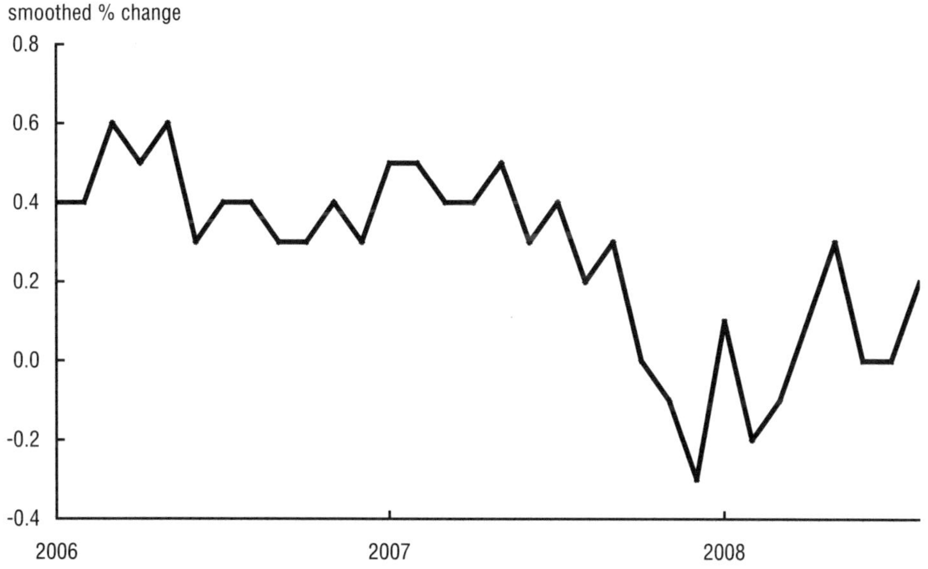

Source: Statistics Canada, CANSIM table 377-0003.

Table 9.1 Gross domestic product, expenditure-based, by province and territory, 1993 to 2007

	1993	1994	1995	1996	1997	1998	1999	2000
	$ millions							
Canada	**727,184**	**770,873**	**810,426**	**836,864**	**882,733**	**914,973**	**982,441**	**1,076,577**
Newfoundland and Labrador	9,771	10,264	10,652	10,417	10,533	11,176	12,184	13,922
Prince Edward Island	2,471	2,521	2,662	2,823	2,800	2,981	3,159	3,366
Nova Scotia	18,343	18,667	19,296	19,512	20,368	21,401	23,059	24,658
New Brunswick	14,693	15,286	16,380	16,626	16,845	17,633	19,041	20,085
Quebec	162,229	170,478	177,331	180,526	188,424	196,258	210,809	224,928
Ontario	293,405	311,096	329,317	338,173	359,353	377,897	409,020	440,759
Manitoba	24,590	25,958	26,966	28,434	29,751	30,972	31,966	34,057
Saskatchewan	22,928	24,480	26,425	28,944	29,157	29,550	30,778	33,828
Alberta	81,179	88,041	92,036	98,634	107,048	107,439	117,080	144,789
British Columbia	94,077	100,512	105,670	108,865	114,383	115,641	120,921	131,333
Yukon	882	910	1,047	1,128	1,107	1,087	1,085	1,190
Northwest Territories (including Nunavut)	2,267	2,387	2,400	2,525	2,691	2,652	..	..
Northwest Territories	..	..	..	..	..	..	2,292	2,515
Nunavut	..	..	..	..	..	..	747	834
Outside Canada	349	273	244	257	273	286	300	313

	2001	2002	2003	2004	2005	2006	2007
	$ millions						
Canada	**1,108,048**	**1,152,905**	**1,213,175**	**1,290,828**	**1,375,080**	**1,446,307**	**1,531,427**
Newfoundland and Labrador	14,179	16,457	18,119	19,302	21,496	25,608	29,034
Prince Edward Island	3,431	3,701	3,798	3,994	4,118	4,304	4,538
Nova Scotia	25,909	27,082	28,851	30,014	31,575	31,997	33,296
New Brunswick	20,684	21,169	22,366	23,534	24,190	25,346	26,410
Quebec	231,624	241,448	250,752	262,890	272,672	282,841	298,157
Ontario	453,701	477,763	493,081	516,792	536,908	557,784	582,019
Manitoba	35,157	36,559	37,451	39,859	41,682	44,851	48,586
Saskatchewan	33,127	34,343	36,653	40,417	43,773	45,922	51,166
Alberta	151,274	150,594	170,113	189,521	222,159	240,025	259,941
British Columbia	133,514	138,193	145,642	157,365	169,404	180,328	190,214
Yukon	1,259	1,254	1,292	1,371	1,478	1,549	1,687
Northwest Territories (including Nunavut)	..	..	..	..	..	..	..
Northwest Territories	2,972	3,033	3,692	4,322	4,128	4,150	4,580
Nunavut	876	951	991	1,073	1,103	1,184	1,371
Outside Canada	341	358	374	374	394	418	428

Note: Dollar amounts in current prices.

Source: Statistics Canada, CANSIM table 384-0002.

Table 9.2 Gross domestic product, income-based, 1993 to 2007

	1993	1994	1995	1996	1997	1998	1999	2000
	$ millions							
Gross domestic product at market prices	**727,184**	**770,873**	**810,426**	**836,864**	**882,733**	**914,973**	**982,441**	**1,076,577**
Net domestic product at basic prices	576,833	613,352	644,818	664,294	700,063	723,487	780,786	863,254
Wages, salaries and supplementary labour income	394,816	404,918	418,825	428,792	453,073	475,335	502,726	545,204
Corporation profits before taxes	41,102	65,464	76,270	80,335	87,932	86,132	110,769	135,978
Government business enterprise profits before taxes	4,694	5,827	6,709	6,143	6,653	7,080	8,401	11,329
Interest and miscellaneous investment income	52,381	52,000	50,981	50,477	48,881	47,134	47,249	55,302
Accrued net income of farm operators from farm production	2,017	1,255	2,702	3,825	1,663	1,724	1,819	1,243
Net income of non-farm unincorporated business, including rent	42,068	44,931	46,363	49,278	54,663	57,936	61,466	64,944
Inventory valuation adjustment	-3,122	-5,372	-2,473	-1,596	-623	-753	-2,317	-2,439
Taxes less subsidies on factors of production	42,877	44,329	45,441	47,040	47,821	48,899	50,673	51,693
Taxes less subsidies on products	54,350	56,721	59,758	61,126	66,025	68,439	72,747	76,647
Capital consumption allowances	94,035	99,631	105,021	110,818	116,574	122,659	128,999	137,425
Statistical discrepancy	1,966	1,169	829	626	71	388	-91	-749

	2001	2002	2003	2004	2005	2006	2007
	$ millions						
Gross domestic product at market prices	**1,108,048**	**1,152,905**	**1,213,175**	**1,290,828**	**1,375,080**	**1,446,307**	**1,531,427**
Net domestic product at basic prices	884,203	912,615	967,051	1,032,534	1,104,917	1,164,344	1,237,131
Wages, salaries and supplementary labour income	570,008	593,307	621,003	654,957	694,041	737,382	782,290
Corporation profits before taxes	127,073	135,229	144,501	169,151	189,357	198,859	210,426
Government business enterprise profits before taxes	10,787	11,661	12,604	12,923	14,578	13,823	15,455
Interest and miscellaneous investment income	52,579	46,693	49,989	54,109	61,070	65,310	68,684
Accrued net income of farm operators from farm production	1,675	1,101	1,439	3,106	1,321	344	582
Net income of non-farm unincorporated business, including rent	68,857	74,292	77,181	81,037	83,636	85,980	89,777
Inventory valuation adjustment	574	-3,584	4,262	-1,747	-933	-1,775	2,968
Taxes less subsidies on factors of production	52,650	53,916	56,072	58,998	61,847	64,421	66,949
Taxes less subsidies on products	75,871	84,139	84,380	89,838	94,334	97,161	100,133
Capital consumption allowances	147,536	155,567	161,817	168,274	176,338	184,750	193,814
Statistical discrepancy	438	584	-73	182	-509	52	349

Note: Dollar amounts in current prices.

Source: Statistics Canada, CANSIM table 380-0016.

Table 9.3 Gross domestic product, expenditure-based, 1993 to 2007

	1993	1994	1995	1996	1997	1998	1999	2000
	$ millions							
Gross domestic product at market prices	**727,184**	**770,873**	**810,426**	**836,864**	**882,733**	**914,973**	**982,441**	**1,076,577**
Personal expenditure on consumer goods and services	428,219	445,857	460,906	480,427	510,695	531,169	560,884	596,009
Durable goods	50,170	54,116	56,169	59,197	67,988	71,325	77,693	81,958
Semi-durable goods	39,263	41,104	42,304	42,766	44,939	47,262	49,548	52,115
Non-durable goods	111,863	112,287	115,024	118,697	123,143	126,253	132,959	143,264
Services	226,923	238,350	247,409	259,767	274,625	286,329	300,684	318,672
Government current expenditure on goods and services	171,163	171,590	172,459	171,161	171,756	179,317	186,054	200,084
Government gross fixed capital formation	19,805	21,634	21,406	20,587	20,104	20,046	23,039	24,524
Government inventories	-4	-1	30	-2	5	-27	-3	24
Business gross fixed capital formation	111,269	123,321	121,592	129,351	154,737	161,790	171,431	181,748
Residential structures	39,666	42,422	36,136	39,538	43,519	42,497	45,100	48,572
Non-residential structures and equipment	71,603	80,899	85,456	89,813	111,218	119,293	126,331	133,176
Non-residential structures	30,192	34,002	34,669	36,360	43,872	45,177	47,229	49,826
Machinery and equipment	41,411	46,897	50,787	53,453	67,346	74,116	79,102	83,350
Business investment in inventories	-1,294	528	8,999	2,271	8,174	4,733	4,990	11,505
Non-farm	-2,153	775	8,705	1,577	9,174	5,409	4,951	11,355
Farm	859	-247	294	694	-1,000	-676	39	150
Exports of goods and services	219,664	262,127	302,480	321,248	348,604	379,203	424,258	490,688
Goods	190,213	228,168	265,334	280,079	303,379	327,160	369,037	429,375
Services	29,451	33,959	37,146	41,169	45,225	52,043	55,221	61,313
Imports of goods and services	219,673	253,014	276,618	287,553	331,271	360,871	388,303	428,754
Goods	177,121	207,875	229,938	237,689	277,727	303,395	327,026	362,337
Services	42,552	45,139	46,680	49,864	53,544	57,476	61,277	66,417
Statistical discrepancy	-1,965	-1,169	-828	-626	-71	-387	91	749
Final domestic demand	**730,456**	**762,402**	**776,363**	**801,526**	**857,292**	**892,322**	**941,408**	**1,002,365**

See note and source at end of table.

Table 9.3 Gross domestic product, expenditure-based, 1993 to 2007 (continued)

	2001	2002	2003	2004	2005	2006	2007
	$ millions						
Gross domestic product at market prices	**1,108,048**	**1,152,905**	**1,213,175**	**1,290,828**	**1,375,080**	**1,446,307**	**1,531,427**
Personal expenditure on consumer goods and services	620,614	655,722	686,552	720,401	760,701	803,502	853,966
Durable goods	84,930	92,085	93,793	95,479	100,014	105,716	111,944
Semi-durable goods	54,565	57,052	58,485	60,608	63,055	66,818	70,364
Non-durable goods	150,305	158,399	168,144	176,939	187,836	195,572	205,652
Services	330,814	348,186	366,130	387,375	409,796	435,396	466,006
Government current expenditure on goods and services	211,706	224,428	238,416	248,868	262,650	279,806	298,067
Government gross fixed capital formation	27,287	28,589	30,107	32,082	36,296	40,336	43,715
Government inventories	13	-45	15	21	27	-41	15
Business gross fixed capital formation	189,978	196,585	208,090	229,434	253,074	277,885	297,636
Residential structures	55,133	65,651	72,714	82,918	89,791	98,386	108,592
Non-residential structures and equipment	134,845	130,934	135,376	146,516	163,283	179,499	189,044
Non-residential structures	52,966	50,659	54,545	62,081	72,674	85,698	92,800
Machinery and equipment	81,879	80,275	80,831	84,435	90,609	93,801	96,244
Business investment in inventories	-4,740	-2,674	4,305	5,589	9,642	7,824	7,152
Non-farm	-3,745	-1,094	2,982	4,098	9,038	8,369	8,378
Farm	-995	-1,580	1,323	1,491	604	-545	-1,226
Exports of goods and services	482,463	479,185	462,473	495,347	520,379	524,706	534,669
Goods	420,733	414,034	399,122	429,064	451,779	455,696	465,237
Services	61,730	65,151	63,351	66,283	68,600	69,010	69,432
Imports of goods and services	418,836	428,301	416,856	440,732	468,197	487,660	503,445
Goods	350,067	356,728	342,711	363,307	388,282	404,391	415,595
Services	68,769	71,573	74,145	77,425	79,915	83,269	87,850
Statistical discrepancy	-437	-584	73	-182	508	-51	-348
Final domestic demand	**1,049,585**	**1,105,324**	**1,163,165**	**1,230,785**	**1,312,721**	**1,401,529**	**1,493,384**

Note: Dollar amounts in current prices.

Source: Statistics Canada, CANSIM table 380-0017.

Table 9.4 Gross domestic product at basic prices, by sector, 1997 to 2007

	1997	1998	1999	2000	2001
	millions of chained 2002 dollars				
All industries[1]	**888,158**	**922,584**	**974,405**	**1,026,242**	**1,040,943**
Goods-producing industries					
Agriculture, forestry, fishing and hunting	22,985	24,471	26,193	26,268	24,674
Mining and oil and gas extraction	49,244	49,991	50,000	51,519	51,236
Manufacturing	151,330	158,819	171,923	188,925	181,084
Construction	45,421	46,928	49,053	51,757	55,542
Utilities	29,045	28,554	28,982	29,050	27,384
Service-producing industries					
Transportation and warehousing	43,048	43,905	46,603	48,921	50,176
Information and cultural industries	26,403	28,255	31,617	34,007	36,498
Wholesale trade	42,823	46,221	49,396	52,519	53,438
Retail trade	44,499	47,210	49,437	52,579	55,234
Finance and insurance, real estate and renting, and leasing and management of companies and enterprises	168,523	173,796	181,851	189,181	196,769
Professional, scientific and technical services	33,859	38,056	41,845	46,307	47,453
Administrative and support, waste management and remediation services	17,582	18,771	20,934	21,809	22,820
Educational services	48,904	49,000	50,162	50,394	50,675
Health care and social assistance	61,114	61,765	63,754	65,968	67,198
Arts, entertainment and recreation	8,669	8,928	9,333	9,718	10,142
Accommodation and food services	21,668	22,931	23,804	24,544	24,950
Public administration	54,293	54,909	56,674	57,968	59,705
Other services (except public administration)	21,262	21,886	23,335	24,627	26,101

See notes and source at end of table.

Table 9.4 Gross domestic product at basic prices, by sector, 1997 to 2007 (continued)

	2002	2003	2004	2005	2006	2007
	millions of chained 2002 dollars					
All industries[1]	**1,068,765**	**1,091,378**	**1,126,802**	**1,160,024**	**1,193,905**	**1,223,949**
Goods-producing industries						
Agriculture, forestry, fishing and hunting	23,293	25,478	27,685	28,437	27,847	27,077
Mining and oil and gas extraction	53,488	54,979	55,849	56,044	57,174	58,342
Manufacturing	182,736	181,349	185,504	188,478	186,631	184,712
Construction	57,775	59,871	63,592	68,527	74,087	76,884
Utilities	28,883	29,057	29,131	30,550	30,128	31,169
Service-producing industries						
Transportation and warehousing	50,066	50,270	51,960	53,802	55,501	56,377
Information and cultural industries	38,229	38,631	40,232	41,848	43,147	44,202
Wholesale trade	55,226	57,767	60,283	63,879	68,383	71,334
Retail trade	58,483	60,515	62,870	65,132	69,015	72,915
Finance and insurance, real estate and renting, and leasing and management of companies and enterprises	202,959	207,544	215,098	221,951	230,362	240,054
Professional, scientific and technical services	48,481	50,797	52,349	53,793	55,377	57,296
Administrative and support, waste management and remediation services	24,853	25,722	27,345	28,756	30,524	31,666
Educational services	51,593	52,566	53,807	55,008	56,221	57,571
Health care and social assistance	68,142	70,324	71,736	72,784	74,780	76,753
Arts, entertainment and recreation	10,398	10,365	10,848	10,940	11,410	11,713
Accommodation and food services	25,408	24,881	25,721	26,418	27,365	27,681
Public administration	61,523	63,314	64,355	65,309	66,758	67,973
Other services (except public administration)	27,230	27,894	28,825	29,346	30,072	30,904

Note: North American Industry Classification System (NAICS), 2002.

1. Aggregates are not always equal to the sum of their components from 1981 to 2001. This is caused by changing the set of relative prices when a new base year is adopted.

Source: Statistics Canada, CANSIM table 379-0027.

Table 9.5 Canada's balance of international payments, 1993 to 2007

	1993	1994	1995	1996	1997	1998	1999	2000
	$ millions							
Current account								
Receipts	**235,576**	**285,601**	**330,978**	**351,038**	**385,415**	**414,777**	**461,219**	**531,961**
Goods and services	218,444	260,917	301,130	319,965	347,134	377,385	422,670	489,090
Goods	190,213	228,167	265,334	280,079	303,378	327,162	369,035	429,372
Services	28,230	32,750	35,796	39,886	43,755	50,223	53,636	59,718
Investment income	13,787	21,100	25,898	26,176	33,252	32,338	32,905	36,755
Transfers	3,346	3,584	3,951	4,897	5,029	5,054	5,644	6,116
Payments	**263,670**	**303,331**	**337,078**	**346,438**	**396,812**	**426,140**	**458,649**	**502,692**
Goods and services	218,964	252,285	275,869	286,650	330,346	359,947	387,298	427,836
Goods	177,123	207,873	229,937	237,689	277,727	303,399	327,026	362,337
Services	41,840	44,413	45,933	48,961	52,619	56,549	60,272	65,500
Investment income	40,619	46,990	57,089	55,571	62,133	61,965	66,518	69,863
Transfers	4,088	4,056	4,120	4,217	4,333	4,228	4,834	4,992
Balance	**-28,093**	**-17,730**	**-6,099**	**4,600**	**-11,397**	**-11,363**	**2,570**	**29,269**
Goods and services	-520	8,632	25,261	33,315	16,788	17,438	35,373	61,254
Goods	13,090	20,295	35,397	42,391	25,652	23,763	42,009	67,036
Services	-13,610	-11,663	-10,136	-9,076	-8,864	-6,325	-6,636	-5,782
Investment income	-26,832	-25,889	-31,191	-29,395	-28,882	-29,627	-33,613	-33,109
Transfers	-742	-472	-169	680	697	826	810	1,124
Capital account, net flow	**10,704**	**10,241**	**6,784**	**7,957**	**7,508**	**4,934**	**5,049**	**5,314**
Financial account, net flow[1]	**23,763**	**7,520**	**-5,489**	**-20,191**	**8,256**	**-405**	**-17,531**	**-27,070**
Canadian assets, net flow	-26,943	-49,029	-38,394	-73,306	-62,546	-67,161	-41,946	-142,039
Canadian direct investments abroad	-7,354	-12,694	-15,732	-17,858	-31,937	-50,957	-25,625	-66,352
Canadian portfolio investments	-17,881	-8,927	-7,331	-19,317	-11,849	-22,497	-23,101	-63,927
Foreign portfolio bonds	-5,071	435	-1,085	-2,070	-6,642	-7,064	-2,477	-3,963
Foreign portfolio stocks	-12,811	-9,362	-6,247	-17,247	-5,207	-15,433	-20,623	-59,965
Foreign money market	..	..	..	..	..	..	..	..
Other Canadian investments	-1,707	-27,408	-15,331	-36,132	-18,760	6,292	6,780	-11,759
Loans	-1,139	123	-3,438	-4,208	-18,923	12,637	2,680	-5,126
Deposits	10,214	-19,889	-7,162	-18,015	-2,898	-6,225	10,592	3,973
Official international reserves	-1,206	489	-3,778	-7,498	3,389	-7,452	-8,818	-5,480
Other assets	-9,576	-8,131	-952	-6,411	-328	7,332	2,326	-5,125
Canadian liabilities, net flow	50,706	56,550	32,905	53,116	70,803	66,757	24,415	114,969
Foreign direct investments in Canada	6,103	11,206	12,703	13,137	15,958	33,828	36,762	99,198
Foreign portfolio investments	52,799	23,312	25,233	18,668	16,181	24,779	3,738	14,598
Canadian portfolio bonds	31,446	15,995	30,730	17,953	6,166	10,337	2,602	-21,458
Canadian portfolio stocks	12,056	6,412	-4,242	8,034	7,645	14,311	14,346	35,232
Canadian money market	9,296	905	-1,254	-7,319	2,369	130	-13,209	824
Other foreign investments	-8,196	22,032	-5,032	21,311	38,664	8,149	-16,086	1,173
Loans	-325	-137	1,129	5,994	1,873	3,181	6,641	3,396
Deposits	-8,180	21,005	-6,009	16,863	34,106	3,375	-24,103	-962
Other liabilities	310	1,165	-151	-1,546	2,685	1,593	1,377	-1,261
Statistical discrepancy	**-6,374**	**-32**	**4,805**	**7,633**	**-4,367**	**6,833**	**9,912**	**-7,514**

See note and source at end of table.

Table 9.5 Canada's balance of international payments, 1993 to 2007 (continued)

	2001	2002	2003	2004	2005	2006	2007
	$ millions						
Current account							
Receipts	**513,754**	**514,913**	**496,899**	**539,081**	**575,151**	**594,207**	**605,933**
Goods and services	480,795	477,522	460,903	493,757	518,762	522,926	532,690
Goods	420,730	414,039	399,122	429,067	451,783	455,696	465,232
Services	60,065	63,483	61,781	64,690	66,979	67,230	67,458
Investment income	25,990	30,502	29,253	38,169	48,213	61,599	63,679
Transfers	6,968	6,890	6,743	7,155	8,176	9,682	9,564
Payments	**488,649**	**495,135**	**482,250**	**510,030**	**547,208**	**570,629**	**591,751**
Goods and services	417,945	427,434	416,011	439,988	467,423	486,789	502,509
Goods	350,071	356,727	342,710	363,308	388,282	404,395	415,599
Services	67,874	70,707	73,302	76,680	79,141	82,394	86,910
Investment income	65,320	60,799	59,284	62,468	70,735	73,446	79,358
Transfers	5,384	6,902	6,955	7,574	9,051	10,394	9,884
Balance	**25,104**	**19,778**	**14,649**	**29,051**	**27,943**	**23,578**	**14,183**
Goods and services	62,850	50,088	44,892	53,769	51,340	36,137	30,181
Goods	70,659	57,311	56,413	65,759	63,501	51,302	49,633
Services	-7,809	-7,224	-11,521	-11,990	-12,162	-15,165	-19,452
Investment income	-39,330	-30,297	-30,031	-24,299	-22,522	-11,847	-15,678
Transfers	1,584	-12	-212	-419	-875	-712	-320
Capital account, net flow	**5,752**	**4,936**	**4,225**	**4,466**	**5,940**	**4,201**	**4,280**
Financial account, net flow[1]	**-21,375**	**-22,144**	**-19,935**	**-37,295**	**-38,287**	**-22,741**	**-22,642**
Canadian assets, net flow	-113,930	-83,631	-67,724	-87,448	-116,081	-165,339	-163,768
Canadian direct investments abroad	-55,800	-42,015	-32,118	-56,841	-40,645	-51,322	-53,130
Canadian portfolio investments	-37,573	-29,319	-19,054	-24,369	-53,279	-78,693	-45,873
Foreign portfolio bonds	-1,920	-6,229	-7,974	-15,290	-29,238	-43,602	-26,732
Foreign portfolio stocks	-35,653	-21,253	-7,699	-8,092	-21,951	-28,291	-30,563
Foreign money market	..	-1,837	-3,381	-987	-2,089	-6,800	11,422
Other Canadian investments	-20,556	-12,297	-16,553	-6,238	-22,157	-35,325	-64,765
Loans	-8,051	-8,587	7,614	3,558	8,217	-12,201	-9,835
Deposits	-2,172	5,844	-19,286	-10,661	-15,817	-8,183	-39,195
Official international reserves	-3,353	298	4,693	3,427	-1,653	-1,013	-4,644
Other assets	-6,980	-9,851	-9,574	-2,561	-12,903	-13,927	-11,091
Canadian liabilities, net flow	92,555	61,487	47,789	50,153	77,793	142,598	141,125
Foreign direct investments in Canada	42,844	34,769	10,483	-474	35,046	78,317	115,407
Foreign portfolio investments	37,779	18,599	19,714	54,762	9,577	32,544	-33,754
Canadian portfolio bonds	41,002	18,297	7,870	19,449	-78	18,015	9,477
Canadian portfolio stocks	4,125	-1,531	13,491	35,742	9,133	10,814	-41,808
Canadian money market	-7,349	1,833	-1,646	-429	522	3,715	-1,424
Other foreign investments	11,932	8,119	17,592	-4,135	33,171	31,737	59,473
Loans	-5,941	1,400	2,192	-2,013	3,496	11,873	8,290
Deposits	23,716	13,565	18,304	-531	28,951	20,724	48,556
Other liabilities	-5,843	-6,846	-2,904	-1,591	723	-860	2,627
Statistical discrepancy	**-9,481**	**-2,570**	**1,062**	**3,778**	**4,404**	**-5,038**	**4,180**

1. A minus sign denotes an outflow of capital resulting from an increase in claims to non-residents or a decrease in liabilities to non-residents.

Source: Statistics Canada, CANSIM tables 376-0001 and 376-0002.

Table 9.6 National balance sheet, assets, 1993 to 2007

	1993	1994	1995	1996	1997	1998	1999	2000
	$ millions							
All assets	**6,836,021**	**7,261,081**	**7,621,198**	**8,105,253**	**8,682,898**	**9,236,089**	**9,885,481**	**10,555,419**
Non-financial assets	2,654,584	2,783,847	2,852,877	2,942,186	3,077,380	3,218,515	3,382,306	3,564,334
Residential structures	707,914	739,526	749,702	770,434	798,876	829,677	871,382	906,034
Non-residential structures	709,197	737,311	759,734	788,612	818,984	845,979	875,800	920,032
Machinery and equipment	266,244	280,939	291,852	295,130	316,413	343,059	362,083	387,713
Consumer durables	218,930	227,097	231,167	236,360	246,692	258,923	277,357	292,519
Inventories	124,483	131,535	146,976	151,010	158,782	170,248	179,202	194,775
Land	627,816	667,439	673,446	700,640	737,633	770,629	816,482	863,261
Financial assets	4,181,437	4,477,234	4,768,321	5,163,067	5,605,518	6,017,574	6,503,175	6,991,085
Official reserves	16,881	17,487	20,769	28,204	25,705	35,920	41,463	47,801
Currency and bank deposits	386,748	414,558	442,188	464,682	504,193	500,298	540,982	605,648
Deposits in other institutions	183,650	173,614	177,209	181,106	168,562	174,625	185,072	147,525
Foreign currency and deposits	43,663	51,390	60,940	80,699	83,313	93,760	106,853	68,843
Consumer credit	104,551	111,166	116,713	124,054	132,826	144,189	158,245	172,093
Trade receivables	139,379	145,109	156,170	164,913	171,371	177,799	193,695	211,106
Bank loans	146,588	152,733	156,407	155,890	165,433	181,953	179,536	187,401
Other loans	92,441	103,787	108,681	116,467	132,026	145,558	163,978	170,401
Government of Canada short-term paper	139,687	129,356	133,524	117,851	95,038	77,955	85,482	72,775
Other short-term paper	63,370	66,829	69,965	80,505	103,581	128,194	160,587	173,781
Mortgages	417,936	433,497	443,906	459,879	478,715	497,928	519,765	544,082
Canada bonds	160,497	196,841	211,323	236,162	257,268	272,808	270,424	275,418
Provincial bonds	172,593	174,398	185,059	189,232	196,566	194,756	212,204	223,209
Municipal bonds	32,413	33,240	32,896	33,851	33,669	30,354	28,140	31,248
Other Canadian bonds	105,496	118,813	121,893	127,457	146,112	165,706	197,381	223,714
Life insurance and pensions	526,636	562,116	606,231	655,736	716,423	788,892	861,409	940,531
Corporate claims	462,841	503,729	545,557	576,758	645,998	734,715	748,271	868,874
Government claims	115,210	118,551	116,629	128,318	127,675	138,481	178,467	194,366
Shares	464,964	514,889	551,957	641,383	747,558	835,134	925,606	1,030,985
Foreign investments	80,452	96,910	104,850	127,767	150,569	172,303	193,275	225,148
Other financial assets	325,441	358,221	405,454	472,153	522,917	526,246	552,340	576,136

See source at end of table.

Table 9.6 National balance sheet, assets, 1993 to 2007 (continued)

	2001	2002	2003	2004	2005	2006	2007
				$ millions			
All assets	**11,160,760**	**11,737,908**	**12,194,457**	**13,046,496**	**14,048,355**	**15,231,434**	**16,465,708**
Non-financial assets	3,737,307	3,965,790	4,167,500	4,483,592	4,794,042	5,157,467	5,570,981
Residential structures	958,361	1,031,276	1,122,515	1,215,119	1,314,745	1,465,798	1,597,176
Non-residential structures	946,214	976,364	1,015,034	1,084,323	1,131,290	1,165,960	1,257,686
Machinery and equipment	408,142	421,169	401,783	403,433	413,633	429,636	434,585
Consumer durables	308,021	330,846	345,088	359,248	374,978	386,824	398,575
Inventories	190,419	192,381	187,661	194,972	206,397	215,949	220,286
Land	926,150	1,013,754	1,095,419	1,226,497	1,352,999	1,493,300	1,662,673
Financial assets	7,423,453	7,772,118	8,026,957	8,562,904	9,254,313	10,073,967	10,894,727
Official reserves	53,327	56,230	45,689	40,314	38,029	40,960	40,593
Currency and bank deposits	637,910	678,791	707,792	782,036	856,234	919,320	1,012,386
Deposits in other institutions	160,118	164,536	180,135	193,269	210,475	225,308	245,627
Foreign currency and deposits	86,488	99,598	89,391	94,779	107,659	137,908	176,808
Consumer credit	187,131	204,792	225,221	248,691	273,869	302,103	336,850
Trade receivables	214,873	220,682	226,005	232,658	254,173	263,727	277,602
Bank loans	183,646	188,161	186,216	204,636	216,670	233,352	273,490
Other loans	176,959	194,674	192,815	209,452	219,123	233,575	240,258
Government of Canada short-term paper	92,290	97,163	108,420	110,734	120,159	113,158	107,002
Other short-term paper	169,597	171,604	156,627	154,342	175,390	214,354	226,562
Mortgages	571,944	601,957	640,838	687,882	748,525	816,121	904,583
Canada bonds	265,727	252,269	256,616	241,593	239,769	233,402	229,976
Provincial bonds	229,529	243,154	249,110	269,554	279,833	277,287	299,627
Municipal bonds	31,468	32,827	34,068	35,633	36,067	38,557	42,480
Other Canadian bonds	244,926	275,042	307,390	349,091	414,970	476,637	550,242
Life insurance and pensions	955,577	979,100	1,012,979	1,080,258	1,165,390	1,262,798	1,361,965
Corporate claims	976,178	1,063,854	1,075,689	1,168,054	1,217,074	1,308,610	1,430,860
Government claims	206,288	211,297	208,916	209,713	209,243	217,751	226,561
Shares	1,083,434	1,112,494	1,146,388	1,201,121	1,313,995	1,463,863	1,580,828
Foreign investments	256,414	280,438	263,886	265,695	295,396	367,418	349,566
Other financial assets	639,629	643,455	712,766	783,399	862,270	927,758	980,861

Source: Statistics Canada, CANSIM table 378-0004.

Table 9.7 National balance sheet, liabilities, 1993 to 2007

	1993	1994	1995	1996	1997	1998	1999	2000
	$ millions							
Liabilities and net worth	**6,836,021**	**7,261,081**	**7,621,198**	**8,105,253**	**8,682,898**	**9,236,089**	**9,885,481**	**10,555,419**
All liabilities	4,505,176	4,810,317	5,092,511	5,474,432	5,895,740	6,317,237	6,746,853	7,199,917
Currency and bank deposits	393,728	423,528	450,727	471,893	513,500	510,176	552,014	618,480
Deposits in other institutions	183,874	173,741	177,332	181,229	168,672	174,732	185,186	147,525
Foreign currency and deposits	72,791	85,759	82,751	94,066	110,575	120,232	124,102	93,582
Consumer credit	104,551	111,166	116,713	124,054	132,826	144,189	158,245	172,093
Trade payables	141,647	147,728	158,491	165,026	171,156	175,277	191,070	211,065
Bank loans	138,914	146,186	149,012	150,255	155,889	174,593	171,523	177,246
Other loans	120,616	126,871	130,736	138,149	149,057	163,928	182,862	185,987
Government of Canada short-term paper	172,479	165,199	164,230	142,128	116,782	97,253	98,203	84,362
Other short-term paper	76,391	78,504	83,360	94,351	122,071	149,783	175,332	189,948
Mortgages	418,319	433,889	444,326	460,199	479,026	498,252	520,095	544,397
Canada bonds	236,552	271,078	297,160	330,359	348,389	360,273	359,966	355,308
Provincial bonds	294,409	321,003	335,365	339,388	342,060	352,913	351,666	354,263
Municipal bonds	37,553	39,007	38,947	39,858	39,432	36,277	33,410	36,071
Other Canadian bonds	179,281	200,766	212,669	226,424	262,779	310,331	343,500	371,832
Life insurance and pensions	526,636	562,116	606,231	655,736	716,423	788,892	861,409	940,531
Corporate claims	194,280	211,810	229,417	244,039	288,752	331,966	324,638	356,884
Government claims	115,210	118,551	116,629	128,318	127,675	138,481	178,467	194,366
Shares	779,751	843,824	906,591	1,027,530	1,157,537	1,285,010	1,397,217	1,599,601
Other liabilities	318,194	349,591	391,824	461,430	493,139	504,679	537,948	566,376
Net worth	2,330,845	2,450,764	2,528,687	2,630,821	2,787,158	2,918,852	3,138,628	3,355,502

See source at end of table.

Table 9.7 National balance sheet, liabilities, 1993 to 2007 (continued)

	2001	2002	2003	2004	2005	2006	2007
				$ millions			
Liabilities and net worth	**11,160,760**	**11,737,908**	**12,194,457**	**13,046,496**	**14,048,355**	**15,231,434**	**16,465,708**
All liabilities	7,626,890	7,980,810	8,243,656	8,743,026	9,420,744	10,172,955	11,050,981
Currency and bank deposits	654,150	692,773	722,022	798,264	872,473	940,210	1,032,928
Deposits in other institutions	160,118	164,536	180,135	193,269	210,475	225,308	245,627
Foreign currency and deposits	110,309	120,120	107,519	103,666	116,274	132,089	170,648
Consumer credit	187,131	204,792	225,221	248,691	273,869	302,103	336,850
Trade payables	219,593	227,139	227,310	231,656	251,353	265,928	286,745
Bank loans	173,216	178,433	180,701	196,762	207,364	217,241	255,592
Other loans	187,799	199,182	196,217	206,014	217,614	222,459	242,914
Government of Canada short-term paper	99,729	107,050	118,941	118,762	129,632	126,307	117,712
Other short-term paper	183,283	186,542	166,356	165,240	185,764	223,451	236,514
Mortgages	572,266	602,323	641,194	688,233	748,873	816,467	904,918
Canada bonds	339,262	331,079	315,027	295,423	285,530	278,641	267,494
Provincial bonds	362,379	376,886	368,899	383,642	391,666	392,391	398,581
Municipal bonds	35,926	36,389	37,202	39,080	39,827	42,664	46,566
Other Canadian bonds	452,086	498,611	519,113	568,588	627,889	710,072	782,006
Life insurance and pensions	955,577	979,100	1,012,979	1,080,258	1,165,390	1,262,798	1,361,965
Corporate claims	399,148	440,710	427,029	429,373	478,062	513,323	581,748
Government claims	206,288	211,297	208,916	209,713	209,243	217,751	226,561
Shares	1,705,341	1,791,515	1,886,844	2,019,868	2,167,565	2,380,209	2,608,066
Other liabilities	623,289	632,333	702,031	766,524	841,881	903,543	947,546
Net worth	3,533,870	3,757,098	3,950,801	4,303,470	4,627,611	5,058,479	5,414,727

Source: Statistics Canada, CANSIM table 378-0004.

Table 9.8 Canada's international investment position, assets, 2002 to 2007

	2002	2003	2004	2005	2006	2007
	$ millions					
All assets	**979,184**	**921,148**	**961,998**	**1,013,424**	**1,190,429**	**1,182,416**
Canadian direct investments abroad	435,494	412,217	448,975	459,606	523,260	508,596
Canadian portfolio investments	270,775	253,788	265,374	292,412	364,664	346,005
Portfolio foreign bonds	45,392	45,809	58,549	82,276	128,505	138,301
Portfolio foreign stocks	216,307	197,025	195,745	197,082	216,194	200,193
Other Canadian investments	272,915	255,143	247,649	261,405	302,504	327,814
Loans	71,731	50,695	49,392	45,957	72,360	77,246
Allowances	-11,918	..	..	..	..	..
Deposits	99,056	103,583	109,442	120,813	131,427	154,137
Official international reserves	56,230	45,690	40,315	38,030	40,959	40,593
Other assets	57,817	55,174	48,500	56,605	57,758	55,838

Note: Data are as of December 31.

Source: Statistics Canada, CANSIM table 376-0037.

Table 9.9 Canada's international investment position, liabilities, 2002 to 2007

	2002	2003	2004	2005	2006	2007
	$ millions					
All liabilities	**1,187,876**	**1,137,847**	**1,142,120**	**1,179,855**	**1,289,417**	**1,338,670**
Foreign direct investments in Canada	356,819	373,685	383,498	407,610	448,858	521,127
Foreign portfolio investments	554,975	507,150	520,432	507,419	541,677	497,745
Portfolio Canadian bonds	449,072	401,050	398,090	380,818	404,590	378,442
Portfolio Canadian stocks	80,617	84,712	102,721	105,818	112,571	97,304
Portfolio Canadian money market instruments	25,285	21,388	19,621	20,783	24,515	21,999
Other foreign investments	276,082	257,012	238,190	264,826	298,882	319,797
Loans	58,772	52,398	40,237	41,645	49,508	52,469
Deposits	195,036	183,125	175,978	201,025	227,149	243,519
Other liabilities	22,275	21,489	21,975	22,156	22,225	23,809
Canada's net international investment position	**-208,692**	**-216,699**	**-180,122**	**-166,431**	**-98,988**	**-156,254**

Note: Data are as of December 31.

Source: Statistics Canada, CANSIM table 376-0037.

Education

10

Overview

Education represents the second largest sector in Canada's economy as measured by the government funding allocated to it. From 1999 to 2008, education spending by the various levels of government increased an average of 6% per year to $91.1 billion in current dollars. Only health sector spending grew faster over the decade.

Under the constitution, the provinces and territories are responsible for education and are the main source of its funding. The federal government funds the education of Aboriginal peoples on reserves, contributes to postsecondary education and supports other educational activities.

Total spending on elementary and secondary public schools in Canada rose 41% from $33.8 billion in 1999 to $47.5 billion in 2008. Meanwhile, $38.8 billion was spent in 2008 on postsecondary education, nearly a 90% increase from the 1999 spending level, which totalled $20.5 billion.

School population

The number of students enrolled in elementary and secondary public schools in Canada fell 3% from the 1999/2000 to 2005/2006 school years to 5.2 million children. Newfoundland and Labrador was the hardest hit province: it experienced a decline in enrolment of 18%, caused largely by ongoing migration to other provinces.

The introduction of provincial examinations in the 2000/2001 school year also contributed to a decline in enrolments. This downward trend was felt across the country, except in Alberta (1.4%) and Ontario (0.6%), where enrolment rates rose.

Chart 10.1
Full-time equivalent educators in public elementary and secondary schools, by province and territory, 1998/1999 to 2004/2005

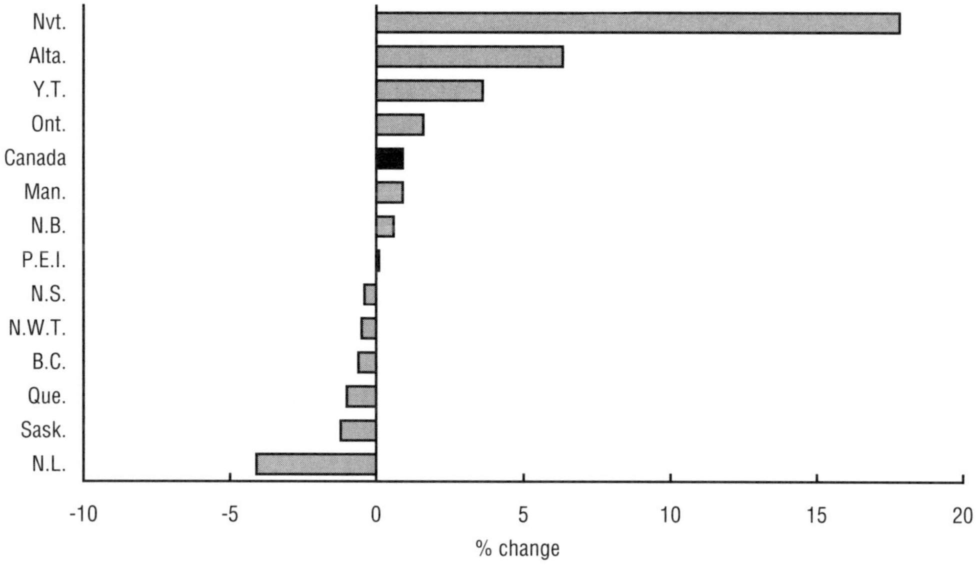

Source: Statistics Canada, Catalogue no. 81-595-XIE.

For a fifth straight year, universities posted record enrolment, with 1.0 million Canadian students in 2005/2006. Enrolment rose 3% from the previous year, the second lowest increase since 2000.

There continued to be proportionally more women than men in universities in 2005/2006. Women accounted for 58% of enrolled students, a proportion that has remained stable since 2001. According to a Statistics Canada study released in September 2007, the main factors explaining the gap in university enrolment between men and women are school performance (45%), work and study habits at age 15 (11%), parental education expectations (9%) and other factors (12%).

Educators

In 2005/2006, there were 329,315 full-time (or equivalent) educators in elementary and secondary public schools. The term 'educator' includes not only teachers, but also all employees in the public school system who hold a teaching certificate, including principals, vice-principals, educational advisors, guidance counsellors, and religious and pastoral advisors.

Chart 10.2
University participation rate, by age

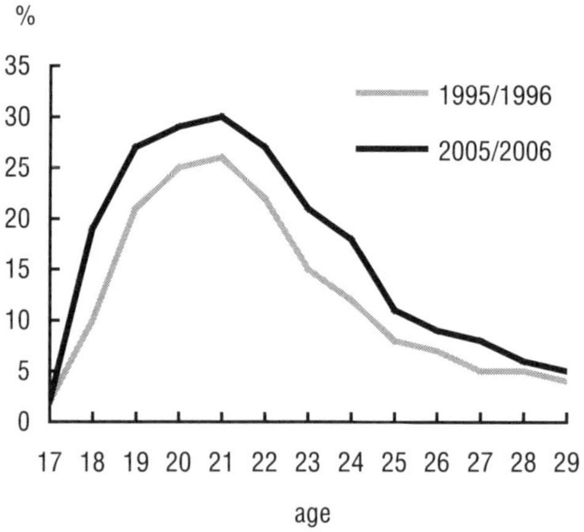

Note: The participation rate is based on a monthly average from September to April.
Source: Statistics Canada, Catalogue no. 81-582-XIE.

Table 10.a
Educators in public elementary and secondary schools, 2004/2005

	Average remuneration per educator	Student–educator ratio
Canada	**64,553**	**15.9**
N.L.	59,809	13.6
P.E.I.	58,412	15.1
N.S.	61,087	15.7
N.B.	56,244	15.9
Que.	55,207	14.2
Ont.	70,977	16.6
Man.	63,466	14.5
Sask.	56,637	15.5
Alta.	68,987	16.9
B.C.	63,904	17.5
Y.T.	77,964	11.5
N.W.T	75,756	15.4
Nvt.	106,676	16.2

Note: The student–educator ratio must not be confused with class size. The former includes personnel outside the class (principals, counsellors and specialists).
Source: Statistics Canada, Catologue no. 81-595-MIE.

From 1998/1999 to 2004/2005, the student-to-educator ratio in elementary and secondary public schools fell nationally from 16.5 to 15.9, which means there were fewer students per educator. Lower ratios occurred in all provinces and territories, except British Columbia. In 2004/2005, the number of students per educator ranged from lows of 13.6 in Newfoundland and Labrador and 11.5 in Yukon to the high of 17.5 in British Columbia.

Educators' salaries accounted for about two-thirds of all elementary and secondary education spending. The average pay of educators (in current dollars) rose from 1998/1999 to 2004/2005, rising from $53,569 to $64,553.

Graduates

Slightly fewer than 313,600 students graduated from public secondary schools in the 2005/2006 school year, up 3% from

1999/2000. This increase was mainly due to the elimination of Grade 13 in Ontario, known as Ontario Academic Courses. Excluding the students in this double cohort, there was little change in the total number of graduates in Canada from 1999/2000 to 2005/2006 (1%).

Universities issued a record 215,400 degrees, diplomas and certificates in 2005, up 2% from 2004 and 43,000 more than in 1998, which had the lowest number of graduates in the past decade. Approximately 172,700 undergraduate students completed their studies, up 2% from 2004. The number of students earning a masters degree rose 50% from 1998 to 2005, to 33,000 students. Some 4,200 students earned a doctorate degree in 2005.

Overall, women are more likely than men to receive a university degree: 128,600 women earned an academic qualification in 2005, or about 60% of all university graduates.

According to the 2004/2005 Survey of Earned Doctorates, 46% of doctorate holders are women. This marks an increase from 43%

Chart 10.3
Undergraduate tuition fees and the Consumer Price Index

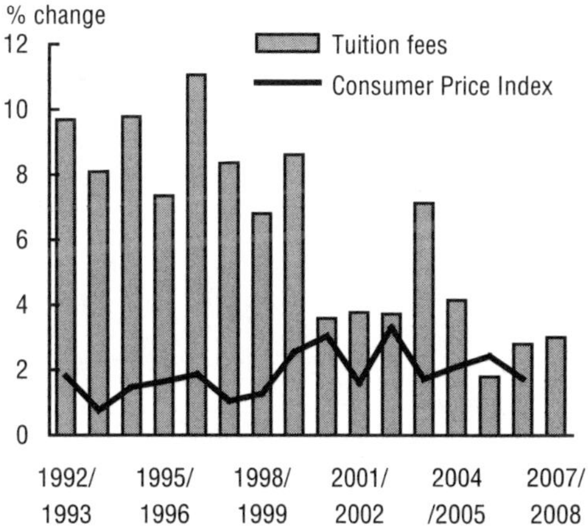

Note: Consumer price index annualized by taking averages from Septermber to August.
Source: Statistics Canada, Culture, Tourism and the Centre for Education Statistics Division.

in 2003/2004. Although the overall gender gap has narrowed, there were still differences in 2004/2005, depending on the field of study. For instance, engineering remains a male-dominated field, while psychology has become dominated by women.

The proportion of women who hold a doctorate has grown considerably in traditionally male-dominated fields. For example, from 2003/2004 to 2004/2005, the percentage of women graduates in computer sciences and mathematics increased 49%. The number of women earning a degree in physics rose 23%.

The relatively high number of foreign male students in Canadian universities contributes to the gap between men and women in terms of doctoral degrees. If foreign students and students with visas are excluded from the data, the percentage of female graduates from a doctoral program is slightly higher than 50%.

Tuition fees

During the 2000s, the rise in tuition fees for undergraduate students slowed to an average of 4%. This slowing followed an average annual rate of increase of 10% throughout the 1990s.

Even with limited hikes, full-time undergraduate tuition fees climbed on average faster than the Consumer Price Index. However, the gap between tuition fees and the general rate of inflation declined from 2001/2002 to 2007/2008.

Full-time Canadian undergraduates paid an average of $4,524 in tuition fees for the 2007/2008 academic year, up from $4,400 in current dollars the previous year. In 1998/1999, they paid on average $3,064, compared with $1,185 in current dollars in 1988/1989.

In 2007/2008, full-time graduate and doctoral students spent $5,447 on average on tuition fees, up 1% from the previous year, representing less than half the increase in fees of undergraduate students.

More apprentices register, but few finish

Apprenticeship training programs represent an important source of new skilled workers. In most provinces, the training of registered apprentices combines classroom technical training with practical work experience.

The length of apprenticeship training programs varies from two to five years, depending on the trade or profession. However, programs can often take longer than the expected time to complete.

The national increase in construction projects resulted in record registrations in apprenticeship training programs in 2005. From 1999 to 2005, the number of registrations rose 53% to 32,210.

This growth occurred primarily in the building construction and the electricity, electronics and related trades. Building construction apprentices accounted for 23% of the total growth in 2005 registrations.

Although the number registering in apprenticeship programs has grown considerably, relatively few Canadian students complete their training. In 2005, 20,555 students earned their diploma, or 2,035 more graduates than in 2003. Except in 2002, when there was a slight decrease, the number of apprentices graduating remained stable from 1999 to 2003.

Many factors can lead an apprentice to discontinue a training program, according to the Registered Apprenticeship Information System. Some of these factors are limited job opportunities, training costs, family reasons, too few tradespersons to provide supervision, literacy level and a lack of jobs once certified.

Chart 10.4
Registrations and completions in apprenticeship programs

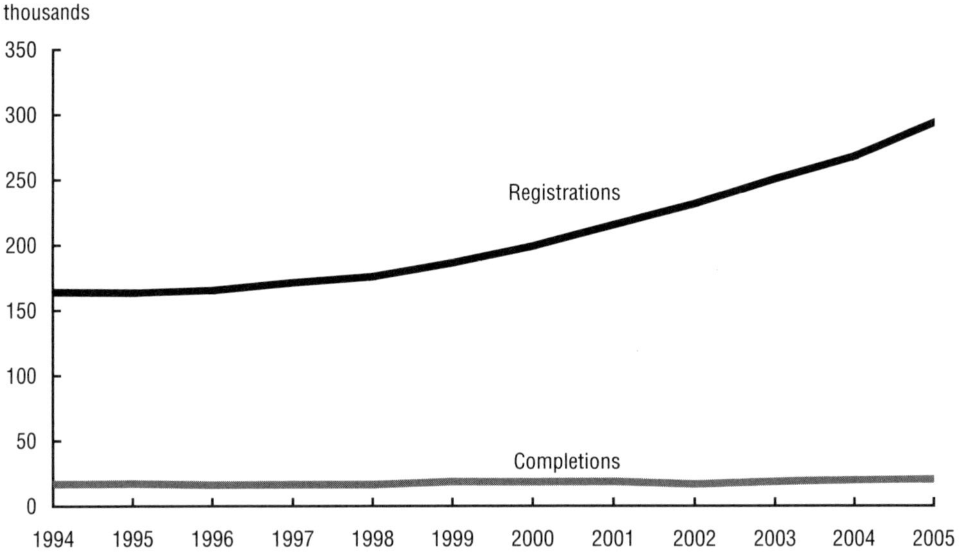

Source: Statistics Canada, CANSIM tables 477-0051 and 477-0052.

Online learning popular

Fully 6.4 million adult Canadians, or 26% of the population aged 18 and older, used the Internet from home for education, training or school work in 2005.

The most common type of education-related use of the Internet is to research information for project assignments or to solve academic problems. A total of 4.2 million adult Canadians—two out of three who went online for education, training or school work in 2005—used the Internet for these activities.

One out of four who used the Internet for education-related purposes went online for distance education, self-directed learning or correspondence courses. Other types of education-related uses are to communicate with administration, to obtain transcripts, and to communicate with teachers or peers, which includes turning in school work.

Eight out of ten full-time and part-time students reported using the Internet for education, training or school work in 2005.

Urban residents are more likely than those in rural areas and small towns to go online to research information for assignments (66% versus 62%). However, urban Canadians are less likely than those from rural areas and small towns to report using the Internet for distance education, self-directed learning or correspondence courses (25% versus 29%).

Although slight, the differences in the percentage of users living in rural areas and small communities and those living in urban areas indicate that rural Canadians have a greater propensity to use the Internet for distance learning. This suggests that online learning may help overcome the barrier of distance that many students face in rural areas.

Chart 10.5
Internet users, by type of education activity, 2005

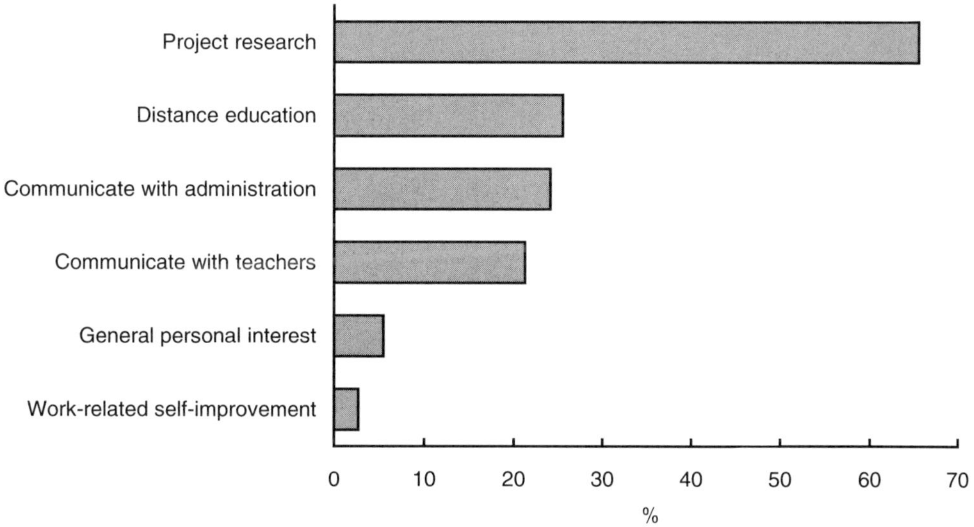

Note: Respondents who reported going online in 2005 for education, training or school work were then asked "For what specific educational purposes did you use the Internet, during the past 12 months?"
Source: Statistics Canada, Catalogue no. 81-004-XIE.

Table 10.1 Educational attainment of working-age population, by sex, 1997 to 2007

	Working-age population	0 to 8 years of study		Some high school		High school graduate		Some postsecondary	
	thousands	thousands	%	thousands	%	thousands	%	thousands	%
Both sexes									
1997	**23,256**	2,747	11.8	4,423	19.0	4,362	18.8	2,121	9.1
1998	**23,523**	2,646	11.2	4,444	18.9	4,460	19.0	2,120	9.0
1999	**23,787**	2,588	10.9	4,395	18.5	4,570	19.2	2,116	8.9
2000	**24,094**	2,502	10.4	4,293	17.8	4,719	19.6	2,275	9.4
2001	**24,444**	2,371	9.7	4,272	17.5	4,740	19.4	2,241	9.2
2002	**24,797**	2,322	9.4	4,205	17.0	4,811	19.4	2,274	9.2
2003	**25,107**	2,262	9.0	4,015	16.0	4,810	19.2	2,453	9.8
2004	**25,443**	2,223	8.7	3,988	15.7	4,906	19.3	2,478	9.7
2005	**25,806**	2,163	8.4	3,918	15.2	5,121	19.8	2,221	8.6
2006	**26,185**	2,122	8.1	3,954	15.1	5,208	19.9	2,117	8.1
2007	**26,553**	2,027	7.6	3,872	14.6	5,238	19.7	2,160	8.1
Males									
1997	**11,404**	1,287	11.3	2,217	19.4	2,013	17.7	1,019	8.9
1998	**11,549**	1,249	10.8	2,226	19.3	2,076	18.0	1,018	8.8
1999	**11,683**	1,227	10.5	2,210	18.9	2,134	18.3	1,020	8.7
2000	**11,843**	1,181	10.0	2,160	18.2	2,210	18.7	1,107	9.3
2001	**12,024**	1,110	9.2	2,166	18.0	2,230	18.5	1,088	9.0
2002	**12,201**	1,092	9.0	2,132	17.5	2,260	18.5	1,117	9.2
2003	**12,352**	1,056	8.5	2,053	16.6	2,266	18.3	1,189	9.6
2004	**12,515**	1,031	8.2	2,041	16.3	2,319	18.5	1,229	9.8
2005	**12,693**	1,012	8.0	2,016	15.9	2,432	19.2	1,106	8.7
2006	**12,883**	983	7.6	2,022	15.7	2,496	19.4	1,060	8.2
2007	**13,065**	943	7.2	1,995	15.3	2,524	19.3	1,070	8.2
Females									
1997	**11,852**	1,459	12.3	2,205	18.6	2,349	19.8	1,102	9.3
1998	**11,974**	1,397	11.7	2,218	18.5	2,385	19.9	1,103	9.2
1999	**12,104**	1,361	11.2	2,185	18.1	2,436	20.1	1,096	9.1
2000	**12,252**	1,321	10.8	2,134	17.4	2,508	20.5	1,168	9.5
2001	**12,420**	1,261	10.2	2,106	17.0	2,510	20.2	1,152	9.3
2002	**12,596**	1,230	9.8	2,072	16.5	2,551	20.2	1,158	9.2
2003	**12,755**	1,206	9.5	1,962	15.4	2,545	20.0	1,264	9.9
2004	**12,928**	1,192	9.2	1,948	15.1	2,587	20.0	1,249	9.7
2005	**13,113**	1,151	8.8	1,902	14.5	2,690	20.5	1,116	8.5
2006	**13,303**	1,140	8.6	1,932	14.5	2,712	20.4	1,057	7.9
2007	**13,488**	1,084	8.0	1,877	13.9	2,714	20.1	1,090	8.1

See note and source at end of table.

Table 10.1 Educational attainment of working-age population, by sex, 1997 to 2007 (continued)

	Postsecondary certificate or diploma		All university degrees		Bachelor's degree		Above bachelor's degree	
	thousands	%	thousands	%	thousands	%	thousands	%
Both sexes								
1997	6,357	27.3	3,247	14.0	2,214	9.5	1,033	4.4
1998	6,513	27.7	3,340	14.2	2,304	9.8	1,036	4.4
1999	6,597	27.7	3,522	14.8	2,402	10.1	1,119	4.7
2000	6,584	27.3	3,722	15.4	2,507	10.4	1,215	5.0
2001	6,916	28.3	3,905	16.0	2,661	10.9	1,244	5.1
2002	7,124	28.7	4,061	16.4	2,790	11.3	1,271	5.1
2003	7,261	28.9	4,306	17.2	2,969	11.8	1,337	5.3
2004	7,458	29.3	4,390	17.3	3,070	12.1	1,320	5.2
2005	7,692	29.8	4,690	18.2	3,227	12.5	1,464	5.7
2006	7,832	29.9	4,952	18.9	3,445	13.2	1,507	5.8
2007	8,101	30.5	5,157	19.4	3,589	13.5	1,568	5.9
Males								
1997	3,132	27.5	1,735	15.2	1,105	9.7	630	5.5
1998	3,197	27.7	1,784	15.4	1,159	10.0	625	5.4
1999	3,247	27.8	1,847	15.8	1,170	10.0	676	5.8
2000	3,259	27.5	1,926	16.3	1,208	10.2	718	6.1
2001	3,406	28.3	2,025	16.8	1,295	10.8	730	6.1
2002	3,505	28.7	2,095	17.2	1,351	11.1	744	6.1
2003	3,586	29.0	2,203	17.8	1,430	11.6	773	6.3
2004	3,675	29.4	2,220	17.7	1,463	11.7	758	6.1
2005	3,783	29.8	2,345	18.5	1,519	12.0	827	6.5
2006	3,857	29.9	2,466	19.1	1,612	12.5	853	6.6
2007	3,978	30.4	2,557	19.6	1,679	12.8	878	6.7
Females								
1997	3,225	27.2	1,512	12.8	1,109	9.4	403	3.4
1998	3,316	27.7	1,556	13.0	1,145	9.6	411	3.4
1999	3,351	27.7	1,675	13.8	1,232	10.2	443	3.7
2000	3,325	27.1	1,796	14.7	1,299	10.6	497	4.1
2001	3,510	28.3	1,881	15.1	1,366	11.0	515	4.1
2002	3,619	28.7	1,967	15.6	1,439	11.4	528	4.2
2003	3,675	28.8	2,103	16.5	1,540	12.1	563	4.4
2004	3,783	29.3	2,170	16.8	1,608	12.4	562	4.3
2005	3,909	29.8	2,345	17.9	1,708	13.0	637	4.9
2006	3,975	29.9	2,487	18.7	1,833	13.8	654	4.9
2007	4,123	30.6	2,600	19.3	1,910	14.2	690	5.1

Note: Population aged 15 and older based on Labour Force Survey estimates.

Source: Statistics Canada, CANSIM table 282-0004.

Table 10.2 School board revenue and expenditures, 1992 to 2006

	1992	1993	1994	1995	1996	1997	1998	1999
	$ thousands							
Revenue	**31,779,197**	**31,603,451**	**32,064,138**	**32,224,966**	**31,899,333**	**32,042,472**	**35,590,628**	**32,933,191**
Own-source revenue	11,383,409	11,779,777	11,312,396	11,359,580	11,640,998	12,157,134	9,186,870	9,593,045
Property and related taxes	10,226,228	10,615,606	10,126,998	10,180,707	10,433,594	10,926,304	7,801,048	8,009,046
Real property taxes	8,920,373	9,304,047	8,862,895	8,913,431	9,152,598	9,617,759	7,602,321	7,814,361
Grants in lieu of taxes	164,648	164,130	150,483	145,988	148,583	152,255	96,439	89,993
Federal government	45,748	41,180	40,222	40,870	39,173	44,341	40,772	36,637
Federal government business enterprises	2,279	1,815	1,900	1,815	1,843	1,962	2,330	2,116
Provincial and territorial governments	101,502	109,377	101,001	96,656	100,548	99,793	48,405	46,928
Provincial and territorial government business enterprises	12,297	9,103	5,732	5,109	5,223	4,054	3,148	3,026
Local governments	0	318	362	383	407	457	484	483
Local government business enterprises	2,822	2,337	1,266	1,155	1,389	1,648	1,300	803
Business taxes	956,251	958,475	976,084	1,006,023	1,015,806	1,047,918	26,780	28,381
Miscellaneous property and related taxes	184,956	188,954	137,536	115,265	116,607	108,372	75,508	76,311
Other taxes	2,113	596	566	930	619	651	599	650
Sales of goods and services	1,083,530	1,094,451	1,107,931	1,094,804	1,130,374	1,157,659	1,304,790	1,492,498
Intergovernment	467,215	450,263	426,572	409,886	395,245	382,141	457,962	483,870
General	616,315	644,188	681,359	684,918	735,129	775,518	846,828	1,008,628
Rentals	49,015	49,479	54,413	40,309	41,443	43,403	49,226	56,675
Other sales of goods and services	567,300	594,709	626,946	644,609	693,686	732,115	797,557	951,953
Investment income	54,233	49,400	55,135	61,675	53,049	46,592	54,598	65,691
Other interest income	5,261	5,711	5,161	4,802	4,857	5,270	4,641	5,892
Other investment income	48,972	43,689	49,974	56,873	48,192	41,322	49,957	59,799
Other revenue from own sources	17,305	19,724	21,766	21,464	23,362	25,927	25,835	25,160
Specific-purpose transfers from other government subsectors	20,395,788	19,823,674	20,751,742	20,865,386	20,258,335	19,885,338	26,403,758	23,340,146
Federal government	76,242	89,919	98,538	132,051	92,000	81,580	82,258	90,975
Provincial and territorial governments	20,165,582	19,584,064	20,502,833	20,585,449	20,015,657	19,650,260	26,161,478	23,088,695
Education transfers	19,440,044	18,856,849	19,761,317	19,860,652	19,253,989	18,960,162	25,637,572	22,688,501
Debt charges (interest)	725,538	727,215	741,516	724,797	761,668	690,098	523,906	400,194
Local governments	153,964	149,691	150,371	147,886	150,678	153,498	160,022	160,476
Expenditures	**31,666,395**	**31,215,122**	**32,133,862**	**31,738,443**	**31,754,347**	**32,212,258**	**32,091,168**	**32,700,627**
Education	30,787,056	30,283,658	31,112,930	30,642,856	30,687,738	31,169,335	31,309,610	31,955,580
Debt charges	879,339	931,464	1,020,932	1,095,587	1,066,609	1,042,923	781,558	745,047
Interest	879,140	931,302	1,020,779	1,095,385	1,066,523	1,042,534	781,414	737,104
Other debt charges	199	162	153	202	86	389	144	7,943
Surplus/deficit (-)	**112,802**	**388,329**	**-69,724**	**486,523**	**144,986**	**-169,786**	**3,499,460**	**232,564**

See note and source at end of table.

Table 10.2 School board revenue and expenditures, 1992 to 2006 (continued)

	2000	2001	2002	2003	2004	2005	2006
	$ thousands						
Revenue	**34,049,949**	**35,230,651**	**36,895,015**	**39,085,203**	**39,348,228**	**41,328,799**	**45,457,819**
Own-source revenue	9,696,626	9,851,322	10,121,370	10,349,619	10,435,931	10,907,645	11,315,980
Property and related taxes	7,999,391	8,105,789	8,197,216	8,355,012	8,483,512	8,902,057	9,233,020
Real property taxes	7,803,833	7,907,445	8,013,090	8,163,446	8,293,159	8,702,948	9,033,628
Grants in lieu of taxes	90,908	84,244	78,233	82,718	81,214	84,155	82,172
Federal government	36,802	32,480	30,971	31,887	32,509	33,603	33,001
Federal government business enterprises	1,447	876	469	376	308	322	313
Provincial and territorial governments	47,941	44,850	40,749	44,254	41,924	43,433	42,144
Provincial and territorial government business enterprises	3,367	3,758	4,322	4,228	4,243	4,452	4,369
Local governments	469	510	527	525	536	543	574
Local government business enterprises	882	1,770	1,195	1,448	1,694	1,802	1,771
Business taxes	29,054	31,123	32,065	33,432	34,535	36,010	34,671
Miscellaneous property and related taxes	75,596	82,977	73,828	75,416	74,604	78,944	82,549
Other taxes	708	723	695	692	715	746	718
Sales of goods and services	1,590,727	1,644,381	1,822,908	1,878,446	1,839,105	1,888,136	1,963,120
Intergovernment	547,924	519,393	515,877	512,769	527,331	540,674	562,263
General	1,042,803	1,124,988	1,307,031	1,365,677	1,311,774	1,347,462	1,400,857
Rentals	58,919	66,368	105,892	117,929	119,779	124,752	129,212
Other sales of goods and services	983,884	1,058,620	1,201,139	1,247,748	1,191,995	1,222,710	1,271,645
Investment income	78,818	74,635	71,844	83,865	81,960	84,756	86,023
Other interest income	5,574	6,324	6,985	5,322	5,498	5,733	5,520
Other investment income	73,244	68,311	64,859	78,543	76,462	79,023	80,503
Other revenue from own sources	26,982	25,794	28,707	31,604	30,639	31,950	33,099
Specific-purpose transfers from other government subsectors	24,353,323	25,379,329	26,773,645	28,735,584	28,912,297	30,421,154	34,141,839
Federal government	84,721	89,923	104,689	98,705	86,519	89,211	93,242
Provincial and territorial governments	24,103,915	25,120,176	26,494,344	28,459,642	28,650,516	30,151,637	33,867,134
Education transfers	23,723,258	24,701,947	26,089,163	28,059,578	28,240,574	29,734,232	33,433,957
Debt charges (interest)	380,657	418,229	405,181	400,064	409,942	417,405	433,177
Local governments	164,687	169,230	174,612	177,237	175,262	180,306	181,463
Expenditures	**34,142,482**	**35,368,073**	**36,873,300**	**38,264,627**	**39,479,158**	**41,439,144**	**45,033,800**
Education	33,416,048	34,624,407	36,150,312	37,528,221	38,759,210	40,735,347	44,356,765
Debt charges	726,434	743,666	722,988	736,406	719,948	703,797	677,035
Interest	721,368	734,845	712,633	729,472	712,874	696,623	669,470
Other debt charges	5,066	8,821	10,355	6,934	7,074	7,174	7,565
Surplus/deficit (-)	**-92,533**	**-137,422**	**21,715**	**820,576**	**-130,930**	**-110,345**	**424,019**

Note: Data not available for New Brunswick, Yukon and Nunavut.

Source: Statistics Canada, CANSIM table 385-0009.

Table 10.3 Enrolment in public elementary and secondary schools, by province and territory, 1999/2000 to 2005/2006

	Canada	Newfoundland and Labrador	Prince Edward Island	Nova Scotia[1]	New Brunswick[2]	Quebec[3]	Ontario[4]
	number						
1999/2000	**5,372,733**	94,118	24,089	158,205	127,003	1,247,757	2,131,626
2000/2001	**5,356,161**	90,287	23,153	155,873	124,942	1,237,981	2,143,599
2001/2002	**5,365,150**	87,019	22,843	153,450	122,792	1,244,689	2,163,108
2002/2003	**5,347,402**	84,397	22,615	150,599	120,600	1,245,339	2,164,940
2003/2004	**5,286,949**	81,545	22,239	148,514	118,869	1,241,143	2,129,742
2004/2005	**5,253,442**	79,508	22,393	145,396	117,145	1,233,100	2,123,904
2005/2006	**5,212,533**	76,827	21,948	142,304	114,820	1,216,293	2,118,544
	% change						
1999/2000	**0.3**	-3.5	-0.2	-1.1	-1.6	-0.2	0.9
2000/2001	**-0.3**	-4.1	-3.9	-1.5	-1.6	-0.8	0.6
2001/2002	**0.2**	-3.6	-1.3	-1.6	-1.7	0.5	0.9
2002/2003	**-0.3**	-3.0	-1.0	-1.9	-1.8	0.1	0.1
2003/2004	**-1.1**	-3.4	-1.7	-1.4	-1.4	-0.3	-1.6
2004/2005	**-0.6**	-2.5	0.7	-2.1	-1.5	-0.6	-0.3
2005/2006	**-0.8**	-3.4	-2.0	-2.1	-2.0	-1.4	-0.3

	Manitoba[4]	Saskatchewan[5]	Alberta	British Columbia[5]	Yukon	Northwest Territories	Nunavut
	number						
1999/2000	192,630	194,797	543,387	629,545	6,102	18,068	...
2000/2001	197,067	192,885	546,402	628,265	5,975	9,753	9,584
2001/2002	189,912	190,711	549,633	625,074	5,764	9,672	9,558
2002/2003	188,907	186,518	548,122	622,838	5,608	9,707	9,548
2003/2004	186,892	182,687	551,375	613,235	5,610	9,747	9,364
2004/2005	186,287	178,932	549,533	605,543	5,520	9,718	9,362
2005/2006	184,352	176,069	550,983	596,174	5,459	9,607	9,354
	% change						
1999/2000	2.3	-1.0	0.6	-0.2	-2.1	...	...
2000/2001	-3.6	-1.1	0.6	-0.5	-3.5	-0.8	-0.3
2001/2002	-0.5	-2.2	-0.3	-0.4	-2.7	0.4	-0.1
2002/2003	-1.1	-2.1	0.6	-1.5	0.0	0.4	-1.9
2003/2004	-0.3	-2.1	-0.3	-1.3	-1.6	-0.3	0.0
2004/2005	-1.0	-1.6	0.3	-1.5	-1.1	-1.1	-0.1
2005/2006	-1.1	-1.1	0.1	-1.1	0.0	-0.4	-3.1

1. Includes enrolments in vocational programs for youth and adults.
2. Includes enrolments in adult programs and vocational programs for youth and adults.
3. Data exclude publicly funded hospital and provincial schools, care, treatment and correctional facilities.
4. Until 2000/2001, includes enrolments in adult programs and professional training under the authority of the school boards or districts.
5. Includes enrolments in adult programs.

Source: Statistics Canada, Catalogue no. 81-595-MIE2008067.

Table 10.4 Graduates of public elementary and secondary schools, by province and territory, 1999/2000 to 2005/2006

	Canada	Newfoundland and Labrador	Prince Edward Island	Nova Scotia	New Brunswick	Quebec	Ontario[1]
				number			
1999/2000	304,472	6,810	1,798	9,914	8,912	69,000	114,404
2000/2001	305,175	6,109	1,717	10,064	8,552	67,710	115,599
2001/2002	314,462	6,079	1,667	10,124	8,574	66,276	124,783
2002/2003	333,733	5,947	1,753	10,387	8,291	64,988	143,187
2003/2004	315,301	5,637	1,734	10,445	7,996	67,896	123,238
2004/2005	318,595	5,505	1,695	10,360	8,200	68,538	124,902
2005/2006	313,580	5,262	1,736	10,241	8,299	69,984	118,099
				% change			
1999/2000	..	-1.2	10.4	-2.3	1.5	..	..
2000/2001	0.2	-10.3	-4.5	1.5	-4.0	-1.9	1.0
2001/2002	3.0	-0.5	-2.9	0.6	0.3	-2.1	7.9
2002/2003	6.1	-2.2	5.2	2.6	-3.3	-1.9	14.7
2003/2004	-5.5	-5.2	-1.1	0.6	-3.6	4.5	-13.9
2004/2005	1.0	-2.3	-2.2	-0.8	2.6	0.9	1.4
2005/2006	-1.6	-4.4	2.4	-1.1	1.2	2.1	-5.4

	Manitoba[2]	Saskat-chewan	Alberta	British Columbia[3]	Yukon	Northwest Territories	Nunavut
				number			
1999/2000	11,807	13,105	28,321	39,716	258	293	134
2000/2001	11,723	12,957	29,303	40,703	283	327	128
2001/2002	11,685	12,739	29,877	41,967	280	275	136
2002/2003	12,282	12,367	31,155	42,635	282	320	139
2003/2004	12,598	11,957	32,159	40,816	332	363	130
2004/2005	12,422	12,625	31,782	41,673	336	384	173
2005/2006	12,446	12,698	32,356	41,534	321	421	183
				% change			
1999/2000	-0.2	2.3	6.6	5.2	-11.0	-7.0	4.7
2000/2001	-0.7	-1.1	3.5	2.5	9.7	11.6	-4.5
2001/2002	-0.3	-1.7	2.0	3.1	-1.1	-15.9	6.3
2002/2003	5.1	-2.9	4.3	1.6	0.7	16.4	2.2
2003/2004	2.6	-3.3	3.2	-4.3	17.7	13.4	-6.5
2004/2005	-1.4	5.6	-1.2	2.1	1.2	5.8	33.1
2005/2006	0.2	0.6	1.8	-0.3	-4.5	9.6	5.8

1. Data exclude publicly funded hospital and provincial schools, care, treatment and correctional facilities.
2. Historical revisions have been made to this table to exclude students that graduated from Adult Learning Centres registered under the *Adult Learning Centres Act*, effective July 2001.
3. The number of graduates in the final year is understated from 2% to 3% because some schools have not submitted course information before the data collection cutoff for this report.

Source: Statistics Canada, Catalogue no. 81-595-MIE2008067.

Table 10.5 University and college revenue and expenditures, 1994 to 2007

	1994	1995	1996	1997	1998	1999	2000
	$ thousands						
Revenue	**16,419,382**	**16,759,086**	**17,260,407**	**16,729,056**	**17,389,686**	**20,064,718**	**20,380,239**
Own-source revenue	5,612,258	5,889,502	6,277,982	6,653,193	7,447,138	7,887,522	8,791,925
Sales of goods and services	4,349,760	4,567,345	4,843,608	5,187,833	5,699,797	6,044,702	6,715,382
Tuition fees	2,339,171	2,507,056	2,690,708	2,889,160	3,179,565	3,506,275	3,881,521
Other sales of goods and services	2,010,590	2,060,289	2,152,900	2,298,673	2,520,232	2,538,427	2,833,861
Investment income	367,552	366,970	427,658	408,272	556,419	476,694	592,797
Other revenue from own sources	894,945	955,187	1,006,716	1,057,088	1,190,922	1,366,126	1,483,746
Transfers from other levels of government	10,807,124	10,869,584	10,982,425	10,075,863	9,942,548	12,177,196	11,588,314
Federal government	1,095,690	1,110,639	1,090,080	1,022,516	980,566	1,112,046	1,352,613
Provincial and territorial governments	9,701,848	9,746,774	9,877,178	9,028,729	8,932,862	11,049,246	10,221,834
Local governments	9,586	12,171	15,167	24,618	29,120	15,904	13,867
Expenditures	**16,749,070**	**16,917,362**	**17,192,872**	**16,804,525**	**17,194,597**	**18,022,802**	**19,478,054**
Postsecondary education	16,451,698	16,559,462	16,747,684	16,381,240	16,762,116	17,679,221	18,800,032
Administration	3,103,484	3,157,017	3,361,662	3,205,490	3,251,008	3,438,931	3,826,107
Education	9,320,107	9,304,767	9,249,982	9,176,367	9,253,953	9,724,860	9,806,404
Support to students	428,626	447,082	453,669	307,665	347,649	407,889	513,845
Other	3,599,481	3,650,595	3,682,371	3,691,718	3,909,506	4,107,541	4,653,676
Special retraining services	..	..	..	..	..	..	240,451
Debt charges	297,372	357,900	445,189	423,285	432,481	343,581	437,571
Surplus/deficit (-)	**-329,689**	**-158,276**	**67,535**	**-75,469**	**195,089**	**2,041,916**	**902,185**

	2001	2002	2003	2004	2005	2006	2007
	$ thousands						
Revenue	**21,732,604**	**23,262,806**	**25,359,135**	**28,096,412**	**29,484,455**	**30,990,494**	**33,847,597**
Own-source revenue	9,630,461	10,339,207	11,244,357	12,752,007	13,336,261	13,976,578	15,413,521
Sales of goods and services	7,371,133	8,132,232	9,026,491	9,906,500	10,520,144	11,024,426	12,168,566
Tuition fees	4,144,097	4,486,787	5,085,897	5,766,539	6,152,681	6,453,724	7,147,470
Other sales of goods and services	3,227,036	3,645,445	3,940,594	4,139,962	4,367,463	4,570,702	5,021,096
Investment income	604,613	396,046	370,231	821,830	645,905	678,871	747,924
Other revenue from own sources	1,654,715	1,810,929	1,847,635	2,023,677	2,170,212	2,273,281	2,497,031
Transfers from other levels of government	12,102,143	12,923,599	14,114,778	15,344,405	16,148,194	17,013,916	18,434,076
Federal government	1,624,714	1,922,197	2,270,560	2,564,931	2,678,489	2,819,458	3,073,356
Provincial and territorial governments	10,451,811	10,947,140	11,817,345	12,750,006	13,444,014	14,167,730	15,330,445
Local governments	25,618	54,262	26,873	29,468	25,691	26,728	30,274
Expenditures	**21,278,479**	**23,454,251**	**25,590,341**	**27,690,208**	**29,609,613**	**31,262,977**	**34,107,650**
Postsecondary education	20,569,831	22,717,330	24,820,214	26,804,032	28,699,579	30,277,775	33,044,907
Administration	4,267,373	4,662,921	4,717,093	4,759,180	5,377,969	5,737,298	6,257,850
Education	10,447,939	11,372,063	12,485,313	13,748,442	14,250,885	15,003,320	16,351,516
Support to students	603,597	718,845	818,445	961,623	1,031,730	1,080,572	1,197,408
Other	5,250,922	5,963,501	6,799,363	7,334,787	8,038,995	8,456,584	9,238,132
Special retraining services	243,966	272,106	271,758	284,984	277,324	288,372	318,114
Debt charges	464,682	464,815	498,369	575,652	606,483	669,187	716,182
Surplus/deficit (-)	**454,125**	**-191,445**	**-231,206**	**406,204**	**-125,158**	**-272,484**	**-260,053**

Notes: Fiscal year ending March 31.
Excludes Yukon College for confidentiality purposes.

Source: Statistics Canada, CANSIM table 385-0007.

Table 10.6 University enrolment, by instructional programs, 1994/1995 to 2005/2006

	1994/1995	1995/1996	1996/1997	1997/1998	1998/1999	1999/2000
	number					
All instructional programs	**858,972**	**846,408**	**829,767**	**822,774**	**826,362**	**847,503**
Personal improvement and leisure	..	..	..	..	..	..
Education	77,472	73,290	70,428	67,623	65,673	66,282
Visual and performing arts and communications technologies	25,494	25,704	24,882	24,984	25,359	25,413
Humanities	139,254	144,522	135,750	130,038	127,392	119,358
Social and behavioural sciences and law	147,720	143,607	136,992	132,135	129,795	132,417
Business, management and public administration	123,222	120,414	121,188	124,626	128,556	134,367
Physical and life sciences and technologies	77,112	78,525	76,842	76,536	75,537	79,353
Mathematics, computer and information sciences	32,454	32,133	32,622	34,407	37,473	41,574
Architecture, engineering and related technologies	63,657	62,259	62,088	63,438	65,223	67,434
Agriculture, natural resources and conservation	14,067	15,135	15,831	16,731	16,362	16,416
Health, parks, recreation and fitness	73,131	73,884	74,694	74,781	74,826	74,841
Personal, protective and transportation services	210	183	189	351	345	372
Other instructional programs	85,173	76,752	78,255	77,118	79,821	89,673
	2000/2001	**2001/2002**	**2002/2003**	**2003/2004**	**2004/2005**	**2005/2006**
	number					
All instructional programs	**850,581**	**886,605**	**933,870**	**993,246**	**1,017,588**	**1,047,705**
Personal improvement and leisure	0	66	69	51	27	372
Education	66,477	69,468	71,973	76,704	72,087	73,455
Visual and performing arts and communications technologies	26,922	27,915	29,877	34,182	36,858	37,242
Humanities	124,047	130,068	140,511	152,718	151,374	161,139
Social and behavioural sciences and law	135,177	138,693	149,742	163,032	176,424	182,784
Business, management and public administration	134,784	141,531	152,295	161,130	165,069	169,293
Physical and life sciences and technologies	79,905	81,411	84,555	92,715	96,423	98,376
Mathematics, computer and information sciences	43,053	46,035	45,837	43,932	40,644	36,594
Architecture, engineering and related technologies	70,038	74,850	81,132	85,809	86,484	85,599
Agriculture, natural resources and conservation	15,423	14,847	14,496	14,619	14,757	15,210
Health, parks, recreation and fitness	74,571	80,838	85,128	92,223	98,370	104,157
Personal, protective and transportation services	1,047	1,185	1,317	1,299	1,827	1,764
Other instructional programs	79,134	79,698	76,953	74,832	77,247	81,723

Source: Statistics Canada, CANSIM table 477-0013.

Table 10.7 University enrolment, by program level, 1994/1995 to 2005/2006

	1994/1995	1995/1996	1996/1997	1997/1998	1998/1999	1999/2000
	number					
All program levels	**858,972**	**846,408**	**829,767**	**822,774**	**826,362**	**847,503**
Trade/vocational and preparatory training certificate or diploma	..	..	..	..	..	147
Community college certificate or diploma and other community college	2,016	2,409	2,457	2,352	2,232	2,811
Undergraduate level	658,284	648,972	639,588	633,018	633,495	650,367
Bachelor's and other undergraduate degree	586,116	580,185	575,886	572,331	571,161	583,146
Other undergraduate level	72,168	68,787	63,702	60,687	62,337	67,221
Graduate level	112,947	112,524	112,068	112,692	113,481	116,304
Master's degree	69,783	69,300	69,093	69,852	71,292	74,331
Earned doctorate	27,147	27,306	27,198	27,003	26,505	26,493
Other graduate levels[1]	16,017	15,918	15,777	15,834	15,681	15,483
Other program levels[2]	85,722	82,503	75,651	74,712	77,154	77,868
	2000/2001	**2001/2002**	**2002/2003**	**2003/2004**	**2004/2005**	**2005/2006**
	number					
All program levels	**850,581**	**886,605**	**933,870**	**993,246**	**1,017,588**	**1,047,705**
Trade/vocational and preparatory training certificate or diploma	204	90	159	168	144	753
Community college certificate or diploma and other community college	2,295	2,088	2,268	2,946	2,379	4,809
Undergraduate level	657,189	680,619	719,058	770,391	787,125	803,493
Bachelor's and other undergraduate degree	589,695	613,473	648,321	696,720	718,278	737,853
Other undergraduate level	67,497	67,146	70,737	73,671	68,847	65,637
Graduate level	118,152	124,605	134,952	142,644	150,435	153,552
Master's degree	75,195	79,533	85,800	89,385	93,633	94,065
Earned doctorate	26,598	27,390	29,340	32,004	34,581	36,702
Other graduate levels[1]	16,356	17,679	19,815	21,249	22,218	22,785
Other program levels[2]	72,741	79,206	77,433	77,103	77,505	85,101

1. Includes master's qualifying year, university graduate level certificate or diploma, PhD (Doctor of Philosophy) qualifying year or probationary, internship (Postgraduate Medical Education known as post-MD.) and residency (medical, dental, veterinary).
2. Includes program levels not applicable and non-program (taking non-credit courses or taking courses without seeking a credit).

Source: Statistics Canada, CANSIM table 477-0013.

Table 10.8 University degrees, diplomas and certificates granted, 1994 to 2005

	1994	1995	1996	1997	1998	1999
	number					
All instructional programs	**178,074**	**178,065**	**178,113**	**173,934**	**172,074**	**173,577**
Personal improvement and leisure	..	..	..	..	..	..
Education	26,304	26,454	25,713	23,742	21,636	22,290
Visual and performing arts and communications technologies	5,310	5,241	5,199	5,205	5,256	5,202
Humanities	23,058	22,386	22,377	20,988	20,364	19,593
Social and behavioural sciences and law	39,423	39,678	38,988	37,872	37,899	36,702
Business, management and public administration	31,620	30,252	30,054	29,916	30,492	31,629
Physical and life sciences and technologies	13,119	13,662	14,631	15,183	15,552	14,607
Mathematics, computer and information sciences	6,825	7,194	6,996	6,867	6,966	7,710
Architecture, engineering and related technologies	12,999	13,293	13,341	12,912	13,026	12,798
Agriculture, natural resources and conservation	2,616	2,754	3,036	3,240	3,258	3,825
Health, parks, recreation and fitness	16,197	16,563	16,734	16,746	16,497	16,920
Personal, protective and transportation services	78	54	75	102	81	90
Other instructional programs	525	537	966	1,158	1,047	2,211
	2000	**2001**	**2002**	**2003**	**2004**	**2005**
	number					
All instructional programs	**176,556**	**178,101**	**186,153**	**198,525**	**210,504**	**215,367**
Personal improvement and leisure	..	..	..	..	3	33
Education	22,542	22,350	23,664	24,864	25,401	25,191
Visual and performing arts and communications technologies	5,373	5,904	5,958	6,708	7,554	7,845
Humanities	20,064	19,902	20,571	22,227	22,485	23,904
Social and behavioural sciences and law	36,315	35,784	37,026	38,613	41,346	42,069
Business, management and public administration	33,213	34,791	37,581	40,944	44,295	45,318
Physical and life sciences and technologies	14,730	14,967	14,460	14,865	15,408	15,921
Mathematics, computer and information sciences	8,448	9,009	10,008	10,602	11,040	9,993
Architecture, engineering and related technologies	13,305	13,842	14,769	16,389	17,502	17,988
Agriculture, natural resources and conservation	4,008	3,888	3,660	3,771	3,615	3,303
Health, parks, recreation and fitness	16,518	16,314	17,286	18,222	20,244	21,903
Personal, protective and transportation services	81	228	270	270	360	327
Other instructional programs	1,959	1,122	900	1,050	1,248	1,581

Source: Statistics Canada, CANSIM table 477-0014.

Table 10.9 University degrees, diplomas and certificates granted, by province, 1994 to 2005

	1994	1995	1996	1997	1998	1999
	number					
Canada	**178,074**	**178,065**	**178,113**	**173,934**	**172,074**	**173,577**
Newfoundland and Labrador	2,718	2,571	2,907	2,952	3,000	3,114
Prince Edward Island	573	585	528	570	405	540
Nova Scotia	8,103	7,887	7,725	7,785	7,812	7,824
New Brunswick	4,005	4,149	4,428	4,311	4,032	3,975
Quebec	57,852	56,856	56,253	53,589	51,066	50,958
Ontario	66,189	66,861	67,668	65,562	65,898	65,697
Manitoba	6,285	6,315	6,030	5,895	5,640	5,442
Saskatchewan	5,415	5,784	5,715	5,337	5,445	5,547
Alberta	12,282	12,270	12,240	12,816	13,002	13,560
British Columbia	14,652	14,784	14,616	15,117	15,780	16,917
	2000	**2001**	**2002**	**2003**	**2004**	**2005**
	number					
Canada	**176,556**	**178,101**	**186,153**	**198,525**	**210,504**	**215,367**
Newfoundland and Labrador	2,931	2,862	2,898	2,976	3,168	3,186
Prince Edward Island	534	606	555	624	672	750
Nova Scotia	7,638	7,680	7,878	8,766	9,579	9,513
New Brunswick	4,032	4,101	4,395	4,557	4,944	5,244
Quebec	50,847	51,153	54,009	57,786	61,212	62,973
Ontario	67,221	68,286	70,749	75,864	80,436	84,138
Manitoba	5,340	5,397	5,580	5,871	6,309	6,345
Saskatchewan	5,793	5,694	5,739	5,868	5,778	3,747
Alberta	14,052	15,087	16,344	17,199	18,189	18,009
British Columbia	18,171	17,238	18,000	19,017	20,214	21,462

Source: Statistics Canada, CANSIM table 477-0014.

Table 10.10 Employment in educational and related services, by province, 2003 to 2007

	2003	2004	2005	2006	2007
			number		
Canada	**996,387**	**1,010,814**	**1,031,380**	**1,055,465**	**1,078,856**
Newfoundland and Labrador	16,612	16,504	15,813	16,127	16,141
Prince Edward Island	4,255	4,464	4,462	4,466	4,636
Nova Scotia	36,449	36,537	36,025	37,134	35,855
New Brunswick	24,206	23,834	24,285	24,952	26,329
Quebec	237,454	238,454	236,586	241,182	244,309
Ontario	362,346	370,804	387,460	397,519	408,014
Manitoba	43,166	44,584	46,156	45,841	45,786
Saskatchewan	37,202	37,977	38,603	38,818	39,897
Alberta	104,806	105,655	107,756	109,537	114,445
British Columbia	125,536	127,590	129,927	135,680	139,081

Note: Excludes owners or partners of unincorporated businesses and professional practices, the self-employed, unpaid family workers, people working outside Canada, military personnel and casual workers for whom a T4 is not required.

Source: Statistics Canada, CANSIM table 281-0024.

Table 10.11 Undergraduate tuition fees for full-time students, by discipline, 2006/2007 and 2007/2008

	2006/2007	2007/2008
	average ($)	
Average undergraduate tuition fees	**4,400**	**4,524**
Education	3,373	3,473
Visual and performing arts, and communications technologies	3,991	4,148
Humanities	4,336	4,459
Social and behavioral science	4,041	4,156
Law	7,155	7,334
Business, management and public administration	4,195	4,271
Physical and life sciences and technology	4,270	4,467
Mathematics, computer and information science	4,650	4,700
Engineering	4,943	5,131
Architecture and related technologies	3,839	3,957
Agriculture, natural resources and conservation	3,869	3,963
Medicine	9,659	9,937
Parks, recreation, health (other than medicine) and fitness	4,996	5,099

Note: Using the most current enrolment data available, average tuition fees have been weighted by the number of students enrolled by institution and field of study. Fees at both public and private institutions are included in the weighted average calculations.

Source: Statistics Canada, Centre for Education Statistics.

Table 10.12 Undergraduate tuition fees for full-time students, by province, 2002/2003 to 2007/2008

	2002/2003	2003/2004	2004/2005	2005/2006	2006/2007	2007/2008
			average ($)			
Canada	**3,711**	**3,975**	**4,141**	**4,211**	**4,400**	**4,524**
Newfoundland and Labrador	2,729	2,606	2,606	2,606	2,633	2,633
Prince Edward Island	3,891	4,132	4,374	4,645	4,920	4,440
Nova Scotia	5,214	5,556	6,003	6,323	6,422	5,878
New Brunswick	4,186	4,457	4,719	5,037	5,470	5,733
Quebec	1,852	1,865	1,888	1,900	1,932	2,025
Ontario	4,572	4,808	4,831	4,933	5,155	5,381
Manitoba	3,144	3,155	3,235	3,333	3,319	3,384
Saskatchewan	4,287	4,645	5,063	5,063	4,774	4,774
Alberta	4,165	4,512	4,953	4,838	4,763	4,964
British Columbia	3,176	4,084	4,735	4,867	4,740	4,855

Note: Using the most current enrolment data available, average tuition fees have been weighted by the number of students enrolled by institution and field of study. Fees at both public and private institutions are included in the weighted average calculations.

Source: Statistics Canada, Centre for Education Statistics.

Table 10.13 Public and private elementary and secondary education expenditures, 1994/1995 to 2002/2003

	1994/1995	1995/1996	1996/1997	1997/1998	1998/1999
			$ thousands		
Canada	**35,936,049**	**36,425,267**	**36,804,814**	**37,163,556**	**38,758,819**
Newfoundland and Labrador	616,810	584,608	597,391	564,714	569,287
Prince Edward Island	129,122	120,901	118,483	127,047	143,263
Nova Scotia	948,279	922,044	937,344	920,575	1,027,450
New Brunswick	822,261	819,655	838,058	847,354	866,150
Quebec	8,123,686	8,141,401	8,063,282	7,600,775	7,772,687
Ontario	14,790,781	14,971,529	15,092,680	15,502,879	16,191,535
Manitoba	1,467,811	1,552,395	1,577,814	1,616,574	1,690,214
Saskatchewan	1,177,760	1,271,038	1,293,069	1,335,093	1,375,143
Alberta	3,191,827	3,197,260	3,296,624	3,528,301	3,882,363
British Columbia	4,267,103	4,534,959	4,681,100	4,802,043	4,907,057
Yukon	81,774	71,169	77,158	82,838	76,779
Northwest Territories including Nunavut	293,087	213,704	208,782	211,662	208,959
Northwest Territories	..	..	..	..	..
Nunavut	..	..	..	..	..
Foreign and undistributed[1]	25,748	24,604	23,029	23,701	47,932

	1999/2000	2000/2001	2001/2002	2002/2003
		$ thousands		
Canada	**39,403,757**	**40,285,311**	**42,294,686**	**43,695,970**
Newfoundland and Labrador	573,908	577,319	608,376	626,405
Prince Edward Island	142,211	150,277	156,399	154,309
Nova Scotia	1,080,247	996,439	1,006,261	1,063,426
New Brunswick	885,836	843,565	864,441	893,478
Quebec	8,554,451	8,860,058	9,628,481	9,507,216
Ontario	15,786,513	15,842,478	16,390,755	17,122,615
Manitoba	1,756,112	1,821,560	1,853,923	1,976,918
Saskatchewan	1,389,976	1,453,208	1,490,336	1,633,710
Alberta	3,922,073	4,139,444	4,401,026	4,724,349
British Columbia	5,005,492	5,294,063	5,552,127	5,621,639
Yukon	81,178	81,289	87,159	90,812
Northwest Territories including Nunavut	..	..	..	..
Northwest Territories	118,246	117,625	140,288	151,824
Nunavut	85,416	85,439	91,986	98,458
Foreign and undistributed[1]	22,098	22,547	23,128	30,811

Note: Data are estimates for the most recent year, budgetary for the second most recent year, and preliminary for the third most recent year.

1. Foreign and undistributed expenditures by the federal government that cannot be attributed to a particular province or territory.

Source: Statistics Canada, CANSIM table 478-0014.

Table 10.14 Registered apprenticeship training, growth in registrations and completions, by major trade group, 2000/2001 to 2004/2005

	2000/2001	2001/2002	2002/2003	2003/2004	2004/2005
	annual % change				
Total major trade groups					
Registrations	8.1	7.5	8.4	6.8	9.7
Completions	0.4	-9.7	11.0	6.4	4.3
Building construction trades					
Registrations	7.7	12.9	13.2	12.6	13.4
Completions	2.7	-1.7	24.7	1.6	14.5
Electrical, electronics and related trades					
Registrations	11.9	8.8	7.0	7.1	8.8
Completions	15.0	-0.5	-8.3	24.2	6.7
Food and service trades					
Registrations	10.1	5.4	8.3	3.8	4.7
Completions	-5.4	-24.9	16.1	6.3	2.2
Industrial and related mechanical trades					
Registrations	7.1	4.9	5.9	1.0	5.9
Completions	8.1	-9.7	18.4	6.5	-4.9
Metal fabricating trades					
Registrations	7.5	5.2	5.6	3.7	10.5
Completions	-0.8	-8.3	15.6	7.6	-1.0
Motor vehicle and heavy equipment trades					
Registrations	4.7	5.0	8.1	5.9	9.3
Completions	-6.7	-13.0	8.1	-3.4	8.2
Other trades[1]					
Registrations	16.8	14.0	12.4	16.1	11.4
Completions	-6.3	-3.3	24.1	0.0	1.4

1. Includes miscellaneous trades and occupations not classified elsewhere. One must also be aware that many of the apprenticeship trades and occupations that have been introduced since the 1990s have been added to this group. Some of the these new trades and occupations include child and youth worker, early childhood educator, pork production technician and those related to motion picture and theatre, such as assistant cameraperson, grip and set dresser.

Source: Statistics Canada, CANSIM tables 477-0051 and 477-0052.

Energy

Overview

Canada ranks among the world's largest producers of energy, is energy self-sufficient and is the largest source of U.S. energy imports. Almost all of Canada's energy exports go to the United States: the two countries trade oil, natural gas, coal and electricity. Our trade surplus in energy—crude oil, refined petroleum and other products, natural gas, coal and electricity—reached $55.9 billion in 2007, almost a 29% increase from 2004.

Oil brings billions to Canada's economy each year. In 2007, the energy industry accounted for 5.6% of the gross domestic product and for nearly 20%, or $90 billion, of the total value of Canadian exports. That year, the industry directly employed 372,200 people, or 2.2% of the labour force.

Exports of crude oil alone reached $41.8 billion, up from $25.6 billion in 2004, and nearly four times the value a decade earlier. Exports of crude accounted for 9.3% of total merchandise trade in 2007, more than twice the proportion in 1995 (3.7%).

The volume of gasoline sales rose 3.9% from 2006 to 2007, despite the higher prices at the pump. Canadian drivers consumed 42.5 billion litres of gasoline in 2007, up 21.3% from 35.1 billion litres in 1995. Forty percent of Canadians' energy appetite is fuelled by refined petroleum products; that proportion has basically not changed since 1990.

Crude oil production rising

In 2007, Canada produced 160.5 million cubic metres of crude oil, up 4.2% from 2006. That amounts to 2.8 million barrels per day. (One cubic metre contains 1,000 litres and equals 6.3 barrels.)

Alberta produced just over two-thirds of the crude oil pumped in 2007. Saskatchewan, a

Chart 11.1
Exports of crude petroleum

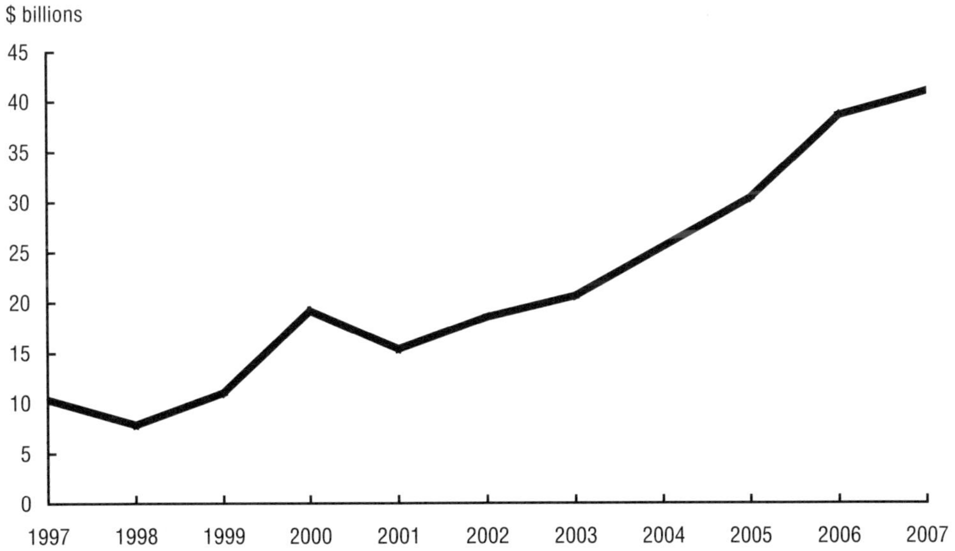

Notes: In current dollars. Data are on a balance of payments basis.
Source: Statistics Canada, CANSIM table 228-0001.

distant second, contributed 16%, while Nova Scotia's and Newfoundland and Labrador's offshore rigs together accounted for nearly 14%. Crude oil flows from wells in seven Canadian provinces.

Discoveries of conventional oil and gas have fallen in recent years, so the industry has increasingly been shifting to non-conventional sites—for example, offshore and the oil sands—to meet demand. In particular, higher oil prices and robust global demand have fuelled an expansion of Alberta's oil sands industry.

Investment in the oil sands reached $18 billion in 2007, up 17% from 2006. Just a decade ago, investment by the industry was less than one-tenth that of the manufacturing sector. In 2008, producers intend to invest $19.7 billion in the oil sands alone, which will surpass the $19.6 billion planned by the entire manufacturing sector.

The oil sands are a large resource: the deposits contain as much as 27.4 billion cubic metres of economically viable oil, or enough to meet the country's current energy needs for 500 years.

Chart 11.2
Production, consumption and exports of crude oil

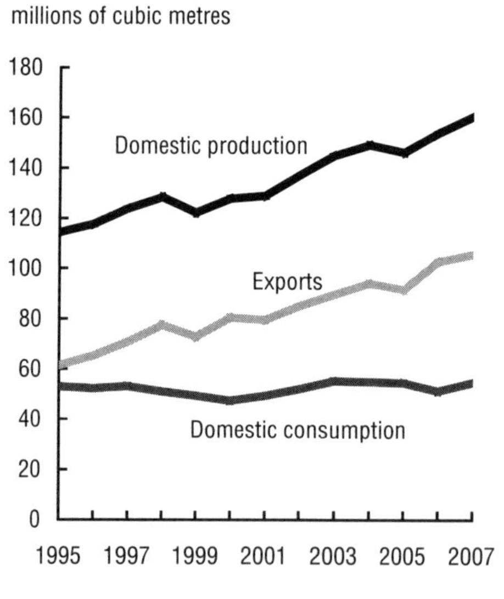

Source: Statistics Canada, CANSIM table 126-0001.

Table 11.a
Energy production by fuel type, 2007

	terajoules
Coal	1,339,754
Crude oil	5,935,706
Natural gas	7,219,725
Natural gas liquids	701,362
Primary electricity, hydro and nuclear	1,599,479
Refined petroleum products	4,676,361

Source: Statistics Canada, CANSIM table 128-0009.

Two-thirds of production is exported

Canada exported an average of 294,411 cubic metres of crude oil per day in 2007. Since 1995, the United States has received 99% of Canada's oil exports.

Alberta is Canada's top energy-exporting province. All of its oil exports go to the United States, facilitated by a network of more than 16,000 kilometres of pipeline. The major beneficiary has been the U.S. Midwest. In 2007, 61.7 million cubic metres of crude oil flowed into states such as Illinois, Minnesota and Oklahoma.

Demand for Canadian crude has been growing in the Rocky Mountain region, which includes Wyoming, Colorado and Utah. This region imported 19.7 million cubic metres of Canadian crude oil in 2007, more than double 1995 totals.

U.S. demand driving oil production increases

From 1995 to 2007, Canada's output of crude oil increased an average of 3.4% annually. Stronger foreign demand—almost exclusively from the United States—has been the driver; domestic demand for Canadian crude has remained fairly stable. In volume terms, Canada's oil exports have grown an average 5.6% annually since 1995.

In 2007, Canada exported 104.8 million cubic metres to the United States, more than did Saudi Arabia, Venezuela and Mexico; our exports covered 10% of America's oil needs.

Some oil stays in Canada

Canadian demand for crude oil reached 106,960 million cubic metres in 2007. Canada has 19 refineries with a total capacity of 324,500 cubic metres a day, according to the National Energy Board; 16 of these refineries produce a full range of refined petroleum products.

In 2006, these refineries operated at an average 90% of capacity. In 2007, 60% of Ontario's crude oil came from Western Canada, 3% from Eastern Canada and 36% from import sources. Refineries in Western Canada process Western Canadian production exclusively, including crude from the oil sands.

Chart 11.3
Exports of oil, natural gas and electricity to the United States

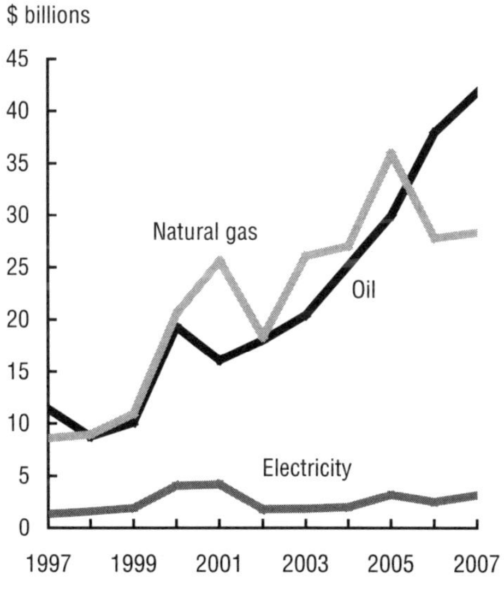

Source: Statistics Canada, Catalogue no. 57-601-XIE.

More electricity flowing south and north

Canada and the United States have an extensive electricity trade, and the two countries' electricity networks are heavily integrated, which became apparent during the Northeast blackout in August 2003. Net electricity exports to the United States in 2007 were nearly double the five-year average of 15.7 terawatt hours, generating $3.1 billion in revenue. Electricity imports from the United States more than tripled from 1995 to 2006, but they make up a small portion of Canada's demand.

Warmer weather, making for less need for heating in the cooler months, and the shrinking manufacturing sector, have curbed electricity generation from primary sources—hydro, steam, nuclear, combustion turbines, wind and tidal. Generation from these sources slipped 0.6% in 2006 from the year before, to 444,299.9 gigawatt hours. From 1995 to 2006, generation from primary sources rose 4.5%.

Nuclear generation increased 6.4% in 2006 from 2005, as Ontario's Pickering station returned Unit 1 to service. Nuclear power supplies 52% of the electricity generated in Ontario, enough to supply all the homes in the province. Nuclear power supplied 16% of Canada's total electricity production in 2006.

Although Canada's utilities are managing to meet domestic demand for electricity, new or upgraded electricity transmission facilities are being planned to serve Canada's growing population and economy.

Electricity from wind, solar and tidal sources continues to grow, but these make up less than 0.5% of the electricity generated. Wind generation projects doubled capacity from 2005 to 2006, to 1,460 megawatts; Ontario added 400 megawatts of that. According to the Canadian Wind Energy Association, Canada ranked twelfth in the world in wind energy capacity at the end of 2006.

Not so conventional anymore

As Alberta's reserves of light crude oil began to decline in the 1990s, so did production: by 2005, it had fallen to just over half its 1990 total. Since 1997, Newfoundland and Labrador have offset some of that decline with the flows of light crude oil from its offshore—'non-conventional'—oil fields.

Conventional crude oil refers to light, medium and heavy hydrocarbons. It has been the traditional source for most oil production. Conventional crude oil is produced by drilling wells and is differentiated from non-conventional crude oil by the extraction methods. Examples are coal bed methane, offshore fields and oil sands.

Alberta's non-conventional crude oil, known as the oil sands, is too thick to flow in its natural state and requires special extraction methods to bring it to the surface. Expensive 'upgraders' are then used to transform the heavy crude into light crude and synthetic oil.

Light oil flows easily through wells and pipelines. When refined, it yields a large quantity of transportation fuels such as gasoline, diesel and jet fuel. Heavy oil requires additional pumping or dilution to flow through wells and pipelines. It yields more heating oil and less transportation fuels when refined. Prices for a light oil called West Texas Intermediate (WTI) are quoted most often, but not all barrels of oil are created equal.

Canadian producers are turning out more and more heavy crude in Alberta that requires more time and energy to refine and that sell at a discount of between US$10 and US$20 a barrel compared with WTI.

Chart 11.4
Conventional and non-conventional oil production

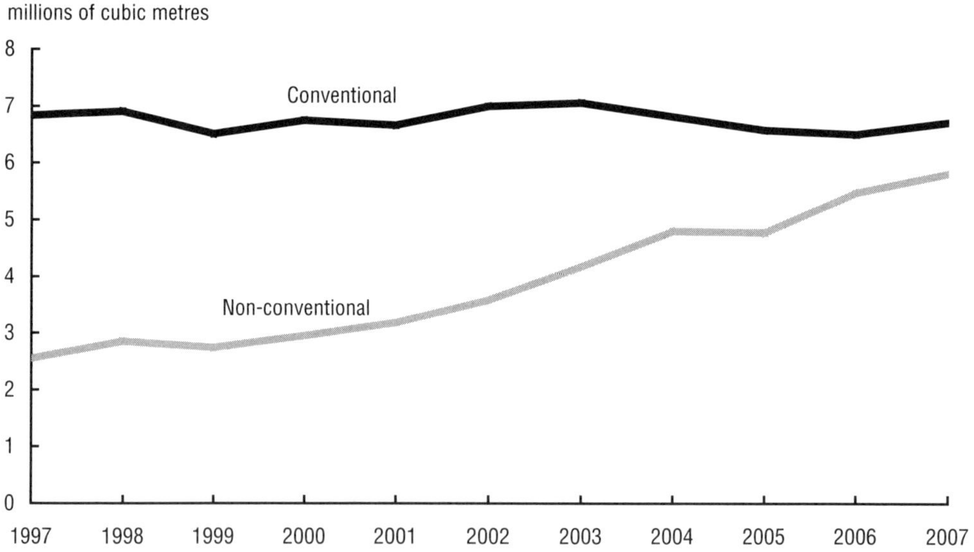

Source: Statistics Canada, CANSIM table 126-0001.

Researching alternative energy

Research and development (R&D) into new and cleaner energy technologies continues to grow. A recent survey looked at energy R&D in five broad areas: fossil fuels, nuclear technologies, energy transportation and transmission, energy conservation and alternative energy sources.

From 1993 to 2003, Canadian industries increased their R&D spending in only one of these areas: alternative energy sources. In 2003, this spending totalled $204 million, and accounted for 31% of industries' total R&D spending on energy, compared with 15% in 1993.

Prior to 1996, Canadian industries were spending more on R&D in energy conservation than for alternative energy sources: that changed completely in 2000.

Of the 2003 spending on alternative energy, more than 40% went to technologies to store energy or to alternative fuels, such as ethanol and biodiesel. Improvements to hydroelectric generation accounted for 14% of R&D spending; solar energy got 11%.

Seven percent went to biomass energy, carbon dioxide capture and wind power technologies combined. Although Canada surpassed 1,000 megawatts of installed wind energy capacity by June 2006—enough electricity to power 315,000 homes—wind power technologies have not made up a large portion of Canadian R&D spending.

Canada's manufacturing sector accounts for most R&D spending on alternative energy—$151 million in 2003. Manufacturing accounted for 75% of all spending on alternative energy research. From 1994 to 2003, manufacturing accounted for virtually all the growth in spending on alternative energy research. (The survey did not cover the spending of governments, universities and private organizations.)

Chart 11.5
Private research and development spending on energy and energy-related components

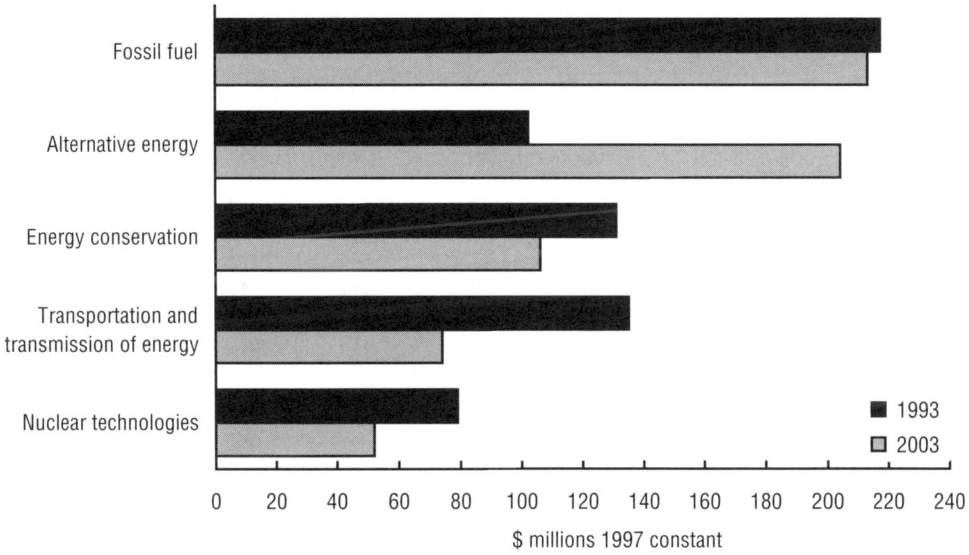

Source: Statistics Canada, Catalogue no. 11-621-MIE.

Table 11.1 Energy supply and demand, 1992 to 2006

	1992	1993	1994	1995	1996	1997	1998	1999
	petajoules							
Primary energy supply[1]								
Availability	9,176.3	9,314.1	9,564.3	9,695.2	10,097.2	10,200.1	10,194.9	10,518.3
Production	12,196.2	13,077.8	13,913.3	14,489.2	14,800.3	15,284.4	15,368.7	15,358.2
Exports	5,246.8	5,653.8	6,348.6	6,878.6	6,950.2	7,496.4	7,818.3	7,824.0
Imports	1,625.0	1,644.9	1,749.7	1,682.5	1,977.2	2,231.8	2,385.3	2,518.5
Primary and secondary energy supply								
Net supply[2]	8,015.7	8,165.2	8,412.4	8,583.6	8,899.6	8,927.6	8,841.3	9,190.7
Producer consumption	978.8	988.3	1,017.2	1,039.8	1,059.1	999.2	1,073.3	1,229.3
Non-energy use	709.2	729.5	740.6	758.8	800.0	833.0	811.8	828.9
Primary and secondary energy demand[3]	**6,327.6**	**6,447.4**	**6,654.7**	**6,785.0**	**7,040.4**	**7,095.5**	**6,956.2**	**7,132.5**
Industrial	1,961.6	1,973.2	2,053.4	2,105.6	2,180.5	2,196.9	2,149.0	2,177.3
Transportation	1,885.8	1,918.2	2,021.3	2,065.1	2,124.7	2,182.9	2,256.6	2,307.3
Agriculture	196.9	198.8	195.8	209.2	222.9	230.0	224.7	229.9
Residential	1,216.3	1,256.7	1,286.7	1,259.1	1,358.2	1,295.1	1,183.5	1,232.3
Public administration	133.7	132.1	143.1	143.3	134.1	135.9	130.3	124.5
Commercial and other institutional	933.4	968.6	954.4	1,002.6	1,020.4	1,054.8	1,012.3	1,061.4

	2000	2001	2002	2003	2004	2005	2006
	petajoules						
Primary energy supply[1]							
Availability	10,831.0	10,950.4	11,163.5	11,478.5	11,527.5	11,307.1	11,216.0
Production	15,768.4	15,894.9	16,171.0	16,170.9	16,553.7	16,489.9	16,796.0
Exports	8,328.4	8,443.8	8,561.9	8,499.0	8,822.7	8,662.2	8,851.3
Imports	2,852.2	3,013.4	2,923.6	3,459.8	3,107.6	3,139.2	2,936.3
Primary and secondary energy supply							
Net supply[2]	9,423.7	9,303.5	9,623.1	9,829.9	10,014.0	9,946.1	9,883.0
Producer consumption	1,257.4	1,264.9	1,344.1	1,340.0	1,303.2	1,274.0	1,279.9
Non-energy use	790.3	863.2	894.3	903.4	1,029.3	983.7	1,042.7
Primary and secondary energy demand[3]	**7,376.0**	**7,175.4**	**7,384.7**	**7,586.5**	**7,681.6**	**7,688.5**	**7,560.4**
Industrial	2,268.6	2,166.3	2,229.5	2,318.6	2,343.2	2,312.8	2,312.5
Transportation	2,279.8	2,240.4	2,250.1	2,266.3	2,347.3	2,388.8	2,373.3
Agriculture	231.9	218.1	206.8	211.8	208.9	208.5	210.8
Residential	1,287.8	1,240.0	1,286.7	1,338.2	1,313.0	1,296.6	1,250.3
Public administration	131.3	126.8	125.2	128.1	131.9	136.1	127.7
Commercial and other institutional	1,176.4	1,184.1	1,286.7	1,323.8	1,337.5	1,346.1	1,286.0

1. Primary energy sources are coal, crude oil, natural gas, natural gas liquids, hydro and nuclear electricity.
2. Primary and secondary sources.
3. Final demand.

Source: Statistics Canada, CANSIM tables 128-0002 and 128-0009.

Table 11.2 Consumer Price Index, energy, 1993 to 2007

	1993	1994	1995	1996	1997	1998	1999	2000
	2002=100							
Electricity	87.2	87.7	87.3	88.3	89.3	90.1	90.8	91.3
Natural gas	61.5	66.7	62.6	61.9	66.5	70.6	77.5	94.2
Fuel oil and other fuel	77.1	76.2	75.1	80.3	85.2	76.5	76.8	108.7
Gasoline	77.4	76.5	80.1	83.6	85.2	77.9	84.9	103.5

	2001	2002	2003	2004	2005	2006	2007
	2002=100						
Electricity	92.9	100.0	98.0	102.0	104.9	110.8	112.9
Natural gas	122.1	100.0	130.1	127.4	136.3	140.5	131.3
Fuel oil and other fuel	108.8	100.0	114.9	126.5	158.7	165.9	172.5
Gasoline	100.8	100.0	106.4	117.6	132.6	139.8	146.1

Source: Statistics Canada, CANSIM table 326-0021.

Table 11.3 Gasoline prices, by selected urban centres, 1992 to 2007

	1992	1993	1994	1995	1996	1997	1998	1999
	cents per litre							
St. John's	60.8	57.0	58.6	62.8	61.4	67.7	64.4	66.2
Charlottetown and Summerside	60.8	56.8	55.0	59.3	59.2	60.6	53.6	52.9
Halifax	..	50.7	52.0	54.3	54.8	60.6	57.1	60.8
Saint John	..	54.7	53.6	56.0	55.1	60.2	55.4	59.2
Québec	61.1	59.0	56.7	58.2	60.6	61.3	55.2	61.5
Montréal	60.2	57.4	55.2	56.8	60.6	61.9	56.3	63.0
Ottawa	57.3	54.2	52.5	53.8	55.1	56.0	51.3	56.2
Toronto	52.4	51.1	49.8	52.4	56.1	56.1	51.6	57.5
Thunder Bay	57.2	56.5	56.2	56.6	61.2	62.6	54.0	58.0
Winnipeg	49.5	52.1	52.3	54.6	56.9	57.4	53.3	57.3
Regina	49.4	53.6	55.6	57.5	59.3	60.0	55.6	60.5
Saskatoon	51.6	55.7	55.3	57.8	60.8	60.6	56.7	59.8
Edmonton	47.6	45.7	45.4	47.6	49.6	52.1	47.0	51.4
Calgary	46.6	47.3	47.4	50.0	51.7	53.2	48.9	52.6
Vancouver	53.8	54.8	55.6	58.4	59.2	58.8	50.6	54.3
Victoria	52.1	51.0	51.8	54.8	57.9	59.0	52.7	59.2
Whitehorse	58.4	58.0	58.1	63.4	67.0	67.9	66.9	67.3
Yellowknife	64.4	65.2	65.7	70.2	73.2	73.9	72.1	73.6

	2000	2001	2002	2003	2004	2005	2006	2007
	cents per litre							
St. John's	83.0	79.1	77.0	82.8	91.7	102.1	107.6	111.0
Charlottetown and Summerside	70.1	71.9	68.2	74.0	84.1	96.4	103.0	104.2
Halifax	76.1	72.8	73.4	78.0	87.5	97.9	103.7	106.8
Saint John	73.3	70.0	72.5	78.8	88.0	97.9	102.2	101.4
Québec	71.9	74.0	72.1	77.8	87.0	97.5	102.4	106.4
Montréal	77.2	73.8	71.4	76.7	85.8	96.4	100.8	104.3
Ottawa	69.0	66.0	65.9	70.2	77.2	88.5	92.2	98.1
Toronto	70.8	67.8	67.3	70.9	76.6	89.0	93.4	97.4
Thunder Bay	72.6	72.5	71.0	76.9	82.8	94.0	98.5	106.2
Winnipeg	66.7	65.0	63.2	67.6	76.7	90.0	96.6	102.2
Regina	71.7	72.2	72.7	76.0	82.5	92.7	99.6	104.7
Saskatoon	71.7	72.2	73.0	75.9	82.8	93.5	99.8	104.5
Edmonton	63.5	61.3	63.4	67.4	75.9	85.1	91.0	96.7
Calgary	64.0	64.5	64.6	66.3	74.8	85.8	92.3	98.5
Vancouver	69.1	68.9	70.4	76.8	86.0	97.1	103.8	108.1
Victoria	73.5	73.9	73.9	81.1	89.9	99.2	105.4	108.3
Whitehorse	81.4	81.7	80.8	83.6	93.9	105.5	107.6	111.2
Yellowknife	85.4	88.2	88.5	92.2	96.8	105.0	109.5	118.0

Note: Average annual price of regular unleaded gasoline at self-service filling stations.
Source: Statistics Canada, CANSIM table 326-0009.

Table 11.4 Household heating fuel prices, by selected urban centres, 1992 to 2007

	1992	1993	1994	1995	1996	1997	1998	1999
	cents per litre							
St. John's	39.7	39.6	36.3	36.5	39.8	44.3	35.1	38.6
Charlottetown and Summerside	35.5	36.0	34.4	36.1	37.5	39.2	32.4	32.8
Halifax	36.5	36.5	33.8	34.0	38.5	42.8	36.9	38.9
Saint John	38.2	38.7	36.2	35.2	41.7	46.4	41.5	40.9
Québec	39.2	39.2	39.6	39.0	41.8	40.9	37.0	38.2
Montréal	37.7	37.0	36.5	33.4	34.6	36.7	32.8	33.6
Ottawa	37.3	37.4	37.3	37.3	39.6	42.8	39.2	39.3
Toronto	36.4	38.0	38.3	38.3	40.6	43.4	41.2	39.1
Thunder Bay	40.9	41.0	40.2	42.0	45.2	43.8	37.7	39.1
Winnipeg	41.0	42.5	41.8	41.9	44.4	47.8	47.0	45.6
Regina	36.1	35.7	35.6	36.9	39.7	42.7	40.9	41.4
Saskatoon	37.6	38.0	39.3	40.9	41.9	44.1	42.1	41.7
Vancouver	40.4	41.4	41.5	41.5	42.5	43.9	41.4	42.2
Victoria	39.0	39.5	39.6	39.6	40.5	44.2	40.7	42.9
Whitehorse	41.8	42.5	42.5	41.9	43.3	46.0	42.4	41.6
Yellowknife	37.1	38.7	38.7	37.9	39.6	38.9	35.0	37.1

	2000	2001	2002	2003	2004	2005	2006	2007
	cents per litre							
St. John's	56.1	54.5	50.1	54.8	62.4	78.6	84.8	87.6
Charlottetown and Summerside	48.8	51.3	46.5	53.4	56.8	73.8	77.6	79.3
Halifax	56.1	54.7	53.3	61.4	68.5	83.6	87.9	84.0
Saint John	59.4	58.7	54.9	62.4	66.0	83.2	84.7	89.7
Québec	50.2	49.1	48.8	56.3	61.3	77.2	79.0	83.3
Montréal	51.3	49.9	46.3	54.3	58.6	75.0	78.6	82.0
Ottawa	53.4	56.8	49.2	57.2	62.9	77.4	81.6	86.8
Toronto	54.3	55.9	50.8	57.9	64.0	78.0	82.2	87.6
Thunder Bay	54.3	54.6	47.9	57.1	62.9	81.4	85.5	91.0
Winnipeg	56.1	60.2	53.0	60.8	64.4	81.6	84.0	91.5
Regina	53.3	55.2	51.8	55.7	62.4	82.0	82.6	91.8
Saskatoon	54.0	56.5	54.6	59.3	65.3	80.0	85.5	91.5
Vancouver	57.1	58.1	54.2	59.2	69.4	88.1	89.0	93.5
Victoria	57.9	58.0	53.6	62.9	72.3	90.8	94.1	99.9
Whitehorse	57.0	63.1	57.5	64.5	72.3	88.4	94.1	102.3
Yellowknife	52.3	51.9	49.0	56.5	62.0	81.3	84.8	96.4

Note: Average annual price.
Source: Statistics Canada, CANSIM table 326-0009.

Table 11.5 Established crude oil reserves, 1991 to 2005

	1991	1992	1993	1994	1995	1996	1997	1998
	millions of cubic metres							
Canada	**614.9**	**590.4**	**582.2**	**544.5**	**553.0**	**526.7**	**532.2**	**673.5**
Newfoundland and Labrador	..	..	..	..	..	..	..	144.3
Ontario	1.3	1.2	1.2	2.0	1.9	1.9	1.8	1.9
Manitoba	7.2	6.7	6.5	6.3	5.6	5.1	4.7	4.2
Saskatchewan	120.2	122.6	130.2	141.9	150.1	156.8	176.6	180.9
Alberta	468.5	442.0	426.8	374.8	374.1	342.0	326.8	315.2
British Columbia	17.7	17.9	17.5	19.4	21.3	20.9	22.3	26.9

	1999	2000	2001	2002	2003	2004	2005
	millions of cubic metres						
Canada	**642.5**	**667.3**	**644.7**	**606.1**	**590.0**	**603.8**	**752.3**
Newfoundland and Labrador	138.0	159.6	151.0	134.4	121.3	138.7	272.9
Ontario	1.9	2.0	1.9	1.8	1.9	1.9	1.6
Manitoba	4.3	4.5	4.0	3.4	4.6	3.9	3.9
Saskatchewan	169.1	182.1	184.9	183.9	184.7	187.9	197.7
Alberta	301.6	291.4	278.3	260.3	253.9	249.2	254.8
British Columbia	27.7	27.6	24.7	22.3	23.6	22.2	21.5

Note: Data are for closing stock of established crude oil reserves.
Source: Statistics Canada, CANSIM table 153-0013.

Table 11.6 Established natural gas reserves, 1991 to 2005

	1991	1992	1993	1994	1995	1996	1997	1998
	billions of cubic metres							
Canada	**1,965.2**	**1,929.1**	**1,859.9**	**1,832.7**	**1,840.9**	**1,725.9**	**1,620.4**	**1,562.2**
Nova Scotia	..	..	..	..	..	..	..	..
Ontario	16.7	16.9	17.2	13.4	12.0	12.5	12.5	12.2
Saskatchewan	82.1	78.4	84.7	86.7	86.6	81.8	76.5	71.5
Alberta	1,626.2	1,594.7	1,534.9	1,490.3	1,488.8	1,378.1	1,284.0	1,239.9
British Columbia	240.1	239.2	223.1	242.2	253.5	253.5	247.4	238.6

	1999	2000	2001	2002	2003	2004	2005
	billions of cubic metres						
Canada	**1,526.8**	**1,614.5**	**1,547.8**	**1,529.6**	**1,469.5**	**1,497.5**	**1,553.7**
Nova Scotia	..	67.1	61.7	56.2	23.2	19.3	15.2
Ontario	12.0	11.6	11.5	11.3	11.5	11.5	13.0
Saskatchewan	68.6	75.6	81.7	76.2	87.4	85.0	91.6
Alberta	1,207.2	1,210.7	1,141.4	1,131.3	1,087.6	1,092.3	1,086.0
British Columbia	239.0	249.5	251.5	254.7	259.9	289.4	347.8

Note: Data are for closing stock of established natural gas reserves.
Source: Statistics Canada, CANSIM table 153-0014.

Table 11.7 Established reserves of natural gas liquids, 1990 to 2004

	1990	1991	1992	1993	1994	1995	1996	1997
	thousands of cubic metres							
Canada	**649,718**	**639,935**	**636,588**	**621,645**	**593,278**	**599,569**	**546,580**	**502,751**
Manitoba	72	65	61	56	52	46	91	0
Saskatchewan	1,976	1,862	1,724	2,035	2,207	2,155	2,086	1,632
Alberta	637,300	626,600	623,700	603,200	574,300	580,600	527,500	483,400
Propane	124,800	121,400	121,100	118,100	111,600	109,400	103,000	91,400
Ethane	320,000	316,000	312,000	305,000	290,000	300,000	264,000	245,000
Butane	71,700	69,900	70,600	67,100	63,900	62,900	58,500	51,900
Pentanes plus	120,800	119,300	120,000	113,000	108,800	108,300	102,000	95,100
British Columbia	10,370	11,408	11,103	16,354	16,719	16,768	16,903	17,719

	1998	1999	2000	2001	2002	2003	2004
	thousands of cubic metres						
Canada	**487,525**	**487,339**	**486,977**	**476,429**	**370,919**	**310,651**	**307,546**
Manitoba	..	..	..	..	..	..	..
Saskatchewan	1,482	1,306	1,010	981	1,000	1,029	888
Alberta	468,900	469,700	473,900	463,600	359,100	298,500	295,000
Propane	88,600	82,600	85,500	84,100	79,300	69,400	71,300
Ethane	238,000	256,000	252,000	252,100	165,100	124,000	122,900
Butane	51,100	48,600	50,400	49,900	46,900	41,900	41,500
Pentanes plus	91,200	82,500	86,000	77,500	67,800	63,200	59,300
British Columbia	17,143	16,333	12,067	11,848	10,819	11,122	11,658

Note: Data are for closing stock of established reserves of natural gas liquids.
Source: Statistics Canada, CANSIM table 153-0015.

Table 11.8 Energy fuel consumption of the manufacturing sector, by subsector, 2001 to 2006

	2001	2002	2003	2004	2005	2006
	terajoules					
All manufacturing	**2,511,331**	**2,511,322**	**2,521,077**	**2,614,696**	**2,502,600**	**2,396,304**
Food	89,116	88,765	89,041	90,928	95,774	96,279
Beverage and tobacco products	12,196	12,896	12,237	12,266	12,475	11,570
Textile mills	8,634	8,238	8,050	8,058	7,745	7,316
Textile product mills	4,275	4,303	3,554	3,545	3,550	3,332
Clothing	5,174	4,985	4,978	3,997	2,154	1,737
Leather and allied products	1,071	966	768	568	309	235
Wood products	118,511	122,595	120,183	124,853	129,219	134,337
Paper	834,855	830,779	835,318	850,894	776,211	682,554
Printing and related support activities	8,754	8,548	8,765	8,521	8,878	8,305
Petroleum and coal products	345,471	366,241	368,429	405,491	358,993	365,385
Chemicals	275,596	252,056	254,575	278,149	272,915	262,051
Plastic and rubber products	33,972	32,592	35,045	37,011	37,846	34,904
Non-metallic mineral products	115,198	118,845	117,924	126,049	126,257	124,283
Primary metals	524,957	519,559	521,073	521,069	524,651	532,833
Fabricated metal products	38,542	41,361	39,784	41,647	40,979	37,104
Machinery	14,070	13,819	15,223	16,042	18,039	16,592
Computer and electronic products	3,682	3,931	4,563	5,100	5,621	5,311
Electrical equipment, appliances and components	6,318	6,011	6,708	7,107	7,282	6,456
Transportation equipment	54,249	57,134	56,725	56,267	55,896	50,560
Furniture and related products	11,058	11,308	11,521	10,908	11,645	10,496
Miscellaneous manufacturing	5,633	6,391	6,610	6,226	6,161	4,665

Note: North American Industry Classification System (NAICS), 2002.
Source: Statistics Canada, CANSIM table 128-0006.

Table 11.9 Energy fuel consumption of the manufacturing sector, by fuel type, 2001 to 2006

	2001	2002	2003	2004	2005	2006
	terajoules					
Energy consumed	**2,511,331**	**2,511,322**	**2,521,077**	**2,614,696**	**2,502,600**	**2,396,304**
Coal	47,572	46,775	50,841	55,381	51,734	51,744
Coal coke	96,338	93,299	92,236	93,389	92,869	102,762
Coke oven gas	27,036	26,824	28,019	28,333	29,530	29,422
Electricity	684,234	696,960	705,419	700,993	724,656	695,986
Heavy fuel oil	139,351	114,653	138,696	150,234	126,431	100,842
Middle distillates	22,736	19,838	18,166	19,896	19,713	17,137
Natural gas	721,897	726,312	672,564	694,866	662,426	626,557
Petroleum coke and coke from catalytic cracking catalyst	75,647	84,085	88,419	94,986	82,019	82,864
Propane	15,358	12,640	11,634	9,448	7,404	7,150
Refinery fuel gas	173,033	175,149	178,996	207,558	186,407	197,698
Spent pulping liquor	288,942	290,859	292,635	299,806	258,505	224,189
Steam	40,076	41,336	47,956	48,029	50,076	55,124
Wood	179,109	182,594	195,495	211,777	210,828	204,828

Note: North American Industry Classification System (NAICS), 2002.
Source: Statistics Canada, CANSIM table 128-0006.

Environment

Overview

The environment has been an issue of concern among Canadians and the subject of debate in the media for years. In 2007, it was the number one issue, and 45% of Canadians rated the quality of the environment as 'fair.' Of issues Canadians say the country is facing, climate change tops the list.

According to the 2007 Canadian Environmental Sustainability Indicators, the pressure on Canada's environment is steady or increasing. From 1990 to 2005, greenhouse gas (GHG) emissions and air quality were ongoing concerns. During the same period, guidelines for protecting aquatic life were not being met, at least occasionally, at many monitoring sites across the country.

While Canadians are changing their activities to protect the environment, reducing the nation's impact on the environment is proving difficult, especially in an era of population and economic growth. From 1990 to 2005, the country's population grew 17%, from 27.7 million people to 32.3 million, while the gross domestic product rose 51.4%, in 2002 constant prices.

Economic activity growth can also lead to industries using more energy and producing more GHGs and air pollutants. Some large energy-consuming industries became more efficient, which offset some of the growth in GHGs. For instance, while the manufacturing industry reduced its energy requirements to produce a unit of goods and services by 33% from 1990 to 2002, energy use still rose 4%.

Greenhouse gases

GHGs occur naturally and help regulate the climate by trapping heat in the atmosphere and reflecting it back to the surface. GHG emissions from human activities amplify the natural greenhouse effect and contribute

Chart 12.1
Greenhouse gas emissions

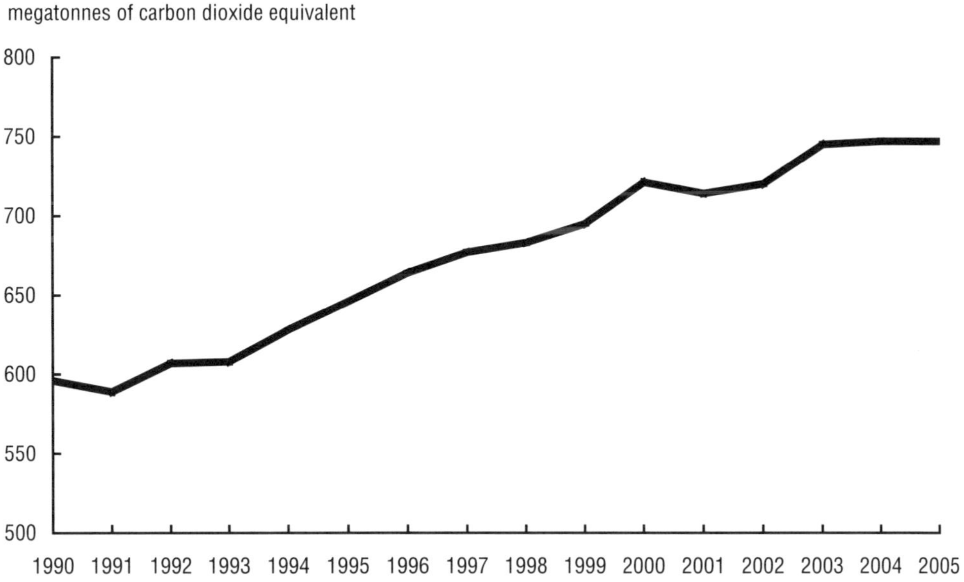

Source: Statistics Canada, Catalogue no. 16-251-XWE.

to climate change. Six GHGs are tracked by Canada's GHG emissions indicator: carbon dioxide (CO_2), methane (CH_4), nitrous oxide (N_2O), sulphur hexafluoride (SF_6), hydrofluorocarbons (HFCs) and perfluorocarbons (PFCs). Canada's GHG emissions increased about 25% from 1990 to 2005. In 1990, 596 megatonnes of CO_2 equivalent were emitted, and in 2005, 747 megatonnes.

While the long-term trend points upwards, emissions stopped growing from 2003 to 2005, primarily as a result of reduced emissions from electricity generation. This reduction was the result of reduced coal and increased hydro and nuclear generation, lower demand for fuels because of warmer winters, and a reduced rate of increase in fossil fuel production.

Energy production and consumption accounted for most (82%) of Canada's total GHG emissions in 2005. GHG emissions from the oil, gas and coal industry increased 48% from 1990 to 2005, as crude oil and natural gas production and export increased. GHG emissions from road transportation rose 33% in the same period, mainly because of a shift in consumer preference from automobiles to less fuel-efficient vehicles and an increase in heavy truck transport. GHG emissions from thermal–electric power and heat generation increased 37%, as electricity production rose to meet demand and more fossil fuels were used to generate electricity.

Chart 12.2
Ground-level ozone exposure

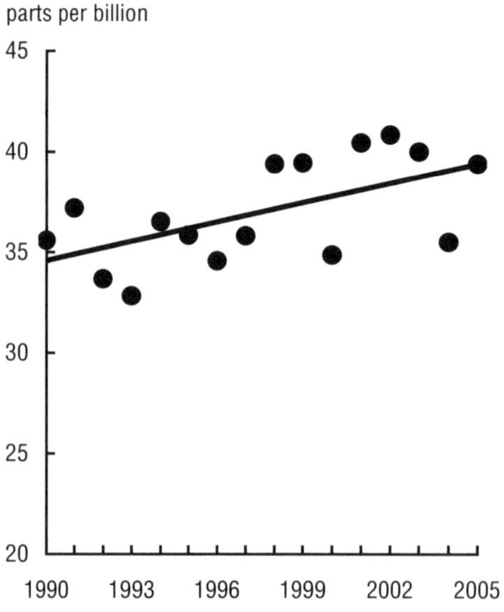

Note: Population weighted.
Source: Statistics Canada, Catalogue no. 16-251-XWE.

Table 12.a
Households affected by swimming restrictions, by province, 2005

	Were aware of any swimming restrictions or closures at a nearby beach[1]	Prevented from swimming by restrictions[2]
	%	
Newfoundland and Labrador	F	F
Prince Edward Island	F	F
Nova Scotia	19	76
New Brunswick	9E	72
Quebec	13	53
Ontario	45	70
Manitoba	44	69
Saskatchewan	6	F
Alberta	15	73
British Columbia	11	64

1. Includes only those households reporting a household member who had swum or had planned to swim at a nearby beach in 2005.
2. Only households reporting awareness of swimming restrictions.

Source: Statistics Canada, Households and the Environment Survey, 2006.

Air quality

Monitoring stations across Canada track air quality indicators for ground-level ozone and fine particulate matter, both key components of smog and two of the most pervasive and widespread air pollutants.

Ground-level ozone is formed by chemical reactions principally involving nitrogen oxides (NO_X) and volatile organic compounds

(VOCs) in the presence of sunlight. The burning of fossil fuels in transportation, industry, and electricity generation and the production and use of paints, cosmetics, and solvents increase concentrations of NO_X and VOCs, creating ground-level ozone.

Ozone exposure increased about 12% from 1990 to 2005, an average 0.8% increase per year. Concentrations increased 17% in southern Ontario and 15% in southern Quebec. In other regions, the ozone exposure showed no significant changes.

Fine particulate matter is emitted directly as a pollutant or is formed in the air as a secondary pollutant from sulphur dioxide, NO_X, VOCs and ammonia. Most fine particulate matter emissions are a result of industry, wood burned for heating and transportation.

Canada's exposure indicator for fine particulate matter showed no significant increase or decrease, either nationally or regionally, from 2000 to 2005.

Chart 12.3
Freshwater quality at sites in southern Canada, 2003 to 2005

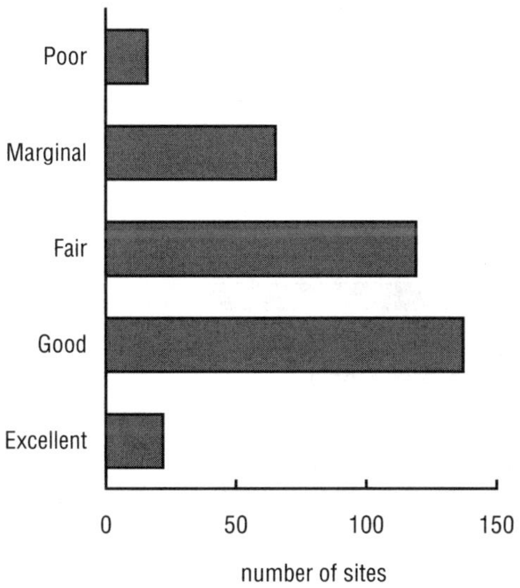

Source: Statistics Canada, Catalogue no. 16-251-XIE.

Water quality

At least 115,000 tonnes of pollutants were directly discharged into Canada's freshwater and coastal surface waters in 2005. Manufacturers, service providers, institutions and households discharge hundreds of different substances into rivers and lakes. Many pollutants make their way into water bodies indirectly, after being released into the air or onto the land.

Runoff from agricultural lands and urban areas, which often have high concentrations of nitrogen or phosphorous, can degrade water quality. Changes in water flows, snow melts and heavy rainfall can also harm water quality by, for example, increasing levels of suspended sediments that are often high in nutrients and metals.

Poor water quality affects aquatic life and human uses of water. For example, high concentrations of nitrogen and phosphorus in the water may result in excessive aquatic plant growth, such as algal blooms, which reduce the amount of dissolved oxygen available for fish and other aquatic animals. Some algal blooms are toxic, killing livestock and harming shellfish.

The quality of Canada's freshwater is measured using the Water Quality Index, an indicator that examines the extent to which water quality guidelines for the protection of aquatic life (plants, invertebrates and fish) are being met at selected lake and river monitoring sites throughout Canada.

Freshwater quality for 359 monitoring sites in southern Canada was rated as 'good' or 'excellent' at 44% of the sites, 'fair' at 33%, and 'marginal' or 'poor' at 23%. Freshwater quality measured at 36 monitoring sites in northern Canada was rated as 'good' or 'excellent' at 56% of the sites, 'fair' at 31%, and 'marginal' or 'poor' at 14%.

Households' impact on the environment

If asked what they do to reduce their impact on the environment, most Canadians probably think of recycling or composting, conserving energy, curbing residential pesticide use or conserving water.

Diverting waste through recycling makes for less waste entering our landfills, helps conserve natural resources and energy, saves landfill space and reduces emissions of methane, which is a greenhouse gas produced in landfills.

In 2006, 93% of Canadian households had access to at least one recycling program, and 97% of these households used at least one of the programs they had access to. Across Canada, 27% of households composted their kitchen waste, their lawn and garden waste or both, up from 23% in 1994.

Some types of household wastes can pose environmental problems. When Canadians were asked how they disposed of leftover paint, disused or expired medication, and computers and other electronics, significant proportions said they were holding onto paint (38%), medication (11%) and computers and communications devices, such as cellphones (35%), because they were unsure how to dispose of them safely.

Conservation is catching on: among households that use thermostats, the proportion with a programmable thermostat increased from 16% in 1994 to 40% in 2006. Among all households with a thermostat, programmable or not, 53% turned down the heat before retiring at night.

The possible negative effects of lawn and garden pesticides have fuelled public debate for several years. In 2005, 29% of Canadian households with a lawn or garden used pesticides, down slightly from 1994. Among the provinces, rates ranged from 14% in Prince Edward Island to 44% in Manitoba.

Chart 12.4
Households with access to at least one recycling program, by province, 2006

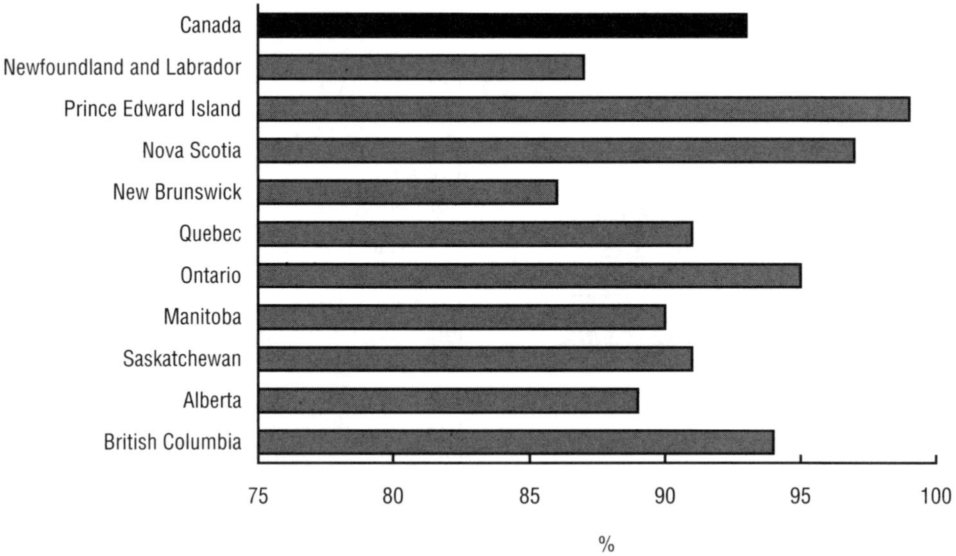

Source: Statistics Canada, Catalogue no. 11-526-XIE.

Protecting and managing the environment

Canadian businesses play a key role in environmental protection. By changing product design, technology, operations and behaviour, firms can curb waste and pollution in manufacturing processes.

Businesses spent $6.8 billion on environmental protection in 2004, about the same as in 2002. Of this, $2.9 billion was for capital expenditures, including pollution prevention.

The most used methods of pollution prevention were pollution prevention training (69%), prevention of leaks and spills (67%), and recirculation, recovery, reuse or recycling (62%). The remaining $3.8 billion was for operating expenses, including $1.5 billion for pollution abatement and control, or 'end-of-pipe' technologies.

To curb the release of substances to air, businesses spent $409 million in capital for end-of-pipe technologies, and $826 million on pollution prevention. They spent $576 million from operating funds and $379 million from capital funds to reduce greenhouse gas emissions.

Energy conservation processes and technologies can reduce emission of pollutants, reduce costs or improve productivity. Over half of businesses (59%) used technologies and processes to reduce energy consumption in 2004. One-third used an energy management or monitoring system, while 29% performed an energy audit sometime during the period from 2002 to 2004.

The petroleum and coal products industry spent the most on environmental protection in 2004, followed by the oil and gas extraction industry. Pulp, paper and paperboard firms were the most likely to use energy conservation technologies.

The federal government funds research and development to care for the environment: $401 milliion in 2005/2006.

Chart 12.5
Environmental protection expenditures, all industries, 2004

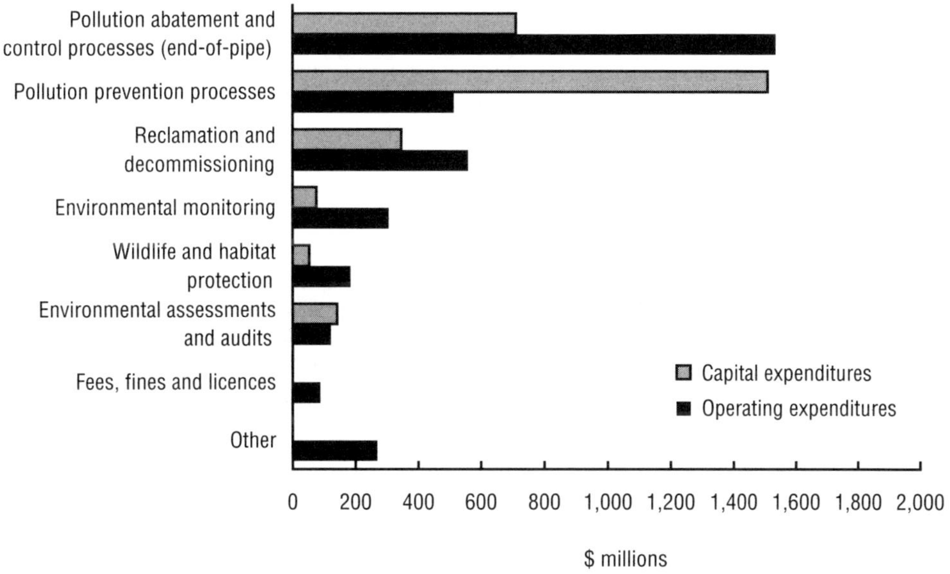

Source: Statistics Canada, Catalogue no. 16F0006XIE.

Table 12.1 Greenhouse gas emissions, by source, 1990 and 2005

	Carbon dioxide		Methane		Nitrous oxide	
	1990	2005	1990	2005	1990	2005
	kilotonnes					
Total[1]	**459,000**	**583,000**	**3,800.00**	**5,200.00**	**150.00**	**140.00**
Energy	428,000	544,000	1,700.00	2,600.00	30.00	30.00
Stationary combustion sources	276,000	338,000	200.00	200.00	7.00	8.00
Electricity and heat generation	94,700	128,000	1.80	5.10	2.00	2.00
Fossil fuel industries	49,600	70,400	80.00	100.00	1.00	2.00
Petroleum refining and upgrading	16,000	18,000	...	...	0.30	0.40
Fossil fuel production	34,100	52,000	80.00	100.00	0.70	1.00
Mining and oil and gas extraction	6,140	15,500	0.10	0.30	0.10	0.40
Manufacturing industries	54,200	45,400	3.00	3.00	2.00	2.00
Iron and steel	6,420	6,460	0.20	0.20	0.20	0.20
Non-ferrous metals	3,170	3,170	0.07	0.07	0.05	0.05
Chemical	7,050	5,320	0.15	0.11	0.10	0.09
Pulp and paper	13,400	7,040	2.00	2.00	0.80	0.80
Cement	3,680	4,570	0.07	0.10	0.04	0.04
Other manufacturing	20,500	18,800	0.40	0.40	0.40	0.40
Construction	1,860	1,300	0.03	0.02	0.05	0.03
Commercial and institutional	25,700	36,600	0.50	0.60	0.50	0.70
Residential	41,300	39,500	100.00	90.00	2.00	2.00
Agriculture and forestry	2,400	1,930	0.04	0.03	0.05	0.06
Transport[2]	142,000	190,000	30.00	30.00	20.00	20.00
Civil aviation (domestic aviation)	6,220	8,420	0.50	0.50	0.60	0.80
Road transportation	97,700	131,000	15.00	9.40	10.00	11.00
Light-duty gasoline vehicles	45,100	39,800	7.80	3.20	6.20	4.10
Light-duty gasoline trucks	20,200	42,800	3.10	3.20	3.20	5.30
Heavy-duty gasoline vehicles	7,950	6,370	1.30	0.38	0.22	0.43
Motorcycles	147	255	0.14	0.16	0.00	0.01
Light-duty diesel automobiles	355	432	0.01	0.01	0.03	0.03
Light-duty diesel trucks	708	2,150	0.02	0.05	0.05	0.20
Heavy-duty diesel vehicles	21,000	38,600	1.00	2.00	0.60	1.00
Propane and natural gas vehicles	2,170	706	1.00	0.70	0.04	0.01
Railways	6,310	5,620	0.30	0.30	3.00	2.00
Navigation (domestic marine)	4,730	6,070	0.30	0.40	1.00	1.00
Other transportation	27,000	38,000	20.00	20.00	6.00	9.00
Off-road gasoline	7,000	7,000	8.00	8.00	0.10	0.20
Off-road diesel	14,000	21,000	0.70	1.00	6.00	9.00
Pipelines	6,700	9,850	6.70	9.80	0.20	0.30
Fugitive sources	11,000	16,000	1,500.00	2,300.00	0.10	0.10
Coal mining	...	...	90.00	30.00	...	...
Oil and natural gas	10,600	16,500	1,440.00	2,310.00	0.10	0.10
Oil	95	170	193.00	260.00	0.10	0.10
Natural gas	23	61	613.00	989.00	...	...
Venting	6,090	10,800	627.00	1,050.00	...	0.01
Flaring	4,400	5,400	2.60	3.70	0.00	0.01

See notes and source at end of table.

Table 12.1 Greenhouse gas emissions, by source, 1990 and 2005 (continued)

	Carbon dioxide		Methane		Nitrous oxide	
	1990	2005	1990	2005	1990	2005
	kilotonnes					
Industrial processes	30,000	39,000	...	...	37.80	12.60
Mineral products	8,300	9,500	...	...	...	...
Cement production	5,400	7,200	...	...	...	...
Lime production	1,700	1,700	...	...	...	...
Mineral product use[3]	1,090	599	...	...	...	...
Chemical industry	3,900	5,000	...	...	37.80	12.60
Ammonia production	3,900	5,000	...	...	...	...
Nitric acid production	...	...	...	...	3.27	4.08
Adipic acid production	...	...	...	...	35.00	8.50
Metal production	9,770	11,900	...	...	...	...
Iron and steel production	7,060	7,010	...	...	...	...
Aluminum production	2,700	4,800	...	...	...	...
Sulfur hexafloride used in magnesium smelters and casters	...	...	...	...	...	...
Consumption of halocarbons and sulfur hexafloride	...	...	...	...	...	...
Other and undifferentiated production	8,300	13,000	...	...	...	...
Solvent and other product use	...	...	...	...	0.56	0.57
Agriculture	...	...	1,000.00	1,300.00	80.00	93.00
Enteric fermentation	...	...	880.00	1,200.00	...	...
Manure management	...	...	120.00	150.00	13.00	17.00
Agricultural soils	...	...	...	...	67.00	76.00
Direct sources	...	...	...	...	39.00	41.00
Pasture, range and paddock manure	...	...	...	...	10.00	14.00
Indirect sources	...	...	...	...	20.00	20.00
Waste	270	190	1,100.00	1,300.00	2.00	2.00
Solid waste disposal on land	...	...	1,000.00	1,300.00	...	...
Wastewater handling	...	...	11.00	12.00	2.00	2.00
Waste incineration	270	190	0.40	0.06	0.40	0.20
Land use, land use change and forestry	-130,000	-26,000	150.00	260.00	6.40	11.00
Forest land	-160,000	-35,000	130.00	240.00	5.50	10.00
Cropland	14,000	180	20.00	9.00	0.80	0.50
Grassland	.	.	.	.	.	.
Wetlands	5,000	1,000	0.40	2.00	0.01	0.07
Settlements	9,000	8,000	5.00	5.00	0.20	0.20

Note: Figures may not add to totals because of rounding.

1. National totals exclude all greenhouse gas emissions from the 'Land use, land use change and forestry' sector.
2. Emissions from ethanol fuel are reported within the gasoline vehicle subcategories under 'Transport.'
3. The category 'Mineral product use' includes carbon dioxide emissions from the use of limestone and dolomite, soda ash and magnesite.

Source: Environment Canada.

Table 12.2 Substances released to land, 2005

	Releases[1]	Share of total
	tonnes	%
Hydrogen sulphide	268,623.7	83.8
Zinc and its compounds	10,077.8	3.1
Asbestos (friable form)	6,354.4	2.0
Ammonia[2]	6,805.6	2.1
Methanol	5,901.4	1.8
Manganese and its compounds	5,366.7	1.7
Phosphorous (total)	4,762.9	1.5
Ethylene glycol	2,633.8	0.8
Lead and its compounds	3,126.4	1.0
Vanadium and its compounds (except when in an alloy)	1,288.4	0.4

Note: Top 10 substances only.

1. Data include disposals.
2. Refers to the total of both ammonia (NH_3) and ammonium ion (NH_4+) in solution.

Source: Statistics Canada, Catalogue no. 16-201-XIE.

Table 12.3 Waste disposal and diversion, by province, 2002, 2004 and 2006

	Total waste disposed			Total materials diverted		
	2002	2004	2006	2002	2004	2006
	tonnes					
Canada	**24,081,371**	**25,226,766**	**27,249,178**	**6,641,546**	**7,112,735**	**7,749,030**
Newfoundland and Labrador	376,594	400,048	407,728	30,386	35,308	30,385
Nova Scotia	389,194	399,967	401,670	192,006	239,845	275,983
New Brunswick	413,606	442,173	450,238	130,728	139,262	252,174
Quebec	5,846,459	6,454,000	6,808,440	1,743,376	2,130,100	2,456,300
Ontario	9,645,633	9,809,264	10,437,780	2,265,968	2,414,552	2,396,856
Manitoba	896,556	928,117	1,024,272	215,815	157,490	152,799
Saskatchewan	795,124	794,933	833,753	116,296	114,182	106,868
Alberta	2,890,294	3,077,311	3,819,872	690,517	620,080	652,637
British Columbia	2,687,882	2,767,657	2,917,080	1,218,475	1,209,216	1,366,191

Note: Data for Prince Edward Island and the territories supressed to meet the confidentiality requirements of the *Statistics Act.*

Source: Statistics Canada, Catalogue no. 16-253-XIE.

Table 12.4 Capital expenditures on pollution prevention, by environmental milieu and by industry, 2004

	All environmental milieu	Air	Surface water	On-site milieu contained solid and liquid waste	Noise, radiation and vibration	Other
	$ millions					
All industries	**1,507.9**	**826.0**	**306.9**	**276.9**	**45.9**	**52.2**
Logging	0.1	0.0	0s	0s	0.0	0.1
Oil and gas extraction	207.3	131.1	18.9	42.8	3.6	11.0
Mining	51.8	6.2	24.3	21.2	0.0	0.1
Electric power generation, transmission and distribution	71.8	36.7	19.4	x	x	x
Natural gas distribution	8.0	2.1	0.2	5.7	0.0	0.0
Food	36.0	11.6	12.3	6.9	0.1	5.2
Beverage and tobacco products	4.5	2.8	0.9	0.1	0.0	0.7
Wood products	46.4	26.7	15.4	x	x	x
Pulp, paper and paperboard mills	53.3	27.7	14.3	4.2	1.3	5.7
Petroleum and coal products	779.5	446.3	170.1	123.5	x	x
Chemicals	38.3	14.3	7.3	10.2	0.4	6.0
Non-metallic mineral products	54.6	31.8	3.7	7.0	0.1	12.1
Primary metals	46.7	17.5	3.4	23.4	0.1	2.3
Fabricated metal products	20.3	19.6	0.1	0.1	0.0	0.5
Transportation equipment	52.0	46.6	1.1	1.8	0.2	2.3
Pipeline transportation	37.3	5.1	15.3	13.4	1.2	2.3

Source: Statistics Canada, Catalogue no. 16-201-XIE.

Table 12.5 Capital expenditures on pollution abatement and control, by environmental milieu and by industry, 2004

	All environmental milieu	Air	Surface water	On-site contained solid and liquid waste	Noise, radiation and vibration
	$ millions				
All industries	**710.0**	**409.4**	**183.0**	**96.4**	**21.2**
Logging	0.5	0.1	0.0	0.4	0.0
Oil and gas extraction	65.5	31.9	13.9	17.0	2.7
Mining	85.9	x	53.1	2.9	x
Electric power generation, transmission and distribution	80.1	x	20.8	9.7	x
Natural gas distribution	2.2	0.4	0.0	1.8	0.0
Food	34.7	12.1	11.4	11.0	0.2
Beverage and tobacco products	6.0	0.5	4.8	0.2	0.6
Wood products	30.7	24.7	4.1	1.7	0.1
Pulp, paper and paperboard mills	99.7	58.9	29.5	10.6	0.7
Petroleum and coal products	93.1	41.1	22.5	22.5	7.1
Chemicals	32.5	16.8	10.2	4.6	0.9
Non-metallic mineral products	25.7	24.3	0.4	0.4	0.6
Primary metals	103.2	82.1	9.9	10.5	0.8
Fabricated metal products	12.3	10.6	1.2	0.3	0.1
Transportation equipment	33.1	x	0.5	0s	x
Pipeline transportation	4.7	1.1	0.9	2.7	0.0

Source: Statistics Canada, Catalogue no. 16-201-XIE.

Table 12.6 Production of selected mineral commodities, 2005 and 2006

	2005	2006p
	carats	
Diamonds	12,314,031	13,233,813
	kilograms	
Gold	120,541	103,807
Platinum group	23,904	24,082
	tonnes	
Zinc	666,664	633,500
Copper	595,383	608,286
Nickel	199,932	234,111
Lead	79,254	82,393
Uranium	11,627	9,862
Molybdenum	7,935	7,842
Cobalt	5,767	6,976
Silver	1,124	982
Cadmium	723	549
Bismuth	170	222
Antimony	79	90
Gemstones	92	109
Tantalum	63	58
	kilotonnes	
Sand and gravel	246,629	236,477
Stone	165,966	164,615
Iron ore	32,513	35,010
Salt	13,496	13,505
Potash	10,594	8,295
Gypsum	9,241	9,138
Quartz	1,914	1,977
Peat	1,363	1,237
Nepheline syenite	743	719
Soapstone, talc, pyrophyllite	90	82
Barite	23	21

Note: Canadian mines only.
Source: Statistics Canada, Catalogue no. 26-202-XIB.

Ethnic diversity and immigration

Overview

Look down the street in most neighbourhoods in Canada and you might see people from all over the world. You may share a class or an office with someone from South America, play sports with someone from Africa, Europe or Asia, or you and your family may be one of the 6.2 million foreign-born people who call Canada home.

On the 2006 Census, people reported more than 200 different ethnic origins. The percentage who reported having more than one ethnic origin rose to 41%, up from 36% a decade earlier in 1996.

The ethnic origins of Canada's population reflect immigration patterns. However, the concept of ethnic origin can also be fluid: how individuals perceive their roots can change with the amount of time spent in Canada, awareness of their family background, or the social context at the time of the census.

As well, people may marry or form unions with people from other ethnic groups, which increases the complexity of gathering ethnic data.

Canadian ethnicity

On the 1996 Census form, 'Canadian' was added to the list of examples of ethnic origins for the first time. By 2006, one out of three—10.1 million people—reported Canadian as either their only ethnic origin or in combination with another ethnic origin. The majority (91%) of the population aged 15 and older who reported a Canadian origin were born in Canada and had both parents born inside Canada.

After Canadian, the ethnic origins that people most frequently reported were English, Irish, French, Scottish, German, Italian, Chinese, North American Indian, Ukrainian and Dutch.

Chart 13.1
Recent immigrants to Canada, by region of origin

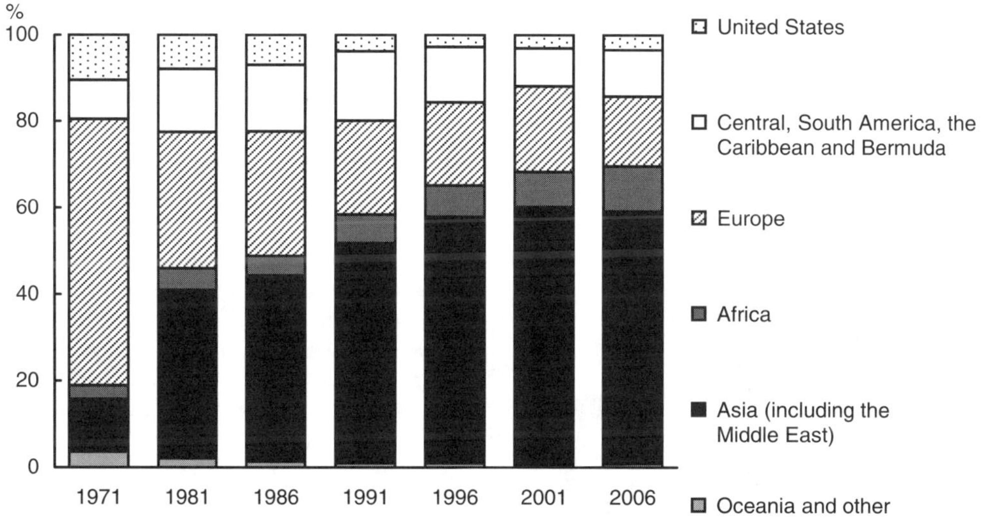

Notes: 'Recent immigrants' refers to landed immigrants who arrived in Canada within five years prior to a given census. "Other" includes Greenland, St Pierre and Miquelon, the category 'other country', as well as a small number of immigrants born in Canada.
Source: Statistics Canada, censuses of population, 1971 to 2006.

In 2006, 20% of Canada's population was foreign-born, the highest proportion since 1931. Canada's proportion was lower than Australia, at 22%, but higher than the United States, at 13%. In the city of Toronto, one in two residents was born outside Canada. In the city of Montréal, one in three was foreign-born. In Richmond, British Columbia, it was three out of five residents.

Immigrants and settlement

The 2006 Census reported that 1.1 million recent immigrants came to Canada from January 1, 2001 to May 16, 2006. Canada's largest group of recent immigrants were from Asia (including the Middle East), accounting for 58% of immigrants in 2006. Europe, in second place, accounted for 16%, compared with 61% in the 1971 Census. Central and South America and the Caribbean accounted for 11%, while 11% came from Africa.

At the turn of the 20th century, many immigrants, particularly Europeans, came to Canada for good farmland. Today's immigrants tend to move to the large cities.

Chart 13.2
Foreign-born population, selected CMAs, 2006

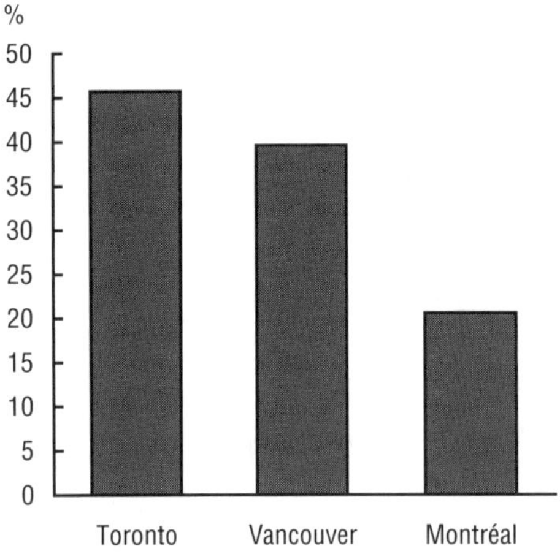

Source: Statistics Canada, Catalogue no. 11-008-XIE.

Table 13.a
Distribution of immigrants in selected CMAs, 2006

	Total population	Total immigrant population[1]	Recent immigrants[2]
	%		
Montréal	11.5	12.0	14.9
Toronto	16.2	37.5	40.4
Vancouver	6.7	13.4	13.7

1. Defined in the 2006 Census as people who are, or have been, landed immigrants in Canada.
2. Immigrants who came to Canada between January 1, 2001 and May 16, 2006.

Source: Statistics Canada, Census of Population 2006.

Toronto, Vancouver and Montréal account for 34% of Canada's total population, but these three census metropolitan areas (CMAs) attracted 69% of all recent immigrants to Canada. Calgary is home to 5% of recent arrivals; 3% call Ottawa–Gatineau home; and 3% chose Edmonton.

The reasons why newcomers choose to settle in Canada's three largest CMAs varies, according to the Longitudinal Survey of Immigrants to Canada (LSIC). The most cited reason for settling in Toronto, Montréal or Vancouver is to join social support networks of family and friends. Among newcomers in Toronto, the second-most cited reason is the job prospects. Among newcomers in Montréal, it is language, while those who settle in Vancouver cite the climate.

Some immigrants do move to smaller centres. After their first year of permanent residence, immigrants who settle in small towns or in rural communities earned a 4% higher average income in 2005 than Canadian-born residents in the same areas. Immigrants who settled in rural areas or small towns had a median income of $19,500, compared with $16,800 for those in larger urban areas.

In the LSIC, recent immigrants were asked about the most important reason for settling permanently in Canada. The most prevalent responses were the quality of life (32%), the desire to be close to family and friends (20%), the future prospects for their family in Canada (18%) and the peaceful nature of the country (9%).

Canada's generational makeup

In the 2006 Census, 61% of respondents aged 15 and older were at least third-generation Canadian; that is, they were born in Canada and both their parents were also born in Canada.

Another 16% of the population was second generation; that is, one or both of their parents was born in another country. The largest proportion, 54%, report European origins, either alone or in combination with other origins. Large numbers of immigrants arrived in Canada from European countries in the early part of the 20th century.

The most commonly reported European origins are German (13%), Italian (11%), Dutch (6%) and Ukrainian (5%). Another 41% of second-generation Canadians report origins in the British Isles (Cornish, English, Irish, Manx, Scottish, Welsh and others.)

First-generation people accounted for 24% of Canada's population aged 15 and older in the 2006 Census. First generation means they were born in another country. The countries reflect Canada's most recent source countries for immigrants. In this group, 24% report East Asian or Southeast Asian origins, either alone or in combination with another origin.

People of European origins make up slightly over one-third (34%) of the first generation population. The leading groups are Italian, comprising 6.0% of all the first generation population, followed by German (5.8%), Polish (3.5%) and Portuguese (3.2%).

An additional 14% of the first generation aged 15 and over report British Isles origins, either alone or with other origins.

Chart 13.3
Number and share of visible minority people

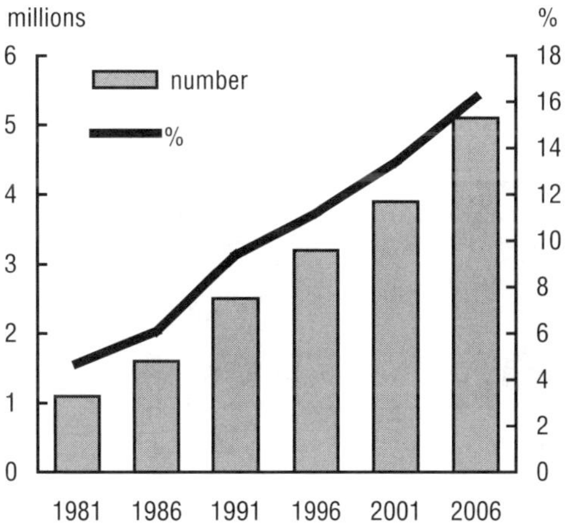

Source: Statistics Canada, Census of Population, 1981 to 2006.

Mixed unions on the rise

Mixed unions made up 3.9% of all unions in Canada in 2006, up from 3.1% in 2001 and 2.6% in 1991. Among all couples, 3.3% were people in unions involving a visible minority person and a non-visible minority person. In contrast, mixed unions involving couples of two different visible minority groups accounted for 0.6% of all couples in Canada in 2006.

The 2006 Census recorded a 33% rise since 2001 in the number of mixed unions (marriage or common-law) involving a visible minority person with either a non-visible minority person or a person of a different visible minority. This was more than five times the increase of 6% for all couples.

The Japanese had the highest proportion of mixed couples. There were 29,700 couples involving at least one Japanese person in the 2006 Census, 75% of these pairings included a non-Japanese partner. The South Asian and Chinese populations were least likely to be involved in a mixed union—13% of all South Asian couples and 17% of all Chinese couples.

Meeting immigrants' expectations

Each year, some 220,000 people take a huge step and immigrate to Canada. They set down roots, often learning a new language or beginning a new career.

Most are happy with their decision. A survey that studies immigrants aged 15 and older during their first years in Canada found that 84% are positive about their decision to immigrate after four years of living here.

Two-thirds say life here has lived up to their expectations. Those who came as refugees or family-class immigrants are more likely than economic immigrants to be content. One in three of family-class immigrants say their expectations of life in Canada have been consistently exceeded, compared with one in six economic immigrants.

The survey also asked immigrants to identify the greatest difficulties encountered here. Two are cited more than any other: 46% say "finding an adequate job" while 26% say "learning French or English."

Six months after landing, the vast majority (91%) intended to settle here permanently and become citizens. Four years later, 15% of the newcomers had done just that.

According to the 2006 Census, 85% of Canada's foreign-born who were eligible had become Canadian citizens, a slight increase from 84% in 2001. Three percent of the population in 2006 had Canadian citizenship and citizenship in at least one other country. Eighty percent of those who had multiple citizenships were foreign-born. The rest of the multiple citizenship holders (20%) were Canadians by birth who also reported citizenship in another country.

The longer immigrants reside in Canada, the more likely they are to hold Canadian citizenship. Of those who came to Canada before 1961, 94% have Canadian citizenship. Among those who arrived during the 1960s and 1970s, 89% have become citizens. Eighty-four percent of those who arrived in the 1990s are now citizens.

Chart 13.4
Citizenship status of new immigrants four years after arrival in Canada, 2005

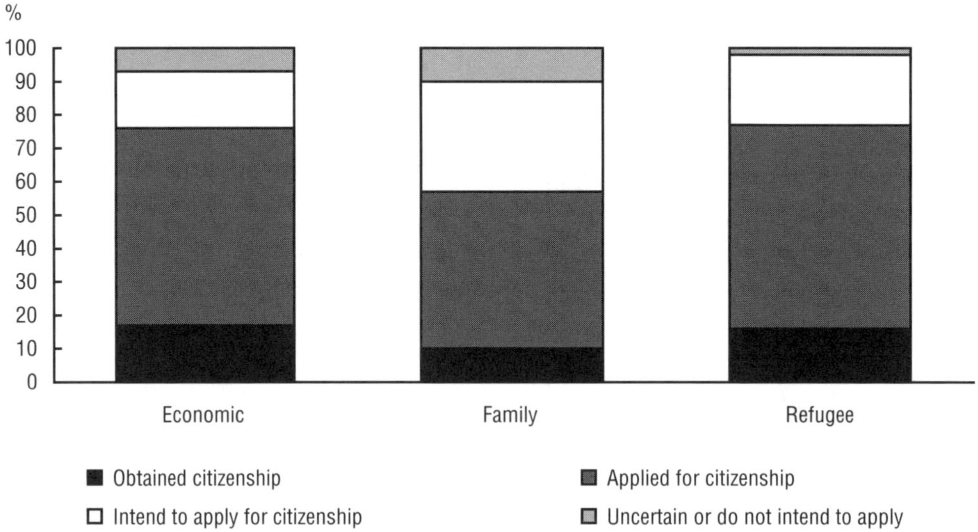

Source: Statistics Canada, Catalogue no. 11-008-XIE.

Educated immigrants face a paradox

Canada has an aging workforce and a low fertility rate, so the government has increasingly turned to highly-educated immigrants to ensure that skilled workers are available. However, these immigrants often encounter a paradox: they are recruited because of their knowledge, but after arriving in Canada, many need to meet re-accreditation requirements and this might be a barrier to fully using their skills.

One in three people aged 25 to 54 who immigrated here from 2001 to 2006 had at least a bachelor's degree, compared with one in six Canadian-born people in the same age group. One in five recent immigrants had a graduate degree, compared with one in twenty Canadians.

Immigrant engineers are an example of the paradox, since engineering was the most popular field of study among recent degree-holding immigrants: 25% in 2006, compared with 6% of Canadian-born degree holders. In a study of 34,000 foreign-trained engineers, 26% of those aged 32 to 54 worked here in engineering occupations in 2001, compared with 41% of Canadian-born engineers.

Underemployment—when people cannot find a job in their field—is most common among foreign-trained immigrants born in Southeast Asia and East Asia. Those born in European countries (other than Eastern Europe) or in South Asian countries are the most likely to find work in Canada as engineers.

Important characteristics for professionals seeking Canadian re-accreditation are the educational system in the source country, the length of schooling, the type of education (including the content of professional degrees and the requirements for specialized degrees), as well as the use of French or English in the educational system or other sectors of the economy.

Chart 13.5
Employment rate of immigrants, by highest certificate, diploma or degree, 2006

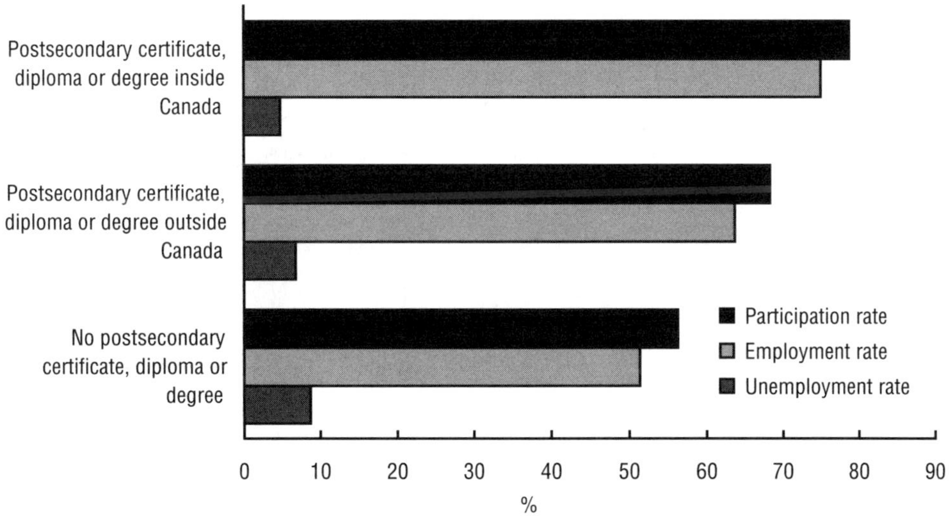

Source: Statistics Canada, Catalogue no. 97-560-XIE.

Table 13.1 Population, by selected ethnic origins, 2006

	Total responses	Single responses[1]	Multiple responses[2]
		number	
Total population	**31,241,030**	**18,319,580**	**12,921,445**
Canadian	**10,066,290**	5,748,725	4,317,570
English	**6,570,015**	1,367,125	5,202,890
French	**4,941,210**	1,230,535	3,710,675
Scottish	**4,719,850**	568,515	4,151,340
Irish	**4,354,155**	491,030	3,863,125
German	**3,179,425**	670,640	2,508,785
Italian	**1,445,335**	741,045	704,285
Chinese	**1,346,510**	1,135,365	211,145
North American Indian	**1,253,615**	512,150	741,470
Ukrainian	**1,209,085**	300,590	908,495
Dutch (Netherlands)	**1,035,965**	303,400	732,560
Polish	**984,565**	269,375	715,190
East Indian	**962,665**	780,175	182,495
Russian	**500,600**	98,245	402,355
Welsh	**440,965**	27,115	413,855
Filipino	**436,190**	321,390	114,800
Norwegian	**432,515**	44,790	387,725
Portuguese	**410,850**	262,230	148,625
Métis	**409,065**	77,295	331,770
British Isles, n.i.e.[3]	**403,915**	94,145	309,770
Swedish	**334,765**	28,445	306,325
Spanish	**325,730**	67,475	258,255
American	**316,350**	28,785	287,565
Hungarian (Magyar)	**315,510**	88,685	226,820
Jewish	**315,120**	134,045	181,070
Greek	**242,685**	145,250	97,435
Jamaican	**231,110**	134,320	96,785
Danish	**200,035**	33,770	166,265
Austrian	**194,255**	27,060	167,195

1. Single ethnic origin response: Occurs when a respondent provides one ethnic origin only.
2. Multiple ethnic response: Occurs when a respondent provides two or more ethnic origins.
3. The abbreviation 'n.i.e.' means 'not included elsewhere'.
Source: Statistics Canada, 2006 Census of Population.

Table 13.2 Visible minority population, by province and territory, 2006

	Canada	Newfoundland and Labrador	Prince Edward Island	Nova Scotia	New Brunswick	Quebec	Ontario
	number						
Total population	**31,241,030**	**500,605**	**134,205**	**903,090**	**719,650**	**7,435,900**	**12,028,895**
Total visible minority population	**5,068,095**	5,720	1,825	37,685	13,345	654,350	2,745,205
Chinese	**1,216,565**	1,325	255	4,300	2,445	79,825	576,980
South Asian	**1,262,865**	1,590	135	3,810	1,960	72,850	794,170
Black	**783,795**	900	645	19,225	4,455	188,070	473,765
Filipino	**410,700**	305	30	700	530	24,200	203,220
Latin American	**304,245**	485	215	950	715	89,510	147,135
Southeast Asian	**239,935**	120	30	815	440	50,460	110,045
Arab	**265,550**	545	265	4,505	840	109,020	111,405
West Asian	**156,695**	115	30	780	550	16,115	96,615
Korean	**141,890**	60	70	800	620	5,310	69,540
Japanese	**81,300**	140	65	505	165	3,540	28,080
Visible minority, n.i.e.[1]	**71,420**	75	65	255	155	4,155	56,845
Multiple visible minority	**133,120**	60	25	1,030	460	11,310	77,405
Not a visible minority	**26,172,940**	494,890	132,375	865,405	706,305	6,781,550	9,283,690

	Manitoba	Saskatchewan	Alberta	British Columbia	Yukon	Northwest Territories	Nunavut
	number						
Total population	**1,133,515**	**953,850**	**3,256,355**	**4,074,380**	**30,195**	**41,055**	**29,325**
Total visible minority population	109,100	33,895	454,200	1,008,855	1,220	2,265	420
Chinese	13,705	9,505	120,270	407,225	320	315	75
South Asian	16,565	5,130	103,885	262,290	195	210	85
Black	15,660	5,090	47,075	28,315	125	375	100
Filipino	37,785	3,770	51,090	88,075	210	690	80
Latin American	6,275	2,520	27,265	28,960	100	85	20
Southeast Asian	5,670	2,555	28,605	40,690	145	355	10
Arab	2,320	1,710	26,180	8,635	20	90	15
West Asian	1,960	1,020	9,655	29,810	0	40	0
Korean	2,190	735	12,045	50,490	10	15	10
Japanese	2,010	645	11,030	35,060	40	15	10
Visible minority, n.i.e.[1]	1,690	405	3,850	3,880	10	30	10
Multiple visible minority	3,265	810	13,250	25,415	35	40	15
Not a visible minority	1,024,415	919,950	2,802,155	3,065,525	28,975	38,790	28,905

1. The abbreviation 'n.i.e.' means 'not included elsewhere.'

Source: Statistics Canada, 2006 Census of Population.

Table 13.3 Visible minority population, by selected visible minority groups and census metropolitan areas, 2006

	Total population	Visible minority population	South Asian	Chinese	Black	Filipino	Latin American	Arab	Southeast Asian
	number								
St. John's	**179,270**	3,460	890	990	620	155	320	190	55
Halifax	**369,455**	27,645	2,900	3,100	13,270	530	690	3,840	655
Moncton	**124,055**	2,425	350	295	1,035	100	95	165	65
Saint John	**120,875**	3,805	485	975	1,250	205	210	125	60
Saguenay	**149,600**	1,280	45	295	330	50	280	195	55
Québec	**704,185**	16,355	535	1,855	5,080	120	3,150	2,800	1,615
Sherbrooke	**183,635**	7,000	340	590	1,830	35	2,060	940	410
Trois-Rivières	**138,555**	2,270	50	210	625	15	540	535	225
Montréal	**3,588,520**	590,380	70,615	72,010	169,065	23,510	75,400	98,880	44,965
Ottawa–Gatineau	**1,117,120**	179,295	27,130	32,445	45,060	7,330	10,630	28,195	11,670
Kingston	**148,475**	8,600	1,785	2,470	1,900	485	1,050	370	330
Peterborough	**115,140**	3,095	665	730	575	110	255	80	180
Oshawa	**328,070**	33,700	6,195	3,690	12,605	2,155	1,665	1,135	670
Toronto	**5,072,075**	2,174,065	684,070	486,325	352,220	171,985	99,290	53,430	70,215
Hamilton	**683,450**	84,295	19,970	11,660	16,480	4,880	6,760	6,500	6,805
St. Catharines–Niagara	**385,035**	25,470	3,595	3,600	5,030	2,130	4,205	1,480	2,090
Kitchener	**446,495**	61,455	16,240	9,150	9,450	1,850	6,805	3,175	6,150
Brantford	**122,830**	6,715	1,785	695	1,700	655	390	240	580
Guelph	**126,085**	16,025	3,875	3,110	1,600	1,965	1,070	510	1,600
London	**452,575**	50,300	6,415	6,545	8,255	1,990	7,920	7,800	4,050
Windsor	**320,730**	51,200	10,265	7,825	9,490	3,145	2,905	9,975	2,945
Barrie	**175,335**	10,130	1,900	1,180	2,310	875	1,165	300	530
Greater Sudbury / Grand Sudbury	**156,400**	3,280	580	620	1,100	150	180	115	145
Thunder Bay	**121,050**	3,275	390	925	450	250	170	50	370
Winnipeg	**686,040**	102,940	15,290	12,810	14,470	36,935	5,480	2,125	5,340
Regina	**192,435**	12,605	1,975	3,335	2,170	1,230	955	475	1,260
Saskatoon	**230,850**	14,870	2,230	4,245	1,900	1,920	1,050	940	1,010
Calgary	**1,070,295**	237,890	57,700	66,375	21,060	25,565	13,410	11,660	15,750
Edmonton	**1,024,825**	175,295	40,200	47,195	20,380	19,630	9,210	11,940	11,025
Kelowna	**160,560**	8,320	2,345	1,470	660	410	525	60	720
Abbotsford	**156,640**	35,715	25,580	2,245	930	730	1,275	150	1,665
Vancouver	**2,097,965**	875,295	207,160	381,535	20,670	78,890	22,695	7,430	33,470
Victoria	**325,060**	33,870	7,210	12,330	2,360	2,760	1,845	500	1,585

Source: Statistics Canada, 2006 Census of Population.

Table 13.4 Visible minority population, by age group, 2006

	All age groups	0 to 14	15 to 24	25 to 44	45 to 64	65 to 74	75 and older
				number			
Total population	**31,241,030**	**5,576,805**	**4,207,815**	**8,781,165**	**8,600,935**	**2,255,640**	**1,818,655**
Total visible minority population	**5,068,095**	1,145,395	785,355	1,674,175	1,094,055	233,060	136,055
Chinese	**1,216,565**	210,930	186,925	385,525	303,440	76,060	53,680
South Asian	**1,262,865**	305,220	181,410	424,850	260,975	61,550	28,865
Black	**783,795**	221,660	130,010	244,805	142,485	29,805	15,030
Filipino	**410,700**	89,780	53,885	141,225	99,690	16,680	9,435
Latin American	**304,245**	59,915	51,885	114,620	65,015	8,360	4,450
Southeast Asian	**239,935**	55,355	38,270	80,410	51,755	8,445	5,700
Arab	**265,550**	69,650	40,985	96,010	46,560	8,125	4,210
West Asian	**156,695**	30,840	29,190	54,015	34,560	5,360	2,725
Korean	**141,890**	27,275	28,945	44,405	32,820	5,745	2,700
Japanese	**81,300**	14,900	10,290	26,860	17,600	6,005	5,630
Visible minority (not indicated elsewhere)	**71,420**	14,305	11,375	24,925	16,175	2,960	1,680
Multiple visible minority	**133,120**	45,550	22,180	36,515	22,975	3,955	1,950
Not a visible minority	**26,172,940**	4,431,410	3,422,455	7,107,000	7,506,885	2,022,585	1,682,600

Source: Statistics Canada, 2006 Census of Population.

Table 13.5 Visible minority groups, generation status in Canada, 2006

	Total generation status	First generation	Second generation	Third generation or more
	number			
Total visible minority population	**3,922,700**	**3,273,070**	**551,740**	**97,890**
Chinese	**1,005,635**	850,335	138,520	16,775
South Asian	**957,645**	820,180	132,190	5,275
Black	**562,135**	403,955	115,090	43,095
Filipino	**320,915**	283,560	35,760	1,595
Latin American	**244,330**	219,440	22,870	2,015
Southeast Asian	**184,575**	159,285	23,450	1,845
Arab	**195,900**	173,015	20,300	2,585
West Asian	**125,855**	120,710	4,580	565
Korean	**114,615**	104,640	9,190	790
Japanese	**66,400**	28,715	18,510	19,170
Visible minority (not indicated elsewhere)	**57,115**	44,965	11,005	1,150
Multiple visible minority	**87,565**	64,260	20,270	3,035

Source: Statistics Canada, 2006 Census of Population.

Families, households and housing

14

Overview

In 2006, 84% of Canada's population lived in a census family, that is, a household comprised either of a married or a common-law couple and with or without children, or a household comprised of a lone parent and at least one child in the home. This proportion has remained relatively stable over the last two decades, but the family portrait has evolved: the structure of Canada's families is more varied today than in the past.

The proportion of census families made up of a couple with children under age 25 and living at home has declined over the last 20 years: in 2006, census families comprised of a couple without children at home slightly outnumbered those with children at home. Also, more and more couples are choosing common-law relationships over marriage, and an increasing number of parents are raising children alone, either by choice or as the result of a broken relationship.

Households in which a person lived alone represented a growing share of the population, but they remained a minority.

Same-sex marriage was legalized across Canada in July 2005 and appeared for the first time on the 2006 census form. The census enumerated 7,500 same-sex married couples, a number that is relatively low compared with the total census count of 45,300 same-sex couples.

Fewer families with children

The 2006 Census was the first time that census families comprised of couples without children outnumbered those with children. Couples without children under 25 living at home accounted for 43% of census families in 2006; couples with children accounted for 41% of census families.

Chart 14.1
Census families, by presence of children at home

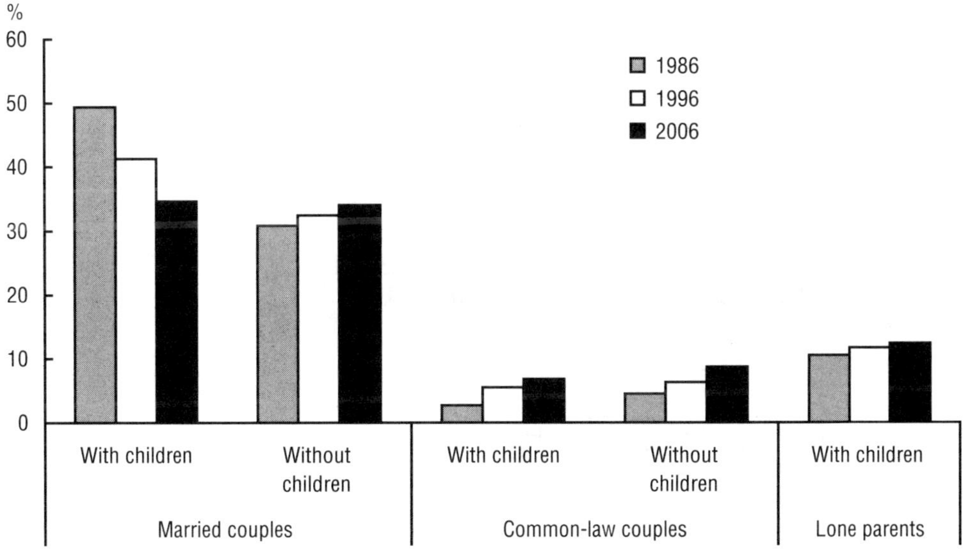

Source: Statistics Canada, Catalogue no. 97-553-XIE.

The proportion of Canada's census families comprised of a couple with children has been declining for two decades. In 1986, 52% of census families were couples with children, whereas 35% were couples without children.

From 1986 to 2006, the proportion of married couples with children declined from 49% in 1986 to 35% in 2006. However, the proportion of married couples without children rose from 31% to 34%.

During the same period, the proportion of common-law couples who had children more than doubled their share, from 3% to 7%, while the proportion of common-law couples without children at home increased from 5% to 9%.

The declining number of couples with children can be attributed to the aging baby boomer population, whose children have for the most part grown and moved out of their parents' home. The decrease is also linked to the fact that baby busters—the generation following the baby boomers—are fewer in number and have lower fertility rates than earlier generations.

Table 14.a
Family characteristics

	2006
	number
No children at home	3,420,850
One child at home	2,429,695
Two children at home	2,132,830
Three or more children at home	913,465
Average number of children at home	1.1

Source: Statistics Canada, 2006 Census of population.

The number of children per family has also dropped. The proportion of census families with one child under age 25 at home increased slightly, from 37% in 2001 to 38% in 2006. In contrast, the proportion of families with three or more children slipped from 20% in 2001 to 19% in 2006. Lower fertility rates may help explain this trend.

Fewer married couples

Although most Canadian couples choose marriage, the proportion of married-couple families declined from 2001 to 2006.

Chart 14.2
One-person households in Canada and selected countries, 2006

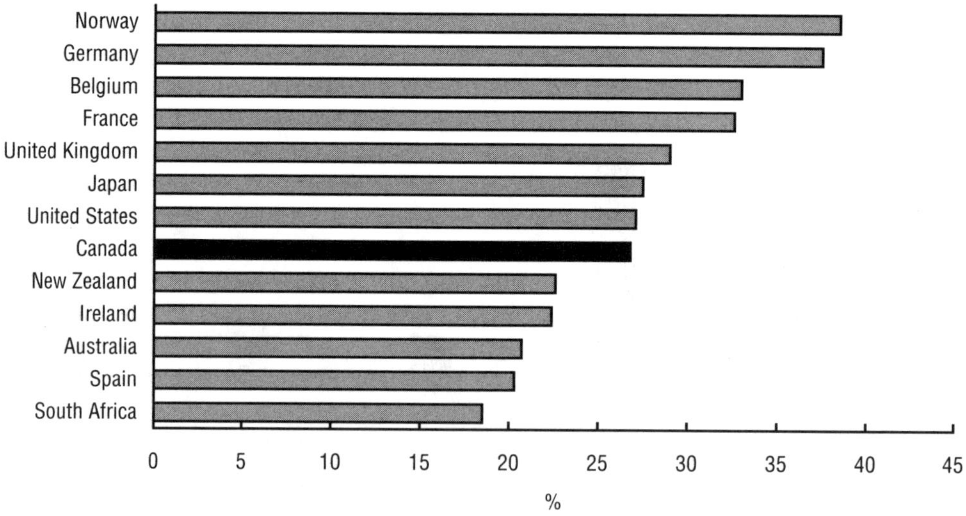

Source: Statistics Canada, Catalogue no. 97-553-XIE.

Married-couple families accounted for 69% of all census families in 2006, down from 71% five years earlier. During the same period, the proportion of common-law-couple families rose from 14% to 16%, and the share of lone-parent families increased from 15.7% to 15.9%.

Two decades ago, common-law-couple families accounted for 7% of all census families, while married-couple families accounted for 80% and lone-parent families, 13%.

Lone-parent families: more women, more never-married and fewer widowed

Eighty percent of the 1.4 million lone-parent families enumerated in 2006 were headed by women. For the past two decades, lone-parent families headed by women have outnumbered those headed by men by about four to one.

However, families headed by men have been growing at a faster pace. From 2001 to 2006, the number of lone-father families increased more than twice as fast as the number of lone-mother families. One explanation for the faster gain among lone-parent families headed by men is that fewer mothers are granted sole custody following a divorce.

Chart 14.3
Couple families, by legal marital status

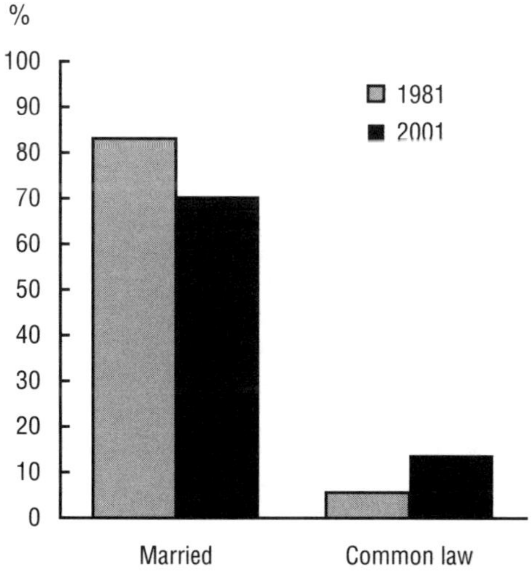

Source: Statistics Canada, Catalogue no. 96F0030XIE.

In 2006, there were more never-married lone parents and fewer widowed lone parents compared with 55 years earlier. In 2006, 30% of lone parents had never been legally married and 19% were widowed. In 1951, 2% had never been legally married and 67% were widowed.

Nearly 30% of lone parents were divorced in 2006, a decline from the 1996 historic peak of 34%. In 1951, 3% of lone parents were divorced. Changes to the *Divorce Act* in 1968 and 1986—the former broadened the grounds for divorce, and the latter reduced the minimum separation required—contributed to the rising number of divorced lone parents.

Household size declining

Throughout the 20th century and into the 21st century, the proportion of large households has decreased, and that of smaller households has increased. In 2006, there were three times as many one-person households as households with five or more people. Of the 12.4 million private households, 27% were one-person households, while 9% were large households of five or more people.

In 1941, 6% of households were comprised of one person, while 38% were comprised of five or more people. The proportion of one-person households surpassed that of large households in 1981.

Household size has declined as people either have fewer children or have no children living at home. Smaller households may also be the product of higher rates of divorce and separation.

More same-sex couples being counted

Following the legalization of same-sex marriage in Canada in July 2005, the 2006 Census enumerated same-sex married couples for the first time. The census counted 45,300 same-sex couples, making up 0.6% of all couples in Canada. Among that 45,300, 17% were same-sex married couples.

Although still few, the number of same-sex couples has increased five times faster than the number of opposite-sex couples. From 2001 to 2006, the number of same-sex couples grew 33%, whereas the number of opposite-sex couples grew 6%.

Quebec has Canada's largest proportion of same-sex couples: 0.8% of all couples in 2006. Half of all same-sex couples lived in the three major census metropolitan areas of Toronto, Montréal and Vancouver.

In 2006, 54% of same-sex married spouses were men; 46% were women. Proportions were similar for same-sex common-law partners in both 2006 and 2001.

About 9% of individuals in same-sex couples had children aged 24 and under living at home in 2006. Children at home were more common for women in same-sex couples than for men. Also, same-sex married spouses were more likely to have children at home than were same-sex common-law partners.

People in same-sex couples were generally younger than their counterparts in opposite-sex couples: 25% of people in same-sex couples were aged 34 and younger, and 4% were seniors 65 or older. In opposite-sex couples, 18% were aged 34 and under, and 16% were seniors.

Chart 14.4
Same-sex couples, by province and territory, 2006

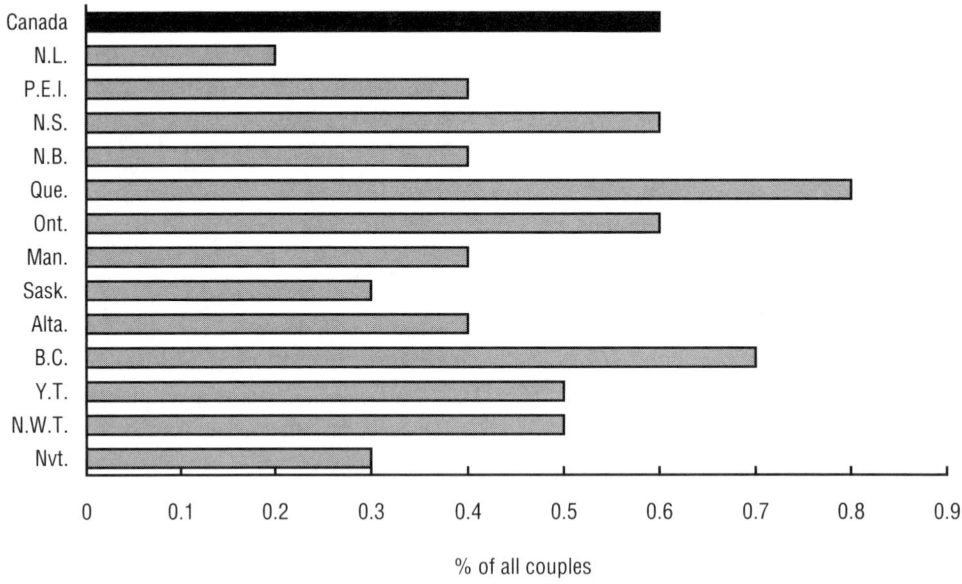

Source: Statistics Canada, 2006 Census of Population.

Home ownership for young adults

Some Canadians see buying a home as a good investment, as a form of forced savings or as a source of satisfaction in just being 'at home.' Whatever the motivation, becoming a homeowner is important for most.

A person's primary activity in the labour market, living arrangements, age and place of residence are the key factors affecting the probability of young adults owning a home, according to the 2006 General Social Survey. Young adults over age 30 who had a permanent job for 12 months, who were married and had children, and who lived in a rural setting were the most likely to own a home.

Household income has the greatest apparent association with home ownership. In 2006, 22% of young adults with an income of less than $30,000 per year were homeowners, whereas 68% of those with an annual income of $50,000 to $80,000, and 82% of those with incomes of $100,000 or more, were homeowners.

Certain family characteristics are also associated with home ownership. In 2006, 79% of young adults who were married and had children owned their own home. Forty percent of young adults living alone were homeowners, and among lone parents 33% were homeowners.

Among young adults who had children and were part of a common-law couple, 63% owned their own home, a smaller proportion than that among young married adults with children. This might be partly because provincial rules on property ownership can be different for common-law couples than married couples. It is also possible that some common-law couples wait until they are married before buying a home.

Chart 14.5
Probability of home ownership, 2006

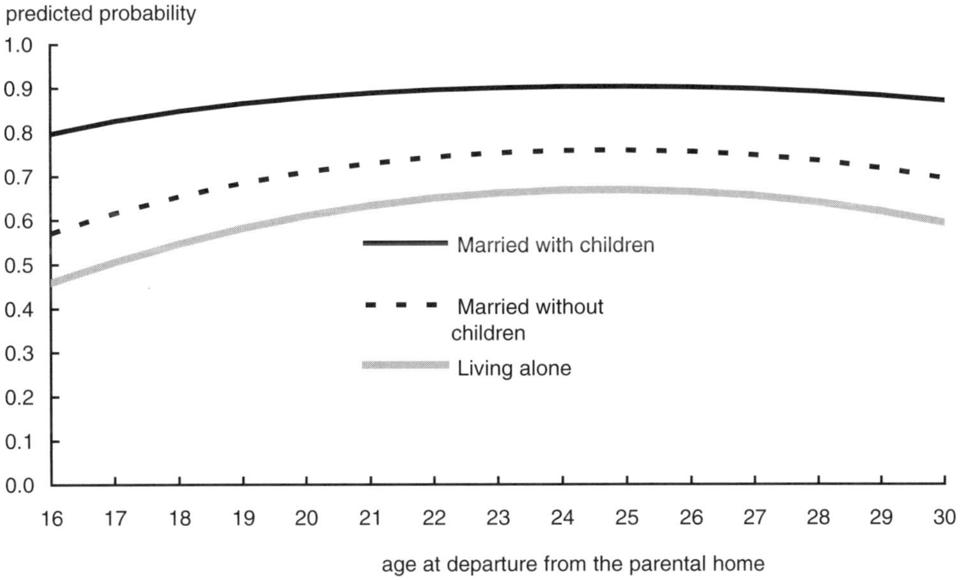

Source: Statistics Canada, Catalogue no. 11-008-XIE.

Table 14.1 Family structure, by census metropolitan area, 2006

	All families			Families of married couples		
	Total	No children at home	Children at home	All married couples	No children at home	Children at home
	number					
St. John's	**52,525**	18,105	34,420	36,695	14,250	22,445
Halifax	**105,200**	42,445	62,755	72,885	32,335	40,550
Moncton	**37,130**	15,930	21,205	25,310	11,970	13,335
Saint John	**35,565**	13,740	21,825	25,010	11,395	13,615
Saguenay	**44,540**	19,065	25,470	24,780	12,890	11,890
Québec	**200,960**	86,955	114,000	100,390	51,280	49,110
Sherbrooke	**51,405**	22,345	29,055	25,795	13,650	12,140
Trois-Rivières	**39,685**	17,400	22,285	20,040	11,190	8,850
Montréal	**994,960**	366,990	627,970	562,050	237,350	324,705
Ottawa–Gatineau	**314,310**	115,535	198,770	211,590	85,020	126,570
Kingston	**42,995**	18,105	24,890	30,595	14,435	16,165
Peterborough	**33,505**	14,690	18,810	24,185	12,035	12,150
Oshawa	**94,575**	30,615	63,955	67,970	24,545	43,430
Toronto	**1,405,845**	418,550	987,295	1,059,125	349,135	709,990
Hamilton	**195,905**	70,425	125,475	144,150	58,375	85,775
St. Catharines–Niagara	**112,550**	45,170	67,380	81,640	38,515	43,125
Kitchener	**126,205**	44,365	81,840	93,250	36,255	56,995
Brantford	**35,680**	13,370	22,315	25,360	11,105	14,260
Guelph	**35,735**	13,160	22,575	25,800	10,400	15,395
London	**127,795**	49,055	78,740	91,330	39,685	51,650
Windsor	**90,350**	31,075	59,280	66,410	26,390	40,025
Barrie	**50,095**	17,400	32,700	35,580	13,680	21,905
Greater Sudbury / Grand Sudbury	**46,340**	18,625	27,715	32,115	15,235	16,880
Thunder Bay	**35,055**	13,580	21,475	24,345	11,070	13,275
Winnipeg	**189,785**	69,515	120,275	134,455	57,005	77,445
Regina	**53,720**	20,455	33,260	37,530	16,875	20,660
Saskatoon	**63,205**	24,465	38,745	45,135	20,215	24,915
Calgary	**295,345**	109,215	186,125	217,520	84,850	132,670
Edmonton	**284,400**	106,890	177,510	203,790	84,555	119,230
Kelowna	**48,280**	23,570	24,710	35,545	19,895	15,650
Abbotsford	**44,365**	16,820	27,545	33,795	14,410	19,385
Vancouver	**580,120**	207,650	372,470	433,180	166,040	267,140
Victoria	**91,935**	42,660	49,275	64,185	33,580	30,600

See note and source at end of table.

Table 14.1 Family structure, by census metropolitan area, 2006 (continued)

	Families of common-law couples			Lone-parent families		
	All common-law couples	No children at home	Children at home	All lone-parent families	Male parent	Female parent
	number					
St. John's	6,060	3,860	2,200	9,775	1,650	8,125
Halifax	14,950	10,110	4,835	17,365	2,900	14,470
Moncton	6,010	3,955	2,055	5,815	975	4,845
Saint John	3,795	2,345	1,445	6,765	1,135	5,625
Saguenay	13,120	6,175	6,945	6,635	1,500	5,135
Québec	69,275	35,675	33,605	31,290	7,700	23,585
Sherbrooke	17,010	8,695	8,315	8,600	2,325	6,275
Trois-Rivières	12,875	6,210	6,665	6,770	1,360	5,410
Montréal	252,685	129,645	123,040	180,220	35,490	144,735
Ottawa–Gatineau	51,105	30,515	20,590	51,610	10,205	41,405
Kingston	5,855	3,670	2,185	6,545	1,250	5,295
Peterborough	4,205	2,655	1,550	5,115	880	4,235
Oshawa	11,020	6,075	4,945	15,585	3,065	12,515
Toronto	109,290	69,420	39,870	237,430	39,835	197,595
Hamilton	19,570	12,055	7,515	32,185	5,630	26,545
St. Catharines–Niagara	11,835	6,650	5,185	19,070	3,705	15,365
Kitchener	14,175	8,105	6,070	18,775	3,625	15,150
Brantford	4,440	2,265	2,175	5,875	1,150	4,730
Guelph	4,585	2,760	1,825	5,350	1,135	4,215
London	15,300	9,370	5,925	21,170	3,880	17,290
Windsor	8,275	4,680	3,595	15,665	2,900	12,760
Barrie	6,910	3,720	3,195	7,600	1,535	6,065
Greater Sudbury / Grand Sudbury	6,410	3,390	3,015	7,820	1,450	6,370
Thunder Bay	4,330	2,505	1,820	6,380	1,215	5,160
Winnipeg	20,325	12,510	7,815	35,010	6,125	28,885
Regina	5,905	3,585	2,320	10,280	1,890	8,390
Saskatoon	6,795	4,250	2,550	11,275	2,250	9,025
Calgary	35,605	24,370	11,235	42,220	8,610	33,610
Edmonton	34,520	22,330	12,185	46,085	9,285	36,800
Kelowna	5,660	3,670	1,990	7,070	1,350	5,720
Abbotsford	4,110	2,415	1,695	6,460	1,145	5,315
Vancouver	58,825	41,610	17,215	88,115	16,870	71,250
Victoria	13,110	9,080	4,030	14,635	2,960	11,675

Note: Census families in private households.

Source: Statistics Canada, 2006 Census of Population.

Table 14.2 Population, by marital status and sex, 2003 to 2007

	2003	2004	2005	2006	2007
	number				
Total marital status	**31,676,077**	**31,995,199**	**32,312,077**	**32,649,482**	**32,976,026**
Males	15,688,977	15,846,832	16,003,804	16,170,723	16,332,277
Females	15,987,100	16,148,367	16,308,273	16,478,759	16,643,749
Single	13,231,209	13,368,674	13,507,149	13,653,059	13,800,997
Males	7,078,089	7,155,622	7,233,428	7,314,611	7,396,835
Females	6,153,120	6,213,052	6,273,721	6,338,448	6,404,162
Married[1]	15,438,972	15,558,054	15,675,089	15,802,300	15,916,860
Males	7,701,393	7,752,882	7,803,419	7,860,087	7,910,554
Females	7,737,579	7,805,172	7,871,670	7,942,213	8,006,306
Widowed	1,532,940	1,544,226	1,553,488	1,563,856	1,573,455
Males	288,816	295,446	301,404	307,050	312,357
Females	1,244,124	1,248,780	1,252,084	1,256,806	1,261,098
Divorced	1,472,956	1,524,245	1,576,351	1,630,267	1,684,714
Males	620,679	642,882	665,553	688,975	712,531
Females	852,277	881,363	910,798	941,292	972,183

Note: Population estimates as of July 1.

1. Includes people who are legally married, legally married and separated, and living in common-law unions.

Source: Statistics Canada, CANSIM table 051-0010.

Table 14.3 Marriages, by province and territory, 2002 to 2006

	2002	2003	2004p	2005p	2006p
	number				
Canada	**146,738**	**147,391**	**148,585**	**148,439**	**149,792**
Newfoundland and Labrador	2,959	2,876	2,850	2,806	2,752
Prince Edward Island	901	823	827	829	828
Nova Scotia	4,899	4,742	4,729	4,698	4,667
New Brunswick	3,818	3,724	3,708	3,686	3,646
Quebec	21,987	21,138	21,279	22,244	21,900
Ontario	61,615	63,485	64,114	64,677	65,170
Manitoba	5,905	5,659	5,710	5,732	5,746
Saskatchewan	5,067	4,977	5,011	5,000	4,995
Alberta	17,981	17,622	17,909	18,392	19,060
British Columbia	21,247	21,981	22,080	20,007	20,660
Yukon	143	158	160	159	160
Northwest Territories	144	139	141	140	138
Nunavut	72	67	67	69	70

Source: Statistics Canada, CANSIM table 053-0001.

Table 14.4 Divorces, by province and territory, 1999 to 2004

	1999	2000	2001	2002	2003	2004
	number					
Canada	**70,910**	**71,144**	**71,110**	**70,155**	**70,828**	**69,644**
Newfoundland and Labrador	892	913	755	842	662	837
Prince Edward Island	291	272	246	258	281	293
Nova Scotia	1,954	2,054	1,945	1,990	1,907	2,000
New Brunswick	1,671	1,717	1,570	1,461	1,450	1,415
Quebec	17,144	17,054	17,094	16,499	16,738	15,999
Ontario	26,088	26,148	26,516	26,170	27,513	26,374
Manitoba	2,572	2,430	2,480	2,396	2,352	2,333
Saskatchewan	2,237	2,194	1,955	1,959	1,992	1,875
Alberta	7,931	8,176	8,252	8,291	7,960	8,317
British Columbia	9,935	10,017	10,115	10,125	9,820	10,049
Yukon	112	68	91	90	87	66
Northwest Territories (including Nunavut)	83	..	..	..	..	..
Northwest Territories	..	94	83	68	62	71
Nunavut	..	7	8	6	4	15

Source: Statistics Canada, CANSIM tables 053-0002 and 101-6501.

Table 14.5 Census families, selected years from 1971 to 2006

	All families		Husband–wife families		Lone-parent families	
	Total	Average number of family members	Total	Average number of family members	Total	Average number of family members
	thousands	number	thousands	number	thousands	number
1971	**5,042.6**	3.7	4,566.3	3.8	476.3	3.1
1976	**5,714.5**	3.5	5,156.7	3.5	557.9	2.9
1981	**6,309.2**	3.3	5,597.2	3.3	712.0	2.7
1986	**6,864.2**	3.1	5,995.0	3.2	869.2	2.6
1991	**7,482.1**	3.1	6,511.8	3.1	970.3	2.6
1996	**7,975.0**	3.1	6,818.5	3.1	1,156.5	2.6
2001	**8,481.4**	3.0	7,149.1	3.1	1,332.3	2.5
2006	**8,859.1**	3.0	7,468.5	3.1	1,390.7	2.5

Source: Statistics Canada, Catalogue no. 91-213-XIB.

Table 14.6 Family structure, by province and territory, 2006

	Canada	Newfoundland and Labrador	Prince Edward Island	Nova Scotia	New Brunswick	Quebec
	number					
All families	**8,896,840**	**155,730**	**39,185**	**267,415**	**217,795**	**2,121,610**
No children at home	**3,420,850**	61,950	15,315	112,190	91,300	853,895
Children at home	**5,475,990**	93,775	23,870	155,230	126,490	1,267,720
Families of married couples	**6,105,910**	114,635	28,695	187,420	151,210	1,156,930
No children at home	**2,662,135**	53,165	12,935	91,125	73,435	555,885
Children at home	**3,443,775**	61,465	15,765	96,295	77,775	601,040
Families of common-law couples	**1,376,870**	16,935	4,085	34,700	31,000	611,850
No children at home	**758,715**	8,785	2,380	21,060	17,865	298,005
Children at home	**618,150**	8,150	1,705	13,645	13,130	313,845
Lone-parent families	**1,414,060**	24,160	6,405	45,290	35,585	352,825
Male parent	**281,775**	4,420	1,135	8,010	6,435	77,940
Female parent	**1,132,290**	19,740	5,265	37,280	29,150	274,890

	Ontario	Manitoba	Saskatchewan	Alberta	British Columbia	Yukon	Northwest Territories	Nunavut
	number							
All families	**3,422,320**	**312,805**	**267,455**	**904,850**	**1,161,420**	**8,335**	**10,880**	**7,035**
No children at home	1,217,845	119,575	110,835	351,300	479,400	3,075	3,130	1,040
Children at home	2,204,470	193,230	156,620	553,550	682,025	5,260	7,750	5,995
Families of married couples	2,530,560	225,880	194,160	658,900	844,430	4,640	5,555	2,890
No children at home	1,008,550	100,490	95,415	278,990	387,780	2,005	1,830	525
Children at home	1,522,015	125,385	98,750	379,910	456,650	2,635	3,725	2,365
Families of common-law couples	351,040	33,715	28,855	115,685	141,830	1,970	2,990	2,205
No children at home	209,300	19,080	15,425	72,310	91,620	1,065	1,300	515
Children at home	141,745	14,635	13,430	43,370	50,205	900	1,690	1,690
Lone-parent families	540,715	53,210	44,445	130,265	175,160	1,725	2,330	1,940
Male parent	99,605	10,275	9,270	27,715	35,390	445	635	495
Female parent	441,105	42,930	35,170	102,555	139,770	1,280	1,695	1,445

Note: Census families in private households.

Source: Statistics Canada, 2006 Census of Population.

Table 14.7 Population, by living arrangements and by province and territory, 2006

	Canada	Newfoundland and Labrador	Prince Edward Island	Nova Scotia	New Brunswick	Quebec	Ontario
	number						
Total population in private households	**31,074,405**	**499,060**	**133,330**	**899,755**	**716,870**	**7,396,275**	**11,981,235**
Persons in family households	**26,727,405**	447,535	116,675	767,785	621,700	6,168,355	10,542,660
Spouses, common-law partners or lone parents	**16,379,620**	287,300	71,965	489,540	400,000	3,890,395	6,303,925
Children in census families	**9,733,765**	150,655	42,595	262,000	209,190	2,173,525	3,977,010
Non-family persons living with relatives[1]	**393,350**	6,610	1,250	10,140	7,580	67,630	174,355
Non-family persons living with census families other than their own	**220,665**	2,970	855	6,105	4,925	36,805	87,375
Persons in non-family households	**4,347,000**	51,525	16,655	131,970	95,165	1,227,920	1,438,570
Living with relatives[1]	**250,670**	3,540	1,025	7,125	4,955	64,820	84,560
Living with non-relatives only	**769,285**	8,150	2,810	24,900	18,270	182,765	249,145
Living alone	**3,327,050**	39,830	12,825	99,945	71,945	980,340	1,104,865

See notes and source at end of table.

Table 14.7 Population, by living arrangements and by province and territory, 2006 (continued)

	Manitoba	Saskatch-ewan	Alberta	British Columbia	Yukon	Northwest Territories	Nunavut
	number						
Total population in private households	**1,119,530**	**945,890**	**3,228,065**	**4,054,605**	**29,855**	**40,725**	**29,200**
Persons in family households	956,425	802,985	2,768,210	3,447,325	24,750	35,905	27,085
Spouses, common-law partners or lone parents	572,400	490,470	1,679,435	2,147,675	14,940	19,430	12,130
Children in census families	364,255	297,165	1,016,850	1,202,140	9,130	15,160	14,085
Non-family persons living with relatives[1]	13,800	9,355	40,375	60,275	420	860	695
Non-family persons living with census families other than their own	5,975	5,990	31,555	37,220	255	450	170
Persons in non-family households	163,100	142,910	459,855	607,280	5,105	4,820	2,115
Living with relatives[1]	11,050	8,850	33,640	30,060	245	545	250
Living with non-relatives only	23,750	22,745	117,525	116,640	960	1,195	425
Living alone	128,295	111,315	308,690	460,580	3,900	3,080	1,435

Note: Population in private households.

1. Non-relatives may be present.

Source: Statistics Canada, 2006 Census of Population.

Table 14.8 Household equipment, 1998 to 2006

	1998	1999	2000	2001	2002	2003	2004	2005	2006
					%				
Washing machine	81.2	80.3	80.6	80.4	80.5	81.2	81.9	82.2	81.3
Clothes dryer	78.9	77.7	78.2	79.3	78.4	78.8	79.5	80.4	80.8
Dishwasher	51.3	50.0	51.4	52.1	54.6	55.0	56.0	57.2	57.7
Refrigerator	99.8	99.7	99.8	99.7	99.9	99.7	99.8	99.7	99.8
Freezer	59.0	57.6	57.9	56.1	56.8	56.1	55.2	56.3	53.9
Microwave oven	88.7	89.6	90.8	91.3	92.4	93.0	93.8	94.1	93.9
Air conditioning	33.2	34.5	34.6	35.8	37.5	39.6	41.7	44.2	48.1
Telephone (regular or cellular)	98.6	98.8	98.8	98.6	98.7	98.8	98.9	98.9	99.2
Cellular telephone	26.5	32.5	42.0	47.6	51.7	54.0	58.9	64.2	67.7
Compact disc (CD) player	66.3	70.5	74.3	71.1	73.9	76.2	79.7	80.4	81.6
Cablevision	72.9	73.0	72.4	68.1	66.1	64.8	66.3	65.4	65.2
Satellite dish	..	..	..	..	..	..	22.0	22.6	24.1
Digital video disc (DVD) player	..	..	..	..	..	..	68.3	77.1	83.0
Compact disc (CD) writer	..	..	..	..	..	..	38.3	43.5	47.9
Digital video disc (DVD) writer	..	..	..	..	..	..	16.0	24.5	31.7
Video cassette recorders	88.0	88.7	89.9	91.6	92.1	90.2	90.0	89.1	82.0
Home computer	45.2	50.0	55.2	59.8	64.1	66.6	68.7	72.0	75.4
Internet use from home	25.0	33.4	42.6	49.9	54.5	56.9	59.8	64.3	68.1
Colour televisions	98.7	98.8	98.9	99.2	99.1	99.0	99.2	99.0	99.0
Vehicle (owned or leased)	82.9	83.0	83.6	83.0	84.0	83.1	83.8	83.6	82.5
Owned vehicles (automobiles, trucks, vans)	79.0	78.6	79.4	78.2	79.3	78.2	79.1	79.0	77.3
Leased vehicles (automobiles, trucks, vans)	8.7	8.9	9.0	9.8	9.8	9.8	9.9	10.1	10.8

Notes: All data refer to December 31 of the reference year.

In every second year starting with 2001, statistics for Canada include the territories. For the other years, Canada-level statistics include only the 10 provinces.

Source: Statistics Canada, CANSIM table 203-0020.

Table 14.9 Owned dwellings, by province and territory, 2001 to 2006

	2001	2002	2003	2004	2005	2006
			%			
Canada	**64.4**	**64.8**	**65.6**	**65.8**	**67.1**	**65.7**
Newfoundland and Labrador	76.4	76.5	77.0	76.6	79.6	78.9
Prince Edward Island	71.3	69.8	73.2	72.7	68.5	70.5
Nova Scotia	72.4	69.5	69.9	71.1	71.2	69.2
New Brunswick	72.6	71.7	73.8	76.9	76.8	76.6
Quebec	57.7	56.8	57.1	56.6	59.2	56.8
Ontario	64.8	66.7	68.0	67.6	68.8	66.7
Manitoba	70.9	68.7	70.6	68.9	73.0	69.2
Saskatchewan	71.3	73.1	72.5	73.9	74.5	72.5
Alberta	70.4	71.1	72.1	72.2	74.0	74.1
British Columbia	63.7	63.3	64.0	66.6	65.3	67.0
Yukon	63.2	..	62.2	..	62.1	..
Northwest Territories	48.8	..	51.9	..	60.9	..
Nunavut	20.8	..	26.9	..	F	..

Notes: All data refer to December 31 of the reference year.
In every second year starting with 2001, statistics for Canada include the territories. For the other years, Canada-level statistics include only the 10 provinces.
Includes owned dwellings with or without a mortgage.

Source: Statistics Canada, CANSIM table 203-0019.

Table 14.10 Average number of rooms per dwelling, by household size, 2006

	All households	One person	Two people	Three people	Four people	Five people	Six people or more
				number			
Canada	**6.4**	**4.8**	**6.3**	**6.9**	**7.7**	**8.1**	**8.2**
Newfoundland and Labrador	7.2	5.8	7.0	7.6	8.2	8.5	8.9
Prince Edward Island	6.8	5.3	6.7	7.1	7.8	8.5	8.9
Nova Scotia	6.7	5.3	6.6	7.3	7.9	8.4	9.0
New Brunswick	6.7	5.4	6.6	7.1	7.8	8.4	8.8
Quebec	5.8	4.4	5.8	6.4	7.2	7.7	7.9
Ontario	6.6	5.0	6.5	7.0	7.7	8.1	8.1
Manitoba	6.3	4.8	6.3	6.9	7.6	7.8	7.7
Saskatchewan	6.8	5.3	7.0	7.5	8.1	8.4	7.9
Alberta	6.8	5.2	6.7	7.3	8.0	8.3	8.5
British Columbia	6.4	4.7	6.4	7.0	7.8	8.3	8.6
Yukon	5.9	4.5	5.9	6.6	7.4	7.7	8.0
Northwest Territories	5.6	4.3	5.3	5.9	6.6	6.6	6.6
Nunavut	5.0	3.9	4.7	5.1	5.2	5.5	5.8

Source: Statistics Canada, Catalogue no. 97-554-XWE2006015.

Geography

15

Overview

"If some countries have too much history, we have too much geography," said former Prime Minister William Lyon Mackenzie King in a speech to the House of Commons in 1936. Canada's total area measures 9,984,670 square kilometres, of which 9,093,507 are land and 891,163 are freshwater. Canada's coastline, which includes the Arctic coast, is the longest in the world, measuring 243,042 kilometres.

Canada stretches 5,500 kilometres from Cape Spear, Newfoundland and Labrador, to the Yukon–Alaska border. From Middle Island in Lake Erie to Cape Columbia on Ellesmere Island, it measures 4,600 kilometres. The southwesternmost point of Canada is at the same latitude as northern California.

If we indeed have too much geography, most Canadians see relatively little of it in their daily lives. Much of Canada's population lives relatively close to the U.S. border, as shown on the population density map below.

Canadians continue to gravitate toward urban areas. From 1996 to 2006, the urban population grew 9%, from 23 to nearly 25 million people. Together, census metropolitan areas (CMAs) and census agglomerations contain 80% of Canada's total population, although they cover only 4% of the land area. Canada now has 33 CMAs, up from 27 CMAs in 2001 and 25 CMAs in 1996.

Physical geography

One of the fundamental aspects of physical geography is land cover—the observed physical and biological cover of the land, such as vegetation or man-made features. (See the full-colour map of Canada's land cover on the inside front cover of this book.) The most pervasive types of land cover are evergreen needleleaf forest, which covers 26% of Canada, and barren and sparsely vegetated land, which covers 29%.

Map 15.1
Population density, 2006

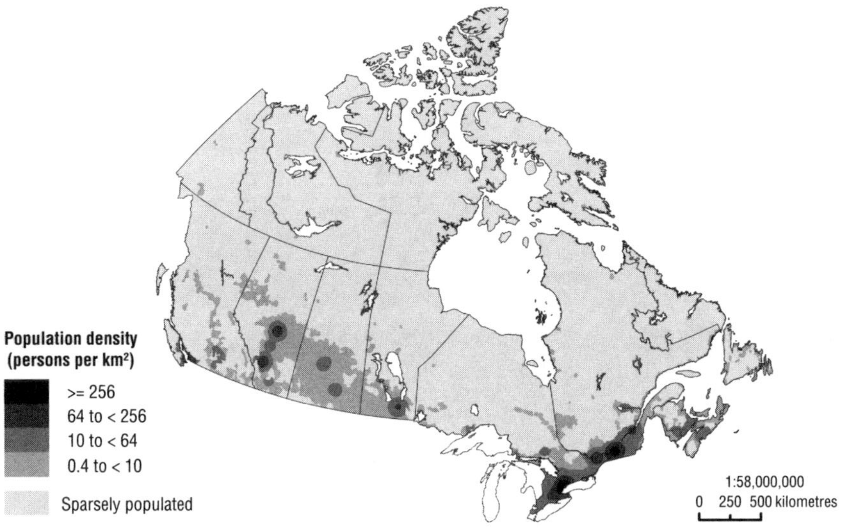

Source: Statistics Canada, Census of Population, 2006.

Facets of climate change

Much of the low vegetation and barren land is found in the Arctic, which makes up 39% of Canada's total surface area—about 3.9 million square kilometres.

Climate change in the Arctic is raising the possibility that the Northwest Passage may become easily navigable. The effect of climate change on Arctic ice is shown in the map accompanying the first Focus article of this chapter.

Another facet of climate change that may affect other parts of Canada is the possibility of changing precipitation patterns. Mapping data showing such shifts, if they are occurring, are not yet available; a map of precipitation patterns that have occured in the recent past is shown on the third page of this chapter.

One type of event that is not associated with climate change is tsunamis; these long high sea waves are usually the result of earthquakes or an underwater disturbance. The second Focus article features a reference map showing recent significant seismic events on the west coast, the edges of the area's major tectonic plates, and the degrees of risk along the coastline in the event of another tsunami.

Table 15.a
Coldest day of the year, 30-year average, selected cities, 1971 to 2000

	degrees Celsius
Whitehorse	-52.2
Regina	-50.0
Edmonton	-48.3
Iqaluit	-45.6
Winnipeg	-45.0
Saint John	-36.7
Québec	-36.1
Ottawa	-36.1
Toronto	-32.8
Halifax	-28.5
St. John's	-23.8
Victoria	-15.6

Source: Environment Canada, Canadian Climate Normals or Averages, 1971 to 2000.

Map 15.2
Climate regions

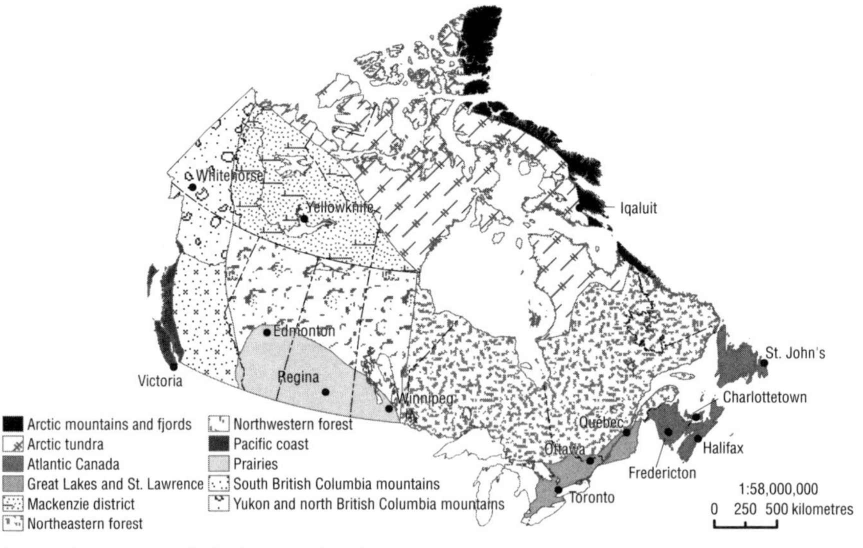

Source: Statistics Canada, Environment Canada.

Map 15.3
Normal precipitation, 1971 to 2000

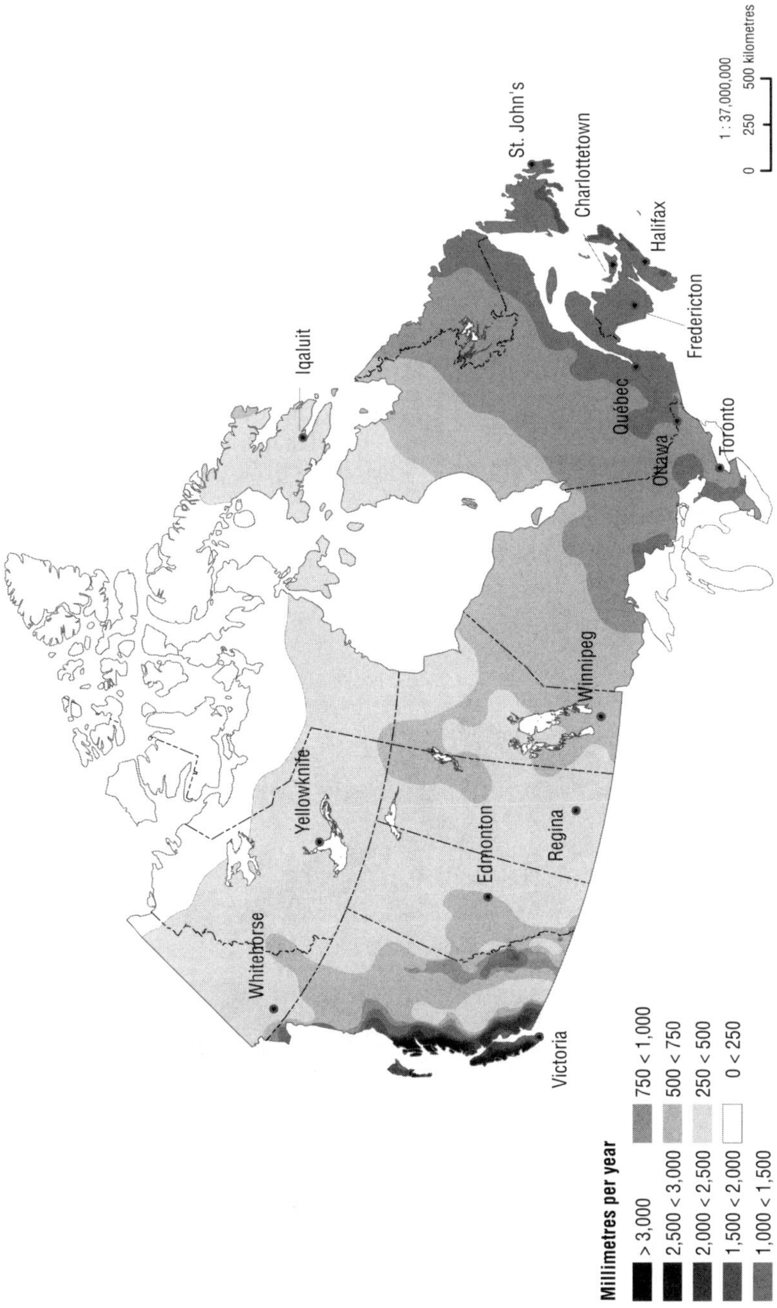

Source: Environment Canada.

Northwest Passage opening or not

Climate change has sparked interest in the possibility of using the Northwest Passage for shipping and other commercial activity.

This is making Arctic sovereignty a hot issue: some countries, including the United States, acknowledge the Arctic islands as Canadian territory, but consider the passage to be international waters.

According to the Canadian Coast Guard, 86 ships entered Canada's Arctic waters in 2007, including research vessels from Denmark, Germany and Russia. There were 11 transits of the Northwest Passage, 5 of them by cruise ships.

Evidence is strong that sea ice is receding, but the long-term consequences are less clear. From 1974 to 2004, the average extent of sea ice cover in summer declined by 15% to 20%. The remaining ice was 10% to 15% thinner overall, and 40% thinner in the central Arctic Ocean, according to the Arctic Climate Impact Assessment, a study commissioned by the Arctic Council, an intergovernmental forum made up of Canada and other nations with Arctic territory. As well, satellite measurements analysed by the U.S. National Snow and Ice Data Centre show that the ice might be melting even more quickly.

In 2001, a U.S. Navy report predicted that "within five to 10 years, the Northwest Passage will be open to non-ice-strengthened vessels for at least one month each summer."

However, the Canadian government has noted that 'multi-year ice', three or four metres thick and nearly as hard as concrete, is being pushed into the Northwest Passage, so passage may still be difficult.

Map 15.4
Polar region ice extents

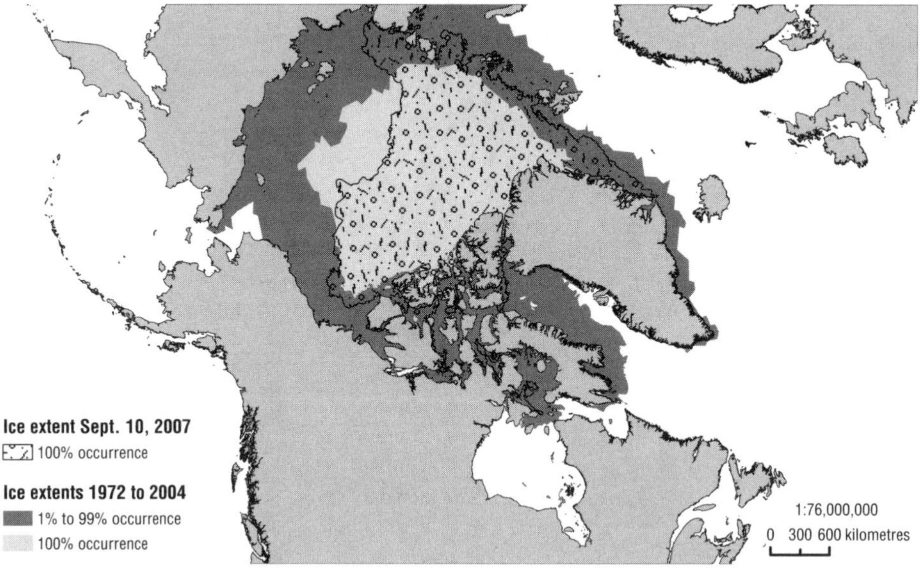

Source: Environment Canada.

On the lookout for the next tsunami

Map 15.5
West coast tsunami run-up risk zones

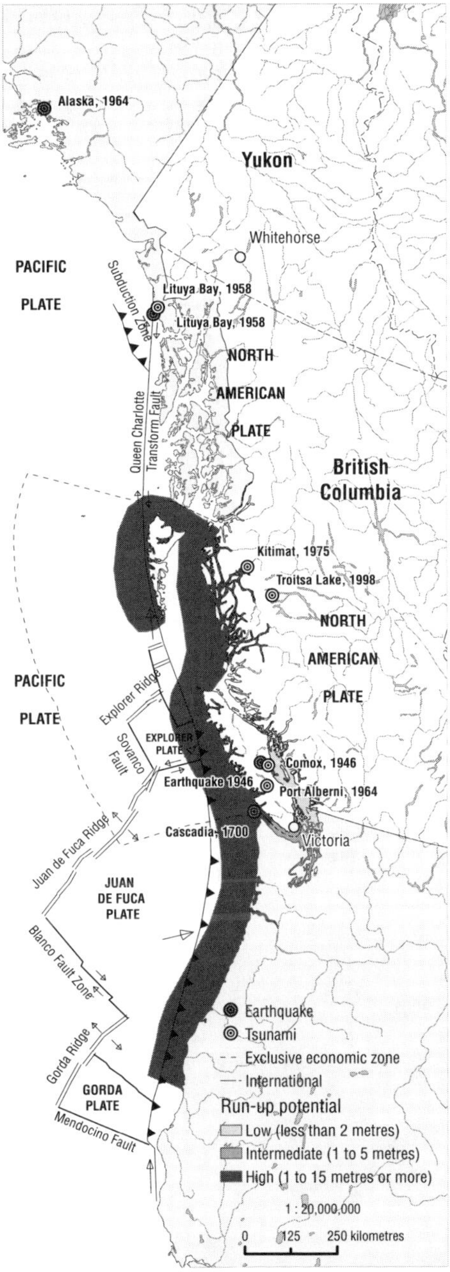

Source: Natural Resources Canada.

Canada's long coastlines make it vulnerable to natural disasters. Tsunamis, for example, can be created by earthquakes, landslides underwater or on land, volcanic eruptions, or meteorite impacts.

If a tsunami occurs in the Pacific Ocean, the first warning will come from an internationally co-ordinated network of seismographs. The Geological Survey of Canada maintains over 30 seismic stations within 300 kilometres of British Columbia's coast. These stations feed real-time data to authorities in areas vulnerable to tsunamis so they can initiate contingency plans.

Canada has not seen, in recorded history, an event on the scale of the tsunami that swept from Indonesia across the Indian Ocean on December 26, 2004. However, on November 18, 1929, a magnitude 7.2 earthquake occurred at the southern edge of the Grand Banks, 280 kilometres south of Newfoundland. The earthquake triggered the largest underwater landslide in recorded Canadian history—a displacement of 200 cubic kilometres of sediment that travelled along the ocean floor.

The resulting tsunami was the worst on record for Canada: waves with heights of between 3 and 8 metres and a run-up of up to 13 metres struck communities on the Burin Peninsula—at peak tide. Twenty-eight people perished; property damage was extensive.

Following the Indonesian crisis, Canada implemented a tsunami warning system on the Atlantic coast. An extensive system was already in place on the Pacific coast—over 70% of tsunamis occur in the Pacific Ocean. Now, the Atlantic Storm Prediction Center's capability to issue surge and other weather-related warnings has been upgraded to include tsunamis, at a cost of about $250,000.

Table 15.1 Weather conditions, selected urban centres

	Extreme maximum temperature		Extreme minimum temperature		Rainfall[1]	Snowfall[1,2]	Precipitation[2,3]
	degrees Celsius	year	degrees Celsius	year	millimetres	centimetres	millimetres
St. John's	31.5	1983	-23.8	1986	1,191.0	322.3	1,513.7
Charlottetown	34.4	1944	-30.5	1982	880.4	311.9	1,173.3
Halifax	35.0	1995	-28.5	1993	1,238.9	230.5	1,452.2
Saint John	34.4	1976	-36.7	1948	1,147.9	256.9	1,390.3
Fredericton	37.2	1975	-37.2	1962	885.5	276.5	1,143.3
Québec	35.6	1953	-36.1	1962	923.8	315.9	1,230.3
Sherbrooke	33.7	1983	-40.0	1979	873.9	294.3	1,144.1
Trois-Rivières	36.1	1975	-41.1	1976	858.6	241.4	1,099.8
Montréal	35.6	1955	-37.2	1933	819.7	220.5	1,046.2
Ottawa	37.8	1944	-36.1	1943	732.0	235.7	943.5
Kingston	34.3	1983	-34.5	1981	794.6	181.0	968.4
Oshawa	36.5	1988	-30.5	1981	759.5	118.4	877.9
Toronto	38.3	1948	-31.3	1981	684.6	115.4	792.7
Hamilton	37.4	1988	-28.0	1994	764.8	161.8	910.1
St. Catharines	37.4	1988	-25.7	1979	745.7	136.6	873.6
London	38.2	1988	-31.7	1970	817.9	202.4	987.1
Windsor	40.2	1988	-29.1	1994	805.2	126.6	918.3
Greater Sudbury / Grand Sudbury	38.3	1975	-39.3	1982	656.5	274.4	899.3
Thunder Bay	40.3	1983	-41.1	1951	559.0	187.6	711.6
Winnipeg	40.6	1949	-45.0	1966	415.6	110.6	513.7
Regina	43.3	1937	-50.0	1885	304.4	105.9	388.1
Saskatoon	40.6	1988	-50.0	1893	265.2	97.2	350.0
Edmonton	34.5	1998	-48.3	1938	365.7	123.5	476.9
Calgary	36.1	1919	-45.0	1893	320.6	126.7	412.6
Abbotsford	37.8	1958	-21.1	1950	1,507.5	63.5	1,573.2
Vancouver	33.3	1960	-17.8	1950	1,154.7	48.2	1,199.0
Victoria	36.1	1941	-15.6	1950	841.4	43.8	883.3
Whitehorse	34.4	1969	-52.2	1947	163.1	145.0	267.4
Yellowknife	32.5	1989	-51.2	1947	164.5	151.8	280.7
Iqaluit	25.8	2001	-45.6	1967	198.3	235.8	412.1

1. Annual average.
2. On average, one centimetre of snow equals one millimetre of rain.
3. Totals may not add up because of different densities of snow.

Source: Environment Canada, Climate Normals or Averages, 1971 to 2001.

Table 15.2 Major sea islands, by region

	Area
	square kilometres
Baffin Island	507,451
Queen Elizabeth Islands	
Ellesmere	196,236
Devon	55,247
Axel Heiberg	43,178
Melville	42,149
Bathurst	16,042
Prince Patrick	15,848
Ellef Ringnes	11,295
Cornwallis	6,995
Amund Ringnes	5,255
Mackenzie King	5,048
Borden	2,794
Cornwall	2,358
Eglinton	1,541
Graham	1,378
Lougheed	1,308
Byam Martin	1,150
Île Vanier	1,126
Cameron	1,059
Arctic islands south of Queen Elizabeth Islands (but north of the Arctic Circle)[1]	
Victoria	217,291
Banks	70,028
Prince of Wales	33,339
Somerset	24,786
King William	13,111
Bylot	11,067
Prince Charles	9,521
Stefansson	4,463
Richards	2,165
Arctic islands south of Queen Elizabeth Islands (but north of the Arctic Circle)[1] (concluded)	
Air Force	1,720
Wales	1,137
Rowley	1,090
Northwest Territories and Nunavut south of the Arctic Circle	
Southampton[2]	41,214
Coats[2]	5,498
Mansel[2]	3,180
Akimiski[2]	3,001
Flaherty[2]	1,585
Nottingham[3]	1,372
Resolution[3]	1,015
Pacific Coast	
Vancouver	31,285
Graham	6,361
Moresby	2,608
Princess Royal	2,251
Pitt	1,375
Atlantic Coast and Gulf of St. Lawrence	
Newfoundland and Labrador (main island)	108,860
Gulf of St. Lawrence	
Cape Breton	10,311
Anticosti	7,941
Prince Edward	5,620
Bay of Fundy	
Grand Manan	137

Note: A major island has a land area greater than 130 square kilometres.

1. There are no islands over 130 square kilometres in Yukon.
2. Formerly the District of Keewatin.
3. Formerly the District of Franklin.

Source: Natural Resources Canada, *Atlas of Canada*.

Table 15.3 Selected principal heights, by province and territory

	Elevation
	metres
Newfoundland and Labrador	
Torngat Mountains	
Mount Caubvick[1,2] (on N.L.–Que. boundary)	1,652
Cirque Mountain	1,568
Mount Cladonia	1,453
Mount Eliot	1,356
Mount Tetragona	1,356
Quartzite Mountain	1,186
Blow Me Down Mountain	1,183
Mealy Mountains	
Unnamed peak (53°37’ N, 58°33’ W)	1,176
Kaumajet Mountains	
Bishops Mitre	1,113
Long Range Mountains	
Lewis Hills	814
Gros Morne	806
Prince Edward Island	
Queen’s County (46°20’ N, 63°25’ W)[2]	142
Nova Scotia	
White Hill (Cape Breton Highlands) (46°42’ N, 60°36’ W)[2]	532
New Brunswick	
Mount Carleton[2]	817
Mount Edward	800
Quebec	
Monts Torngat	
Mont D’Iberville[1,2] (on N.L.–Que. boundary)	1,652
Les Appalaches	
Mont Jacques-Cartier	1,268
Mont Gosford	1,192
Mont Richardson	1,185
Mont Mégantic	1,105
Les Laurentides	
Unnamed peak (47°19’ N, 70°50’ W)	1,166
Mont Tremblant	968
Mont Sainte-Anne	800
Mont Sir-Wilfrid	783
Quebec (concluded)	
Monts Otish	
Mont Yapeitso	1,135
Collines Montérégiennes	
Mont Brome	554
Ontario	
Ishpatina Ridge[2]	693
Ogidaki Mountain	665
Batchawana Mountain	653
Tip Top Mountain	640
Niagara Escarpment	600
Blue Mountains	541
Osler Bluff	526
Caledon Mountain	427
Manitoba	
Baldy Mountain[2]	832
Highest point in Porcupine Hills	823
Riding Mountain	610
Saskatchewan	
Cypress Hills[2]	1,392
Wood Mountain	1,013
Vermilion Hills	785
Alberta	
Rocky Mountains	
Mount Columbia[2] (on Alta.–B.C. boundary)	3,747
North Twin	3,733
Mount Alberta	3,620
Mount Assiniboine (on Alta.–B.C. boundary)	3,618
Mount Forbes	3,612
South Twin	3,581
Mount Temple	3,547
Mount Brazeau	3,525
Snow Dome (on Alta.–B.C. boundary)	3,520
Mount Lyell (on Alta.–B.C. boundary)	3,504
Mount Athabasca	3,491
Mount King Edward (on Alta.–B.C. boundary)	3,490
Mount Kitchener	3,490

See notes and source at end of table.

Table 15.3 Selected principal heights, by province and territory (continued)

	Elevation
	metres
Alberta (concluded)	
Mount Kitchener	3,490
British Columbia	
St. Elias Mountains	
Fairweather Mountain[2] (on Alaska–B.C. boundary)	4,663
Mount Quincy Adams (on Alaska–B.C. boundary)	4,133
Mount Root (on Alaska–B.C. boundary)	3,901
Coast Mountains	
Mount Waddington	4,016
Mount Tiedemann	3,848
Combatant Mountain	3,756
Asperity	3,716
Serra Peaks	3,642
Monarch Mountain	3,459
Rocky Mountains	
Mount Robson	3,954
Mount Columbia (on Alta.–B.C. boundary)	3,747
Mount Clemenceau	3,642
Mount Assiniboine (on Alta.–B.C. boundary)	3,618
Mount Goodsir, North Tower	3,581
Mount Goodsir, South Tower	3,520
Snow Dome (on Alta.–B.C. boundary)	3,520
Mount Bryce	3,507
Selkirk Mountains	
Mount Sir Sandford	3,522
Cariboo Mountains	
Mount Sir Wilfrid Laurier	3,520
Purcell Mountains	
Mount Farnham	3,481
Monashee Mountains	
Torii Mountain	3,429
Yukon	
St. Elias Mountains	
Mount Logan[2,3]	5,959
Mount St. Elias (on Alaska–Yukon boundary)	5,489
Mount Lucania	5,226
Yukon (concluded)	
King Peak	5,173
Mount Steele	5,067
Mount Wood	4,838
Mount Vancouver (on Alaska–Yukon boundary)	4,785
Mount Macaulay	4,663
Mount Slaggard	4,663
Mount Hubbard (on Alaska–Yukon boundary)	4,577
Northwest Territories	
Mackenzie Mountains	
Unnamed peak (61°52' N, 127°42' W)[2]	2,773
Mount Sir James MacBrien	2,762
Franklin Mountains	
Cap Mountain	1,577
Mount Clark	1,462
Pointed Mountain	1,405
Nahanni Butte	1,396
Melville Island	
Unnamed peak (75°25' N, 114°47' W)	776
Banks Island	
Durham Heights	732
Victoria Island	
Unnamed peak (71°51' N, 112°36' W)	655
Nunavut	
Axel Heiberg Island	
Outlook Peak	2,210
Baffin Island	
Mount Odin	2,147
Devon Island	
Summit Devon Ice Cap	1,908
Ellesmere Island	
Barbeau Peak[2]	2,616

1. Known as Mont D'Iberville in Quebec and as Mount Caubvick in Newfoundland and Labrador.
2. Highest point in province or territory.
3. Highest point in Canada.

Source: Natural Resources Canada, *Atlas of Canada*.

Table 15.4 Principal rivers and their tributaries

	Drainage area	Length
	square kilometres	kilometres
Flowing into the Pacific Ocean		
Yukon (international boundary to head of Nisutlin)	323,800	1,149
Porcupine	61,400	721
Stewart	51,000	644
Pelly	51,000	608
Teslin	35,500	393
White	38,000	265
Columbia (international boundary to head of Columbia Lake)	102,800	801
Kootenay	37,700	780
Kettle (to head of Holmes Lake)	4,700	336
Okanagan (to head of Okanagan Lake)	21,600	314
Fraser	232,300	1,370
Thompson (to head of North Thompson)	55,400	489
North Thompson	20,700	338
South Thompson (to head of Shuswap)	17,800	332
Nechako (to head of Eutsuk Lake)	47,100	462
Stuart (to head of Driftwood)	16,200	415
Skeena	54,400	579
Stikine	49,800	539
Nass	21,100	380
Flowing into the Arctic Ocean		
Mackenzie (to head of Finlay)	1,805,200	4,241
Peace (to head of Finlay)	302,500	1,923
Smoky	51,300	492
Athabasca	95,300	1,231
Pembina	12,900	547
Liard	277,100	1,115
South Nahanni	36,300	563
Fort Nelson (to head of Sikanni Chief)	55,900	517
Petitot	23,200	404
Hay	48,200	702
Peel (mouth of west Channelto head of Ogilvie)	73,600	684
Arctic Red	23,200	499
Slave (from Peace River to Great Slave Lake)	616,400	415
Fond du Lac (to outlet of Wollaston Lake)	66,800	277
Back (to outlet of Muskox Lake)	106,500	974
Coppermine	..	845
Anderson	..	692
Horton	..	618
Flowing into Hudson Bay and Hudson Strait		
Nelson (to head of Bow)	892,300	2,575
Nelson (to outlet of Lake Winnipeg)	802,900	644
Saskatchewan (to head of Bow)	334,100	1,939
South Saskatchewan (to head of Bow)	144,300	1,392
Red Deer	45,100	724
Bow	26,200	587
Oldman	26,700	362
North Saskatchewan	112,800	1,287
Battle (to head of Pigeon Lake)	30,300	570
Red (to head of Sheyenne)	138,600	877
Assiniboine	160,600	1,070
Winnipeg (to head of Firesteel)	106,500	813
English	52,300	615
Fairford (to head of Manitoba Red Deer)	80,300	684
Churchill (to head of Churchill Lake)	281,300	1,609
Beaver (to outlet of Beaver Lake)	..	491
Severn (to head of Black Birch)	102,800	982

See source at end of table.

Table 15.4 Principal rivers and their tributaries (continued)

	Drainage area	Length
	square kilometres	kilometres
Flowing into Hudson Bay and Hudson Strait (continued)		
Albany (to head of Cat)	135,200	982
Thelon	142,400	904
Dubawnt	57,500	842
La Grande-Rivière (Fort George River)	97,600	893
Koksoak (to head of Caniapiscau)	133,400	874
Nottaway (via Bell to head of Mégiscane)	65,800	776
Rupert (to head of Témiscamie)	43,400	763
Eastmain	46,400	756
Attawapiskat (to head of Bow Lake)	50,500	748
Kazan (to head of Ennadai Lake)	71,500	732
Grande rivière de la Baleine	42,700	724
George	41,700	565
Moose (to head of Mattagami)	108,500	547
Abitibi (to head of Louis Lake)	29,500	547
Mattagami (to head of Minisinakwa Lake)	37,000	443
Missinaibi	23,500	426
Harricana/Harricanaw	29,300	533
Hayes	108,000	483
aux Feuilles	42,500	480
Winisk	67,300	475
Broadback	20,800	450
à la Baleine	31,900	428
de Povungnituk	28,500	389
Innuksuac	11,400	385
Petite rivière de la Baleine	15,900	380
Arnaud	49,500	377
Nastapoca	13,400	360
Kogaluc	11,600	304
Flowing into the Gulf of Mexico		
Milk	21,600	1,005
Frenchman	5,500	341
Battle Creek	2,600	203
Lodge Creek	2,100	126
Flowing into the Atlantic Ocean		
St. Lawrence River	839,200	3,058
Nipigon (to head of Ombabika)	25,400	209
Spanish	14,000	338
Trent (to head of Irondale)	12,400	402
Ottawa River	146,300	1,271
Gatineau	23,700	386
du Lièvre	10,400	330
Saguenay (to head of Péribonca)	88,000	698
Péribonca	28,200	451
Mistassini	21,900	298
Ashuapmushuan	15,700	266
Saint-Maurice	43,300	563
Manicouagan (to head Mouchalagane)	45,800	560
aux Outardes	19,000	499
Romaine	14,350	496
Betsiamites (to head of Manouanis)	18,700	444
Moisie	19,200	410
St-Augustin	9,900	233
Richelieu (to mouth of Lake Champlain)	3,800	171
Churchill (to head of Ashuanipi)	79,800	856
Saint John	35,500	673
Little Mecatina	19,600	547
Natashquan	16,100	410

Source: Natural Resources Canada, *Atlas of Canada.*

Table 15.5 Principal lakes, elevation and area, by province and territory

	Elevation	Area
	metres	square kilometres
The Great Lakes[1]		
Superior	184	28,700
Michigan	176	0
Huron	177	36,000
Erie	174	12,800
Ontario	75	10,000
Newfoundland and Labrador		
Smallwood Reservoir	471	6,527
Melville Lake	tidal[2]	3,069
Nova Scotia		
Bras d'Or Lake	tidal[2]	1,099
Quebec		
Lac Mistassini	372	2,335
Réservoir Manicouagan	366	1,950
Réservoir Gouin	404	1,570
Lac à l'Eau-Claire	241	1,383
Lac Bienville	426	1,249
Lac Saint-Jean	98	1,003
Réservoir Pipmuacan	396	978
Lac Minto	168	761
Réservoir Cabonga	361	677
Ontario		
Lake Nipigon	260	4,848
Lake of the Woods[3]	323	3,150
Lac Seul	357	1,657
Ontario (concluded)		
Lake Abitibi[3]	265	931
Lake Nipissing	196	832
Lake Simcoe	219	744
Rainy Lake[3]	338	741
Big Trout Lake	213	661
Lake St. Clair	175	490
Manitoba		
Lake Winnipeg	217	24,387
Lake Winnipegosis	254	5,374
Lake Manitoba	248	4,624
Southern Indian Lake	254	2,247
Cedar Lake	253	1,353
Island Lake	227	1,223
Gods Lake	178	1,151
Cross Lake	207	755
Playgreen Lake	217	657
Saskatchewan		
Lake Athabasca[3]	213	7,935
Reindeer Lake[3]	337	6,650
Wollaston Lake	398	2,681
Cree Lake	487	1,434
Lac La Rouge	364	1,413
Peter Pond Lake	421	778
Doré Lake	459	640

See notes and sources at end of table.

Table 15.5 Principal lakes, elevation and area, by province and territory (continued)

	Elevation	Area
	metres	square kilometres
Alberta		
Lake Claire	213	1,436
Lesser Slave Lake	577	1,168
British Columbia		
Williston Lake	671	1,761
Atlin Lake[3]	668	775
Yukon		
Kluane Lake	781	409
Northwest Territories		
Great Bear Lake[3]	156	31,328
Great Slave Lake	156	28,568
Lac la Martre	265	1,776
Kasba Lake	336	1,341
MacKay Lake	431	1,061
Hottah Lake	180	918
Aylmer Lake	375	847
Nonacho Lake	354	784
Clinton-Colden Lake	375	737
Selwyn Lake	398	717
Point Lake	375	701
Northwest Territories (concluded)		
Wholdaia Lake	364	678
Lac de Gras	396	633
Buffalo Lake	265	612
Nunavut		
Nettilling Lake	30	5,542
Dubawnt Lake	236	3,833
Amadjuak Lake	113	3,115
Nueltin Lake[3]	278	2,279
Baker Lake	2	1,887
Yathkyed Lake	140	1,449
Aberdeen Lake	80	1,100
Napaktulik Lake	381	1,080
Garry Lake	148	976
Contwoyto Lake	564	957
Ennadai Lake	311	681
Tulemalu Lake	279	668
Kamilukuak Lake	266	638
Kaminak Lake	53	600

Notes: A principal lake has an area larger than 400 square kilometres.
New Brunswick and Prince Edward Island have no principal lakes.
Area of lakes includes islands.

1. Data for the Great Lakes represent the area on the Canadian side of the Canada–U.S. border only.
2. Daily, monthly and seasonal variations in the time and heights of tides.
3. Spans provincial or territorial boundary. Listed under province or territory containing larger portion.

Sources: Natural Resources Canada, *Atlas of Canada*; and International Lake Environment Committee, *World Lakes Database*.

Table 15.6 Land and freshwater area, Canada and selected countries

	Area	Land	Fresh water
	square kilometres		
Russia	17,075,200	16,995,800	79,400
Canada	9,984,670	9,093,507	891,163
United States	9,826,630	9,161,923	664,707
China	9,596,960	9,326,410	270,550
Brazil	8,511,965	8,456,510	55,455
Australia	7,686,850	7,617,930	68,920
India	3,287,590	2,973,190	314,400
Argentina	2,766,890	2,736,690	30,200
Kazakhstan	2,717,300	2,669,800	47,500
Sudan	2,505,810	2,376,000	129,810
Algeria	2,381,740	2,381,740	0
Democratic Republic of the Congo	2,345,410	2,267,600	77,810
Saudi Arabia	2,149,690	2,149,690	0
Mexico	1,972,550	1,923,040	49,510
Indonesia	1,919,440	1,826,440	93,000
Libya	1,759,540	1,759,540	0
Iran	1,648,000	1,636,000	12,000
Mongolia	1,564,116	1,564,116	0
Peru	1,285,220	1,280,000	5,220
Chad	1,284,000	1,259,200	24,800

Source: Central Intelligence Agency, Office of Public Affairs. *The World Factbook 2007,* Washington.

Table 15.7 Land and freshwater area, by province and territory

	Area		Land	Fresh water
	%	square kilometres		
Canada	**100.0**	**9,984,670**	**9,093,507**	**891,163**
Newfoundland and Labrador	4.1	405,212	373,872	31,340
Prince Edward Island	0.1	5,660	5,660	.
Nova Scotia	0.6	55,284	53,338	1,946
New Brunswick	0.7	72,908	71,450	1,458
Quebec	15.4	1,542,056	1,365,128	176,928
Ontario	10.8	1,076,395	917,741	158,654
Manitoba	6.5	647,797	553,556	94,241
Saskatchewan	6.5	651,036	591,670	59,366
Alberta	6.6	661,848	642,317	19,531
British Columbia	9.5	944,735	925,186	19,549
Yukon	4.8	482,443	474,391	8,052
Northwest Territories	13.5	1,346,106	1,183,085	163,021
Nunavut	21.0	2,093,190	1,936,113	157,077

Source: Natural Resources Canada, *Atlas of Canada.*

Government

16

Overview

Managing a country as large, diverse and dynamic as Canada presents a big challenge—just imagine delivering services to 33 million people who are spread across 10 million square kilometres.

The task is so large that it takes 3.2 million people working in hundreds of public sector organizations at three levels of government. Federal public servants process social security benefits such as Employment Insurance. Provincial public servants ensure that hospitals and clinics provide the health services Canadians need. Local government employees provide services such as the supply of safe drinking water, garbage removal, parks, policing and firefighting.

Most employees work at a provincial or local level

Provincial, territorial and local government employees make up the majority of public servants, and include general government (ministries and departments) as well as universities, colleges, school boards, and health and social service institutions. All told, these organizations account for about 80% of public sector employees, about 2.5 million people.

The federal government accounts for about 12% of all public sector workers. The remainder work in government business enterprises—in activities such as delivering the mail, selling alcohol in provincial liquor stores and providing electricity through local utilities.

Renewal in the public service

All three levels of government scaled back their workforces in the early to mid-1990s to cut budgets and eliminate deficits. However, since 1997 the number of public sector employees has grown by 16% and the private

Chart 16.1
Government sector employees as a percentage of total employment

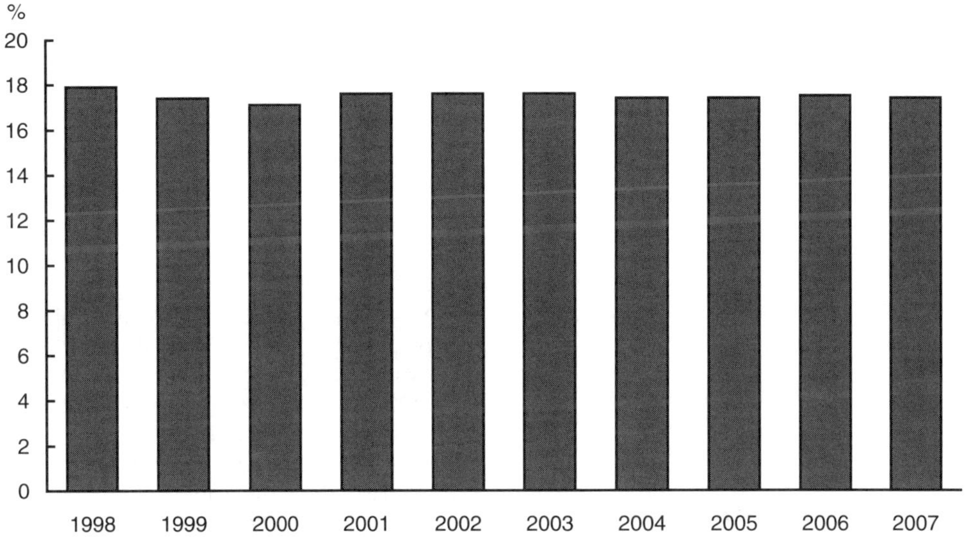

Note: Data are on a calendar year basis.
Source: Statistics Canada, Catalogue no. 68-213-XIE.

sector labour force has also grown. As such, the proportion of government sector workers among all working Canadians has remained essentially unchanged at 18%.

Delivering essential government services and other programs is expensive work. In 2007, our three levels of government managed budgets totalling $604.5 billion. This spending includes all departments, ministries and government programs, as well as the Canada Pension Plan and Quebec Pension Plan accounts.

How each level of government spends taxpayers' dollars is partly determined by the constitution. The federal level is responsible for activities that benefit the nation as a whole, such as nationwide social service programs or international relations.

Of the $223.9 billion in federal spending in 2007, about one-third was dedicated to social security payments, family allowances and income assistance. International activities such as national defense, foreign diplomacy and international assistance totalled 10% of federal spending, as did health care and general purpose transfer payments to other levels of government.

Chart 16.2
Net debt, by level of government

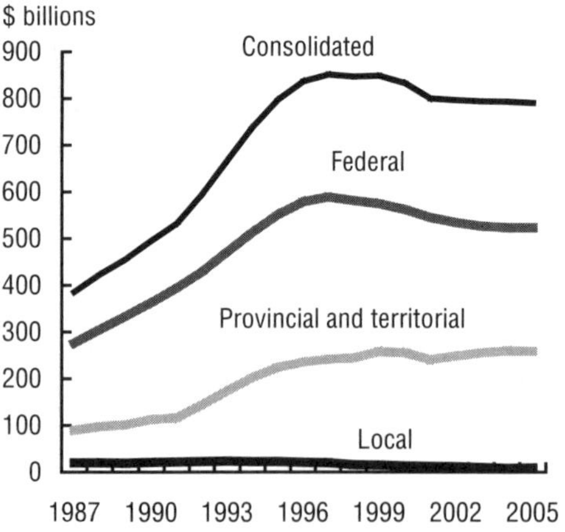

Source: Statistics Canada, CANSIM table 385-0014.

Table 16.a
Public sector employment, wages and salaries

	2006	2007
	number	
Employees[1]	3,164,593	3,225,700
	$ thousands	
Wages and salaries[2]	151,863,218	160,985,860

1. Annual average.
2. Annual total.
Source: Statistics Canada, CANSIM table 183-0002.

The provinces have the main responsibility for health care and education of the $278.4 billon the provinces spent in 2007, more than one-half was devoted to these two areas. Social services account for about one-sixth of provincial spending.

Of the $62.9 billion spent at the local level in 2006, transportation and communication services—such as roads, snow removal and public transit—made up the largest single area of expenditure, absorbing about one-fifth of municipal budgets. Environmental services such as water purification, sewage treatment and garbage disposal were another major item (18% of all spending), as was the protection of people and property—firefighting, policing and the courts (16%).

Spending on priorities

Health and education are the services that have been given priority in recent years. From 2003 to 2007, total government spending on health care jumped 28%, outpacing the 20% growth rate in overall government spending over the same period.

The 23% increase in spending on education also outpaced expenditure growth; spending on postsecondary education jumped 31% from 2003 to 2007. Social services spending rose 20%, keeping pace with overall growth. Other areas saw little growth or even decreases over the same period, such as resource conservation and industrial development, labour, employment and immigration, housing, regional planning and research establishments.

Reducing the debt burden

Governments have recently reduced spending in another key area: interest charges on debt. By reducing or eliminating deficits—the shortfalls governments face in a given year—and paying lower interest rates, interest charges as a portion of government expenditures have fallen, from 11% in 2002 to 8% in 2007.

Success in fighting the deficit and debt has not been shared equally by all levels of government. The federal government has posted surpluses every year since 1998. The provinces and territories have seen mixed results, however. Quebec, Ontario, Newfoundland and Labrador, and the three territories have mostly seen deficits, but the commodities boom has helped oil-rich Alberta record sizeable surpluses—$9.5 billion in 2007. Taken together, local governments across Canada have experienced five consecutive years of deficit since 2003.

The 25% overall increase in government spending from 2002 to 2007 has been possible in large part because revenues grew 29% during that period.

Chart 16.3
Consolidated federal, provincial, territorial and local government revenue

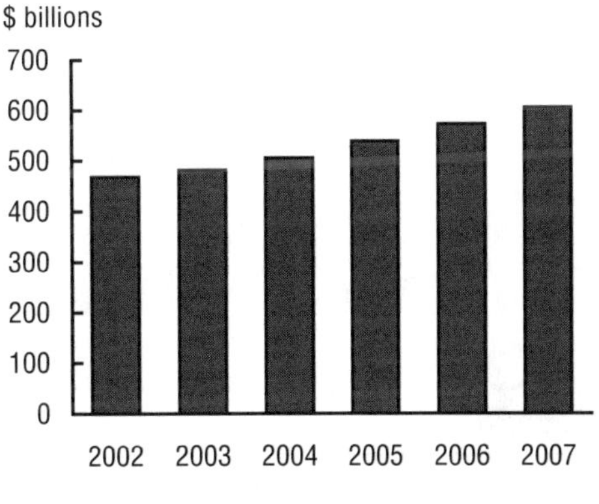

Note: Data for consolidated, federal, provincial and territorial governments are as at March 31, local government data are at December 31.
Source: Statistics Canada, CANSIM table 385-0001.

Seventy percent of total government income is generated by income taxes, consumption taxes and contributions to social insurance plans. The federal government is most reliant on taxation for revenue, 84% of its income is generated by tax measures. A further 9% is earned through contributions to social insurance plans. The provincial and local levels use taxation less; 57% and 40% of their income, respectively, comes from taxes.

Government income growing

Thanks to robust economic growth over the past decade, government income has seen 29% growth since 2002. With more Canadians working and salaries rising, the total amount of income tax collected jumped 31% from 2002 to 2007 to $246.2 billion. Contributions to government social insurance plans also rose, by 24% to $74.5 billion.

Strong growth in consumer and business spending has pushed income from consumption taxes up 18% to $105.4 billion, although the reduction of the Goods and Services Tax in 2006 has slowed this growth. As well, the booming commodities sector and a steadily rising stock market increased income from government investments by 58% to $51.1 billion.

Rejuvenating Canada's infrastructure

On the road, over waterways and under the ground, governments have been upgrading and replacing infrastructure at a rate not seen in decades.

Much of our infrastructure is the product of the last great boom in infrastructure spending during the 1950s, 1960s and 1970s. But governments have sparked a new cycle of investment in the 2000s, reducing the average age of our roads, bridges, water systems, wastewater facilities and sewers to 16.3 years in 2007, down from its peak of 17.5 years in 2000.

Rapidly growing Ontario had the youngest infrastructure in the country in 2007, followed by Prince Edward Island and Alberta. The oldest belonged to Nova Scotia, Manitoba and Saskatchewan.

The largest re-investment has been made in our highways and roads. Since 2001, Quebec alone accounted for more than half of the reduction in the national average age of roads, which was 14.9 years in 2007. Over the same period, the average age of roads fell in all provinces except Prince Edward Island and Newfoundland and Labrador.

Water supply systems have also seen sustained heavy investment, especially in Ontario and British Columbia, which now own the country's youngest systems. Wastewater treatment facilities, however, are still significantly aged, particularly in Quebec and Prince Edward Island.

Infrastructure investment has also been focused on community recreation. For example, the number of sports facilities grew by nearly 4% a year from 1961 to 2005, particularly in Western Canada for the 1988 Olympic Games in Calgary and the 2010 Olympic Games in Vancouver.

Quebec, unlike other regions, has boosted investment in cultural facilities rather than in sports facilities. Since the 1960s, Quebec has spent approximately $100 per person (in 1997 dollars) on libraries, museums, theatres and historic sites.

Chart 16.4
Average annual growth of government infrastructure capital, by period

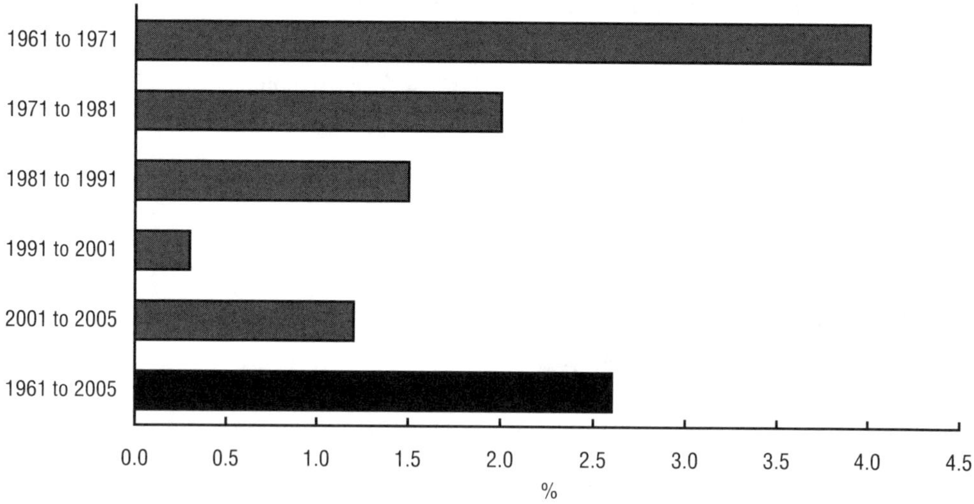

Source: Statistics Canada, Catalogue no. 11-624-MIE.

Changes in social services spending

Keeping up with Canada's rapidly changing society over the past two decades has involved some shifts in government spending. As all levels of government grapple with the effects of a stronger economy, growing populations and an aging workforce, they have changed the ways they support their citizens with social services.

In some areas, spending on social services—programs that aim to improve the well-being of individuals or families—has slowed. While it remains the single largest component of government spending, social services spending is growing at a slower pace than other areas. Spending on health rose an average 6% each year from 2003 to 2007 and environment spending 9%, but social service spending rose 5%.

In other areas, social services as a proportion of all spending has decreased. The strong Canadian economy and the lowest unemployment rate in over three decades combined to reduce spending on Employment Insurance to 6% of federal government expenditures in 2007, from 10% in 1989.

Other parts of the social services system have boosted spending to keep up with growing demand. To keep up with Canada's aging population, the Old Age Security program has expanded. In 1989, spending in this area amounted to $15.2 billion, or 14% of program expenditures; by 2007 the federal government was spending $31.1 billion on Old Age Security, or 14% of total spending.

Equally, as more Canadians retire, more people draw pension benefits. Annual spending under the Canada Pension Plan and Quebec Pension Plan has more than tripled from $11.3 billion in 1989 to $35.1 billion in 2007.

Chart 16.5
Social services spending, by province

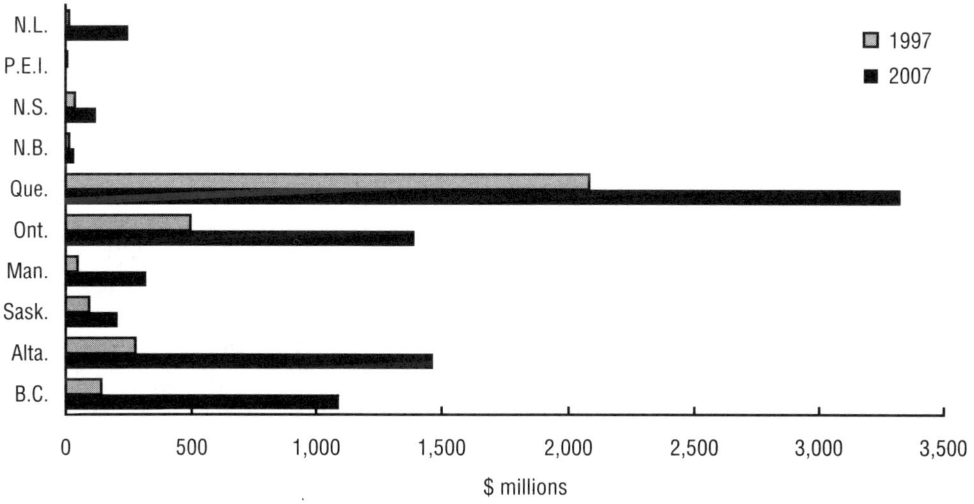

Source: Statistics Canada, CANSIM table 385-0008.

Table 16.1 Consolidated government revenue and expenditures, 1995 to 2008

	1995	1996	1997	1998	1999	2000	2001
	$ millions						
Revenue	**335,313**	**352,416**	**366,764**	**390,484**	**404,976**	**436,558**	**475,137**
Income taxes	123,417	134,343	143,578	160,204	164,593	178,423	191,144
Personal income taxes	102,144	108,649	113,750	123,029	127,763	138,443	143,116
Corporation income taxes	19,525	23,604	26,758	33,897	33,621	36,155	43,262
Mining and logging taxes	308	479	223	304	307	326	454
Taxes on payments to non-residents	1,439	1,611	2,847	2,974	2,901	3,499	4,312
Consumption taxes	65,647	66,951	69,372	73,065	76,697	80,088	87,870
General sales tax	40,050	40,320	42,222	44,620	47,566	51,323	55,523
Alcoholic beverages and tobacco taxes	5,389	5,459	5,581	5,801	6,235	6,190	6,203
Amusement tax	309	351	411	485	627	630	598
Gasoline and motive fuel taxes	9,984	10,710	10,873	11,227	11,602	11,789	11,745
Custom duties	3,576	2,971	2,677	2,766	2,359	2,104	2,807
Liquor profits	2,356	2,658	2,519	2,727	2,807	2,747	3,475
Remitted gaming profits	2,814	3,200	3,517	3,730	4,175	4,183	6,315
Other consumption taxes	1,170	1,282	1,573	1,709	1,325	1,121	1,205
Property and related taxes	35,491	35,846	36,935	38,546	38,557	40,255	41,063
Other taxes	12,455	13,039	13,080	13,333	14,054	14,334	15,157
Health and drug insurance premiums	1,589	1,579	1,648	1,700	2,018	1,950	2,178
Contributions to social security plans	42,571	43,272	45,212	45,874	49,552	51,946	57,530
Sales of goods and services	24,978	25,744	27,763	27,409	29,097	32,202	34,415
Investment income	24,555	26,285	26,153	26,377	24,560	29,588	38,836
Other revenue from own sources	4,609	5,357	3,022	3,976	5,849	7,773	6,943
Expenditures	**389,155**	**397,616**	**389,359**	**391,673**	**407,343**	**422,402**	**446,505**
General government services	12,227	12,157	12,255	12,496	13,238	13,752	15,968
Protection of persons and property	29,248	29,330	28,501	27,984	29,366	31,749	32,978
Transportation and communication	18,150	19,680	17,422	17,062	17,823	18,117	17,979
Health	51,753	53,105	53,427	56,762	59,378	64,317	70,465
Social services	117,133	118,048	120,176	122,256	126,240	129,704	135,793
Education	55,644	55,602	54,269	55,390	57,970	60,457	63,522
Resource conservation and industrial development	15,473	15,029	13,072	11,670	12,992	14,353	15,713
Environment	8,398	8,666	8,381	8,703	8,566	8,672	9,222
Recreation and culture	8,906	9,189	9,010	8,751	9,277	9,909	10,871
Labour, employment and immigration	2,575	2,805	2,237	2,930	2,996	2,951	2,882
Housing	3,885	3,948	4,053	3,733	3,816	3,519	3,723
Foreign affairs and international assistance	4,634	3,954	3,761	3,676	4,035	4,291	4,477
Regional planning and development	1,564	1,558	1,527	1,562	1,688	1,762	1,847
Research establishments	2,135	1,933	1,623	1,522	1,724	1,951	1,419
Debt charges	56,994	62,056	59,114	56,011	56,900	56,397	57,790
Other expenditures	436	556	530	1,166	1,334	501	1,857
Surplus/deficit (-)	-53,842	-45,200	-22,595	-1,189	-2,367	14,156	28,632

See note and source at end of table.

Table 16.1 Consolidated government revenue and expenditures, 1995 to 2008 (continued)

	2002	2003	2004	2005	2006	2007	2008
				$ millions			
Revenue	**468,149**	**481,412**	**505,434**	**538,265**	**571,678**	**604,541**	**635,664**
Income taxes	188,011	178,173	188,619	207,415	225,218	246,175	267,360
Personal income taxes	144,746	139,836	145,324	155,136	167,409	180,034	193,491
Corporation income taxes	38,819	33,608	38,925	46,928	50,893	58,240	65,995
Mining and logging taxes	297	352	215	530	757	1,005	994
Taxes on payments to non-residents	4,150	4,377	4,156	4,822	6,159	6,896	6,879
Consumption taxes	88,987	96,431	98,918	104,495	107,844	105,396	111,461
General sales tax	56,076	60,210	62,169	66,352	69,460	67,397	72,162
Alcoholic beverages and tobacco taxes	7,201	8,800	9,260	9,673	9,024	8,430	8,711
Amusement tax	592	592	552	561	563	518	508
Gasoline and motive fuel taxes	11,743	12,337	12,760	12,700	13,013	13,079	13,575
Custom duties	3,018	3,189	2,804	3,041	3,429	3,651	3,728
Liquor profits	3,144	3,334	3,544	3,703	3,976	4,207	4,408
Remitted gaming profits	5,926	6,095	5,969	6,395	6,438	6,152	6,229
Other consumption taxes	1,288	1,873	1,860	2,070	1,941	1,961	2,139
Property and related taxes	41,730	42,529	44,244	46,721	49,404	51,220	52,993
Other taxes	14,940	16,083	17,037	18,018	18,885	20,549	21,092
Health and drug insurance premiums	2,282	3,000	3,132	3,206	3,258	3,268	3,424
Contributions to social security plans	59,953	63,489	67,568	69,039	71,132	74,489	76,505
Sales of goods and services	34,594	37,299	38,704	40,822	42,459	45,541	47,840
Investment income	32,269	34,838	37,267	40,525	47,528	51,125	51,074
Other revenue from own sources	5,381	9,570	9,946	8,022	5,950	6,779	3,916
Expenditures	**461,306**	**480,915**	**501,884**	**516,576**	**544,753**	**576,182**	**607,589**
General government services	15,765	17,520	18,633	18,792	19,796	20,612	21,110
Protection of persons and property	35,218	37,193	39,154	41,096	43,534	46,752	49,125
Transportation and communication	18,628	19,148	20,258	21,172	24,723	25,913	29,516
Health	76,935	83,315	89,479	94,497	99,126	106,919	115,358
Social services	141,751	145,398	150,827	156,762	164,524	173,812	183,278
Education	66,559	70,533	74,246	77,140	82,685	86,837	91,144
Resource conservation and industrial development	16,329	18,784	19,430	18,652	19,754	20,978	21,379
Environment	9,853	10,259	11,391	11,903	12,935	14,464	16,082
Recreation and culture	11,347	11,690	13,143	13,476	14,207	14,891	15,880
Labour, employment and immigration	3,019	3,395	3,440	2,328	2,480	2,498	2,590
Housing	3,420	3,624	3,833	3,880	4,244	4,435	4,575
Foreign affairs and international assistance	4,562	5,128	4,611	5,556	5,585	6,500	5,942
Regional planning and development	2,099	2,111	2,133	2,057	2,217	2,385	2,665
Research establishments	1,767	1,881	1,890	1,823	1,859	2,165	2,354
Debt charges	52,075	49,475	46,917	45,506	44,755	45,844	45,181
Other expenditures	1,979	1,463	2,499	1,935	2,329	1,176	1,410
Surplus/deficit (-)	6,842	496	3,550	21,689	26,925	28,360	28,075

Note: Data for the federal, provincial and territorial governments are as of March 31 and the local government data are as of December 31.

Source: Statistics Canada, CANSIM table 385-0001.

Table 16.2 Government transfer payments to individuals, 1992 to 2005

	1992	1993	1994	1995	1996	1997	1998
				$ millions			
All levels of government	**93,077**	**98,323**	**98,495**	**98,512**	**98,865**	**100,431**	**104,558**
Federal government	49,317	51,600	50,166	48,879	48,752	49,234	50,739
Family and youth allowances	2,870	37	37	38	39	43	58
Child Tax Benefit or Credit	658	5,252	5,259	5,214	5,228	5,310	5,600
Pensions (First and Second World Wars)	856	848	864	909	914	921	918
War veterans' allowances	443	441	417	397	383	387	387
Grants to Aboriginal people	2,573	2,886	3,027	3,566	3,564	3,730	4,447
Goods and Services Tax Credit	2,557	2,655	2,833	2,810	2,866	2,905	2,924
Employment Insurance benefits	18,648	17,591	15,012	12,889	11,859	10,874	10,713
Old Age Security payments	18,776	19,479	20,170	20,622	21,221	21,798	22,398
Scholarships and research grants	726	727	780	687	686	700	519
Miscellaneous and other transfers	1,210	1,684	1,767	1,747	1,992	2,566	2,775
Provincial governments	23,651	24,603	24,815	25,406	25,576	25,945	26,717
Social assistance, income maintenance	9,371	9,660	9,863	9,854	9,258	8,723	8,050
Social assistance, other	1,213	2,239	2,316	2,308	2,371	2,408	2,241
Workers' Compensation benefits	4,091	3,925	3,811	3,992	4,198	4,067	3,886
Grants to benevolent associations	6,848	5,506	5,577	5,962	6,123	6,714	7,196
Miscellaneous transfers	2,128	3,273	3,248	3,290	3,626	4,033	5,344
Local governments	3,410	3,899	3,949	3,738	2,950	2,640	3,523
Canada Pension Plan	12,808	14,058	15,132	15,777	16,559	17,327	18,054
Quebec Pension Plan	3,891	4,163	4,433	4,712	5,028	5,285	5,525
	1999	**2000**	**2001**	**2002**	**2003**	**2004**	**2005**
				$ millions			
All levels of government	**106,006**	**110,487**	**117,633**	**121,047**	**124,775**	**130,044**	**134,766**
Federal government	51,575	53,479	57,965	60,857	62,949	65,438	67,282
Family and youth allowances	84	99	116	133	140	157	165
Child Tax Benefit or Credit	5,939	6,577	7,379	7,824	8,051	8,547	9,174
Pensions (First and Second World Wars)	910	973	1,196	1,398	1,463	1,527	1,571
War veterans' allowances	414	404	267	212	223	266	292
Grants to Aboriginal people	4,271	4,511	4,448	4,800	4,951	5,191	5,584
Goods and Services Tax Credit	2,943	2,974	3,099	3,140	3,264	3,346	3,472
Employment Insurance benefits	10,150	9,615	11,361	12,837	13,361	13,269	12,937
Old Age Security payments	22,907	23,790	24,789	25,747	26,931	27,992	29,085
Scholarships and research grants	519	531	560	585	612	668	692
Miscellaneous and other transfers	3,438	4,005	4,750	4,181	3,953	4,475	4,310
Provincial governments	27,170	28,574	29,662	29,781	30,066	31,074	32,551
Social assistance, income maintenance	7,048	6,538	6,547	6,603	6,641	6,788	6,893
Social assistance, other	2,546	2,906	2,966	2,936	3,061	3,180	3,252
Workers' Compensation benefits	4,073	4,434	4,840	5,150	5,036	5,081	5,295
Grants to benevolent associations	7,322	7,953	8,406	8,500	8,667	8,920	9,155
Miscellaneous transfers	6,181	6,743	6,903	6,592	6,661	7,105	7,956
Local governments	2,990	3,248	3,641	2,637	2,747	2,903	2,912
Canada Pension Plan	18,540	19,183	20,023	21,076	21,986	23,129	24,225
Quebec Pension Plan	5,731	6,003	6,342	6,696	7,027	7,500	7,796

Source: Statistics Canada, CANSIM table 384-0009.

Table 16.3 Federal government debt, 1994 to 2007

	1994	1995	1996	1997	1998	1999	2000
	$ millions						
Gross federal debt	**557,604**	**595,877**	**634,939**	**651,124**	**645,725**	**648,389**	**648,212**
Unmatured debt	414,942	441,991	470,581	477,940	468,024	461,004	457,331
Marketable bonds	208,464	233,621	262,279	295,022	309,256	315,421	315,854
Treasury bills	166,000	164,450	166,100	135,400	112,300	96,950	99,850
Notes and loans	5,649	9,046	7,296	10,557	12,533	16,353	11,302
Canada Savings Bonds	31,331	31,386	31,428	33,493	30,479	28,217	26,899
Bonds issued to the Canada Pension Plan	3,498	3,488	3,478	3,468	3,456	4,063	3,426
Superannuation accounts	94,097	101,033	107,882	114,205	117,456	122,407	128,346
Dominion notes and coins in circulation	2,464	2,570	2,805	3,243	3,346	3,428	3,601
Other liabilities	46,101	50,283	53,671	55,736	56,899	61,550	58,934
Unmatured debt payable in foreign currencies	10,668	16,921	16,809	23,016	27,183	36,000	32,589
Financial assets	44,385	45,192	56,221	62,722	64,144	73,921	86,479
Net federal debt[1]	**513,219**	**550,685**	**578,718**	**588,402**	**581,581**	**574,468**	**561,733**
	2001	**2002**	**2003**	**2004**	**2005**	**2006**	**2007**
	$ millions						
Gross federal debt	**644,900**	**640,526**	**629,638**	**628,830**	**626,217**	**619,701**	**618,790**
Unmatured debt	447,741	444,058	441,366	437,946	432,996	428,354	419,646
Marketable bonds	316,651	314,685	303,689	292,145	276,676	269,577	264,664
Treasury bills	88,700	94,201	104,600	113,400	127,200	131,600	134,100
Notes and loans	12,570	7,765	7,124	7,720	6,705	6,740	3,965
Canada Savings Bonds	26,416	24,021	22,584	21,330	19,080	17,342	15,175
Bonds issued to the Canada Pension Plan	3,404	3,386	3,369	3,351	3,335	3,095	1,742
Superannuation accounts	129,185	126,921	125,708	127,560	129,579	131,062	134,726
Dominion notes and coins in circulation	3,763	3,914	4,122	4,193	4,310	4,533	4,750
Other liabilities	64,211	65,633	58,442	59,131	59,332	55,752	59,668
Unmatured debt payable in foreign currencies	33,664	27,547	21,603	20,827	16,543	14,333	10,617
Financial assets	99,600	105,836	103,146	105,182	102,873	105,602	110,681
Net federal debt[1]	**545,300**	**534,690**	**526,492**	**523,648**	**523,344**	**514,099**	**508,109**

Note: Fiscal year ending March 31.

1. Net federal debt equals gross federal debt minus financial assets.

Source: Statistics Canada, CANSIM table 385-0010.

Table 16.4 Local government revenue and expenditures, 1996 to 2007

	1996	1997	1998	1999	2000	2001
	$ thousands					
Revenue	**71,091,614**	**71,653,094**	**79,762,114**	**79,451,699**	**79,592,734**	**82,975,700**
Own source revenue	42,158,810	43,769,168	44,636,875	47,105,477	48,166,738	50,195,967
Consumption taxes	53,752	54,984	57,688	77,824	83,450	91,430
Property and related taxes	29,978,851	31,082,662	31,003,224	32,175,113	32,347,101	33,321,793
Other taxes	389,097	440,650	458,448	511,733	513,763	556,465
Sales of goods and services	9,074,083	9,654,961	10,436,005	11,498,887	12,094,702	12,861,473
Investment income	2,206,610	2,064,419	2,163,079	2,272,428	2,441,897	2,609,744
Other revenue from own sources	456,417	471,492	518,431	569,492	685,825	755,062
General purpose transfers from other government subsectors	1,520,974	1,238,912	1,424,893	1,183,535	1,165,153	1,335,653
Specific purpose transfers from other government subsectors	27,411,830	26,645,014	33,700,346	31,162,687	30,260,843	31,444,080
Expenditures	**71,137,903**	**72,064,460**	**74,180,972**	**75,934,368**	**78,889,423**	**81,923,239**
General government services	3,877,000	4,014,048	4,237,621	4,711,618	3,836,904	4,359,578
Protection of persons and property	6,113,280	6,195,067	6,767,336	6,819,085	7,194,115	7,707,272
Transportation and communication	7,936,934	8,390,888	8,492,782	8,822,465	8,918,128	9,094,338
Health	723,213	674,411	860,300	763,441	914,879	1,142,819
Social services	4,263,112	4,213,551	5,171,253	4,982,959	5,532,077	5,187,874
Education	30,687,738	31,198,727	31,335,434	31,969,447	33,442,064	34,679,067
Resource conservation and industrial development	720,586	796,395	813,459	912,009	940,118	970,859
Environment	6,299,724	6,442,329	6,250,761	6,388,056	6,797,043	7,168,290
Recreation and culture	4,846,077	4,649,903	4,741,202	5,003,778	5,538,033	5,846,720
Housing	550,909	558,536	1,098,613	1,142,914	1,481,658	1,721,882
Regional planning and development	623,945	648,769	696,463	742,136	780,654	859,517
Debt charges	4,175,801	3,951,100	3,585,330	3,413,081	3,174,753	3,071,983
Other expenditures	319,584	330,736	130,418	263,379	338,997	113,040
Surplus (+) / deficit (-)	**-46,289**	**-411,366**	**5,581,142**	**3,517,331**	**703,311**	**1,052,461**

See note and source at end of table.

Table 16.4 Local government revenue and expenditures, 1996 to 2007 (continued)

	2002	2003	2004	2005	2006	2007
	$ thousands					
Revenue	**86,250,076**	**90,692,440**	**94,606,314**	**99,512,869**	**108,429,815**	**109,667,285**
Own source revenue	51,548,535	53,541,264	56,642,305	59,652,013	63,258,309	65,333,614
Consumption taxes	96,387	97,623	98,885	102,297	110,859	114,747
Property and related taxes	34,263,273	35,821,903	37,759,412	39,901,677	41,646,452	43,075,562
Other taxes	620,433	632,025	717,411	733,215	770,098	786,673
Sales of goods and services	13,464,364	13,599,140	14,344,044	14,976,225	16,243,751	16,712,824
Investment income	2,332,801	2,579,762	2,868,614	3,062,347	3,508,467	3,603,756
Other revenue from own sources	771,277	810,811	853,939	876,252	978,682	1,040,052
General purpose transfers from other government subsectors	1,474,235	1,545,596	1,657,222	1,827,974	1,842,701	1,879,803
Specific purpose transfers from other government subsectors	33,227,306	35,605,580	36,306,787	38,032,882	43,328,805	42,453,868
Expenditures	**85,368,021**	**91,633,360**	**94,878,259**	**100,461,389**	**108,704,519**	**112,166,933**
General government services	5,165,139	5,853,617	5,854,126	6,037,124	6,414,515	6,887,145
Protection of persons and property	8,096,465	8,981,806	9,232,645	9,843,695	10,358,766	10,960,292
Transportation and communication	9,245,703	10,186,898	10,799,284	11,716,661	12,685,486	13,821,798
Health	1,248,668	1,342,148	1,471,662	1,622,440	1,670,285	1,676,049
Social services	5,285,551	5,547,707	5,777,432	5,996,978	6,179,661	6,095,391
Education	36,178,085	37,557,661	38,709,529	40,125,158	44,316,435	43,499,985
Resource conservation and industrial development	937,830	1,094,150	1,155,389	1,257,949	1,386,869	1,464,293
Environment	7,432,848	8,591,633	9,012,248	10,065,411	11,135,736	12,461,375
Recreation and culture	5,751,152	6,546,538	6,774,704	7,502,875	7,914,672	8,563,751
Housing	1,901,034	1,950,566	2,009,372	2,240,100	2,402,429	2,347,563
Regional planning and development	903,391	944,251	1,012,986	1,080,641	1,195,225	1,370,169
Debt charges	3,014,306	2,958,402	2,958,169	2,910,791	2,971,221	2,938,687
Other expenditures	207,849	77,983	110,713	61,566	73,219	80,435
Surplus (+) / deficit (-)	**882,055**	**-940,920**	**-271,945**	**-948,520**	**-274,704**	**-2,499,648**

Note: Year ending December 31.

Source: Statistics Canada, CANSIM table 385-0003.

Table 16.5 Public sector employment, wages and salaries, 2003 to 2007

	2003	2004	2005	2006	2007
			number		
Employment[1]	**3,031,830**	**3,054,125**	**3,101,494**	**3,164,593**	**3,225,700**
Government	2,756,850	2,771,572	2,819,798	2,880,763	2,936,738
Federal general government[2]	366,428	366,733	370,477	386,765	387,636
Provincial and territorial general government	345,684	343,772	348,521	351,893	357,949
Health and social service institutions, provincial and territorial	752,279	753,450	766,773	780,390	800,669
Universities, colleges, vocational and trade institutions, provincial and territorial	320,542	326,118	334,720	340,289	348,734
Local general government	367,627	368,713	377,603	385,621	395,167
Local school boards	604,290	612,786	621,703	635,806	646,583
Government business enterprises	274,980	282,553	281,696	283,831	288,962
Federal government business enterprises	92,084	94,634	95,436	96,310	99,121
Provincial and territorial government business enterprises	131,314	134,859	131,543	130,963	131,252
Local government business enterprises	51,582	53,060	54,717	56,558	58,589
			$ thousands		
Wages and salaries[3]	**132,743,725**	**137,457,424**	**144,018,454**	**151,863,218**	**160,985,860**
Government	119,780,111	123,636,733	129,908,952	137,057,274	145,215,977
Federal general government[2]	21,018,975	21,318,865	23,641,854	24,607,268	25,826,946
Provincial and territorial general government	17,047,909	17,312,214	17,704,886	18,605,108	19,547,493
Health and social service institutions, provincial and territorial	29,142,154	30,118,469	31,061,851	32,952,374	35,726,591
Universities, colleges, vocational and trade institutions, provincial and territorial	13,174,934	13,955,697	14,854,839	15,826,476	16,678,163
Local general government	14,826,207	15,468,000	16,314,796	17,258,817	18,276,605
Local school boards	24,569,925	25,463,489	26,330,725	27,807,232	29,160,183
Government business enterprises	12,963,614	13,820,691	14,109,503	14,805,943	15,769,884
Federal government business enterprises	3,741,516	4,021,975	4,072,449	4,316,943	4,634,364
Provincial and territorial government business enterprises	6,659,890	7,109,667	7,207,753	7,505,088	7,981,573
Local government business enterprises	2,562,206	2,689,052	2,829,299	2,983,915	3,153,947

Notes: As of August 24, 2005, minor revisions were brought to some estimates prior to 2005: the Nunavut general government data have been revised from 2000 on; the federal government business enterprise data for Nova Scotia and Manitoba have been revised from 2003 on; the Ontario provincial government business enterprise data have been revised from 2003 on. The corresponding totals have changed for total government, total government business enterprises and total public sector.

As of December 31.

1. Employment data are not in full-time equivalent and do not distinguish between full-time and part-time employees. The data are an annual average. Includes employees both in and outside of Canada.
2. Federal general government data include reservists and full-time military personnel.
3. Wages and salaries data are an annual sum. Includes employees both in and outside of Canada.

Source: Statistics Canada, CANSIM table 183-0002.

Table 16.6 Military personnel and pay, 2003 to 2007

	2003	2004	2005	2006	2007
			number		
Employees[1]					
Canada and outside Canada	**83,766**	**84,059**	**85,706**	**87,730**	**89,332**
Newfoundland and Labrador	1,295	1,402	1,375	1,226	1,227
Prince Edward Island	262	266	284	213	230
Nova Scotia	10,598	10,696	10,830	10,520	10,536
New Brunswick	4,949	4,959	5,084	5,300	5,763
Quebec	15,384	15,402	16,121	17,663	18,200
Ontario	27,751	27,681	28,413	29,741	29,904
Manitoba	3,960	3,908	3,927	3,824	4,002
Saskatchewan	1,100	1,104	1,150	1,108	1,112
Alberta	9,052	9,209	9,078	9,090	9,217
British Columbia	7,741	7,776	7,793	7,298	7,305
Yukon	x	x	x	x	x
Northwest Territories	148	153	150	166	174
Nunavut	x	x	x	x	x
Outside Canada	1,521	1,496	1,494	1,577	1,656
			$ thousands		
Annual wages and salaries[2]					
Canada and outside Canada	**4,072,576**	**4,130,991**	**4,635,783**	**4,738,238**	**4,914,600**
Newfoundland and Labrador	44,635	45,623	55,668	53,914	55,117
Prince Edward Island	4,516	4,838	6,299	5,862	6,986
Nova Scotia	571,509	577,900	645,756	656,543	667,479
New Brunswick	218,997	224,507	257,565	268,851	305,644
Quebec	667,067	691,148	777,348	801,439	873,722
Ontario	1,365,989	1,377,531	1,552,523	1,616,418	1,646,513
Manitoba	200,137	196,817	220,550	215,275	224,931
Saskatchewan	45,867	47,793	50,570	51,691	53,794
Alberta	426,726	433,678	483,977	485,571	490,258
British Columbia	399,413	406,287	448,902	440,776	447,203
Yukon	x	x	x	x	x
Northwest Territories	11,920	12,102	13,807	14,303	14,824
Nunavut	x	x	x	x	x
Outside Canada	115,550	112,388	122,103	126,492	125,769

Notes: Employment data are not in full-time equivalents and do not distinguish between full-time and part-time employees. Civilian employees are excluded.

1. Average annual number.
2. Wages and salaries data are an annual sum.

Source: Statistics Canada, CANSIM table 183-0004.

Table 16.7 Health and social services institutions' revenue and expenditures, 2003 to 2007

	2003	2004	2005	2006	2007
			$ thousands		
Revenue	**53,363,118**	**57,163,948**	**60,362,742**	**63,712,802**	**69,039,362**
Own-source revenue	8,066,583	8,417,204	8,985,511	9,508,376	10,326,873
Sales of goods and services	6,742,844	7,236,310	7,748,671	8,202,267	8,909,139
Investment income	122,103	146,341	115,278	120,579	130,779
Other revenue from own sources	1,201,636	1,034,552	1,121,562	1,185,531	1,286,956
Transfers from all levels of government	45,296,535	48,746,744	51,377,231	54,204,425	58,712,489
Federal government	857	6,334	6,868	5,282	5,848
Provincial governments	45,105,809	48,475,693	51,148,536	53,962,320	58,449,620
Local governments	189,869	264,718	221,827	236,823	257,022
Expenditures	**55,064,854**	**59,121,941**	**61,907,633**	**63,972,758**	**69,301,721**
Health	48,856,865	52,582,587	55,037,326	56,800,899	61,568,320
Hospital care	25,624,256	27,357,155	28,647,459	30,126,928	32,716,547
Medical care	11,272,160	12,110,118	13,164,745	12,842,837	13,902,999
Preventive care	953,514	1,077,248	1,167,437	1,224,864	1,327,722
Other health services	11,006,935	12,038,066	12,057,686	12,606,270	13,621,052
Social services	5,998,135	6,315,931	6,641,924	6,938,575	7,484,622
Social assistance	58,051	47,541	41,312	4,471	4,906
Other social services	5,940,084	6,268,390	6,600,611	6,934,104	7,479,716
Debt charges	205,220	218,531	224,545	233,223	248,713
Housing	4,634	4,893	3,838	61	67
Surplus/deficit (-)	**-1,701,734**	**-1,957,994**	**-1,544,891**	**-259,957**	**-262,359**

Note: Fiscal year ending March 31.
Source: Statistics Canada, CANSIM table 385-0008.

Health

17

Overview

Canada has made considerable progress in the health of its population over the last few decades. There has been a steady increase in life expectancy—due in part to repeated success in the battle against infectious diseases—as well as a decline in the number of deaths caused by respiratory diseases and falling infant mortality.

There is also good news about lifestyles and healthy behaviour. Fewer Canadians are smoking regularly, and more of them are active in their free time.

Still, many problems continue to affect Canadians' health. Nutrition is one area where there is room for improvement: most Canadians consume too much salt. Obesity and activity limitations due to chronic conditions are also common among Canadians. And cardiovascular disease and cancer remain the leading causes of death in Canada.

Healthy Canadians

Most Canadians today consider themselves to be in good or excellent health. In 2005, 60% of Canadians said their health was either very good or excellent. The figure for those aged 20 to 34 was 70%; it was 40% for seniors.

Life expectancy at birth was 80 years in 2005, compared with 78 years in 1995. A girl born in 2005 can expect to live 83 years; a boy can expect to live 78 years. The difference in average lifespan between the sexes has narrowed recently, from 6 years in 1995 to 5 years in 2005.

Chart 17.1
Life expectancy at birth, by sex

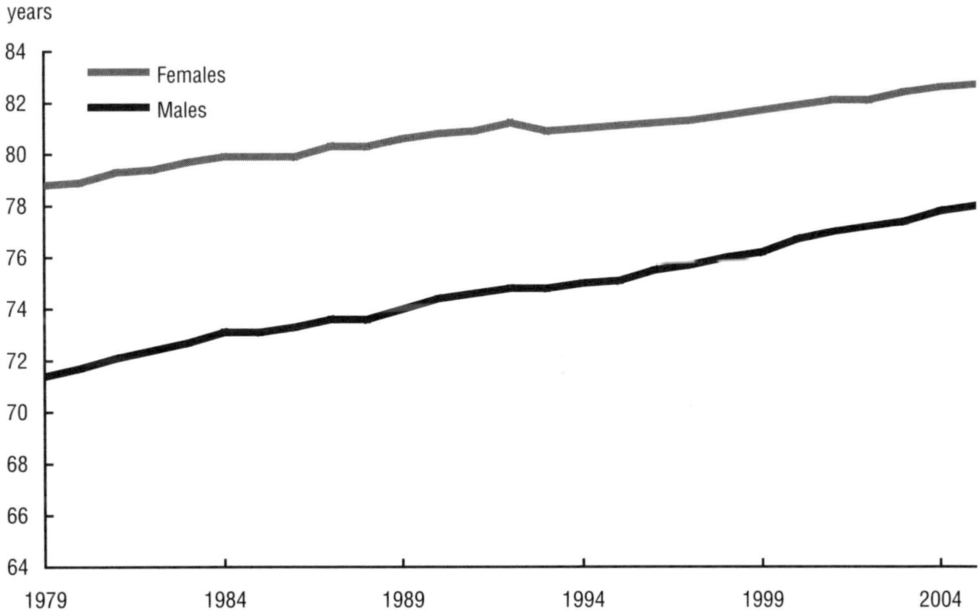

Note: Life expectancy is the remaining years of life.
Source: Statistics Canada, CANSIM tables 102-0025 and 102-0511.

Some health disparities and concerns

There are significant disparities in health across the Canadian population. For example, in northern areas where the Inuit live (Nunavut, Nunavik, Inuvialuit region and Nunatsiavut), life expectancy in 2001 was 67 years, about the same as in developing countries such as the Dominican Republic, Egypt and Guatemala.

In the 1990s, life expectancy at birth in areas where the Inuit live did not increase as it did in the rest of Canada. In fact, it declined by one year: the average life expectancy for both sexes combined was 68 years in 1991.

The level of obesity in the Canadian population—using measured height and weight of an individual to calculate the body mass index (BMI)—is an increasing concern. In 2005, 12% of adults were obese and 27% were overweight. Over the past 30 years, the BMI has increased for both adults and children. The rates for Aboriginal people were generally higher than for the Canadian population as a whole. A study of Aboriginal people aged 19 to 50 in Ontario and the western provinces (excluding reserves) found that, in 2004, they were 2.5 times more likely to be obese or overweight as their non-Aboriginal contemporaries.

Chart 17.2
Obesity rate by age group, 2005

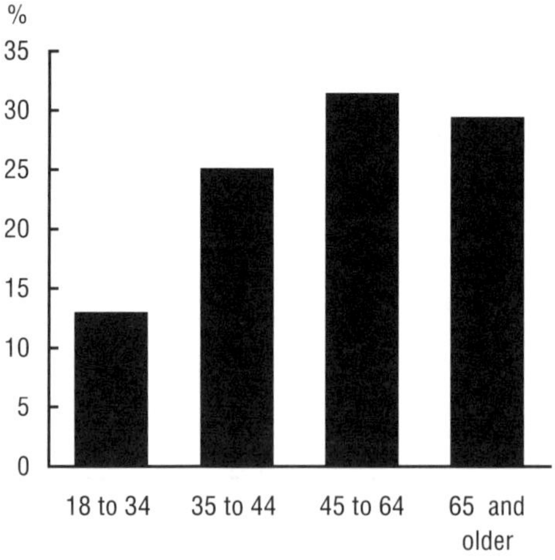

Source: Statistics Canada, Catalogue no. 82-620-XIE.

Table 17.a
Health indicators, 2005

	Males	Females
Life expectancy at birth (years)	78.0	82.7
Infant mortality rate, (deaths per 1,000 live births)	5.9	5.0
Babies with low birth weight (%)	5.6	6.4
Total fertility rate, (number of live births per woman)	...	1.5
Daily smokers (%)	18.2	14.9

Source: Statistics Canada, CANSIM tables 102-0506, 102-0511, 102-4505, 102-4511 and 105-0427.

More have a disability

A growing number of Canadians today are suffering from limitations that affect their day-to-day activities. In 2006, 4.4 million Canadians who were in a household had activity limitations. That is a disability rate of 14%, up from 12% in 2001, when about 3.6 million people reported activity limitations.

Population aging may account for some of the increase. Another factor may be greater social acceptance of reporting disabilities.

Limitations associated with pain and mobility or agility problems are the most common types of disabilities affecting people aged 15 and older. Nearly 3 million Canadians aged 15 and older, or 11% of that age group, reported one of those conditions in 2006.

More are practising healthy behaviours

Practising healthy habits such as engaging in regular physical activity, avoiding smoking and not consuming too much salt is generally good for people's health.

From 2000/2001 to 2005, the proportion of Canadians aged 12 and older who were active or moderately active during their free time increased from 43% to 52%.

Walking is the physical activity that Canadians engage in most during their free time. Recreational activities also include gardening, doing exercises at home, swimming, bicycling, running, dancing and weightlifting.

People who are active in their free time are more likely to rate their health as either very good or excellent. Active people also report lower levels of stress than less active people, and they are less likely to have high blood pressure or to be overweight or obese.

From 2000/2001 to 2007, the proportion of Canadians aged 12 and older who smoked daily or occasionally dropped by 4 percentage points, from 26% to 22%.

The proportion of non-smokers aged 12 and older exposed to second-hand smoke at home fell as well, from 10.5% to 7.4% from 2003 to 2007, while over the same period, the number of smokers asked to refrain from smoking in the house increased from 56% to 67%

Despite these improvements in behaviour, most Canadians consume much more salt in a typical day than is recommended, according to the 2004 Canadian Community Health Survey (CCHS) on nutrition. Excessive salt consumption is linked with an increase in the risk of undesirable health effects, such as high blood pressure.

In 2004, 85% of men and 60% of women aged 19 to 70 in Canada exceeded the maximum daily intake of 2,300 mg of sodium recommended by the Institute of Medicine, an independent American organization.

The average salt intake of Canadians as a whole in 2004 was 3,092 mg a day, one-third more than the maximum recommended by the organization.

The amount of salt added to food was not measured in the CCHS, nor was it included in the calculation of daily sodium intake. However, the average daily dose of sodium for people who add salt to their meals was 3,396 mg, compared with 2,927 mg for people who never add salt.

Chart 17.3
Deaths due to cardiovascular disease and cancer

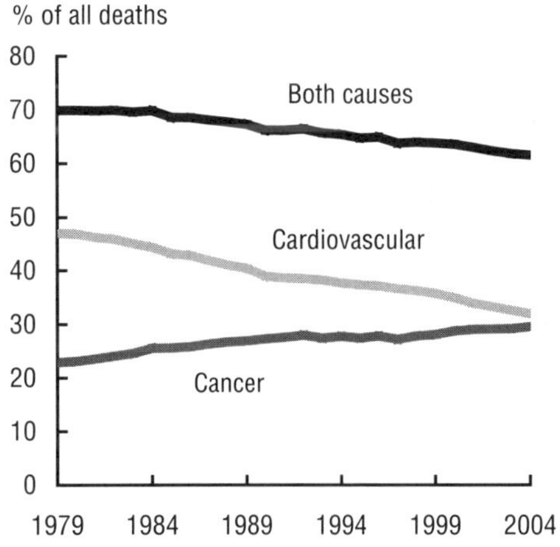

Source: Statistics Canada, Catalogue no. 84F0209XWE.

Deaths on the rise as the population ages

The population is aging, so the number of deaths in Canada has been increasing steadily in recent years, up to 226,584 deaths in 2004. Deaths due to cardiovascular disease and cancer made up 62% of all deaths in 2004.

Cardiovascular disease has been the leading cause of death in Canada over the past 25 years. In 1979, cardiovascular disease was responsible for 47% of all deaths in Canada; by 2004, the proportion had fallen to 32%.

Cancer has been the second leading cause of death in Canada over the past 25 years. From 1979 to 2004, the proportion of deaths due to cancer rose from 23% to 30%.

More Canadians having the flu shot

Despite increases in influenza vaccination rates across the country, many Canadians considered high-risk for serious complications from influenza infection—specifically, younger people with chronic health conditions and healthy seniors—are still not being vaccinated.

Nationally, influenza vaccination rates nearly doubled from 1996/1997 to 2000/2001, rising from 15% to 27%. After plateauing from 2000/2001 to 2003, the rates rose again, to 34% in 2005. Why this pattern occurred is a matter of speculation. The past decade has seen outbreaks of new respiratory diseases. As well, public health officials have stepped up planning for an influenza pandemic. This has included educating the public about the importance of an annual vaccination.

Ontario, which introduced free flu shots for all residents aged six months and older in 2000, led the provinces: vaccination rates rose from 18% in 1996/1997 to 42% in 2005. Nunavut had the highest vaccination rates among seniors and healthy young people, even before introducing universal immunization. Newfoundland and Labrador had the lowest rates, though they doubled from 11% in 1996/1997 to 22% in 2005. And Nova Scotia, even without a universal vaccination program, has matched Ontario's vaccination rates among high-risk groups.

In 2005, vaccination rates among individuals aged 65 and older compared favourably with the 70% target set in 1993. However, the new 80% target set in 2005 was reached only by seniors aged 75 and older with chronic conditions.

Vaccination rates are much lower among people younger than 65 with chronic conditions. Just 56% of individuals aged 50 to 64 with chronic conditions were vaccinated in 2005, while only one-third of those younger than 50 with chronic conditions were vaccinated.

Chart 17.4
Percentage vaccinated for influenza, by age group and presence of chronic conditions, 2005

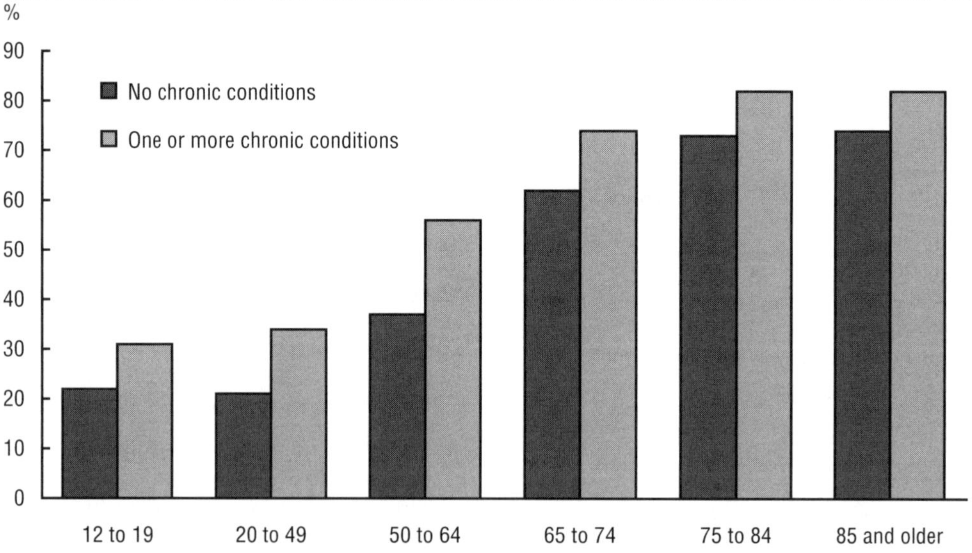

Source: Statistics Canada, Catalogue no. 82-003-XIE.

Surfing the Internet for health

The Internet has changed the way many of us obtain health information and, potentially, our relationship with physicians.

More than one out of three Canadian adults aged 18 and older, 8.7 million adults, used the Internet to search for health information in 2005. These 'health users' had higher levels of education and income, and more than half of them were women.

More than one-third of all health users later discussed the information they found with a family physician or with some other health care provider.

Fifty-six percent of these Internet health users searched for information on specific medical conditions in 2005. Meanwhile, half of them were looking for lifestyle information—especially on diet, nutrition and exercise. In all age groups, women were more likely than men to search for information on specific diseases.

People aged 18 to 44 were more likely to do research on lifestyle and the health care system. In that age group, a higher proportion of women than men looked for information about drugs or medications and about alternative therapies.

People aged 45 and older were more inclined to search for data on specific diseases and drugs or medications. As well, more men than women in that age group looked for information about the health care system or health care delivery.

Internet health users were more likely to surf the Web daily, spending at least five hours a week online. They engaged in more online activities, and they were more likely to have been using the Internet for at least five years.

Chart 17.5
Health users who discussed online health information with family doctor, by type of search, 2005

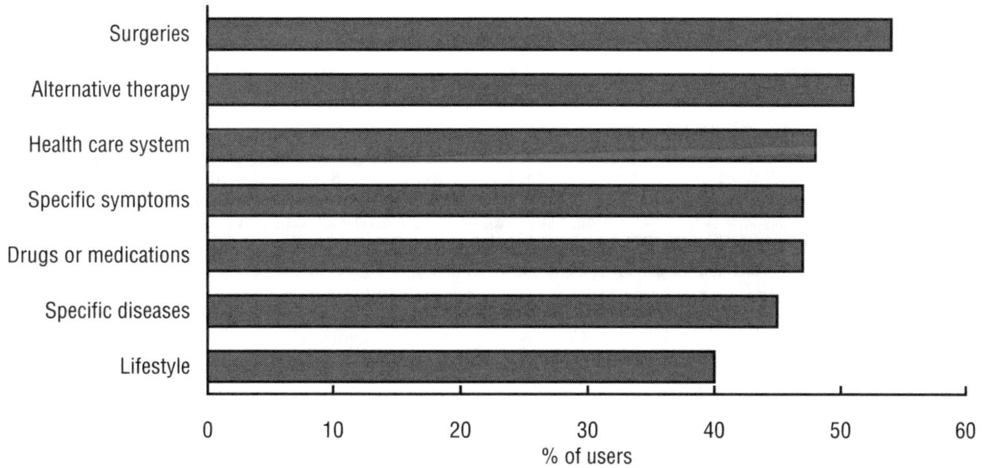

Note: Household population aged 18 or older.
Source: Statistics Canada, Catalogue no. 82-003-XIE.

Table 17.1 Mortality rates, by selected causes and by sex, 2000 and 2004

	2000			2004		
	Both sexes	Males	Females	Both sexes	Males	Females
	rate per 100,000 population					
All causes of death	**615.5**	**778.3**	**493.2**	**571.9**	**710.0**	**465.6**
Septicaemia	**3.8**	4.6	3.3	**4.0**	4.6	3.6
Viral hepatitis	**0.4**	0.6	0.2	**1.0**	1.4	0.7
Human immunodeficiency virus	**1.6**	2.6	0.5	**1.2**	1.9	0.4
Malignant neoplasms	**180.4**	225.3	149.4	**173.7**	212.1	147.0
Colon, rectum and anus	**19.0**	24.0	15.1	**18.7**	23.5	15.0
Pancreas	**8.9**	10.1	7.8	**9.3**	10.4	8.2
Trachea, bronchus and lung	**47.1**	64.3	34.4	**46.6**	60.6	36.2
Breast	**13.9**	0.3	25.0	**12.8**	0.2	23.1
Prostate[1]	...	26.7	...	...	23.4	...
Diabetes mellitus	**18.9**	22.9	15.7	**19.6**	24.8	15.8
Alzheimer's disease	**13.2**	11.7	13.8	**12.7**	10.5	13.7
Heart diseases	**152.0**	202.9	113.4	**126.8**	168.1	94.6
Ischaemic heart diseases	**117.5**	163.1	82.9	**96.2**	133.3	67.6
Other heart diseases	**31.6**	37.3	27.3	**27.7**	32.0	24.1
Cerebrovascular diseases	**42.2**	46.4	38.8	**34.9**	37.9	32.4
Influenza and pneumonia	**13.2**	17.0	11.0	**13.4**	17.0	11.3
Influenza	**1.5**	1.6	1.4	**0.7**	0.8	0.6
Pneumonia	**11.7**	15.4	9.6	**12.7**	16.2	10.6
Chronic lower respiratory diseases	**27.2**	39.8	19.8	**24.8**	33.8	19.4
Chronic liver disease and cirrhosis	**6.5**	9.4	3.9	**6.0**	8.4	3.9
Alcoholic liver disease	**3.3**	5.2	1.5	**3.0**	4.5	1.6
Other chronic liver disease and cirrhosis	**3.2**	4.2	2.4	**3.0**	3.9	2.3
Renal failure	**8.4**	11.3	6.7	**8.3**	11.6	6.5
Certain conditions originating in the perinatal period	**3.9**	4.3	3.5	**4.3**	4.5	4.2
Congenital malformations, deformations and chromosomal abnormalities	**3.4**	3.7	3.1	**3.1**	3.1	3.1
Accidents (unintentional injuries)	**25.8**	35.8	16.6	**24.7**	33.8	16.0
Motor vehicle accidents	**8.6**	12.4	5.0	**8.7**	12.7	4.9
Falls	**4.3**	5.9	3.1	**5.4**	6.8	4.3
Accidental poisoning and exposure to noxious substances	**3.0**	4.3	1.7	**2.8**	4.1	1.6
Suicide	**11.4**	18.0	5.0	**10.8**	16.6	5.1
Homicide	**1.6**	2.3	0.8	**1.7**	2.4	0.9

Note: Rates are age-standardized to the 1991 Census of Population.

1. A combined rate is not calculated for gender-specific causes of death.

Source: Statistics Canada, CANSIM table 102-0552.

Table 17.2 Life expectancy at birth, by sex and by province and territory, 2005

	Males	Females
	age in years	
Canada	**78.0**	**82.7**
Newfoundland and Labrador	75.6	80.9
Prince Edward Island	77.4	82.1
Nova Scotia	76.7	81.8
New Brunswick	77.2	82.4
Quebec	77.7	82.9
Ontario	78.5	82.7
Manitoba	76.6	81.4
Saskatchewan	76.6	82.1
Alberta	77.8	82.7
British Columbia	78.8	83.5
Yukon	74.5	78.6
Northwest Territories	78.4	81.7
Nunavut	66.8	74.2

Source: Statistics Canada, CANSIM table 102-0511 and Catalogue no. 89-506-XPB.

Table 17.3 Residents of care facilities for the aged, by sex and by province and territory, 2000/2001 and 2005/2006

	2000/2001			2005/2006		
	Both sexes	Males	Females	Both sexes	Males	Females
	number					
Canada[1]	**168,816**	**38,629**	**97,710**	**196,242**	**46,943**	**110,555**
Newfoundland and Labrador	**3,803**	1,202	2,601	**4,246**	1,327	2,919
Prince Edward Island	**1,589**	444	1,145	**1,555**	409	1,146
Nova Scotia	**6,682**	1,805	4,877	**6,585**	1,746	4,839
New Brunswick	**5,854**	1,737	4,117	**6,333**	1,959	4,374
Quebec[1]	**32,477**	..	..	**38,744**	..	..
Ontario	**68,707**	18,676	50,031	**84,365**	24,598	59,767
Manitoba	**8,893**	2,402	6,491	**9,541**	2,918	6,623
Saskatchewan	**8,403**	2,625	5,778	**7,873**	2,450	5,423
Alberta	**13,539**	4,274	9,265	**15,676**	5,057	10,619
British Columbia	**18,676**	5,397	13,279	**21,015**	6,367	14,648
Territories[2]	**193**	67	126	**309**	112	197

Notes: Data are as of March 31.

Care facilities in which the predominant group of residents are elderly; residents of these facilities are not exclusively the aged.

1. Data for Quebec are derived from administrative sources of the Ministère de la santé et des services sociaux; these sources do not provide the age and sex distribution of residents, therefore, the Canada totals for males and females exclude Quebec.
2. Includes data for Yukon, Northwest Territories and Nunavut.

Source: Statistics Canada, CANSIM table 107-5504.

Table 17.4 Measured adult weight classes, by age group and sex, 2005

	Under-weight	Normal weight	Over-weight	Obese			
				Total	Class I	Class II	Class III
	%						
Both sexes							
18 to 34 years	3.5E	56.2	27.3	12.9	8.5	3.0E	F
18 to 24 years	5.4E	63.6	22.9	8.0E	6.7E	F	F
18 to 19 years	F	63.0	25.3E	F	F	F	F
20 to 24 years	5.6E	63.9	21.8	8.6E	7.2E	F	F
25 to 34 years	1.9E	50.4	30.7	16.7	10.0E	4.5E	F
35 to 44 years	F	43.5	29.9	25.0	17.5	5.4E	2.1E
45 to 64 years	F	26.1	41.7	31.3	22.8	5.3	3.2E
45 to 54 years	F	28.9	40.1	29.9	22.0	4.5E	3.4E
55 to 64 years	F	22.6	43.6	33.1	23.9	6.3E	F
65 years and older	1.2E	28.9	40.6	29.3	21.6	6.3E	1.4E
65 to 74 years	F	25.0	39.4	34.4	25.6	7.2E	F
75 years and older	F	34.0	42.3	22.4	16.3	5.0E	F
Males							
18 to 34 years	F	51.2	34.6	12.6E	9.1E	F	F
18 to 24 years	F	62.5	28.1E	6.6E	5.3E	F	F
18 to 19 years	F	61.3	31.2E	F	F	F	F
20 to 24 years	F	63.2	26.4E	8.1E	F	F	F
25 to 34 years	F	41.5	40.2	17.8E	12.4E	F	F
35 to 44 years	F	34.7	37.7	27.2	21.7	F	F
45 to 64 years	F	17.5	47.6	33.8	27.9	4.2E	F
45 to 54 years	F	21.4	47.0	30.1	24.0	F	F
55 to 64 years	F	13.4	48.4	37.8	32.0	4.8E	F
65 years and older	F	24.0	44.2	31.2	26.9	3.0E	F
65 to 74 years	F	19.8E	42.8	36.4	31.6	F	F
75 years and older	F	33.1	47.0	19.9E	16.5E	F	F
Females							
18 to 34 years	5.4E	61.5	19.5	13.2	7.9E	2.9E	F
18 to 24 years	8.5E	64.8	16.8E	9.7E	8.3E	F	F
18 to 19 years	F	65.5	F	F	F	F	F
20 to 24 years	F	64.6	17.0E	F	F	F	F
25 to 34 years	3.3E	59.1	21.5	15.6	7.6E	4.1E	F
35 to 44 years	F	52.9	21.6	22.7	13.0E	6.9E	F
45 to 64 years	F	34.6	35.8	28.8	17.8	6.4E	4.6E
45 to 54 years	F	35.4	34.2	29.6	20.2E	F	F
55 to 64 years	F	33.3	38.1	27.6	14.4E	8.0E	F
65 years and older	F	32.8	37.8	27.7	17.4	8.9E	F
65 to 74 years	F	31.1	35.4	32.2	18.6E	12.1E	F
75 years and older	F	34.4	40.0	23.7	16.2E	5.9E	F

Notes: Weight categories based on measured body mass index.
Household population aged 18 and older excluding pregnant females.
Source: Statistics Canada, CANSIM table 105-0407.

Table 17.5 Injuries causing limitation of normal activities, by age group and sex, 2005

	Sought medical attention	Did not seek medical attention	Medical attention not stated	No injuries	Not stated
	%				
Both sexes					
12 to 19	13.8	10.2	1.3	74.8	1.2
20 to 34	9.7	5.7	1.9	82.7	1.8
35 to 44	7.3	5.0	2.7	85.0	2.7
45 to 64	6.6	4.2	2.4	86.8	2.3
65 and older	5.1	2.7	3.7	88.5	3.6
Males					
12 to 19	16.3	12.1	1.4	70.2	1.3
20 to 34	12.5	7.8	2.0	77.7	1.9
35 to 44	8.7	6.6	2.7	81.9	2.6
45 to 64	6.4	4.7	2.5	86.3	2.5
65 and older	4.0	2.4	3.7	89.9	3.6
Females					
12 to 19	11.1	8.1	1.2	79.6	1.1
20 to 34	7.0	3.6	1.8	87.7	1.7
35 to 44	5.9	3.3	2.8	88.1	2.7
45 to 64	6.8	3.7	2.3	87.3	2.2
65 and older	6.0	3.0	3.8	87.3	3.7

Notes: Household population aged 12 and older who sustained injuries in the past 12 months.
Excludes repetitive strain injuries.

Source: Statistics Canada, CANSIM table 105-0418.

Table 17.6 Pain or discomfort that affects activities, by age group and sex, 2003 and 2005

	Affects activities		Does not prevent activity		Affects a few, some or most activities		Not stated	
	2003	2005	2003[E]	2005[E]	2003[E]	2005[E]	2003[E]	2005[E]
	%							
Both sexes								
12 to 14 years	96.7	95.9	0.9[E]	1.6[E]	2.0[E]	1.1[E]	F	F
15 to 19 years	93.1	92.4	2.6	2.6	4.1	3.3[E]	F	1.7[E]
20 to 24 years	91.0	91.2	4.1[E]	2.7[E]	4.4	4.9	F	1.2[E]
25 to 34 years	89.8	88.3	3.1	3.6	6.7	5.7	F	2.4
45 to 54 years	81.0	77.8	5.0	6.2	13.2	13.9	0.8[E]	2.1
55 to 64 years	77.6	74.9	5.9	6.4	15.3	16.2	1.2[E]	2.4[E]
65 to 74 years	76.8	73.6	5.7	6.1	15.9	16.5	1.5[E]	3.9
75 years and older	71.3	66.1	5.6	7.0	20.4	22.1	2.6[E]	4.9
Males								
12 to 14 years	98.5	95.9	0.8[E]	1.9[E]	F	F	F	F
15 to 19 years	95.2	93.2	2.6[E]	1.7[E]	2.1[E]	3.1[E]	F	2.1[E]
20 to 24 years	93.7	90.7	3.4[E]	2.5[E]	2.5[E]	5.3[E]	F	F
25 to 34 years	90.7	88.3	3.7[E]	3.9	5.3[E]	5.2	F	2.5[E]
45 to 54 years	84.9	79.4	5.0	6.1	9.7	12.3	0.4[E]	2.2[E]
55 to 64 years	80.6	77.2	6.0	6.5	11.9	12.9	F	3.4[E]
65 to 74 years	84.0	77.6	3.6[E]	6.1	11.4	11.9	1.0[E]	4.5[E]
75 years and older	76.2	73.0	5.8[E]	6.5	15.1	15.0	2.9[E]	5.5[E]
Females								
12 to 14 years	94.7	95.9	F	F	3.5[E]	F	F	F
15 to 19 years	90.9	91.6	2.5[E]	3.5[E]	6.1[E]	3.5[E]	F	1.4[E]
20 to 24 years	88.2	91.6	4.8[E]	3.0[E]	6.5[E]	4.5[E]	F	F
25 to 34 years	88.8	88.2	2.5[E]	3.3	8.1	6.3	F	2.2[E]
45 to 54 years	77.2	76.3	5.1	6.2	16.5	15.4	F	2.1[E]
55 to 64 years	74.6	72.6	5.8	6.4	18.7	19.6	0.9[E]	1.4[E]
65 to 74 years	70.3	69.8	7.6	6.1	20.0	20.8	F	3.3[E]
75 years and older	68.3	61.7	5.5	7.3	23.8	26.6	2.4[E]	4.5

Note: Household population aged 12 and older who experience pain or discomfort.
Source: Statistics Canada, CANSIM table 105-0203.

Table 17.7 Health expenditures, 2002 to 2006

	2002	2003	2004	2005p	2006p
			$ millions		
Health expenditures	**114,912.4**	**123,382.0**	**131,380.2**	**139,836.3**	**148,014.1**
Hospitals	34,887.5	37,162.1	39,863.8	42,098.8	44,131.3
Other institutions	10,751.1	11,501.9	12,326.1	13,204.3	13,962.2
Physicians	15,048.9	16,124.6	17,167.9	18,127.8	19,413.2
Other professionals	13,096.8	13,190.3	14,197.9	14,904.6	15,616.4
Dental services	8,264.8	8,447.1	8,983.1	9,486.1	9,943.3
Vision care services	2,792.1	2,675.0	3,054.2	3,117.5	3,247.7
Other	2,040.0	2,068.2	2,160.6	2,301.0	2,425.5
Drugs	18,441.3	20,139.3	21,829.0	23,721.6	25,155.4
Prescribed drugs	14,839.9	16,482.7	18,009.8	19,735.8	21,090.3
Non-prescribed drugs	3,601.4	3,656.6	3,819.1	3,985.8	4,065.1
Other expenditures	22,686.6	25,263.8	25,995.5	27,779.1	29,735.4
			% of gross domestic product		
Health expenditures	**10.0**	**10.1**	**10.2**	**10.2**	**10.3**

Note: Health expenditures include spending by federal, provincial, territorial and local governments, the Workers' Compensation Board and the private sector.

Source: Canadian Institute for Health Information.

Table 17.8 Capital and repair expenditures by the health care and social assistance sector, by province and territory, 1996, 2001 and 2006

	1996	2001	2006p
		$ millions	
Canada	**2,742.5**	**5,333.0**	**8,369.5**
Newfoundland and Labrador	25.6	108.3	74.9
Prince Edward Island	7.2	x	14.4
Nova Scotia	37.9	123.1	131.3
New Brunswick	97.7	101.8	263.6
Quebec	x	1,014.5	1,648.9
Ontario	1,146.8	2,093.1	3,170.9
Manitoba	79.5	189.5	274.6
Saskatchewan	101.0	204.2	212.6
Alberta	152.6	761.3	1,160.7
British Columbia	424.9	649.6	1,375.0
Yukon	6.7	14.7	6.3
Northwest Territories (including Nunavut)	20.0	..	..
Northwest Territories	..	x	8.4
Nunavut	..	10.9	28.0

Source: Statistics Canada, CANSIM table 029-0005.

Table 17.9 Average weekly earnings of workers in the health care and social assistance sector, selected groups, 1997, 2002 and 2007

	1997	2002	2007
		$	
All health care and social assistance	**545.57**	**604.07**	**703.04**
Ambulatory health care services	503.20	557.45	692.68
Offices of physicians	468.96	519.09	707.36
Offices of dentists	504.41	561.39	718.18
Hospitals	653.12	712.67	812.00
Nursing and residential care facilities	466.54	543.99	615.95
Social assistance	403.05	482.43	568.12
Child daycare services	352.56	426.50	497.99

Note: Data include overtime.
Source: Statistics Canada, CANSIM table 281-0027.

Income, pensions, spending and wealth

Overview

Earning money, purchasing a home, a car and other assets, these activities are central to the lives of families. Thanks to economic growth, many Canadians have seen significant economic progress over the last decade. As incomes have grown, spending is near record levels, and family net worth has grown.

Gains for all families

From 1997 to 2006, the median after-tax annual income of families composed of two or more people grew 18%, from $49,400 to $58,300 (2006 constant dollars). This period of sustained growth follows two decades where the median after-tax income for most families grew very little or even declined.

Elderly families, married couples, and two-parent families with children closely reflected the median after-tax overall growth rate of 18% of the past decade. Other families saw bigger growth: the median after-tax incomes of unattached individuals expanded 24% to $22,800 in 2006, with non-elderly women seeing their income grow 36%. Despite this growth, unattached, non-elderly women earned 22% less than unattached, non-elderly men.

Median after-tax incomes for unattached elderly men and women grew the slowest from 1997 to 2006, at 11% and 14% respectively. Lone-parent families saw the most income growth during the past decade: their median after-tax income increased by almost half, from $23,800 in 1997 to $34,900 in 2006.

Incomes follow trends

Incomes across Canada follow regional economic trends, so families in different parts of the country have experienced growth

Chart 18.1
Family median after-tax income, by province

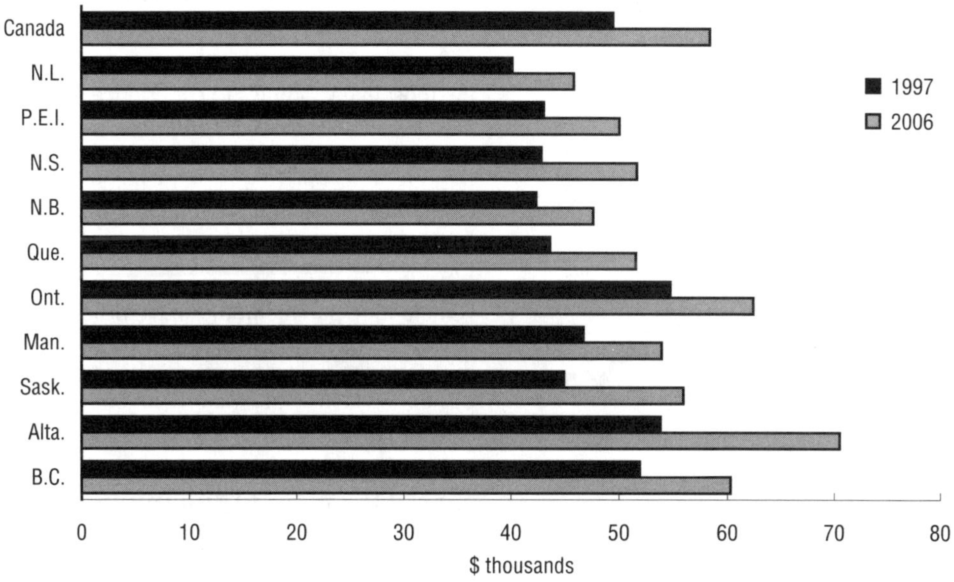

Note: Measured in 2006 constant dollars; economic families of two or more people.
Source: Statistics Canada, Catalogue no. 75-202-XIE.

at varying levels since 1997. The western economic boom, particularly since 2003, has helped families in Alberta to pull in 31% more over the last decade. In 2006, Alberta had Canada's highest median after-tax family income for a third consecutive year. From 2005 to 2006 alone, the median income there grew by $4,600.

After Alberta, Canada's highest median incomes in 2006 were found in Ontario ($62,400) and British Columbia ($60,300). All other provinces saw median incomes below the national average of $58,300.

Government transfers reduce income inequality

Government transfers can make up a sizeable portion of family income. From 2005 to 2006, unattached individuals and families of two or more people saw their median transfers rise from $3,100 to $3,500.

Chart 18.2
Low-income rates, by family type

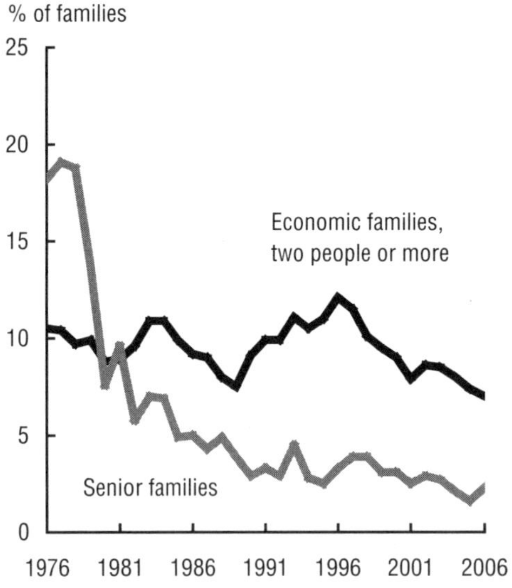

Note: After-tax income 1992 base.
Source: Statistics Canada, CANSIM table 202-0804.

Table 18.a
Average household spending, selected expenditures, 2006

	$
Personal taxes	13,634
Shelter	12,986
Transportation	9,240
Food	7,046
Household operation	3,251
Clothing	2,870
Health care	1,867
Personal care	1,158

Source: Statistics Canada, CANSIM table 203-0001.

Child tax benefit programs were changed and new federal and provincial benefits were introduced in 2006, increasing not only the amounts transferred to families, but also the proportion of families receiving transfers. In 2006, 7.9 million families (88% of all Canadian families) and 3.8 million unattached individuals (83%) received government transfers.

While government transfer programs help to reduce income inequality, 633,000 families, or 7% of all families, remained below the low income cut-off after taxes in 2006. This proportion was unchanged from 2005.

In the late 1970s, Canada's seniors were the most likely families to experience low income, with nearly 20% earning less than the low income cut-off. Pension program reforms at the end of the 1970s helped this rate to decline sharply, so that by 2006 senior families had Canada's lowest incidence of low income, at 2.3%.

Female lone-parent families have historically recorded high incidences of low income. But this has been reduced considerably: from a peak of 53% in 1996, the low-income rate for single mothers stood at 28% in 2006.

Taxes take most of the budget

Income brings income taxes. Taxes remained the single largest share of Canadians' household budgets in 2006. Across all types of households nationwide, families paid an average of $13,634 in taxes, accounting for about 20% of all household expenditures. Taxes were followed closely by shelter costs at 19% and transportation at 14%. Spending on shelter increased from 2005 to 2006 by 5%, to an average of $12,986, largely as a result of the hot housing market out West. Renters also saw their costs increase over the year, by about 10%. Canadian families spent 4% more getting to and from work or around town, to an average of $9,240.

Higher shelter and transportation spending has not stopped Canadians from opening their wallets on other items. With incomes up and the economy booming, households have been spending significantly more on wireless communications, clothing, household furnishings and equipment.

How Canadians spend can depend in large part on their financial situation. The one-fifth of households with the highest incomes, for example, spent 28% of their budget on food, shelter and clothing in 2006, and 29% on personal income taxes. By contrast, the one-fifth of households with the lowest incomes spent 50% of their budget on food, shelter and clothing, with taxes claiming 3%.

Chart 18.3
Registered Retirement Savings Plan, median contributions, 2006

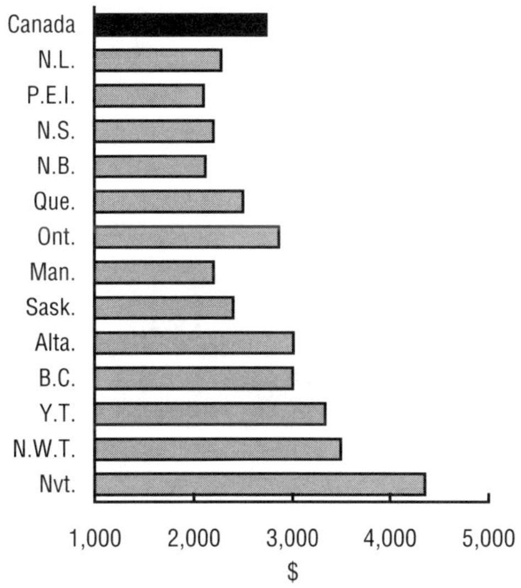

Source: Statistics Canada, CANSIM table 111-0039.

Record contributions to retirement savings plans

Canadians did not spend all their earnings at the mall in 2006. They also set money aside for the future by investing in shares and financial programs. The number of people reporting investment income increased for a third straight year in 2006, to 8.2 million. The year was profitable for investors: the total amount earned from their investments grew 16%, reaching $40.9 billion.

Registered Retirement Savings Plans were also popular in 2006: 6.2 million Canadians made contributions totalling $32.4 billion—the highest amount ever reported. The median contribution nationwide was $2,730.

Albertans took advantage of their larger incomes in 2006 and made the largest median contribution among the provinces, at $3,010. Historically, Canadians in the three territories have put much more into retirement savings plans; in 2006 in Nunavut, the median contribution was $4,350.

About 5.8 million people were also members of employer-sponsored Registered Pension Plans (RPPs), which added 77,700 new members in 2006. Contributions to RPPs climbed 17% to a record high of $43.8 billion. Employers accounted for 72% of total contributions. Although RPPs add members every year, they have grown more slowly than the number of paid workers, so the proportion of paid workers with an RPP has been declining.

With incomes, spending and savings on the rise over the past few years—not to mention rising home values—the net worth of Canadian families has been climbing steadily. The median net worth of all families rose from $120,500 in 1999 to $148,400 in 2005.

Afferding a home in today's market

Home ownership in 2006 reached its highest level since 1971. However, the rise of house prices in recent years has Canadians in some markets concerned about housing affordability.

Affordability means different things to different people. A commonly used benchmark comes from Canada Mortgage and Housing Corporation: Does the household spend less or more than 30% of its income on shelter costs? Shelter costs include rent or mortgage payments, utilities, property taxes and condo fees.

As of 2006, one in four Canadian households spent 30% or more of their income on shelter—a slight gain from 2001 but lower than the proportion in 1996 following the economic downturn in the early 1990s.

Fifty-one percent of the households that exceeded the benchmark in 2006 were renters, 41% were homeowners with a mortgage, and the rest were households that owned a home without a mortgage.

A study on the dynamics of housing affordability found that 3 out of 10 Canadians spent more than 30% of their household income on shelter at some point during the three years from 2002 to 2004. However, only 1 out of 10 persistently spent more than 30% in all three years.

The poorest 40% of Canadians represented 80% of the households that exceeded the budgetary benchmark of housing affordability. Conversely, the richest 40% of Canadians accounted for 7% of the households exceeding the benchmark.

The households most likely to exceed the 30% benchmark were those with people living alone, female lone parents, renters or immigrants. They were also most likely to be living in two of Canada's most expensive cities: Vancouver and Toronto.

Chart 18.4
Home ownership, by province and territory, 2006

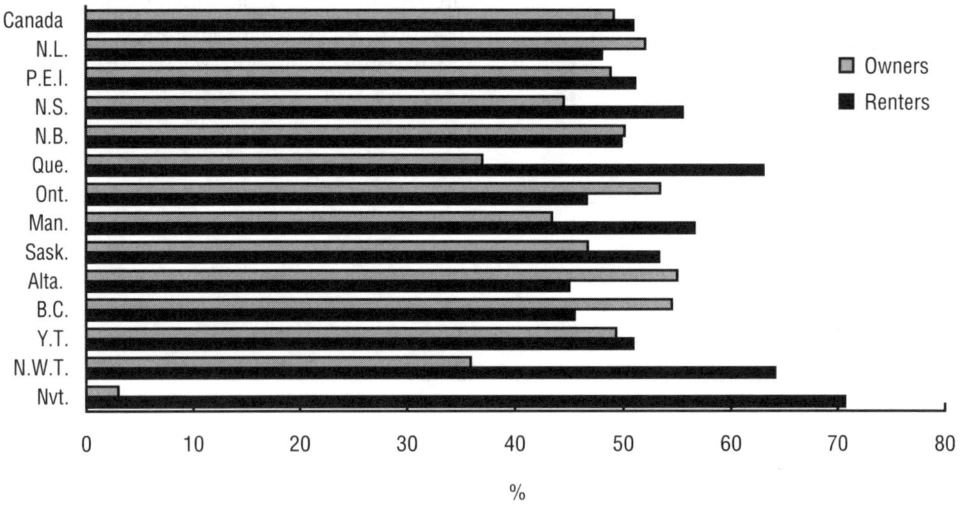

Notes: Private households with household income greater than zero in non-farm, non-reserve private occupied dwellings.
Households spending 30% or more of household income on shelter costs.
Source: Statistics Canada, Catalogue no. 97-554-XWE.

Profiling the high-income Canadian

What does it take to be among Canada's richest people in terms of annual income? It seems the number of millionaires increases every year, but a recent study suggests the group is still fairly small.

Membership in the most exclusive group—the richest one-hundredth of a percent (0.01%) comes with a hefty price tag: an annual income of $2,833,000 or more.

You do not need to be making a million dollars a year to be among the 237,000 Canadians who make up the richest 1% of the population, but it still requires a sizeable annual income: $181,000 or more. Joining the richest 5%—about 1.2 million Canadians—requires an annual income of $89,000 or more.

People with Canada's highest incomes share many characteristics. Most are men and most are married, although the number of women in the top 5% increased from one in seven in 1982 to one in four in 2004. Most rich Canadians are also aged 45 to 64; three out of five individuals in the top 0.01% are in this age group.

Almost half of the richest 1.2 million Canadians live in Ontario. Quebec is home to 18%, followed by Alberta with 15%, and British Columbia with 13%. Canada's richest also tend to reside in its larger urban centres.

Incomes among the top 5% rose much faster than for the rest of the Canadian population from 1992 to 2004. As income increases, so do the taxes on that income. In 2004, the bottom 95% of the taxfiler population received 75% of income and paid 64% of taxes, whereas the top 5% received 25% of income and paid 36% of taxes.

Chart 18.5
Proportion of individual income tax filers, by total income group

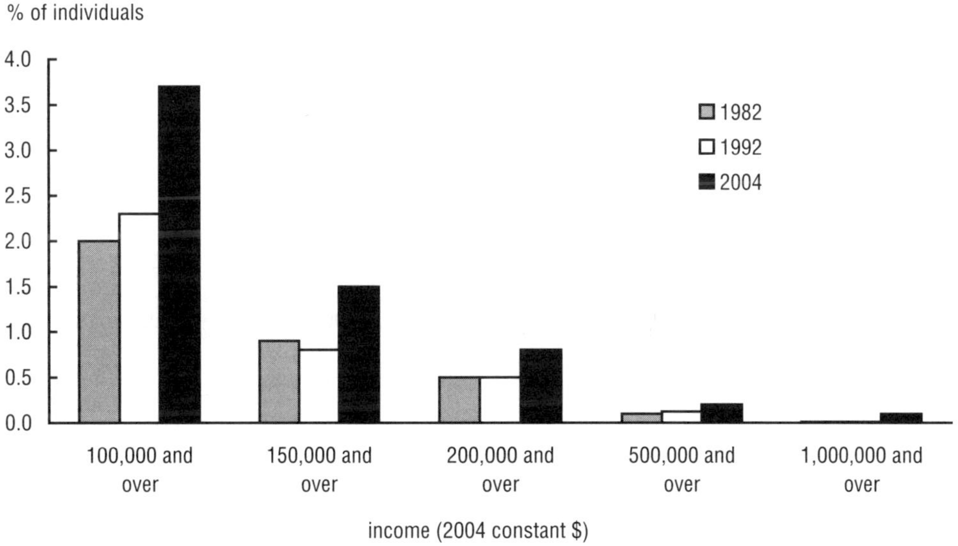

Note: Excluding the value of Registered Pension Plans.
Source: Statistics Canada, Catalogue no. 75F0002MIE.

Table 18.1 Average total income, by economic family type, 1992 to 2006

	1992	1993	1994	1995	1996	1997	1998
	$ 2006 constant						
Economic families	**68,400**	**67,200**	**67,900**	**68,300**	**68,600**	**70,100**	**72,600**
Elderly families[1]	50,200	50,500	50,400	52,800	49,200	49,500	50,200
Married couples	45,200	46,300	46,300	47,100	48,000	48,300	49,100
Other elderly families	61,100	59,400	60,100	66,400	53,200	53,400	54,000
Non-elderly families[2]	71,500	70,000	70,900	71,000	71,700	73,400	76,300
Married couples	70,200	68,300	66,200	67,500	70,400	73,600	74,600
No earner	32,500	33,200	32,600	31,400	34,000	35,600	33,600
One earner	54,200	54,500	55,300	55,500	54,300	57,900	59,200
Two earners	80,800	79,500	76,400	77,900	83,200	84,900	87,400
Two-parent families with children[3]	77,300	75,000	76,600	76,500	76,600	79,100	82,800
No earner	21,800	23,600	22,800	21,300	23,100	25,300	24,300
One earner	57,000	55,700	58,100	55,200	59,000	58,000	65,400
Two earners	79,600	77,800	79,700	80,000	80,000	82,100	85,100
Three or more earners	96,100	95,900	96,800	97,600	99,000	101,600	101,600
Married couples with other relatives	93,200	94,500	95,200	93,100	98,600	98,000	100,200
Lone-parent families[3]	33,300	31,800	33,700	33,700	31,900	31,900	34,800
Male lone-parent families	50,900	45,000	46,100	45,800	49,200	48,700	51,800
Female lone-parent families	31,100	29,700	31,700	31,800	29,200	29,200	31,800
No earner	18,300	18,900	18,600	18,900	17,500	16,500	17,100
One earner	34,300	32,300	33,800	34,000	34,300	32,800	34,000
Two or more earners	48,400	47,600	54,200	53,900	47,300	49,700	52,700
Other non-elderly families	51,000	54,400	54,200	54,300	61,900	60,500	65,300
Unattached individuals	**28,500**	**28,500**	**28,400**	**28,700**	**28,100**	**28,000**	**28,700**
Elderly male	28,100	26,000	30,100	28,800	29,800	30,100	31,000
Non-earner	27,700	24,600	26,400	26,400	27,100	27,600	27,500
Earner	32,900	38,400	62,400	50,600	50,900[E]	45,200	52,700[E]
Elderly female	22,500	21,300	21,700	23,300	24,200	24,800	24,400
Non-earner	22,100	20,800	21,300	22,800	23,500	23,800	23,500
Earner	30,000	37,300	33,300	36,300	41,400	39,100	37,400
Non-elderly male	32,300	32,700	33,000	32,300	31,600	31,100	32,300
Non-earner	13,700	13,500	14,200	13,100	11,800	11,100	11,100
Earner	36,600	38,400	37,900	37,100	36,700	36,900	37,800
Non-elderly female	27,400	28,400	26,300	27,700	25,300	25,200	26,100
Non-earner	14,400	14,000	16,300	14,300	11,500	12,400	11,700
Earner	32,000	33,200	30,500	32,400	30,700	30,400	32,000

See notes and source at end of table.

Table 18.1 Average total income, by economic family type, 1992 to 2006 (continued)

	1999	2000	2001	2002	2003	2004	2005	2006
	$ 2006 constant							
Economic families	**74,200**	**76,900**	**78,100**	**77,900**	**77,300**	**79,200**	**79,900**	**81,700**
Elderly families[1]	52,100	52,400	52,700	53,300	53,100	54,100	56,200	57,400
Married couples	51,400	50,800	51,700	51,700	52,100	53,900	54,400	55,600
Other elderly families	54,600	58,100	56,200	59,500	56,900	55,000	62,900	64,100
Non-elderly families[2]	77,800	81,000	82,300	81,900	81,400	83,600	84,000	86,000
Married couples	73,800	74,800	79,500	78,000	75,800	76,600	79,300	81,200
No earner	35,400	36,400	41,600	38,100	36,300	36,000	36,200	39,400
One earner	61,400	60,000	65,200	59,600	60,400	64,000	66,200	64,500
Two earners	84,900	85,200	89,400	89,500	85,600	85,300	89,000	91,400
Two-parent families with children[3]	84,800	88,000	89,300	89,800	90,900	94,200	91,300	93,500
No earner	23,700	23,500	25,800	26,200	23,900	25,200	21,900	26,200
One earner	64,400	64,400	65,700	69,500	71,300	68,900	65,500	66,300
Two earners	86,500	89,900	90,400	90,600	91,000	94,300	92,700	93,300
Three or more earners	105,100	109,500	112,100	109,500	110,900	117,500	113,400	117,800
Married couples with other relatives	104,900	112,100	108,000	107,200	107,300	110,300	115,900	119,500
Lone-parent families[3]	36,000	39,200	40,000	38,100	38,900	38,900	45,400	45,800
Male lone-parent families	52,800	57,500	54,100	54,300	58,800	54,900	65,500	67,100
Female lone-parent families	32,900	35,400	37,100	34,300	34,500	35,400	40,900	40,900
No earner	18,000	17,000	18,000	17,200	16,900	18,300	18,100	20,500
One earner	34,300	35,400	36,900	34,700	34,100	35,500	42,100	40,800
Two or more earners	51,900	57,200	59,300	51,800	54,300	51,600	54,100	55,300
Other non-elderly families	66,000	68,600	68,900	70,700	65,200	68,600	66,800	68,200
Unattached individuals	**30,500**	**30,500**	**31,400**	**32,000**	**32,600**	**32,500**	**32,900**	**34,200**
Elderly male	29,800	28,500	30,400	30,100	31,400	30,800	31,800	32,400
Non-earner	28,000	26,600	28,500	27,300	27,500	28,600	27,300	28,100
Earner	42,000	39,200	41,800	42,000	45,200	39,100	49,600	48,400
Elderly female	24,400	25,000	26,000	26,500	26,300	27,400	26,400	28,400
Non-earner	23,600	24,200	24,800	25,900	25,400	26,200	25,300	27,400
Earner	35,900	36,600	41,000	34,000	33,800	37,500	37,200	37,700
Non-elderly male	34,000	35,300	35,800	36,000	37,000	36,100	37,500	39,300
Non-earner	10,800	10,700	12,700	12,400	13,100	12,800	13,100	13,300
Earner	38,800	39,800	40,200	40,900	42,000	40,600	42,800	43,700
Non-elderly female	29,900	28,100	28,800	30,400	30,600	30,600	30,400	31,000
Non-earner	11,500	11,400	12,900	12,800	13,800	13,700	15,500	14,500
Earner	36,500	33,700	34,200	35,900	35,500	35,700	34,300	35,300

Note: "Average total income" refers to income from all sources, including government transfers and before deduction of federal and provincial income taxes. It may also be called 'income before tax' (but after transfers).

1. Families in which the major income earner is 65 years of age and older; for data prior to 1996, the head of family is 65 years of age or older.
2. Families in which the major income earner is less than 65 years of age.
3. Families with children less than 18 years of age.

Source: Statistics Canada, CANSIM table 202-0403.

Table 18.2 Average total income, by economic family type and by province, 2006

	Canada	Newfoundland and Labrador	Prince Edward Island	Nova Scotia	New Brunswick	Quebec
	$ 2006 constant					
Economic families	**81,700**	**63,900**	**66,200**	**71,100**	**64,500**	**72,200**
Elderly families[1]	**57,400**	40,200	51,000	50,600	46,400	48,100
Married couples	**55,600**	40,500	48,200	51,800	43,600	46,100
Other elderly families	**64,100**	39,200	F	47,100	55,200	55,400
Non-elderly families[2]	**86,000**	68,800	69,000	75,300	68,000	76,400
Married couples	**81,200**	60,600	67,300	66,800	63,100	71,000
No earner	**39,400**	F	F	40,000	31,600	38,700
One earner	**64,500**	52,100	51,000	56,300	49,900	63,600
Two earners	**91,400**	68,400	74,000	74,700	73,500	77,600
Two-parent families with children[3]	**93,500**	80,000	76,400	84,500	77,500	87,000
No earner	**26,200**	F	F	F	F	F
One earner	**66,300**	65,200[E]	F	59,400[E]	48,600	60,800
Two earners	**93,300**	81,800	76,300	82,200	79,000	89,300
Three or more earners	**117,800**	92,700	86,300	112,600	96,000	103,500
Married couples with other relatives	**119,500**	92,000	96,100	106,600	92,800	103,600
Lone-parent families[3]	**45,800**	34,500	32,200	40,300	33,200	47,700
Male lone-parent families	**67,100**	F	F	F	F	73,700[E]
Female lone-parent families	**40,900**	32,100	31,200	35,300	31,400	39,300
No earner	**20,500**	F	F	F	F	19,200
One earner	**40,800**	30,500	28,800	36,200	29,500	37,600
Two or more earners	**55,300**	F	F	F	F	55,000
Other non-elderly families	**68,200**	60,500	56,600	64,300	50,600	56,200
Unattached individuals	**34,200**	**25,900**	**25,000**	**26,900**	**25,300**	**30,300**
Elderly male	**32,400**	24,300	F	26,200	25,900	26,900
Non-earner	**28,100**	23,900	F	25,000	22,700	22,900
Earner	**48,400**	F	F	F	F	43,000
Elderly female	**28,400**	19,400	24,600	27,200	21,600	27,600
Non-earner	**27,400**	19,400	24,100	26,200	21,200	26,500
Earner	**37,700**	F	F	F	F	37,600
Non-elderly male	**39,300**	30,600	24,200	29,000	28,400	33,400
Non-earner	**13,300**	F	F	15,300[E]	8,900[E]	13,300[E]
Earner	**43,700**	37,400	28,200	31,900	33,300	37,300
Non-elderly female	**31,000**	24,900	25,000	24,800	23,400	28,700
Non-earner	**14,500**	F	F	12,200	13,200[E]	15,500[E]
Earner	**35,300**	32,500	28,900	27,800	26,500	33,000

See notes and source at end of table.

Table 18.2 Average total income, by economic family type and by province, 2006 (continued)

	Ontario	Manitoba	Saskatchewan	Alberta	British Columbia
	$ 2006 constant				
Economic families	**87,700**	**75,000**	**76,000**	**97,000**	**80,700**
Elderly families[1]	62,300	57,600	53,100	60,800	64,500
Married couples	60,100	55,800	53,600	59,400	62,100
Other elderly families	69,500	64,400	50,800	68,800	73,800
Non-elderly families[2]	92,300	78,100	80,600	102,200	83,900
Married couples	85,300	72,000	81,100	105,900	85,800
No earner	41,000	F	F	F	F
One earner	63,900	52,600	61,500	80,200	69,300
Two earners	98,500	82,600	87,700	113,700	96,100
Two-parent families with children[3]	97,600	80,700	90,200	108,500	89,500
No earner	41,000	F	F	F	F
One earner	59,000	57,500	60,000	120,200E	59,600
Two earners	100,000	77,400	85,400	94,700	91,700
Three or more earners	122,400	105,800	118,100	137,100	113,400
Married couples with other relatives	132,100	121,600	107,000	139,600	102,200
Lone-parent families[3]	48,000	39,500	34,100	53,400	40,500
Male lone-parent families	67,000	49,300	41,000E	78,000	55,300E
Female lone-parent families	44,100	37,400	32,600	47,500	37,700
No earner	22,400	F	F	F	F
One earner	46,500	35,100	31,700	44,800	35,400
Two or more earners	56,500	F	45,600	63,100	51,600
Other non-elderly families	74,700	75,200	67,900	71,200	68,700
Unattached individuals	**37,100**	**29,100**	**29,400**	**42,300**	**35,200**
Elderly male	40,100	28,300	30,000	27,700	32,800
Non-earner	33,700	24,900	28,500	29,500	28,200
Earner	61,400E	F	F	F	F
Elderly female	30,300	24,900	26,400	26,700	31,200
Non-earner	29,400	24,600	23,700	24,700	30,600
Earner	38,600	F	45,700E	37,900	36,300
Non-elderly male	41,400	33,300	34,100	52,200	39,800
Non-earner	14,300	20,700E	6,800E	F	10,500E
Earner	46,800	34,900	38,000	54,900	44,200
Non-elderly female	34,200	26,800	25,400	34,200	30,900
Non-earner	15,400	9,800E	11,100E	12,800	12,600E
Earner	39,400	30,300	27,700	36,600	35,100

Note: "Average total income" refers to income from all sources, including government transfers and before deduction of federal and provincial income taxes. It may also be called 'income before tax' (but after transfers).

1. Families in which the major income earner is 65 years of age and older.
2. Families in which the major income earner is less than 65 years of age.
3. Families with children less than 18 years of age.

Source: Statistics Canada, CANSIM table 202-0403.

Table 18.3 Average income after tax, by economic family type, 1992 to 2006

	1992	1993	1994	1995	1996	1997	1998	1999
	$ 2006 constant							
Economic families	**55,200**	**54,300**	**54,600**	**54,700**	**55,100**	**56,200**	**58,000**	**59,800**
Elderly families[1]	43,900	44,000	43,800	45,500	42,200	42,600	42,900	44,700
Married couples	39,900	40,400	40,400	40,800	40,900	41,200	41,600	43,800
Other elderly families	52,800	51,600	52,000	56,600	46,500	46,900	47,300	48,100
Non-elderly families[2]	57,200	56,000	56,500	56,400	57,200	58,400	60,500	62,200
Married couples	55,300	53,500	52,200	53,000	54,900	57,000	57,900	57,800
No earner	28,700	28,700	28,700	27,700	29,000	29,900	28,900	29,700
One earner	44,200	43,800	44,200	44,000	43,100	45,900	46,700	48,500
Two earners	62,800	61,400	59,500	60,500	64,200	65,100	67,000	66,100
Two-parent families with children[3]	61,300	59,600	60,400	60,200	60,500	62,300	65,000	67,200
No earner	21,500	23,000	22,400	21,000	22,700	24,600	23,600	23,200
One earner	45,300	45,100	46,000	44,300	46,300	44,800	50,100	50,700
Two earners	62,700	61,200	62,300	62,300	63,000	64,500	66,700	68,000
Three or more earners	76,700	76,300	76,700	77,100	78,700	81,000	80,800	84,400
Married couples with other relatives	75,200	76,000	76,000	74,100	78,500	78,300	79,700	84,300
Lone-parent families[3]	29,300	28,500	29,700	29,600	28,400	28,400	30,800	31,900
Male lone-parent families	40,900	37,700	37,600	37,300	40,600	40,100	42,600	42,600
Female lone-parent families	27,800	27,000	28,400	28,300	26,600	26,500	28,700	29,900
No earner	18,200	18,800	18,400	18,600	17,400	16,400	16,900	17,500
One earner	30,000	28,600	29,800	29,700	30,300	29,300	30,200	30,800
Two or more earners	41,400	41,900	46,400	45,900	41,700	43,700	46,700	46,800
Other non-elderly families	43,100	45,100	45,000	45,200	52,000	51,100	54,300	55,400
Unattached individuals	**23,700**	**23,500**	**23,400**	**23,600**	**23,200**	**23,200**	**23,700**	**24,900**
Elderly male	24,600	23,100	25,500	24,800	25,400	25,700	26,500	25,600
Non-earner	24,300	22,100	23,400	23,400	23,600	24,000	24,000	24,500
Earner	27,700	31,600	44,400	38,200	39,700	35,700	41,200	33,000
Elderly female	20,500	19,600	20,000	20,900	21,500	21,900	21,700	21,700
Non-earner	20,200	19,300	19,700	20,600	21,100	21,200	21,100	21,200
Earner	26,000	30,100	27,800	29,600	33,100	31,100	30,200	28,900
Non-elderly male	25,900	25,900	26,000	25,600	25,200	25,000	25,700	27,000
Non-earner	12,800	12,600	13,100	12,200	11,000	10,400	10,500	10,100
Earner	28,900	29,900	29,400	29,000	28,900	29,300	29,700	30,500
Non-elderly female	22,500	23,000	21,700	22,600	21,000	20,900	21,500	23,800
Non-earner	13,100	12,900	14,700	13,300	10,800	11,500	10,800	10,300
Earner	25,800	26,400	24,600	25,900	25,000	24,800	25,900	28,700

See notes and source at end of table.

Table 18.3 Average income after tax, by economic family type, 1992 to 2006 (continued)

	2000	2001	2002	2003	2004	2005	2006
				$ 2006 constant			
Economic families	**61,600**	**64,100**	**64,200**	**63,600**	**65,200**	**66,000**	**67,600**
Elderly families[1]	44,400	45,900	46,500	46,300	47,200	49,100	50,100
Married couples	43,100	44,800	45,100	45,200	46,700	47,200	48,300
Other elderly families	49,200	50,200	51,900	50,200	49,000	56,000	56,600
Non-elderly families[2]	64,500	67,100	67,000	66,600	68,300	69,000	70,800
Married couples	58,600	63,300	62,500	60,900	61,500	63,900	65,800
No earner	30,300	34,900	31,300	31,400	29,800	31,200	34,200
One earner	47,500	52,600	48,900	48,700	51,300	53,300	52,600
Two earners	66,300	70,800	71,200	68,400	68,500	71,500	73,700
Two-parent families with children[3]	69,600	72,100	72,900	73,400	76,100	74,500	76,400
No earner	22,700	25,500	25,400	23,600	25,000	21,600	26,000
One earner	50,800	52,900	55,600	56,400	55,700	53,700	54,900
Two earners	70,600	72,800	73,100	73,400	75,900	75,200	75,800
Three or more earners	87,900	91,300	90,200	90,700	95,400	93,400	96,700
Married couples with other relatives	89,400	88,900	88,100	88,500	90,600	94,800	97,700
Lone-parent families[3]	34,500	35,800	34,200	34,800	35,000	39,600	40,300
Male lone-parent families	46,000	44,800	45,400	48,300	46,000	52,500	54,500
Female lone-parent families	32,100	33,900	31,500	31,800	32,500	36,700	37,000
No earner	17,000	17,900	17,100	16,800	18,200	18,100	20,000
One earner	31,800	33,500	31,700	31,500	32,400	37,000	36,400
Two or more earners	51,100	53,400	46,700	48,700	46,800	49,300	50,300
Other non-elderly families	55,900	58,900	60,400	56,200	59,000	57,600	59,100
Unattached individuals	**25,100**	**26,300**	**26,900**	**27,100**	**27,000**	**27,500**	**28,500**
Elderly male	24,600	26,400	26,300	27,100	26,800	27,500	27,800
Non-earner	23,400	25,100	24,500	24,300	25,500	24,500	25,000
Earner	31,200	34,400	34,200	36,600	31,400	39,600	38,200
Elderly female	22,000	23,400	23,900	23,300	24,300	23,600	25,500
Non-earner	21,500	22,500	23,500	22,800	23,500	22,700	24,700
Earner	30,000	35,000	29,000	27,700	31,500	31,400	32,300
Non-elderly male	28,200	29,100	29,500	30,000	29,400	30,500	31,700
Non-earner	10,000	11,800	11,500	12,100	11,600	11,800	11,900
Earner	31,500	32,400	33,200	33,800	32,800	34,600	35,100
Non-elderly female	22,900	24,100	25,200	25,400	25,300	25,700	26,000
Non-earner	10,300	11,900	11,800	12,600	12,500	14,100	13,300
Earner	27,100	28,100	29,400	29,100	29,200	28,700	29,300

Note: "Average income after tax" refers to total income, which includes government transfers, minus income tax.

1. Families in which the major income earner is 65 years of age and older; for data prior to 1996, the head of family is 65 or older.
2. Families in which the major income earner is less than 65 years of age.
3. Families with children less than 18 years of age.

Source: Statistics Canada, CANSIM table 202-0603.

Table 18.4 Average income after tax, by economic family type and by province, 2006

	Canada	Newfoundland and Labrador	Prince Edward Island	Nova Scotia	New Brunswick	Quebec
	$ 2006 constant					
Economic families	**67,600**	**53,200**	**56,000**	**58,900**	**54,600**	**59,100**
Elderly families[1]	**50,100**	36,600	45,800	44,200	42,000	42,500
Married couples	**48,300**	36,500	43,100	44,800	39,700	40,400
Other elderly families	**56,600**	36,700	F	42,600	49,500	50,400
Non-elderly families[2]	**70,800**	56,700	57,900	62,000	56,900	62,000
Married couples	**65,800**	49,900	55,500	54,500	52,200	56,700
No earner	**34,200**	F	F	35,700	26,900	33,300
One earner	**52,600**	43,800	42,700	46,100	41,600	50,300
Two earners	**73,700**	56,000	60,800	60,400	60,500	61,800
Two-parent families with children[3]	**76,400**	64,000	63,400	68,700	64,300	70,100
No earner	**26,000**	F	F	F	F	F
One earner	**54,900**	52,900	F	49,400	42,600	50,000
Two earners	**75,800**	65,200	62,300	67,000	64,900	71,500
Three or more earners	**96,700**	74,400	73,000	89,900	79,800	84,100
Married couples with other relatives	**97,700**	76,100	80,900	87,800	77,200	84,000
Lone-parent families[3]	**40,300**	31,500	29,800	35,500	30,800	40,900
Male lone-parent families	**54,500**	F	F	F	F	56,600[E]
Female lone-parent families	**37,000**	29,900	29,200	32,500	29,600	35,900
No earner	**20,000**	F	F	F	F	19,100
One earner	**36,400**	28,300	27,400	33,200	28,000	34,100
Two or more earners	**50,300**	F	F	F	F	49,700
Other non-elderly families	**59,100**	52,600	49,700	55,400	45,200	48,800
Unattached individuals	**28,500**	**22,200**	**21,400**	**23,100**	**21,900**	**25,100**
Elderly male	**27,800**	21,700	F	23,600	23,600	23,800
Non-earner	**25,000**	21,400	F	22,900	21,400	21,200
Earner	**38,200**	F	F	F	F	34,400
Elderly female	**25,500**	18,400	21,500	24,200	19,700	25,100
Non-earner	**24,700**	18,400	21,100	23,300	19,400	24,400
Earner	**32,300**	F	F	F	F	31,200
Non-elderly male	**31,700**	25,400	20,600	24,200	23,800	26,500
Non-earner	**11,900**	F	F	13,600[E]	8,700	11,600
Earner	**35,100**	30,500	23,600	26,400	27,600	29,400
Non-elderly female	**26,000**	20,900	21,100	21,300	20,200	23,800
Non-earner	**13,300**	F	F	11,700	12,200	14,000
Earner	**29,300**	26,700	24,300	23,700	22,600	27,000

See notes and source at end of table.

Table 18.4 Average income after tax, by economic family type, by province, 2006 (continued)

	Ontario	Manitoba	Saskatch-ewan	Alberta	British Columbia
	$ 2006 constant				
Economic families	**72,400**	**62,100**	**63,200**	**80,400**	**68,000**
Elderly families[1]	53,900	50,200	46,500	53,300	55,800
Married couples	51,900	48,400	46,700	51,800	53,500
Other elderly families	60,200	57,000	45,600	61,900	64,600
Non-elderly families[2]	75,700	64,200	66,500	84,200	70,400
Married couples	69,400	58,500	65,500	85,600	70,200
No earner	35,500	F	F	F	F
One earner	53,100	42,600	49,900	64,900	56,900
Two earners	79,400	67,000	70,600	91,700	78,300
Two-parent families with children[3]	79,600	66,400	74,000	88,900	74,900
No earner	F	F	F	F	F
One earner	49,900	47,200	50,100	92,800E	51,700
Two earners	80,900	63,900	70,100	78,900	75,700
Three or more earners	100,200	86,500	96,000	112,800	95,900
Married couples with other relatives	106,700	98,100	88,500	115,200	87,000
Lone-parent families[3]	42,000	35,100	31,500	47,000	36,800
Male lone-parent families	56,100	40,100	34,700E	65,300	47,400E
Female lone-parent families	39,200	34,000	30,800	42,600	34,800
No earner	21,500	F	F	F	F
One earner	40,300	31,600	30,100	39,600	32,700
Two or more earners	51,300	F	41,900	57,400	47,400
Other non-elderly families	64,400	62,700	59,000	62,300	60,300
Unattached individuals	**30,600**	**24,800**	**25,100**	**35,100**	**29,600**
Elderly male	32,800	25,200	26,500	25,100	29,000
Non-earner	29,000	22,800	25,400	26,500	25,500
Earner	45,300	F	F	F	F
Elderly female	26,800	22,800	24,000	25,000	26,900
Non-earner	26,200	22,600	21,800	23,500	26,400
Earner	33,000	F	40,500E	33,400	31,300
Non-elderly male	33,500	27,200	27,900	42,100	32,700
Non-earner	12,800	16,800E	6,600E	F	9,700E
Earner	37,500	28,500	30,800	44,100	36,200
Non-elderly female	28,300	22,700	21,700	29,200	26,500
Non-earner	14,300	9,100E	10,100E	12,200	11,800E
Earner	32,100	25,500	23,500	31,100	29,900

Note: "Average income after tax" refers to total income, which includes government transfers, minus income tax.

1. Families in which the major income earner is 65 years of age and older.
2. Families in which the major income earner is less than 65 of age.
3. Families with children less than 18 years of age.

Source: Statistics Canada, CANSIM table 202-0603.

Table 18.5 People with low income after tax, by age group, sex and economic family type, 1992 to 2006

	1992	1993	1994	1995	1996	1997	1998
				%			
Both sexes	**13.3**	**14.3**	**13.8**	**14.6**	**15.7**	**15.3**	**13.7**
0 to 17 years	14.9	16.7	15.8	17.6	18.5	17.8	15.5
18 to 64 years	13.2	13.9	13.9	14.6	15.7	15.5	14.0
65 and older	9.8	11.5	8.6	8.6	9.8	9.1	8.6
Males	12.2	13.1	12.5	13.7	14.9	14.3	12.9
0 to 17 years	15.1	16.4	15.4	17.3	19.0	18.0	16.1
18 to 64 years	12.2	12.8	12.7	13.8	14.7	14.3	12.9
65 and older	5.1	7.2	4.1	3.8	5.6	5.6	5.4
Females	14.3	15.5	14.9	15.6	16.5	16.3	14.5
0 to 17 years	14.8	17.1	16.3	17.9	18.1	17.5	14.9
18 to 64 years	14.2	14.9	15.1	15.4	16.6	16.7	15.0
65 and older	13.4	14.8	12.0	12.3	13.0	11.8	11.1
Economic families	**10.1**	**11.2**	**10.6**	**11.6**	**12.5**	**11.9**	**10.4**
Males	9.2	10.1	9.6	10.8	11.7	10.9	9.6
Females	11.0	12.3	11.6	12.4	13.2	12.8	11.1
0 to 17 years	14.9	16.7	15.8	17.6	18.5	17.8	15.5
Two-parent families	9.1	10.6	10.2	11.8	12.4	11.6	9.9
Female lone-parent families	48.7	49.5	48.9	51.9	55.8	53.2	46.1
Other economic families	14.0	19.5	21.5	20.5	20.4	23.6	20.0
18 to 64 years	9.0	9.8	9.5	10.3	11.2	10.6	9.2
Males	7.4	8.0	8.0	9.1	9.8	8.9	7.8
Females	10.5	11.4	10.8	11.5	12.5	12.1	10.6
65 and older	2.6	3.6	2.3	1.9	2.8E	3.4E	3.3E
Males	2.5	3.9	2.1	1.9	2.5E	3.0E	2.7E
Females	2.7	3.3	2.5	1.9	3.1E	3.8E	3.9E
Unattached individuals	**35.1**	**35.5**	**35.0**	**35.0**	**37.2**	**37.9**	**35.2**
Males	33.4	34.1	32.5	33.8	35.6	36.7	33.8
Females	36.6	36.8	37.4	36.2	38.7	39.2	36.5
0 to 64 years	38.5	38.4	39.9	39.7	41.7	43.8	40.4
Males	36.0	36.3	35.7	37.5	38.2	39.8	36.5
Females	41.9	41.4	45.7	42.5	46.8	49.5	45.8
65 and older	25.9	28.1	22.3	23.1	25.4	22.1	20.9
Males	16.9	21.3	13.1	12.1	19.8	17.3	17.5
Females	28.8	30.4	25.3	26.8	27.2	23.7	22.1

See note and source at end of table.

Table 18.5 People with low income after tax, by age group, sex and economic family type, 1992 to 2006 (continued)

	1999	2000	2001	2002	2003	2004	2005	2006
	%							
Both sexes	**13.0**	**12.5**	**11.2**	**11.6**	**11.6**	**11.4**	**10.8**	**10.5**
0 to 17 years	14.4	13.8	12.1	12.3	12.5	13.0	11.7	11.3
18 to 64 years	13.4	12.9	11.7	12.1	12.2	11.9	11.4	11.3
65 and older	7.9	7.6	6.7	7.6	6.8	5.6	6.1	5.4
Males	12.4	11.4	10.3	10.7	11.0	10.8	10.5	10.1
0 to 17 years	14.7	13.4	12.0	12.7	12.8	13.1	12.2	11.3
18 to 64 years	12.8	11.8	10.6	11.0	11.5	11.3	11.1	10.9
65 and older	4.8	4.6	4.6	4.9	4.4	3.5	3.3	3.4
Females	13.6	13.6	12.1	12.4	12.2	11.9	11.2	10.9
0 to 17 years	14.1	14.2	12.2	11.8	12.2	12.8	11.1	11.3
18 to 64 years	14.1	14.1	12.8	13.1	12.9	12.6	11.8	11.6
65 and older	10.4	10.0	8.3	9.7	8.7	7.3	8.4	7.0
Economic families	**9.7**	**9.3**	**8.1**	**8.6**	**8.7**	**8.2**	**7.5**	**7.3**
Males	9.2	8.4	7.4	8.0	8.1	7.7	7.1	6.9
Females	10.3	10.1	8.7	9.2	9.2	8.8	7.9	7.8
0 to 17 years	14.4	13.8	12.1	12.3	12.5	13.0	11.7	11.3
Two-parent families	9.4	9.5	8.3	7.4	7.9	8.4	7.8	7.7
Female lone-parent families	41.9	40.1	37.4	43.0	41.4	40.4	33.4	32.3
Other economic families	21.4	12.8	9.1E	9.1E	12.2E	13.0E	11.8E	9.5E
18 to 64 years	8.8	8.4	7.3	8.1	8.1	7.5	6.9	6.8
Males	7.8	7.4	6.3	7.0	7.2	6.4	6.0	6.1
Females	9.8	9.5	8.3	9.2	9.0	8.4	7.7	7.4
65 and older	2.3E	2.1E	1.9E	2.4	2.2	1.7E	1.2E	1.4E
Males	2.1E	1.7E	1.9E	2.3E	2.0E	1.7E	1.1E	1.1E
Females	2.4E	2.5E	1.9E	2.4E	2.3E	1.6E	1.3E	1.7E
Unattached individuals	**34.1**	**32.9**	**30.8**	**29.5**	**29.7**	**30.1**	**30.4**	**29.2**
Males	33.0	30.0	28.4	27.1	28.4	29.2	29.8	28.8
Females	35.2	35.7	33.3	32.0	30.9	31.0	31.0	29.6
0 to 64 years	38.8	37.3	35.3	33.2	33.9	35.0	34.3	33.7
Males	35.5	32.1	30.3	29.0	30.7	32.0	32.3	31.2
Females	43.6	44.3	42.2	39.0	38.1	39.3	37.1	37.1
65 and older	21.1	20.6	18.1	19.4	17.7	15.4	18.5	15.5
Males	17.2	17.6	16.8	15.9	14.7	11.5	13.6	14.0
Females	22.5	21.7	18.6	20.7	18.9	16.9	20.3	16.1

Note: Prevalence of low income shows the proportion of people living below the low-income cut-offs within a given group; these cut-offs were determined from an analysis of the 1992 Family Expenditure Survey data.

Source: Statistics Canada, CANSIM table 202-0802.

Table 18.6 Average household expenditures, by province and territory, 2006

	Canada	Newfoundland and Labrador	Prince Edward Island	Nova Scotia	New Brunswick	Quebec	Ontario
				$			
Total expenditures	**67,736**	**53,939**	**54,689**	**56,319**	**54,101**	**56,559**	**73,318**
Total current consumption	**48,765**	39,520	41,700	41,613	39,675	41,122	52,664
Food	**7,046**	6,322	6,557	6,210	6,082	6,935	7,331
Shelter	**12,986**	8,605	9,966	10,234	9,093	10,048	15,163
Household operations	**3,251**	2,973	3,045	3,206	2,872	2,616	3,529
Household furnishings and equipment	**2,131**	1,831	1,789	1,876	1,615	1,834	2,234
Clothing	**2,870**	2,622	2,215	2,323	2,193	2,401	3,185
Transportation	**9,240**	7,824	8,145	7,951	8,571	7,536	9,645
Health care	**1,867**	1,510	1,981	1,695	1,724	1,946	1,609
Personal care	**1,158**	1,021	1,018	1,040	969	1,072	1,233
Recreation	**3,975**	3,350	3,128	3,066	3,082	3,275	4,232
Reading materials and other printed matter	**264**	199	261	246	216	238	268
Education	**1,157**	705	915	1,064	946	665	1,402
Tobacco products and alcoholic beverages	**1,475**	1,628	1,714	1,567	1,246	1,441	1,391
Games of chance (net amount)	**258**	280	246	251	243	235	262
Miscellaneous	**1,087**	652	719	885	825	881	1,180
Personal income taxes	**13,634**	10,074	8,046	10,074	9,590	11,218	14,869
Personal insurance payments and pension contributions	**3,832**	3,202	3,661	3,325	3,489	3,453	3,977
Gifts of money and contributions	**1,505**	1,143	1,282	1,308	1,346	765	1,808

See source at end of table.

Table 18.6 Average household expenditures, by province and territory, 2006 (continued)

	Manitoba	Saskatchewan	Alberta	British Columbia	Yukon	Northwest Territories	Nunavut
				$			
Total expenditures	**59,230**	**59,364**	**85,236**	**71,580**	..	..	..
Total current consumption	41,001	42,244	59,736	52,334	..	..	..
Food	6,101	5,765	7,449	7,156	..	..	..
Shelter	10,176	10,333	14,690	14,521	..	..	..
Household operations	2,782	2,928	3,984	3,453	..	..	..
Household furnishings and equipment	1,696	1,900	3,036	2,095	..	..	..
Clothing	2,346	2,366	3,588	2,896	..	..	..
Transportation	8,113	8,730	12,162	10,200	..	..	..
Health care	1,728	1,724	2,435	2,178	..	..	..
Personal care	1,017	1,031	1,374	1,098	..	..	..
Recreation	3,287	3,580	5,890	3,894	..	..	..
Reading materials and other printed matter	257	238	323	291	..	..	..
Education	909	855	1,341	1,529	..	..	..
Tobacco products and alcoholic beverages	1,382	1,490	1,837	1,515	..	..	..
Games of chance (net amount)	300	272	280	260	..	..	..
Miscellaneous	907	1,031	1,347	1,246	..	..	..
Personal income taxes	12,282	11,920	18,616	13,929	..	..	..
Personal insurance payments and pension contributions	3,700	3,609	4,851	3,725	..	..	..
Gifts of money and contributions	2,248	1,592	2,032	1,592	..	..	..

Source: Statistics Canada, CANSIM table 203-0001.

Table 18.7 Assets and debts held by family units, median amounts, 1999 and 2005

	1999			2005		
	$ 2005 constant	thousands of family units	% holding assets and debts	$ 2005 constant	thousands of family units	% holding assets and debts
Assets	**184,622**	**12,216**	**100.0**	**229,930**	**13,348**	**100.0**
Private pension assets[1]	57,602	8,511	69.7	68,020	9,417	70.6
RRSPs, LIRAs, RRIFs and other[2]	23,041	7,197	58.9	30,000	7,748	58.0
EPPs[3]	56,214	5,611	45.9	68,305	6,490	48.6
Financial assets, non-pension	5,299	10,965	89.8	6,100	11,932	89.4
Deposits in financial institutions	2,880	10,685	87.5	3,600	11,613	87.0
Mutual funds, investment funds and income trusts	14,976	1,706	14.0	24,200	1,641	12.3
Stocks	10,368	1,207	9.9	11,500	1,321	9.9
Bonds (savings and other)	2,880	1,715	14.0	2,500	1,394	10.4
Other financial assets[4]	5,530	1,615	13.2	6,000	2,329	17.5
Non-financial assets	115,204	12,216	100.0	141,700	13,348	100.0
Principal residence	144,005	7,278	59.6	180,000	8,265	61.9
Other real estate	72,578	1,987	16.3	85,000	2,142	16.1
Vehicles	10,368	9,346	76.5	11,557	10,062	75.4
Other non-financial assets[5]	11,520	12,216	100.0	10,000	13,348	100.0
Equity in business	10,368	2,325	19.0	15,794	2,221	16.6
Debts	**32,257**	**8,215**	**67.3**	**44,500**	**9,263**	**69.4**
Mortgages	79,490	4,191	34.3	93,000	4,870	36.5
Principal residence	76,610	3,908	32.0	90,000	4,557	34.1
Other real estate	69,122	563	4.6	90,000	624	4.7
Line of credit	5,760	1,880	15.4	9,000	3,323	24.9
Credit card and installment debt[6]	2,074	4,648	38.0	2,400	5,252	39.3
Student loans	8,295	1,435	11.7	9,000	1,574	11.8
Vehicle loans	10,368	2,541	20.8	11,000	3,449	25.8
Other debt	4,608	1,983	16.2	6,000	1,878	14.1

Note: Family units include economic families.

1. Excludes public plans administered or sponsored by governments: Old Age Security including the Guaranteed Income Supplement and the Spouse's Allowance, as well as the Canada Pension Plan / Quebec Pension Plan.
2. Registered Retirement Savings Plans (RRSPs), Locked-in-Retirement Accounts (LIRAs), Registered Retirement Income Funds (RRIFs). Other includes Deferred Profit Sharing Plans (DPSPs), annuities and other miscellaneous pension assets.
3. Employer-sponsored Registered Pension Plans (EPPs). Valued on a termination basis. Only plan membership to the time of the Survey of Financial Security was considered. Interest rates are assumed based on current market rates.
4. Includes Registered Education Savings Plans (RESPs), treasury bills, mortgage-backed securities, money held in trust, money owed to the respondent and other miscellaneous financial assets, including shares of privately-held companies.
5. The value of the contents of the respondent's principal residence, valuables and collectibles, copyrights and patents, etc.
6. Includes major credit cards and retail store cards, gasoline station cards, etc. Instalment debt is the total amount owing on deferred payment or instalment plans where the purchased item is to be paid for over a period of time.

Source: Statistics Canada, Survey of Financial Security.

Table 18.8 Assets and debts held by family units, by education level, median amounts, 1999 and 2005

	1999		2005	
	$ 2005 constant	thousands of family units	$ 2005 constant	thousands of family units
All education levels[1]				
Assets[2]	184,622	12,216	229,930	13,348
Debts	32,257	8,215	44,500	9,263
Net worth (assets less debts)	120,451	12,209	148,350	13,342
Less than high school				
Assets[2]	118,660	3,375	114,198	2,813
Debts	13,248	1,723	14,400	1,408
Net worth (assets less debts)	87,901	3,370	92,433	2,806
Graduated high school				
Assets[2]	168,773	2,869	202,000	3,508
Debts	32,031	2,007	42,073	2,470
Net worth (assets less debts)	103,039	2,868	120,007	3,508
Non-university postsecondary certificate				
Assets[2]	191,579	3,434	251,125	3,737
Debts	38,017	2,579	45,500	2,907
Net worth (assets less debts)	117,841	3,432	171,000	3,737
University degree or certificate				
Assets[2]	313,354	2,539	370,500	3,290
Debts	54,155	1,907	78,130	2,478
Net worth (assets less debts)	220,161	2,539	237,400	3,290

Note: Family units include economic families.

1. "Education level" refers to the education level of an unattached individual or, for families, the major income recipient.
2. Includes Employer-sponsored Registered Pension Plans. These plans were valued on a termination basis. Only plan membership to the time of the Survey of Financial Security was considered. Interest rates are assumed based on current market rates. Excludes public plans administered or sponsored by governments: Old Age Security including the Guaranteed Income Supplement and the Spouse's Allowance, as well as the Canada Pension Plan / Quebec Pension Plan.

Source: Statistics Canada, Survey of Financial Security.

Table 18.9 Net worth of family units, by sex and age group, median amounts, 2005

	Family units	Net worth[1]		
	%	%	median amount[2]	debt-to-asset ratio
Both sexes, all ages	**100.0**	**100.0**	**148,350**	**0.14**
Less than 65	82.0	76.0	120,200	0.17
Less than 35	25.0	5.3	18,750	0.39
35 to 44	21.8	18.2	135,408	0.24
45 to 54	20.7	26.6	231,900	0.13
55 to 64	14.5	25.9	407,417	0.07
65 and older	18.0	24.0	303,167	0.02
Males, all ages	**100.0**	**100.0**	**184,964**	**0.14**
Less than 65	83.4	75.9	151,471	0.17
Less than 35	23.9	5.2	28,203	0.41
35 to 44	22.5	18.1	150,225	0.25
45 to 54	21.7	25.9	273,483	0.13
55 to 64	15.3	26.8	448,795	0.07
65 and older	16.6	24.1	405,000	0.07
Females, all ages	**100.0**	**100.0**	**105,470**	**0.13**
Less than 65	79.9	76.2	76,499	0.16
Less than 35	26.6	5.6	9,900	0.37
35 to 44	20.7	18.6	96,856	0.22
45 to 54	19.2	28.1	178,650	0.14
55 to 64	13.4	24.0	345,877	0.07
65 and older	20.1	23.8	204,833	F

Notes: Family units include economic families.
Sex and age groups refer to an unattached individual or, for families, the major income recipient.
1. Net worth includes Employer-sponsored Registered Pension Plans valued on a termination basis.
2. $ 2005 constant.
Source: Statistics Canada, Survey of Financial Security.

Table 18.10 Family units and net worth, by net worth group, 2005

	Family units		Net worth[1]	
	thousands	%	$ millions 2005 constant	%
All family units' net worth groups[2]	13,348	100.0	4,862,486	100.0
Negative net worth	872	6.5	-12,751	-0.3
Less than $5,000	1,220	9.1	2,068	0.0
$5,000 to $14,999	854	6.4	7,762	0.2
$15,000 to $29,999	791	5.9	17,149	0.4
$30,000 to $49,999	602	4.5	23,235	0.5
$50,000 to $74,999	760	5.7	46,275	1.0
$75,000 to $99,999	583	4.4	51,702	1.1
$100,000 to $149,999	1,020	7.6	127,010	2.6
$150,000 to $249,999	1,487	11.1	293,647	6.0
$250,000 to $499,999	2,253	16.9	813,922	16.7
$500,000 to $999,999	1,807	13.5	1,233,616	25.4
$1,000,000 and over	1,098	8.2	2,258,851	46.5

Note: Family units include economic families.
1. Net worth includes Employer-sponsored Registered Pension Plans valued on a termination basis.
2. Includes family units with net worth of $0.
Source: Statistics Canada, Survey of Financial Security.

Table 18.11 RPP members, by type of plan, contributory status and province, 2001 to 2007

	2001	2002	2003	2004	2005	2006	2007
	% of total						
Newfoundland and Labrador	**1.8**	**1.8**	**1.8**	**1.8**	**1.8**	**1.8**	**1.6**
Defined benefit	1.5	1.5	1.5	1.5	1.4	1.4	1.4
Defined contribution	3.8	3.7	3.8	3.7	3.8	3.9	2.7
Contributory	2.1	2.1	2.1	2.1	2.0	2.0	1.7
Non-contributory	1.0	1.1	1.1	1.1	0.9	1.0	1.0
Prince Edward Island	**0.3**	**0.3**	**0.3**	**0.4**	**0.4**	**0.4**	**0.3**
Defined benefit	0.3	0.3	0.3	0.3	0.4	0.3	0.3
Defined contribution	0.5	0.4	0.4	0.5	0.4	0.4	0.5
Contributory	0.4	0.4	0.4	0.4	0.4	0.4	0.4
Non-contributory	0.2	0.1	0.1	0.1	0.1	0.1	0.1
Nova Scotia	**3.0**	**3.0**	**2.9**	**2.9**	**3.0**	**3.0**	**2.9**
Defined benefit	2.9	2.9	2.8	2.9	2.9	2.9	2.8
Defined contribution	3.7	3.7	3.6	3.5	3.7	3.8	4.0
Contributory	3.2	3.3	3.1	3.1	3.2	3.2	3.1
Non-contributory	2.3	2.3	2.3	2.4	2.2	2.2	2.1
New Brunswick	**2.2**	**2.3**	**2.3**	**2.3**	**2.3**	**2.3**	**2.1**
Defined benefit	2.1	2.2	2.2	2.2	2.2	2.1	1.9
Defined contribution	2.5	2.8	2.9	2.8	3.0	3.2	3.0
Contributory	2.6	2.7	2.6	2.6	2.6	2.5	2.3
Non-contributory	1.1	1.2	1.3	1.3	1.3	1.3	1.3
Quebec	**24.0**	**24.4**	**24.1**	**24.8**	**25.0**	**25.1**	**25.1**
Defined benefit	25.3	25.9	25.8	26.7	27.0	27.2	27.1
Defined contribution	15.6	15.7	15.9	16.1	15.8	16.0	17.0
Contributory	28.1	28.2	28.0	28.9	28.7	28.2	28.2
Non-contributory	13.0	14.0	13.0	12.7	13.0	13.6	12.2
Ontario	**39.2**	**38.7**	**39.2**	**38.8**	**38.8**	**38.4**	**38.2**
Defined benefit	39.8	39.7	40.4	39.7	39.7	39.2	38.8
Defined contribution	37.0	36.6	36.6	37.6	37.9	37.1	37.7
Contributory	34.8	34.3	34.8	34.5	34.3	34.5	34.9
Non-contributory	51.2	50.7	52.1	51.9	53.6	53.3	52.1
Manitoba	**4.3**	**4.3**	**4.2**	**4.3**	**4.3**	**4.2**	**4.2**
Defined benefit	3.8	3.8	3.4	3.4	3.4	3.4	3.4
Defined contribution	6.1	6.1	5.9	5.8	5.8	6.0	5.8
Contributory	4.8	4.8	4.7	4.7	4.7	4.5	4.4
Non-contributory	3.1	3.1	2.8	2.8	2.9	3.2	3.3
Saskatchewan	**3.5**	**3.6**	**3.6**	**3.6**	**3.6**	**3.6**	**3.5**
Defined benefit	2.5	2.5	2.5	2.4	2.4	2.4	2.6
Defined contribution	9.9	10.2	10.3	10.1	10.2	10.1	8.8
Contributory	4.1	4.1	4.2	4.1	4.0	3.9	3.8
Non-contributory	1.8	2.0	2.0	2.0	2.0	2.2	2.3
Alberta	**8.5**	**8.9**	**9.0**	**9.1**	**9.1**	**9.4**	**9.7**
Defined benefit	8.1	8.6	8.8	8.9	8.8	9.3	9.5
Defined contribution	10.1	10.6	10.9	10.7	10.5	10.5	11.0
Contributory	8.1	8.4	8.5	8.5	8.5	8.7	8.6
Non-contributory	9.4	10.1	10.3	11.0	11.0	12.2	14.4
British Columbia	**12.7**	**12.2**	**11.9**	**11.5**	**11.4**	**11.4**	**11.7**
Defined benefit	13.1	12.0	11.7	11.4	11.2	11.2	11.5
Defined contribution	10.4	9.7	9.2	8.9	8.6	8.7	9.1
Contributory	11.3	11.2	10.9	10.5	11.1	11.6	11.9
Non-contributory	16.5	15.1	14.6	14.5	12.5	10.5	10.9

Note: The reference date for number of registered pension plans and their terms and conditions is January 1. However, the data on plan members' contributions and assets are as of the plan's year end in the previous calendar year.

Source: Statistics Canada, CANSIM table 280-0008.

Table 18.12 RRSP contributions, by contributor characteristics, 2000 to 2006

	2000	2001	2002	2003	2004	2005	2006
				number			
Taxfilers	21,611,830	21,886,860	21,979,210	22,465,770	22,725,310	23,311,690	23,338,370
				%			
Male taxfilers	49	49	49	49	48	48	48
Female taxfilers	51	51	51	51	52	52	52
				number			
Total RRSP contributors	6,291,170	6,241,050	5,991,440	5,948,340	6,002,350	6,135,980	6,196,050
				%			
Male RRSP contributors	55	55	54	54	54	54	54
Female RRSP contributors	45	45	46	46	46	46	46
				years			
Average age of RRSP contributors	43	43	43	43	44	44	44
				%			
Age groups of RRSP contributors							
0 to 24 years	5	5	4	4	4	4	4
25 to 34 years	21	21	21	20	20	20	20
35 to 44 years	30	30	29	28	28	27	26
45 to 54 years	28	28	28	29	29	30	30
55 to 64 years	14	14	15	16	16	17	18
65 years and over	2	2	2	2	2	3	3
Income level of RRSP contributors							
Less than $20,000	11	10	10	9	8	8	7
$20,000 or more	89	90	90	91	92	92	93
$40,000 or more	54	56	58	60	62	64	67
$60,000 or more	26	27	29	31	34	36	39
$80,000 or more	12	13	14	15	17	19	21
				$ thousands			
Total RRSP contributions	29,280,163	28,438,914	27,072,812	27,561,305	28,788,102	30,581,252	32,350,792
				%			
Male RRSP contributions	61	62	61	62	62	62	62
Female RRSP contributions	39	38	39	38	38	38	38
Income level of RRSP contributions							
Less than $20,000	4	3	3	3	3	2	2
$20,000 or more	96	97	97	97	97	98	98
$40,000 or more	76	77	79	80	82	84	85
$60,000 or more	50	52	54	57	60	62	65
$80,000 or more	31	33	35	37	40	44	47

Source: Statistics Canada, CANSIM table 111-0039.

Information and communications technology

19

Overview

Look back 30 years and you will see a world where the telephone, television and radio were the most visible information and communications technologies (ICTs).

The telecommunications services industry has changed significantly as a result of increased competition in all markets. New players have joined the industry. For instance, cable companies are delivering telecommunications services such as Internet access and local telephone service in addition to television services.

Now personal computers, cellphones and the Internet are the ICTs central to how we live our lives and conduct our business. New ICTs are being developed and marketed, older ones are being improved and transformed, and we are devoting more money and time working, playing and communicating with them.

In 2006, cable companies accounted for 54% of high-speed residential Internet subscribers. Cable companies started offering local telephone service in 2005 and, by the end of 2006, served 12% of local residential lines.

In 2006, over 99% of Canadian households had landline or mobile telephone service. Sixty-eight percent of households had home Internet access, the large majority with high-speed service; 1 in 10 households used dial-up. Canada has the highest broadband subscription rate among the G8 countries.

More than three-quarters of Canadian households reported owning a computer in 2006, while 31% of households reported buying new computer hardware.

As for businesses, 87% of private-sector organizations used the Internet in 2007, while 81% used e-mail and 41% had a

Chart 19.1
Business use of information and communications technologies

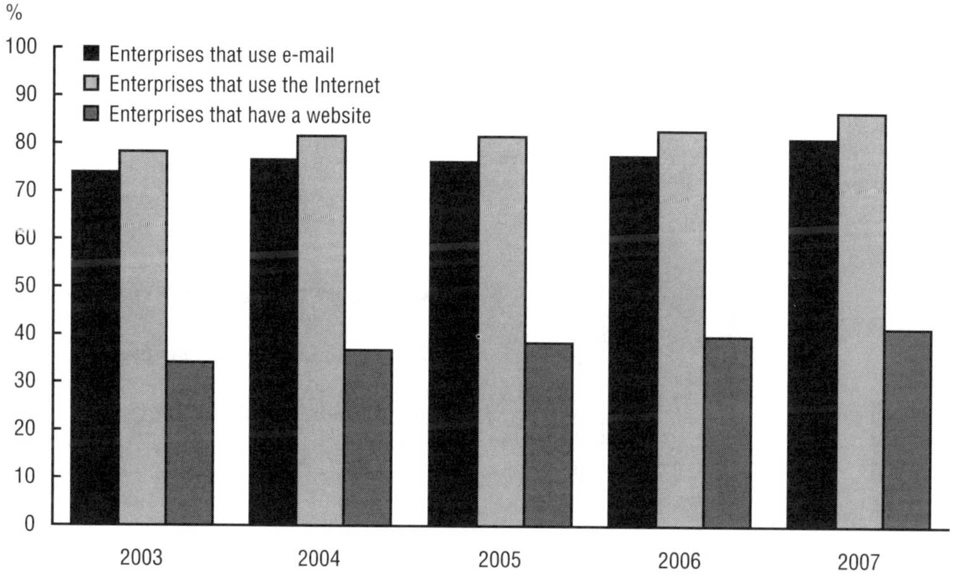

Source: Statistics Canada, CANSIM tables 358-0007 and 358-0008

website. All these rates have increased by close to 8 percentage points since 2003. Internet usage in 2007 varied significantly: from 100% for the educational services sector to 73% for the forestry sector.

Selling online

With the widespread use of the Internet, electronic commerce continues to gain strength; 2007 marked the sixth consecutive year of double-digit growth for online sales.

Total private- and public-sector Internet sales totalled $62.7 billion, up 26% from 2006. Customers outside Canada generated an estimated 19% of the value of online private-sector sales in 2007.

However, Internet sales still account for slightly less than 2% of total operating revenue of private sector firms. The private sector reported $58.2 billion in e-commerce; the public sector nearly $4.5 billion. In the private sector, while the majority of online sales are business-to-business, that dominance is decreasing: in 2007, business-to-business accounted for 62% of online sales, down from 68% in 2006, while business-to-consumer sales climbed from 32% to 38%.

Chart 19.2
Internet sales with or without online payment

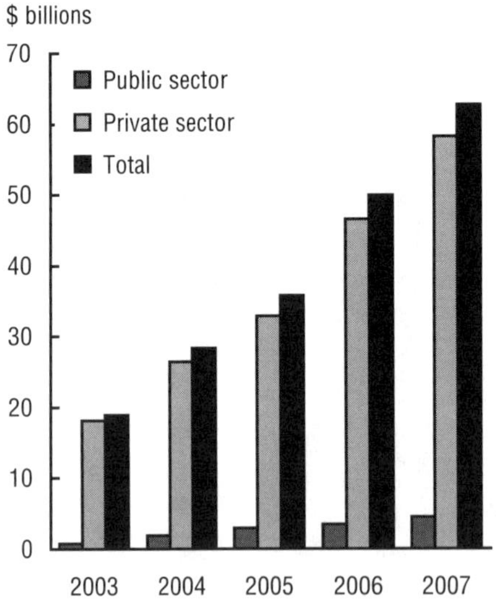

Source: Statistics Canada, CANSIM table 358-0010.

Table 19.a
Internet users, by sex and age group, 2007

	Men	Women
	%	
16 and older	74.1	72.3
34 and younger	92.3	94.0
35 to 54	78.5	81.0
55 to 64	60.8	60.9
65 and older	34.6	24.0

Source: Statistics Canada, CANSIM table 358-0124.

However, the proportion of online business-to-business versus business-to-consumer sales varied by sector. For example, in the retail trade, accommodation and food services, educational services, and arts, entertainment and recreational sectors most sales were to consumers.

Four sectors accounted for the majority of the value of online sales: wholesale trade (17%), transportation and warehousing (16%), manufacturing (15%) and retail trade (10%). Still, not all companies in those sectors are selling online. In 2007, 27% of firms in the information and cultural industries sectors, and 24% of those in the arts, entertainment and recreational industries sold goods or services online.

Spending personal time online

Almost three-quarters of Canadians aged 16 or older went online for personal reasons over the 12-month period ending in October/November 2007. Those 19.2 million people used the Internet from home for a diverse range of activities. The most popular were e-mail and general browsing.

Other common activities were finding government or health information, making travel arrangements, banking, paying bills, and ordering goods and services.

As well, 20% of home Internet users reported contributing content by posting images, writing blogs or participating in discussion groups. Of that 20%, more than half were under the age of 30.

Different age groups showed distinct differences in Internet use. For example, in 2007, 96% of people aged 16 to 24 went online, compared with 29% of those aged 65 and older.

Nearly three-quarters of both men and women used the Internet in 2007, but men were online more often and for longer periods than women.

Ongoing change in telecommunications services

The importance of telecommunications services in our lives is reflected in the revenues earned by service providers. In 2006, those revenues reached $36.1 billion, up $1.6 billion or 4.5% over 2005. This was largely attributable to the increased revenue growth from mobile phone and Internet services. Mobile phone service revenues showed 15% year-over-year growth, while Internet service revenues jumped 18%.

Change in our use of services continues to escalate, with technological improvements and increased availability of phone service alternatives. In December 2007, 24% of Canadian households reported using only a traditional landline service, down from 29% a year earlier. Conversely in December 2007, 72% of households reported having at least one cellphone, up from 67% a year earlier. Over the year, the number of cellphone-only households grew from 5% to 6%.

Chart 19.3
International trade in commercial services

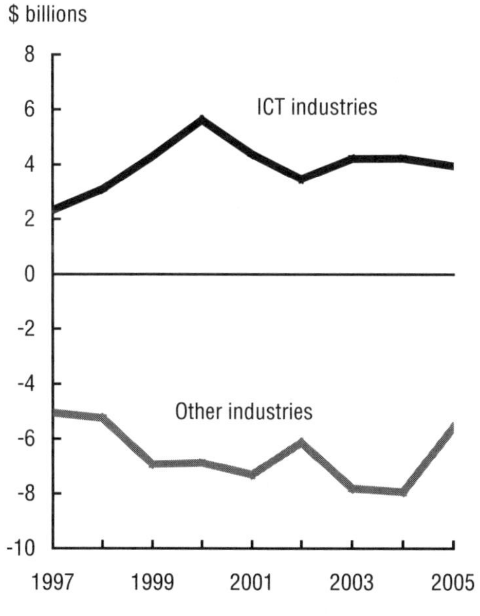

Source: Statistics Canada, Catalogue no. 11-621-MIE.

International markets for ICT services

Canada's ICT services sector does not share the usual trade balance pattern for services. Services—which comprise the four major categories of travel, transportation, commercial and government services—had a trade deficit of $12.2 billion in 2005. However, trade in ICT commercial services posted a trade surplus of $4.0 billion.

Commercial services cover a broad range of activities such as insurance, management, architecture, royalties, fees and licences, informatics and information, engineering and technical services, and research and development. ICT commercial services transactions were in such areas as computer services, software publishing and telecommunications. Within the ICT sector, the information and cultural industries accounted for 54% of the 2005 ICT commercial services trade surplus.

Internet users use other media too

There are only 24 hours in a day, but heavy Internet users still manage to fit traditional media—watching television and reading books, magazines and newspapers—into their day.

Canadians' activities were surveyed during the course of a day in 2005. It found that we spend 150 minutes of a typical day consuming traditional media, with television taking up the lion's share of that time.

Heavy Internet users (those logging more than 60 minutes a day for personal use) watch as much television as those not using the Internet: an average 121 minutes a day versus 125 minutes a day. This similarity questions the extent to which Internet users consider the Internet a replacement for television, or simply another form of information and entertainment. Heavy Internet users actually averaged 152 minutes a day of leisure time online in 2005.

Internet users are avid consumers of other media, including printed materials. They tend to spend slightly more time during the day reading books than non-users, and also tend to read books and magazines with greater frequency. Non-Internet users, though, are just as likely to be regular newspaper readers as Internet users are.

As well as reading more, Internet users are more likely to go to the movies or watch rented or purchased movies at home on a regular basis. Internet users are also keen about music: 51% listen to music they downloaded on their computer at least once a week. They are also more likely than non-Internet users to listen to music CDs, DVDs, cassettes and records.

Non-users of the Internet are more likely to say that they never read books or magazines, or watch films.

Chart 19.4
Media use for leisure, Internet users and non-users, 2005

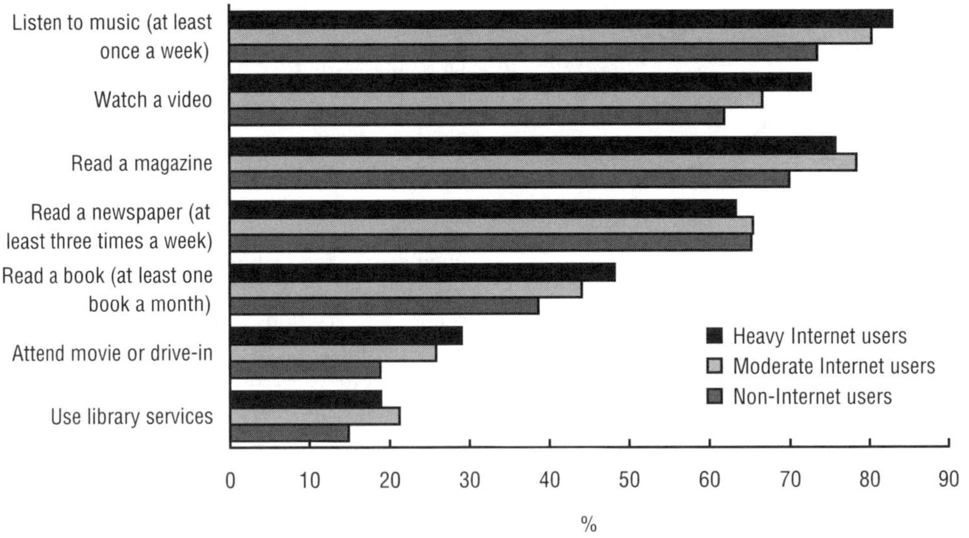

Note: Activities occur at least once a month unless otherwise stated.
Source: Statistics Canada, Catalogue no. 88-003-XIE.

Call centres: A growth industry

The annual growth in Canada's telephone call centres outstripped overall economic expansion by more than four times from 1998 to 2006. The industry's average revenue growth in that period was 28% per year, compared with 6% for the economy in general. That marks a climb in revenues from $424 million to $2.76 billion, which represents 48% of the revenues for the entire business support services industry.

Call centre revenue growth has been accompanied by employment growth. From 1991 to 2005, employment climbed 13% in the goods-producing sector and 25% in the services sector as a whole; employment in business support services rose 190%.

Business services used to be provided where they are consumed, but advances in information and communications technologies allow many services to be provided over longer distances. During the 1990s and early 2000s, more telephone call centres set up shop in areas with higher unemployment and a relatively educated population, often in smaller cities.

Canada's telephone call centres are most prevalent in the eastern provinces and in Ontario. Ontario centres generated two-thirds of 2006 call centre revenues. Nationwide, there were an average 6.8 call centres per 10,000 business establishments in 2006. However, the averages were 15.8 for Prince Edward Island, 13.1 for New Brunswick and 8.4 for Ontario.

From 2000 to 2005, there was a net increase of 96 call centres in Canada: the number of small call centres (0 to 10 employees) decreased by 73; but the number of medium-sized centres (10 to 49 employees) grew by 72 and large call centres (50 employees or more) increased by 97.

Chart 19.5
Call centres per 10,000 business establishments, 2005

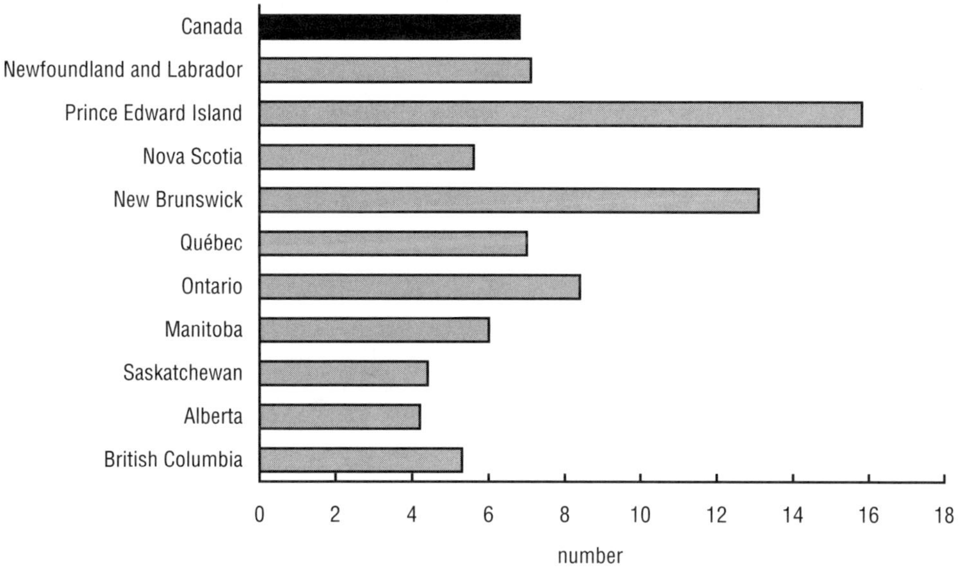

Source: Statistics Canada, Catalogue no. 63F0002MIE.

Table 19.1 Employment, information and cultural industries, 1994 to 2007

	1994	1995	1996	1997	1998	1999
	number					
Information and cultural industries	**279,777**	**284,566**	**283,051**	**288,372**	**297,503**	**304,067**
Publishing industries	68,555	68,679	69,542	72,250	75,475	76,656
Newspaper, periodical, book and database publishers	60,559	59,939	59,531	60,229	61,348	59,589
Software publishers	7,996	8,740	10,010	12,021	14,127	17,066
Motion picture and sound recording industries	25,210	25,234	26,895	29,912	32,735	34,306
Motion picture and video industries	23,552	23,488	24,944	27,791	30,430	31,954
Sound recording industries	1,657	1,746	1,950	2,121	2,305	2,351
Broadcasting (excluding Internet)	36,051	36,381	37,064	37,008	37,837	37,453
Radio and television broadcasting	35,071	35,429	36,098	36,074	36,897	36,550
Pay and specialty television	980	953	966	934	941	902
Telecommunications	121,025	125,257	119,481	119,674	122,521	124,379
Wired telecommunications carriers	84,663	87,274	83,303	83,105	85,002	85,603
Wireless telecommunications carriers (excluding satellite)	22,734	23,567	22,339	22,355	22,367	22,257
Satellite telecommunications	2,560	2,606	2,425	2,502	2,574	2,571
Other telecommunications	11,067	11,810	11,414	11,712	12,578	13,948
Data processing, hosting and related services	4,728	5,304	5,905	7,033	8,248	10,233
Other information services	24,208	23,711	24,165	22,496	20,686	21,040

See note and source at end of table.

Table 19.1 Employment, information and cultural industries, 1994 to 2007 (continued)

	2000	2001	2002	2003	2004	2005	2006	2007
	number							
Information and cultural industries	**318,783**	**328,509**	**329,770**	**335,202**	**335,136**	**341,786**	**349,519**	**354,263**
Publishing industries	83,152	85,653	86,087	x	82,512	85,371	85,787	90,801
Newspaper, periodical, book and database publishers	62,964	63,030	62,694	x	59,546	60,252	58,638	61,595
Software publishers	20,188	22,623	23,393	22,526	22,966	25,119	27,148	29,206
Motion picture and sound recording industries	36,622	38,228	38,694	37,872	35,549	36,065	34,037	31,960
Motion picture and video industries	34,213	35,872	36,260	35,256	32,659	33,023	31,346	29,407
Sound recording industries	2,409	2,356	2,434	2,616	2,890	3,041	2,691	2,553
Broadcasting (excluding Internet)	37,634	37,436	37,822	39,006	39,888	39,103	42,369	44,141
Radio and television broadcasting	36,764	35,975	36,125	37,005	37,775	37,035	40,122	41,276
Pay and specialty television	870	1,460	1,698	2,000	2,113	2,068	2,247	2,866
Telecommunications	127,934	128,951	126,824	131,658	135,658	139,559	143,667	141,830
Wired telecommunications carriers	86,991	85,961	87,018	92,426	95,572	98,665	100,305	99,029
Wireless telecommunications carriers (excluding satellite)	22,837	23,176	22,661	23,206	23,142	23,351	24,689	23,763
Satellite telecommunications	2,641	3,300	3,759	4,883	5,731	6,202	6,792	6,976
Other telecommunications	15,464	16,515	13,387	11,144	11,214	11,341	11,881	12,063
Data processing, hosting and related services	11,939	14,344	13,963	13,628	13,715	13,156	13,733	14,009
Other information services	21,502	23,897	26,380	x	27,814	28,533	29,927	31,522

Note: North American Industry Classification System (NAICS), 2002.
Source: Statistics Canada, CANSIM table 281-0024.

Table 19.2 Internet use at home by individuals, by type of activity, 2007

	All Canadians[1]	Internet users at home[2]
	%	
E-mail	63.1	92.0
Using an instant messenger	34.3	49.9
Searching for information on Canadian municipal, provincial or federal governments	35.3	51.4
Communicating with Canadian municipal, provincial or federal governments	17.5	25.5
Searching for medical or health-related information	40.2	58.6
Education, training or school work	34.0	49.5
Travel information or making travel arrangements	45.4	66.1
Searching for employment	22.2	32.3
Paying bills and electronic banking	42.9	62.5
Researching investments	17.5	25.5
Playing games	26.5	38.7
Obtaining or saving music	30.5	44.5
Obtaining or saving software	22.3	32.5
Viewing the news or sports	43.7	63.7
Obtaining weather reports or road conditions	47.9	69.8
Listening to the radio over the Internet	19.3	28.1
Downloading or watching television	10.8	15.7
Downloading or watching a movie	8.6	12.5
Researching community events	30.4	44.3
General browsing (surfing)	52.1	76.0
Contributing content (blogs, photos, discussion, groups)	13.9	20.3
Researching other matters (family history, parenting)	47.7	69.5
Making telephone calls	6.0	8.7
Selling goods or services (through auction sites)	6.1	8.9

1. Percentage of all individuals aged 16 years and older.
2. Percentage of all individuals aged 16 years and older who responded that they had used the Internet in the previous 12 months for personal non-business use from home.

Source: Statistics Canada, CANSIM table 358-0130.

Table 19.3 Internet use by individuals, by location of access, 2007

	%
All locations	**73.2**
Home	68.6
Work	30.0
School	14.5
Public library	10.8
Other location	22.0

Notes: Percentage of all individuals aged 16 and older who responded that they had used the Internet in the previous 12 months for personal non-business use from any location.

Internet access from any location includes use from home, school, work, public library or other, and counts an individual only once, regardless of use from multiple locations.

Source: Statistics Canada, CANSIM table 358-0122.

Table 19.4 Radio broadcasting industry, by operating and financial detail, 2001 to 2006

	2001	2002	2003	2004	2005	2006
	$ thousands					
Radio broadcasting						
Operating revenue	1,414,445	1,456,949	1,555,689	1,582,608	1,697,414	1,795,786
Sales of air time	1,062,288	1,096,744	1,187,259	1,227,759	1,335,295	1,406,789
Operating expenses	1,251,331	1,302,466	1,353,557	1,454,583	1,515,956	1,594,254
Profit before interest and taxes	163,114	154,483	202,132	128,025	181,458	201,532
Private radio broadcasting						
Operating revenue	1,074,782	1,105,836	1,196,514	1,234,694	1,345,799	1,419,489
Sales of air time	1,051,483	1,084,058	1,174,971	1,214,197	1,319,467	1,389,459
Operating expenses	902,879	932,772	969,288	1,011,782	1,062,958	1,135,495
Profit before interest and taxes	171,903	173,063	227,226	222,911	282,840	283,994
Public and non-commercial radio broadcasting						
Operating revenue	339,663	351,114	359,175	347,915	351,615	376,297
Sales of air time	10,804	12,686	12,288	13,562	15,828	17,329
Operating expenses	348,453	369,694	384,269	442,801	452,997	458,759
Profit before interest and taxes	-8,790	-18,580	-25,094	-94,886	-101,382	-82,462

Note: North American Industry Classification System (NAICS), 2007.
Source: Statistics Canada, CANSIM table 357-0002.

Table 19.5 Television broadcasting industry, 2002 to 2007

	2002	2003	2004	2005	2006	2007
	$ thousands					
Operating revenue						
Private conventional television	1,900,887	2,069,920	2,082,902	2,166,063	2,163,622	2,187,197
Public and non-commercial television	1,172,534	1,212,567	1,238,192	1,173,731	1,337,943	1,267,134
Pay and specialty television	1,702,287	1,884,772	2,065,201	2,222,092	2,499,033	2,725,214
Pay television	332,513	349,759	384,375	409,795	482,314	547,437
Specialty television	1,369,773	1,535,013	1,680,826	1,812,297	2,016,719	2,177,777
Operating expenses						
Private conventional television	1,722,242	1,769,596	1,850,365	1,923,407	2,072,679	2,071,160
Public and non-commercial television	1,249,383	1,297,583	1,429,466	1,309,461	1,469,512	1,372,744
Pay and specialty television	1,509,795	1,601,538	1,651,105	1,666,203	1,926,152	2,078,078
Pay television	252,125	259,851	298,906	301,812	357,498	430,716
Specialty television	1,257,670	1,341,687	1,352,199	1,364,391	1,568,654	1,647,362
Profit before interest and taxes						
Private conventional television	178,644	300,324	232,537	242,656	90,943	116,037
Public and non-commercial television	-76,849	-85,016	-191,273	-135,730	-131,569	-105,610
Pay and specialty television	192,492	283,234	414,095	555,889	572,881	647,135
Pay television	80,388	89,908	85,469	107,983	124,816	116,720
Specialty television	112,103	193,326	328,627	447,906	448,065	530,415

Note: North American Industry Classification System (NAICS), 2007.
Source: Statistics Canada, CANSIM table 357-0001.

Table 19.6 Use of information and communication technologies, 2002 to 2007

	2002	2003	2004	2005	2006	2007
			%			
E-mail	71.2	73.9	76.6	76.2	77.5	81.1
Wireless communication	57.7	56.5	56.6	59.5	74.0	76.7
Internet	75.7	78.3	81.6	81.6	82.8	86.7
Intranet	14.9	16.4	17.6	18.8	19.7	21.2
Extranet	5.3	6.1	6.3	7.3	7.5	9.4
Sales of goods or services over the Internet	7.6	7.1	7.4	7.3	8.0	8.2
Purchase of goods or services over the Internet	24.6	32.3	25.2	28.6	32.5	37.7

Notes: North American Industry Classification System (NAICS), 2007.
Percentage of private sector enterprises that use the technology.

Source: Statistics Canada, CANSIM table 358-0007 and 358-0010.

International merchandise trade

20

Overview

The rise of the loonie has made Canada's exports relatively more expensive and imports relatively cheaper.

In 2007, exporters and importers in all sectors of Canada's international merchandise trade felt the effect of the loonie's climb.

The Canadian dollar reached parity with the U.S. dollar in 2007 for the first time in more than a generation. The dollar appreciated 17% during the year, as measured by the Bank of Canada's monthly noon spot rate.

The dollar also appreciated against three other currencies important to international traders: the pound, the euro and the yen.

Other factors had an impact on merchandise trade, such as rising commodity and energy prices and the housing slowdown in the United States.

Trade surplus lowest in eight years

Canada's annual merchandise trade surplus with the world shrank to $48.1 billion in 2007, its lowest value since 1999. The trade surplus has been in decline for three years since reaching $65.8 billion in 2004. Exports rose 2.1% to $463.1 billion, but imports grew more, 2.7% to $415.0 billion, leading to the decline in the surplus.

Without the energy sector in 2007, Canada would have had a trade deficit with the world.

The trade surplus in industrial goods and materials, as well as in agricultural and fishing products, grew in 2007, but the trade surplus in forestry contracted. Trade in automotive products slipped into deficit for the first time since 1987.

Chart 20.1
Merchandise trade balance

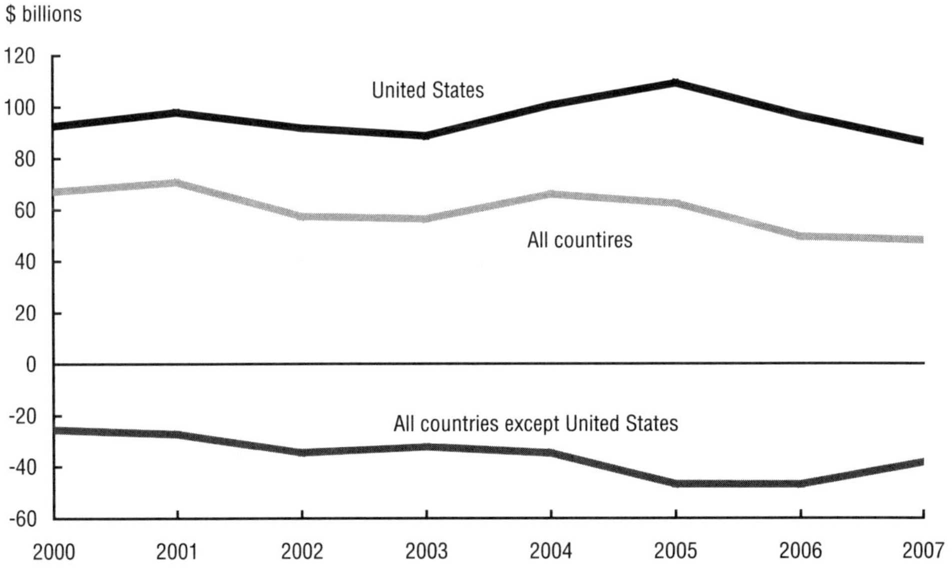

Source: Statistics Canada, CANSIM table 228-0003.

The United States remains Canada's key trading partner, accounting for 77% of exports and 65% of imports. With the rising loonie, Canada's merchandise trade surplus with the United States continued to shrink in 2007, reaching $86.3 billion, the lowest it has been since 1999.

In 2007, Canada's trade gap with other countries narrowed to a deficit of $35.5 billion. This was the smallest trade deficit with countries other than the United States since 2004: in 2007, Canadian exports to non-U.S. countries advanced 16.0%; imports rose 4.2%.

High commodity prices

Sharply higher commodity prices since 2002 have helped to lift the loonie: its rise has, in turn, helped to lower prices of imported goods. A slowing American economy in 2007 was largely confined to housing, autos and the financial sector.

Chart 20.2
Share of Canada's goods exports

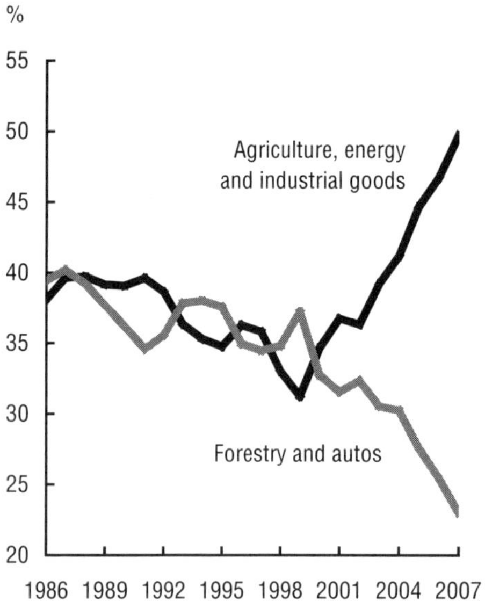

Source: Statistics Canada, CANSIM table 228-0041.

Table 20.a
Canada's international trade partners, 2007

	Imports	Exports
	$ billions	
Total	**406.7**	**450.4**
United States	220.4	356.0
China	38.3	9.3
Japan	15.4	9.2
Mexico	17.2	4.9
United Kingdom	11.5	12.8
Other European Union countries	37.9	21.9
Other countries	65.9	36.3

Note: Customs basis.
Source: Statistics Canada, CANSIM table 228-0003 and Catalogue no. 65-208-XIE.

Export earnings from forestry fell 13%, and auto products, 6%. Thanks largely to earnings from resources—exports of oil, natural gas, metal ores, metal alloys, and potash, for instance—Canada's economy has maintained steady growth. Energy is the biggest contributor to Canada's trade surplus today. Energy prices and trade volumes have grown, while the influence of other sectors like forestry and autos has declined.

Industrial goods led exports

Merchandise exports rose 2% to a record $463.1 billion in 2007. Export volumes increased 1%; prices rose 1%. Industrial goods and materials led the way for a second year in a row, climbing 11% to $104.5 billion.

Automotive and forestry products were the exceptions, as the depressed U.S. housing market cut both sectors' exports. Forestry was also challenged by the mountain pine beetle, the strong loonie, labour disputes, and adjusting to the new softwood lumber agreement. Automotive exports have been declining since 2005.

The export value of metal ores and alloys has been rising annually since 2004, largely due to higher prices. In 2007, industrial demand from Asia propelled prices for a wide range of primary metals to record levels. Demand from China for potash-based fertilizers rose; global potash supplies dwindled and Saskatchewan mines resumed production.

Energy exports rose 6% in 2007 to $91.6 billion. Largely, this reflected strong crude oil exports, which climbed 7% to $41.2 billion. The price of crude rose 6% while export volume increased 1%, as the oil sands industry continued to boom.

Exports of agricultural and fishing products grew 10% to $34.5 billion in 2007. Exports of barley, used as animal feed, jumped 87%. Wheat exports remained strong, rising 27%, based in part on higher prices, lower world supplies, and robust demand from India and China. Canola exports climbed 29% on upward price pressures.

Chart 20.3
Import values and volumes, 2000 to 2007

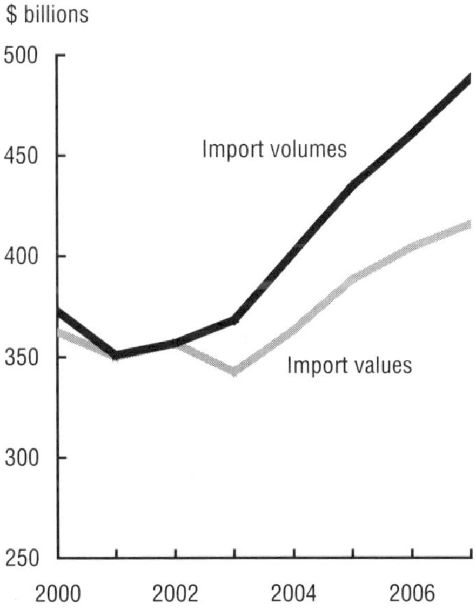

Source: Statistics Canada, International Trade Division.

Imports advanced in all sectors

Canada's imports rose 3% in 2007 to a record $415.1 billion: all sectors posted growth. The prices of imports fell, but record volumes pushed up the value of imports.

Leading import growth in terms of value were 'other consumer goods,' particularly imported pharmaceutical products, toys, clothing and house furnishings. The value of these imports has advanced 18% during the last four years, but their volume is up 45%.

Imports of agricultural and fishing products hit a record high in 2007. Corn imports grew by 70% as the biofuels industry continued to expand in Canada. Energy imports were up for a fifth straight year. Machinery and equipment imports were strong, as industrial and agricultural machinery continued to pour into the robust economy of Western Canada to support mining, exploration and farming activities.

Aircraft, engines and parts imports rose as airlines and the military built up fleets and switched to more fuel-efficient planes. Imports of cars and trucks have risen in recent years, but the same cannot be said for vehicle parts. After exceeding $45 billion in 1999, vehicle parts imports have been falling, to $36.2 billion in 2007.

Diversifying the trade portfolio

The trading patterns of Canadian companies have recently shifted. Exports to non-U.S. countries have greatly expanded, up 16% in 2007 alone. These countries now comprise one-fifth of Canada's export market.

Canada's trade is expanding with Europe—particularly the United Kingdom, Norway and the Netherlands—and with China, India and Mexico. Uranium exports to Europe nearly tripled in 2007. Exports of oil drilling platforms increased to the United Kingdom. Imports of pharmaceutical products from Europe have doubled in the last five years.

Exports to China are growing

Canada's merchandise trade with China has grown quickly this decade. China emerged as Canada's second largest trading partner in 2003; by 2007, our total trade with China—exports and imports—reached $47.6 billion, and accounted for 6% of Canada's world trade. That still pales next to Canada's $625.9 billion worth of trade with the United States, which made up 70% of Canada's world trade of $878.1 billion in 2007. However, it marks strong expansion.

Exports to China comprised 17% of Canada's export growth in 2007. This growth lifted China to overtake Japan as Canada's third largest export market, behind the United States and the United Kingdom.

China has become a manufacturing powerhouse: the industrialization process and its citizens' newfound affluence have put pressure on world prices for natural resources, including Canada's.

Canadian exports to China jumped 21% in 2007 from 2006, and surpassed $9 billion, nearly twice their value in 2003. Industrial goods dominated the advance: metals to manufacture stainless steel, infrastructure, machinery and electronics; fertilizers to raise crops; synthetic rubber and plastics to make toys and consumer goods; and organic chemicals to produce polyester for clothing. Forest products, such as pulp for paper and cardboard, were also a key export in 2007, as were agricultural products, especially canola seed and oil.

Imports from China—up 11% to $38 billion in 2007—have been boosted by the higher loonie: it gained 10% against the Chinese yuan in 2007 alone. Since 2002, China has been the second largest supplier of foreign goods to Canadians. Mostly, Canadians are importing high-tech products and equipment from China. Also popular are games, toys, apparel, footwear, furniture and fixtures.

Chart 20.4
Canada's merchandise trade with China

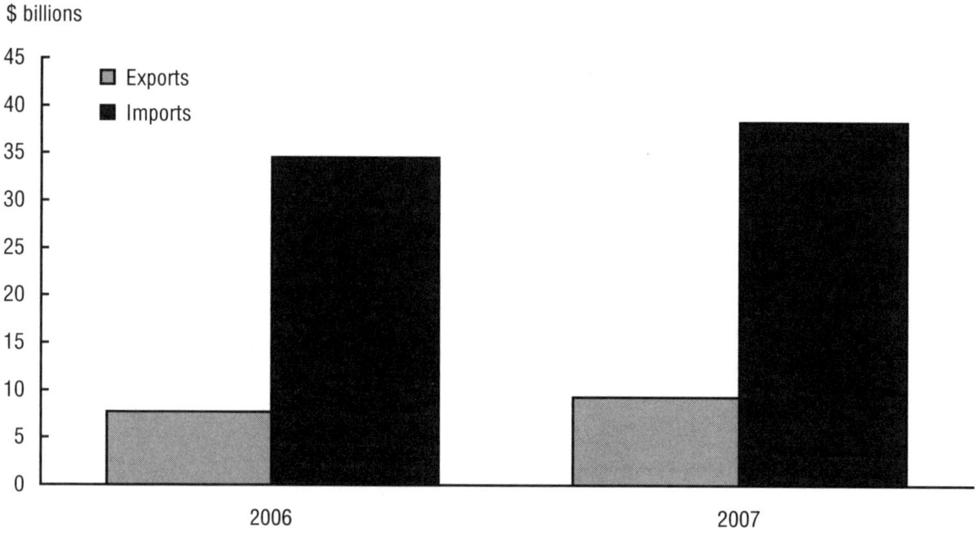

Source: Statistics Canada, Catalogue no. 65-208-XIE.

Russia an emerging trade partner

Canadian companies are turning to Russia as a trade partner with potential. Canada's exports to Russia grew to $1.1 billion in 2007 from $288.1 million in 1997. Imports arriving in Canada rose to $1.1 billion in 2007 from $730.6 million in 1998. The growth in Canadian exports to Russia is remarkable, given that the Canadian dollar appreciated against the ruble an average 21% annually from 1998 to 2007.

From 1998 to 2007, Canada's merchandise trade with Russia climbed 117% to $2.3 billion. This growth rate was four times the growth in Canada's total world trade over that period. Still, Russia accounted for just 0.3% of Canadian international trade in 2007; the United States accounted for 67%.

Canada was in a trade deficit position with Russia throughout the period. The deficit peaked at $1.2 billion in 2005, then shrank to a $289.0 million in 2007. Manufactured goods accounted for 84% of exports to Russia in 2007, and 7 of the top 10 products. The leaders were: industrial and agricultural machinery, automotive products, meat products, and aircraft and parts.

Canada's leading imports from Russia are mineral fuels, precious stones and metals, fertilizers, beverages, iron and steel products, fish and seafood. In 1998, imports of mineral fuels, mainly crude oil, made up 15% of those imports. By 2007, they represented more than two-thirds—however, most of that growth reflects higher prices. Beverage imports from Russia have expanded twenty-fold since 1998, to $52.4 million in 2007.

In recent years, our trade deficit with Russia has been driven mainly by mineral fuels. Excluding mineral fuels, Canada had a trade surplus of $704 million with Russia.

Chart 20.5
Canada's merchandise trade with Russia

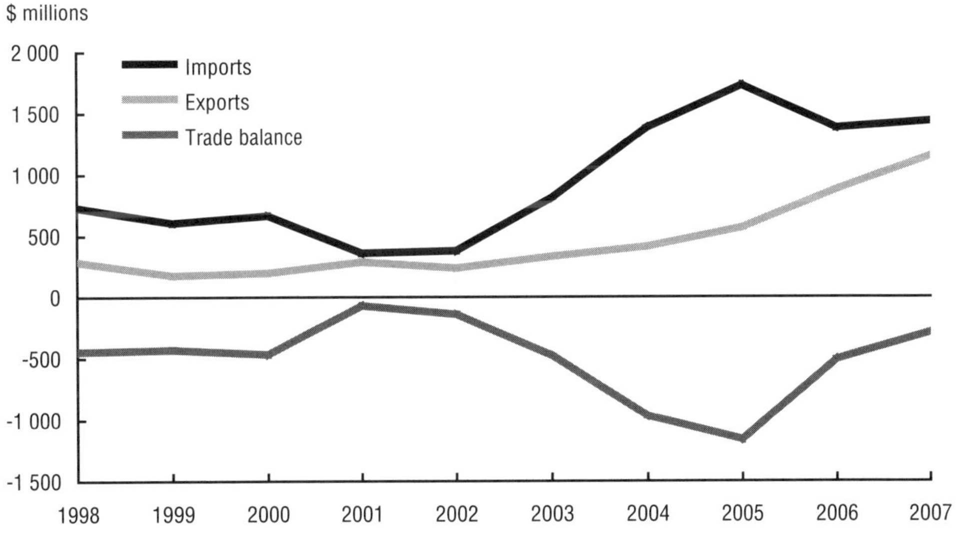

Source: Statistics Canada, Catalogue no. 65-508-XIE.

Table 20.1 Merchandise imports, by commodity, 1993 to 2007

	1993	1994	1995	1996	1997	1998	1999	2000
	$ millions							
Imports, all merchandise	**177,123.2**	**207,872.5**	**229,936.5**	**237,688.6**	**277,726.5**	**303,398.6**	**327,026.0**	**362,336.7**
Live animals	174.0	215.4	188.3	171.1	183.8	235.0	302.7	410.2
Food, feed, beverages and tobacco	10,114.3	11,597.4	12,222.4	12,954.6	14,363.5	15,858.3	16,249.3	16,978.4
Meat and meat preparations	992.2	1,137.4	1,133.7	1,033.7	1,200.0	1,251.4	1,279.8	1,404.0
Fish and marine animals	996.1	1,126.4	1,286.5	1,469.6	1,434.0	1,635.8	1,869.7	1,928.8
Fresh fruits and berries	1,283.9	1,303.4	1,387.5	1,418.3	1,503.0	1,581.3	1,645.8	1,679.4
Dried fruits, fruits and fruit preparations	648.0	693.4	745.6	861.1	900.8	935.3	1,020.3	1,003.8
Fresh vegetables	944.7	949.6	1,054.4	971.7	1,112.5	1,233.8	1,213.6	1,386.6
Other vegetables and vegetable preparations	643.9	700.3	718.3	761.1	838.2	963.5	1,050.0	1,048.8
Cocoa, coffee, tea and other food preparations	1,452.9	2,089.3	2,056.9	2,131.7	2,589.7	2,948.9	2,865.0	2,817.4
Dairy produce, eggs and honey	245.2	265.5	276.1	352.0	355.0	409.7	437.8	487.6
Corn (maize), shelled	157.6	158.5	216.9	251.0	250.3	283.6	228.1	300.0
Other cereals and cereal preparations	632.9	750.1	805.1	891.1	998.0	1,136.6	1,164.1	1,243.6
Sugar and sugar preparations	759.7	866.5	879.4	970.7	1,035.6	1,100.9	991.6	1,034.0
Fodder and feed, except unmilled cereals	551.1	613.7	628.4	728.6	809.9	796.4	734.0	825.3
Beverages	746.2	872.8	959.4	1,015.3	1,214.7	1,455.8	1,669.2	1,735.1
Tobacco	60.0	70.4	74.2	98.6	121.6	125.2	80.3	84.1
Crude materials, inedible	9,143.2	9,898.0	11,531.4	13,048.1	14,171.5	12,476.7	14,316.0	21,462.6
Metals in ores, concentrates and scrap	1,983.6	2,326.2	2,989.1	2,863.0	2,950.2	2,788.4	2,747.4	3,067.1
Coal and other related products	476.9	548.0	591.6	751.4	910.3	1,116.3	1,098.1	1,270.2
Crude petroleum	4,687.9	4,609.3	4,833.2	6,707.8	7,189.4	5,227.4	7,160.3	13,436.6
Crude animal products	163.9	221.8	239.1	248.0	293.2	256.2	242.1	272.9
Crude vegetable products	638.4	663.1	815.2	843.9	949.6	939.3	965.5	995.8
Crude wood products	293.3	406.8	560.4	435.7	544.1	618.8	626.9	695.2
Cotton	86.8	101.6	149.2	168.3	154.0	221.3	138.0	172.4
Wool and man-made fibres	204.8	260.0	296.5	279.9	328.5	343.7	348.6	389.8
Crude non-metallic minerals	607.5	761.2	1,057.1	750.0	852.1	965.4	989.1	1,162.4
Fabricated materials, inedible	32,279.3	38,823.1	44,277.2	45,967.5	54,508.4	60,113.0	62,411.8	69,870.4
End products, inedible	114,407.5	136,993.1	151,331.7	153,330.6	181,930.0	202,489.8	221,180.5	240,462.0
Special transactions, trade	4,349.2	4,877.0	5,441.4	7,075.9	6,954.9	6,339.2	6,343.1	6,653.7
Other balance of payments adjustments	6,655.7	5,468.5	4,944.0	5,140.8	5,614.5	5,886.5	6,222.5	6,499.5

See note and source at end of table.

Table 20.1 Merchandise imports, by commodity, 1993 to 2007 (continued)

	2001	2002	2003	2004	2005	2006	2007
	$ millions						
Imports, all merchandise	**350,071.2**	**356,727.1**	**342,709.5**	**363,157.8**	**387,804.0**	**404,252.6**	**415,005.7**
Live animals	398.0	236.7	174.3	137.7	144.3	165.3	181.4
Food, feed, beverages and tobacco	18,687.0	20,195.2	19,945.4	19,862.2	20,666.0	22,053.2	24,076.8
Meat and meat preparations	1,635.9	1,681.4	1,596.7	1,311.4	1,454.5	1,650.9	1,934.2
Fish and marine animals	1,945.3	1,935.4	1,812.2	1,804.4	1,822.7	1,815.9	1,890.5
Fresh fruits and berries	1,815.3	2,020.1	2,013.5	2,070.8	2,206.9	2,318.5	2,501.0
Dried fruits, fruits and fruit preparations	992.1	1,075.6	1,061.9	1,099.8	1,134.8	1,234.0	1,349.6
Fresh vegetables	1,502.3	1,700.3	1,638.7	1,633.7	1,718.0	1,786.5	1,921.6
Other vegetables and vegetable preparations	1,133.4	1,275.1	1,211.3	1,240.2	1,337.2	1,359.9	1,469.0
Cocoa, coffee, tea and other food preparations	2,948.7	3,340.3	3,427.6	3,590.2	3,697.5	3,921.2	4,062.6
Dairy produce, eggs and honey	581.4	583.3	567.3	638.9	616.8	539.2	625.4
Corn (maize), shelled	555.3	733.0	599.9	366.4	342.5	322.4	547.9
Other cereals and cereal preparations	1,380.1	1,484.5	1,416.3	1,453.9	1,488.7	1,558.8	1,726.0
Sugar and sugar preparations	1,218.1	1,179.2	1,220.2	1,176.9	1,228.2	1,412.7	1,326.8
Fodder and feed, except unmilled cereals	981.0	1,041.2	968.0	1,007.1	891.2	984.3	1,130.1
Beverages	1,910.2	2,035.3	2,294.9	2,359.4	2,605.7	2,888.0	3,197.2
Tobacco	88.0	110.6	116.9	109.1	121.3	261.0	394.7
Crude materials, inedible	20,936.6	20,405.7	22,813.6	27,950.5	34,391.1	35,828.0	38,994.4
Metals in ores, concentrates and scrap	2,991.7	2,980.1	3,029.2	4,103.6	4,357.1	6,097.9	7,675.7
Coal and other related products	1,430.5	1,932.9	2,838.8	3,715.0	5,073.3	3,871.4	4,305.9
Crude petroleum	12,814.3	11,722.3	13,300.9	16,439.0	21,581.9	22,562.0	23,670.5
Crude animal products	300.3	317.6	302.7	285.6	256.9	265.8	315.9
Crude vegetable products	1,119.2	1,214.3	1,229.4	1,256.4	1,151.2	1,179.0	1,198.9
Crude wood products	703.6	686.0	619.2	632.2	611.9	563.5	530.1
Cotton	168.5	133.7	159.1	142.4	78.6	56.6	39.1
Wool and man-made fibres	380.2	370.7	361.4	343.3	326.0	289.4	279.1
Crude non-metallic minerals	1,028.4	1,048.0	972.9	1,032.9	954.2	942.3	979.1
Fabricated materials, inedible	69,411.3	69,538.7	66,667.4	74,912.7	82,219.9	87,135.6	86,940.0
End products, inedible	227,417.2	233,889.6	221,481.5	229,178.2	238,793.3	246,527.0	251,428.3
Special transactions, trade	6,851.6	5,973.8	5,309.7	4,967.1	4,649.6	4,771.3	5,192.1
Other balance of payments adjustments	6,369.5	6,487.3	6,317.6	6,149.4	6,939.9	7,772.2	8,192.9

Note: On a balance of payments basis.

Source: Statistics Canada, CANSIM table 228-0003.

Table 20.2 Merchandise exports, by commodity, 1993 to 2007

	1993	1994	1995	1996	1997	1998	1999	2000
	$ millions							
Exports, all merchandise	**190,213.1**	**228,167.1**	**265,333.9**	**280,079.3**	**303,378.2**	**327,161.5**	**369,034.9**	**429,372.2**
Live animals	1,393.5	1,338.3	1,517.7	1,888.4	1,905.3	1,975.8	1,567.8	1,742.7
Food, feed, beverages and tobacco	13,233.3	14,890.6	17,014.1	18,884.6	20,380.4	19,814.5	21,312.6	23,268.6
Fish, fresh, frozen, preserved and canned	2,867.5	3,258.5	3,496.2	3,444.1	3,497.8	3,664.5	4,260.8	4,560.6
Barley	460.7	590.5	564.5	847.8	683.0	340.3	256.9	377.9
Wheat	2,952.4	3,547.3	4,325.2	4,658.6	5,051.5	3,642.3	3,356.2	3,608.9
Wheat flour	24.8	46.2	50.6	33.8	39.7	35.3	54.8	60.1
Other cereals unmilled	220.3	250.9	318.6	432.5	489.8	348.4	400.3	263.5
Other cereal preparations	567.7	678.5	798.5	1,017.1	1,115.2	1,290.5	1,449.8	1,593.3
Meat and meat preparations	1,456.8	1,603.0	1,845.2	2,161.0	2,641.8	2,669.5	3,247.8	4,005.1
Alcoholic beverages	853.0	1,026.2	980.0	1,071.0	1,166.7	1,217.5	1,366.4	1,310.6
Other food, feed, beverages and tobacco	3,830.2	3,889.4	4,635.4	5,218.7	5,695.0	6,606.1	6,919.8	7,488.5
Crude materials, inedible	20,880.4	23,584.9	26,469.0	30,266.3	31,655.2	29,854.0	34,562.6	53,398.2
Rapeseed	735.1	1,571.5	1,265.3	1,158.0	1,126.1	1,638.5	1,332.8	1,147.5
Other crude vegetable products	790.3	1,013.2	1,169.0	1,236.7	1,362.1	1,610.9	1,399.1	1,441.7
Iron ores, concentrates and scrap	998.5	1,272.0	1,386.0	1,440.2	1,841.5	1,830.9	1,493.3	1,532.1
Copper in ores, concentrates and scrap	822.5	774.0	1,196.3	872.0	928.5	614.4	452.1	792.6
Nickel in ores, concentrates and scrap	618.0	592.9	981.5	1,117.7	907.3	917.4	807.1	1,071.9
Zinc in ores, concentrates and scrap	324.6	349.1	486.8	536.6	695.4	509.2	479.0	481.2
Other ores, concentrates and scrap	1,127.9	1,346.8	1,812.5	1,949.3	1,534.2	1,499.0	1,917.0	2,073.8
Crude petroleum	6,222.5	6,507.1	8,263.5	10,497.2	10,366.3	7,829.8	11,017.1	19,165.9
Natural gas	5,903.4	6,427.8	5,649.1	7,432.8	8,625.6	8,967.1	10,951.4	20,536.8
Coal and other crude bituminous substances	1,194.8	1,298.5	1,384.7	1,433.7	1,515.1	1,343.7	1,228.7	1,194.4
Unmanufactured asbestos	265.2	303.3	323.3	343.3	226.7	172.5	164.7	149.4
Other crude animal products	474.8	523.0	579.2	610.8	664.7	677.2	652.6	711.0
Other crude wood products	394.0	322.6	347.9	346.2	432.6	523.0	671.4	846.1
Other crude non-metallic minerals	484.5	625.9	714.1	694.5	652.9	847.4	1,496.7	1,707.0
Other crude materials, inedible	524.3	657.1	909.7	597.3	776.1	873.1	499.9	546.8
Fabricated materials, inedible	56,994.3	69,826.7	84,003.2	85,042.6	89,749.4	91,817.6	97,976.8	113,102.1
End products, inedible	91,064.8	110,410.1	127,264.6	134,806.7	149,130.3	171,731.0	199,953.3	223,135.3
Special transactions, trade	2,164.9	2,564.1	2,865.1	3,154.5	4,074.5	5,563.4	7,348.2	7,980.0
Other balance of payments adjustments	4,481.9	5,552.5	6,200.3	6,036.2	6,483.1	6,405.3	6,313.7	6,745.3

See note and source at end of table.

Table 20.2 Merchandise exports, by commodity, 1993 to 2007 (continued)

	2001	2002	2003	2004	2005	2006	2007
				$ millions			
Exports, all merchandise	**420,730.4**	**414,038.5**	**399,122.1**	**429,005.8**	**450,149.9**	**453,732.4**	**463,051.4**
Live animals	2,394.3	2,506.9	1,318.7	873.0	1,542.7	2,015.5	2,428.0
Food, feed, beverages and tobacco	25,911.5	25,843.1	25,046.9	26,842.0	25,704.5	25,832.8	27,730.6
Fish, fresh, frozen, preserved and canned	4,722.3	5,239.5	4,987.1	4,857.7	4,673.1	4,434.3	4,292.6
Barley	383.9	194.1	172.1	321.9	360.1	257.5	485.1
Wheat	3,807.2	3,052.6	2,809.2	3,481.4	2,697.2	3,609.2	4,637.4
Wheat flour	64.0	91.4	81.3	85.0	78.8	81.5	75.8
Other cereals unmilled	279.8	288.5	299.2	310.1	303.2	407.0	606.5
Other cereal preparations	1,830.6	2,048.0	2,138.6	2,214.0	2,248.5	2,328.8	2,536.5
Meat and meat preparations	4,885.6	4,840.8	4,203.5	4,980.1	5,083.1	4,268.3	4,142.7
Alcoholic beverages	1,357.6	1,185.4	1,300.2	1,226.8	1,036.6	995.0	871.3
Other food, feed, beverages and tobacco	8,580.5	8,902.9	9,055.8	9,365.0	9,223.8	9,451.1	10,082.7
Crude materials, inedible	54,713.5	50,980.7	61,268.0	69,594.4	85,698.7	88,541.4	95,728.8
Rapeseed	1,275.8	921.1	1,298.0	1,414.3	1,297.6	1,750.5	2,259.4
Other crude vegetable products	1,496.4	1,601.7	1,570.3	1,545.2	1,552.0	1,611.5	1,952.3
Iron ores, concentrates and scrap	1,381.2	1,634.5	1,743.5	2,043.6	2,591.8	3,191.1	3,311.6
Copper in ores, concentrates and scrap	661.9	577.2	592.3	844.5	1,370.6	2,367.5	2,195.8
Nickel in ores, concentrates and scrap	1,010.6	1,139.1	1,143.9	1,829.4	1,700.0	2,441.1	5,092.0
Zinc in ores, concentrates and scrap	436.7	388.4	228.4	233.9	230.3	325.0	387.3
Other ores, concentrates and scrap	2,177.7	2,147.6	2,081.5	2,377.2	2,879.9	3,023.0	3,418.7
Crude petroleum	15,370.2	18,550.8	20,644.2	25,570.4	30,418.3	38,574.6	40,997.6
Natural gas	25,595.1	18,372.0	26,083.4	27,382.1	35,988.6	27,804.7	28,377.6
Coal and other crude bituminous substances	1,217.5	1,212.1	1,199.1	1,293.3	2,655.6	2,624.5	2,730.9
Unmanufactured asbestos	122.9	100.7	70.7	71.6	66.4	62.2	55.0
Other crude animal products	784.9	802.2	720.5	733.8	817.2	890.0	826.1
Other crude wood products	848.5	1,027.9	902.9	832.6	927.3	880.3	763.8
Other crude non-metallic minerals	1,842.9	2,014.3	2,495.1	2,853.1	2,678.2	2,488.3	2,790.8
Other crude materials, inedible	491.2	491.1	494.1	569.4	525.1	507.1	569.8
Fabricated materials, inedible	111,908.3	108,291.9	103,445.4	118,841.6	124,524.7	128,846.4	133,814.3
End products, inedible	211,387.0	211,446.2	193,248.4	198,762.1	198,147.4	193,380.3	189,469.5
Special transactions, trade	8,168.1	8,232.5	7,689.1	7,985.0	8,288.2	8,732.4	8,175.9
Other balance of payments adjustments	6,247.7	6,737.2	7,105.5	6,107.6	6,243.6	6,383.6	5,704.4

Note: On a balance of payments basis.

Source: Statistics Canada, CANSIM table 228-0003.

Table 20.3 Merchandise imports and exports, by origin and destination, 1993 to 2007

	All merchandise		United States		United Kingdom		Japan	
	$ millions	% change from previous year	$ millions	% change from previous year	$ millions	% change from previous year	$ millions	% change from previous year
Imports								
1993	**177,123.2**	14.7	130,244.3	18.0	4,484.0	11.7	8,477.4	-4.9
1994	**207,872.5**	17.4	155,661.3	19.5	4,854.4	8.3	8,315.4	-1.9
1995	**229,936.5**	10.6	172,516.5	10.8	4,899.1	0.9	8,427.6	1.3
1996	**237,688.6**	3.4	180,010.1	4.3	5,581.1	13.9	7,227.4	-14.2
1997	**277,726.5**	16.8	211,450.8	17.5	6,126.5	9.8	8,711.0	20.5
1998	**303,398.6**	9.2	233,777.6	10.6	6,083.1	-0.7	9,671.8	11.0
1999	**327,026.0**	7.8	249,485.3	6.7	7,685.4	26.3	10,592.2	9.5
2000	**362,336.7**	10.8	266,511.1	6.8	12,289.3	59.9	11,729.8	10.7
2001	**350,071.2**	-3.4	254,330.7	-4.6	11,954.1	-2.7	10,571.9	-9.9
2002	**356,727.1**	1.9	255,232.5	0.4	10,181.3	-14.8	11,732.6	11.0
2003	**342,709.5**	-3.9	240,356.3	-5.8	9,183.0	-9.8	10,645.5	-9.3
2004	**363,157.8**	6.0	250,038.3	4.0	9,460.0	3.0	10,094.5	-5.2
2005	**387,804.0**	6.8	259,348.2	3.7	9,061.2	-4.2	11,210.8	11.1
2006	**404,252.6**	4.2	265,023.0	2.2	9,549.2	5.4	11,858.3	5.8
2007	**415,005.7**	2.7	269,752.5	1.8	9,894.3	3.6	11,972.3	1.0
Exports								
1993	**190,213.1**	16.4	149,099.7	20.8	3,211.5	-6.0	9,184.5	11.3
1994	**228,167.1**	20.0	181,049.3	21.4	3,677.1	14.5	10,788.5	17.5
1995	**265,333.9**	16.3	205,690.6	13.6	4,377.0	19.0	13,286.1	23.2
1996	**280,079.3**	5.6	222,461.3	8.2	4,608.5	5.3	12,423.4	-6.5
1997	**303,378.2**	8.3	242,542.3	9.0	4,689.5	1.8	11,925.5	-4.0
1998	**327,161.5**	7.8	269,318.9	11.0	5,323.3	13.5	9,745.8	-18.3
1999	**369,034.9**	12.8	309,116.8	14.8	6,002.9	12.8	10,125.9	3.9
2000	**429,372.2**	16.4	359,021.2	16.1	7,273.3	21.2	11,297.4	11.6
2001	**420,730.4**	-2.0	352,165.0	-1.9	6,910.3	-5.0	10,120.8	-10.4
2002	**414,038.5**	-1.6	347,051.8	-1.5	6,161.5	-10.8	10,115.0	-0.1
2003	**399,122.1**	-3.6	328,983.3	-5.2	7,695.3	24.9	9,799.5	-3.1
2004	**429,005.8**	7.5	350,576.3	6.6	9,364.0	21.7	9,846.4	0.5
2005	**450,149.9**	4.9	368,414.7	5.1	9,355.4	-0.1	10,168.2	3.3
2006	**453,732.4**	0.8	361,440.4	-1.9	11,281.2	20.6	10,279.2	1.1
2007	**463,051.4**	2.1	356,094.2	-1.5	14,154.8	25.5	9,989.2	-2.8

See note and source at end of table.

Table 20.3 Merchandise imports and exports, by origin and destination, 1993 to 2007 (continued)

	Other Organisation for Economic Co-operation and Development countries		Other		Other European Economic Community countries	
	$ millions	% change from previous year	$ millions	% change from previous year	$ millions	% change from previous year
Imports						
1993	4,683.9	1.5	19,691.1	18.6	9,542.4	-3.7
1994	7,364.7	57.2	20,126.9	2.2	11,549.9	21.0
1995	7,942.3	7.8	20,761.0	3.2	15,390.0	33.2
1996	9,040.6	13.8	20,834.6	0.4	14,994.7	-2.6
1997	11,376.7	25.8	21,948.7	5.3	18,112.9	20.8
1998	11,398.8	0.2	23,326.1	6.3	19,141.2	5.7
1999	13,257.2	16.3	25,240.1	8.2	20,765.8	8.5
2000	19,067.6	43.8	31,602.5	25.2	21,136.5	1.8
2001	18,649.8	-2.2	31,367.6	-0.7	23,197.1	9.7
2002	19,686.6	5.6	34,027.1	8.5	25,867.0	11.5
2003	19,696.9	0.1	36,826.8	8.2	26,001.0	0.5
2004	22,283.6	13.1	44,274.4	20.2	27,007.0	3.9
2005	24,304.5	9.1	54,422.3	22.9	29,457.0	9.1
2006	23,673.3	-2.6	61,618.9	13.2	32,529.8	10.4
2007	25,034.2	5.7	65,949.4	7.0	32,402.9	-0.4
Exports						
1993	3,361.7	5.8	16,557.6	4.3	8,798.0	-6.0
1994	4,536.0	34.9	18,753.5	13.3	9,362.7	6.4
1995	4,563.4	0.6	23,537.6	25.5	13,879.3	48.2
1996	5,087.8	11.5	22,702.0	-3.6	12,796.3	-7.8
1997	8,849.0	73.9	22,111.6	-2.6	13,260.4	3.6
1998	9,120.9	3.1	19,652.2	-11.1	14,000.5	5.6
1999	9,947.2	9.1	19,458.4	-1.0	14,383.8	2.7
2000	12,059.0	21.2	22,875.1	17.6	16,846.3	17.1
2001	12,172.5	0.9	22,672.9	-0.9	16,688.9	-0.9
2002	12,670.7	4.1	21,745.2	-4.1	16,294.3	-2.4
2003	12,754.1	0.7	23,466.4	7.9	16,423.4	0.8
2004	14,189.1	11.3	27,496.2	17.2	17,533.8	6.8
2005	14,528.0	2.4	29,052.9	5.7	18,630.6	6.3
2006	16,773.9	15.5	33,057.6	13.8	20,900.2	12.2
2007	19,690.5	17.4	38,935.8	17.8	24,187.0	15.7

Note: On a balance of payments basis.

Source: Statistics Canada, CANSIM table 228-0003.

Table 20.4 International trade in services, selected years from 1991 to 2006

	1991	1996	2001	2006
	$ millions			
Receipts				
Travel	**7,691**	**11,749**	**16,437**	**16,598**
Business travel	1,482	2,226	2,658	2,889
Personal travel	6,209	9,523	13,779	13,708
Transportation	**4,883**	**7,905**	**10,625**	**12,129**
Water transport	1,528	1,905	2,399	3,811
Air transport	2,041	3,274	4,826	4,834
Land and other transport	1,314	2,726	3,400	3,485
Commercial services	**9,814**	**19,357**	**31,545**	**36,708**
Communications services	1,291	1,748	2,338	2,611
Construction services	46	141	276	226
Insurance services	2,096	2,988	3,711	3,921
Other financial services	496	993	1,160	2,150
Computer and information services	636	1,074	3,609	4,575
Royalties and license fees	210	1,196	3,735	3,680
Non-financial commissions	295	565	687	830
Equipment rentals	191	217	388	341
Management services	918	1,774	3,681	4,977
Advertising and related services	128	223	505	453
Research and development	803	1,703	3,118	3,185
Architectural, engineering and other technical services	890	2,896	2,939	4,609
Miscellaneous services to business	1,322	2,610	3,308	2,561
Audiovisual services	349	1,069	1,891	2,351
Personal, cultural and recreational services	144	160	199	240
Payments				
Travel	**13,753**	**15,353**	**18,487**	**23,311**
Business travel	2,127	3,409	3,405	3,739
Personal travel	11,626	11,943	15,082	19,572
Transportation	**6,760**	**10,567**	**13,970**	**19,194**
Water transport	2,159	3,346	5,248	8,067
Air transport	3,293	4,976	6,124	8,745
Land and other transport	1,308	2,245	2,598	2,382
Commercial services	**13,208**	**22,381**	**34,477**	**38,865**
Communications services	1,183	1,695	2,154	2,218
Construction services	38	93	95	111
Insurance services	2,397	3,934	5,466	5,524
Other financial services	950	1,675	2,563	3,246

See source at end of table.

Table 20.4 International trade in services, selected years from 1991 to 2006 (continued)

	1991	1996	2001	2006
	$ millions			
Payments				
Computer and information services	488	721	1,435	2,291
Royalties and license fees	2,049	2,659	5,856	8,301
Non-financial commissions	370	460	697	776
Equipment rentals	305	440	705	711
Management services	1,513	3,031	5,234	4,939
Advertising and related services	238	487	531	484
Research and development	496	767	1,442	1,345
Architectural, engineering and other technical services	599	1,194	1,668	2,897
Miscellaneous services to business	1,803	3,573	4,321	3,509
Audiovisual services	659	1,506	2,137	2,302
Personal, cultural and recreational services	122	145	174	211
Balance				
Travel	**-6,062**	**-3,604**	**-2,050**	**-6,713**
Business travel	-645	-1,183	-747	-849
Personal travel	-5,417	-2,421	-1,303	-5,864
Transportation	**-1,877**	**-2,662**	**-3,345**	**-7,065**
Water transport	-631	-1,441	-2,849	-4,256
Air transport	-1,252	-1,702	-1,297	-3,911
Land and other transport	6	481	802	1,102
Commercial services	**-3,394**	**-3,023**	**-2,932**	**-2,157**
Communications services	108	53	184	393
Construction services	8	48	180	114
Insurance services	-300	-946	-1,755	-1,603
Other financial services	-454	-682	-1,402	-1,096
Computer and information services	147	354	2,174	2,284
Royalties and license fees	-1,840	-1,463	-2,121	-4,621
Non-financial commissions	-75	104	-10	54
Equipment rentals	-113	-223	-316	-370
Management services	-595	-1,257	-1,553	37
Advertising and related services	-111	-264	-26	-31
Research and development	308	936	1,675	1,840
Architectural, engineering and other technical services	291	1,702	1,271	1,711
Miscellaneous services to business	-481	-963	-1,013	-947
Audiovisual services	-309	-438	-246	50
Personal, cultural and recreational services	22	15	26	28

Source: Statistics Canada, CANSIM tables 376-0031, 376-0032 and 376-0033.

Table 20.5 International trade, by province and territory, selected years from 1987 to 2007

	1987	1992	1997	2002	2007
	$ millions				
Imports to Canada	**143,316**	**192,393**	**331,271**	**428,301**	**503,445**
Newfoundland and Labrador	1,119	1,410	3,159	5,140	7,544
Prince Edward Island	219	301	529	864	1,034
Nova Scotia	3,358	3,933	6,981	9,212	9,598
New Brunswick	3,021	3,900	6,414	9,554	12,209
Quebec	30,286	41,324	66,358	87,078	105,767
Ontario	73,429	96,463	168,003	212,016	229,226
Manitoba	3,722	4,923	9,271	11,079	13,258
Saskatchewan	3,311	4,072	8,425	9,623	12,501
Alberta	10,654	14,333	29,097	43,267	59,829
British Columbia	13,382	20,514	31,953	38,855	50,353
Yukon	95	149	193	294	343
Northwest Territories (including Nunavut)	152	225	486	..	..
Northwest Territories	..	..	..	737	1,052
Nunavut	..	..	..	249	361
Outside Canada	568	846	402	332	371
Exports from Canada	**149,913**	**189,784**	**348,604**	**479,185**	**534,669**
Newfoundland and Labrador	2,005	1,833	3,404	6,530	11,928
Prince Edward Island	264	342	636	1,080	1,140
Nova Scotia	2,861	3,201	5,171	7,324	7,777
New Brunswick	3,516	3,723	6,048	9,920	12,160
Quebec	25,982	34,540	65,694	92,929	96,393
Ontario	71,679	91,677	172,384	233,884	225,636
Manitoba	3,718	4,935	8,872	11,383	14,591
Saskatchewan	5,071	6,168	12,160	14,278	21,341
Alberta	14,021	20,634	38,079	58,811	91,941
British Columbia	19,884	21,573	35,345	41,624	49,621
Yukon	447	515	288	175	211
Northwest Territories (including Nunavut)	342	441	515	..	..
Northwest Territories	..	..	..	1,047	1,864
Nunavut	..	..	..	200	65
Outside Canada	123	202	8	2	2

Note: Expenditure-based gross domestic product.
Source: Statistics Canada, CANSIM table 384-0002.

Labour

21

Overview

Canada's job picture improved in 2007. The unemployment rate—the percentage of Canadians looking for work—averaged 6.0% over the 12 months of 2007, the lowest average annual rate in 33 years.

The number of working Canadians rose 2.3% in 2007, a net increase of 382,000 jobs. It was Canada's fifteenth consecutive year of job growth. More than three-quarters of the newly created jobs were full time. Half of the new jobs were held by older workers (aged 55 and older), who accounted for 30% of the working-age population.

The employment growth rate of 2.3% far surpassed that of the United States, which saw employment rise by 0.8% in 2007. Historically, Canada's unemployment rate has been higher than that of the United States.

For people unable to find work, the time spent unemployed in 2007 was the shortest since 1976: an average of 14.0 weeks.

Still, the brightening prospects for work did not seem to lure more people to the job market. In 2007, the annual average labour force participation rate—the proportion of working-age Canadians who had a job or were looking for one—was 67.6%, up slightly from 67.2% in 2006.

Several regions and industries continued to experience labour shortages, primarily the result of the strong national economy. Atlantic Canada had shortages for the first time in decades: more than 12% of employers reported having trouble finding skilled labour.

Jobs: Provincial variation

Every province recorded higher employment in 2007, for the first time since 2004. Alberta continued its job expansion, though not at such a fast pace as the year before. In 2007, Alberta's workforce grew by a nation-leading 4.7%, compared with a 4.8% rise in 2006.

Chart 21.1
Unemployment rate

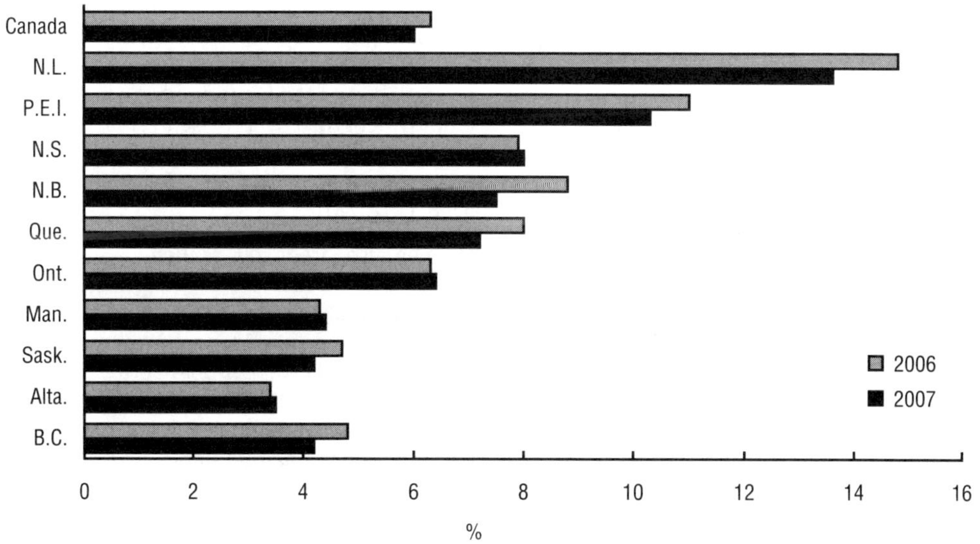

Source: Statistics Canada, CANSIM table 282-0002.

The gains were again fuelled by job growth in natural resources, construction and a number of service-producing industries.

British Columbia posted the second-highest employment gain, 3.2%. Quebec also saw above-average job growth, at 2.3%, thanks to construction; utilities; accommodation and food services; and 'other services' that offset declines in manufacturing employment. Among the provinces with below-average job growth was Ontario, at 1.6% in 2007, partly because of losses in manufacturing.

Table 21.a
Labour force characteristics, 2007

	Men	Women
	thousands	
Population age 15 and older	**13,065.4**	**13,488.0**
Labour force	9,492.8	8,453.0
Employment	8,888.9	7,977.5
Unemployment	603.9	475.5
Not in labour force	3,572.5	5,035.0
	%	
Unemployment rate	6.4	5.6
Participation rate	72.7	62.7
Employment rate	68.0	59.1

Source: Statistics Canada, CANSIM table 282-0002.

Job changes by sector

Several sectors saw dramatic gains in employment in 2007, including utilities, up 13.1% from the end of 2006; mining, oil and gas, 5.9%; accomodation and food services, up 5.4%; and construction, up 6.0%.

But the labour market news was not good for all industries: some continued to struggle. Manufacturing, for example, lost 3.4% of its workforce in 2007, after shedding 4.1% of jobs in 2006. The sector's job losses were partly blamed on the higher Canadian dollar, rising energy costs and tougher competition from other countries. From November 2002 to December 2007, manufacturing jobs declined by 347,000, or 14.9% of the previous total workforce.

Other sectors that saw employment shrink in 2007 included agriculture (down 2.7% from 2006) and fishing, hunting, and trapping, (down 9.1%).

Chart 21.2
Employment, by selected industries, 2006 to 2007

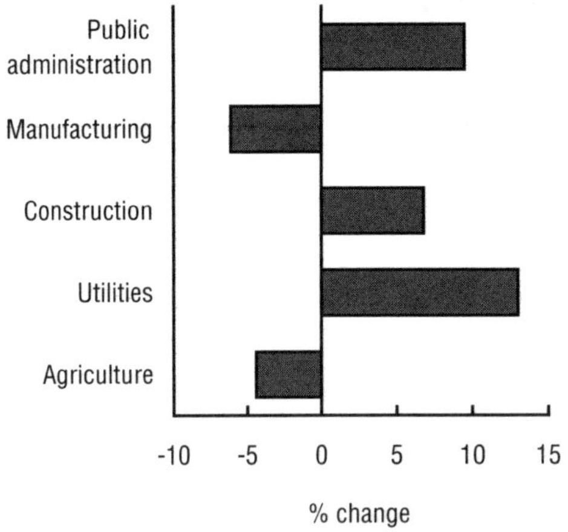

Source: Statistics Canada, CANSIM : table 282-0008.

Older workers fared better

The employment situation improved for most demographic groups in 2007, measured by comparing the 12-month annual average for 2007 with that for 2006. Among them were workers aged 55 and older, whose employment rose by a revised 7.1%, more than triple the national average growth, 2.3%. Employment increased 2.1% for youth (those aged 15 to 24).

Women also fared well, as their unemployment rate fell 0.5 percentage points, to 5.6%. The unemployment rate for Aboriginal people living off-reserve in Western Canada was 9.5% in 2007, down from 12.2% in 2005. Employment rates for immigrants who arrived in Canada within the past five years remained stable in 2007, but increased slightly for immigrants who had arrived more than five years ago.

A changing labour market

The 2006 Census reveals interesting changes in Canada's labour market since the 2001 Census. For example, Canada's employment growth averaged 1.7% in each of the five years, higher than the average among members of the Group of Seven (G7).

There was a shift in employment away from manufacturing (which shed an average of 1.4% of its jobs each year between censuses) and toward mining and oil and gas extraction (which grew an average of 7.5% a year), construction (4.5%), and retail trade (1.8%), among others.

There were corresponding changes in occupations. For example, there were drops in manufacturing-related occupations, such as sewing machine operators (whose ranks decreased by 32.7% from 2001 to 2006) and metal fabricators, including steelworkers (whose numbers fell by 34.4%). Meanwhile, occupations in the expanding construction industry formed one of the fastest-growing categories, as the number of trades helpers and labourers jumped by 57.2% from 2001 to 2006.

An increase in the percentage of foreign-born people living in Canada was reflected in the labour market, which saw the proportion of immigrants rise from 19.9% of workers in 2001 to 21.2% in 2006.

Employee earnings have changed little. The 2006 Census found that the median earnings of Canadians working full-time for a full year was $41,401 in 2005, compared with $41,348 in 1980 (in 2005 constant dollars).

Chart 21.3
Labour force participation rate, aged 55 to 64 years

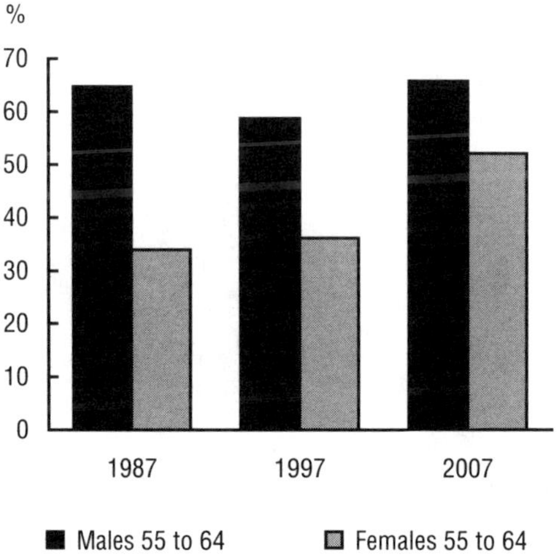

Source: Statistics Canada, CANSIM table 282-0002.

Shift in hours

Recent years have seen the continuation of a 30-year shift—the average weekly hours worked by full-time employees has steadily dropped, while those worked by part-timers has increased.

A dwindling number of people are working part-time jobs because they can't find full-time work—another sign of a hot labour market. In 2007, fewer than one-third of part-time workers did so because of poor economic conditions.

Wage growth gallops

The booming economy and labour shortages saw wages recording their fastest growth in 2007 in a decade. For employees on payroll, average weekly earnings rose 3.2% to $771 for all industries. The average hourly wage in 2007 was $18.80, a 6.0% rise in real terms from $17.68 (in 2002 dollars) in 1997.

In the private sector, managers saw the greatest wage growth since the late 1990s. Their average hourly wages grew 20% from 1997/1998 to 2006/2007, compared with 5% for other private sector employees. Blue-collar workers in manufacturing, clerical employees and salespersons in retail trade (accounting for 26% of private sector employment in 2006/2007) saw virtually no wage growth.

Fewer employees work at home

With the widespread technology in Canadian homes, teleworking would presumably be an option for many workers. The numbers show, however, that the trend has gathered some momentum, but has not taken off.

The practice of employees doing some or all of their regularly scheduled work at home has levelled off in recent years, slipping from 10.2% of employees in 2000 to 9.8% in 2005, or about 1.3 million workers.

The desire to telework can come from the employer or employee, or both. One in four teleworkers said in 2005 that working at least some of the time at home was a requirement of their job. Others cited personal advantages to working at home, such as saving time and money on commuting, and more easily balancing work and family demands. On the negative side, working at home may reduce an employee's social circle, stifle career advancement, or even increase workload.

For employers, telework arrangements may boost employee productivity, reduce expenses for work space, improve recruitment and retention of employees, and reduce absenteeism. The most commonly cited disadvantages are difficulties co-ordinating work and communicating with the employee, lack of control over quality of work, and information security.

The technology that makes telework possible in the first place is becoming so portable that employees can use laptops, cell phones and other devices to work almost anywhere—such as in cars or airports—and thus they do not need to use a home office.

Telework is more pervasive among the self-employed, who generally have more flexibility in choosing their workplace: it rose from 49.5% of the self-employed in 2000 to 54.6% in 2005.

Chart 21.4
People working from home

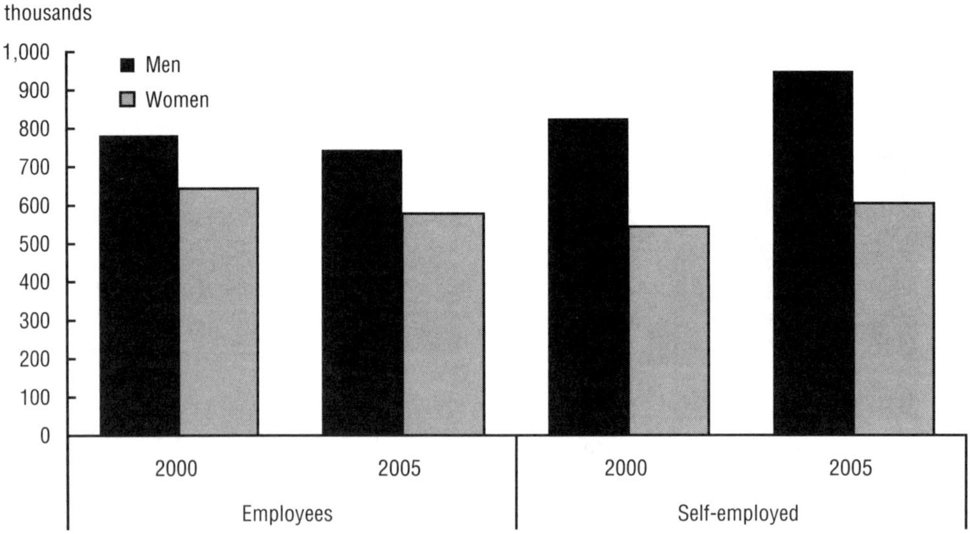

Source: Statistics Canada, Catalogue no. 75-001-XIE.

Work stress reduces job performance

Canadians with stressful jobs might get plenty of work done while they're under pressure, but eventually, their productivity declines. A recent study analysed 2002 data regarding job strain, a major source of work stress, and the findings confirm what many employees and employers know first-hand: stress has considerable consequences.

Job strain is found among workers who have high psychological demands—they need to think at a high pace and intensity, use high levels of skills and must try hard to keep up with colleagues—but have little control over what to do and when to do it.

Over a two-year period, those with high job strain showed reduced work activities; that is, they were limited in the kind or amount of activity they could do at work. They were twice as likely to show reduced work activities as those with low-strain jobs.

Workers with high-strain jobs were also much more likely to take a disability day in the two weeks before being surveyed, meaning that they were in hospital or stayed in bed all day, cut down on normal activities or found their daily activities more difficult because of illness or injury.

Physically stressful jobs can take a toll as well. Workers in physically demanding jobs were twice as likely as those in non-physical jobs to be absent from work. They were also around 1.6 times more likely to have reduced work activities two years later.

The study found some good news, however: a supportive environment both at home and at work and positive coping mechanisms (such as getting more exercise, talking with others and doing enjoyable things to relax) can all but eliminate the chances of having reduced work activities over time.

Chart 21.5
Work stress among employed women and men, 2002

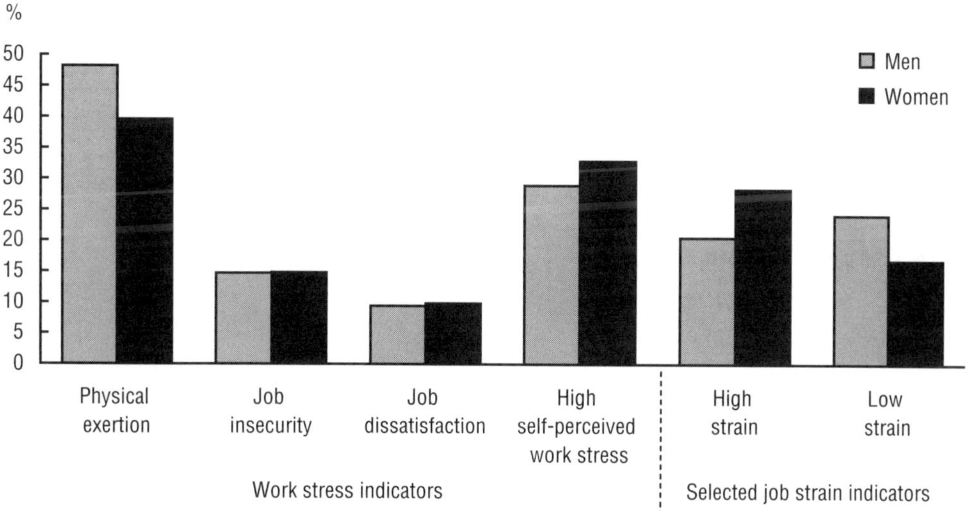

Note: Employed population 15 to 75, Canada excluding territories.
Source: Statistics Canada, Catalogue no. 75-001-XIE.

Table 21.1 Labour force characteristics, by sex and by province, 2007

	Canada	Newfoundland and Labrador	Prince Edward Island	Nova Scotia	New Brunswick	Quebec
			thousands			
Population						
Both sexes	**26,553.4**	424.3	113.3	764.3	613.2	6,314.5
Males	**13,065.4**	206.4	54.6	368.6	299.0	3,105.0
Females	**13,488.0**	217.9	58.6	395.7	314.2	3,209.5
Labour force						
Both sexes	**17,945.8**	251.2	77.3	486.7	392.4	4,150.1
Males	**9,492.8**	131.4	39.2	249.9	204.2	2,191.1
Females	**8,453.0**	119.8	38.1	236.8	188.2	1,959.0
Employed						
Both sexes	**16,866.4**	217.1	69.3	447.6	362.8	3,851.7
Males	**8,888.9**	111.8	34.8	226.7	186.3	2,017.4
Females	**7,977.5**	105.3	34.5	220.9	176.6	1,834.3
Unemployed						
Both sexes	**1,079.4**	34.1	8.0	39.1	29.6	298.4
Males	**603.9**	19.6	4.4	23.2	17.9	173.7
Females	**475.5**	14.5	3.5	15.8	11.7	124.7
Not in the labour force						
Both sexes	**8,607.5**	173.1	35.9	277.7	220.8	2,164.4
Males	**3,572.5**	75.0	15.4	118.7	94.8	913.9
Females	**5,035.0**	98.1	20.5	158.9	126.0	1,250.5
			%			
Participation rate						
Both sexes	**67.6**	59.2	68.2	63.7	64.0	65.7
Males	**72.7**	63.7	71.8	67.8	68.3	70.6
Females	**62.7**	55.0	65.0	59.8	59.9	61.0
Employment rate						
Both sexes	**63.5**	51.2	61.2	58.6	59.2	61.0
Males	**68.0**	54.2	63.7	61.5	62.3	65.0
Females	**59.1**	48.3	58.9	55.8	56.2	57.2
Unemployment rate						
Both sexes	**6.0**	13.6	10.3	8.0	7.5	7.2
Males	**6.4**	14.9	11.2	9.3	8.8	7.9
Females	**5.6**	12.1	9.2	6.7	6.2	6.4

See note and source at end of table.

Table 21.1 Labour force characteristics, by sex and by province, 2007 (continued)

	Ontario	Manitoba	Saskatchewan	Alberta	British Columbia
	thousands				
Population					
Both sexes	10,361.6	898.7	751.4	2,740.7	3,571.4
Males	5,078.2	442.3	370.7	1,381.8	1,758.7
Females	5,283.4	456.4	380.7	1,358.9	1,812.6
Labour force					
Both sexes	7,043.5	623.9	523.8	2,030.6	2,366.4
Males	3,687.3	333.7	281.9	1,112.6	1,261.5
Females	3,356.2	290.2	241.9	918.0	1,104.9
Employed					
Both sexes	6,593.8	596.5	501.8	1,959.4	2,266.3
Males	3,437.2	318.7	269.9	1,075.4	1,210.9
Females	3,156.6	277.8	231.9	884.1	1,055.4
Unemployed					
Both sexes	449.7	27.4	22.0	71.1	100.0
Males	250.1	15.0	12.0	37.2	50.6
Females	199.7	12.4	10.0	33.9	49.4
Not in the labour force					
Both sexes	3,318.1	274.8	227.6	710.2	1,205.0
Males	1,390.9	108.6	88.8	269.2	497.2
Females	1,927.2	166.2	138.8	441.0	707.8
	%				
Participation rate					
Both sexes	68.0	69.4	69.7	74.1	66.3
Males	72.6	75.4	76.0	80.5	71.7
Females	63.5	63.6	63.5	67.6	61.0
Employment rate					
Both sexes	63.6	66.4	66.8	71.5	63.5
Males	67.7	72.1	72.8	77.8	68.9
Females	59.7	60.9	60.9	65.1	58.2
Unemployment rate					
Both sexes	6.4	4.4	4.2	3.5	4.2
Males	6.8	4.5	4.3	3.3	4.0
Females	6.0	4.3	4.1	3.7	4.5

Note: Population aged 15 and older.

Source: Statistics Canada, CANSIM table 282-0002.

Table 21.2 Labour force participation rates, by sex and age group, 1982 to 2007

	Labour force			Participation rates		
	15 and older			15 and older		
	Both sexes	Males	Females	Both sexes	Males	Females
	thousands			%		
1982	**12,301.8**	7,245.7	5,056.2	**64.4**	77.0	52.1
1983	**12,527.6**	7,319.8	5,207.8	**64.7**	76.9	53.0
1984	**12,747.9**	7,392.8	5,355.1	**65.0**	76.7	53.8
1985	**13,012.4**	7,478.9	5,533.5	**65.6**	76.7	54.9
1986	**13,272.1**	7,585.4	5,686.7	**66.1**	76.8	55.7
1987	**13,526.0**	7,680.2	5,845.8	**66.5**	76.8	56.5
1988	**13,779.1**	7,754.3	6,024.8	**66.8**	76.6	57.4
1989	**14,057.0**	7,872.4	6,184.6	**67.3**	76.8	58.1
1990	**14,244.6**	7,924.1	6,320.6	**67.1**	76.1	58.5
1991	**14,336.3**	7,924.6	6,411.8	**66.6**	75.0	58.4
1992	**14,336.1**	7,911.2	6,425.0	**65.7**	73.9	57.8
1993	**14,435.0**	7,943.2	6,491.9	**65.3**	73.3	57.7
1994	**14,573.7**	8,014.3	6,559.4	**65.2**	73.1	57.5
1995	**14,689.2**	8,049.5	6,639.8	**64.8**	72.5	57.5
1996	**14,853.5**	8,129.1	6,724.4	**64.7**	72.2	57.4
1997	**15,079.1**	8,233.8	6,845.3	**64.8**	72.2	57.8
1998	**15,316.3**	8,324.3	6,992.0	**65.1**	72.1	58.4
1999	**15,588.3**	8,457.6	7,130.7	**65.5**	72.4	58.9
2000	**15,847.0**	8,569.2	7,277.8	**65.8**	72.4	59.4
2001	**16,109.8**	8,690.9	7,418.9	**65.9**	72.3	59.7
2002	**16,579.3**	8,906.2	7,673.1	**66.9**	73.0	60.9
2003	**16,958.5**	9,067.7	7,890.9	**67.5**	73.4	61.9
2004	**17,182.3**	9,166.0	8,016.3	**67.5**	73.2	62.0
2005	**17,342.6**	9,243.7	8,098.8	**67.2**	72.8	61.8
2006	**17,592.8**	9,335.4	8,257.3	**67.2**	72.5	62.1
2007	**17,945.8**	9,492.8	8,453.0	**67.6**	72.7	62.7

See source at end of table.

Table 21.2 Labour force participation rates, by sex and age group, 1982 to 2007 (continued)

	Participation rates							
	15 to 24		25 to 44		45 and older		65 and older	
	Males	Females	Males	Females	Males	Females	Males	Females
	%							
1982	70.7	63.8	94.3	66.1	61.8	30.5	12.7	4.0
1983	70.6	64.5	94.0	67.6	61.3	30.8	12.1	3.7
1984	70.8	65.0	94.1	69.4	60.3	30.8	11.8	3.9
1985	71.1	65.6	94.2	70.9	59.4	31.8	11.8	4.1
1986	72.3	67.0	94.4	73.1	58.6	30.9	11.1	3.4
1987	73.0	67.5	94.3	74.0	58.1	32.0	11.2	3.3
1988	73.1	68.0	94.2	75.3	57.5	33.0	10.7	3.6
1989	73.8	68.5	94.2	76.6	57.4	33.4	10.5	3.9
1990	72.4	67.3	93.8	77.7	56.8	33.9	10.8	3.6
1991	70.1	66.1	93.1	77.8	56.3	34.6	11.1	3.4
1992	67.8	64.5	92.0	76.8	55.9	35.4	10.6	3.4
1993	66.5	62.2	92.1	77.1	55.5	36.1	9.7	3.5
1994	65.9	61.9	91.8	76.9	55.9	36.6	10.7	3.4
1995	64.9	61.3	91.6	77.1	55.4	36.9	9.9	3.4
1996	64.1	60.3	91.6	77.8	55.4	37.1	9.8	3.4
1997	63.6	59.2	91.9	78.4	55.8	38.1	9.8	3.6
1998	63.4	60.2	92.2	79.0	55.8	39.3	10.2	3.5
1999	65.3	61.5	92.2	79.6	56.4	39.9	9.8	3.4
2000	65.9	62.8	92.1	79.9	56.7	40.9	9.5	3.3
2001	66.1	63.2	92.1	80.4	56.9	41.6	9.4	3.4
2002	67.8	65.3	92.3	81.3	58.1	43.2	10.3	3.8
2003	68.3	66.5	92.5	81.7	59.2	45.0	11.5	4.2
2004	67.8	66.2	92.4	82.2	59.6	45.5	11.8	4.4
2005	66.1	65.8	92.3	81.8	59.9	45.9	12.1	5.0
2006	66.4	66.4	92.0	81.8	59.6	46.8	12.1	5.2
2007	67.4	66.5	92.1	82.6	60.0	47.8	13.0	5.6

Source: Statistics Canada, CANSIM table 282-0002.

Table 21.3 Labour force characteristics, by sex and age group, 2007

	Population	Labour force	Employed	Unemployed	Participation rate	Employment rate	Unemployment rate
	thousands				%		
Both sexes	**26,553.4**	**17,945.8**	**16,866.4**	**1,079.4**	**67.6**	**63.5**	**6.0**
15 to 24	**4,353.5**	2,915.1	2,589.4	325.7	67.0	59.5	11.2
15 to 19	**2,136.7**	1,177.8	1,003.0	174.8	55.1	46.9	14.8
20 to 24	**2,216.8**	1,737.3	1,586.4	150.9	78.4	71.6	8.7
25 and older	**22,199.9**	15,030.8	14,277.0	753.8	67.7	64.3	5.0
25 to 44	**9,266.0**	8,092.9	7,658.9	434.0	87.3	82.7	5.4
25 to 34	**4,395.6**	3,819.4	3,603.6	215.9	86.9	82.0	5.7
35 to 44	**4,870.4**	4,273.4	4,055.3	218.1	87.7	83.3	5.1
45 to 64	**8,813.1**	6,571.5	6,264.8	306.7	74.6	71.1	4.7
45 to 54	**5,062.7**	4,317.0	4,123.9	193.1	85.3	81.5	4.5
55 to 64	**3,750.4**	2,254.5	2,140.9	113.6	60.1	57.1	5.0
55 and older	**7,871.2**	2,620.9	2,494.3	126.6	33.3	31.7	4.8
65 and older	**4,120.8**	366.4	353.4	13.0	8.9	8.6	3.5
Males	**13,065.4**	**9,492.8**	**8,888.9**	**603.9**	**72.7**	**68.0**	**6.4**
15 to 24	**2,220.9**	1,496.7	1,313.3	183.4	67.4	59.1	12.3
15 to 19	**1,092.8**	588.2	491.4	96.9	53.8	45.0	16.5
20 to 24	**1,128.1**	908.5	821.9	86.6	80.5	72.9	9.5
25 and older	**10,844.5**	7,996.1	7,575.7	420.4	73.7	69.9	5.3
25 to 44	**4,641.5**	4,274.7	4,032.6	242.0	92.1	86.9	5.7
25 to 34	**2,205.9**	2,024.7	1,896.5	128.3	91.8	86.0	6.3
35 to 44	**2,435.7**	2,249.9	2,136.2	113.7	92.4	87.7	5.1
45 to 64	**4,358.5**	3,482.1	3,312.4	169.7	79.9	76.0	4.9
45 to 54	**2,513.8**	2,244.1	2,138.5	105.6	89.3	85.1	4.7
55 to 64	**1,844.7**	1,238.0	1,173.9	64.1	67.1	63.6	5.2
55 and older	**3,689.1**	1,477.3	1,404.5	72.8	40.0	38.1	4.9
65 and older	**1,844.5**	239.3	230.6	8.7	13.0	12.5	3.6
Females	**13,488.0**	**8,453.0**	**7,977.5**	**475.5**	**62.7**	**59.1**	**5.6**
15 to 24	**2,132.6**	1,418.4	1,276.1	142.2	66.5	59.8	10.0
15 to 19	**1,043.9**	589.5	511.6	77.9	56.5	49.0	13.2
20 to 24	**1,088.6**	828.8	764.5	64.3	76.1	70.2	7.8
25 and older	**11,355.5**	7,034.7	6,701.4	333.3	61.9	59.0	4.7
25 to 44	**4,624.4**	3,818.2	3,626.2	192.0	82.6	78.4	5.0
25 to 34	**2,189.7**	1,794.8	1,707.2	87.6	82.0	78.0	4.9
35 to 44	**2,434.7**	2,023.5	1,919.0	104.4	83.1	78.8	5.2
45 to 64	**4,454.7**	3,089.4	2,952.5	137.0	69.4	66.3	4.4
45 to 54	**2,548.9**	2,072.9	1,985.4	87.5	81.3	77.9	4.2
55 to 64	**1,905.8**	1,016.5	967.1	49.5	53.3	50.7	4.9
55 and older	**4,182.1**	1,143.6	1,089.8	53.8	27.3	26.1	4.7
65 and older	**2,276.3**	127.0	122.8	4.3	5.6	5.4	3.4

Note: Population aged 15 and older.

Source: Statistics Canada, CANSIM table 282-0002.

Table 21.4 Labour force characteristics, by selected census metropolitan area, 2007

	Population	Labour force	Employed	Unemployed	Participation rate	Employment rate	Unemployment rate
	thousands				%		
St. John's	**152.0**	101.5	94.5	7.0	66.8	62.2	6.9
Halifax	**313.3**	220.0	208.4	11.5	70.2	66.5	5.2
Saint John	**103.9**	69.4	66.0	3.4	66.8	63.5	4.9
Saguenay	**125.6**	77.0	70.2	6.8	61.3	55.9	8.8
Québec	**605.4**	406.1	385.7	20.4	67.1	63.7	5.0
Sherbrooke	**136.8**	89.7	84.1	5.7	65.6	61.5	6.4
Trois-Rivières	**120.5**	76.8	70.8	6.0	63.7	58.8	7.8
Montréal	**3,036.5**	2,045.4	1,902.6	142.9	67.4	62.7	7.0
Ottawa–Gatineau	**951.5**	687.1	651.5	35.6	72.2	68.5	5.2
Quebec part	**240.0**	172.8	163.3	9.4	72.0	68.0	5.4
Ontario part	**711.5**	514.3	488.2	26.2	72.3	68.6	5.1
Kingston	**125.9**	82.7	78.3	4.4	65.7	62.2	5.3
Oshawa	**282.1**	193.4	181.5	11.9	68.6	64.3	6.2
Toronto	**4,452.7**	3,074.8	2,865.5	209.3	69.1	64.4	6.8
Hamilton	**592.5**	397.9	374.0	23.9	67.2	63.1	6.0
St. Catharines–Niagara	**328.1**	207.6	193.5	14.1	63.3	59.0	6.8
Kitchener	**377.1**	265.0	250.3	14.7	70.3	66.4	5.5
London	**381.3**	263.5	247.4	16.1	69.1	64.9	6.1
Windsor	**271.8**	174.7	158.4	16.3	64.3	58.3	9.3
Greater Sudbury / Grand Sudbury	**132.8**	85.8	80.9	4.9	64.6	60.9	5.7
Thunder Bay	**104.1**	67.8	63.2	4.5	65.1	60.7	6.6
Winnipeg	**576.4**	409.6	390.5	19.1	71.1	67.7	4.7
Regina	**163.1**	115.4	109.8	5.6	70.8	67.3	4.9
Saskatoon	**191.0**	141.1	135.5	5.7	73.9	70.9	4.0
Calgary	**923.9**	703.2	680.6	22.7	76.1	73.7	3.2
Edmonton	**866.7**	623.0	599.1	23.9	71.9	69.1	3.8
Abbotsford	**131.5**	88.5	84.8	3.8	67.3	64.5	4.3
Vancouver	**1,898.1**	1,273.6	1,222.7	50.8	67.1	64.4	4.0
Victoria	**283.1**	189.1	182.9	6.2	66.8	64.6	3.3

Note: Population aged 15 and older.

Source: Statistics Canada, CANSIM table 282-0053.

Table 21.5 Full-time and part-time employment, by sex and age group, 2002 to 2007

	2002	2003	2004	2005	2006	2007
	thousands					
Total employed, both sexes	**15,310.4**	**15,672.3**	**15,947.0**	**16,169.7**	**16,484.3**	**16,866.4**
15 to 24	2,399.1	2,449.4	2,461.0	2,472.5	2,535.8	2,589.4
25 to 44	7,575.6	7,571.5	7,594.0	7,597.5	7,610.7	7,658.9
45 and older	5,335.7	5,651.4	5,892.0	6,099.7	6,337.8	6,618.2
Full-time	12,439.3	12,705.3	12,998.1	13,206.2	13,509.7	13,803.1
15 to 24	1,323.1	1,344.3	1,361.4	1,370.2	1,419.8	1,435.1
25 to 44	6,627.0	6,624.7	6,671.2	6,684.7	6,730.9	6,774.4
45 and older	4,489.1	4,736.3	4,965.5	5,151.3	5,359.0	5,593.6
Part-time	2,871.1	2,967.0	2,948.9	2,963.5	2,974.7	3,063.3
15 to 24	1,076.0	1,105.1	1,099.6	1,102.3	1,116.0	1,154.3
25 to 44	948.5	946.8	922.8	912.8	879.9	884.5
45 and older	846.6	915.0	926.5	948.4	978.8	1,024.5
Total employed, males	**8,184.4**	**8,348.1**	**8,480.6**	**8,594.7**	**8,727.1**	**8,888.9**
15 to 24	1,224.3	1,243.2	1,248.3	1,239.0	1,276.9	1,313.3
25 to 44	4,028.4	4,029.0	4,023.8	4,032.1	4,035.3	4,032.6
45 and older	2,931.7	3,075.8	3,208.4	3,323.6	3,414.9	3,543.0
Full-time	7,287.9	7,423.0	7,559.3	7,664.0	7,781.0	7,909.9
15 to 24	763.9	774.9	781.2	782.5	809.2	828.5
25 to 44	3,831.1	3,832.2	3,834.1	3,832.6	3,845.6	3,840.2
45 and older	2,692.9	2,815.9	2,944.1	3,048.9	3,126.2	3,241.3
Part-time	896.5	925.0	921.3	930.7	946.1	979.0
15 to 24	460.4	468.3	467.1	456.5	467.7	484.8
25 to 44	197.4	196.9	189.8	199.5	189.7	192.5
45 and older	238.8	259.8	264.4	274.7	288.7	301.7
Total employed, females	**7,126.0**	**7,324.2**	**7,466.4**	**7,575.0**	**7,757.2**	**7,977.5**
15 to 24	1,174.8	1,206.2	1,212.6	1,233.5	1,258.9	1,276.1
25 to 44	3,547.1	3,542.5	3,570.2	3,565.4	3,575.4	3,626.2
45 and older	2,404.0	2,575.6	2,683.5	2,776.2	2,922.9	3,075.2
Full-time	5,151.4	5,282.3	5,438.8	5,542.3	5,728.7	5,893.2
15 to 24	559.2	569.4	580.2	587.8	610.5	606.6
25 to 44	2,796.0	2,792.5	2,837.2	2,852.1	2,885.3	2,934.2
45 and older	1,796.2	1,920.4	2,021.4	2,102.4	2,232.8	2,352.4
Part-time	1,974.6	2,041.9	2,027.6	2,032.8	2,028.5	2,084.3
15 to 24	615.6	636.8	632.4	645.8	648.4	669.5
25 to 44	751.2	749.9	733.0	713.3	690.1	692.0
45 and older	607.8	655.2	662.1	673.7	690.0	722.8

Source: Statistics Canada, CANSIM table 282-0002.

Table 21.6 Reasons for part-time work, by sex and age group, 2007

	All ages	15 to 24	25 to 44	45 and older
	thousands			
All persons employed part time	**3,063.3**	**1,154.3**	**884.5**	**1,024.5**
All males employed part time	**979.0**	484.8	192.5	301.7
All females employed part time	**2,084.3**	669.5	692.0	722.8
	%			
Both sexes				
Own illness	**3.5**	0.6	3.4	6.7
Caring for children	**10.7**	0.9	30.4	4.8
Other personal/family responsibilities	**2.8**	0.5	3.9	4.5
Going to school	**32.3**	76.6	11.0	0.9
Personal preference	**27.7**	5.8	19.2	59.6
Other voluntary	**0.8**	0.4	1.2	0.9
Involuntary (no full-time work available)	**22.2**	15.2	31.0	22.5
Males				
Own illness	**3.5**	0.7	5.6	6.5
Caring for children	**1.1**	x	3.7	1.2
Other personal/family responsibilities	**1.1**	0.4	1.6	1.9
Going to school	**43.0**	78.3	19.8	1.1
Personal preference	**26.8**	5.7	21.9	63.7
Other voluntary	**1.0**	0.4	2.1	1.3
Involuntary (no full-time work available)	**23.5**	14.4	45.2	24.3
Females				
Own illness	**3.5**	0.6	2.7	6.8
Caring for children	**15.2**	1.5	37.8	6.3
Other personal/family responsibilities	**3.7**	0.6	4.5	5.6
Going to school	**27.3**	75.5	8.5	0.8
Personal preference	**28.1**	5.8	18.5	58.0
Other voluntary	**0.7**	0.4	0.9	0.7
Involuntary (no full-time work available)	**21.5**	15.7	27.0	21.8

Note: Expressed as a percentage of total part-time employment.
Population aged 15 and older.

Source: Statistics Canada, CANSIM table 282-0014.

Table 21.7 Employment, by sector, 1992 to 2007

	1992	1993	1994	1995	1996	1997	1998	1999
	thousands							
All sectors	**12,730.9**	**12,792.7**	**13,058.7**	**13,295.4**	**13,421.4**	**13,706.0**	**14,046.2**	**14,406.7**
Goods-producing sector	3,390.6	3,325.2	3,397.5	3,467.6	3,476.0	3,561.0	3,657.9	3,742.5
Agriculture	439.4	445.5	437.2	419.3	422.5	417.0	424.2	406.0
Forestry, fishing, mining, oil and gas extraction	280.1	271.8	285.6	294.8	294.0	296.7	293.5	263.8
Utilities	143.5	137.4	127.0	123.5	124.1	115.3	114.7	114.3
Construction	713.1	691.2	724.6	726.4	709.7	721.0	731.9	766.9
Manufacturing	1,814.5	1,779.2	1,823.2	1,903.8	1,925.7	2,010.9	2,093.5	2,191.5
Services-producing sector	9,340.3	9,467.6	9,661.2	9,827.7	9,945.4	10,145.1	10,388.4	10,664.3
Trade	2,038.4	2,027.0	2,061.1	2,077.5	2,087.7	2,106.1	2,125.4	2,218.2
Transportation and warehousing	609.6	618.6	644.9	660.8	674.0	694.6	712.7	737.0
Finance, insurance, real estate and leasing	840.5	839.8	832.7	846.1	861.4	865.0	847.9	859.9
Professional, scientific and technical services	590.0	615.9	642.5	674.3	706.7	777.8	849.8	900.7
Business, building and other support services	322.8	342.8	365.4	402.5	420.8	441.8	478.1	504.7
Educational services	886.5	905.5	927.2	928.3	913.0	916.6	930.0	970.7
Health care and social assistance	1,326.9	1,348.5	1,364.2	1,388.6	1,390.9	1,388.4	1,428.5	1,436.0
Information, culture and recreation	492.9	503.2	537.4	567.7	579.1	603.5	615.8	630.5
Accommodation and food services	769.6	772.1	799.1	816.1	847.9	871.0	911.4	913.6
Public administration	865.0	861.7	834.8	818.6	807.8	797.2	781.9	776.3
Other services	598.0	632.5	651.9	647.2	656.0	683.0	706.8	716.5

	2000	2001	2002	2003	2004	2005	2006	2007
	thousands							
All sectors	**14,764.2**	**14,946.2**	**15,310.4**	**15,672.3**	**15,947.0**	**16,169.7**	**16,484.3**	**16,866.4**
Goods-producing sector	3,822.0	3,779.9	3,878.6	3,925.7	3,989.8	4,002.4	3,985.9	3,993.0
Agriculture	372.1	323.3	325.4	332.4	326.0	343.7	346.4	337.2
Forestry, fishing, mining, oil and gas extraction	275.4	278.9	270.3	281.6	286.6	306.4	330.1	339.3
Utilities	114.9	124.4	131.9	130.5	133.3	125.3	122.0	138.0
Construction	810.1	824.3	865.2	906.0	951.7	1,019.5	1,069.7	1,133.5
Manufacturing	2,249.4	2,229.0	2,285.9	2,275.2	2,292.1	2,207.4	2,117.7	2,044.9
Services-producing sector	10,942.2	11,166.2	11,431.8	11,746.6	11,957.2	12,167.3	12,498.4	12,873.5
Trade	2,293.3	2,363.3	2,409.3	2,467.8	2,507.1	2,574.6	2,633.5	2,682.4
Transportation and warehousing	772.3	775.8	760.7	790.9	799.4	793.6	802.2	822.8
Finance, insurance, real estate and leasing	857.9	876.7	895.1	917.0	960.6	987.8	1,040.5	1,060.4
Professional, scientific and technical services	932.2	986.5	987.1	1,003.6	1,018.3	1,050.0	1,089.9	1,136.9
Business, building and other support services	537.0	537.2	579.6	608.7	630.2	654.4	690.0	702.1
Educational services	974.1	981.6	1,007.4	1,027.1	1,035.7	1,106.1	1,158.4	1,183.2
Health care and social assistance	1,514.0	1,540.4	1,617.3	1,679.2	1,733.4	1,734.6	1,785.5	1,846.1
Information, culture and recreation	662.1	709.4	715.1	714.6	738.0	735.1	745.0	782.0
Accommodation and food services	938.2	943.2	985.1	1,005.5	1,012.4	1,004.5	1,015.0	1,069.4
Public administration	772.6	785.4	788.9	819.0	825.5	833.1	837.4	864.6
Other services	688.5	666.8	686.2	713.1	696.6	693.4	701.0	723.5

Note: North American Industry Classification System (NAICS), 2002.
Source: Statistics Canada, CANSIM table 282-0008.

Table 21.8 Employment, by sector and by province, 2007

	Canada	Newfoundland and Labrador	Prince Edward Island	Nova Scotia	New Brunswick	Quebec
	thousands					
All sectors	**16,866.4**	**217.1**	**69.3**	**447.6**	**362.8**	**3,851.7**
Goods-producing sector	**3,993.0**	48.6	17.9	88.2	83.4	872.1
Agriculture	**337.2**	1.3	3.6	5.6	6.3	65.3
Forestry, fishing, mining, oil and gas extraction	**339.3**	16.2	2.4	12.2	11.1	35.8
Utilities	**138.0**	1.7	0.3	1.9	4.1	32.3
Construction	**1,133.5**	13.5	5.0	27.2	24.0	195.5
Manufacturing	**2,044.9**	15.9	6.7	41.4	37.9	543.2
Services-producing sector	**12,873.5**	168.6	51.4	359.4	279.4	2,979.6
Trade	**2,682.4**	36.8	10.5	77.0	57.2	646.0
Transportation and warehousing	**822.8**	10.2	2.3	18.4	19.1	178.4
Finance, insurance, real estate and leasing	**1,060.4**	7.3	2.7	23.2	16.4	231.6
Professional, scientific and technical services	**1,136.9**	8.2	2.2	17.5	15.5	256.7
Business, building and other support services	**702.1**	8.6	2.8	27.1	20.2	147.4
Educational services	**1,183.2**	17.1	4.7	36.3	26.8	259.3
Health care and social assistance	**1,846.1**	31.5	8.3	61.5	48.0	455.2
Information, culture and recreation	**782.0**	8.3	2.7	19.5	13.4	171.9
Accommodation and food services	**1,069.4**	14.8	5.9	30.2	24.2	236.5
Public administration	**864.6**	16.5	6.6	28.1	21.4	219.8
Other services	**723.5**	9.3	2.8	20.5	17.1	176.7

	Ontario	Manitoba	Saskatchewan	Alberta	British Columbia
	thousands				
All sectors	**6,593.8**	**596.5**	**501.8**	**1,959.4**	**2,266.3**
Goods-producing sector	1,552.4	144.8	132.8	557.0	495.7
Agriculture	96.1	28.7	43.8	50.4	36.2
Forestry, fishing, mining, oil and gas extraction	34.8	6.4	22.1	151.0	47.3
Utilities	58.3	5.4	4.2	19.6	10.3
Construction	412.6	33.8	32.1	193.1	196.9
Manufacturing	950.6	70.6	30.7	142.9	205.1
Services-producing sector	5,041.4	451.7	368.9	1,402.4	1,770.6
Trade	1,027.2	89.4	82.6	290.6	365.0
Transportation and warehousing	304.1	34.3	24.6	105.7	125.6
Finance, insurance, real estate and leasing	474.4	34.9	26.6	98.4	145.0
Professional, scientific and technical services	477.8	25.4	21.1	146.3	166.3
Business, building and other support services	294.9	17.1	11.5	73.9	98.5
Educational services	466.1	46.5	40.2	130.0	156.1
Health care and social assistance	671.0	79.8	61.7	189.5	239.7
Information, culture and recreation	328.2	24.1	19.9	76.2	117.8
Accommodation and food services	399.7	38.0	30.8	116.8	172.7
Public administration	331.0	37.4	27.7	80.1	95.9
Other services	267.1	24.8	22.4	94.9	88.0

Note: North American Industry Classification System (NAICS), 2002.
Source: Statistics Canada, CANSIM table 282-0008.

Table 21.9 Employment and average weekly earnings, public administration and all industries, 1994 to 2007

	1994	1995	1996	1997	1998	1999	2000
	thousands[1]						
All industries[2]	**10,973.7**	**11,208.7**	**11,292.5**	**11,624.9**	**11,885.4**	**12,055.8**	**12,460.9**
Public administration	760.5	746.8	722.7	707.6	702.3	705.0	713.0
Federal administration[3]	278.1	265.0	251.9	236.8	234.7	237.9	240.9
Provincial and territorial administration	224.5	222.6	208.9	202.7	202.1	206.1	208.0
Local administration	227.2	228.4	230.1	234.8	231.5	226.6	229.9
	average weekly earnings[1] ($)						
All industries[2]	**592.88**	**598.67**	**611.01**	**623.43**	**632.72**	**640.47**	**655.55**
Public administration	732.69	729.83	725.35	729.12	734.1	761.05	781.15
Federal administration[3]	803.86	804.63	801.01	813.34	830.71	886.01	926.60
Provincial and territorial administration	723.31	721.99	728.45	741.41	750.14	758.82	767.44
Local administration	683.45	678.67	670.12	666.15	657.34	671.37	680.57
	2001	**2002**	**2003**	**2004**	**2005**	**2006**	**2007**
	thousands						
All industries[2]	**12,770.2**	**12,961.2**	**13,226.3**	**13,425.7**	**13,692.9**	**14,032.7**	**14,306.8**
Public administration	743.7	746.7	782.1	785.0	795.3	813.7	822.7
Federal administration[3]	247.5	248.0	258.0	257.0	257.5	269.2	269.0
Provincial and territorial administration	208.4	207.0	222.5	224.4	226.3	229.7	233.2
Local administration	252.8	255.5	260.9	261.6	268.4	272.9	279.4
	average weekly earnings[1] ($)						
All industries[2]	**664.88**	**678.91**	**688.11**	**702.61**	**725.26**	**746.89**	**770.82**
Public administration	787.87	829.33	855.15	872.05	899.05	930.85	969.04
Federal administration[3]	931.57	1,014.45	1,043.49	1,066.43	1,110.61	1,165.74	1,230.98
Provincial and territorial administration	780.45	804.34	833.63	846.09	862.93	890.59	908.19
Local administration	688.62	710.44	732.21	747.87	767.95	776.45	812.56

Notes: North American Industry Classification System (NAICS), 2002.
Data include overtime.

1. Excludes owners or partners of unincorporated businesses and professional practices, the self-employed, unpaid family workers, people working outside of Canada, military personnel and casual workers for whom a T4 is not required.
2. Excludes agriculture, fishing and trapping, private household services, religious organizations and the military.
3. Excludes the military.

Source: Statistics Canada, CANSIM tables 281-0024 and 281-0027.

Table 21.10 Average hourly wages of employees, by selected characteristics and professions, 2006 and 2007

	2006		2007		2006 to 2007
	thousands	average hourly wage ($)	thousands	average hourly wage ($)	% change in average hourly wage
All employed people[1]	**13,986.3**	**19.72**	**14,251.4**	**20.41**	**3.50**
Age 15 to 24	2,443.4	11.36	2,500.2	11.81	3.96
Age 25 to 54	9,863.9	21.49	9,959.1	22.28	3.68
Age 55 and older	1,679.0	21.50	1,792.2	22.03	2.47
Males	7,105.7	21.43	7,185.8	22.17	3.45
Females	6,880.6	17.96	7,065.6	18.62	3.67
Full-time workers	11,526.9	20.99	11,716.2	21.73	3.53
Part-time workers	2,459.4	13.80	2,535.2	14.33	3.84
Union coverage[2]	4,428.6	22.73	4,491.5	23.51	3.43
No union coverage[3]	9,557.7	18.33	9,759.8	18.98	3.55
Permanent job[4]	12,163.1	20.38	12,408.8	21.07	3.39
Temporary job[5]	1,823.2	15.30	1,842.6	15.99	4.51
Management occupations	1,005.9	31.13	1,006.4	31.93	2.57
Business, finance and administrative occupations	2,729.8	18.79	2,753.5	19.44	3.46
Natural and applied sciences and related occupations	1,001.0	27.78	1,050.5	28.62	3.02
Health occupations	860.3	23.11	864.5	24.27	5.02
Occupations in social science, education, public administration and religion	1,239.6	25.64	1,276.5	26.29	2.54
Occupations in art, culture, recreation and sport	323.0	19.71	324.1	20.62	4.62
Sales and service occupations	3,514.2	13.10	3,686.8	13.65	4.20
Trade, transport and equipment operators and related occupations	2,032.4	19.52	2,065.9	20.38	4.41
Occupations unique to primary industry	299.6	16.20	293.0	17.57	8.46
Occupations unique to processing, manufacturing and utilities	980.8	17.18	930.2	17.59	2.39

Note: Data are not seasonally adjusted.

1. Those who work as employees of a private firm or business or the public sector.
2. Employees who are members of a union and employees who are not members of a union, but who are covered by a collective agreement or a union contract.
3. Employees who are not members of a union or not covered by a collective agreement or a union contract.
4. A job that is expected to last as long as the employee wants it (given that business conditions permit) and has no predetermined end date.
5. A job that has a predetermined end date or will end as soon as a specified project is completed. This includes seasonal jobs; temporary, term or contract jobs including work done through a temporary help agency; casual jobs; and other temporary work.

Source: Statistics Canada, CANSIM tables 282-0069 and 282-0073.

Table 21.11 Average earnings, by sex and work pattern, 1992 to 2006

	All earners			Full-year, full-time workers		
	Females	Males	Earnings ratio[1]	Females	Males	Earnings ratio[1]
	$ 2006 constant		%	$ 2006 constant		%
1992	23,400	37,900	61.9	36,400	51,700	70.4
1993	23,700	37,900	62.5	36,500	51,200	71.3
1994	23,500	38,900	60.5	35,700	52,100	68.5
1995	24,300	38,300	63.4	37,000	51,200	72.3
1996	24,200	38,300	63.1	36,400	50,400	72.3
1997	24,300	39,300	61.9	36,100	52,800	68.3
1998	25,400	40,400	62.8	38,700	53,800	71.9
1999	25,800	41,200	62.6	37,200	54,400	68.4
2000	26,300	42,500	61.7	38,400	54,400	70.6
2001	26,400	42,400	62.1	38,800	55,500	69.9
2002	26,700	42,500	62.8	39,000	55,600	70.2
2003	26,400	41,900	62.9	38,900	55,400	70.2
2004	26,700	42,100	63.4	40,100	57,400	69.9
2005	27,300	42,700	64.0	40,000	56,800	70.5
2006	27,700	42,900	64.7	41,300	57,400	71.9

1. Represents female-to-male earnings ratio.

Source: Statistics Canada, CANSIM table 202-0102.

Table 21.12 Earners, by sex and work pattern, 1992 to 2006

	All earners			Full-year, full-time workers		
	Both sexes	Females	Males	Both sexes	Females	Males
	thousands					
1992	**15,048**	6,867	8,181	**8,326**	3,271	5,055
1993	**14,905**	6,795	8,110	**8,386**	3,316	5,070
1994	**15,006**	6,800	8,206	**8,590**	3,327	5,263
1995	**15,346**	6,993	8,352	**8,771**	3,458	5,314
1996	**15,187**	6,880	8,307	**7,881**	3,044	4,837
1997	**15,577**	7,122	8,455	**8,008**	3,135	4,873
1998	**15,896**	7,298	8,599	**8,178**	3,239	4,939
1999	**16,403**	7,590	8,813	**8,497**	3,431	5,066
2000	**16,858**	7,830	9,028	**8,305**	3,349	4,956
2001	**17,226**	8,004	9,221	**8,713**	3,518	5,194
2002	**17,445**	8,121	9,324	**8,483**	3,477	5,006
2003	**17,830**	8,336	9,494	**8,725**	3,650	5,075
2004	**18,163**	8,454	9,709	**9,006**	3,743	5,263
2005	**18,393**	8,615	9,779	**9,342**	3,946	5,396
2006	**18,863**	8,850	10,013	**9,072**	3,804	5,268

Note: Data before 1996 are taken from the Survey of Consumer Finances (SCF) and data from 1996 on are taken from the Survey of Labour and Income Dynamics (SLID). The surveys use different definitions and, as a result, the number of people working full year, full time in the SLID is smaller than in the SCF.

Source: Statistics Canada, CANSIM table 202-0101.

Table 21.13 Employment rate, by educational attainment, age group and sex, 2001 and 2007

	2001			2007		
	Both sexes	Males	Females	Both sexes	Males	Females
	%					
All education levels	**61.1**	**66.8**	**55.6**	**63.5**	**68.0**	**59.1**
15 to 24	**56.3**	56.5	56.2	**59.5**	59.1	59.8
25 to 44	**80.6**	85.9	75.3	**82.7**	86.9	78.4
45 and older	**46.2**	53.7	39.4	**51.2**	57.1	45.7
Less than Grade 9	**20.8**	29.1	13.5	**21.3**	29.1	14.4
15 to 24	**24.3**	28.1	19.4	**29.7**	32.6	26.3
25 to 44	**50.8**	62.6	38.0	**52.2**	60.5	41.7
45 and older	**16.5**	24.1	10.3	**16.8**	24.2	10.9
Some high school	**44.5**	51.7	37.1	**45.2**	51.5	38.4
15 to 24	**42.1**	43.3	40.7	**44.5**	44.7	44.3
25 to 44	**67.7**	76.1	57.0	**68.4**	75.7	58.0
45 and older	**33.9**	43.8	25.8	**36.4**	45.8	27.9
High school graduate	**65.4**	73.6	58.2	**65.5**	72.5	59.1
15 to 24	**68.5**	70.6	66.0	**70.1**	70.9	69.3
25 to 44	**80.1**	87.0	73.3	**80.6**	86.4	74.0
45 and older	**50.7**	60.4	43.7	**54.0**	61.7	48.3
Some postsecondary	**63.0**	66.6	59.7	**64.2**	66.5	62.0
15 to 24	**59.3**	59.1	59.5	**61.0**	59.7	62.3
25 to 44	**76.8**	83.1	71.0	**77.7**	82.3	72.7
45 and older	**51.6**	56.6	47.1	**55.6**	59.4	52.1
Postsecondary certificate or diploma[1]	**72.4**	77.0	68.1	**72.9**	76.4	69.6
15 to 24	**75.3**	74.7	75.9	**77.3**	77.4	77.1
25 to 44	**84.6**	89.0	80.2	**86.6**	90.2	83.1
45 and older	**57.5**	63.0	52.2	**60.1**	64.0	56.4
Bachelor's degree	**77.3**	79.9	74.8	**77.0**	79.5	74.8
15 to 24	**74.9**	75.5	74.6	**72.3**	74.6	71.0
25 to 44	**85.0**	89.1	81.5	**86.2**	90.0	83.1
45 and older	**66.0**	68.3	63.3	**66.1**	68.6	63.5
Above bachelor's degree	**78.1**	78.3	77.7	**76.5**	76.8	76.1
15 to 24	**67.0**	72.4	64.2	**73.0**	67.3	75.8
25 to 44	**87.3**	89.7	84.7	**85.7**	89.7	81.6
45 and older	**69.4**	69.5	69.0	**68.6**	68.0	69.7

1. Includes trades certificate.

Source: Statistics Canada, CANSIM table 282-0004.

Table 21.14 Self-employment, by sex, 1977 to 2007

	Both sexes	Males	Females
		thousands	
1977	**1,210.3**	880.4	329.8
1978	**1,263.4**	910.3	353.1
1979	**1,324.7**	944.6	380.1
1980	**1,363.6**	971.9	391.7
1981	**1,425.2**	1,020.6	404.6
1982	**1,483.2**	1,056.7	426.5
1983	**1,543.2**	1,094.5	448.7
1984	**1,569.7**	1,096.4	473.3
1985	**1,726.0**	1,188.9	537.2
1986	**1,674.2**	1,175.6	498.5
1987	**1,699.1**	1,185.8	513.3
1988	**1,774.1**	1,233.1	541.0
1989	**1,800.3**	1,240.7	559.6
1990	**1,836.6**	1,263.6	573.0
1991	**1,895.8**	1,313.2	582.6
1992	**1,927.5**	1,316.7	610.8
1993	**2,011.1**	1,361.7	649.4
1994	**2,028.5**	1,351.7	676.7
1995	**2,083.1**	1,381.8	701.3
1996	**2,171.6**	1,426.8	744.8
1997	**2,349.4**	1,522.2	827.2
1998	**2,405.7**	1,550.6	855.1
1999	**2,433.0**	1,582.8	850.2
2000	**2,373.7**	1,538.7	835.1
2001	**2,276.7**	1,503.3	773.4
2002	**2,314.5**	1,499.7	814.7
2003	**2,401.8**	1,571.1	830.7
2004	**2,453.4**	1,614.5	838.9
2005	**2,511.6**	1,645.6	866.0
2006	**2,498.0**	1,621.4	876.6
2007	**2,615.0**	1,703.2	911.9

Source: Statistics Canada, CANSIM table 282-0012.

Table 21.15 Days lost annually per worker, by province, 2002 to 2007

	2002	2003	2004	2005	2006	2007
	average number					
Canada	**9.1**	**9.2**	**9.2**	**9.6**	**9.7**	**10.2**
Newfoundland and Labrador	8.6	10.5	10.3	9.5	9.7	9.8
Prince Edward Island	8.5	7.7	7.6	8.6	8.5	8.4
Nova Scotia	10.4	9.8	11.0	10.8	10.7	12.0
New Brunswick	9.7	10.2	9.6	10.3	11.5	10.5
Quebec	9.9	10.8	10.8	11.2	11.5	12.0
Ontario	8.4	8.3	8.5	8.6	8.8	9.3
Manitoba	10.1	9.4	9.8	9.9	10.1	10.8
Saskatchewan	10.3	10.4	10.3	11.1	11.0	10.5
Alberta	8.5	8.0	7.5	8.6	9.0	9.0
British Columbia	9.5	9.9	8.8	10.3	9.4	10.1

Notes: Excludes maternity leave.
Includes full-time paid workers only.
Source: Statistics Canada, CANSIM table 279-0029.

Table 21.16 Days lost annually per worker, by sector, 2002 to 2007

	2002	2003	2004	2005	2006	2007
	average number					
Goods-producing sector	**9.2**	**9.3**	**9.1**	**9.3**	**9.6**	**9.8**
Primary industries	8.3	7.9	7.9	7.6	8.3	8.5
Utilities	8.3	10.0	10.2	9.1	12.4	11.2
Construction	9.2	8.6	7.2	8.3	9.5	9.4
Manufacturing	9.4	9.7	9.9	9.9	9.7	10.2
Services-producing sector	**9.1**	**9.2**	**9.2**	**9.8**	**9.8**	**10.3**
Trade	7.4	8.1	7.6	8.2	8.5	9.3
Transportation and warehousing	10.2	11.4	11.1	12.2	11.6	12.2
Finance, insurance, real estate and leasing	8.0	8.8	7.8	8.9	7.5	8.9
Professional, scientific and technical services	6.1	5.3	5.6	5.3	5.6	6.6
Business, building and other support services	9.1	8.7	9.6	11.0	11.5	10.6
Educational services	9.8	9.5	8.8	9.8	10.7	10.6
Health care and social assistance	13.7	13.0	14.4	14.2	14.4	14.3
Information, culture and recreation	8.2	7.6	7.9	8.5	8.7	9.3
Accommodation and food services	7.7	7.8	7.9	9.1	8.2	8.1
Public administration	11.1	10.9	10.9	12.2	12.0	12.2
Other services	6.7	7.0	7.5	6.8	7.3	9.5

Notes: North American Industry Classification System (NAICS), 2002.
Excludes maternity leave.
Includes full-time paid workers only, who were not at work because of illness, disability and personal or family responsibility.
Source: Statistics Canada, CANSIM table 279-0030.

Table 21.17 Days lost annually per worker because of illness or disability, by province, 2002 to 2007

	2002	2003	2004	2005	2006	2007
	average number					
Canada	**7.4**	**7.5**	**7.5**	**7.8**	**7.6**	**8.1**
Newfoundland and Labrador	6.9	9.1	8.8	8.1	8.2	8.2
Prince Edward Island	6.9	6.4	6.0	6.9	6.9	6.8
Nova Scotia	8.8	8.1	9.1	9.0	8.9	9.9
New Brunswick	8.4	8.8	8.0	8.5	9.7	8.8
Quebec	8.4	9.3	9.4	9.6	9.3	9.8
Ontario	6.6	6.5	6.7	6.7	6.6	7.2
Manitoba	8.4	7.8	8.0	7.9	8.1	8.7
Saskatchewan	8.3	8.6	8.1	8.9	8.7	8.3
Alberta	6.7	6.2	5.6	6.5	6.6	6.9
British Columbia	7.8	8.1	7.3	8.5	7.6	8.2

Note: Includes full-time paid workers only.

Source: Statistics Canada, CANSIM table 279-0029.

Table 21.18 Labour force and paid workers covered by a Registered Pension Plan, by sex, selected years from 1985 to 2005

	1985	1991	1995	2000	2005
	number				
Registered pension plan[1] members					
Both sexes	4,668,381	5,318,090	5,149,912	5,431,578	5,690,580
Males	3,047,160	3,129,263	2,894,564	2,984,444	2,977,758
Females	1,621,221	2,188,827	2,255,348	2,447,134	2,712,822
	%				
Labour force covered by a registered pension plan					
Both sexes	35.3	36.7	34.7	34.0	32.5
Males	39.9	38.9	35.5	34.4	31.9
Females	29.0	33.9	33.8	33.4	33.3
Paid workers[2] covered by a registered pension plan					
Both sexes	44.2	45.3	42.8	40.8	38.5
Males	50.5	49.1	44.5	41.9	38.3
Females	35.7	40.8	40.9	39.5	38.7

Note: The data used from the Labour Force Survey (labour force and paid workers) are annual averages to which the number of Canadian Forces members was added.

1. Plans are established by either employers or unions to provide retirement income to employees.
2. Refers to employees in the public and private sector and includes self-employed workers in incorporated business (with and without paid help).

Source: Statistics Canada, Pension Plans in Canada and Labour Force Survey.

Languages

22

Overview

Ninety-eight percent of Canadians can speak one or both of the country's official languages, but that does not necessarily mean that English or French is their 'mother tongue'—the language a person learns first and still understands. According to the 2006 Census, about 58% of Canadians reported English as their mother tongue and about 22% reported French. The third largest mother-tongue group, 3% of the population, reported Chinese languages, including Mandarin and Cantonese.

In 2006, Canada had 18.0 million anglophones, 3% more than in 2001, and 6.9 million francophones, 2% more than in 2001. Although the numbers of people in these groups are rising, their share of the Canadian population is declining. Anglophones saw their share of the Canadian population decline from 59% in 2001 to 58% in 2006. Francophones saw their share decline from 23% in 2001 to 22% in 2006. These decreases are largely attributable to the growing allophone population.

An 'allophone' is a person whose mother tongue is not English or French. Canada's allophone population neared 6.3 million in 2006, up 18% since 2001. As a group, allophones made up 20% of Canada's population in 2006, up from 18% in 2001 and 17% in 1996.

What's learned first, what's spoken at home

The language people first learn and the language they speak in their daily home lives are not always the same. Also, in many households many languages are spoken.

English and French, however, are the most commonly used languages at home: 94% of Canadians speak one of the official languages at home regularly, and 89% use English or

Chart 22.1
Population, by mother tongue, 2001 to 2006

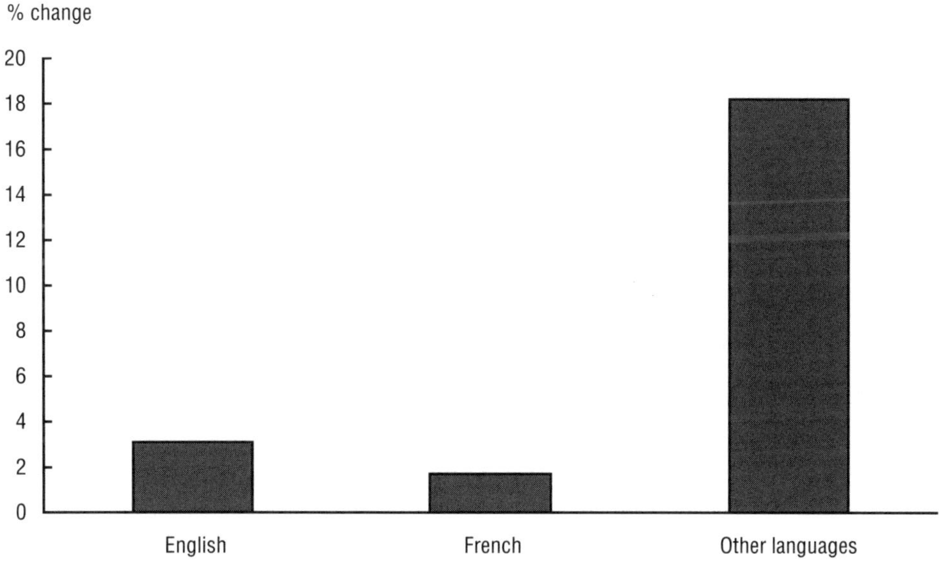

Source: Statistics Canada, 2006 Census of Population.

French at home most often, sometimes in combination with a non-official language.

Speaking English or French in the home regularly does not mean that other languages are not spoken as well. The rapid rise in the allophone population has boosted the proportion of people who speak a non-official language at home to 12% in 2006 from 10% in 2001. Of Canada's 6.3 million allophones, 46% reported speaking English or French most often at home in 2006; another 22% reported that they speak English or French regularly at home, but use another language most often.

Mother-tongue mosaic

Of the 1.1 million immigrants who settled in Canada between the 2001 and 2006 censuses, 901,300, or 80%, were allophones. Canadians reported more than 200 different mother-tongue languages in the 2006 Census, including languages associated with historic immigration patterns, such as German, Italian, Ukrainian and Dutch, as well as languages that characterize more recent immigration, such as Chinese languages, Punjabi and Spanish.

Chart 22.2
Allophone population, selected census metropolitan areas, 2006

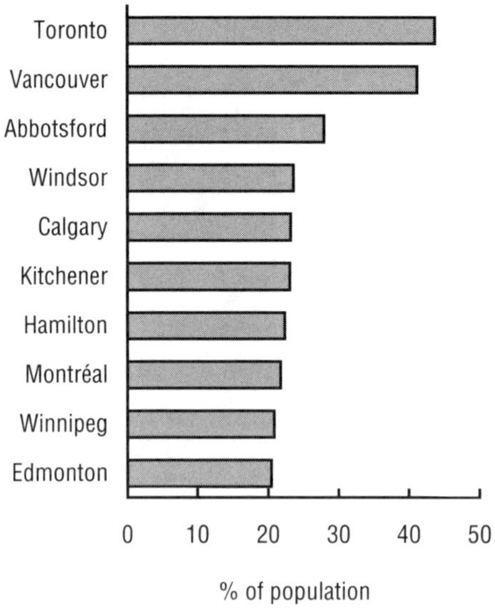

Source: Statistics Canada, 2006 Census of Population.

Table 22.a
Most common non-official mother tongues

	1971		2006
	number		number
German	558,965	Chinese languages[1]	1,034,090
Italian	538,765	Italian	476,905
Ukrainian	309,890	German	466,650
Polish	136,540	Punjabi	382,585
Chinese languages[1]	95,915	Spanish	362,120
Portuguese	85,845	Arabic	286,785
Arabic	28,520	Tagalog	266,440
Spanish	23,950	Portuguese	229,280
Punjabi	..	Polish	217,605
Tagalog	..	Urdu	156,415
Urdu	..	Ukrainian	141,805

1. Includes Mandarin, Cantonese, Hakka, Taiwanese, and other Chinese languages.

Source: Statistics Canada, censuses of population, 1971 and 2006.

Of the 1,034,000 people in Canada in 2006 whose mother tongue is a Chinese language, two-thirds arrived in Canada within the last 25 years. This number rose 19% from 2001 to 2006, the largest increase since 2001 of any allophone group in Canada. It was followed by Spanish, Punjabi, Urdu, Tagalog and Arabic.

The Chinese languages accounted for the largest proportion of non-official mother-tongue groups in 2006, 16%. The next largest groups were Italian (8%) and German (7%).

While some non-official language mother-tongue groups have grown, others have shrunk. As a smaller share of our new immigrants are arriving from Italy, Ukraine and Poland, those mother tongues are losing ground, being replaced by languages such as Chinese and Punjabi. For example, the number of people in Canada with Italian as a mother tongue declined by more than 17,000, or 4%, from 2001 to 2006. The decline of Ukrainian was similar, a loss of nearly 15,600. German-speakers, however were on the increase: after declining from 1961 to 2001, their numbers rose by 11,000 from 2001 to 2006.

Canada's census metropolitan areas (CMAs) are home to 87% of allophones: 72% of whom reside in Toronto, Vancouver, Montréal, Calgary, Edmonton and Ottawa–Gatineau. Another 6% live in Hamilton, Winnipeg and Kitchener.

Toronto had the largest proportion of allophones in 2006—44% of Toronto residents had a mother tongue other than English or French, followed by Vancouver (41%), Calgary (23%), Montréal (22%), Edmonton (21%) and Ottawa–Gatineau (17%).

Language is a tool

When immigrants arrive in Canada, their ability to express themselves in one of the official languages can have a major impact on how successfully they integrate.

Chart 22.3
Immigrants' most-cited difficulties since arrival in Canada, 2004/2005

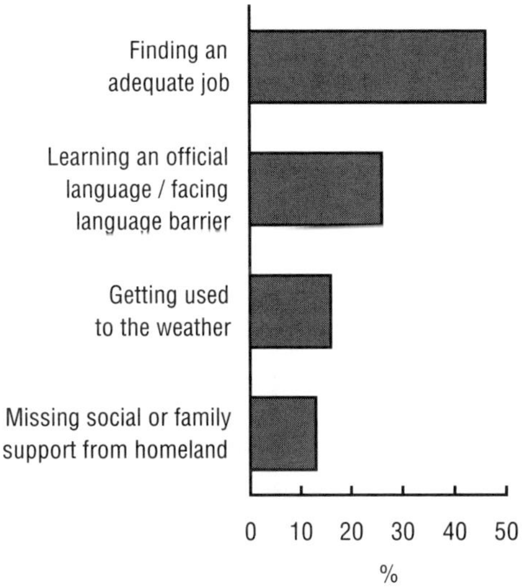

Note: Four years after their arrival in Canada in 2000/2001.
Source: Statistics Canada, Catalogue no. 89-624-XWE.

In 2004/2005, four years after their arrival in Canada in 2000/2001, finding an 'appropriate' job—one that was a good match with the person's skills—was the top-ranked difficulty reported by 46% of immigrants who participated in the Longitudinal Survey of Immigrants to Canada (LSIC). The second-ranked difficulty, reported by 26% of immigrants surveyed, was overcoming the language barrier.

Six months after their arrival in Canada, 58% of immigrants who participated in the survey reported being able to speak English well or very well; 11% reported the same for French. These percentages rose to 69% and 14% after spending four years in Canada.

In Quebec, 55% of immigrants reported speaking French well or very well six months after their arrival—a percentage that climbed to 73% after four years in Canada. Of immigrants to Quebec, 40% could speak English well or very well six months after their arrival, and 54% could do so four years after arrival.

Many immigrants stated that it was important for them to learn or improve their English or, in Quebec, both official languages. About 45% of immigrants who participated in the LSIC said they had taken language training in English since coming to Canada; 10% had done so in French. Most benefited from their language training. Of those immigrants who took training in English, 38% found it very useful and 47% found it useful.

In Quebec, of those who took training in French, 55% found it very useful and 35% found it useful.

Language training helped them with daily communication, adjusting to life in Canada, making new friends and looking for work.

Aboriginal languages

More than 50 different Aboriginal languages exist across Canada, yet only three of them—Cree, Inuktitut and Ojibway—have a large enough population base to make their long-term survival likely.

Among the nearly 1.2 million people who identified themselves as an Aboriginal person in the 2006 Census, the third-largest group, Inuit, had the largest proportion of people who speak an Aboriginal language: 69% of the 50,845 Inuit could speak Inuktitut.

North American Indians, or First Nations, were the largest Aboriginal census group, with 698,025 people. Of these people, 29% could speak an Aboriginal language well enough to carry on a conversation. This compares with the Métis, the second-largest Aboriginal group, at 4%.

While Inuktitut remains strong overall, fewer Inuit are reporting it as their mother tongue. In 2006, 64% of Inuit reported Inuktitut as their mother tongue, down from 68% in 1996. Knowledge and use of the language are also declining: 69% of Inuit could converse in Inuktitut in 2006, down from 72% in 1996. Fewer speak it as their main language at home: 50% in 2006, down from 58% in 1996.

As with the Inuit, more First Nations people could speak an Aboriginal language (29%) than reported one as a mother tongue (25%), suggesting many have learned an Aboriginal language as a second language.

The most commonly spoken First Nations language is Cree. The number of Cree speakers increased 7% from 2001 to 2006. In 2006, 87,285 First Nations people could converse in Cree, 30,255 in Ojibway, 12,435 in Oji-Cree and 11,080 in Montagnais–Naskapi. Four percent of Métis spoke an Aboriginal language in 2006, compared with 5% in 2001.

Chart 22.4
Mother tongue, selected Aboriginal languages, 2006

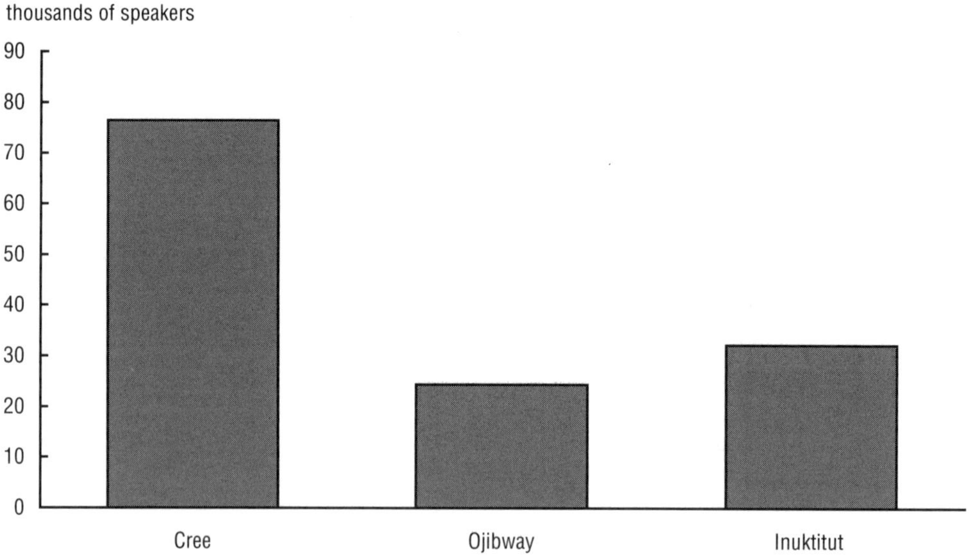

Source: Statistics Canada, 2006 Census of Population.

Official-language minorities

An official-language minority is either a French-speaker or French-speaking population living outside of Quebec, where English is predominant, or an English-speaker or English-speaking population living in Quebec, where French is predominant. The government, in its *Official Languages Act* of 1988, committed to "enhancing the vitality of the English and French linguistic minority communities in Canada."

In 2006, 8% of Quebec's population had English as their mother tongue and 4% of Canada excluding Quebec, had French.

Most adult French-speakers living outside Quebec (78%) and most adult English-speakers inside Quebec (87%) felt that being able to use their language in their daily life was important, according to the 2006 Survey on the Vitality of Official-Language Minorities. Most French-speakers outside Quebec and English-speakers in Quebec felt it was important to have their linguistic rights respected with regard to, for example, receiving an education or accessing federal government services.

How much people care about these rights varies: 91% of French-speakers who did not feel comfortable using English felt strongly about these rights, while 79% of French-speakers who feel equally comfortable in both languages felt the same way.

French-speakers outside Quebec seemed generally optimistic about the continuing presence of French in their community: only 25% of French-speaking adults outside Quebec believed that French will lose ground during the next 10 years. Their English-speaking counterparts in Quebec are more pessimistic about the future presence of English in their community: 36% believed the presence of English will decline.

Chart 22.5
Adults belonging to the official-language minority, by the first official language spoken, Quebec and Canada less Quebec, 2006

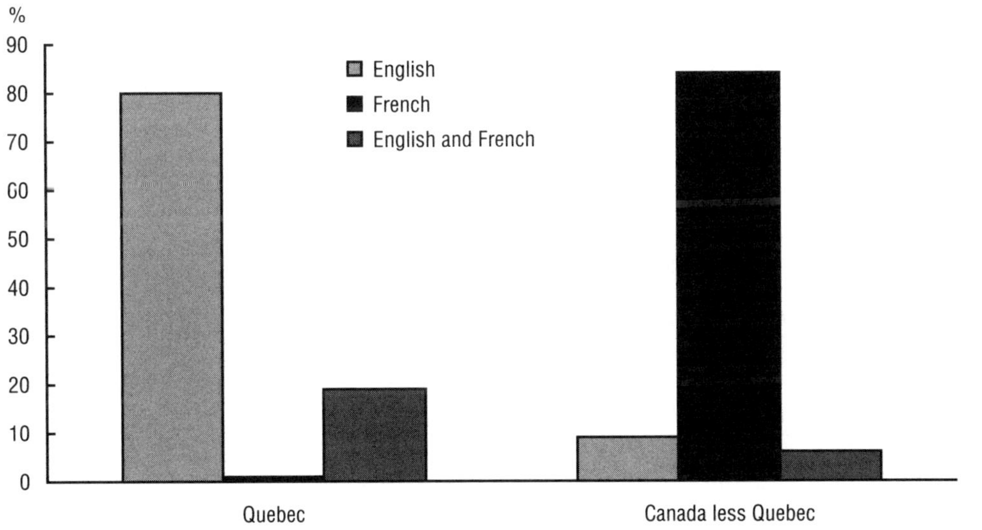

Source: Statistics Canada, Catalogue no. 91-548-XIE.

Table 22.1 Population, by mother tongue and by province and territory, 2006

	Canada	Newfoundland and Labrador	Prince Edward Island	Nova Scotia	New Brunswick	Quebec
	number					
Population	**31,241,030**	**500,610**	**134,205**	**903,090**	**719,650**	**7,435,905**
Mother tongue, single response[1]	**30,848,270**	499,830	133,570	899,270	714,490	7,339,495
English	**17,882,775**	488,405	125,260	832,105	463,190	575,555
French	**6,817,655**	1,885	5,345	32,540	232,975	5,877,660
Non-official languages	**6,147,840**	9,540	2,960	34,620	18,320	886,280
Chinese	**1,012,065**	1,080	190	3,370	2,160	63,415
Cantonese	**361,450**	185	15	505	295	9,850
Mandarin	**170,950**	120	45	595	505	7,770
Hakka	**4,415**	0	0	0	10	85
Chinese (not otherwise specified)	**456,705**	760	115	2,240	1,270	44,740
Italian	**455,040**	195	55	905	590	124,820
German	**450,570**	655	275	4,045	1,935	17,855
Polish	**211,175**	115	70	1,570	220	17,305
Spanish	**345,345**	670	220	1,305	1,040	108,790
Portuguese	**219,275**	150	10	560	210	34,710
Punjabi	**367,505**	120	0	420	55	11,905
Ukrainian	**134,500**	60	20	440	140	5,395
Arabic	**261,640**	540	150	4,425	970	108,105
Dutch	**128,900**	300	865	2,440	1,290	3,620
Tagalog (Pilipino)	**235,615**	180	15	415	330	11,785
Greek	**117,285**	70	30	1,035	275	41,845
Vietnamese	**141,630**	15	10	500	205	25,370
Cree	**78,855**	20	0	15	0	13,340
Inuktitut (Inuit)	**32,380**	595	15	15	0	9,615
Other non-official languages	**1,956,060**	4,775	1,035	13,160	8,900	288,405
Mother tongue, multiple responses[2]	**392,760**	780	635	3,820	5,160	96,405
English and French	**98,625**	295	495	2,100	4,450	43,335
English and non-official language	**240,005**	435	105	1,440	560	16,200
French and non-official language	**43,335**	30	25	140	120	31,350
English, French and non-official language	**10,790**	10	10	145	30	5,520

See notes and source at end of table.

Table 22.1 Population, by mother tongue and by province and territory, 2006 (continued)

	Ontario	Manitoba	Saskat-chewan	Alberta	British Columbia	Yukon	Northwest Territories	Nunavut
	number							
Population	**12,028,895**	**1,133,510**	**953,850**	**3,256,355**	**4,074,385**	**30,195**	**41,055**	**29,325**
Mother tongue, single response[1]	11,853,565	1,118,690	946,250	3,221,420	4,022,045	29,940	40,680	29,025
English	8,230,705	838,415	811,725	2,576,670	2,875,770	25,655	31,545	7,765
French	488,815	43,955	16,060	61,225	54,745	1,105	975	370
Non-official languages	3,134,045	236,320	118,465	583,530	1,091,530	3,180	8,165	20,885
Chinese	482,570	11,045	7,475	97,275	342,920	260	260	40
Cantonese	181,820	3,105	1,720	32,485	131,245	85	120	10
Mandarin	75,335	1,470	715	12,135	72,155	70	15	10
Hakka	2,805	10	15	425	1,075	0	0	0
Chinese (not otherwise specified)	215,345	6,345	4,970	51,145	129,560	90	110	20
Italian	282,750	4,775	735	13,095	27,020	25	55	10
German	158,000	67,030	28,555	84,505	86,690	775	190	40
Polish	140,890	8,870	2,510	21,990	17,565	20	30	15
Spanish	160,275	6,850	2,735	29,125	34,075	130	90	30
Portuguese	155,310	6,295	380	7,205	14,385	15	25	10
Punjabi	152,645	6,340	850	36,320	158,750	80	10	10
Ukrainian	48,310	21,950	16,350	29,455	12,285	40	40	10
Arabic	114,730	2,125	1,525	20,495	8,440	15	105	10
Dutch	68,180	3,835	1,785	19,980	26,355	140	95	15
Tagalog (Pilipino)	117,365	22,490	2,170	29,740	50,425	145	505	45
Greek	61,330	1,635	1,060	3,305	6,670	10	0	0
Vietnamese	67,150	2,740	1,305	19,350	24,560	105	305	0
Cree	3,495	19,105	24,255	17,215	1,145	50	190	20
Inuktitut (Inuit)	390	140	35	155	110	60	750	20,480
Other non-official languages	1,120,655	51,095	26,740	154,320	280,135	1,310	5,515	150
Mother tongue, multiple responses[2]	175,330	14,825	7,600	34,930	52,335	250	380	305
English and French	32,690	2,630	1,130	5,405	5,920	110	45	20
English and non-official language	131,290	11,675	6,080	27,725	43,785	130	320	260
French and non-official language	7,790	435	245	1,325	1,840	10	15	20
English, French and non-official language	3,565	85	140	480	790	0	0	0

1. The respondent reported only one language as a mother tongue.

2. The respondent reported more than one language as a mother tongue.

Source: Statistics Canada, 2006 Census of Population.

Table 22.2 Population, by mother tongue and by census metropolitan area, 2006

	Total population	Single responses	English	French	Non-official languages
	number				
St. John's	**179,270**	178,880	174,480	535	3,860
Halifax	**369,455**	367,520	337,715	10,085	19,725
Moncton	**124,055**	122,830	77,345	42,925	2,555
Saint John	**120,875**	120,300	111,215	5,510	3,570
Saguenay	**149,600**	149,230	1,100	146,435	1,700
Québec	**704,185**	700,810	10,250	671,140	19,410
Sherbrooke	**183,635**	182,345	8,850	165,115	8,385
Trois-Rivières	**138,560**	138,055	1,300	134,255	2,495
Montréal	**3,588,520**	3,514,485	425,635	2,328,400	760,445
Ottawa–Gatineau	**1,117,120**	1,096,315	550,260	360,175	185,875
Kingston	**148,475**	147,440	129,770	4,305	13,360
Peterborough	**115,140**	114,630	106,510	1,295	6,825
Oshawa	**328,070**	325,510	283,475	6,820	35,215
Toronto	**5,072,075**	4,965,405	2,746,480	58,590	2,160,335
Hamilton	**683,450**	675,780	516,360	9,725	149,695
St. Catharines–Niagara	**385,035**	381,310	307,350	13,490	60,475
Kitchener	**446,495**	441,780	334,620	5,975	101,180
Brantford	**122,825**	122,115	107,720	1,310	13,085
Guelph	**126,080**	124,875	100,365	1,755	22,755
London	**452,580**	448,750	363,885	6,055	78,805
Windsor	**320,730**	315,780	230,920	11,105	73,755
Barrie	**175,335**	174,055	154,535	3,720	15,800
Greater Sudbury / Grand Sudbury	**156,395**	154,170	99,445	42,950	11,775
Thunder Bay	**121,050**	120,185	101,305	3,100	15,780
Winnipeg	**686,040**	676,315	507,530	29,020	139,765
Regina	**192,440**	190,890	169,720	2,675	18,495
Saskatoon	**230,850**	228,865	197,260	3,490	28,120
Calgary	**1,070,295**	1,056,760	797,555	16,310	242,895
Edmonton	**1,024,820**	1,011,725	785,755	21,980	203,990
Kelowna	**160,560**	159,490	136,025	2,530	20,935
Abbotsford	**156,640**	154,770	110,265	1,625	42,885
Vancouver	**2,097,960**	2,060,350	1,190,560	24,130	845,660
Victoria	**325,065**	322,655	274,950	5,580	42,120

See source at end of table.

Table 22.2 Population, by mother tongue and by census metropolitan area, 2006 (continued)

	Multiple responses	English and French	English and non-official language	French and non-official language	English, French and non-official language
	number				
St. John's	390	110	235	30	15
Halifax	1,935	1,015	710	85	125
Moncton	1,225	1,085	70	60	15
Saint John	575	495	80	0	0
Saguenay	365	270	0	80	0
Québec	3,375	2,120	85	1,015	155
Sherbrooke	1,295	830	25	400	40
Trois-Rivières	505	320	25	120	30
Montréal	74,035	26,855	15,225	27,005	4,950
Ottawa–Gatineau	20,810	10,495	6,785	2,890	635
Kingston	1,035	365	630	20	15
Peterborough	505	220	265	15	0
Oshawa	2,555	540	1,875	100	45
Toronto	106,670	7,955	92,670	3,865	2,180
Hamilton	7,670	1,135	6,020	380	140
St. Catharines–Niagara	3,725	1,020	2,505	155	45
Kitchener	4,715	695	3,690	255	75
Brantford	710	105	570	20	15
Guelph	1,205	180	975	40	15
London	3,830	730	2,860	170	65
Windsor	4,955	1,115	3,420	330	80
Barrie	1,280	415	815	10	35
Greater Sudbury / Grand Sudbury	2,225	1,675	490	40	15
Thunder Bay	870	190	590	70	15
Winnipeg	9,720	1,830	7,525	310	50
Regina	1,545	225	1,220	70	30
Saskatoon	1,990	265	1,630	50	45
Calgary	13,535	1,845	10,920	600	165
Edmonton	13,100	1,830	10,600	485	185
Kelowna	1,075	175	805	90	0
Abbotsford	1,870	135	1,680	40	10
Vancouver	37,615	2,855	32,880	1,285	595
Victoria	37,615	700	1,530	115	60

Source: Statistics Canada, 2006 Census of Population.

Table 22.3 Population, by knowledge of official language and by province and territory, 2006

	Total	English only	French only	Both English and French	Neither English nor French
	number				
Canada	**31,241,030**	**21,129,945**	**4,141,850**	**5,448,850**	**520,380**
Newfoundland and Labrador	**500,610**	475,985	90	23,675	850
Prince Edward Island	**134,205**	116,990	60	17,100	55
Nova Scotia	**903,090**	805,690	1,000	95,010	1,385
New Brunswick	**719,650**	405,045	73,750	240,085	765
Quebec	**7,435,905**	336,785	4,010,880	3,017,860	70,375
Ontario	**12,028,895**	10,335,705	49,210	1,377,325	266,660
Manitoba	**1,133,510**	1,017,560	1,930	103,520	10,500
Saskatchewan	**953,850**	902,655	485	47,450	3,260
Alberta	**3,256,355**	2,990,805	2,200	222,885	40,470
British Columbia	**4,074,385**	3,653,365	2,070	295,645	123,305
Yukon	**30,195**	26,515	105	3,440	130
Northwest Territories	**41,055**	37,010	50	3,665	325
Nunavut	**29,325**	25,830	20	1,170	2,305

Source: Statistics Canada, 2006 Census of Population.

Table 22.4 Mother tongue, frequency of language used at work, 2006

	Total	Most often	Regularly	Never
	number			
Total	**18,418,100**	**14,414,245**	**1,234,245**	**2,769,615**
Single responses	**18,208,410**	14,232,070	1,220,545	2,755,795
English	**10,717,070**	10,612,740	76,000	28,330
French	**3,992,820**	621,310	917,420	2,454,085
Non-official languages	**3,498,520**	2,998,015	227,115	273,385
Multiple responses	**209,690**	182,175	13,700	13,815
English and French	**49,580**	37,715	6,900	4,960
English and non-official language	**131,950**	128,560	2,040	1,345
French and non-official language	**22,920**	11,465	4,330	7,120
English, French and non-official language	**5,245**	4,430	420	390

Note: Population 15 years and older who had worked since January 1, 2005, regardless of whether or not they were in the labour force in the reference week.

Source: Statistics Canada, 2006 Census of Population.

Manufacturing industries

23

Overview

Manufacturing runs the gamut from frozen french fries to fine paper, cars to aluminum cans, microprocessors to motor oil—thousands of products for sale at home and abroad. In 2007, Canada's manufacturing sales totalled $607.3 billion, and 2 million Canadians were employed in the sector. Although manufacturing remains a powerhouse in our economy, contributing 15% to gross domestic product (GDP) in 2007, the sector is undergoing fundamental change.

Employment in the sector has declined, industrial capacity is underutilised, and output in 2007 was down 1% for a second straight year, leaving it slightly higher than in 2002. Even so, increased industrial product prices and demand for resource-based goods have meant little change in either the value or volume of manufacturing sales. And with high demand for raw materials and record prices for specific natural resources, operating profits in 2007 halted a two-year downward trend, rising 5% to $45.0 billion, the highest it has been since 2004.

A sector in transition

The manufacturing sector has faced significant challenges in 2007, including fierce global competition, rising demand for key resources and the rapid strengthening of the Canadian dollar. The loonie's value exceeded that of the U.S. dollar in September 2007 for the first time in 30 years, making Canadian-made exports to the United States more expensive and thus less competitive. For exporters of manufactured goods, that challenge was compounded by the U.S. subprime mortgage crisis and beckoning recession. For a second consecutive year, exports to the United States fell; this was partly offset by higher exports overseas and strong consumer demand in Canada.

Chart 23.1
Manufacturers' sales

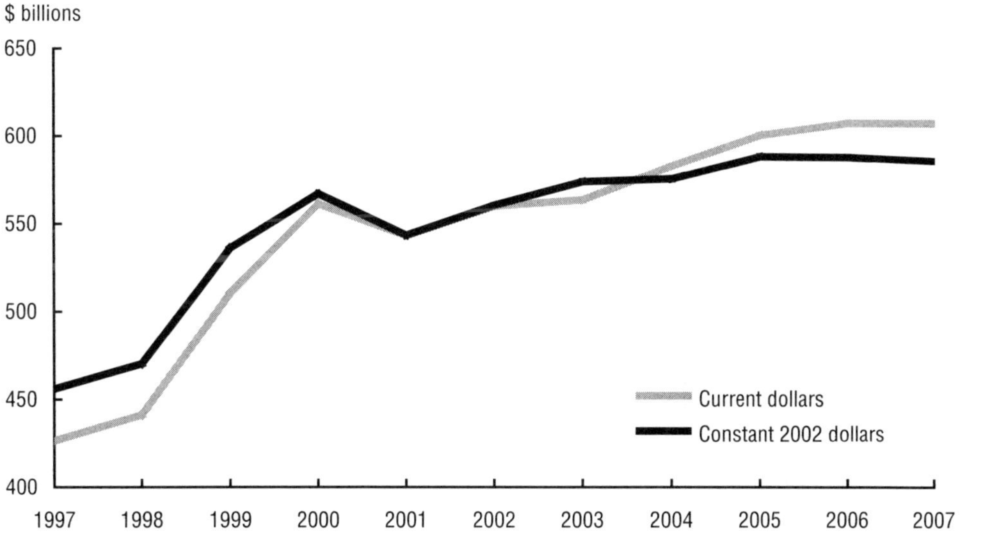

Source: Statistics Canada, CANSIM tables 304-0014 and 377-0008.

Some industries benefit, others struggle

The changing dynamics in Canadian manufacturing highlight the changes the sector is undergoing. In 2007, 10 of 21 manufacturing industries reported improved sales. Benefiting from rising global demand, the petroleum and coal products industry reported sizeable gains, which were boosted by average annual prices that increased by about 65% from 2003 to 2007. With sales of $66.7 billion, petroleum and coal products accounted for 11% of total manufacturing sales in 2007. For the first time, this industry overtook motor vehicle manufacturing, becoming second only to the food industry in total manufacturing sales.

The second-biggest gainer in 2007 was primary metals. Sales by primary metal manufacturers reached $53.0 billion, as prices within the industry rose 10% compared with 2006. As well, 2007 saw a resurgence in Canada's aerospace industry, a result of re-investment in global airline fleets and the awarding of several major defence contracts. Aerospace product and parts manufacturers reported a 3% gain in 2007, reaching a record $16.3 billion in production.

Chart 23.2
Capacity utilization rate, manufacturing

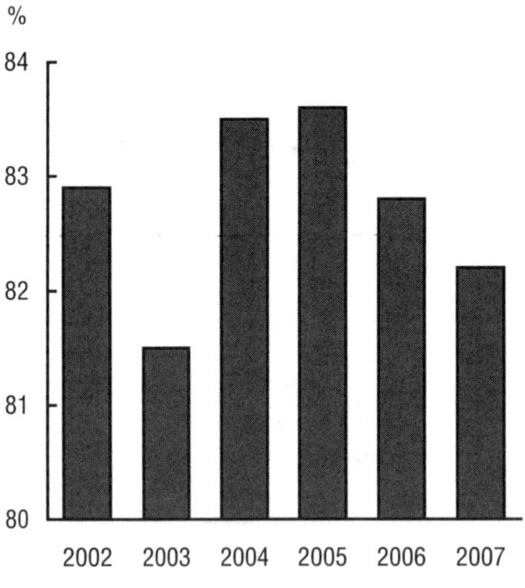

Source: Statistics Canada, CANSIM table 028-0002.

Table 23.a
Manufacturing sales, by region, 2007

	$ billions	% of total
Atlantic provinces	32.2	5.3
Quebec	148.3	24.5
Ontario	291.7	48.0
Prairies	91.2	15.2
British Columbia	42.9	7.1

Note: Data for the territories represent less than 1%.
Source: Statistics Canada, CANSIM table 304-0015.

The hardest hit in a rapidly changing sector in 2007 was the wood products industry, where year-over-year sales fell 18% to $25.0 billion, the lowest since 1996. This industry in particular has been buffeted by the higher Canadian dollar, the decline in the U.S. housing market, rising energy costs and falling wood prices. Since 2004, wood product sales have dropped 30%.

The motor vehicle industry also continues to wane: 2007 saw its third consecutive annual decline. Sales fell 2.2% to $60.6 billion in 2007, less than the 7.5% sales drop in 2006. However, manufacturing sales of motor vehicles have fallen 23% from their peak of $78.3 billion in 1999. This trend results from the cumulative effect of the economic downturn in the United States, where approximately 90% of Canadian-made motor vehicles are sold; high gasoline prices; and the growing demand for more fuel-efficient vehicles rather than the larger autos and trucks that are among the models assembled in Canada.

Operating below capacity

Manufacturing plants are operating below capacity, a sign of the slowdown. The 'capacity utilization rate' is the ratio of actual output in a sector to its estimated potential output. In 2007, the average rate in the manufacturing sector was 82%, down slightly from 2006. Wood products manufacturing, in particular, operated well below capacity: the annual average rate in this industry in 2007 was 77%, well short of the record 92% in 2004. But wood product manufacturers were not alone; 18 of the 21 major industry groups in manufacturing saw reductions in 2007.

But making a profit

Despite the challenges, operating profits have stayed consistent in nominal terms since 1999. What has changed is the source of the profits. In 1999, the petroleum and primary metals industries accounted for 13% of total manufacturing profits. By 2007, their share had almost tripled to 37%. By contrast, motor vehicle and vehicle parts, and wood and paper products manufacturers, which made up 33% of total profits in 1999, dropped to 6% in 2007.

Chart 23.3
Manufacturing sales, by region

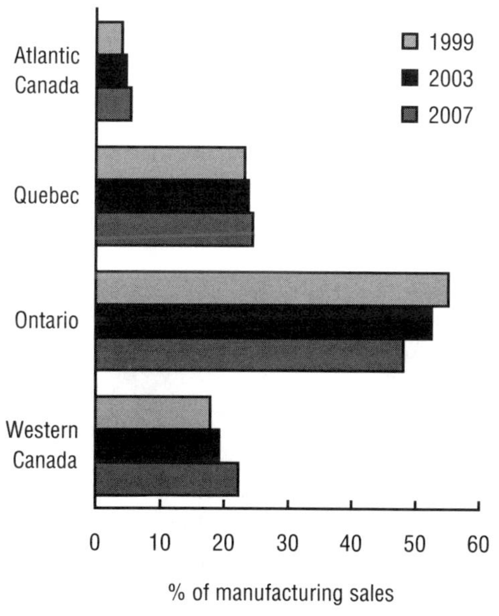

Source: Statistics Canada, CANSIM table 304-0015.

Provincial patterns

The changing nature of manufacturing is echoed in the provincial patterns. Ontario remains the manufacturing heavyweight. However, as the centre of Canada's challenged auto industry, the province has been losing strength. Ontario still accounted for 48% of national manufacturing sales in 2007, but this was down seven percentage points from its 55% share in 1999. As well, while most provinces reported higher manufacturing sales in 2007 than the year before, Ontario posted its second straight decline, slipping 1.5% to $291.7 billion. This was Ontario's lowest level since 2001.

Unlike Ontario, Quebec has enjoyed continued growth in manufacturing sales. In 2007, Quebec posted its sixth consecutive year of rising sales, buoyed by gains in primary metals, food and aerospace. At $148.3 billion, its share of the national total was 24%, up from 23% in 2005.

The four provinces west of Ontario accounted for 22% of total sales in Canada, up from 19% in 2003. Alberta is enjoying the impact of the petroleum and coal products industry on manufacturing sales: it leads the western provinces in sales growth. Alberta posted manufacturing sales of $65.6 billion in 2007, for its fifth successive annual increase. Alberta accounted for nearly one-half of Western Canada's manufacturing sales.

In Newfoundland and Labrador, sales rose 20.7% in 2007 to $5.3 billion, making the province the main contributor to Atlantic growth.

How do they know that? Innovation in manufacturing

Information helps power innovation. To develop new and improved products and processes, firms need knowledge and technology. To get that knowledge and technology from outside, they generally have three options: buying information; buying advanced machinery, hardware and software; or collaborating.

Four out of five manufacturers that introduced a new or significantly improved product or process from 2002 to 2004 cited buying machinery, equipment and software as their most common innovative activity. One out of five manufacturers reported purchasing external research and development, and roughly the same number purchased other external knowledge.

Companies get information relevant to their innovative activities from multiple sources. For a strong majority of companies, clients or customers are a highly important source of information. Many cite suppliers of equipment, materials, components or software, and competitors or other firms in their sector. Other sources include consultants' commercial and public research organizations, universities, colleges and other higher education institutions.

For many, the route to innovation is collaboration. From 2002 to 2004, one in five innovative companies had some kind of collaborative arrangement and many had overlapping collaborations. Three-quarters identified suppliers as their partners. Nearly as many also reported partnerships with clients. Forty percent reported collaborations with other plants in the same firm; one-third teamed with industrial associations.

Chart 23.4
Innovative manufacturing establishments, by type of knowledge and technology purchased, 2002 to 2004

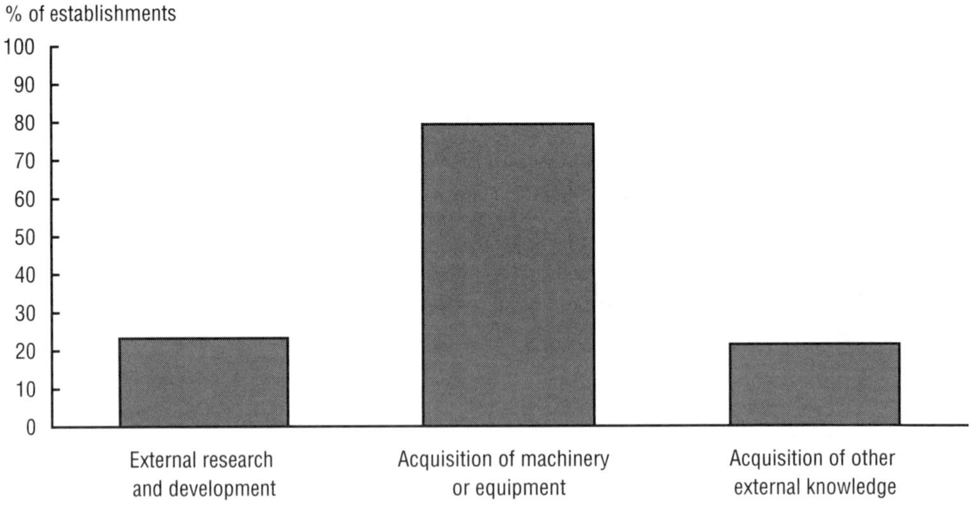

Source: Statistics Canada, Catalogue no. 88-003-XIE.

Lumber a challenged industry

The lumber industry helped shape Canada, with a mill once the dominant feature in many towns across the country. In recent years, though, the lumber industry has faced challenges and extensive restructuring. The industry has lost thousands of jobs since 2000, and seen declining sales and operating profits.

Lumber is essentially an export industry with one major market—80% of output is shipped outside the country, and, in 2006, 80% of lumber exports went to the United States. The industry has been hurt by U.S. duties imposed from 2002 to 2006, the higher Canadian dollar and the downturn in housing construction. As well, rising energy and raw materials prices and declining lumber prices have had a negative impact.

Despite these challenges, lumber is still an important industry. In 2006, it contributed $7.6 billion to Canada's GDP, comprising 4.4% of the manufacturing sector and 0.7% of overall GDP, and it accounted for 4% of total merchandise exports.

Nonetheless, the impact of the challenges is striking. From 2000 to 2006, lumber industry employment dropped by 27%, from 74,000 to 54,000. In 2007, sales of wood products dipped 15.6% from the previous year, the biggest decline among all manufacturing industries. Sales of $24.9 billion were the lowest since 1996. As well in 2007, profits for wood products and paper manufacturers fell for the sixth time in seven years.

In 2006, Canada and the United States signed a new pact on softwood lumber exports. It included an agreement to reimburse most of the duties collected since 2002, and it set a new base price over which Canadian exporters will not have to pay duties.

Chart 23.5
Lumber exports to selected countries

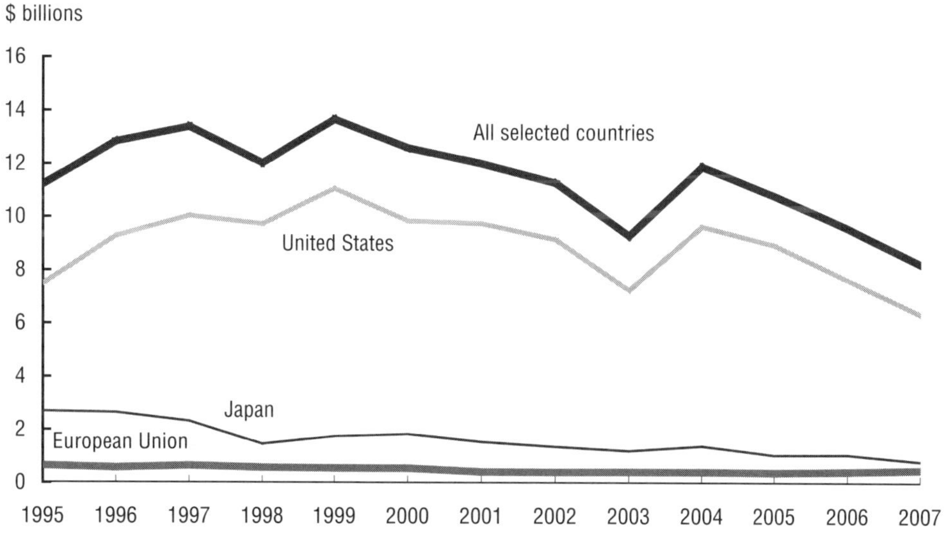

Source: Statistics Canada, special tabulation, International Trade Division.

Table 23.1 Gross domestic product at basic prices, by manufacturing subsector, 1998 to 2006

	1998	1999	2000	2001	2002
	chained (1997) $ millions				
Manufacturing sector	**149,314**	**161,634**	**177,618**	**170,247**	**171,800**
Food	14,520	14,883	15,499	16,627	16,528
Beverage and tobacco products	5,186	4,729	4,896	4,690	4,679
Textile mills and textile product mills	2,431	2,458	2,703	2,555	2,539
Clothing	3,266	3,164	3,778	3,655	3,419
Leather and allied products	388	371	437	372	362
Paper	10,559	11,606	12,035	11,430	12,007
Printing and related support activities	4,313	4,411	5,042	5,608	5,252
Petroleum and coal products	1,805	1,737	1,741	1,950	1,981
Chemicals	12,958	13,470	14,926	15,307	16,052
Plastics and rubber products	7,343	7,989	9,138	9,123	9,845
Wood products	9,669	10,390	11,524	11,016	12,281
Non-metallic mineral products	4,121	4,152	4,566	4,772	4,869
Primary metals and fabricated metal products	20,186	21,300	24,815	24,135	24,875
Machinery	10,111	9,938	11,383	11,184	10,896
Computer and electronic products	8,841	12,384	14,963	8,854	7,620
Electrical equipment, appliances and components	3,625	3,803	4,573	4,519	3,825
Transportation equipment	23,181	27,779	28,104	25,345	25,241
Furniture and related products	4,102	4,487	5,241	5,461	5,405
Miscellaneous manufacturing	2,768	2,734	3,142	3,123	3,479

	2003	2004	2005	2006
	chained (1997) $ millions			
Manufacturing sector	**170,465**	**173,726**	**174,987**	**172,638**
Food	16,316	16,665	16,879	17,030
Beverage and tobacco products	4,478	4,593	4,706	4,136
Textile mills and textile product mills	2,211	2,153	1,993	1,724
Clothing	3,290	3,054	2,758	2,615
Leather and allied products	310	248	179	173
Paper	12,101	12,077	11,711	10,934
Printing and related support activities	5,106	5,023	4,979	4,867
Petroleum and coal products	2,002	2,044	1,987	1,999
Chemicals	16,473	17,109	17,202	17,389
Plastics and rubber products	9,772	9,643	9,349	8,819
Wood products	12,482	13,280	13,488	13,217
Non-metallic mineral products	5,120	5,145	5,149	5,159
Primary metals and fabricated metal products	24,309	24,430	24,932	24,984
Machinery	10,605	10,686	10,983	11,363
Computer and electronic products	8,731	8,915	9,496	9,726
Electrical equipment, appliances and components	3,340	3,288	3,236	3,161
Transportation equipment	25,196	26,736	27,342	26,934
Furniture and related products	4,954	4,952	5,031	4,794
Miscellaneous manufacturing	3,500	3,480	3,470	3,652

Note: North American Industry Classification System (NAICS), 2002.
Source: Statistics Canada, CANSIM table 379-0017.

Table 23.2 Manufacturing sales, by manufacturing subsector, 1995 to 2007

	1995	1996	1997	1998	1999	2000	2001
	$ millions						
Manufacturing sector	**389,779.5**	**400,085.1**	**426,519.4**	**441,152.6**	**510,549.9**	**561,300.9**	**543,272.0**
Food	45,170.0	48,246.0	50,513.4	51,468.6	55,104.9	57,278.7	61,609.3
Beverage and tobacco products	9,317.9	9,610.4	10,154.4	11,190.5	11,250.8	11,625.5	11,699.1
Textile mills and textile product mills	5,558.6	5,621.5	5,960.2	6,371.0	6,602.4	6,966.1	6,848.8
Clothing	6,568.4	6,677.7	6,947.0	6,967.6	7,429.3	7,936.6	7,685.0
Leather and allied products	985.9	942.8	1,001.3	944.2	967.1	956.4	967.2
Paper	36,013.7	30,663.2	29,761.6	29,790.5	33,236.4	38,213.2	35,852.9
Printing and related support activities	8,447.9	8,841.4	8,961.8	9,341.9	10,436.0	11,079.3	11,633.8
Petroleum and coal products	17,969.3	20,688.6	20,932.8	16,325.6	21,347.3	33,918.0	33,407.5
Chemicals	30,074.0	30,252.6	32,486.3	31,374.1	34,194.7	37,205.8	38,391.4
Plastics and rubber products	14,048.1	15,045.3	16,504.1	17,362.1	21,108.8	21,858.0	22,986.9
Wood products	22,621.5	24,000.3	25,960.2	25,994.4	31,214.5	31,669.8	30,074.1
Non-metallic mineral products	7,220.7	7,851.9	8,487.7	8,930.3	9,653.4	9,926.8	10,324.3
Primary metals	26,178.1	26,781.9	28,743.2	29,596.9	30,755.1	36,352.2	34,115.3
Fabricated metal products	17,505.8	19,174.5	21,082.6	22,850.8	27,625.0	29,685.8	30,189.5
Machinery	18,060.8	19,548.5	21,835.9	23,097.3	24,284.6	26,283.4	26,422.0
Computer and electronic products	22,845.0	22,072.9	23,154.3	25,356.4	27,295.3	37,273.3	27,040.1
Electrical equipment, appliances and components	7,587.9	7,834.5	8,085.3	8,486.9	10,488.1	11,595.5	11,637.6
Transportation equipment	82,992.4	84,548.0	92,822.9	101,064.1	130,037.5	132,252.5	122,560.4
Furniture and related products	6,140.3	6,839.8	7,892.6	9,013.0	10,995.4	12,608.2	13,054.9
Miscellaneous manufacturing	4,473.0	4,843.2	5,231.8	5,626.2	6,523.2	6,615.9	6,771.9

	2002	2003	2004	2005	2006	2007
	$ millions					
Manufacturing sector	**559,902.7**	**562,551.7**	**586,779.4**	**606,254.5**	**611,044.4**	**613,470.6**
Food	64,089.5	67,065.8	68,254.9	67,518.3	72,138.0	74,208.3
Beverage and tobacco products	12,074.4	12,191.5	12,567.7	12,643.5	11,196.7	10,939.8
Textile mills and textile product mills	7,211.0	6,672.8	6,323.3	5,988.8	5,003.9	4,558.4
Clothing	8,024.4	7,893.8	6,452.3	5,537.9	5,309.9	4,474.4
Leather and allied products	933.6	849.6	665.3	529.8	459.1	510.3
Paper	34,284.4	33,359.4	33,840.2	32,536.1	31,422.4	31,071.6
Printing and related support activities	12,155.3	12,435.5	11,701.7	12,224.7	10,868.4	10,728.9
Petroleum and coal products	33,690.1	37,585.3	45,736.1	57,073.5	61,219.4	66,359.8
Chemicals	40,469.2	43,088.5	47,266.6	51,432.2	53,046.1	51,226.2
Plastics and rubber products	25,286.6	26,464.1	25,791.5	27,329.3	27,808.9	25,987.0
Wood products	32,801.6	32,360.0	36,020.3	33,704.4	29,465.4	24,886.7
Non-metallic mineral products	11,630.8	12,029.4	12,339.8	12,900.2	13,945.7	15,246.4
Primary metals	36,074.9	36,897.8	42,954.7	43,760.4	51,273.6	53,842.9
Fabricated metal products	32,210.5	33,313.1	33,255.7	35,393.9	35,411.5	36,898.6
Machinery	27,448.5	28,070.2	28,143.2	30,694.6	31,424.7	32,675.7
Computer and electronic products	22,656.3	20,826.3	20,818.4	20,103.8	19,560.7	19,154.4
Electrical equipment, appliances and components	10,135.9	9,482.2	9,526.6	9,869.9	10,520.1	10,624.5
Transportation equipment	126,451.6	120,565.8	123,322.0	124,810.1	118,449.0	116,426.9
Furniture and related products	13,916.5	13,719.5	13,374.3	13,407.6	13,358.9	13,917.8
Miscellaneous manufacturing	8,357.6	8,702.3	8,424.6	8,795.3	9,161.9	9,732.0

Note: North American Industry Classification System (NAICS), 2002.

Source: Statistics Canada, CANSIM table 304-0014.

Table 23.3 Employment, by manufacturing subsector, 1995 to 2007

	1995	1996	1997	1998	1999	2000	2001
	number						
Manufacturing sector	**1,739,096**	**1,779,368**	**1,845,808**	**1,906,843**	**1,946,466**	**2,036,697**	**1,996,202**
Food	206,340	213,999	216,006	222,195	224,202	232,653	229,448
Beverage and tobacco products	32,984	29,736	32,068	34,255	33,791	35,424	35,901
Textile mills	26,813	27,035	28,225	29,449	29,520	30,133	29,181
Textile product mills	16,512	17,890	19,845	20,500	20,417	20,928	19,707
Clothing	86,510	85,882	88,569	90,422	89,465	93,347	86,689
Leather and allied products	12,160	12,218	12,391	11,473	11,241	12,219	12,129
Paper	104,450	103,394	104,098	100,821	103,110	110,144	103,835
Printing and related support activities	80,375	76,787	76,948	79,810	82,459	85,537	83,529
Petroleum and coal products	13,414	13,990	13,747	13,753	15,454	15,879	15,305
Chemicals	88,054	86,874	88,774	89,227	91,385	95,493	93,412
Plastics and rubber products	96,902	104,354	111,754	115,525	117,688	123,469	125,864
Wood products	108,431	116,544	124,299	127,559	134,177	141,872	134,714
Non-metallic mineral products	47,077	45,687	48,554	52,166	53,286	56,440	53,719
Primary metals	102,127	101,727	98,828	100,957	100,529	104,253	91,936
Fabricated metal products	139,590	146,910	157,630	165,626	173,072	183,246	187,521
Machinery	116,450	124,562	131,871	134,419	132,486	136,397	134,897
Computer and electronic products	88,905	88,310	92,754	97,905	101,630	106,289	105,716
Electrical equipment, appliances and components	46,669	45,178	45,477	45,898	48,538	53,780	50,375
Transportation equipment	204,534	214,530	215,751	229,476	235,548	244,196	242,725
Furniture and related products	69,149	71,094	81,566	86,086	88,698	94,350	98,819
Miscellaneous manufacturing	51,648	52,668	56,652	59,319	59,772	60,648	60,780

	2002	2003	2004	2005	2006	2007
	number					
Manufacturing sector	**1,953,247**	**1,933,510**	**1,892,330**	**1,857,939**	**1,840,025**	**1,784,722**
Food	232,358	234,410	236,266	232,876	234,164	232,355
Beverage and tobacco products	36,022	33,314	31,991	28,097	28,114	27,119
Textile mills	28,324	27,902	24,011	19,651	16,541	14,595
Textile product mills	19,022	18,414	18,073	17,685	16,477	15,164
Clothing	80,093	74,579	65,703	54,521	48,494	41,958
Leather and allied products	13,100	12,782	10,685	9,279	8,272	7,524
Paper	95,981	96,994	93,718	87,689	83,810	79,380
Printing and related support activities	79,678	78,593	73,774	72,829	73,148	75,206
Petroleum and coal products	15,401	15,674	15,301	15,758	16,336	16,657
Chemicals	92,246	92,797	92,761	93,030	90,823	88,960
Plastics and rubber products	127,635	128,741	129,825	127,830	127,230	120,387
Wood products	132,261	131,686	135,261	133,447	128,385	121,163
Non-metallic mineral products	52,547	53,351	53,307	53,066	55,521	54,577
Primary metals	90,322	85,394	79,703	78,731	80,681	78,802
Fabricated metal products	183,980	183,364	178,988	178,727	183,051	178,760
Machinery	137,332	137,162	136,049	140,411	144,467	139,714
Computer and electronic products	95,263	89,091	87,200	85,422	84,727	83,139
Electrical equipment, appliances and components	47,002	46,362	43,898	43,044	43,157	43,661
Transportation equipment	233,603	231,268	229,245	229,337	222,798	217,255
Furniture and related products	99,742	99,371	94,505	95,731	91,967	86,841
Miscellaneous manufacturing	61,334	62,261	62,065	60,778	61,863	61,505

Note: North American Industry Classification System (NAICS), 2002.
Annual number of salaried and hourly employees on payroll.

Source: Statistics Canada, CANSIM table 281-0024.

Table 23.4 Manufacturing sector and workers, by province and territory, 2005 and 2006

	Canada	Newfoundland and Labrador	Prince Edward Island	Nova Scotia	New Brunswick	Quebec	Ontario
	number						
Establishments							
2005	**85,724**	765	351	1,944	1,533	23,042	34,184
2006	**83,545**	729	348	1,818	1,463	22,615	32,700
Production workers							
2005	**1,351,014**	13,885	4,422	29,967	27,349	354,269	627,182
2006	**1,314,983**	12,549	4,766	27,468	26,858	340,533	603,631

	Manitoba	Saskatch-ewan	Alberta	British Columbia	Yukon	Northwest Territories	Nunavut
	number						
Establishments							
2005	2,307	1,804	7,750	11,942	59	28	15
2006	2,266	1,772	7,739	12,010	52	21	12
Production workers							
2005	46,185	20,699	103,828	122,776	185	183	84
2006	45,670	20,227	109,439	123,384	199	173	86

Note: The number of establishments represents a count of locations that perform manufacturing activities and normally correspond to plants, factories and mills. It excludes sales offices and warehouses that support manufacturing activities.

Source: Statistics Canada, CANSIM table 301-0006.

Table 23.5 Industrial capacity utilization rates, 2007

	First quarter	Second quarter	Third quarter	Fourth quarter
		%		
All industries	**83.9**	**84.2**	**83.4**	**81.8**
Manufacturing	82.6	83.3	82.4	80.3
Food	80.3	80.8	80.4	79.0
Beverage and tobacco products	74.1	76.7	72.9	72.8
Textile mills and textile products	77.9	79.3	75.6	73.6
Clothing	73.8	75.2	76.9	70.4
Leather and allied products	78.8	82.4	76.5	84.6
Paper	88.9	89.5	88.2	86.6
Printing and related support activities	72.6	76.3	79.3	80.6
Petroleum and coal products	86.4	87.7	85.3	78.8
Chemical	78.0	81.2	79.3	78.3
Plastics and rubber products	74.4	77.0	77.6	73.4
Wood products	81.3	80.6	76.2	71.0
Non-metallic mineral products	82.1	84.4	81.6	79.0
Primary metals	90.8	91.8	89.6	91.4
Fabricated metal products	82.5	85.5	83.0	82.2
Machinery	83.2	84.9	83.8	82.2
Computer and electronic products	88.2	89.8	88.3	86.1
Electrical equipment, appliances and components	79.8	79.9	77.2	74.3
Transportation equipment	87.0	83.6	86.4	83.4
Furniture and related products	84.0	83.2	79.9	77.8
Miscellaneous manufacturing	87.5	87.3	81.8	79.4

Note: North American Industry Classification System (NAICS), 2002.
Source: Statistics Canada, CANSIM table 028-0002.

Population and demography

Overview

Canada had the fastest growth among the G8 nations from 2001 to 2006: our population rose 5.2%. The United States ranked second, with a 5.0% growth. On July 1, 2007, Canada's population had reached 33.0 million, 2.0 million more people than in 2001.

Two-thirds of Canada's population growth is due to international migration: an average of 240,000 newcomers have arrived each year since 2001. By contrast, 60% of the population growth in the United States stems from natural increase—that is, more births than deaths. Births in the United States averaged 2.0 children per woman over the last few years, the highest of the G8; Canadian women have an average of 1.5 children.

Canada extends across a vast territory of nearly 10 million square kilometres and has 3.5 people per square kilometre. However, in the country's large census metropolitan areas (CMAs), population density reaches, on average, 238 inhabitants per square kilometre. Most of these CMAs are located in the southern part of the country. Vast northern areas are sparsely populated: the Northwest Territories, Yukon and Nunavut makes up 39% of Canada's total area but had only 0.3% of its population in 2007.

Growth is uneven across the country

Two-thirds of Canada's population growth from 2001 to 2006 was concentrated in Alberta and Ontario.

Alberta is enjoying an economic boom, and its population grew 10% from 2001 to 2006, making it the fastest-growing province in the country. On July 1, 2007, 3.5 million people lived in Alberta and the province made up 11% of the Canadian population.

Chart 24.1
Population growth rates of G8 countries, annual average, 2001 to 2006

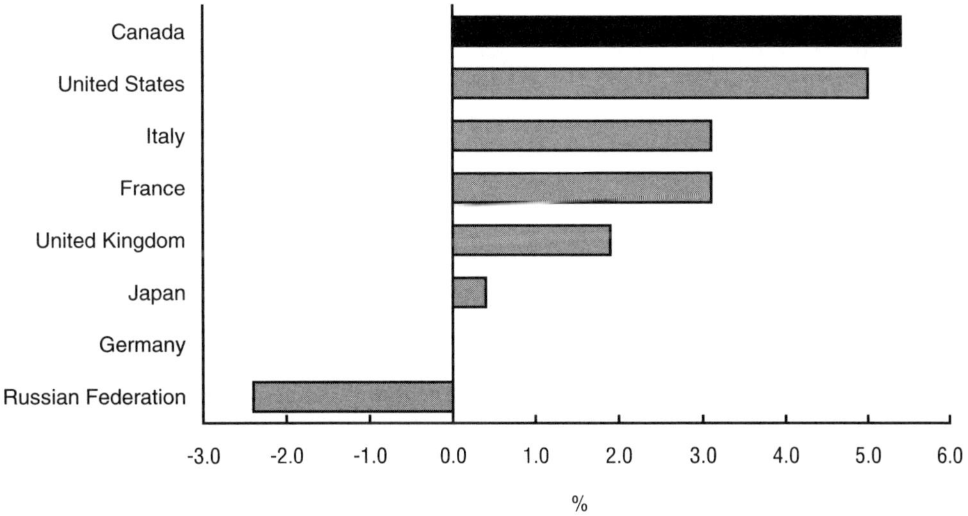

Note: Population as of July 1.
Sources: Statistics Canada; U.S. Census Bureau; Eurostat; U.K. Office of National Statistics; Statistics Bureau of Japan and Russian Federal State Statistics Service.

Gains from migration from the rest of Canada are still the main component of growth. Natural increase in Alberta, which is relatively higher than in other provinces, is generating growth, too; immigration, to a lesser degree, is also a contributing factor.

Ontario is Canada's most populous province. In 2007, Ontario had 12.8 million people and the province made up 39% of the Canadian population. From 2001 to 2006, half of the country's population growth was in Ontario.

During 2006/2007, however, Ontario saw a net loss of 36,200 people who left for other regions, and the province welcomed 17,600 fewer immigrants than the previous year. The province's slower population growth in 2006/2007 was the weakest on record since 1980/1981.

Quebec, the second most populous province, had a population of 7.7 million people on July 1, 2007, and had 23% of the Canadian population. In 1971, 28% of the Canadian population lived in Quebec.

Chart 24.2
Urban–rural variation in population growth, 2001 to 2006

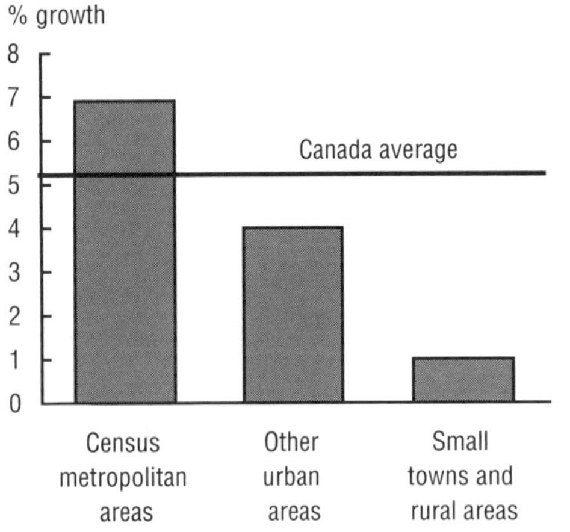

Source: Statistics Canada, Census of Population, 2001 and 2006.

Table 24.a
Components of population growth

	1990/1991	2000/2001	2006/2007
	number		
Births	402,929	327,107	352,848
Deaths	192,439	219,114	237,931
Immigrants	221,382	252,533	238,127
Emigrants	43,692	47,766	41,349

Note: Estimates for the period from July 1 to June 30.
Source: Statistics Canada, CANSIM table 051-0004.

From 2001 to 2006, Quebec's population grew 3%—three times faster than during the period from 1996 to 2001. This was the second highest growth since the end of the baby boom in the mid-1960s. This upswing is due to an increase in international migration and to smaller losses in migration exchanges with other provinces.

Quebec's population growth was slower during 2006/2007 than in the previous year, despite the gains in births and immigrants.

Population fluctuations

The populations in Saskatchewan and in Newfoundland and Labrador continued to decline from 2001 to 2006.

From 2001 to 2006, the former had a 1% population decline, while the latter saw its population fall 2%. This decline continued until June 30, 2006 in Saskatchewan and until June 30, 2007 in Newfoundland and Labrador.

From July 1, 2006, to October 1, 2007, Saskatchewan's population grew to one million. The population of Newfoundland and Labrador was estimated at 507,500 at October 1, 2007, up 1,200 people from July 1, 2007.

In 2007, the total population of the three territories, that is, the Northwest Territories, Yukon and Nunavut, surpassed 100,000. In all three territories, natural increase is usually the main growth factor.

An increasingly urban population

According to the 2006 Census, 68% of Canadians live in one of the country's 33 CMAs. Moreover, 45% of Canada's population lives in the six largest CMAs: Toronto, Montréal, Vancouver, Ottawa–Gatineau, Calgary and Edmonton. From 2001 to 2006, two-thirds of the population growth was in one of these six CMAs.

Almost 90% of the growth in population took place in Canada's 33 CMAs. In the CMAs, this growth was 7%, whereas the growth was 4% in mid-size urban centres and 1% in small towns and rural regions.

From 2001 to 2006, some mid-size urban centres posted growth rates of more than 10%, twice as high as the rate for all of Canada. For example, Okotoks, Alberta, south of Calgary, grew 47%. Elsewhere in Alberta, Wood Buffalo's population, which includes Fort McMurray, grew 24%; Red Deer, 22%; Grande Prairie, 22%; and Lloydminster, 13%. Yellowknife, Northwest Territories, also grew 13% from 2001 to 2006.

Chart 24.3
Population projections, children and seniors

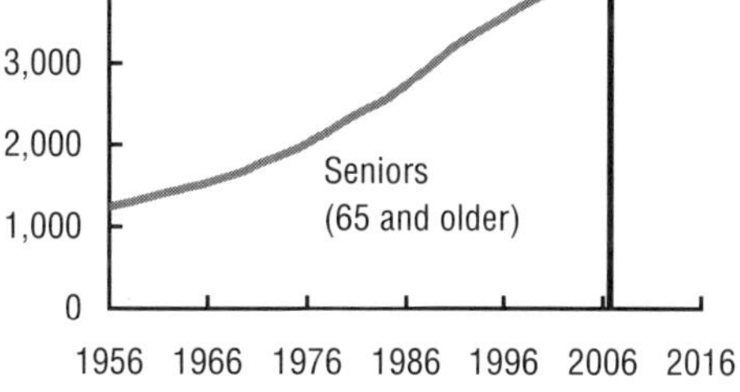

1. Medium growth scenario.
Source: Statistics Canada, CANSIM tables 051-0026, 051-0001 and 052-0004.

An aging population

Canada may be one of the youngest G8 countries, but its population is aging considerably. Mainly, this is a result of decreasing fertility rates and longer life expectancy. On July 1, 2007, the median age among Canadians was 39 years, an increase compared with 26 years in 1971.

In 2007, the number of people aged 65 and older reached 4.4 million, an increase from 2001. Seniors made up 13% of the population as a whole, a proportion that has risen progressively over the years. In 1971, the proportion of seniors was 8%.

The proportion of children under the age of 15 has continued to decline; it was 17% in 2007, compared with 29% in 1971.

According to recent population projections, Canada could soon have more people at the age where they can leave the labour force than people at the age where they can begin working.

These rapid changes present many challenges for Canadian employers and for society as a whole: a high turnover rate in labour, knowledge transfer, employee retention, health among older workers and continuing education for employees, for example.

A slight baby boom

During 2006/2007, there were 352,800 births recorded in Canada. The number of births had declined throughout the 1990s, until it reached about 327,100 in 2000/2001, its lowest level since the end of the Second World War. Since then, the number of births has increased every year.

Quebec and Alberta had the largest increase in births from 2005/2006 to 2006/2007. During this period, the number of births increased 6% in Quebec and 4% in Alberta. This was the most births in Alberta since 1983/1984.

Aging: Regional variations

The aging of the population, which results from declining fertility rates and an ever-increasing life expectancy, affects the entire country. However, the effect of this aging varies from one region to the next. The proportion of people aged 65 and older ranged from 2.7% in Nunavut to 15.4% in Saskatchewan, according to the 2006 Census.

As in 2001, the population east of Ontario was generally older than average in 2006, and it was distinctly younger in the Northwest Territories, Nunavut and Alberta, the provinces where seniors are proportionally fewer.

The Atlantic region is the oldest of all Canada's major regions. It has proportionally more people aged 65 and older (14.7%) and fewer children under 15 years (16.1%) than anywhere else. In 1956, seniors made up 7.8% of the population in the Atlantic provinces—a proportion that was smaller than in Ontario, the Prairies and British Columbia.

In Quebec, the number of seniors has more than quadrupled in the last 50 years. In 2006, Quebec had one million people aged 65 and older, accounting for 14.3% of that province's population. In 1956, 5.7% of Quebec's population was 65 and older, the lowest proportion of all the provinces.

British Columbia's population has been one of the oldest in Canada for the last 50 years. In 2006, 14.6% of that province's population had reached the age of 65, compared with 13.7% in Canada as a whole. People younger than 15 years in British Columbia made up 16.5% of the population, a smaller proportion than the national average of 17.7%. In 1956, British Columbia's population was the oldest in Canada.

Chart 24.4
Population aged 65 and older, by province

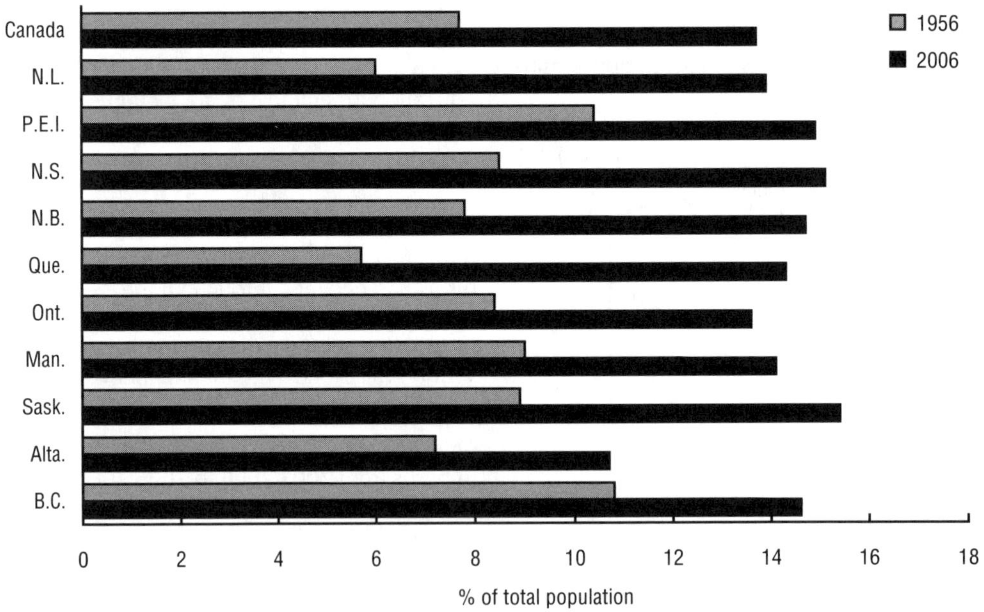

Source: Statistics Canada, Census of population, 1956 and 2006.

Spreading suburbs

The increasingly urbanized Canadian population has meant urban spread: more rapid growth around the edges than in the centre of census metropolitan areas (CMAs). Urban population spread poses many challenges, notably transportation, delivery of services and environmental issues.

From 2001 to 2006, the growth of peripheral municipalities surrounding Canada's 33 CMAs was 11%, or double the national average of 5%. Growth in the central municipalities was slower, at 4%.

Urban population spread usually occurs along major transportation routes. For example, in the Toronto CMA, peripheral municipalities have developed along a network of expressways.

Around Montréal, municipalities like Saint-Jérôme, north of Montréal, and Boucherville on the South Shore have all experienced rapid growth as a result of the developing transportation infrastructure.

In 2006, almost 20% of the population in the suburbs was under the age of 15, compared with 17% in central municipalities. The suburbs also account for a greater population of residents aged 40 to 59, many of whom likely live among families with children.

The population of 20- to 34-year-olds is higher in the CMAs of Toronto, Montréal and Vancouver than in the suburbs. This might stem from an influx of young migrants from other parts of the country and large numbers of immigrants.

The proportion of seniors is higher in central municipalities than in the suburbs: 14% compared with 12%. In Toronto, Montréal and Vancouver, the higher proportion of seniors may be linked to the presence of seniors' residences and health services intended to meet the needs of the senior population.

Chart 24.5
Population aged 14 and younger and 65 and older in central and peripheral municipalities of all CMAs

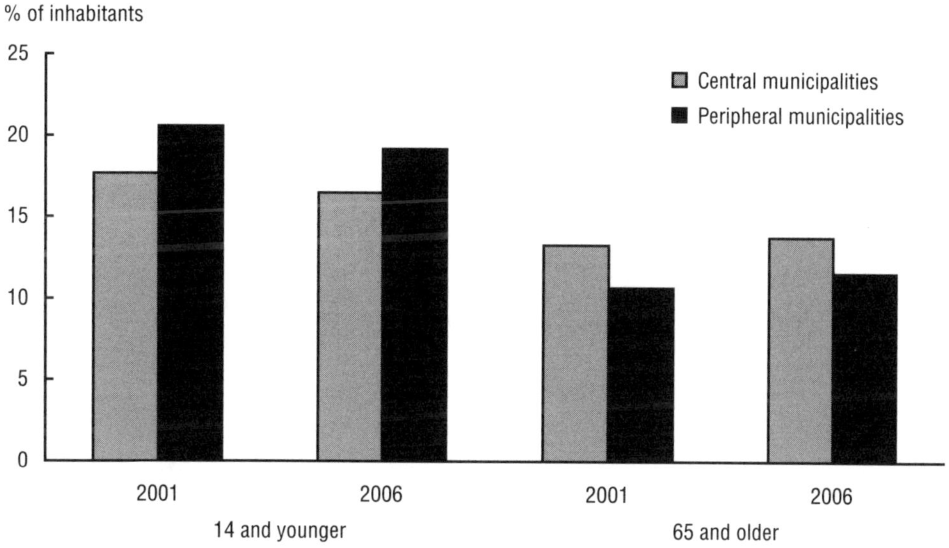

Source: Statistics Canada, 2006 Census of Population.

Table 24.1 Population, by province and territory, selected census years from 1861 to 2001 and 2007

	1861	1871	1881	1891	1901	1911	1921	1931
	number							
Canada[1]	**3,229,633**	**3,689,257**	**4,324,810**	**4,833,239**	**5,371,315**	**7,206,643**	**8,787,949[2]**	**10,376,786**
Newfoundland and Labrador[1]	..	..	..	..	..	..	..	..
Prince Edward Island	80,857	94,021	108,891	109,078	103,259	93,728	88,615	88,038
Nova Scotia	330,857	387,800	440,572	450,396	459,574	492,338	523,837	512,846
New Brunswick	252,047	285,594	321,233	321,263	331,120	351,889	387,876	408,219
Quebec	1,111,566	1,191,516	1,359,027	1,488,535	1,648,898	2,005,776	2,360,510	2,874,662
Ontario	1,396,091	1,620,851	1,926,922	2,114,321	2,182,947	2,527,292	2,933,662	3,431,683
Manitoba	..[3]	25,228	62,260	152,506	255,211	461,394	610,118	700,139
Saskatchewan	..[3]	..[3]	..[3]	..[3]	91,279	492,432	757,510	921,785
Alberta	..[3]	..[3]	..[3]	..[3]	73,022	374,295	588,454	731,605
British Columbia	51,524	36,247	49,459	98,173	178,657	392,480	524,582	694,263
Yukon	..	..	..	..	27,219	8,512	4,157	4,230
Northwest Territories (including Nunavut)	6,691	48,000	56,446	98,967	20,129	6,507	8,143	9,316
Northwest Territories[4]	..	..	..	..	..	..	..	..
Nunavut[4]	..	..	..	..	..	..	..	..

See notes and source at end of table.

Table 24.1 Population, by province and territory, selected census years from 1861 to 2001 and 2007 (continued)

	1941	1951	1961	1971	1981	1991	2001	2007
	number							
Canada[1]	**11,506,655**	**14,009,429**	**18,238,247**	**21,961,999**	**24,820,393**	**28,031,394**	**31,021,251**	**32,976,026**
Newfoundland and Labrador[1]	..	361,416	457,853	530,851	574,775	579,518	521,986	506,275
Prince Edward Island	95,047	98,429	104,629	112,591	123,741	130,306	136,672	138,627
Nova Scotia	577,962	642,584	737,007	797,291	854,646	915,102	932,389	934,147
New Brunswick	457,401	515,697	597,936	642,469	706,325	745,528	749,890	749,782
Quebec	3,331,882	4,055,681	5,259,211	6,137,306	6,547,705	7,064,586	7,396,990	7,700,807
Ontario	3,787,655	4,597,542	6,236,092	7,849,002	8,811,312	10,428,132	11,897,647	12,803,861
Manitoba	729,744	776,541	921,686	998,874	1,036,433	1,109,614	1,151,285	1,186,679
Saskatchewan	895,992	831,728	925,181	932,037	975,867	1,002,686	1,000,134	996,869
Alberta	796,169	939,501	1,331,944	1,665,717	2,294,198	2,592,626	3,056,739	3,473,984
British Columbia	817,861	1,165,210	1,629,082	2,240,472	2,823,933	3,373,464	4,078,447	4,380,256
Yukon	4,914	9,096	14,628	18,991	23,903	28,907	30,129	30,989
Northwest Territories (including Nunavut)	12,028	16,004	22,998	36,398	47,555	..	..	..
Northwest Territories[4]	..	..	..	..	..	38,746	40,822	42,637
Nunavut[4]	..	..	..	..	..	22,179	28,121	31,113

Note: Prior to 1961, data are as of census day; from 1961 onward, data are as of July 1.

1. Beginning in 1951, Newfoundland and Labrador is included in Canada total.

2. Includes 485 members of the Royal Canadian Navy whose province of residence is not known.

3. Included with Northwest Territories.

4. Prior to July 1, 1991, only data for Northwest Territories and Nunavut combined are available.

Source: Statistics Canada, CANSIM table 051-0001.

Table 24.2 Population, by sex and age group and by province and territory, 2007

	Both sexes				Males				Females			
	All ages	0 to 14	15 to 64	65 and older	All ages	0 to 14	15 to 64	65 and older	All ages	0 to 14	15 to 64	65 and older
	thousands											
Canada	**32,976.0**	**5,613.0**	**22,939.6**	**4,423.4**	**16,332.3**	**2,875.0**	**11,518.9**	**1,938.4**	**16,643.7**	**2,738.1**	**11,420.7**	**2,485.0**
Newfoundland and Labrador	506.3	76.6	359.1	70.6	247.8	39.4	176.7	31.7	258.5	37.2	182.4	38.9
Prince Edward Island	138.6	23.5	95.1	20.1	67.5	12.0	46.7	8.8	71.1	11.4	48.3	11.3
Nova Scotia	934.1	144.7	651.1	138.4	456.4	73.7	322.6	60.1	477.8	71.0	328.5	78.3
New Brunswick	749.8	115.5	525.7	108.6	369.5	59.1	263.4	47.0	380.3	56.4	262.2	61.6
Quebec	7,700.8	1,230.9	5,364.3	1,105.5	3,802.1	630.9	2,701.9	469.3	3,898.7	600.1	2,662.4	636.2
Ontario	12,803.9	2,240.7	8,877.4	1,685.7	6,315.8	1,145.5	4,430.0	740.2	6,488.1	1,095.2	4,447.4	945.5
Manitoba	1,186.7	227.8	798.1	160.8	589.4	116.8	403.6	69.1	597.2	111.0	394.5	91.8
Saskatchewan	996.9	190.0	658.6	148.3	494.9	97.4	332.8	64.8	501.9	92.6	325.8	83.5
Alberta	3,474.0	648.1	2,463.9	361.9	1,763.2	332.3	1,268.0	162.9	1,710.8	315.8	1,195.9	199.0
British Columbia	4,380.3	689.5	3,072.9	617.8	2,172.2	354.8	1,535.8	281.6	2,208.1	334.7	1,537.1	336.2
Yukon	31.0	5.4	23.2	2.4	15.6	2.6	11.7	1.3	15.4	2.7	11.5	1.2
Northwest Territories	42.6	10.1	30.4	2.2	22.0	5.2	15.6	1.2	20.7	4.9	14.8	1.0
Nunavut	31.1	10.3	19.8	1.0	15.9	5.3	10.1	0.5	15.2	5.0	9.7	0.4

Note: Population as of July 1.

Source: Statistics Canada, CANSIM table 051-0001.

Table 24.3 Population counts, by census metropolitan areas, 1996, 2001 and 2006

	1996	2001	2006
		number	
St. John's	174,051	172,918	181,113
Halifax	342,966[1]	359,183	372,858
Moncton	..	118,678[1]	126,424
Saint John	125,705	122,678	122,389
Saguenay	160,454	154,938	151,643
Québec[2]	671,889	686,569[1]	715,515
Sherbrooke	149,569[1]	175,950[1]	186,952
Trois-Rivières	139,956	137,507	141,529
Montréal[2]	3,326,447[1]	3,451,027[1]	3,635,571
Ottawa–Gatineau	998,718[1]	1,067,800[1]	1,130,761
Kingston	144,528[1]	146,838	152,358
Peterborough	..	110,876[1]	116,570
Oshawa	268,773	296,298	330,594
Toronto	4,263,759[1]	4,682,897	5,113,149
Hamilton	624,360	662,401	692,911
St. Catharines–Niagara	372,406	377,009	390,317
Kitchener	382,940	414,284	451,235
Brantford[2]	..	118,086[1]	124,607
Guelph	..	117,344	127,009
London	416,546[1]	435,600[1]	457,720
Windsor	286,811[1]	307,877	323,342
Barrie	..	148,480	177,061
Greater Sudbury / Grand Sudbury	165,618[1]	155,601	158,258
Thunder Bay	126,643[1]	121,986	122,907
Winnipeg	667,093[1]	676,594[1]	694,668
Regina	193,652	192,800	194,971
Saskatoon	219,056	225,927	233,923
Calgary[2]	821,628	951,494[1]	1,079,310
Edmonton	862,597	937,845	1,034,945
Kelowna	..	147,739	162,276
Abbotsford	136,480	147,370	159,020
Vancouver	1,831,665	1,986,965	2,116,581
Victoria[2]	304,287	311,902	330,088

1. Figure adjusted because of boundary change.
2. Excludes census data for one or more incompletely enumerated Indian reserves or Indian settlements.

Source: Statistics Canada, censuses of population, 1996, 2001 and 2006.

Table 24.4 Mid-size urban centres with the fastest population growth from 2001 to 2006

	2001	2006	Growth
	number		%
Okotoks, Alberta	11,689	17,145	46.7
Wood Buffalo, Alberta	42,581	52,643	23.6
Grande Prairie, Alberta	58,787	71,868	22.3
Red Deer, Alberta	67,829	82,772	22.0
Yellowknife, Northwest Territories	16,541	18,700	13.1
Lloydminster, Saskatchewan/Alberta	23,964	27,023	12.8
Canmore, Alberta	10,792	12,039	11.6
Medicine Hat, Alberta	61,735	68,822	11.5
Saint-Jean-sur-Richelieu, Quebec	79,600	87,492	9.9
Joliette, Quebec	39,720	43,595	9.8
Chilliwack, British Columbia	74,003	80,892	9.3
Fort St. John, British Columbia	23,007	25,136	9.3
Parksville, British Columbia	24,285	26,518	9.2
Lethbridge, Alberta	87,388	95,196	8.9
Courtenay, British Columbia	45,205	49,214	8.9
Granby, Quebec	63,069	68,352	8.4
Nanaimo, British Columbia	85,664	92,361	7.8
Collingwood, Ontario	16,039	17,290	7.8
Kawartha Lakes, Ontario	69,179	74,561	7.8
Vernon, British Columbia	51,530	55,418	7.5

Source: Statistics Canada, censuses of population, 2001 and 2006.

Table 24.5 Mid-size urban centres with the most significant population decline from 2001 to 2006

	2001	2006	Decline
	number		%
Kitimat, British Columbia	10,285	8,987	12.6
Prince Rupert, British Columbia	15,302	13,392	12.5
Quesnel, British Columbia	24,426	22,449	8.1
Terrace, British Columbia	19,980	18,581	7.0
Williams Lake, British Columbia	19,768	18,760	5.1
Campbellton, New Brunswick / Quebec	18,820	17,888	5.0
North Battleford, Saskatchewan	18,590	17,765	4.4
Kenora, Ontario	15,838	15,177	4.2
Elliot Lake, Ontario	11,956	11,549	3.4
Bathurst, New Brunswick	32,523	31,424	3.4
Edmundston, New Brunswick	22,173	21,442	3.3
Cape Breton, Nova Scotia	109,330	105,928	3.1
La Tuque, Quebec	15,725	15,293	2.7
Thetford Mines, Quebec	26,721	26,107	2.3
Dolbeau-Mistassini, Quebec	14,879	14,546	2.2
Prince George, British Columbia	85,035	83,225	2.1
Miramichi, New Brunswick	25,274	24,737	2.1
Amos, Quebec	18,302	17,918	2.1
Baie-Comeau, Quebec	30,401	29,808	2.0
Prince Albert, Saskatchewan	41,460	40,766	1.7

Source: Statistics Canada, censuses of population, 2001 and 2006.

Table 24.6 Components of population growth, 1861 to 2006

	1861 to 1871	1871 to 1881	1881 to 1891	1891 to 1901	1901 to 1911
			thousands		
Census population at end of period[1]	3,689	4,325	4,833	5,371	7,207
Total population growth[2]	459	636	508	538	1,836
Births	1,370	1,480	1,524	1,548	1,925
Deaths	760	790	870	880	900
Immigration[1]	260	350	680	250	1,550
Emigration[1]	410	404	826	380	740
	1911 to 1921	**1921 to 1931**	**1931 to 1941**	**1941 to 1951[3]**	**1951 to 1956**
			thousands		
Census population at end of period[1]	8,788	10,377	11,507	13,648	16,081
Total population growth[2]	1,581	1,589	1,130	2,141	2,433
Births	2,340	2,415	2,294	3,186	2,106
Deaths	1,070	1,055	1,072	1,214	633
Immigration[1]	1,400	1,200	149	548	783
Emigration[1]	1,089	970	241	379	185
	1956 to 1961	**1961 to 1966**	**1966 to 1971**	**1971 to 1976**	**1976 to 1981**
			thousands		
Census population at end of period[1]	18,238	20,015	21,568	23,450	24,820
Total population growth[2]	2,157	1,777	1,553	1,488	1,371
Births	2,362	2,249	1,856	1,760	1,820
Deaths	687	731	766	824	843
Immigration[1]	760	539	890	1,053	771
Emigration[1]	278	280	427	358	278
	1981 to 1986	**1986 to 1991**	**1991 to 1996**	**1996 to 2001**	**2001 to 2006**
			thousands		
Census population at end of period[1]	26,101	28,031	29,611	31,021	32,623
Total population growth[2]	1,281	1,930	1,579	1,410	1,602
Births	1,872	1,933	1,936	1,705	1,679
Deaths	885	946	1,024	1,089	1,143
Immigration[1]	678	1,164	1,118	1,217	1,384
Emigration[1]	278	213	338	376	317

1. Population based on census counts prior to 1971; from 1971 on, based on adjusted population estimates.
2. The change in population numbers between two censuses.
3. Beginning in 1951, Newfoundland and Labrador is included.

Source: Statistics Canada, censuses of population, CANSIM tables 051-0001, 051-0004 and 071-0001, and Catalogue no. 11-516-XIE.

Table 24.7 Components of population growth, by province and territory, 2005/2006

	Canada	Newfoundland and Labrador	Prince Edward Island	Nova Scotia	New Brunswick	Quebec	Ontario
	number						
Births	**352,848**	4,326	1,348	8,382	6,728	83,150	134,141
Deaths	**237,931**	4,549	1,282	8,654	6,589	55,950	89,737
Immigration	**238,127**	506	732	2,715	1,630	45,082	115,497
Emigration	**41,349**	203	27	825	464	6,687	19,523
Net temporary emigration	**25,567**	107	33	375	225	4,072	10,626
Returning emigrants	**22,532**	62	23	454	241	3,466	9,548
Net non-permanent residents	**17,884**	86	105	-199	380	353	-4,571
Net interprovincial migration	...	-3,786	-266	-2,401	-1,144	-15,568	-36,196

	Manitoba	Saskatchewan	Alberta	British Columbia	Yukon	Northwest Territories	Nunavut
	number						
Births	14,166	11,918	44,661	42,306	311	678	733
Deaths	10,272	9,079	20,581	30,761	182	163	132
Immigration	10,789	3,086	20,116	37,810	55	98	11
Emigration	1,767	579	5,082	6,152	13	14	13
Net temporary emigration	560	515	2,933	6,068	25	17	11
Returning emigrants	811	322	3,643	3,957	5	0	0
Net non-permanent residents	872	197	12,391	8,263	-3	0	10
Net interprovincial migration	-5,852	3,999	51,169	10,646	-370	-346	115

Notes: Period from July 1, 2005 to June 30, 2006.
Preliminary data.

Source: Statistics Canada, CANSIM table 051-0004.

Table 24.8 Population growth rate for Canada, by province and territory, 1956 to 2006

	Canada	Newfoundland and Labrador	Prince Edward Island	Nova Scotia	New Brunswick	Quebec	Ontario
				%			
1956 to 1961	**13.4**	10.3	5.3	6.1	7.8	13.6	15.4
1961 to 1966	**9.7**	7.8	3.7	2.6	3.2	9.9	11.6
1966 to 1971	**7.8**	5.8	2.9	4.4	2.9	4.3	10.7
1971 to 1976	**6.8**	6.0	5.4	4.8	7.3	4.2	7.2
1976 to 1981	**5.8**	2.2	4.3	2.3	2.4	2.4	4.7
1981 to 1986	**5.2**	0.3	3.8	4.1	2.7	2.5	7.1
1986 to 1991	**7.4**	0.5	1.5	2.9	2.8	5.3	10.5
1991 to 1996	**5.6**	-3.4	4.2	1.8	0.9	2.6	6.3
1996 to 2001	**4.8**	-6.8	0.7	0.1	-0.3	2.1	7.3
2001 to 2006	**5.2**	-2.3	1.0	0.3	-0.1	3.4	6.8

	Manitoba	Saskatchewan	Alberta	British Columbia	Yukon	Northwest Territories	Nunavut
				%			
1956 to 1961	8.4	5.1	18.6	16.5	19.7	...	...
1961 to 1966	4.5	3.3	9.9	15.0	-1.4	...	...
1966 to 1971	2.6	-3.0	11.3	16.6	27.9	...	...
1971 to 1976	3.3	0.0	12.2	13.1	18.3	...	...
1976 to 1981	0.5	4.7	22.7	11.5	6.4	...	...
1981 to 1986	5.3	5.5	6.0	6.4	2.4	...	...
1986 to 1991	1.6	-2.6	6.7	12.3	18.1	...	...
1991 to 1996	2.2	1.6	7.0	14.8	8.6	7.7	15.7
1996 to 2001	1.5	-1.9	10.1	5.3	-4.0	-2.2	9.6
2001 to 2006	2.4	-1.3	10.3	5.9	3.6	3.9	8.1

Note: Population estimates as of July 1.

Source: Statistics Canada, CANSIM tables 051-0001 and 051-0026.

Table 24.9 Births, by province and territory, 2001/2002 to 2006/2007

	2001/2002	2002/2003	2003/2004	2004/2005	2005/2006	2006/2007p
	number					
Canada	**328,155**	**330,523**	**337,762**	**339,270**	**345,355**	**352,848**
Newfoundland and Labrador	4,636	4,596	4,598	4,543	4,443	4,326
Prince Edward Island	1,313	1,374	1,403	1,371	1,343	1,348
Nova Scotia	8,693	8,635	8,713	8,575	8,499	8,382
New Brunswick	6,971	7,104	7,072	6,874	6,840	6,728
Quebec	72,602	72,273	74,364	75,422	78,471	83,150
Ontario	128,947	129,256	132,874	132,796	133,961	134,141
Manitoba	13,746	13,765	13,981	14,031	14,136	14,166
Saskatchewan	11,996	11,794	12,121	11,915	11,925	11,918
Alberta	37,602	39,450	40,635	41,345	42,875	44,661
British Columbia	39,932	40,534	40,205	40,631	41,135	42,306
Yukon	344	322	374	340	319	311
Northwest Territories	651	658	697	705	699	678
Nunavut	722	762	725	722	709	733

Note: Period from July 1 to June 30.
Source: Statistics Canada, CANSIM table 051-0004.

Table 24.10 Birth rate, by province and territory, 2001 to 2007

	2001/2002	2002/2003	2003/2004	2004/2005	2005/2006	2006/2007p
	rate per 1,000 population					
Canada	**10.5**	**10.5**	**10.6**	**10.5**	**10.6**	**10.7**
Newfoundland and Labrador	8.9	8.9	8.9	8.8	8.7	8.5
Prince Edward Island	9.6	10.0	10.2	9.9	9.7	9.7
Nova Scotia	9.3	9.2	9.3	9.2	9.1	9.0
New Brunswick	9.3	9.5	9.4	9.1	9.1	9.0
Quebec	9.8	9.7	9.9	9.9	10.3	10.8
Ontario	10.7	10.6	10.7	10.6	10.6	10.5
Manitoba	11.9	11.9	12.0	12.0	12.0	12.0
Saskatchewan	12.0	11.9	12.2	12.0	12.1	12.0
Alberta	12.1	12.5	12.7	12.7	12.8	12.9
British Columbia	9.7	9.8	9.6	9.6	9.6	9.7
Yukon	11.4	10.6	12.1	11.0	10.2	10.1
Northwest Territories	15.8	15.7	16.3	16.5	16.5	16.0
Nunavut	25.6	26.2	24.7	24.2	23.4	23.8

Note: Period from July 1 to June 30.
Source: Statistics Canada, CANSIM tables 051-0004 and 051-0005.

Table 24.11 Deaths, by province and territory, 2001/2002 to 2006/2007

	2001/2002	2002/2003	2003/2004	2004/2005	2005/2006	2006/2007p
	number					
Canada	**220,494**	**223,905**	**228,829**	**229,372**	**230,687**	**237,931**
Newfoundland and Labrador	4,126	4,276	4,254	4,357	4,453	4,549
Prince Edward Island	1,205	1,217	1,225	1,236	1,260	1,282
Nova Scotia	7,922	7,944	8,269	8,329	8,491	8,654
New Brunswick	6,065	6,181	6,373	6,319	6,453	6,589
Quebec	54,735	54,896	56,411	56,041	53,350	55,950
Ontario	80,993	83,410	84,155	84,495	87,181	89,737
Manitoba	9,720	9,852	9,894	9,989	10,130	10,272
Saskatchewan	8,650	8,880	9,130	8,900	8,975	9,079
Alberta	17,937	18,098	18,775	19,004	19,757	20,581
British Columbia	28,697	28,694	29,863	30,254	30,174	30,761
Yukon	150	145	158	169	177	182
Northwest Territories	164	183	188	155	159	163
Nunavut	130	129	134	124	127	132

Note: Period from July 1 to June 30.
Source: Statistics Canada, CANSIM table 051-0004.

Table 24.12 Death rate, by province and territory, 2001 to 2007

	2001/2002	2002/2003	2003/2004	2004/2005	2005/2006	2006/2007p
	rate per 1,000 population					
Canada	**7.1**	**7.1**	**7.2**	**7.1**	**7.1**	**7.2**
Newfoundland and Labrador	7.9	8.2	8.2	8.5	8.7	9.0
Prince Edward Island	8.8	8.9	8.9	9.0	9.1	9.3
Nova Scotia	8.5	8.5	8.8	8.9	9.1	9.3
New Brunswick	8.1	8.2	8.5	8.4	8.6	8.8
Quebec	7.4	7.3	7.5	7.4	7.0	7.3
Ontario	6.7	6.8	6.8	6.8	6.9	7.0
Manitoba	8.4	8.5	8.5	8.5	8.6	8.7
Saskatchewan	8.7	8.9	9.2	9.0	9.1	9.2
Alberta	5.8	5.7	5.9	5.8	5.9	6.0
British Columbia	7.0	6.9	7.1	7.1	7.0	7.0
Yukon	5.0	4.8	5.1	5.5	5.7	5.9
Northwest Territories	4.0	4.5	4.4	3.6	3.8	3.9
Nunavut	4.6	4.4	4.6	4.2	4.2	4.3

Note: Period from July 1 to June 30.
Source: Statistics Canada, CANSIM tables 051-0004 and 051-0005.

Table 24.13 Interprovincial migration, by province or territory of origin and destination, 2006/2007

	Destination						
	Newfoundland and Labrador	Prince Edward Island	Nova Scotia	New Brunswick	Quebec	Ontario	Manitoba
	number						
Net migration	**-3,786**	**-266**	**-2,401**	**-1,144**	**-15,568**	**-36,196**	**-5,852**
In-migrants	11,815	3,575	19,598	14,722	26,263	71,394	17,325
Out-migrants	15,601	3,841	21,999	15,866	41,831	107,590	23,177
Origin							
Newfoundland and Labrador	.	232	1,504	741	257	3,391	231
Prince Edward Island	194	.	793	427	104	932	23
Nova Scotia	1,600	503	.	2,863	797	6,003	342
New Brunswick	533	497	2,555	.	1,860	3,934	175
Quebec	206	451	959	2,383	.	20,942	666
Ontario	4,847	1,022	7,524	4,282	16,827	.	5,053
Manitoba	192	66	404	223	454	4,995	.
Saskatchewan	85	24	291	85	262	2,014	2,528
Alberta	3,318	568	3,719	2,588	2,910	14,474	5,449
British Columbia	608	212	1,744	991	2,546	14,099	2,495
Yukon	57	0	13	9	99	113	0
Northwest Territories	96	0	60	73	23	284	177
Nunavut	79	0	32	57	124	213	186

	Destination					
	Saskatchewan	Alberta	British Columbia	Yukon	Northwest Territories	Nunavut
	number					
Net migration	**3,999**	**51,169**	**10,646**	**-370**	**-346**	**115**
In-migrants	25,903	131,441	67,334	1,597	2,808	1,332
Out-migrants	21,904	80,272	56,688	1,967	3,154	1,217
Origin						
Newfoundland and Labrador	268	7,543	998	14	210	212
Prince Edward Island	27	1,024	259	3	39	16
Nova Scotia	299	7,731	1,457	53	272	79
New Brunswick	150	5,203	903	15	28	13
Quebec	728	10,944	4,315	26	114	97
Ontario	3,010	45,114	19,128	201	356	226
Manitoba	2,985	9,349	4,262	35	121	91
Saskatchewan	.	12,940	3,501	32	89	53
Alberta	14,350	.	31,189	546	873	288
British Columbia	3,752	29,213	.	549	403	76
Yukon	52	705	819	.	100	0
Northwest Territories	233	1,495	418	114	.	181
Nunavut	49	180	85	9	203	.

Note: Period from July 1, 2006 to June 30, 2007.

Source: Statistics Canada, Catalogue no. 91-215-XIE.

Table 24.14 Interprovincial migration, by age group and by province and territory, 2006/2007

	Newfoundland and Labrador	Prince Edward Island	Nova Scotia	New Brunswick	Quebec	Ontario	Manitoba
	number						
In-migrants, all ages	**11,815**	**3,575**	**19,598**	**14,722**	**26,263**	**71,394**	**17,325**
0 to 17	2,474	681	3,936	2,999	4,872	14,049	4,143
18 to 24	1,738	636	3,462	2,529	4,486	11,940	3,168
25 to 44	5,104	1,327	8,348	6,130	11,786	31,524	6,755
45 to 64	2,123	729	3,014	2,410	3,877	9,969	2,324
65 and older	376	202	838	654	1,242	3,912	935
Out-migrants, all ages	**15,601**	**3,841**	**21,999**	**15,866**	**41,831**	**107,590**	**23,177**
0 to 17	2,701	625	4,222	3,156	8,374	23,356	5,299
18 to 24	4,584	1,181	5,401	3,781	6,047	18,174	4,461
25 to 44	5,765	1,407	8,973	6,490	19,799	45,754	8,986
45 to 64	2,211	488	2,719	1,919	5,370	15,507	3,305
65 and older	340	140	684	520	2,241	4,799	1,126
Net-migration, all ages	**-3,786**	**-266**	**-2,401**	**-1,144**	**-15,568**	**-36,196**	**-5,852**
0 to 17	-227	56	-286	-157	-3,502	-9,307	-1,156
18 to 24	-2,846	-545	-1,939	-1,252	-1,561	-6,234	-1,293
25 to 44	-661	-80	-625	-360	-8,013	-14,230	-2,231
45 to 64	-88	241	295	491	-1,493	-5,538	-981
65 and older	36	62	154	134	-999	-887	-191

	Saskatchewan	Alberta	British Columbia	Yukon	Northwest Territories	Nunavut
	number					
In-migrants, all ages	**25,903**	**131,441**	**67,334**	**1,597**	**2,808**	**1,332**
0 to 17	6,610	29,281	11,850	320	580	239
18 to 24	4,732	30,402	11,887	266	579	243
25 to 44	9,581	52,356	26,280	662	1,165	596
45 to 64	3,700	15,200	12,904	283	448	249
65 and older	1,280	4,202	4,413	66	36	5
Out-migrants, all ages	**21,904**	**80,272**	**56,688**	**1,967**	**3,154**	**1,217**
0 to 17	4,744	17,169	10,939	400	770	279
18 to 24	5,372	14,308	11,724	435	474	126
25 to 44	7,708	32,035	22,167	679	1,307	544
45 to 64	2,898	13,210	8,409	395	543	256
65 and older	1,182	3,550	3,449	58	60	12
Net-migration, all ages	**3,999**	**51,169**	**10,646**	**-370**	**-346**	**115**
0 to 17	1,866	12,112	911	-80	-190	-40
18 to 24	-640	16,094	163	-169	105	117
25 to 44	1,873	20,321	4,113	-17	-142	52
45 to 64	802	1,990	4,495	-112	-95	-7
65 and older	98	652	964	8	-24	-7

Note: Period from July 1, 2006 to June 30, 2007.
Source: Statistics Canada, CANSIM table 051-0012.

Table 24.15 Population projections, by age group, selected years from 2006 to 2031

	2006	2011	2016	2021	2026	2031
	thousands					
All ages[1]	**32,547.2**	**33,909.7**	**35,266.8**	**36,608.5**	**37,882.7**	**39,029.4**
0 to 4	1,697.5	1,724.7	1,781.9	1,816.8	1,812.8	1,781.3
5 to 9	1,842.6	1,780.8	1,810.7	1,871.9	1,910.9	1,910.9
10 to 14	2,084.6	1,916.4	1,858.1	1,892.0	1,956.8	1,999.4
15 to 19	2,164.8	2,170.4	2,006.4	1,952.7	1,990.3	2,058.4
20 to 24	2,252.9	2,295.3	2,304.1	2,145.8	2,096.8	2,138.2
25 to 29	2,226.1	2,330.2	2,376.7	2,391.9	2,241.4	2,198.8
30 to 34	2,222.6	2,354.8	2,462.8	2,518.1	2,542.1	2,402.7
35 to 39	2,351.1	2,327.1	2,462.6	2,576.9	2,639.6	2,671.1
40 to 44	2,698.3	2,409.3	2,390.6	2,530.6	2,649.3	2,717.1
45 to 49	2,671.5	2,711.2	2,431.6	2,418.6	2,561.7	2,683.3
50 to 54	2,363.9	2,651.5	2,695.4	2,425.9	2,417.8	2,563.0
55 to 59	2,082.5	2,327.4	2,614.1	2,662.9	2,404.5	2,401.4
60 to 64	1,583.3	2,027.9	2,272.3	2,557.8	2,612.4	2,367.8
65 to 69	1,227.3	1,513.1	1,942.1	2,184.7	2,466.6	2,527.6
70 to 74	1,044.2	1,130.8	1,401.5	1,806.8	2,044.1	2,318.2
75 to 79	878.0	907.6	993.3	1,241.0	1,610.8	1,837.3
80 to 84	638.3	692.2	724.3	804.0	1,016.1	1,332.1
85 to 89	342.8	422.2	465.5	494.6	560.3	719.8
90 to 94	137.3	169.2	211.2	237.4	257.2	299.2
95 to 99	33.1	42.4	54.4	68.6	79.0	87.4
100 and older	4.7	5.4	7.1	9.5	12.1	14.4

Note: Of the six population projection scenarios, based on population estimates as of July 1, 2005, results from scenario 3 medium growth and medium migration trends are presented in this table.

1. Figures may not add to totals because of rounding.

Source: Statistics Canada, CANSIM table 052-0004.

Table 24.16 Population projections, by province and territory, selected years from 2006 to 2031

	2006	2011	2016	2021	2026	2031
	thousands					
Canada	**32,547.2**	**33,909.7**	**35,266.8**	**36,608.5**	**37,882.7**	**39,029.4**
Newfoundland and Labrador	515.2	512.5	511.3	510.7	509.1	505.6
Prince Edward Island	138.7	141.2	143.7	146.1	148.2	149.5
Nova Scotia	939.6	948.5	958.4	968.2	975.8	979.4
New Brunswick	752.9	757.4	762.2	766.4	768.5	767.2
Quebec	7,641.6	7,841.4	8,018.7	8,176.8	8,306.8	8,396.4
Ontario	12,682.0	13,374.7	14,071.4	14,776.6	15,472.0	16,130.4
Manitoba	1,183.1	1,214.8	1,250.9	1,288.1	1,323.7	1,355.7
Saskatchewan	991.5	982.0	978.2	977.4	977.0	975.8
Alberta	3,295.0	3,483.2	3,667.1	3,841.9	4,002.2	4,144.9
British Columbia	4,302.9	4,545.0	4,792.0	5,040.0	5,280.0	5,502.9
Yukon	31.1	31.6	32.1	32.7	33.4	34.0
Northwest Territories	43.6	46.4	48.9	51.1	52.9	54.4
Nunavut	30.2	31.1	31.9	32.5	33.0	33.3

Note: Of the six population projection scenarios, based on population estimates as of July 1, 2005, results from scenario 3 medium growth and medium migration trends are presented in this table.

Source: Statistics Canada, CANSIM table 052-0004.

Prices and price indexes

25

Overview

Whether it is the price that a farmer pays for inputs such as seed and fertilizer, the price a manufacturer pays for essential raw materials or the price a consumer pays for a good or service, prices affect everyone in an economy.

Rising prices for raw materials and inputs into production generally lead to higher prices for final products and services. This erodes the purchasing power of money over time.

Statistics Canada produces several key price indexes, which are closely monitored by consumers, businesses and governments.

The Consumer Price Index (CPI) is the main economic indicator used to measure inflation. It is consulted by those establishing and evaluating economic policies and setting wage increases. The CPI is also used by economists to deflate current dollar estimates—to remove the effects of price changes over time.

The CPI measures price changes of a fixed 'shopping basket' of consumer goods and services that a typical household would purchase. The basket contains over 600 items: on average more than 70,000 price quotes are collected each month to compute the CPI.

Mortgage interest costs and gasoline prices climb

Consumer prices advanced 2.2% in 2007, up from 2.0% in 2006. Owned accommodation and gasoline prices continued to drive up consumer prices in 2007. Owned accommodation is mainly made up of mortgage interest cost and replacement cost—the worn-out structural portion of housing—and is estimated using new housing prices and property taxes. Partly offsetting these increases were lower prices for computer equipment and supplies, the purchase and leasing of passenger vehicles, and natural gas.

Chart 25.1
Selected price indexes

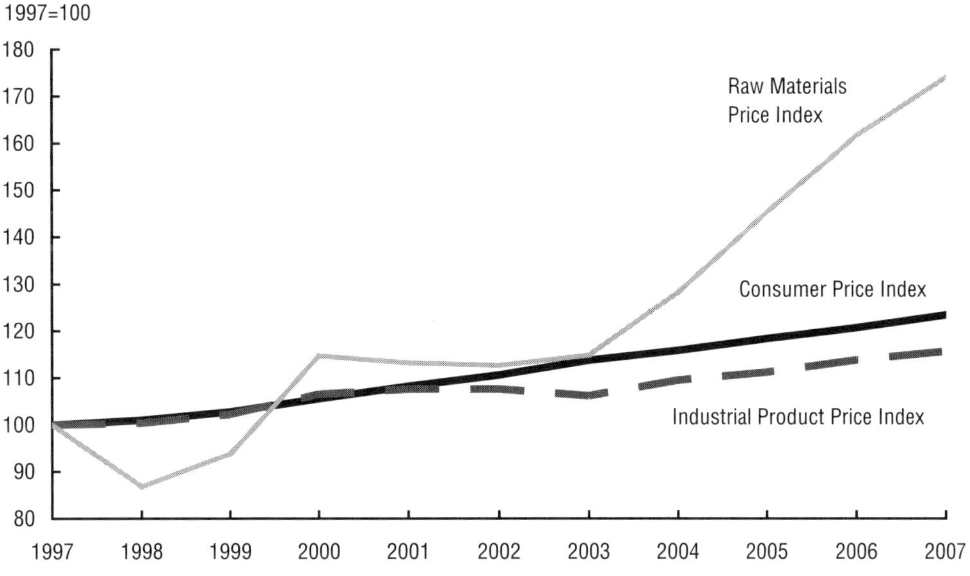

Source: Statistics Canada, CANSIM tables 326-0021, 329-0038 and 330-0006.

Core index surpasses central bank's target

The core index is a special aggregate of the CPI. It is computed by removing the eight most volatile components, and the effect of changes in indirect taxes, from the CPI. These components are fruit, fruit preparations and nuts; vegetables and vegetable preparations; mortgage interest cost; natural gas; heating oil and other fuels; gasoline; intercity transportation; and tobacco products and smokers' supplies. The core index is used by the Bank of Canada as an instrument to conduct monetary policy: the Bank's stated aim is to keep overall inflation at 2.0%.

During the first eight months of 2007, the core index advanced an average 2.3% compared with the same months of 2006. For the last four months of the year, however, the average year-over-year core index eased to a 1.7% rate of growth.

To moderate the rise in the core index during the first eight months of the year, the Bank of Canada increased its key 'overnight rate' by one-quarter of a percentage point in July. In December, the Bank reversed the increase when the core index showed signs of easing. Over the course of 2007, the core index advanced 2.1%—slightly above the Bank's operating target and the 1.9% growth rate posted in 2006. Similarly, the CPI excluding energy (gasoline, natural gas, fuel oil and other fuels, and electricity) advanced 2.1% in 2007, up from 1.7% recorded a year earlier.

Chart 25.2
Consumer Price Index (CPI), core CPI and all-items CPI excluding energy

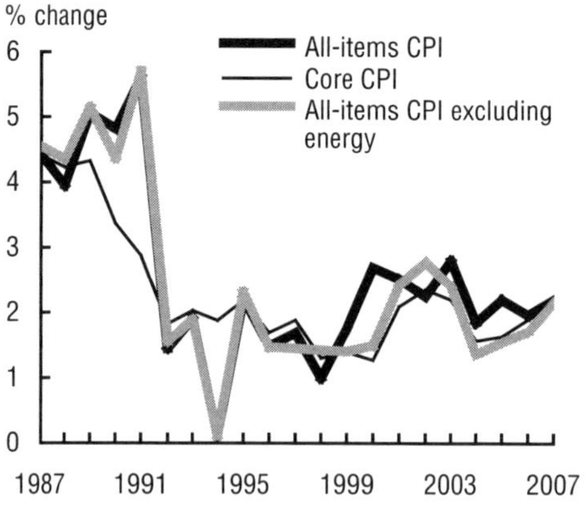

Note: Core CPI excludes from the all-items CPI the effect of changes in indirect taxes and eight of the most volatile components identified by the Bank of Canada.
Source: Statistics Canada, CANSIM table 326-0020.

Table 25.a
Selected special aggregates, goods and services

	1987	1997	2007
		2002=100	
Goods and services	**68.5**	**90.4**	**111.5**
Goods	72.6	91.2	108.0
Services	64.1	89.5	114.8

Source: Statistics Canada, CANSIM table 326-0021.

Western provinces fuel growth in new housing prices

In 2007, Canada's major housing markets turned in strong performances for the sixth consecutive year. According to the New Housing Price Index (NHPI), new housing prices rose 7.7% in 2007, after rising an average 5.8% over the previous five years.

Although gains were posted in most major regions of Canada, new housing prices climbed most sharply in commodity-rich western regions: Saskatoon, 38.8%; Edmonton, 32.1%; Regina, 22.2%; Calgary, 16.2%; and Winnipeg, 11.8%. Windsor (-2.1%) was the only region to see declining new housing prices in 2007.

The NHPI measures changes over time in the contractors' selling prices of new residential houses in 21 metropolitan areas.

Commodity price gains continue

Commodity prices continued to boost the Industrial Product Price Index (IPPI) in 2007. This index kept rising despite a U.S. economic slowdown, which was due directly or indirectly to the meltdown in the U.S. subprime mortgage market. The IPPI is both a measure of the economic performance of Canada's manufacturing sector and another measure of inflation. It reflects the prices that producers receive for goods sold at the factory gate, rather than the prices consumers pay. Manufacturers received an average 1.6% more for their products in 2007 than in 2006, largely the result of higher prices for primary metal products.

Emerging Asia continues to drive up raw material prices

Canadian firms have been grappling with higher prices for their raw material inputs. These higher costs, however, have not been fully reflected in retail prices, thanks in part to the appreciation of the Canadian dollar. The Raw Materials Price Index (RMPI) measures price changes for raw materials that industries in Canada buy for further processing: this index advanced 7.7% in 2007—well short of the 11.3% rise seen in 2006, and its lowest gain since 2003. The rise in raw material prices was largely attributable to non-ferrous metals. After rising 63.5% in 2006, the price of non-ferrous metals advanced another 23.5% in 2007, a sign that Asian demand is levelling off but still greatly affecting commodity prices.

The RMPI includes all costs a purchaser incurs to bring the commodity to the plant, including transportation, net taxes paid, customs and duties, and the effects of subsidies.

Chart 25.3
Price indexes

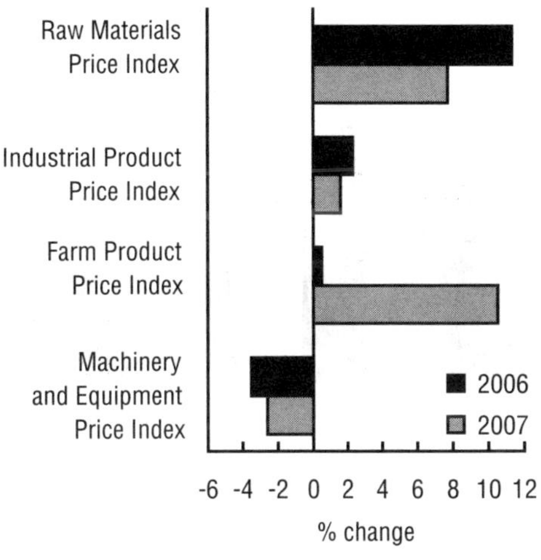

Source: Statistics Canada, CANSIM tables 002-0022, 327-0042, 329-0038 and 330-0006.

Price declines for imported machinery and equipment

Prices for imported machinery and equipment fell 4.0% in 2007. This decline was partly the result of the appreciating Canadian dollar against the American. Prices for domestically produced machinery and equipment slipped 0.1%. The overall Machinery and Equipment Price Index fell 2.5% in 2007, continuing a trend that began in 2003.

Growing importance for measuring changes in prices of service industries

In 2007, Canadian businesses paid 4.6% more for courier and messenger services as measured by the Couriers and Messengers Services Price Index, down from 7.8% in 2006. This index measures price changes for courier and messenger services provided by long- and short-distance delivery companies to Canadian-based business clients.

As service industries become increasingly important in the economy, Statistics Canada is developing new service price indexes that cover, for example, wholesaling and retailing margins, truck transportation and non-residential rent.

Commodity prices fuel Canadian economy

The Canadian economy has rediscovered natural resources thanks to commodity prices, which are having their longest and strongest upswing ever. Firm commodity prices have helped fuel the domestic economy and have contributed to the appreciation of the Canadian dollar.

Commodity markets will likely remember 2007 as the year in which prices for crude oil, wheat, metals and minerals climbed to record highs.

Energy prices dropped in January, then climbed steadily over the rest of 2007. The main driving factor was rising crude oil prices. The West Texas Intermediate price of crude oil reached record highs in 2007, averaging US$75.60 a barrel—up more than 9% from 2006. Rising global demand, continuing geopolitical issues, hurricanes and tight supplies were the key reasons for the spike in crude oil prices.

According to the Raw Materials Price Index, crude mineral oil prices rose 4.8%, despite posting double-digit growth from September through December 2007 when compared with the same months of 2006. Rising raw material costs also contributed to a 5.6% rise in prices for manufactured petroleum and coal products, as measured by the Industrial Product Price Index.

The rise in crude oil prices was partly offset by persistently low prices for natural gas in 2007. Over the course of 2007, natural gas prices fell 11.4%.

A strong Canadian dollar partly limited the impact of these increases. According to the price index for merchandise imports (an international index that measures trade prices), prices for imports were 10.5% lower in 2007 than in 2002, when the Canadian dollar began appreciating.

Chart 25.4
Commodity Price Index

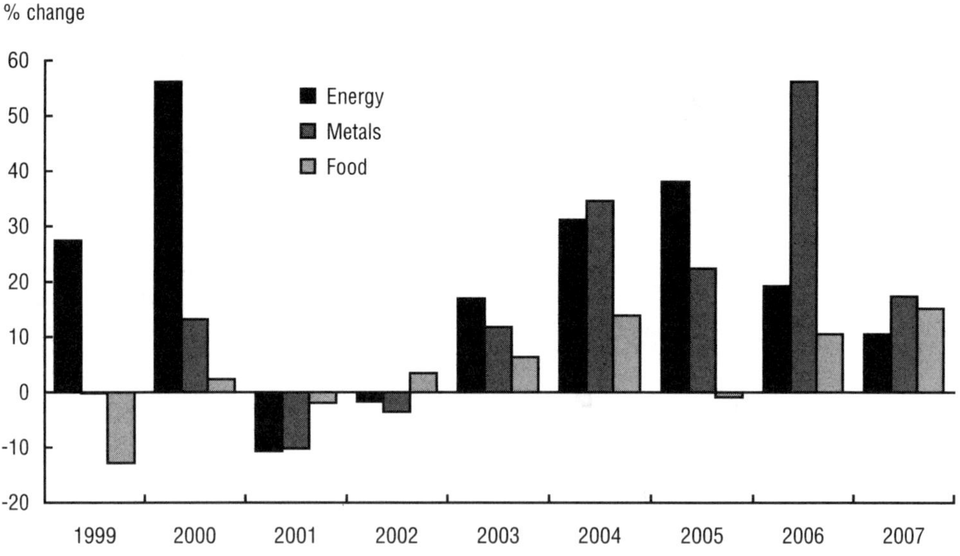

Source: Statistics Canada, CANSIM table 176-0001 and International Monetary Fund.

Food inflation drives global prices

Price increases for the basic commodities, such as food, are fuelling consumer prices, and sometimes fuelling our perceptions of inflation beyond the rates measured by statistical agencies. In 2007, Canadians saw a 2.7% rise in prices for food purchased from stores, as measured by the Consumer Price Index (CPI). Besides the 4.8% rise posted in 2001, a gain of this magnitude has not been seen since 1995.

Consumers in other countries faced higher food inflation in 2007: 3.5% in the European Union, 4.2% in the United States, 4.5% in the United Kingdom, 6.5% in Mexico and 12.3% in China. The high Canadian dollar has helped insulate Canadian consumers from rising food prices.

The recent increase in world food prices follows decades of declining prices after the high inflation of the 1970s. Today, higher transportation costs, climate change, rising ethanol production and growing Asian demand for food are among the reasons for higher food prices.

Crop farmers have benefited from greater cash receipts. Led by a 51.4% annual climb in prices for grains—the highest since monthly grain price data were first published in 1981—prices received by farmers for crops, measured by the Farm Product Price Index, climbed 24.3% in 2007.

Higher grain prices mean higher input costs and higher prices at the factory gate. Manufacturers of grain and oilseed milling products paid 10.3% more in 2007, and bread and bakery goods paid 2.3% more, as measured by the Industrial Product Price Index.

Consumer prices for grain-based products also rose in 2007: rice products rose 2.5%; pasta products, 6.4%; and bakery products, 4.6%, as measured by the CPI.

Chart 25.5
Selected agricultural, industrial and food-related price indexes

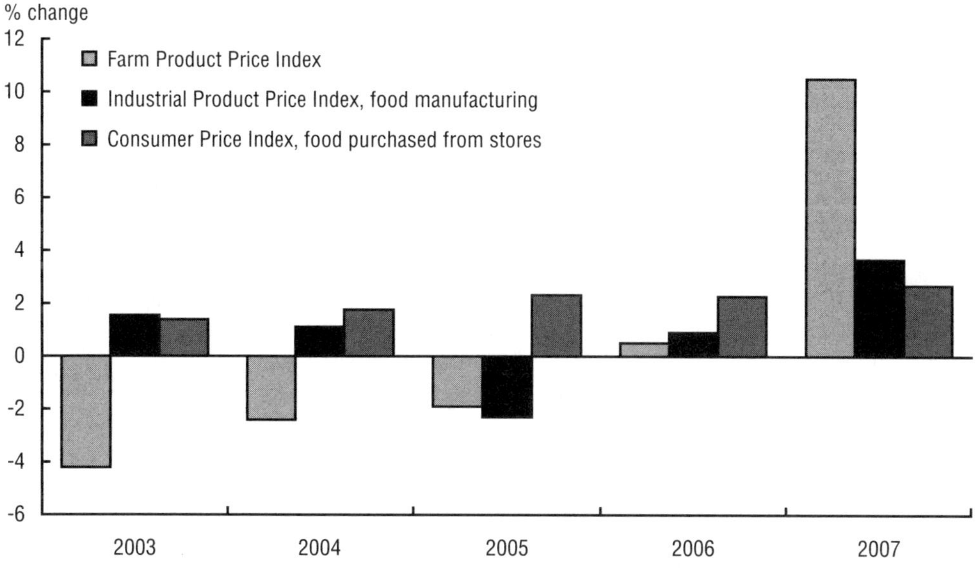

Source: Statistics Canada, CANSIM tables 002-0022, 329-0038 and 326-0021.

Table 25.1 Consumer Price Index, 1998 to 2007

	1998	1999	2000	2001	2002	2003	2004	2005	2006	2007
	2002=100									
All-items	**91.3**	**92.9**	**95.4**	**97.8**	**100.0**	**102.8**	**104.7**	**107.0**	**109.1**	**111.5**
Food	90.9	92.0	93.3	97.4	100.0	101.7	103.8	106.4	108.9	111.8
Shelter	91.1	92.3	95.6	99.1	100.0	103.2	105.8	109.2	113.1	116.9
Household operations and furnishings	95.1	95.8	96.7	98.6	100.0	100.7	101.2	101.7	102.2	103.2
Clothing and footwear	98.8	100.1	100.3	100.7	100.0	98.2	98.0	97.6	95.8	95.7
Transportation	89.6	92.6	97.2	97.3	100.0	105.2	107.7	112.0	115.2	117.1
Health and personal care	93.6	95.4	97.0	98.9	100.0	101.4	102.8	104.6	105.9	107.3
Recreation, education and reading	93.0	94.7	97.0	98.4	100.0	100.8	101.1	100.8	100.6	101.8
Alcoholic beverages and tobacco products	74.9	76.5	79.0	85.0	100.0	110.1	116.0	119.1	121.7	125.5
Core Consumer Price Index (CPI)[1]	93.2	94.5	95.7	97.7	100.0	102.2	103.8	105.5	107.5	109.8
Special aggregates										
All-items excluding food	91.3	93.0	95.8	97.9	100.0	103.0	104.8	107.1	109.2	111.4
All-items excluding shelter	91.3	93.0	95.3	97.3	100.0	102.5	104.1	106.1	107.6	109.4
All-items excluding energy	92.3	93.6	95.0	97.3	100.0	102.4	103.8	105.4	107.2	109.5
All-items excluding gasoline	91.9	93.2	95.0	97.6	100.0	102.6	104.2	106.0	107.9	110.1
Shelter[2]	91.3	92.7	96.1	99.4	100.0	102.7	105.0	108.1	111.8	115.7
Goods	91.4	93.1	96.0	98.4	100.0	101.9	103.4	105.8	107.1	108.0
Services	91.1	92.6	94.8	97.1	100.0	103.6	105.9	108.2	111.1	114.8
	annual % change									
All-items	**1.0**	**1.8**	**2.7**	**2.5**	**2.2**	**2.8**	**1.8**	**2.2**	**2.0**	**2.2**
Food	1.7	1.2	1.4	4.4	2.7	1.7	2.1	2.5	2.3	2.7
Shelter	0.3	1.3	3.6	3.7	0.9	3.2	2.5	3.2	3.6	3.4
Household operations and furnishings	1.5	0.7	0.9	2.0	1.4	0.7	0.5	0.5	0.5	1.0
Clothing and footwear	1.1	1.3	0.2	0.4	-0.7	-1.8	-0.2	-0.4	-1.8	-0.1
Transportation	-0.8	3.3	5.0	0.1	2.8	5.2	2.4	4.0	2.9	1.6
Health and personal care	2.1	1.9	1.7	2.0	1.1	1.4	1.4	1.8	1.2	1.3
Recreation, education and reading	2.2	1.8	2.4	1.4	1.6	0.8	0.3	-0.3	-0.2	1.2
Alcoholic beverages and tobacco products	3.6	2.1	3.3	7.6	17.6	10.1	5.4	2.7	2.2	3.1
Core Consumer Price Index (CPI)[1]	1.3	1.4	1.3	2.1	2.4	2.2	1.6	1.6	1.9	2.1
Special aggregates										
All-items excluding food	0.8	1.9	3.0	2.2	2.1	3.0	1.7	2.2	2.0	2.0
All-items excluding shelter	1.2	1.9	2.5	2.1	2.8	2.5	1.6	1.9	1.4	1.7
All-items excluding energy	1.4	1.4	1.5	2.4	2.8	2.4	1.4	1.5	1.7	2.1
All-items excluding gasoline	..	1.4	1.9	2.7	2.5	2.6	1.6	1.7	1.8	2.0
Shelter[2]	0.6	1.5	3.7	3.4	0.6	2.7	2.2	3.0	3.4	3.5
Goods	0.2	1.9	3.1	2.5	1.6	1.9	1.5	2.3	1.2	0.8
Services	1.8	1.6	2.4	2.4	3.0	3.6	2.2	2.2	2.7	3.3

Note: Annual average indexes are obtained by averaging the indexes for the 12 months of the calendar year.

1. Bank of Canada definition.

2. 1986 definition.

Source: Statistics Canada, CANSIM table 326-0021.

Table 25.2 Consumer Price Index, all-items, by province and territory, 2001 to 2007

	2001	2002	2003	2004	2005	2006	2007
				2002=100			
Canada	**97.8**	**100.0**	**102.8**	**104.7**	**107.0**	**109.1**	**111.5**
Newfoundland and Labrador	97.7	100.0	102.9	104.8	107.6	109.5	111.1
Prince Edward Island	97.4	100.0	103.5	105.8	109.1	111.6	113.6
Nova Scotia	97.1	100.0	103.4	105.3	108.2	110.4	112.5
New Brunswick	96.8	100.0	103.4	104.9	107.4	109.2	111.3
Quebec	98.0	100.0	102.5	104.5	106.9	108.7	110.4
Ontario	98.0	100.0	102.7	104.6	106.9	108.8	110.8
Manitoba	98.5	100.0	101.8	103.8	106.6	108.7	110.9
Saskatchewan	97.2	100.0	102.3	104.6	106.9	109.1	112.2
Alberta	96.7	100.0	104.4	105.9	108.1	112.3	117.9
British Columbia	97.7	100.0	102.2	104.2	106.3	108.1	110.0
Yukon	99.3	100.0	101.9	103.0	105.3	106.8	109.5
Northwest Territories	97.1	100.0	102.3	103.8	106.2	107.7	110.8
Nunavut	..	..	100.2	101.2	102.9	104.6	107.9
				annual % change			
Canada	**2.5**	**2.2**	**2.8**	**1.8**	**2.2**	**2.0**	**2.2**
Newfoundland and Labrador	1.1	2.4	2.9	1.8	2.7	1.8	1.5
Prince Edward Island	2.6	2.7	3.5	2.2	3.1	2.3	1.8
Nova Scotia	1.9	3.0	3.4	1.8	2.8	2.0	1.9
New Brunswick	1.8	3.3	3.4	1.5	2.4	1.7	1.9
Quebec	2.3	2.0	2.5	2.0	2.3	1.7	1.6
Ontario	3.0	2.0	2.7	1.9	2.2	1.8	1.8
Manitoba	2.7	1.5	1.8	2.0	2.7	2.0	2.0
Saskatchewan	3.0	2.9	2.3	2.2	2.2	2.1	2.8
Alberta	2.3	3.4	4.4	1.4	2.1	3.9	5.0
British Columbia	1.7	2.4	2.2	2.0	2.0	1.7	1.8
Yukon	1.8	0.7	1.9	1.1	2.2	1.4	2.5
Northwest Territories	1.6	3.0	2.3	1.5	2.3	1.4	2.9
Nunavut	..	..	..	1.0	1.7	1.7	3.2

Note: Annual average indexes are obtained by averaging the indexes for the 12 months of the calendar year.
Source: Statistics Canada, CANSIM table 326-0021.

Table 25.3 Raw Materials Price Index, 2001 to 2007

	2001	2002	2003	2004	2005	2006	2007
				1997=100			
All raw materials	**113.2**	**112.6**	**114.8**	**128.3**	**145.3**	**161.7**	**174.1**
Mineral fuels	157.5	154.5	165.6	193.9	244.7	258.7	264.5
Vegetable products	84.8	97.7	92.2	88.8	80.3	84.8	102.4
Animals and animal products	108.9	103.6	100.3	101.4	104.6	104.3	106.6
Wood	85.0	83.9	82.2	83.0	75.1	77.8	84.6
Ferrous materials	87.0	92.8	95.9	125.0	125.0	125.7	134.5
Non-ferrous metals	82.0	81.3	82.0	104.8	119.7	195.7	241.7
Non-metallic minerals	109.0	110.5	116.4	122.6	133.9	141.1	148.5
All raw materials excluding mineral fuels	92.7	93.2	91.4	97.9	99.3	116.8	132.3

Note: Annual average indexes are obtained by averaging the indexes for the 12 months of the calendar year.
Source: Statistics Canada, CANSIM table 330-0006.

Table 25.4 Consumer Price Index, food, 2003 to 2007

	2003	2004	2005	2006	2007
			2002=100		
All-items	**102.8**	**104.7**	**107.0**	**109.1**	**111.5**
Food	101.7	103.8	106.4	108.9	111.8
Food purchased from stores	101.4	103.2	105.6	108.0	110.9
Meat	101.8	106.2	108.2	107.9	111.1
Fresh or frozen meat (excluding poultry)	100.9	105.0	106.9	105.8	107.9
Fresh or frozen poultry meat	104.8	112.2	113.0	113.4	120.9
Processed meat	100.7	103.2	106.4	106.7	108.1
Fish and other seafood	99.7	99.1	99.1	98.0	100.1
Fish	99.5	99.4	100.4	100.3	103.0
Seafood and other marine products	100.2	98.3	95.8	92.0	92.7
Dairy products and eggs	103.1	105.7	111.0	115.5	119.8
Dairy products	102.9	105.5	111.1	115.7	119.9
Eggs	104.9	107.7	109.1	111.9	118.4
Bakery and other cereal products	104.3	107.0	109.8	113.6	118.1
Bakery products	105.8	109.3	113.1	118.2	123.6
Cereal products	101.6	102.8	103.9	105.3	108.4
Fruit, fruit preparations and nuts	98.2	99.3	98.8	101.3	105.7
Fresh fruit	96.5	97.9	96.2	98.4	99.6
Preserved fruit and fruit preparations	100.9	101.3	102.6	105.9	116.2
Nuts	99.4	101.6	103.0	103.5	104.9
Vegetables and vegetable preparations	94.3	92.1	93.6	98.4	98.6
Fresh vegetables	92.1	88.9	89.9	95.3	95.2
Preserved vegetables and vegetable preparations	101.8	103.4	106.8	109.2	111.0
Other food products and non-alcoholic beverages	103.3	104.4	107.0	108.9	110.1
Sugar and confectionery	106.0	107.5	107.8	112.1	112.9
Fats and oils	103.8	106.9	108.6	110.3	114.2
Coffee and tea	100.8	102.7	106.1	109.8	110.3
Condiments, spices and vinegars	100.6	100.8	103.0	103.8	104.9
Other food preparations	104.7	106.5	109.0	111.1	111.1
Non-alcoholic beverages	99.4	99.2	103.4	103.8	106.4
Food purchased from restaurants	102.5	105.2	108.2	111.1	114.1

Note: Annual average indexes are obtained by averaging the indexes for the 12 months of the calendar year.
Source: Statistics Canada, CANSIM table 326-0021.

Table 25.5 Farm Product Price Index, 2001 to 2007

	2001	2002	2003	2004	2005	2006	2007
				1997=100			
Canada	**101.8**	**105.7**	**101.3**	**98.9**	**97.0**	**97.5**	**107.7**
Total crops	92.9	108.4	104.5	99.5	87.8	92.1	114.5
Grains	95.2	111.0	105.8	94.1	76.5	84.3	127.6
Oilseeds	74.5	94.1	92.7	95.2	74.5	72.2	97.5
Specialty crops	101.6	124.4	113.3	102.6	84.7	82.1	121.2
Fruit	96.6	104.3	106.7	105.5	107.5	113.3	117.1
Vegetables excluding potatoes	106.1	111.1	111.9	111.9	113.4	118.0	114.3
Potatoes	124.2	166.4	135.7	119.7	126.0	148.7	132.5
Total livestock and animal products	110.3	103.4	98.5	98.4	104.8	102.2	102.4
Cattle and calves	126.0	117.4	98.6	87.7	105.3	105.0	101.3
Hogs	93.7	76.1	75.8	90.1	83.7	72.9	69.4
Poultry	95.5	91.8	95.6	97.9	96.5	93.0	101.9
Eggs	98.9	102.8	102.0	105.5	96.4	98.9	100.9
Dairy	109.7	112.2	119.1	119.8	127.8	130.0	136.9
Eastern Canada	**102.9**	**103.2**	**101.3**	**102.7**	**102.5**	**103.4**	**107.2**
Total crops	94.5	104.9	101.6	99.8	94.5	99.6	105.9
Grains	77.2	89.3	86.0	82.2	65.9	71.8	98.2
Oilseeds	71.6	80.9	89.9	95.2	75.1	66.2	84.3
Specialty crops	123.8	112.4	108.3	127.3	116.2	103.6	131.0
Fruit	103.8	109.5	109.4	104.1	106.9	114.5	115.8
Vegetables excluding potatoes	108.7	111.8	109.9	110.4	113.3	119.7	115.8
Potatoes	126.6	186.1	137.0	115.1	127.3	163.5	133.8
Total livestock and animal products	108.1	101.9	100.8	104.3	107.5	105.7	107.9
Cattle and calves	134.7	126.6	102.3	88.7	106.1	111.8	108.6
Hogs	92.4	73.4	72.7	88.0	80.9	69.3	66.3
Poultry	95.9	92.3	96.1	98.4	95.5	91.4	101.4
Eggs	100.9	105.2	102.2	106.6	96.7	99.6	103.9
Dairy	110.1	112.0	119.5	122.0	130.9	133.7	139.8
Western Canada	**101.1**	**107.8**	**101.4**	**95.9**	**94.3**	**94.5**	**110.2**
Total crops	92.2	110.9	106.4	99.2	83.3	87.1	119.8
Grains	98.9	115.6	110.0	96.1	78.4	86.7	134.9
Oilseeds	75.6	98.8	93.8	95.3	74.4	74.3	102.1
Specialty crops	99.9	124.4	113.0	100.7	82.4	80.5	120.5
Fruit	82.6	94.2	102.0	104.2	104.1	106.6	114.1
Vegetables excluding potatoes	98.9	112.9	117.4	115.8	113.6	113.2	110.2
Potatoes	120.0	135.0	131.4	123.4	122.5	129.8	128.6
Total livestock and animal products	113.3	105.3	96.4	92.7	106.7	103.1	101.4
Cattle and calves	123.6	114.3	97.2	87.2	113.3	111.0	106.9
Hogs	95.6	80.1	80.6	92.7	85.6	76.1	72.0
Poultry	94.4	90.7	94.5	96.7	98.4	96.3	102.9
Eggs	95.3	98.6	101.6	105.2	96.0	97.5	95.1
Dairy	108.1	113.0	117.9	113.0	117.9	118.3	127.7

Source: Statistics Canada, CANSIM table 002-0022.

Table 25.6 Farm Input Price Index, Eastern and Western Canada, 2001 to 2007

	2001	2002	2003	2004	2005	2006	2007
				1992=100			
Canada	**129.5**	**128.5**	**132.8**	**129.6**	**134.9**	**139.3**	**149.7**
Building and fencing	120.0	122.8	122.4	137.7	136.3	137.7	138.7
Machinery and motor vehicles	143.7	143.5	157.0	155.3	163.6	168.7	171.8
Crop production	137.6	135.7	154.7	151.1	156.1	161.9	183.2
Animal production	135.1	132.3	128.2	114.4	124.2	126.5	143.6
Supplies and services	121.1	120.7	127.5	126.9	129.8	131.1	130.8
Hired farm labour	125.4	128.2	129.0	135.4	137.7	142.7	149.7
Property taxes	112.6	118.9	126.4	129.5	132.5	129.9	134.7
Interest	90.5	84.9	83.9	80.7	81.3	90.1	98.2
Farm rent	113.8	121.8	131.9	135.8	129.3	132.1	144.5
Eastern Canada	**126.6**	**126.2**	**129.0**	**127.5**	**131.3**	**135.7**	**145.3**
Building and fencing	121.9	124.3	124.2	136.2	138.6	141.4	144.2
Machinery and motor vehicles	144.4	145.9	159.3	156.4	163.6	167.7	170.4
Crop production	130.1	128.3	137.0	139.8	148.0	154.8	163.2
Animal production	129.3	128.0	125.4	117.6	120.4	122.9	143.6
Supplies and services	123.4	121.8	129.8	129.1	132.9	135.3	134.0
Hired farm labour	127.2	130.4	128.9	135.2	137.8	140.6	146.3
Property taxes	79.7	84.8	90.0	93.8	97.4	101.9	105.6
Interest	92.6	86.7	85.8	83.2	84.2	93.9	102.2
Farm rent	85.2	93.5	97.8	101.4	102.4	106.4	111.4
Western Canada	**132.9**	**130.9**	**137.5**	**131.6**	**138.9**	**143.5**	**154.5**
Building and fencing	118.5	121.6	120.9	138.8	134.2	134.6	133.1
Machinery and motor vehicles	143.3	140.7	154.4	154.3	164.1	170.7	174.0
Crop production	142.7	140.6	167.1	158.4	161.0	165.9	195.7
Animal production	141.0	136.6	131.0	111.4	127.4	129.4	143.2
Supplies and services	118.6	119.6	125.0	124.4	126.5	126.6	127.4
Hired farm labour	123.8	126.0	129.9	136.5	138.3	146.4	155.2
Property taxes	121.4	127.9	136.0	138.7	141.3	135.9	140.9
Interest	89.2	83.7	82.7	79.1	79.4	87.7	95.5
Farm rent	128.0	135.6	148.9	152.8	141.9	143.9	159.5

Source: Statistics Canada, CANSIM table 328-0014.

Table 25.7 Machinery and Equipment Price Index, domestic and imported, by industry, 2001 to 2007

	2001	2002	2003	2004	2005	2006	2007
	1997=100						
Total machinery and equipment	**107.6**	**109.0**	**100.8**	**96.8**	**93.9**	**90.6**	**88.3**
Crop and animal production	115.1	117.4	109.0	105.9	103.6	99.6	98.0
Forestry and logging	113.4	116.3	107.8	104.7	103.0	100.3	97.6
Fishing, hunting and trapping	104.0	106.4	104.2	107.5	106.4	105.6	106.3
Support activities for agriculture and forestry	112.8	114.6	106.8	104.0	101.6	97.5	95.8
Mines, quarries and oil wells	112.8	115.4	107.0	104.4	103.0	101.9	101.0
Utilities	109.9	112.6	103.6	98.5	95.6	93.8	93.2
Construction	111.8	114.9	105.6	101.6	98.9	96.0	94.0
All manufacturing	112.3	113.9	105.0	101.2	98.8	96.2	94.4
Trade	102.8	103.5	96.7	94.0	91.7	88.4	86.1
Transportation (excluding pipeline transportation)	113.8	116.0	108.8	106.6	105.1	103.0	101.4
Pipeline transportation	112.2	115.0	108.6	104.6	103.2	101.3	100.6
Warehousing and storage	110.2	111.8	106.0	104.6	103.9	101.9	100.6
Finance, insurance and real estate	105.7	106.3	97.8	93.8	90.0	84.9	81.4
Private education services	99.1	100.2	90.7	85.6	81.6	77.6	73.9
Education services (excluding private), health care and social assistance	104.1	105.4	97.6	93.4	90.1	86.4	83.6
Other services (excluding public administration)	101.2	101.7	93.3	87.2	83.5	79.9	77.0
Public administration	100.9	102.4	94.8	90.2	86.7	83.5	81.4
	annual % change						
Total machinery and equipment	**3.0**	**1.3**	**-7.5**	**-4.0**	**-3.0**	**-3.5**	**-2.5**
Crop and animal production	4.1	2.0	-7.2	-2.8	-2.2	-3.9	-1.6
Forestry and logging	2.3	2.6	-7.3	-2.9	-1.6	-2.6	-2.7
Fishing, hunting and trapping	3.2	2.3	-2.1	3.2	-1.0	-0.8	0.7
Support activities for agriculture and forestry	4.0	1.6	-6.8	-2.6	-2.3	-4.0	-1.7
Mines, quarries and oil wells	3.7	2.3	-7.3	-2.4	-1.3	-1.1	-0.9
Utilities	3.9	2.5	-8.0	-4.9	-2.9	-1.9	-0.6
Construction	2.9	2.8	-8.1	-3.8	-2.7	-2.9	-2.1
All manufacturing	3.9	1.4	-7.8	-3.6	-2.4	-2.6	-1.9
Trade	2.0	0.7	-6.6	-2.8	-2.4	-3.6	-2.6
Transportation (excluding pipeline transportation)	4.8	1.9	-6.2	-2.0	-1.4	-2.0	-1.6
Pipeline transportation	4.3	2.5	-5.6	-3.7	-1.3	-1.8	-0.7
Warehousing and storage	3.2	1.5	-5.2	-1.3	-0.7	-1.9	-1.3
Finance, insurance and real estate	2.6	0.6	-8.0	-4.1	-4.1	-5.7	-4.1
Private education services	2.6	1.1	-9.5	-5.6	-4.7	-4.9	-4.8
Education services (excluding private), health care and social assistance	3.3	1.2	-7.4	-4.3	-3.5	-4.1	-3.2
Other services (excluding public administration)	2.4	0.5	-8.3	-6.5	-4.2	-4.3	-3.6
Public administration	2.1	1.5	-7.4	-4.9	-3.9	-3.7	-2.4

Source: Statistics Canada, CANSIM table 327-0042.

Table 25.8 Industrial Product Price Index, 1988 to 2007

	1988	1989	1990	1991	1992	1993	1994	1995	1996	1997
	1997=100									
All industrial products	**82.3**	**84.0**	**84.2**	**83.3**	**83.8**	**86.8**	**92.0**	**98.9**	**99.3**	**100.0**
Intermediate goods	84.5	86.1	85.1	82.6	82.2	85.1	91.8	101.1	100.1	100.0
First-stage intermediate goods	95.2	97.3	90.5	81.8	79.5	76.2	92.1	118.5	100.1	100.0
Second-stage intermediate goods	81.1	82.6	83.2	82.5	82.6	86.5	91.7	98.3	100.1	100.0
Finished goods	78.9	80.7	82.9	84.4	86.1	89.4	92.5	95.4	98.0	100.0
Finished foods and feeds	81.9	84.6	87.1	88.9	89.8	91.4	93.7	95.9	98.2	100.0
Capital equipment	77.0	78.8	80.6	82.0	84.8	89.1	92.7	96.0	98.0	100.0
All other finished goods	78.5	79.8	82.1	83.4	85.0	88.6	91.8	95.0	97.9	100.0
Aggregation, by commodities										
Meat, fish and dairy products	79.1	79.7	82.0	82.8	83.7	88.3	90.3	92.5	97.0	100.0
Fruits, vegetables, feeds and other food products	83.3	86.4	86.6	86.3	87.4	88.6	93.0	95.8	99.6	100.0
Beverages	79.3	84.0	86.5	89.5	90.8	92.2	92.8	94.9	97.4	100.0
Tobacco and tobacco products	58.3	61.2	66.2	73.4	78.9	84.1	86.9	89.6	93.4	100.0
Rubber, leather and plastic fabricated products	85.9	88.9	89.3	89.0	88.1	87.7	91.4	100.2	99.4	100.0
Textile products	88.5	90.3	91.4	91.4	91.2	92.3	94.1	97.8	99.2	100.0
Knitted products and clothing	86.6	88.9	91.1	92.2	92.6	92.8	94.2	96.7	99.0	100.0
Lumber and other wood products	63.4	65.9	65.5	64.4	69.8	87.1	97.8	94.0	99.3	100.0
Furniture and fixtures	81.0	84.4	87.4	88.4	87.9	89.8	92.1	98.3	99.3	100.0
Pulp and paper products	90.5	93.4	91.9	83.0	79.7	77.3	85.8	119.5	105.7	100.0
Printing and publishing	69.2	72.7	74.8	77.4	79.1	82.9	87.7	98.6	99.4	100.0
Primary metal products	98.1	97.8	88.6	81.2	79.0	78.2	92.4	105.4	97.9	100.0
Metal fabricated products	80.6	83.3	84.0	83.9	83.7	85.6	89.1	96.4	98.5	100.0
Machinery and equipment	81.6	85.5	87.4	88.7	90.0	92.8	95.6	97.6	99.2	100.0
Motor vehicles and other transport equipment	76.6	76.3	76.7	78.2	82.3	87.8	92.2	94.9	97.5	100.0
Electrical and communications products	90.6	93.8	94.0	93.6	94.4	97.0	99.8	102.2	101.1	100.0
Non-metallic mineral products	89.1	90.5	91.5	90.8	90.3	91.0	94.5	98.9	100.1	100.0
Petroleum and coal products	84.7	86.4	97.3	94.0	86.7	85.8	85.6	90.4	100.5	100.0
Chemicals and chemical products	86.5	87.7	85.4	86.5	85.3	87.0	93.2	101.8	99.8	100.0
Miscellaneous manufactured products	82.3	84.1	85.1	86.6	86.9	90.0	95.8	98.7	100.0	100.0
Miscellaneous non-manufactured products	123.7	104.6	95.0	84.5	83.2	91.3	102.9	120.3	111.1	100.0

See note and source at end of table.

Table 25.8 Industrial Product Price Index, 1988 to 2007 (continued)

	1998	1999	2000	2001	2002	2003	2004	2005	2006	2007
	1997=100									
All industrial products	**100.4**	**102.2**	**106.5**	**107.6**	**107.6**	**106.2**	**109.5**	**111.2**	**113.8**	**115.6**
Intermediate goods	98.4	99.9	105.3	105.0	104.2	103.8	109.9	112.8	117.5	120.5
First-stage intermediate goods	93.8	96.5	111.9	104.5	101.8	105.6	118.0	123.1	141.9	157.3
Second-stage intermediate goods	99.0	100.4	104.3	105.1	104.6	103.5	108.7	111.2	113.8	115.0
Finished goods	103.4	105.6	108.3	111.3	112.6	109.7	108.9	108.7	108.2	108.1
Finished foods and feeds	100.9	102.2	104.3	106.4	108.0	110.3	112.0	112.1	113.5	115.6
Capital equipment	104.9	106.6	107.3	110.7	112.6	107.1	104.5	102.5	100.2	98.3
All other finished goods	103.5	106.4	110.7	113.8	114.7	111.1	110.3	111.0	110.7	110.8
Aggregation, by commodities										
Meat, fish and dairy products	98.7	100.4	104.6	107.7	107.2	108.5	109.7	107.1	107.2	110.0
Fruits, vegetables, feeds and other food products	97.9	95.6	95.6	98.2	101.6	103.6	104.9	102.8	104.6	109.4
Beverages	102.4	105.6	109.0	111.4	114.6	117.7	120.4	121.3	122.5	125.0
Tobacco and tobacco products	103.8	109.4	114.2	127.4	139.5	162.7	169.3	176.3	190.4	213.0
Rubber, leather and plastic fabricated products	99.8	100.2	105.2	106.1	105.0	106.2	108.1	114.3	118.4	116.4
Textile products	101.2	99.6	99.1	100.5	100.4	99.4	98.9	99.9	100.3	99.8
Knitted products and clothing	101.6	102.2	102.8	103.2	103.8	104.1	104.5	104.3	104.7	104.7
Lumber and other wood products	95.9	105.1	95.9	94.6	94.0	90.3	101.1	92.5	87.2	84.2
Furniture and fixtures	101.1	102.3	104.8	106.3	107.5	109.2	111.8	115.1	118.3	120.0
Pulp and paper products	103.5	101.7	115.2	115.0	106.0	102.8	104.1	103.5	105.0	104.0
Printing and publishing	103.5	105.8	109.2	111.8	114.1	113.0	114.0	115.3	115.4	116.6
Primary metal products	96.0	95.2	100.6	94.4	96.3	96.2	113.4	116.5	138.6	145.9
Metal fabricated products	102.6	103.0	104.7	104.9	106.5	107.2	117.0	121.5	123.1	124.4
Machinery and equipment	102.3	103.7	104.8	105.9	106.9	105.9	106.0	107.3	107.0	105.7
Motor vehicles and other transport equipment	107.1	108.5	109.0	113.5	115.1	106.3	101.2	96.5	92.4	89.3
Electrical and communications products	100.1	100.2	98.5	99.4	101.3	95.8	94.7	93.7	93.7	92.1
Non-metallic mineral products	100.2	102.0	105.2	107.4	108.7	109.7	111.6	114.9	119.7	122.8
Petroleum and coal products	82.3	96.1	140.3	133.7	125.5	138.4	161.8	199.9	218.1	230.4
Chemicals and chemical products	96.9	98.6	104.8	107.4	107.3	110.4	113.8	121.0	122.9	126.5
Miscellaneous manufactured products	101.4	103.0	104.3	105.5	107.5	107.2	109.6	110.7	112.9	113.9
Miscellaneous non-manufactured products	90.3	90.3	86.4	86.6	90.8	95.8	125.1	163.7	248.1	443.2

Note: Annual average indexes are obtained by averaging the indexes for the 12 months of the calendar year.

Source: Statistics Canada, CANSIM tables 329-0039, 329-0040, 329-0041, 329-0042, 329-0044, 329-0045, 329-0046 and 329-0048.

Table 25.9 New Housing Price Index, 2001 to 2007

	2001	2002	2003	2004	2005	2006	2007
	1997=100						
Canada	**107.0**	**111.3**	**116.7**	**123.2**	**129.4**	**142.0**	**153.0**
Atlantic Region	105.4	108.7	112.5	115.9	120.5	124.9	129.6
Quebec	111.0	117.3	126.2	134.2	140.8	147.0	153.2
Ontario	110.8	114.9	120.0	126.7	132.6	137.5	141.1
Prairie Region	114.8	121.0	127.3	134.0	143.2	192.5	235.6
British Columbia	90.6	92.9	96.3	101.4	106.3	113.2	120.5
	annual % change						
Canada	**2.8**	**4.0**	**4.9**	**5.6**	**5.0**	**9.7**	**7.7**
Atlantic Region	1.8	3.1	3.5	3.0	4.0	3.7	3.8
Quebec	4.6	5.7	7.6	6.3	4.9	4.4	4.2
Ontario	3.2	3.7	4.4	5.6	4.7	3.7	2.6
Prairie Region	2.3	5.4	5.2	5.3	6.9	34.4	22.4
British Columbia	0.8	2.5	3.7	5.3	4.8	6.5	6.4

Source: Statistics Canada, CANSIM table 327-0005.

Retail and wholesale trade

26

Overview

Canadians' enthusiasm for shopping is swelling the revenues of retailers and wholesalers and spurring employment in the sector. Indeed, the number of people working in retail nearly equals employment in manufacturing, as the retail sector continues to grow while manufacturing contracts.

In 2006, retail operating profits reached $21.1 billion, a 9.5% increase over 2005 and the highest level since 2002.

Operating revenues of $413.8 billion represented a gain of 5.7%, well above the annual average growth rate of 4.7% from 2002 to 2006.

Retail employment expanded an average of 1.8% a year from 2001 to 2006. This was an addition of 156,000 workers to the workforce, bringing the number of jobs to 1.8 million. This was 81,000 workers shy of total employment in manufacturing, the largest employment sector, which shed 137,000 workers over the five-year period.

Meanwhile, wholesalers saw their operating revenues total $660.0 billion in 2006, up 5.8% over 2005. While this growth was lower than the 7.1% in 2005 and the 9.1% in 2004, wholesalers' operating profit margins as a percentage of total operating revenues continued to rise.

In 2006, wholesalers had an operating profit margin increase of 4.7%, up from 4.4% in 2005. Growth in investment and consumer spending, with a healthy construction sector, all contributed to higher revenues and profits.

Most of Canada's shopping is still done the traditional way, in a store. Internet sales have doubled in less than five years, but they still account for less than 2% of the operating revenues of private-sector firms.

Chart 26.1
GDP of retail and wholesale trade

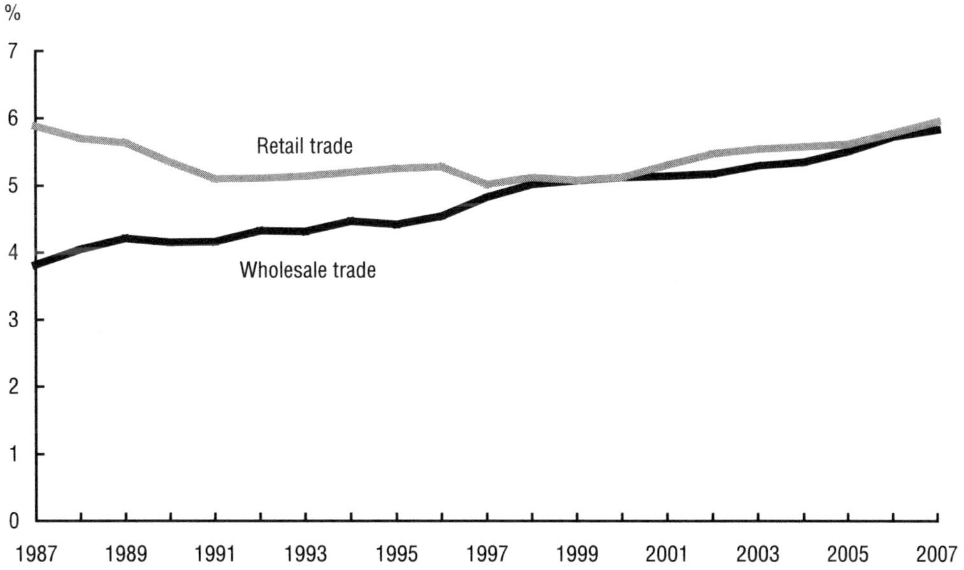

Source: Statistics Canada, CANSIM table 379-0027.

Home products lead retail growth

If shopping patterns reflect interests, then Canadians are focused on their homes. In 2006, all retail trade groups except gas stations reported rising gross margins (total operating revenues less cost of goods sold), as home and garden retailers made major gains. The gross margins of specialized building materials and garden stores increased 26.8% to $1.9 billion, while those of home furnishing stores rose 22.9% to $2.7 billion.

Meanwhile, home centres and hardware stores realized gross margins of $6.0 billion, home electronics and appliance stores, $3.4 billion, and furniture stores, $4.0 billion. It was also a good year for used and recreational motor vehicles and parts dealers, who saw a 20.8% rise in gross margins, up to $4.9 billion.

Gas stations posted a decline of 1.4% from 2005, as they were affected by increased product costs. Their operating revenues rose 8.9% over 2005, but they were hit by an 11.2% increase in the cost of goods sold.

Despite the virtually across-the-board growth in gross margins in 2006, Canada's store-based retailers were dealing with a 9.5% increase in operating expenses over 2005, for a total of $89.2 billion. Operating expenses represented 39.0% of operating revenues for home furnishing stores, up from 34.6% the year before. For specialized building materials and garden stores, the ratio rose from 26.7% to 29.9%.

Half of these operating expenses were for labour, with rental and leasing second at 12.0%, up 12.7% from 2005. Half of the 18 retail trade groups reported double-digit increases in advertising expenses.

Gas stations were again the exception: they were the only retail group to have lower costs for labour. The 16% decline in their labour costs was partly attributable to the growing trend of drivers paying at the pump.

Table 26.a
Retail trade by selected trade group, 2006

	Operating revenues	Operating expenses	Gross margins	Operating profits
	$ millions			
Total	**413,802**	**89,197**	**110,284**	**21,087**
New cars	80,423	9,446	11,262	1,816
Supermarkets	65,299	14,113	16,067	1,954
General merchandise	46,635	10,476	12,362	1,886
Gas stations	42,932	4,442	7,336	2,894
Pharmacies, personal care	27,475	7,290	8,331	1,042
Home centres and hardware	20,235	4,886	6,012	1,126
Used and recreational vehicles and parts	19,710	4,322	4,904	583
Clothing	18,009	7,571	9,124	1,553
Beer, wine and liquor	14,814	2,296	6,588	4,292
Convenience and specialty food stores	14,148	3,244	3,728	484

Source: Statistics Canada, CANSIM table 080-0011.

Chart 26.2
Non-store retail operating revenues, by industry group, 2006

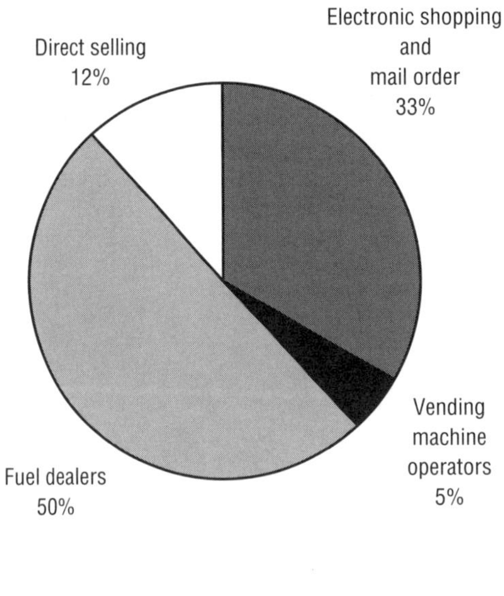

Source: Statistics Canada, CANSIM table 080-0012.

Differing provincial patterns

In 2006, the sales of Canada's store retailers totalled $389.5 billion, an increase of 5.8% over the previous year, as profitability increased an average of 10% nationally.

In the western provinces, both sales growth and profitability were above the national average. In Alberta, sales rose 15.4% to $55.9 billion, while operating profits grew 27.2%. Manitoba and Saskatchewan also saw strong gains in operating profits, enjoying increases of 23.5% and 21.5% respectively. In British Columbia, where operating expenses increased 11.4% over 2005, profits increased 16.2%.

Ontario has lagged behind the rest of Canada over the past few years. Sales there edged up 4.0% in 2006. Combined with a 7.5% rise in operating expenses, this resulted in a 2.3% decline in operating profits. Newfoundland and Labrador was the only other province to see a decline in 2006, down 9.6%.

Chart 26.3
Wholesalers' operating revenues

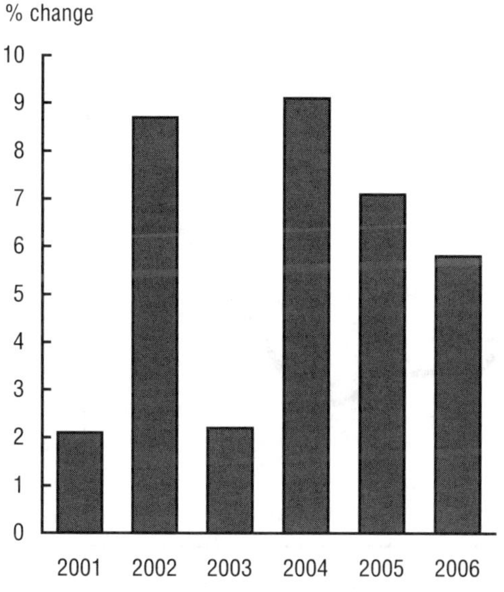

Source: Statistics Canada CANSIM table 081-0005.

Favourable factors benefit wholesale trade

Wholesalers continued to benefit from a variety of favourable factors in 2006: increased business investment, vigorous consumer spending, growth in imports of consumer goods, record construction levels, and lower prices on certain products because of the higher loonie.

The provincial pattern in wholesalers' operating profits differed from that of retailers. For example, Ontario was behind on the retail side, but its wholesalers had a 16.7% gain in operating profits in 2006, well above the Canadian average (10.9%).

Ontario's wholesalers account for 42% of all wholesale revenues. Their average gross margin (21.6%) was above the national average (19.1%), largely because of high margins in apparel, household and personal goods, and office and professional equipment.

Other provinces posted above-average growth in operating profits in 2006: Manitoba led the country with a gain of 51.6%, Nova Scotia was up 20.2% and Alberta had a gain of 16.0%.

Posting the sharpest declines in operating profits were Prince Edward Island, down 22.8%, and New Brunswick, down 22.1%. Saskatchewan also had lower wholesale operating profits, down 8.9% from 2005.

Cross-border shopping now a trickle

Cross-border shopping has not taken flight with the loonie. In fact, today's cross-border shopping volumes pale compared with the flood of shoppers in the late 1980s, when the exchange rate was also rising.

Whether measured by the number of same-day car trips across the border, the average spending on these trips or the amount of online shopping, the recent increases in cross-border shopping have been minimal or, outside of Ontario, insignificant relative to total retail sales.

Americans' cross-border shopping in Canada has tumbled 50% or by 11.3 million trips since the loonie began to rise in 2003. However, Canadians' same-day car trips to the United States increased by 2.2 million.

Americans' overnight visits to Canada have also dropped; this has been partly offset by more overseas visitors. Ontario has borne the brunt of the steep slide in trips here by Americans. Foreign arrivals in Ontario have not been this low since the 1970s.

In 2007, the equivalent of 5.9% of Canada's population made same-day U.S. car trips each month, compared with 5.5% in 2002. These trips hit a peak equal to 17.6% in 1991. Besides tighter border security and higher gas prices, other factors might be dampening enthusiasm for cross-border shopping such as the aging of the population, growth of big-box chains here and today's stronger economy.

This time as the loonie has risen, new and used vehicles have been the fastest-growing segment of cross-border shopping, though the dollar amount—nearly $1 billion in 2007, or five times its 2002 value—still represents less than 2% of the vehicles purchased annually by Canadians.

Chart 26.4
Cross-border shopping and the exchange rate, Canada to the United States

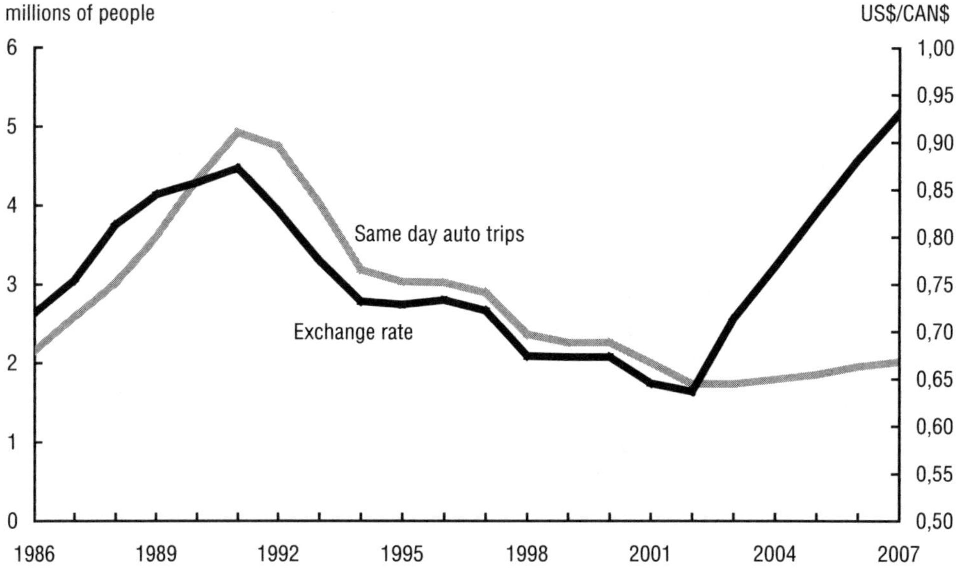

Source: Statistic Canada, CANSIM tables 427-0005 and 176-0064.

Motor vehicle sales shifting, not stalled

The auto industry is in a state of flux with rising energy prices and concerns about climate change. Still, Canadians' vehicle buying patterns in 2007 may not seem consistent with those concerns.

The truck category—including minivans, sport-utility vehicles, light and heavy trucks, vans and buses—posted record-setting sales in 2007. Units sold were at an all-time high of 831,535 units, up 3.5% from 2006.

Overall, dealers sold 1.7 million new vehicles in 2007, a 1.5% increase over 2006 and the second-highest number sold since record-keeping began in 1946.

Newfoundland and Labrador saw the largest growth for new vehicles sold in 2007, at 16.8%. Alberta, which had held the number one spot for sales growth since 2003, posted unit sales percentage growth of 3.3%.

The types of vehicles Canadians are buying have changed in the past decade or so. For example, cars accounted for 65% of sales in 1992, but made up half of 2007 purchases. The 859,003 cars sold in 2007 were 0.5% fewer than in 2006.

This decline continued to come at the expense of the traditional Big Three North-American automakers—General Motors, Ford and Chrysler. In 2007, these automakers accounted for 49.1% of sales, compared with 67.9% in 2000.

Despite the increased sales, the $53.6 billion that Canadian households and business spent on new vehicles in 2007 represented a slight decline (0.6%) from the previous year.

For the first time since 2001, the average amount spent on a new vehicle in Canada fell from the previous year, down 2.0% from $32,386 in 2006 to $31,723 in 2007.

Chart 26.5
Sales of new motor vehicles, 2007

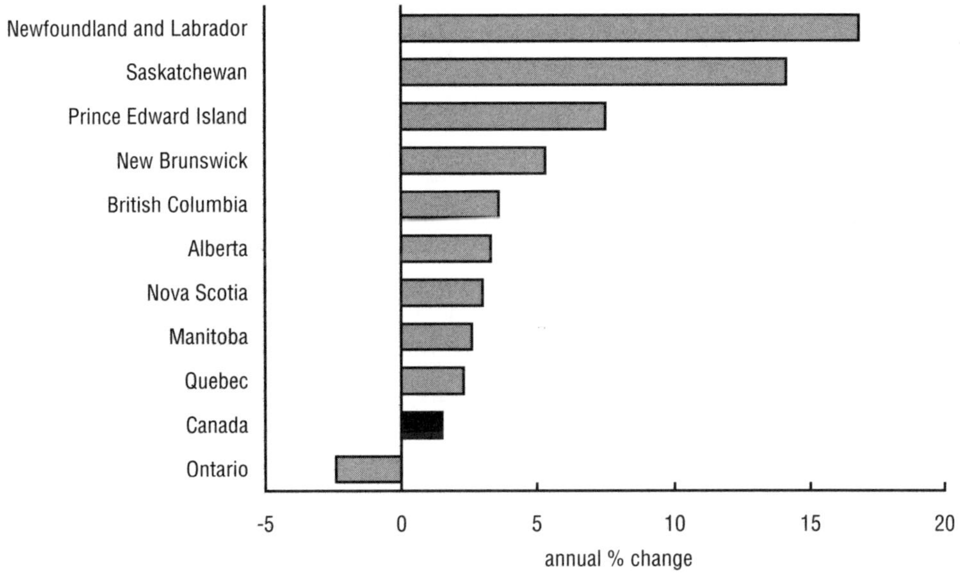

Source: Statistics Canada, Catalogue no. 11-621-MIE.

Table 26.1 Interprovincial trade, by province and territory, 2007

	All goods and services	Goods	Services
	$ millions		
Imports to provinces	**302,105**	.	.
Newfoundland and Labrador	**7,221**	3,290	3,931
Prince Edward Island	**2,345**	1,218	1,127
Nova Scotia	**11,481**	6,102	5,379
New Brunswick	**12,721**	7,455	5,266
Quebec	**60,334**	32,867	27,467
Ontario	**82,520**	51,468	31,052
Manitoba	**16,801**	9,652	7,149
Saskatchewan	**17,945**	9,102	8,843
Alberta	**48,009**	25,768	22,241
British Columbia	**38,784**	20,252	18,532
Yukon	**744**	302	442
Northwest Territories	**2,059**	903	1,156
Nunavut	**950**	429	521
Outside Canada	**189**	137	52
Exports from provinces	**302,105**	.	.
Newfoundland and Labrador	**9,342**	8,345	997
Prince Edward Island	**1,113**	713	400
Nova Scotia	**7,097**	4,273	2,824
New Brunswick	**8,780**	6,077	2,703
Quebec	**57,146**	34,035	23,111
Ontario	**106,838**	47,098	59,740
Manitoba	**14,325**	7,379	6,946
Saskatchewan	**14,869**	11,575	3,294
Alberta	**52,614**	35,173	17,441
British Columbia	**28,532**	13,599	14,933
Yukon	**221**	77	144
Northwest Territories	**1,079**	595	484
Nunavut	**143**	7	136
Outside Canada	**7**	0	7

Note: Expenditure-based gross domestic product.
Source: Statistics Canada, CANSIM table 384-0002.

Table 26.2 Wholesale trade, sales by trade group, 2003 to 2007

	2003	2004	2005	2006	2007
	$ millions				
All trade groups	**415,597.5**	**442,880.3**	**467,469.9**	**490,855.5**	**517,776.4**
Farm products	4,837.0	5,179.8	5,719.7	5,372.2	5,609.2
Food products	72,646.6	73,668.8	75,069.1	77,119.3	81,589.0
Alcohol and tobacco	7,601.0	7,555.2	7,398.9	7,652.4	7,596.4
Apparel	9,260.8	8,733.0	9,006.1	9,019.8	9,377.6
Home and personal products	25,954.9	27,773.5	30,024.0	30,769.1	33,005.2
Pharmaceuticals	24,921.8	28,624.0	30,285.4	32,299.2	34,865.1
Motor vehicles	72,286.5	72,632.7	73,251.8	75,439.7	77,001.3
Motor vehicle parts and accessories	14,596.9	17,431.0	17,961.5	18,455.2	18,680.9
Building supplies	31,207.4	35,605.3	39,687.1	42,997.3	45,330.3
Metal products	11,273.5	14,883.2	16,072.5	17,711.1	17,774.9
Lumber and millwork	10,814.1	13,832.8	13,762.0	13,222.6	12,894.5
Machinery and equipment	35,734.6	40,030.6	46,488.4	50,966.0	54,540.6
Computers and other electronic equipment	27,122.5	26,432.7	27,812.2	29,631.9	31,604.0
Office and professional equipment	18,452.6	19,112.7	20,725.9	22,625.1	24,296.1
Other products	48,887.0	51,385.0	54,205.2	57,574.7	63,611.3

Note: North American Industry Classification System (NAICS), 2002.
Source: Statistics Canada, CANSIM table 081-0007.

Table 26.3 Wholesale trade, sales by province and territory, 2003 to 2007

	2003	2004	2005	2006	2007
	$ millions				
Canada	**415,597.5**	**442,880.3**	**467,469.9**	**490,855.5**	**517,776.4**
Newfoundland and Labrador	2,211.5	2,285.0	2,405.2	2,595.5	2,973.0
Prince Edward Island	497.0	592.2	544.5	448.5	478.4
Nova Scotia	6,688.2	6,456.4	6,642.1	6,582.8	6,748.8
New Brunswick	4,527.8	4,683.5	4,838.1	4,859.1	5,075.9
Quebec	78,702.8	84,488.2	89,192.5	91,973.0	96,762.7
Ontario	223,637.1	235,402.6	242,633.6	251,943.3	262,523.0
Manitoba	9,933.3	10,058.7	10,765.4	11,271.6	12,603.7
Saskatchewan	10,912.5	11,039.0	12,073.0	12,105.6	14,480.0
Alberta	39,967.0	44,965.6	52,266.0	59,073.4	61,725.1
British Columbia	38,165.5	42,364.8	45,447.4	49,328.3	53,547.7
Yukon	72.0	77.7	91.9	118.4	140.1
Northwest Territories	260.9	439.7	544.9	533.0	667.0
Nunavut	21.9	27.0	25.3	23.1	50.9

Source: Statistics Canada, CANSIM table 081-0007.

Table 26.4 Retail store sales, by selected commodities, 2002 to 2007

	2002	2003	2004	2005	2006	2007
	$ thousands					
Total commodities	**320,372,749**	**332,027,040**	**347,703,971**	**367,182,509**	**390,635,726**	**413,384,210**
Food[1]	51,657,937	53,903,751	56,652,229	59,473,338	62,132,248	65,057,277
Non-alcoholic beverages	3,983,295	4,171,140	4,487,664	4,652,653	4,985,585	5,285,446
Alcoholic beverages	14,408,373	15,208,713	15,728,696	16,323,670	17,219,597	18,254,774
Personal care, health and beauty products (non-electric)[2]	8,005,008	8,243,691	9,136,351	9,348,340	9,834,835	10,361,197
Eyewear, prescription and non-prescription	1,234,260	1,220,881	1,299,106	1,327,230	1,427,845	1,519,217
Drugs,[3] vitamins and other health supplements	16,258,706	17,689,289	18,847,652	19,865,191	21,759,867	23,956,879
Luggage and jewellery	2,669,784	2,729,653	2,922,966	2,965,483	3,324,691	3,439,557
Clothing and accessories	21,064,469	21,330,150	22,193,535	23,034,034	24,444,857	25,413,303
Footwear	4,015,217	4,096,491	4,089,528	4,415,258	4,759,675	4,978,438
Furniture (indoor), household appliances and electronics	20,830,879	21,968,969	23,216,362	24,370,225	26,310,634	27,833,964
Home furnishings	7,615,669	7,905,124	8,388,694	8,831,770	9,659,818	10,774,704
New automotive vehicles	42,609,510	42,110,185	42,135,933	44,224,747	46,259,505	47,012,704
Used automotive vehicles	20,921,130	19,211,016	18,939,461	19,171,846	20,283,142	21,782,208
Automotive parts and accessories, labour receipts and rental receipts	13,904,854	14,949,971	15,524,002	16,721,968	17,788,682	18,562,228
Automotive fuels	22,963,371	24,498,428	28,204,465	33,428,907	36,329,833	40,543,775
Automotive oils and additives	756,394	826,626	811,850	856,575	988,814	1,004,925
Tableware, kitchenware, cookware and bakeware	1,592,461	1,630,403	1,748,933	1,805,303	1,943,240	2,001,819
Household cleaning supplies, chemicals and paper products	3,266,793	3,385,810	3,464,650	3,563,878	3,672,636	3,791,473
Other household supplies	1,918,349	2,022,554	2,073,350	2,110,729	2,249,110	2,253,256
Hardware and home renovation products	14,816,055	16,609,941	18,369,582	19,638,889	21,453,768	22,748,965
Lawn and garden products, equipment and plants	3,996,625	4,388,176	4,819,370	5,166,713	5,813,678	6,067,556
Sporting goods	3,836,514	3,881,883	3,844,770	3,958,831	4,218,088	4,346,877
Toys, games and hobby supplies[4]	2,531,502	2,595,763	2,642,719	2,797,038	3,026,285	3,679,376
Fabrics, yarns, sewing supplies and notions	735,625	722,810	740,717	682,495	668,933	670,193
Craft and artists' supplies	340,664	348,376	382,897	377,425	407,946	421,055
Prerecorded media[5]	1,757,464	1,830,651	1,940,899	2,068,737	2,073,218	2,036,142
Books, newspapers and other periodicals	2,596,982	2,658,077	2,740,443	2,863,095	2,923,416	2,982,527
Musical instruments, parts, accessories and supplies	461,840	469,330	502,270	499,416	455,247	437,431
Recreational vehicles	5,920,353	6,078,357	5,826,704	6,114,308	6,679,180	7,563,799
Pet food, supplies and accessories	1,447,161	1,606,080	1,767,702	1,947,399	2,060,048	2,240,947
Tobacco products and supplies	8,091,879	8,882,966	8,844,281	8,540,035	8,294,852	8,144,689
Giftware, novelties and souvenirs	1,555,145	1,401,010	1,297,702	1,200,563	1,347,984	1,357,834
Stationery, office supplies, cards, gift wrap and party supplies	2,814,674	3,105,829	3,329,898	3,534,022	3,659,177	3,760,354
Used and second-hand merchandise and antiques	1,353,210	1,400,177	1,394,336	1,471,636	1,651,632	1,833,107
Meals and lunches	764,193	831,503	889,098	927,755	1,050,087	1,142,950

1. Excludes pet food, meals and lunches.
2. Includes home health care sick room equipment and supplies.
3. Includes both prescription and over-the-counter drugs.
4. Includes electronic games.
5. Includes compact discs (CDs), digital video discs (DVDs) and video and audio tapes (excluding rentals).

Source: Statistics Canada, CANSIM table 080-0018.

Table 26.5 Retail trade, sales by trade group, 2003 to 2007

	2003	2004	2005	2006	2007
			$ millions		
All trade groups	**331,143.4**	**346,721.5**	**366,170.7**	**389,485.1**	**412,037.3**
New car dealers	68,183.6	68,141.1	71,515.6	74,531.3	76,884.4
Used and recreational motor vehicle and parts dealers	14,393.9	14,559.2	15,301.4	17,286.5	18,673.8
Gasoline stations	29,951.3	33,363.8	38,356.8	41,753.3	46,387.6
Furniture stores	7,923.8	8,506.5	8,914.4	9,558.0	10,052.5
Home furnishings stores	3,971.6	4,438.9	4,686.3	5,337.6	5,990.9
Computer and software stores	1,883.9	1,581.8	1,557.5	1,502.1	1,421.3
Home electronics and appliance stores	9,089.7	9,443.1	10,164.8	11,146.2	12,305.9
Home centres and hardware stores	14,595.2	16,597.8	18,220.7	20,121.3	21,412.7
Specialized building materials and garden stores	4,316.0	4,372.8	4,340.4	4,640.9	5,057.1
Supermarkets	56,874.1	59,760.9	62,196.3	63,764.7	65,842.5
Convenience and specialty food stores	8,371.4	8,806.9	9,128.6	9,324.6	9,885.0
Beer, wine and liquor stores	13,293.7	13,789.8	14,343.9	15,095.1	16,140.0
Pharmacies and personal care stores	21,266.6	22,769.3	23,642.7	26,055.0	28,249.4
Clothing stores	14,567.1	15,311.6	16,069.3	17,226.6	18,247.5
Shoe, clothing accessories and jewellery stores	4,903.8	4,876.8	4,981.3	5,399.6	5,606.5
General merchandise stores	40,011.0	42,123.7	43,758.4	46,497.7	48,590.8
Department stores	20,800.8	21,849.9	x	..	..
Other general merchandise stores[1]	19,210.2	20,273.8	x	..	..
Sporting goods, hobby, music and book stores	8,676.1	8,831.4	9,379.3	9,994.3	10,553.9
Miscellaneous store retailers[2]	8,870.7	9,446.1	9,613.1	10,250.3	10,735.4

Note: North American Industry Classification System (NAICS), 2002.

1. Includes warehouse clubs and superstores and all other general merchandise stores.
2. Includes florists; office supply and stationary stores; gift, novelty and souvenir stores; used merchandise stores; pet and pet supply stores; art dealers; mobile home dealers; and all other miscellaneous store retailers.

Source: Statistics Canada, CANSIM table 080-0014.

Table 26.6 Retail trade sales, by province and territory, 2003 to 2007

	2003	2004	2005	2006	2007
			$ millions		
Canada	**331,143.4**	**346,721.5**	**366,170.7**	**389,485.1**	**412,037.3**
Newfoundland and Labrador	5,736.3	5,755.5	5,825.9	6,026.1	6,566.7
Prince Edward Island	1,382.6	1,384.7	1,423.9	1,512.2	1,628.9
Nova Scotia	10,014.9	10,296.5	10,526.9	11,162.5	11,636.1
New Brunswick	7,826.8	7,962.7	8,326.1	8,813.7	9,318.4
Quebec	75,325.7	78,517.9	82,532.5	86,708.9	90,663.3
Ontario	125,122.5	129,085.8	135,320.6	140,807.8	146,252.3
Manitoba	10,953.2	11,691.6	12,381.3	12,869.6	14,008.0
Saskatchewan	9,858.1	10,259.4	10,796.1	11,494.8	12,984.0
Alberta	39,317.8	43,371.6	48,493.0	55,941.8	61,159.8
British Columbia	44,421.0	47,216.6	49,286.3	52,837.1	56,365.4
Yukon	421.6	414.0	433.9	451.3	500.3
Northwest Territories	529.9	532.1	574.8	599.5	679.1
Nunavut	232.9	233.2	249.2	259.8	275.0

Source: Statistics Canada, CANSIM table 080-0014.

Table 26.7 Non-store retailers, financial estimates, by trade group, 2006

	All non-store retailers	Electronic shopping and mail-order houses	Vending machine operators and coffee service operators	Fuel dealers	Other direct selling establishments
			$ thousands		
Total operating revenue	**13,376,734**	**4,449,763**	**637,910**	**6,713,235**	**1,575,826**
Sales of goods for resale	**12,515,771**	4,072,459	613,020	6,505,486	1,324,806[E]
Opening inventory	**654,526**	374,656	39,470	120,001	120,399
Purchases	**9,300,495**	2,752,126	286,605	5,508,519	753,245
Closing inventory	**606,962**	337,248	31,963	123,669	114,083
Cost of goods sold	**9,348,058**	2,789,534	294,112	5,504,851	759,561
Total operating expenses	**3,278,056**	1,381,866	306,854	900,163	689,173
Total labour remuneration	**1,122,475**	335,059	143,164	399,112	245,139

Note: North American Industry Classification System (NAICS), 2002.
Source: Statistics Canada, CANSIM table 080-0012.

Science and technology

27

Overview

Scientific innovation has transformed our lives in ways our grandparents likely never imagined. At home, work and play, yesterday's marvels are today's commonplaces. We reheat last night's dinner in the microwave and have injuries repaired with microsurgery, we share documents as easily with colleagues across the globe as with those in the next office, we go online to find the lyrics to our favourite song or the partner of our dreams. Small wonder, then, that the Organisation for Economic Co-operation and Development (OECD) tells us innovation is integral to competitiveness and national progress.

The OECD says innovative effort, including formal research and development, is the indispensable element of growth. That's why most OECD countries have invested more rapidly in knowledge than in machinery and equipment since the mid-1990s. Canada sits in the middle of the pack of the 30 OECD member nations in terms of gross domestic expenditures on research and development (R&D) as a percentage of gross domestic product (GDP). Canada invested nearly 2% of GDP on R&D in 2007; Sweden posted the highest percentage in the OECD, more than 4%. The United States invested slightly more than 3%.

Who's taking part?

Canada's domestic spending on R&D neared $29.0 billion in 2007, according to preliminary figures, compared with just over $16.0 billion in 1998. That investment comes from businesses, governments, universities, private non-profit groups, institutions of higher education and foreign sources.

The business sector is the biggest R&D player in Canada, investing $13.8 billion in 2007, almost half of the total. The federal government places second, at $5.4 billion, or 19% of all R&D funding, according to

Chart 27.1
Gross domestic expenditures of research and development (GERD) and gross domestic product (GDP)

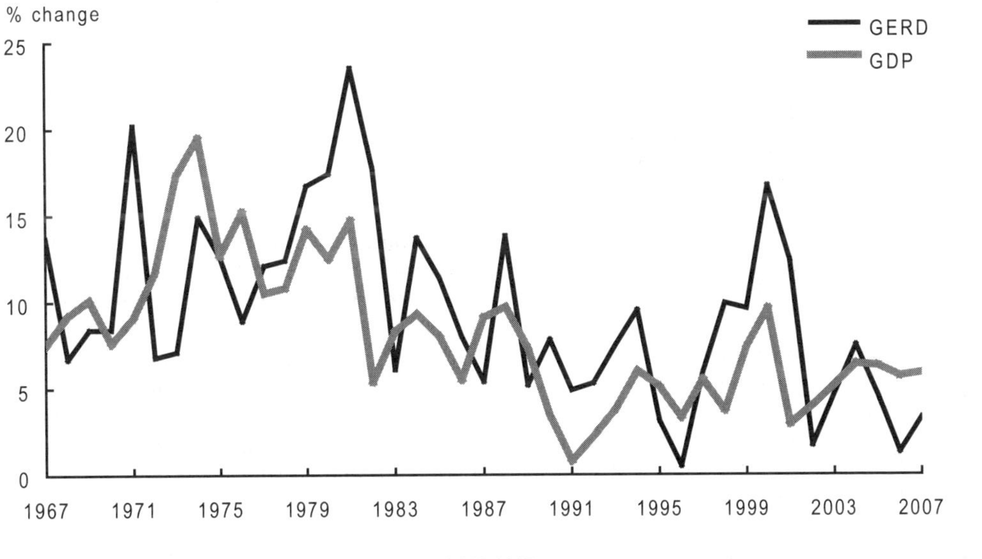

Source: Statistics Canada, CANSIM tables 358-0001 and 380-0017.

2007 preliminary figures. R&D investment intentions in 2007/2008 were 2.9% of the total federal government's budget. While this is down from the 3.3% peak in 2005/2006, it is still ahead of the 2.1% that was invested in the mid-1990s.

Business also performs the majority of R&D in Canada—in 2007, the value of business-performed R&D was $15.8 billion, more than half of all R&D undertaken. Together, business and higher education perform about 90% of the country's R&D year after year. The higher education sector, which includes all affiliated research hospitals, experimental stations and clinics, undertook $10.4 billion worth of R&D in 2007. The federal government, Canada's other major R&D force, conducted $2.3 billion worth of R&D in 2007, primarily at the National Research Council, Agriculture and Agri-Food Canada, National Defence and Natural Resources Canada.

What's being researched?

Chart 27.2
Gross domestic expenditures on research and development, by sector, 2007

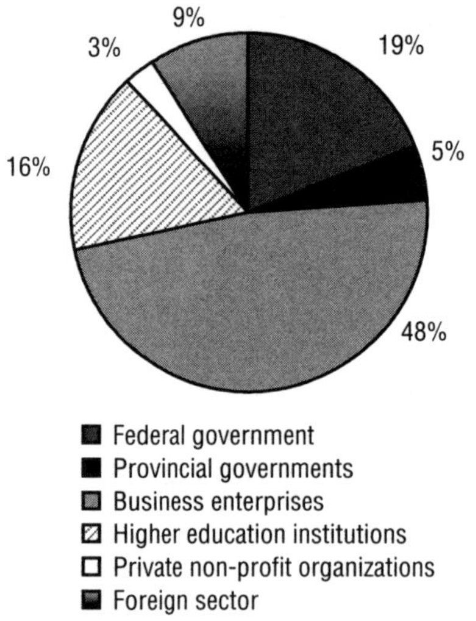

Source: Statistics Canada, CANSIM table 358-0001.

Table 27.a
Personnel engaged in research and development, by sector

	1997	2007
	number	
Total	**143,760**	**213,930**
Federal government	14,840	15,250
Provincial governments[1]	2,880	2,620
Business enterprises[2]	79,380	137,690
Higher education	45,430	56,950
Private non-profit organizations[3]	1,230	1,420

Note: Personnel counts are reported as full-time equivalents (rounded to the nearest 10).
1. Includes provincial research organizations.
2. Natural sciences and engineering only.
3. Counts may fluctuate because of intramural research and development activities.

Source: Statistics Canada, Catalogue no. 88-001-XIE.

R&D spending falls into two major categories: natural sciences and engineering, and social sciences and humanities. In 2007, of the $28.9 billion invested, $26.7 billion went to natural sciences and engineering; $2.2 billion was spent in the social sciences and humanities. This funding allocation is consistent with previous years.

Research in the health sector takes the lion's share of Canada's total R&D spending, accounting for $6.6 billion in 2006, up 6.8% from 2005. This was slightly more than 23% of all R&D spending, compared with 17% a decade earlier. By far the largest proportion, 63%, of health sector research was conducted by the higher education sector.

In the business sector, six industries led in performing R&D: information and cultural industries, communication equipment, scientific research and development, computer system design and related services, pharmaceutical and medicine manufacturing, and aerospace products and parts manufacturing. Together they accounted for one-half of the estimated $15.8 billion worth of R&D performed in the sector in 2007.

Who's in the science workforce?

While a country's innovation climate—one of the key elements for economic health, growth and international competitiveness—is often gauged by the proportion of the GDP devoted to research and development, that's not the only measure.

Another measure of the economic resources devoted to innovation is the size of an economy's science and engineering workforce. Comparing Canada and the United States, the size of the science and engineering workforce in the two countries is proportionally very similar—and it has been that way for the past 30 years. In 2001, the science and engineering workforce comprised 13.6% of total employment in both countries.

The workforce measured includes two groups: a core group, made up of computer and mathematical scientists, life scientists, physical scientists, social scientists and engineers; and a related group made up of workers in health-related occupations, as well as science and engineering managers, science and engineering technologists, other science and engineering workers, and postsecondary educators in science and engineering fields.

The Canada–U.S. percentages are still comparable if just the core group of scientists and engineers is counted: in both countries it equalled 4.5% of total employment in 2000/2001. However, there are differences. In Canada one-quarter of scientists and engineers work in the professional, scientific and technical industries, compared with one-fifth in the United States. In the United States, however, scientists and engineers make up 8.1% of manufacturing employment, compared with 4.8% in Canada.

Chart 27.3
Science and technology workforce, 2006

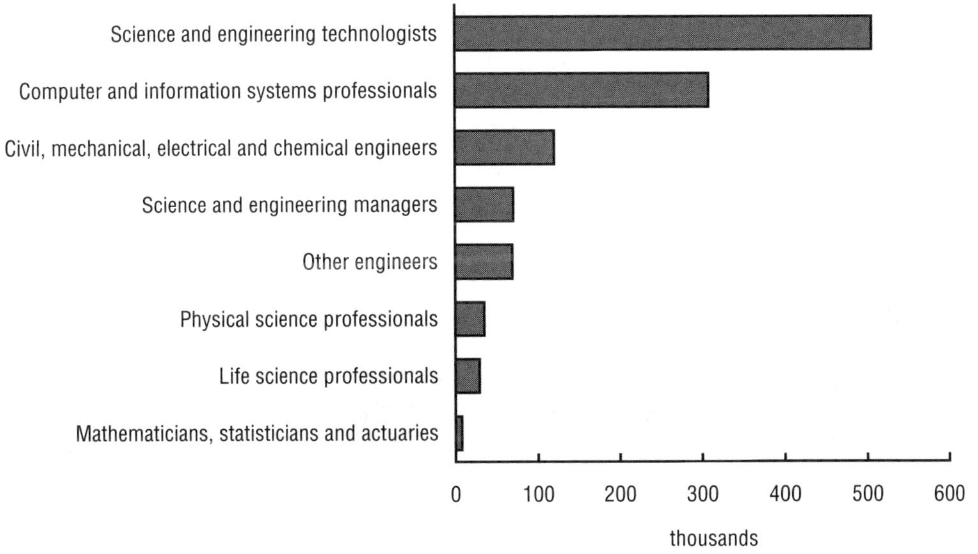

Source: Statistics Canada, Catalogue no. 97-559-XWE.

Outsourcing and innovations

Outsourcing manufacturing is nothing new. For decades firms have outsourced to save costs and focus on their core competencies. But today, companies are also outsourcing many professional services, including R&D, and that is new.

Close to 11% of Canadian manufacturers outsourced at least some of their R&D from 2002 to 2004. Sixty-eight percent outsourced to Canadian establishments—65% outsourced only within their own province—while close to 30% used both Canadian and foreign suppliers. Just 1.7% of outsourcing manufacturers went exclusively to establishments outside Canada.

A look at firms that are comparable in terms of size, industry, location, workforce educational attainment and other factors showed that outsourcing companies produced significantly more innovations, and were more successful in commercializing their innovations. Seventy-four percent of R&D outsourcers produced more than one innovation from 2002 to 2004, compared with 67% of non-outsourcers. Companies that produced at least five innovations in that period showed an even greater difference: 45% of firms that outsourced R&D reported five or more new innovations, compared with 37% of firms that did not outsource R&D.

An assessment of only the companies that innovated showed that while their outsourcing of R&D did not result in their producing more innovations, they did produce more world-first innovations: 24% compared with 19%. These manufacturers tended to have more of their revenue coming from innovations they were already selling. This suggests that they used R&D outsourcing as a strategy to improve competitiveness, while concentrating on innovations.

Chart 27.4
Innovations for establishments that outsourced and did not outsource research and development (R&D), 2002 to 2004

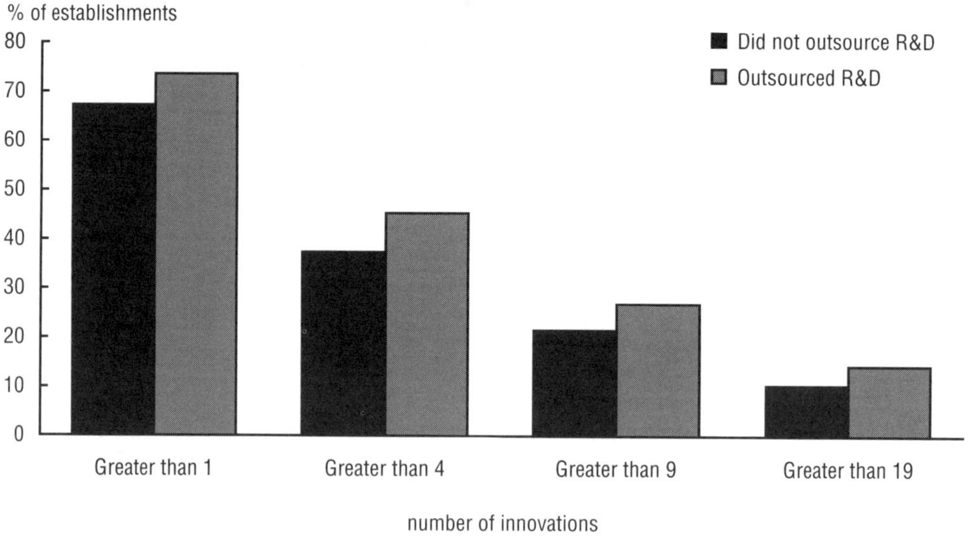

Source: Statistics Canada, Catalogue no. 88-003-XIE.

The nature of nanotechnology

The word 'nanotechnology' evokes visions of the cutting-edge, tiny robots put to work to aid everything from health care to communications. Nanotechnologies can be found in areas as diverse as biotechnology and health, agriculture, electronics and computer technology, environment and energy, optics, and materials and manufacturing.

Nanotechnology involves a suite of technologies enabling direct manipulation, study or exploitation of systems or structures that have at least one dimension on the nanometre (nm) length scale, typically less than 100 nm. The nanometre is equal to one-billionth of a metre.

In 2005, 88 Canadian firms reported involvement in nanotechnology. Of these, 91% were active in R&D, but 27% did report being in the production or market stage. Together nanomaterials, at 43%, and nanobiotechnology, at 42%, accounted for the vast majority of firm activity. Other areas of activity were nanomedicine, nanophotonics and nanoelectronics.

Canadian nanotechnology revenues amounted to $28.2 million in 2005, up 19% from the previous year. Revenues for 2007 were forecast to nearly double, to $55.9 million.

In 2005, Quebec firms accounted for 52% of revenues, with Ontario firms accounting for 22%, British Columbia firms for just under 14% and Alberta firms for 12%.

While the sector is still small, 34 Canadian nanotechnology firms racked up a total of 559 intellectual property instruments in 2005, including patents, patents pending, technology transfer agreements and licensing agreements. More than 70% of the nanotechnology firms reported that they had collaborative arrangements with universities, other companies or government.

Chart 27.5
Nanotechnology firms, 2005

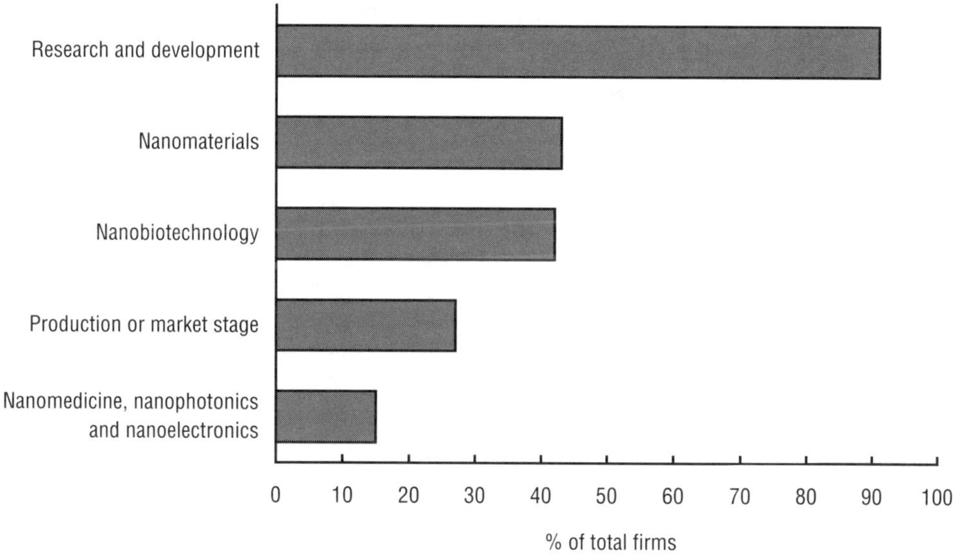

Source: Statistics Canada, Catalogue no. 88-003-XWE.

Table 27.1 Federal expenditures on science and technology, by province and territory, 1999/2000 to 2005/2006

	1999/2000	2000/2001	2001/2002	2002/2003	2003/2004	2004/2005	2005/2006
	$ millions						
Canada (including the National Capital Region)	**5,640**	**6,084**	**7,476**	**7,300**	**7,976**	**8,156**	**8,682**
National Capital Region[1]	1,981	2,130	2,603	2,608	2,642	2,708	2,912
Canada (excluding the National Capital Region)	**3,659**	**3,954**	**4,873**	**4,692**	**5,333**	**5,448**	**5,770**
Newfoundland and Labrador	87	101	95	117	121	137	128
Prince Edward Island	20	29	26	24	33	39	47
Nova Scotia	197	220	225	247	257	294	261
New Brunswick	72	68	82	102	100	122	93
Quebec[2]	833	1,017	1,381	1,243	1,328	1,352	1,485
Ontario[2]	1,309	1,347	1,653	1,582	2,038	1,967	2,102
Manitoba	161	190	211	214	194	226	254
Saskatchewan	131	148	165	151	159	157	193
Alberta	301	327	476	395	469	474	484
British Columbia	528	479	525	582	588	645	673
Yukon, Northwest Territories and Nunavut	20	28	34	35	46	35	51

1. Federal intramural expenditures only.
2. Includes extramural expenditures of the National Capital Region executed within the province.

Source: Statistics Canada, Catalogue no. 88-001-XIE.

Table 27.2 Federal expenditures on research and development, by activity, 2001/2002 to 2007/2008

	2001/2002	2002/2003	2003/2004	2004/2005	2005/2006	2006/2007p	2007/2008p
	$ millions						
Research and development and related scientific activities	**8,169**	**8,014**	**8,765**	**8,935**	**9,449**	**9,662**	**9,534**
Research and development	4,989	4,927	5,462	5,455	6,042	6,062	6,067
Current expenditures	4,571	4,492	5,033	5,033	5,611	5,633	5,635
Administration of extramural programs	213	227	257	269	285	281	296
Capital expenditures	205	208	172	152	146	149	136
Related scientific activities	3,180	3,087	3,303	3,480	3,407	3,600	3,467
Data collection	1,611	1,498	1,618	1,702	1,715	1,770	1,603
Information services	618	679	663	679	676	756	803
Special services and studies	513	588	615	666	627	662	658
Education support	286[1]	177	206	230	259	272	266
Administration of extramural programs	49	54	56	58	59	63	65
Capital expenditures	103	91	145	146	70	78	73

1. Includes a $125 million grant to the Pierre Elliott Trudeau Foundation.

Source: Statistics Canada, Catalogue no. 88-001-XIE.

Table 27.3 Gross domestic expenditures on research and development, by the performing sector and funding sector, 1996 to 2007

	Total[1]	Federal government	Provincial governments	Business enterprise	Higher education	Foreign sources
	$ millions					
Performing sector						
1996	**13,817**	1,792	242	7,997	3,697	...
1997	**14,635**	1,720	214	8,739	3,879	...
1998	**16,088**	1,743	216	9,682	4,370	...
1999	**17,637**	1,859	233	10,399	5,082	...
2000	**20,580**	2,080	255	12,395	5,793	...
2001	**23,132**	2,103	276	14,266	6,424	...
2002	**23,532**	2,190	282	13,541	7,455	...
2003	**24,635**	2,083	278	14,039	8,143	...
2004	**26,480**	2,083	290	14,947	9,058	...
2005p	**27,699**	2,414	300	15,356	9,518	...
2006p	**28,067**	2,298	318	15,360	9,974	...
2007e	**28,984**	2,338	324	15,773	10,433	...
Funding sector						
1996	**13,817**	2,814	629	6,395	1,905	1,714
1997	**14,635**	2,813	657	7,030	1,971	1,794
1998	**16,088**	2,830	640	7,355	2,339	2,552
1999	**17,637**	3,216	770	7,917	2,649	2,705
2000	**20,580**	3,560	879	9,224	2,892	3,580
2001	**23,132**	4,096	1,043	11,618	2,928	2,911
2002	**23,532**	4,250	1,172	12,098	3,462	1,921
2003	**24,635**	4,524	1,378	12,371	3,589	2,136
2004	**26,480**	4,648	1,392	13,082	4,147	2,476
2005p	**27,699**	5,243	1,367	13,431	4,340	2,541
2006p	**28,067**	5,265	1,428	13,463	4,549	2,548
2007e	**28,984**	5,437	1,482	13,840	4,758	2,618

1. Includes private non-profit organizations.

Source: Statistics Canada, Catalogue no. 88-001-XIE.

Table 27.4 Federal expenditures on research and development, by the performing province and funding province, 1996 to 2005

	Canada[1]	National Capital Region	Canada[2]	Newfoundland and Labrador	Prince Edward Island	Nova Scotia
	$ millions					
Performing province						
1996	**1,792**	771	**1,021**	25	10	79
1997	**1,720**	757	**963**	23	10	70
1998	**1,743**	812	**931**	26	10	77
1999	**1,859**	808	**1,051**	25	12	72
2000	**2,080**	889	**1,191**	30	16	88
2001	**2,103**	926	**1,177**	27	16	70
2002	**2,190**	1,015	**1,175**	32	8	76
2003	**2,083**	999	**1,084**	23	12	66
2004	**2,083**	960	**1,123**	23	10	81
2005	**2,414**	1,123	**1,290**	28	28	66
Funding province						
1996[r]	**2,814**	755	**2,059**	42	12	112
1997	**2,813**	740	**2,073**	40	11	107
1998[r]	**2,830**	798	**2,032**	44	12	113
1999	**3,216**	796	**2,420**	48	14	113
2000	**3,560**	872	**2,688**	54	19	129
2001[r]	**4,096**	907	**3,189**	53	19	121
2002[r]	**4,250**	994	**3,256**	63	13	131
2003[r]	**4,524**	983	**3,541**	61	20	131
2004[r]	**4,648**	945	**3,703**	60	18	157
2005	**5,244**	1,103	**4,141**	80	37	150

See notes and source at end of table.

Table 27.4 Federal expenditures on research and development, by the performing province and funding province, 1996 to 2005 (continued)

	New Brunswick	Quebec[3]	Ontario[3]	Manitoba	Saskatchewan	Alberta	British Columbia
	$ millions						
Performing province							
1996	32	226	348	77	47	94	78
1997	29	212	302	59	74	96	83
1998	31	226	276	49	54	94	85
1999	32	250	322	58	60	108	106
2000	27	350	314	69	62	116	111
2001	26	372	328	77	63	98	96
2002	46	370	324	72	53	92	99
2003	30	314	351	63	54	87	80
2004	26	320	329	73	54	110	91
2005	26	368	395	83	68	130	91
Funding province							
1996r	44	546	719	108	75	191	206
1997	41	547	741	88	96	195	200
1998r	44	540	737	82	77	183	198
1999	49	665	868	98	103	218	238
2000	42	806	899	113	121	234	263
2001r	45	999	1,126	124	123	282	290
2002r	68	993	1,114	130	113	281	338
2003r	61	1,053	1,286	131	121	320	340
2004r	57	1,067	1,322	146	123	326	409
2005	62	1,168	1,497	157	126	400	417

1. Includes the National Capital Region, Yukon, Northwest Territories and Nunavut.
2. Includes the Yukon, Northwest Territories and Nunavut; excludes the National Capital Region.
3. Quebec and Ontario figures exclude federal government expenditures performed in the National Capital Region.

Source: Statistics Canada, Catalogue no. 88-001-XIE.

Table 27.5 Gross domestic expenditure on research and development, by province, 1993, 1997, 2001 and 2005

	1993	1997	2001	2005
	$ millions			
Canada (including the National Capital Region)[1]	**12,184**	**14,635**	**23,132**	**27,699**
National Capital Region	774	757	926	1,123
Canada (excluding the National Capital Region)[1]	**11,410**	**13,878**	**22,206**	**26,576**
Newfoundland and Labrador	111	103	142	267
Prince Edward Island	17	17	37	63
Nova Scotia	245	259	376	464
New Brunswick	130	129	162	243
Quebec[2]	3,294	3,933	6,376	7,192
Ontario[2]	5,331	6,788	10,848	12,447
Manitoba	296	271	457	578
Saskatchewan	233	288	396	450
Alberta	834	1,051	1,587	2,286
British Columbia	916	1,038	1,760	2,462

1. Includes Yukon, Northwest Territories and Nunavut.
2. Quebec and Ontario figures exclude federal government expenditures performed in the National Capital Region.
Source: Statistics Canada, Catalogue no. 88-001-XIE.

Table 27.6 Gross domestic expenditures on research and development, health sector compared with all sectors, 1989 to 2006

	All sectors	Health sector		
	$ millions	$ millions	% of all sectors	$ per capita
1989	**9,516**	1,365	14.3	50
1990	**10,260**	1,551	15.1	56
1991	**10,767**	1,665	15.5	59
1992	**11,338**	1,783	15.7	63
1993	**12,184**	2,006	16.5	70
1994	**13,342**	2,105	15.8	73
1995	**13,754**	2,196	16.0	75
1996	**13,816**	2,317	16.8	78
1997	**14,634**	2,447	16.7	82
1998	**16,088**	2,692	16.7	89
1999	**17,637**	2,967	16.8	98
2000	**20,635**	3,560	17.3	116
2001	**23,206**	4,159	17.9	134
2002	**23,382**	5,050	21.6	161
2003	**24,635**	5,168	21.0	163
2004	**26,480**	5,926	22.4	185
2005	**27,699**	6,128	22.1	189
2006p	**28,067**	6,084	21.7	186

Source: Statistics Canada, CANSIM tables 051-0001, 358-0001 and 384-0036, and Catalogue no. 88-001-XIE.

Table 27.7 Business enterprises' research and development expenditures, by province and territory, 2001 to 2006

	2001	2002	2003	2004	2005	2006
	$ millions					
Canada	**14,266**	**13,540**	**14,123**	**15,299**	**15,791**	**16,137**
Newfoundland and Labrador	21	22	31	30	86	99
Prince Edward Island	6	4	7	7	11	13
Nova Scotia	91	93	79	94	102	106
New Brunswick	41	62	64	82	96	102
Quebec	4,158	4,154	4,202	4,340	4,199	4,598
Ontario	7,899	7,064	7,468	7,871	8,250	8,033
Manitoba	173	155	150	183	199	184
Saskatchewan	87	112	88	113	152	167
Alberta	710	782	861	1,131	1,193	1,236
British Columbia[1]	1,080	1,094	1,174	1,447	1,503	1,600

Note: Expenditures on performing research and development.

1. Includes the Yukon Territory, Northwest Territories and Nunavut.

Source: Statistics Canada, Catalogue no. 88-001-XIE.

Table 27.8 Intellectual property management at universities and research hospitals, 1999 to 2006

	1999	2001	2003	2004	2005	2006p
	%					
Institutions engaged in intellectual property management	61	66	72	76	80	82
	number					
Full-time equivalent employees engaged in intellectual property management	178	221	255	280	292	323
Research contracts	5,748	8,247	11,432	14,324	15,877	13,996
Invention disclosures	893	1,105	1,133	1,432	1,452	1,356
Inventions protected[1]	549	682	527	629	761	707
Inventions declined by the institution	..	..	256	355	322	353
Patent applications	656	932	1,252	1,264	1,410	1,442
Patents issued	349	381	347	397	376	339
Patents held	1,915	2,133	3,047	3,827	3,961	4,784
New licences and options	232	354	422	494	621	437
Active licences and options	1,165	1,424	1,756	2,022	2,836	2,038
	$ thousands					
Operational expenditures for intellectual property management	22,018	28,505	36,419	36,927	41,544	42,492
Value of research contracts	393,358	527,051	810,431	940,993	1,001,270	1,154,268
Income from intellectual property	24,745	52,510	55,525	51,210	55,173	59,689
Value of remaining equity held by the institution in publicly traded spin-offs	54,560	45,120	52,351	49,872	41,336	41,524
Investment in spin-offs raised with the assistance of the institution	..	..	54,640	56,421	23,002	..

Note: Data were not collected for 2000 and 2002 since the Survey of Intellectual Property Commercialization in the Higher Education Sector was conducted on an occasional basis from 1998 to 2003.

1. Resulted in protection activity.

Source: Statistics Canada, CANSIM table 358-0025.

Table 27.9 University enrolment in natural and applied science and technology programs, by sex, 2001/2002 to 2005/2006

	2001/2002	2002/2003	2003/2004	2004/2005	2005/2006
	number				
All instructional programs					
Both sexes[1]	886,605	933,870	993,246	1,017,588	1,047,705
Men	376,884	397,167	419,463	430,449	442,419
Women	509,586	536,640	573,531	586,908	604,920
Physical and life sciences and technologies					
Both sexes[1]	81,411	84,555	92,715	96,423	98,376
Men	36,561	37,530	40,896	42,639	44,148
Women	44,847	47,022	51,807	53,781	54,225
Mathematics, computer and information sciences					
Both sexes[1]	46,035	45,837	43,932	40,644	36,594
Men	32,847	33,120	32,115	29,679	26,658
Women	13,182	12,714	11,796	10,920	9,930
Architecture, engineering and related technologies					
Both sexes[1]	74,850	81,132	85,809	86,484	85,599
Men	57,444	62,400	66,543	67,353	67,587
Women	17,403	18,726	19,257	19,125	18,006
Agriculture, natural resources and conservation					
Both sexes[1]	14,847	14,496	14,619	14,757	15,210
Men	6,933	6,672	6,585	6,627	6,747
Women	7,914	7,821	8,028	8,124	8,457

Notes: Historical data coded with the University Student Information System classification have been converted to the Classification of Instructional Programs 2000.

1. Figures may not add to the totals because of the exclusion of the 'sex unknown' category in the table or because of rounding.

Source: Statistics Canada, CANSIM table 477-0013.

Seniors

28

Overview

Canada's elderly population is growing, a trend that began several decades ago. In 2007, the population aged 65 and older was 4.4 million and seniors made up 13% of the total population. That compares with 11% in 1987 and 8% in 1972.

Canada is one of the 'youngest' of the G8 countries, despite the aging of its population. Only the United States had a smaller proportion of elderly people in 2006.

Aging is expected to accelerate over the next few years, particularly when the baby boomers start turning 65. According to a medium-growth scenario, the proportion of seniors in the Canadian population will reach 27% by 2056. The older segments of the population have the fastest growth rates. In 2007, 3% of the population was aged 80 and older. This group could account for 10% of the total population by 2056. Low fertility rates and rising life expectancy are all contributing to the steady increase in the elderly population.

Seniors are generally in better health than a quarter century ago, are more comfortable financially, and lead more active lives than their predecessors. However, as they advance in age, seniors are more likely to be affected by disabilities that prevent them from going about their day-to-day activities normally.

Most seniors are in good health

Life expectancy at age 65 has increased in the last 20 years. In 1985, a 65-year-old could expect to live another 17 years; in 2005, a person the same age could anticipate living another 20 years. The increase was larger for men than for women.

Most seniors consider themselves to be in very good or excellent health, though they are less likely to report being in good health

Chart 28.1
People aged 65 years and older among the G8 countries, 2006

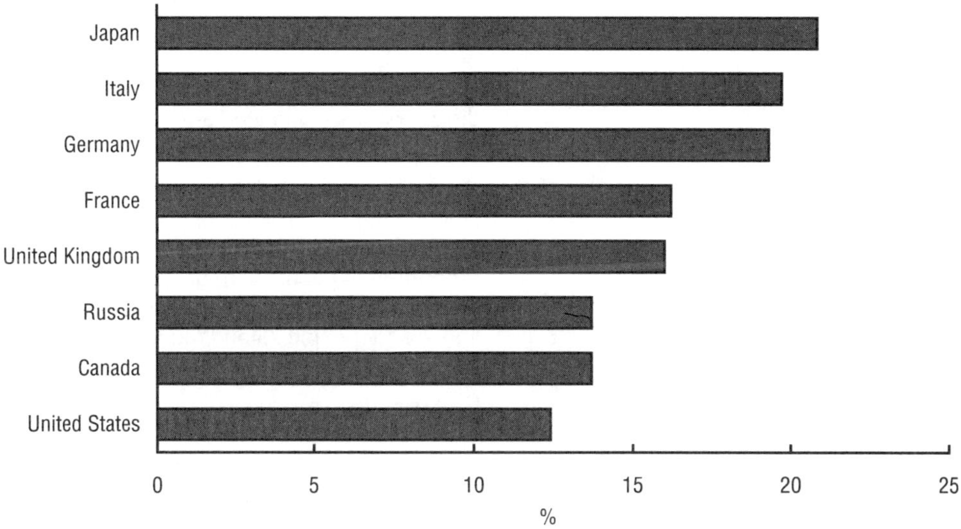

Sources: Statistics Canada, U.S. Census Bureau, Istituto Nazionale di Statistica, Institut National des Statistiques et des Études Économiques, U.K. Office of National Statistics, Statistics Bureau of Japan, Federal Statistical Office of Germany and Federal State Statistics Service of Russia.

than are younger people. In 2005, 44% of people aged 65 to 74 described their health as either very good or excellent. Another 34% considered their health good.

In comparison, among people aged 20 to 34—one of the most positive age groups when it came to self-evaluating their health—70% reported being in very good or excellent health, and 25% in good health.

Moreover, 6 out of 10 seniors reported very little or no stress in their lives, compared with about 3 out of 10 people from 25 to 54 years of age.

Many seniors engage in more or less regular physical activity. In 2005, 52% of men aged 65 to 74 were active or moderately active physically, compared with 53% of men aged 25 to 34 and 48% of men aged 35 to 64. Among senior women, 44% of those aged 65 to 74 reported being either active or moderately active physically.

Chart 28.2
Disability rates, by age group, 2006

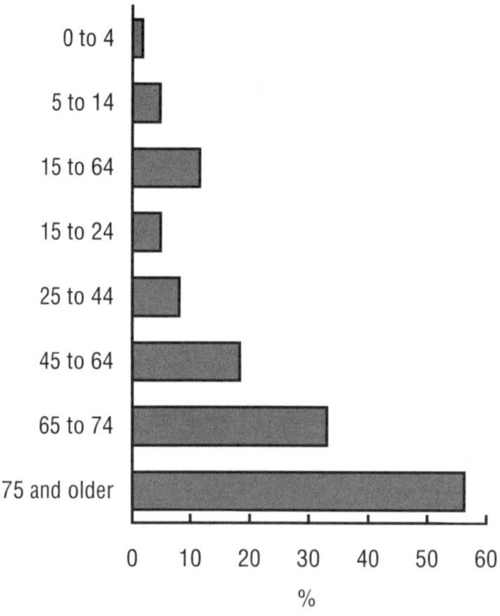

Source: Statistics Canada, Catalogue no. 89-628-XWE.

Table 28.a
Population aged 65 and older, by age group

	1985		2007	
	Men	Women	Men	Women
	number			
Total	**1,115,104**	**1,534,450**	**1,938,407**	**2,484,997**
65 to 69	405,605	484,712	614,494	660,080
70 to 74	321,735	410,188	492,229	555,700
75 to 79	205,793	294,450	398,597	496,055
80 to 84	113,459	189,838	257,633	393,173
85 to 89	47,643	101,476	125,527	243,733
90 and older	20,869	53,786	49,927	136,256

Source: Statistics Canada, CANSIM table 051-0001.

Limitations increase with age

In 2006, 43% of people aged 65 and older had a disability, compared with 12% in the 15-to-64 population. In the 75-and-older age group, 56% were affected by a disability.

The prevalence of most types of disabilities—those related to mobility, agility, hearing, vision and pain—increases with age. In 2006, for example, less than 2% of Canadians aged 15 to 24 had a mobility-related disability, compared with 33% of the 65-and-older group. The proportion jumped to 44% among people aged 75 and older. The percentage of Canadians with memory and speech disorders was 1% in the 15-to-24 age group and 5% in the 75-and-older group in 2006.

The incidence of disabilities related to emotional, psychological or psychiatric conditions declines with age. In 2006, the proportion of people with one of those disabilities was 3% for people aged 45 to 64 and 2% for people 75 and older.

Seniors keep busy

Canadians aged 65 to 74 spend the largest part of their day engaging in leisure activities: 7.8 hours for men and 7.2 hours for women in 2005. In the 75-and-older population, the figures are 8.0 hours a day for men and 7.9 hours for women.

Many seniors take part in social activities or do volunteer work. In 2004, just over half of the population aged 65 to 74 were members of a group or organization, and 39% did volunteer work.

Seniors also provide informal assistance. In 2004, for example, 26% of the 65-to-74 age group helped someone outside their home do housework, maintenance or outdoor work. In addition, 22% of the age group helped care for children.

Seniors are using the Internet more often nowadays. In 2004, 23% of households headed by an elderly person had Internet access, compared with 3% in 1997.

From 2000 to 2003, the proportion of Canadians aged 65 to 74 using the Internet more than doubled from 11% to 28%. The same upward trend occurred among the 75-and-older population, though to a lesser degree. Despite this trend, younger people were more likely to use the Internet: 80% of those aged 25 to 54 used it in 2003.

Chart 28.3
People with low income, by age group

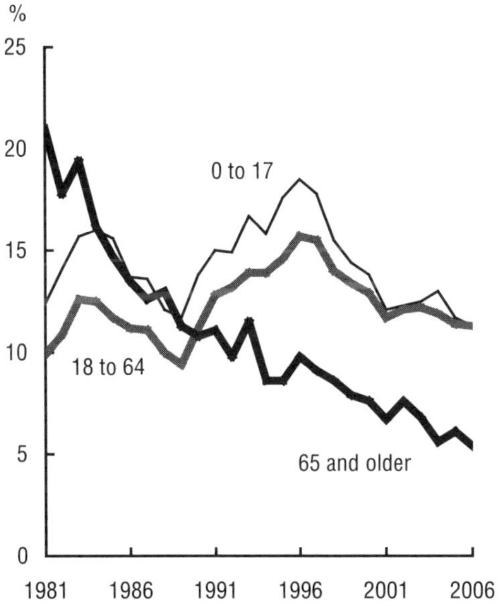

Source: Statistics Canada, CANSIM table 202-0802.

Finances are stabilizing

From 1996 to 2006, the average after-tax income of married elderly couples rose 18%, from $40,900 to $48,300.

The increase benefited seniors with the lowest incomes, helping to reduce the incidence of low income in those groups. The proportion of seniors with low income after taxes fell from 10% in 1996 to 5% in 2006. Despite the decline, the incidence of low income remains higher among elderly women living alone (16%). Quebec and British Columbia are the provinces with the highest levels of low income among seniors.

The extent to which seniors maintain their income after retirement varies with age and income level, according to data gathered from 1983 to 2004. For instance, among people with an average income, family income starts falling after age 60, declines until age 68, and then stabilizes at about 80% of what their income was at age 55.

In contrast, seniors with the lowest 20% of incomes saw little variation in their incomes after age 55 and during their retirement years. After retirement, they maintain almost 100% of their disposable income, since their earnings in the years before retirement are replaced with income from a public pension plan, Old Age Security or the Guaranteed Income Supplement.

Financially better off workers—those with the highest 20% of incomes—receive an average of 70% of their pre-retirement income after age 70. For a family of two, this group's average family income at age 75 was $90,000 after taxes. Forty percent of that income comes from private pension plans and registered retirement savings plans, 28% stems from investment income and capital gains, and 18% is from a public pension plan or Old Age Security.

Still working after retirement

Not all Canadians retire at age 65. A growing number of people are continuing to work well past the usual retirement age, and more seniors can be expected to do so in the coming years.

In 2007, 366,400 Canadians aged 65 or older were in the labour force: 353,400 of them were employed, and the other 13,000 were actively looking for work. The labour force participation rate in the 65-and-older population aged 65 and older was 9% in 2007, up from 7% in 1994.

The labour force participation rate in the 55-to-64 age group has also risen, from 48% in 1994 to 60% in 2007. In the future, elderly workers' share of the labour force is expected to rise further, since a growing number of baby boomers will turn 60 in the next 10 years. The fact that seniors are remaining in the labour force longer could reduce the risk of a labour shortage as the baby boomers start retiring.

In 2007, women were in the majority among the 65-and-older population in 2007, but they made up only 35% of the elderly people in the labour force. When elderly women were younger, comparatively few of them were in the labour force because social expectations were different from what they are for young women today. As the baby boomers advance in age, the proportion of elderly women in the labour force will probably approach the proportion of elderly men in the labour force.

Canadians with a university degree are much more likely than others to continue working after age 65. As well, self-employment and part-time work are more common among seniors than in younger age groups.

Chart 28.4
Participation rate, aged 65 years and older, by sex

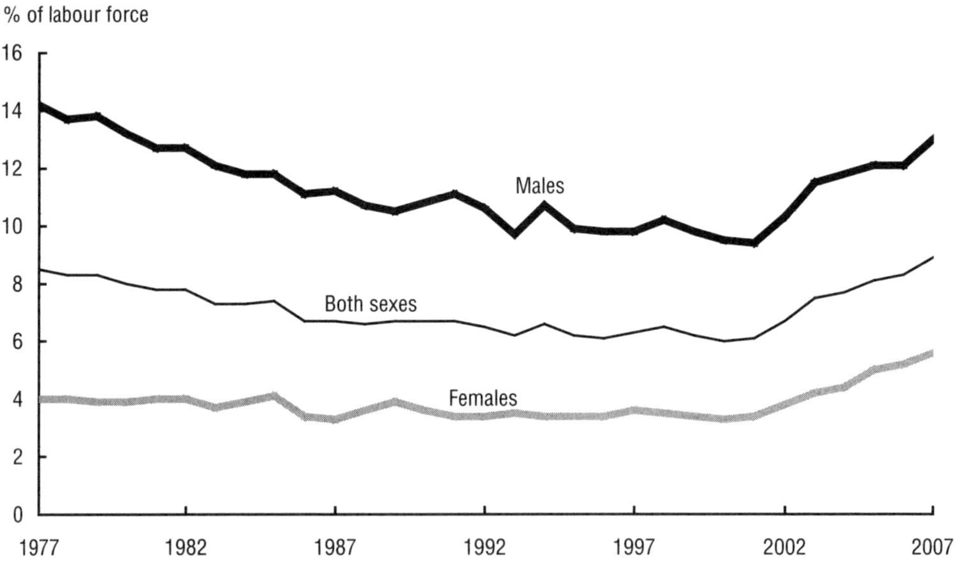

Source: Statistics Canada, CANSIM table 282-2002.

Chronic pain curbs the quality of life for seniors

Most people experience pain at some point in their lives, whether it is temporary discomfort or chronic pain from an injury or illness. However, chronic pain is more likely to affect elderly people than younger adults, and it can diminish their quality of life.

More than 1 out of 4 seniors living in private households and nearly 4 out of 10 seniors living in institutions experience chronic pain.

Chronic pain interferes with the daily activities of many elderly people and can make their lives difficult. The more intense the pain, the more likely it is to interfere with their activities.

Among the seniors living at home and experiencing severe pain, 53% reported that their condition interfered with most activities. Similarly, 64% of institutional residents affected by severe pain reported that it interfered with many activities. An increase in pain over a two-year period was also associated with higher odds of being unhappy or having a negative self-assessment of personal health.

Elderly women are more likely than men to report chronic pain, regardless of their age or whether they are institutionalized. The largest gender gap in reports of chronic pain occurs among seniors who live at home: 31% of the women report chronic pain, compared with 21% of the men.

There is a strong relationship between pain and other chronic health conditions in the elderly population. In addition, seniors with at least two chronic conditions are more likely to experience chronic pain than are seniors with fewer conditions.

Chart 28.5
Population aged 65 and older with chronic pain, 2005 (people living at home) and 1996/1997(people living in institutions)

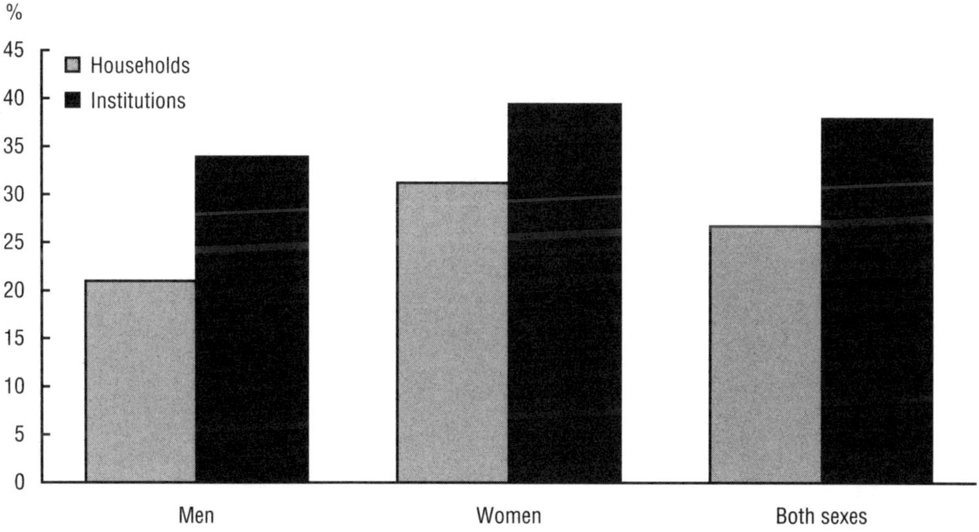

Note: Canada excluding territories.
Source: Statistics Canada, Catalogue no. 82-003-XIE.

Table 28.1 Population estimates and projections, by age group and by province and territory, selected years from 1982 to 2027

	1982			1992			2002		
	0 to 14	15 to 64	65 and older	0 to 14	15 to 64	65 and older	0 to 14	15 to 64	65 and older
	thousands								
Canada	**5,525.3**	**17,150.4**	**2,441.7**	**5,868.1**	**19,203.2**	**3,295.5**	**5,825.4**	**21,554.0**	**3,993.2**
Newfoundland and Labrador	164.0	365.3	45.3	125.7	397.6	56.7	86.9	368.2	64.4
Prince Edward Island	30.3	78.3	15.2	29.2	84.3	17.2	26.0	92.1	18.8
Nova Scotia	196.7	568.1	95.2	185.8	618.0	115.7	162.8	642.8	128.9
New Brunswick	171.7	463.9	72.6	152.4	505.0	90.6	128.9	520.8	100.6
Quebec	1,395.2	4,595.0	589.2	1,404.3	4,902.8	801.0	1,296.0	5,167.8	982.0
Ontario	1,898.9	6,126.0	897.4	2,144.8	7,186.7	1,238.3	2,314.2	8,267.8	1,520.1
Manitoba	239.2	683.0	124.6	243.7	719.6	149.3	236.1	762.0	157.5
Saskatchewan	241.4	626.4	119.4	238.2	622.9	142.9	205.5	642.4	148.0
Alberta	562.0	1,636.7	169.6	619.8	1,772.6	240.5	626.4	2,171.5	318.3
British Columbia	603.1	1,958.8	311.0	696.6	2,331.5	440.4	715.4	2,849.6	550.4
Yukon	6.3	17.3	0.8	7.4	21.5	1.2	6.0	22.3	1.8
Northwest Territories (including Nunavut)	16.5	31.6	1.4	..	..	..	..	..	..
Northwest Territories	..	..	..	11.3	26.9	1.2	10.8	29.0	1.7
Nunavut	..	..	..	8.8	13.7	0.5	10.3	17.8	0.6
	%								
Canada	**22.0**	**68.3**	**9.7**	**20.7**	**67.7**	**11.6**	**18.6**	**68.7**	**12.7**
Newfoundland and Labrador	28.5	63.6	7.9	21.7	68.6	9.8	16.7	70.9	12.4
Prince Edward Island	24.5	63.2	12.3	22.4	64.5	13.2	19.0	67.2	13.8
Nova Scotia	22.9	66.1	11.1	20.2	67.2	12.6	17.4	68.8	13.8
New Brunswick	24.2	65.5	10.3	20.4	67.5	12.1	17.2	69.4	13.4
Quebec	21.2	69.8	9.0	19.8	69.0	11.3	17.4	69.4	13.2
Ontario	21.3	68.7	10.1	20.3	68.0	11.7	19.1	68.3	12.6
Manitoba	22.8	65.2	11.9	21.9	64.7	13.4	20.4	65.9	13.6
Saskatchewan	24.5	63.5	12.1	23.7	62.0	14.2	20.6	64.5	14.9
Alberta	23.7	69.1	7.2	23.5	67.3	9.1	20.1	69.7	10.2
British Columbia	21.0	68.2	10.8	20.1	67.2	12.7	17.4	69.2	13.4
Yukon	25.8	70.9	3.3	24.6	71.4	3.9	20.0	73.9	6.1
Northwest Territories (including Nunavut)	33.3	63.8	2.9	..	..	..	..	..	..
Northwest Territories	..	..	..	28.7	68.1	3.2	26.0	69.8	4.2
Nunavut	..	..	..	38.3	59.7	2.0	35.9	61.9	2.1

See source at end of table.

Table 28.1 Population estimates and projections, by age group and by province and territory, selected years from 1982 to 2027 (continued)

	2007			2027		
	0 to 14	15 to 64	65 and older	0 to 14	15 to 64	65 and older
	thousands					
Canada	**5,613.0**	**22,939.6**	**4,423.4**	**5,689.7**	**24,150.7**	**8,283.2**
Newfoundland and Labrador	76.6	359.1	70.6	62.5	307.8	138.4
Prince Edward Island	23.5	95.1	20.1	21.1	90.9	36.5
Nova Scotia	144.7	651.1	138.4	127.2	596.3	253.4
New Brunswick	115.5	525.7	108.6	98.1	468.4	202.2
Quebec	1,230.9	5,364.3	1,105.5	1,165.8	5,193.8	1,968.5
Ontario	2,240.7	8,877.4	1,685.7	2,378.8	10,048.9	3,179.5
Manitoba	227.8	798.1	160.8	231.2	828.8	270.4
Saskatchewan	190.0	658.6	148.3	165.0	585.4	226.4
Alberta	648.1	2,463.9	361.9	663.8	2,574.2	794.2
British Columbia	689.5	3,072.9	617.8	748.7	3,378.9	1,198.4
Yukon	5.4	23.2	2.4	5.5	21.8	6.3
Northwest Territories (including Nunavut)	..	..	..	..	..	..
Northwest Territories	10.1	30.4	2.2	11.1	34.9	7.3
Nunavut	10.3	19.8	1.0	10.6	20.8	1.8
	%					
Canada	**17.0**	**69.6**	**13.4**	**14.9**	**63.3**	**21.7**
Newfoundland and Labrador	15.1	70.9	13.9	12.3	60.5	27.2
Prince Edward Island	16.9	68.6	14.5	14.2	61.2	24.6
Nova Scotia	15.5	69.7	14.8	13.0	61.0	25.9
New Brunswick	15.4	70.1	14.5	12.8	60.9	26.3
Quebec	16.0	69.7	14.4	14.0	62.4	23.6
Ontario	17.5	69.3	13.2	15.2	64.4	20.4
Manitoba	19.2	67.3	13.6	17.4	62.3	20.3
Saskatchewan	19.1	66.1	14.9	16.9	59.9	23.2
Alberta	18.7	70.9	10.4	16.5	63.8	19.7
British Columbia	15.7	70.2	14.1	14.1	63.4	22.5
Yukon	17.3	74.8	7.9	16.4	64.9	18.8
Northwest Territories (including Nunavut)	..	..	..	..	..	..
Northwest Territories	23.6	71.2	5.2	20.9	65.6	13.7
Nunavut	33.2	63.8	3.1	32.0	62.8	5.4

Source: Statistics Canada, CANSIM table 051-0001.

Table 28.2 Senior population proportion, by selected census metropolitan areas, selected years from 1987 to 2007

	1987	1992	1997	2002	2007
			%		
All census metropolitan areas	**10.2**	**11.0**	**11.6**	**11.9**	**12.5**
St. John's	9.6	9.4	10.1	10.5	11.0
Halifax	9.1	9.8	10.3	10.9	11.8
Saint John	12.3	12.3	12.7	12.9	13.4
Québec	9.6	10.8	11.9	13.1	14.5
Sherbrooke	10.6	11.6	12.3	13.1	14.2
Montréal	10.3	11.3	12.2	12.8	13.6
Ottawa–Gatineau	9.0	9.5	10.3	10.6	11.6
Toronto	9.6	10.3	10.9	10.9	11.3
Thunder Bay	11.0	13.2	14.0	14.8	15.9
Winnipeg	12.2	12.9	13.3	13.4	13.3
Regina	10.5	11.0	11.8	12.5	13.0
Calgary	7.2	7.9	8.7	8.9	9.1
Vancouver	12.0	12.0	11.6	11.9	12.3
Victoria	18.2	18.2	17.5	17.2	17.2

Note: Seniors are people aged 65 and older.
Source: Statistics Canada, CANSIM table 051-0036.

Table 28.3 Life expectancy at birth and at age 65, by sex, selected years from 1921 to 2005

	Life expectancy at birth			Life expectancy at age 65		
	Both sexes	Males	Females	Both sexes	Males	Females
			years			
1921	59.7	58.8	60.6	13.3	13.0	13.6
1931	61.0	60.0	62.1	13.3	13.0	13.7
1941	64.6	63.0	66.3	13.4	12.8	14.1
1951	68.5	66.4	70.9	14.1	13.3	15.0
1961	71.1	68.4	74.3	14.8	13.6	16.1
1971	72.7	69.4	76.5	15.7	13.8	17.6
1981	75.4	71.9	79.1	16.8	14.6	18.9
1992	78.0	74.8	81.2	18.2	16.0	20.1
2002	79.7	77.2	82.1	19.1	17.2	20.6
2003	79.9	77.4	82.4	19.2	17.4	20.8
2004	80.2	77.8	82.6	19.5	17.7	21.0
2005	80.4	78.0	82.7	19.6	17.9	21.1

Notes: Life expectancy estimates for 1921 to 1981 are based on complete life tables.
Newfoundland and Labrador is not included in the 1921 to 1946 life expectancy estimates.
Quebec is not included in the 1921 estimates.
Source: Statistics Canada, CANSIM table 102-0511 and Catalogue no. 89-506-XPB.

Table 28.4 Income of seniors, by sex and selected income sources, selected years from 1981 to 2006

	1981	1986	1991	1996	2001	2006
	%					
Males						
Earnings	22.7	16.5	13.7	15.9	21.1	26.6
Investment income	67.7	61.6	60.8	61.5	58.4	56.0
Retirement income	40.2	48.0	51.0	63.0	69.3	70.6
Old Age Security and Guaranteed Income Supplement, Spouse's Allowance	97.2	97.5	98.9	96.8	93.6	95.8
Canada Pension Plan and Quebec Pension Plan benefits	72.5	79.1	85.5	91.8	94.6	95.5
	aggregate income in $ million 2006 constant					
Earnings	4,537	4,651	5,000	3,631	3,444	5,911
Investment income	6,344	5,843	6,456	5,518	5,844	6,118
Retirement income	4,051	6,135	9,484	15,239	19,895	24,298
Old Age Security and Guaranteed Income Supplement, Spouse's Allowance	6,463	7,729	9,042	9,576	9,801	11,425
Canada Pension Plan and Quebec Pension Plan benefits	3,004	4,998	7,257	9,605	10,823	11,987
	average income in $ 2006 constant					
Earnings	20,700	25,700	28,300	15,700	10,100	12,200
Investment income	9,700	8,600	8,200	6,200	6,200	6,000
Retirement income	10,400	11,600	14,400	16,600	17,800	18,900
Old Age Security and Guaranteed Income Supplement, Spouse's Allowance	6,900	7,200	7,100	6,800	6,500	6,600
Canada Pension Plan and Quebec Pension Plan benefits	4,300	5,800	6,600	7,200	7,100	6,900
	%					
Females						
Earnings	7.4	5.4	4.7	5.2	8.1	11.5
Investment income	55.4	55.3	55.5	57.6	59.6	58.7
Retirement income	17.6	23.5	28.4	39.4	50.0	54.7
Old Age Security and Guaranteed Income Supplement, Spouse's Allowance	97.7	98.3	99.1	97.0	97.4	97.2
Canada Pension Plan and Quebec Pension Plan benefits	35.6	46.8	60.2	74.0	81.9	83.9
	aggregate income in $ million 2006 constant					
Earnings	1,129	1,028	1,067	1,155[E]	1,181	2,398
Investment income	6,038	6,113	7,938	6,541	6,426	5,896
Retirement income	1,575	2,664	4,183	7,111	10,936	15,189
Old Age Security and Guaranteed Income Supplement, Spouse's Allowance	9,154	11,554	13,167	14,042	14,318	15,860
Canada Pension Plan and Quebec Pension Plan benefits	1,468	2,815	4,765	6,995	8,864	10,199
	average income in $ 2006 constant					
Earnings	12,200	13,100	13,300	11,800	7,100	9,200
Investment income	8,800	7,600	8,400	6,000	5,300	4,500
Retirement income	7,200	7,800	8,600	9,500	10,600	12,300
Old Age Security and Guaranteed Income Supplement, Spouse's Allowance	7,500	8,100	7,800	7,600	7,200	7,200
Canada Pension Plan and Quebec Pension Plan benefits	3,300	4,100	4,600	5,000	5,300	5,400

Note: Seniors are people aged 65 and older.

Source: Statistics Canada, CANSIM table 202-0407.

Table 28.5 Members or participants in an organization in the past 12 months, by age group and type of organization, 2003

	Political party or group	Sports or recreational organization	Cultural, educational or hobby organization	Religious affiliated group	School group, neighbourhood, civic or community association	Service club or fraternal organization	Other groups	Member or participant of at least one organization
	%							
Total								
25 to 54	4.2	30.1	17.1	15.5	17.1	6.5	5.6	54.3
55 to 64	7.2	22.0	21.5	20.3	14.4	12.5	7.7	55.5
65 to 74	6.1	20.6	19.0	23.4	12.0	15.9	7.9	54.4
75 and older	5.6	12.4	13.9	21.1	7.5	14.4	5.6	45.9
65 and older	5.8	17.0	16.8	22.4	10.1	15.3	6.9	50.6
Women								
25 to 54	3.6	26.2	18.6	17.9	20.2	5.4	6.7	54.1
55 to 64	6.1	19.7	24.3	22.9	14.9	10.1	8.4	54.8
65 to 74	3.9	18.6	19.8	25.0	11.3	11.9	9.1	52.6
75 and older	3.1	10.2	14.1	22.0	7.1	9.3	5.1	41.9
65 and older	3.5	14.6	17.2	23.6	9.3	10.6	7.2	47.5
Men								
25 to 54	4.7	34.0	15.7	13.1	14.1	7.6	4.4	54.6
55 to 64	8.3	24.3	18.5	17.6	13.8	14.9	6.9	56.2
65 to 74	8.4	22.8	18.1	21.6	12.9	20.5	6.6	56.3
75 and older	9.3	15.7	13.5	19.7	8.2	22.1	6.4	52.0
65 and older	8.8	20.0	16.3	20.8	11.0	21.1	6.5	54.6

Source: Statistics Canada, General Social Survey, 2003.

Table 28.6 Volunteer rate and distribution of volunteer hours, by age group, 2004

	Volunteer rate	Average annual volunteer hours[1]	Median annual volunteer hours[1]
	%	number	
25 to 54	46.6	156	60
55 to 64	42.4	202	80
65 to 74	38.7	250	120
75 and older	22.8	234	102
65 and older	32.4	245	119

1. Estimates of average and median age. Volunteer hours are calculated for volunteers only.

Source: Statistics Canada, Canada Survey of Giving, Volunteering and Participating, 2004.

Society and community

29

Overview

Social, economic and demographic changes are constantly reshaping Canadian society. Today, young adults are taking longer to achieve their independence. More women are self-employed and more are bettering their job opportunities with higher levels of education. Seniors are finding the path to retirement is no longer direct or one way.

Baby boomers are becoming a 'sandwich generation' as they care for both children and aging parents. Parents of children with disabilities are reporting unmet needs and difficulty accessing special education services. Gays, lesbians and bisexuals are enjoying new legal protections, but are still experiencing discrimination at higher rates than heterosexuals.

Social scientists are calling it 'delayed transitions.' Today's young adults are leaving school later, staying longer in their parents' home, entering the labour market later, and postponing conjugal unions and childbearing. Along with delaying marriage, some Canadians are staying single.

Delayed transitions, fewer transitions

In 1971, three out of four 22-year-olds were out of school. Half were married and one in four had children. Thirty years later, just half of the 22-year-olds in 2001 were out of school. Only one in five was in a conjugal union (usually a common-law relationship) and just one in eleven had a child.

Chart 29.1
Average number of transitions by young adults

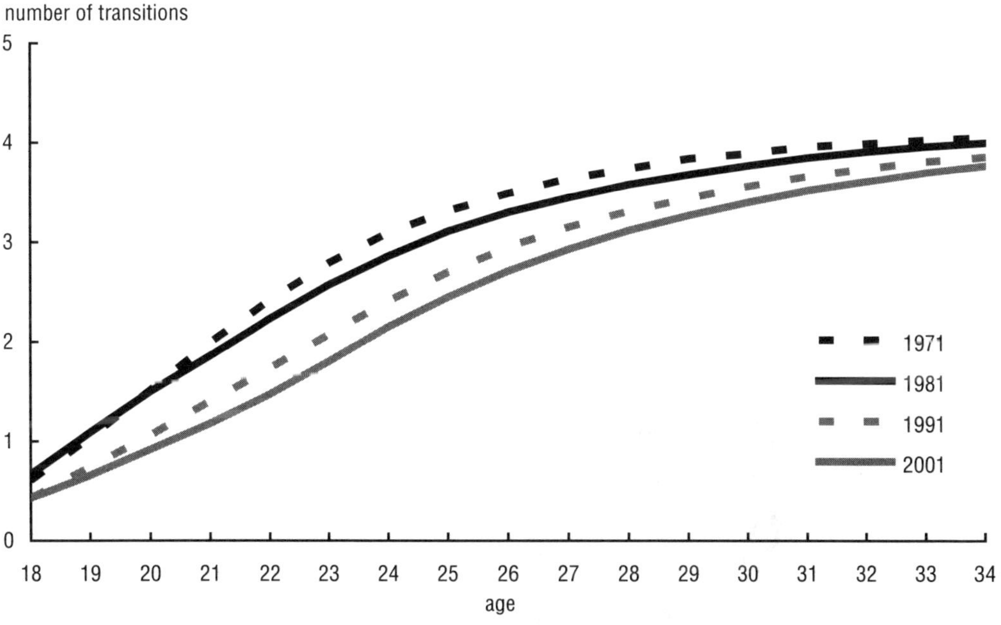

Note: The number of transitions includes five markers: leaving school, leaving home, working full-year full-time, finding a conjugal partner and having children. These markers of adulthood are snapshots taken on the Census reference dates and do not represent completed or irreversible social changes: they simply record the state of transition young adults were in on those dates.

Source: Statistics Canada, Catalogue no. 11-008-XIE.

The delays vary for men and women. In 2001, men at age 34 had made fewer transitions than their counterparts had in 1971. For example, they were less likely to have full-year full-time work. Partly, this may stem from economic changes that made the labour market more dynamic but also more unstable. Work today is less likely to be full-time and tends to offer fewer benefits, which has contributed to insecurity, especially among young men. It is also contributing to delays at other stages of life.

As well, both men and women have upgraded their level of education to take advantage of the premium that university graduates enjoy in the labour market. This by itself has delayed other transitions to adulthood.

By contrast, 34-year-old women in 2001 had made just as many transitions as 34-year-old women did in 1971. However, those transitions were less likely to include marriage and childbearing and they were more likely to include full-year full-time work.

More women are self-employed

A growing number of women are self-employed. In 2006, close to 900,000

Chart 29.2
Self-employment, 1976 to 2006

Source: Statistics Canada, Labour Force Survey.

Table 29.a
Women employed, by age group

	1976	1986	1996	2006
	%			
All women	**41.9**	**50.2**	**52.1**	**58.3**
15 to 24	51.4	58.1	52.0	59.5
25 to 44	50.0	66.4	70.9	77.2
45 to 54	45.6	55.9	66.3	76.8
55 to 64	30.3	30.3	33.5	48.7

Source: Statistics Canada, Catalogue no. 89F0133XIE.

women, or 11% of all those with jobs, were self-employed, up from 9% in 1976. Self-employment has grown about as fast among women as it has among men over the past quarter century, though women are still less likely than men to be self-employed: 11% versus 19% in 2006.

The likelihood of women being employed rises with higher levels of education. In 2006, 75% of women with a university degree and 69% of those with a certificate or diploma from a community college worked for pay or profit, compared with 61% of those with some postsecondary training and 59% of high school graduates. By contrast, 38% of women who had attended but not completed high school had a job, while 15% of women who had not gone beyond Grade 8 had one.

The majority of employed women continue to work in occupations where women have traditionally been concentrated. In 2006, 67% of employed women were working in teaching, nursing or a related health occupation, in a clerical or administrative job, or in a sales or service position. This compared with 30% of employed men.

Path to retirement is not so direct anymore

For many seniors, the straight line of school-work-retirement is less certain these days. Seniors are more likely to move in and out of the workforce than ever before. From 1998 to 2005, leisure time declined and hours in full-time labour increased for Canadians aged 55 to 64. Both men and women were spending to 64. Both men and women were spending roughly an hour a day more in paid work than they were in 1998. Among women, the biggest impact was a decline of more than half an hour a day in the time they devoted to leisure activities.

Studies have found that women are much more likely than men to see retirement as involving more than just getting a pension or stopping paid work. Women tend to include in their concept of work the time they spend doing unpaid work, such as care-giving and volunteering.

Delayed marriage, postponed children and long-lived parents have given rise to a 'sandwich generation' among baby boomers. These individuals are caught between the often-conflicting demands of still caring for children while also caring for parents

Disability rising among children

The prevalence of disability among children has increased in Canada. In 2006, 4.6% of children aged 5 to 14 had one or more disabilities, up from 4.0% in 2001. The rate was higher among boys.

Chart 29.3
Disabilities among children aged 5 to 14, 2006

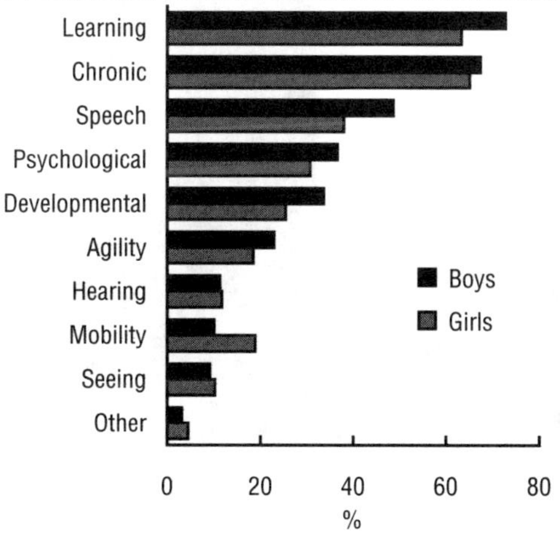

Source: Statistics Canada, Catalogue no. 89-628-XWE.

In the 2005/2006 school year, 163,730 children with disabilities were attending school, most on a part-time basis. Of this group, 43%, or 70,600 children, were attending special education classes. Almost two out of three attended these classes part-time. Learning disabilities are the most common condition requiring special education. Some children have more than one activity limitation such as speech or language difficulties, developmental disabilities, or emotional, psychological or behavioural conditions.

Unmet needs are an issue. In 2006, not all children aged 5 to 14 with disabilities received special education when they needed it, in the opinion of their parents. Nearly half the children in this group had severe or very severe disabilities.

Two-thirds of parents of children with very severe disabilities reported challenges in obtaining special education.

Discrimination persists

Although Canada has recently protected the legal rights of individuals of all sexual orientations, including recognizing legal marriage for same-sex couples, discrimination is still being experienced by gays, lesbians and bisexuals at higher rates than among heterosexuals.

In a 2004 study, the proportion of gays, lesbians and bisexuals who felt they had experienced discrimination was about three times higher than that of heterosexuals. Moreover, 78% of gays and lesbians who experienced discrimination believed it was because of their sexual orientation, compared with 29% of bisexuals and 2% of heterosexuals. Gays, lesbians and bisexuals were most likely to report its occurrence at work or when applying for a job or a promotion, though discrimination was more common for them in all locations than it was for heterosexuals.

More work, less sleep

A higher salary, a longer commute, a long work day, a high stress level: all can mean less sleep.

The 2005 General Social Survey asked 19,500 Canadians aged 15 and older to keep a diary of activities on a given day, including the time they fell asleep that evening and the time they awoke the next morning.

On average, someone who makes $60,000 or more a year sleeps 40 minutes less than someone who makes $20,000. High-income Canadians tend to dedicate more time to their paid work, spend less time with their children and less time at leisure activities.

Men slept for an average of 8 hours and 7 minutes, about 11 minutes less than women. However, about 35% of women reported trouble falling asleep or staying asleep, compared with only 25% of men.

People who commute an hour or more per day sleep 7 hours and 41 minutes on average. People with short commutes (1 to 30 minutes) average 22 minutes more sleep. Again, men tend to sleep less than women.

Time stress reduces the amount of sleep everyone gets. Time-crunched men get 35 minutes less sleep than those who report little time stress; similarly, stressed women get 25 minutes less sleep. Men still sleep fewer minutes per night than women, regardless of their time stress.

Working long hours means less sleep. On average, people who work more than 9 hours a day sleep for 7 hours and 32 minutes. This is 41 minutes fewer per night than people who work less than 4 hours. And it is 55 minutes less than the sleep reported by people who do not work any paid hours.

Chart 29.4
Amount of sleep per night in relation to employment status, 2005

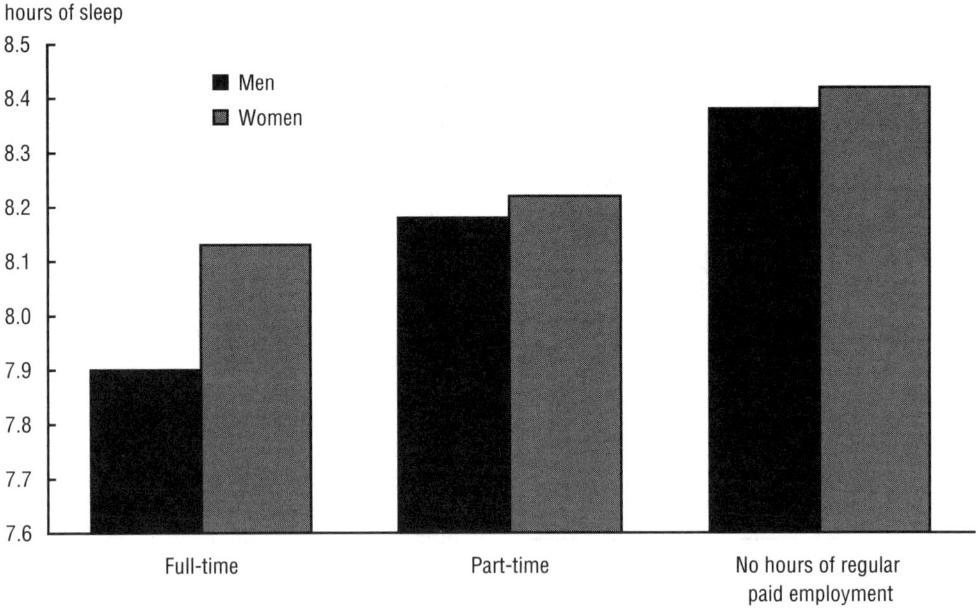

Source: Statistics Canada, Catalogue no. 11-008-XIE.

Workaholics' lives not much fun

What distinguishes the one-third of working adults who see themselves as workaholics? Besides leading lives that are less satisfying and out of balance, they are not having as much fun as their non-workaholic colleagues.

In the 2005 General Social Survey on time use, 31% of employed Canadians aged 19 to 64 identified themselves as workaholics. Among this group of workaholics, 39% reported working 50 or more hours per week. That compares with 20% of non-workaholics who worked that many hours.

More than half of workaholics (56%) feel they do not have time for fun anymore, compared with 34% of non-workaholics. But workaholics do not enjoy their work more than non-workaholics do. Moreover, they are less satisfied with life. Workaholics say they wish they could spend more time with family and friends, and are more likely than non-workaholics to say they are in poor health and have trouble sleeping.

A higher proportion of workaholics report that they usually feel rushed trying to get through the day. Over half feel they are trapped in a daily routine.

Pop culture presents workaholics as high octane over-achievers. But among technical and clerical workers and professionals, much lower percentages of people self-identified as workaholics. People who worked in management and trade were more likely to say they were workaholics. The survey did not find significant differences between workaholics and non-workaholic in terms of their personal income, education, marital status, family structure or place of residence.

However, one key difference emerged: workaholics were more likely to say that their work and home lives are out of kilter. One in three workaholics was dissatisfied with their work–life balance, compared with one in five non-workaholics.

Chart 29.5
Hours worked by workaholics and non-workaholics, 2005

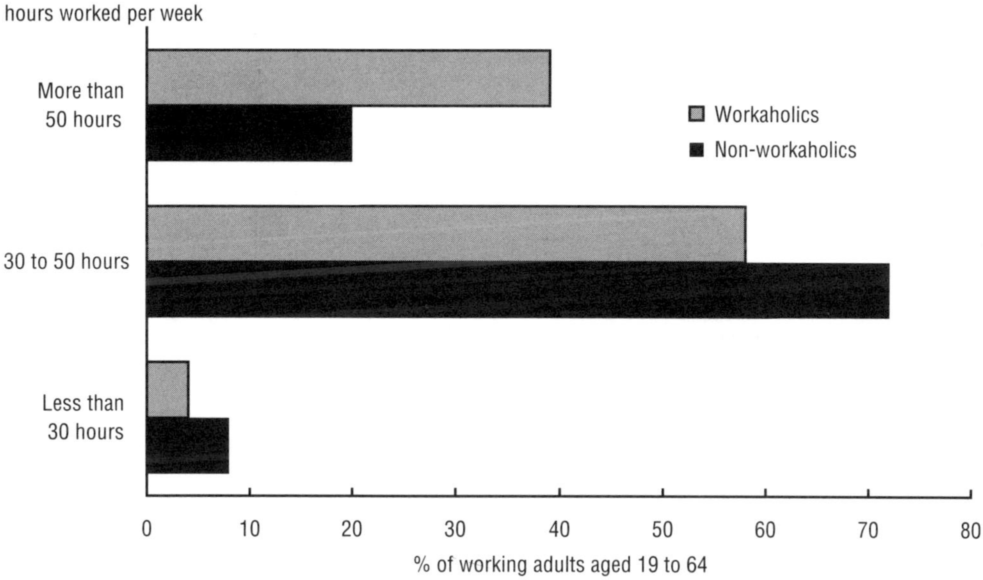

Source: Statistics Canada, Catalogue no. 11-008-XIE.

Table 29.1 Charitable giving, by selected characteristics of donors and by province and territory, 2006

	Canada	Newfoundland and Labrador	Prince Edward Island	Nova Scotia	New Brunswick	Quebec	Ontario
	number						
All taxfilers[1]	**23,338,370**	386,510	102,000	676,600	558,670	5,792,170	8,789,320
All donors	**5,752,630**	83,450	26,850	160,770	127,540	1,286,190	2,335,890
	%						
Males							
Taxfilers[1]	**48**	49	48	48	49	48	48
Donors	**56**	59	53	55	56	57	55
Females							
Taxfilers[1]	**52**	51	52	52	51	52	52
Donors	**44**	41	47	45	44	43	45
	years						
Average age of donors[2]	**52**	54	54	55	54	53	52
	%						
Age group of donors[2]							
0 to 24	**3**	1	2	2	2	3	3
25 to 34	**12**	9	10	9	11	11	13
35 to 44	**19**	18	17	17	17	18	20
45 to 54	**24**	24	23	23	23	25	23
55 to 64	**19**	24	22	21	22	20	18
65 and older	**24**	24	25	28	25	23	24
	$						
Average donation by age group of donors[2]							
0 to 24	**530**	380	220	310	410	160	610
25 to 34	**930**	590	410	650	660	300	1,100
35 to 44	**1,300**	770	710	960	1,000	530	1,600
45 to 54	**1,600**	920	930	1,200	1,300	590	1,900
55 to 64	**1,600**	1,000	1,100	1,300	1,500	610	1,900
65 and older	**1,800**	1,200	1,700	1,700	1,700	890	2,000
Median total income of donors[3,4]	**47,400**	35,400	38,000	41,900	39,700	44,200	50,200
Median donation, both sexes[4]	**250**	330	350	300	290	130	310
Males	**270**	360	410	330	330	140	340
Females	**220**	300	300	270	250	110	280
	$ thousands						
Total charitable donations, both sexes	**8,529,976**	79,652	28,386	203,904	163,515	780,058	4,089,748
Males	**5,723,000**	54,841	16,238	132,392	107,725	522,197	2,725,273
Females	**2,806,976**	24,811	12,148	71,512	55,790	257,861	1,364,475

See notes and source at end of table.

Table 29.1 Charitable giving, by selected characteristics of donors and by province and territory, 2006 (continued)

	Manitoba	Saskatchewan	Alberta	British Columbia	Yukon	Northwest Territories	Nunavut
	number						
All taxfilers[1]	828,920	707,150	2,404,650	3,028,210	21,620	27,070	15,500
All donors	233,270	182,690	600,160	705,080	4,470	4,660	1,630
	%						
Males							
Taxfilers[1]	48	48	50	48	50	51	50
Donors	54	55	57	54	46	52	47
Females							
Taxfilers[1]	52	52	50	52	50	49	50
Donors	46	45	43	46	54	48	53
	years						
Average age of donors[2]	52	54	50	53	49	45	45
	%						
Age group of donors[2]							
0 to 24	4	3	5	3	2	4	4
25 to 34	12	11	15	11	12	19	23
35 to 44	18	17	20	18	22	25	23
45 to 54	23	24	25	23	30	28	23
55 to 64	18	18	17	20	22	18	20
65 and older	24	28	19	25	12	6	7
	$						
Average donation by age group of donors[2]							
0 to 24	840	630	680	630	320	240	440
25 to 34	1,100	890	1,200	1,100	690	660	940
35 to 44	1,500	1,300	1,700	1,500	740	900	1,300
45 to 54	2,100	1,500	2,500	1,900	1,400	1,500	2,300
55 to 64	2,000	1,600	2,600	1,800	1,500	1,700	2,200
65 and older	1,900	1,700	2,900	2,000	1,600	1,900	1,100
Median total income of donors[3,4]	41,700	42,900	53,900	47,600	58,800	78,000	78,300
Median donation, both sexes[4]	310	310	320	320	240	220	450
Males	370	340	370	360	280	230	500
Females	270	280	260	280	200	210	420
	$ thousands						
Total charitable donations, both sexes	407,691	266,325	1,289,145	1,208,068	5,294	5,581	2,608
Males	277,257	173,467	925,094	780,752	2,948	3,424	1,390
Females	130,434	92,858	364,051	427,316	2,346	2,157	1,218

Notes: Charitable giving is the allowable portion of total donations, as reported on the income tax return.

A donor is defined as a taxfiler reporting a charitable donation amount on line 340 of the personal income tax form.

1. Taxfilers are people who filed a tax return for the reference year and were alive at the end of the year.
2. Characteristics such as age are as of December 31 of the reference year.
3. Total income is income from all sources. Median income is rounded to the nearest hundred dollars.
4. Zero values are not included in the calculation of medians for individuals.

Source: Statistics Canada, CANSIM tables 111-0001 and 111-0002.

Table 29.2 Charitable giving, by selected characteristics of donors, 2001 to 2006

	2001	2002	2003	2004	2005	2006
	number					
All taxfilers[1]	21,886,860	21,979,210	22,465,770	22,725,310	23,311,690	23,338,370
All donors	5,521,780	5,520,560	5,588,590	5,781,250	5,833,930	5,752,630
	%					
Males						
Taxfilers[1]	49	49	49	48	48	48
Donors	57	57	57	56	56	56
Females						
Taxfilers[1]	51	51	51	52	52	52
Donors	43	43	43	44	44	44
	years					
Average age of donors[2]	52	52	52	52	52	52
	%					
Age group of donors[2]						
0 to 24	3	3	3	3	3	3
25 to 34	12	12	12	12	12	12
35 to 44	22	21	21	20	20	19
45 to 54	23	23	23	23	23	24
55 to 64	16	16	17	18	18	19
65 and older	24	24	24	24	24	24
	$					
Average donations by age group of donors[2]						
0 to 24	360	380	470	460	490	530
25 to 34	520	590	700	700	820	930
35 to 44	860	940	1,000	1,000	1,200	1,300
45 to 54	1,100	1,100	1,200	1,300	1,400	1,600
55 to 64	1,100	1,200	1,300	1,300	1,500	1,600
65 and older	1,300	1,300	1,400	1,500	1,700	1,800
Median total income of donors[3,4]	40,300	41,200	42,400	43,700	45,400	47,400
Total median donations, both sexes[4]	200	210	220	230	240	250
Males	220	230	240	250	260	270
Females	180	180	200	200	210	220
	$ thousands					
Total charitable donations, both sexes	5,514,371	5,847,068	6,513,013	6,922,616	7,879,588	8,529,976
Males	3,715,250	3,940,147	4,389,106	4,591,471	5,293,624	5,723,000
Females	1,799,121	1,906,921	2,123,908	2,331,145	2,585,965	2,806,976

Notes: Charitable giving is the allowable portion of total donations, as reported on the income tax return.
A donor is defined as a taxfiler reporting a charitable donation amount on line 340 of the personal income tax form.
1. Taxfilers are people who filed a tax return for the reference year and were alive at the end of the year.
2. Characteristics such as age are as of December 31 of the reference year.
3. Total income is income from all sources. Median income is rounded to the nearest hundred dollars.
4. Zero values are not included in the calculation of medians for individuals.
Source: Statistics Canada, CANSIM tables 111-0001 and 111-0002.

Table 29.3 Characteristics of workaholics and non-workaholics, 2005

	Non-workaholics	Workaholics
	years	
Average age	40.7	39.8
	%	
Male	56	59
Female	44	41
Education		
High school diploma or less	29	27
College diploma / some postsecondary	45	45
University degree	26	28
Marital Status		
Married/common-law	69	67
Other	31	33
Household Structure		
Alone	11	11
Couple only	24	23
Couple and children	39	40
Single parent and children	6	6
Other	20	20
Live in a census metropolitan area		
No	33	33
Yes	67	67
Personal income		
Less than $30,000	28	26
$30,000 to $60,000	45	45
More than $60,000	27	29
Occupation		
Management	8	12
Professional	21	18
Technical	8	6
Clerical	17	12
Sales and service	23	24
Trades	13	17
Industry	10	11

Source: Statistics Canada, General Social Survey, 2005.

Table 29.4 Work–life balance of workaholics and non-workaholics, by level of satisfaction, 2005

	Overall	Non-workaholics	Workaholics
		maximum = 10.0	
Average level of satisfaction with			
Life overall	7.7	7.8	7.5
Non-work time	7.1	7.3	6.6
Finances	6.6	6.6	6.5
Work	7.4	7.4	7.4
		maximum = 5.0	
Average level of enjoyment of work	3.8	3.8	3.9
		%	
Satisfied with work–life balance			
No	24	19	34
Yes	76	81	66
Self-rated health			
Poor to fair	10	9	12
Good to excellent	90	91	88
Experience trouble going to or staying asleep			
No	72	74	66
Yes	28	26	34
Cut back on sleep when feel pressed for time			
No	45	50	35
Yes	55	50	65
Feel under stress to accomplish more than you can handle			
No	59	67	42
Yes	41	33	58
Worry about spending enough time with family or friends			
No	49	55	35
Yes	51	45	65

Source: Statistics Canada, General Social Survey, 2005.

Table 29.5 Perception of time by workaholics and non-workaholics, 2005

	Overall	Non-workaholics	Workaholics
		%	
Feel rushed			
Usually	77	73	86
Occasionally	20	23	12
Never	3	3	2
Feel stressed when pressed for time			
No	38	42	29
Yes	62	58	71
Feel trapped in a daily routine			
No	57	61	48
Yes	43	39	52
Feel you do not have time for fun anymore			
No	59	66	44
Yes	41	34	56
Would like to spend more time alone			
No	70	73	65
Yes	30	27	35
Feel like you have not accomplished what you set out to do			
No	52	56	44
Yes	48	44	56
Plan to slow down in the coming year			
No	76	80	68
Yes	24	20	32

Source: Statistics Canada, General Social Survey, 2005.

Table 29.6 Distribution of employment, by occupation, 1987, 1996 and 2006

	1987			1996			2006		
	Women	Men	Women as a percentage of total employed in occupation	Women	Men	Women as a percentage of total employed in occupation	Women	Men	Women as a percentage of total employed in occupation
	thousands								
Total employed	5,307.7	7,025.3	...	6,099.0	7,322.4	...	7,757.2	8,727.1	...
	%								
Total[1]	**100.0**	**100.0**	**43.0**	**100.0**	**100.0**	**45.4**	**100.0**	**100.0**	**47.1**
Clerical and administrative	29.7	7.9	73.9	25.6	7.2	74.9	24.1	7.1	75.0
Sales and service	30.0	18.4	55.2	28.6	19.2	55.4	28.6	19.3	56.8
Primary	2.3	7.2	19.7	2.1	6.5	20.9	1.5	5.3	20.5
Trades, transport and construction	2.1	28.9	5.2	2.1	26.4	6.1	2.1	26.3	6.5
Processing, manufacturing and utilities	5.8	9.1	32.4	4.7	8.8	30.6	4.1	8.1	31.1
Management	**6.0**	**10.5**	**30.1**	**8.2**	**11.6**	**37.0**	**7.1**	**11.0**	**36.3**
Senior management	0.3	0.8	21.0	0.3	0.7	27.2	0.3	0.8	26.3
Other management	5.7	9.7	30.7	7.8	10.9	37.5	6.7	10.2	36.9
Professional	**24.1**	**18.0**	**50.4**	**28.8**	**20.3**	**54.2**	**32.5**	**22.9**	**55.9**
Business and finance	1.9	2.3	38.3	2.8	2.7	46.9	3.3	2.8	51.6
Natural sciences/engineering/mathematics	2.3	7.0	19.6	2.3	8.0	19.1	3.2	10.1	22.0
Social sciences/religion	4.3	2.0	61.4	6.0	2.3	68.8	6.7	2.4	71.3
Teaching	3.8	2.6	52.3	5.1	2.8	60.1	5.6	2.8	63.9
Doctors/dentists/other health	0.9	0.9	43.1	1.2	1.1	48.1	1.4	1.0	55.3
Nursing/therapy/other health-related	8.3	0.9	87.1	8.3	1.0	87.0	8.9	1.1	87.4
Artistic/literary/recreational	2.7	2.1	48.4	3.1	2.4	51.5	3.4	2.6	54.1

1. Includes occupations that are not classified.
Source: Statistics Canada, Catalogue no. 89F0133XIE.

Table 29.7 Distribution of young adults aged 25 to 39 no longer living with their parents, by selected characteristics, 2006

	%		%
Sex		**Highest level of educational attainment**	
Women	52	Less than high school	7
Men	48	High school diploma	25
		College or trade diploma	33
Age group		University degree	34
25 to 27 years	15		
28 to 30 years	20	**Place of residence**	
31 to 33 years	20	Toronto	17
34 to 36 years	22	Montréal	12
37 to 39 years	23	Vancouver	7
		Ottawa–Gatineau	4
Household living arrangements		Calgary	4
Married without children	12	Edmonton	4
Common-law union without children	9	CMA with population 250,000 to 750,000	15
Married with children	42	CMA or CA with population 100,000 to 250,000	9
Common-law union with children	11	CA with population 10,000 to 100,000	12
Lone parent	6	Rural areas and small towns	17
Alone	10		
Other	11	**Always lived with both parents until age 15**	
		No	22
Main activity during the previous 12 months		Yes	78
Permanent employment	62		
Self-employed	9	**Time since immigration**	
Temporary employment	6	Less than 4 years	6
Looking for work	2	5 to 9 years	5
Student	5	10 to 24 years	7
Caring for children / keeping house	14	25 to 39 years	4
Other activity	2	Born in Canada	79
Household income			
Less than $30,000	11		
$30,000 to $49,999	16		
$50,000 to $79,999	26		
$80,000 to $99,999	13		
$100,000 or more	20		

Source: Statistics Canada, Catalogue no. 11-008-XWE.

Table 29.8 Annual admissions, by facility type and by province and territory, 2005/2006

	All facility types			Transition house		
	Total	Women	Children	Total	Women	Children
	number					
Canada	**105,711**	**60,057**	**41,717**	**49,375**	**27,432**	**19,332**
Newfoundland and Labrador	1,125	697	428	894	508	386
Prince Edward Island	162	77	85	0	0	0
Nova Scotia	1,766	1,062	704	1,569	971	598
New Brunswick	2,296	1,447	757	1,626	915	619
Quebec	18,250	10,908	6,553	14,799	8,586	5,698
Ontario	31,858	18,608	12,389	10,889	6,168	4,633
Manitoba	7,936	4,113	3,803	921	419	482
Saskatchewan	6,380	3,141	3,015	1,852	927	925
Alberta	14,326	7,702	6,607	904	484	420
British Columbia	18,604	10,603	6,077	14,370	7,522	4,972
Yukon	857	549	288	727	462	245
Northwest Territories and Nunavut	2,151	1,150	1,001	824	470	354

	Women's emergency centre			Emergency shelter		
	Total	Women	Children	Total	Women	Children
	number					
Canada	**25,532**	**13,947**	**11,513**	**18,556**	**10,720**	**6,863**
Newfoundland and Labrador	25	25	0	81	31	0
Prince Edward Island	0	0	0	143	67	76
Nova Scotia	0	0	0	59	27	32
New Brunswick	0	0	0	339	306	33
Quebec	947	383	494	324	286	38
Ontario	5,216	3,198	2,018	11,532	6,762	4,021
Manitoba	4,025	2,005	2,020	2,025	962	1,063
Saskatchewan	3,784	1,975	1,809	623	191	208
Alberta	8,811	4,078	4,733	2,076	1,257	819
British Columbia	2,409	2,110	287	486	316	170
Yukon	113	77	36	0	0	0
Northwest Territories and Nunavut	202	96	106	868	465	403

See notes and source at end of table.

Table 29.8 Annual admissions, by facility type and by province and territory, 2005/2006 (continued)

	Second stage housing			Family centre		
	Total	Women	Children	Total	Women	Children
	number					
Canada	**3,644**	**1,749**	**2,054**	**1,638**	**920**	**713**
Newfoundland and Labrador	90	49	41	0	0	0
Prince Edward Island	19	10	9	0	0	0
Nova Scotia	138	54	74	0	0	0
New Brunswick	122	59	53	0	0	0
Quebec	490	259	231	0	0	0
Ontario	1,172	519	629	1,638	920	718
Manitoba	308	211	97	0	0	0
Saskatchewan	121	48	73	0	0	0
Alberta	1,000	355	628	0	0	0
British Columbia	362	154	208	0	0	0
Yukon	17	10	7	0	0	0
Northwest Territories and Nunavut	5	1	4	0	0	0

	Safe home network			Other[1]		
	Total	Women	Children	Total	Women	Children
	number					
Canada	**1,395**	**669**	**690**	**5,371**	**4,620**	**547**
Newfoundland and Labrador	0	0	0	35	34	1
Prince Edward Island	0	0	0	0	0	0
Nova Scotia	0	0	0	0	0	0
New Brunswick	0	0	0	209	157	52
Quebec	0	0	0	1,690	1,394	92
Ontario	166	50	116	1,245	991	254
Manitoba	0	0	0	657	516	141
Saskatchewan	0	0	0	0	0	0
Alberta	0	0	0	1,535	1,528	7
British Columbia	977	501	440	0	0	0
Yukon	0	0	0	0	0	0
Northwest Territories and Nunavut	252	118	134	0	0	0

Notes: The woman–child distribution of annual admissions was unknown for about 3% of admissions; in such cases shelters only provided the total number of admissions for the year but were unable to provide a breakdown for women and children. Therefore, total admissions may not equal the sum of admissions for women and children.

Precise reporting period may vary. Shelters were asked to provide information for the twelve-month period ending March 31, 2006 or their own twelve month fiscal period. Because the number and type of shelters participating in each cycle of the Transition Home Survey may vary, comparisons of admissions from 2005/2006 to results from previous survey cycles are not advisable.

1. Includes all other facilities not otherwise classified. This category may include Rural Family Violence Prevention Centres in Alberta, Interim Housing in Manitoba and other types of emergency shelters like the YWCA. These services may not be exclusive to abused women.

Source: Statistics Canada, Cataloge no. 85-002-XIE.

Table 29.9 Employed women with children, by age of youngest child, 1976 to 2006

	Youngest child under age 3	Youngest child aged 3 to 5	Youngest child aged 6 to 15	Total with children under age 16	No children at home[1]
	%				
1976	27.6	36.8	46.4	39.1	60.9
1977	29.3	37.9	47.5	40.4	61.2
1978	32.0	40.6	49.2	42.6	62.3
1979	34.6	42.9	50.9	44.6	64.1
1980	36.9	45.2	53.5	47.1	65.2
1981	39.3	46.7	56.2	49.3	66.0
1982	39.4	46.5	55.3	48.8	64.9
1983	42.2	47.9	55.0	49.8	65.7
1984	44.1	49.1	57.0	51.6	66.1
1985	46.7	52.0	59.1	53.9	67.7
1986	49.3	54.4	61.8	56.6	69.1
1987	50.2	56.1	63.8	58.2	69.8
1988	51.8	58.2	66.5	60.4	71.7
1989	52.9	59.2	69.0	62.3	72.7
1990	53.4	59.5	70.1	63.0	73.5
1991	54.4	60.1	69.0	62.8	72.6
1992	54.0	59.4	68.0	62.1	71.6
1993	54.4	59.4	68.5	62.4	71.6
1994	55.6	59.1	68.5	62.8	72.1
1995	56.0	60.2	69.8	63.8	73.0
1996	57.8	60.5	69.8	64.5	72.4
1997	58.8	62.1	71.1	65.9	73.4
1998	59.2	63.9	72.1	67.0	74.8
1999	60.1	66.0	73.4	68.4	76.0
2000	60.3	67.3	74.4	69.2	76.3
2001	61.3	67.0	75.3	70.1	76.8
2002	61.9	68.1	77.0	71.4	77.9
2003	62.7	68.5	76.7	71.6	79.0
2004	64.5	69.4	77.0	72.4	79.3
2005	64.7	70.6	77.4	72.8	78.7
2006	64.3	69.4	78.2	72.9	79.9

1. Women age 55 and younger with no children 16 and younger living at home.
Source: Statistics Canada, Catalogue no. 89F0133XWE.

Transportation

30

Overview

In Canada, railways, trucks, ships and airplanes transport everything from food to automobiles, and serve almost every segment of the economy: consumers, retailers, wholesalers, manufacturers, importers and exporters.

The system has more kilometres of road per person than almost any other nation, and also includes 1,111 airports, 72,245 km of operating railroad tracks, and more than 300 commercial ports and harbours.

The transportation sector continues to be a strong economic force in the marketplace, and service demand remains strong. In 2006, transportation contributed $55.5 billion, or about 5%, of Canada's gross domestic product (GDP), a slight increase over 2005.

Growth in the sector has been consistent since 2004: 3.2% growth in 2006 followed a 3.5% increase in 2005 and a 3.4% increase in 2004.

Trucking is the sector's largest contributor to GDP: 27% in 2006 came from trucking, about the same as in 2005. Air, water and rail combined contributed another 21% in 2006.

Employment in the transportation sector posted an overall increase of 1% in 2005 compared with 2004, but not every category saw growth. The transportation industry in 2005 employed 547,000 persons, or 4% of Canada's workforce.

The sector's strong showing in 2005 contrasted with slow growth from 2001 to 2003. Slower economic growth throughout the Canadian economy, the September 11, 2001 attacks in the United States, the outbreak of SARS (Severe Acute Respiratory Syndrome), and the start of the war in Iraq in 2003 all hurt the transportation sector. Recovery began in 2004 and 2005, thanks to a strong economy that boosted trucking, rail and air traffic.

Map 30.1
National highway system

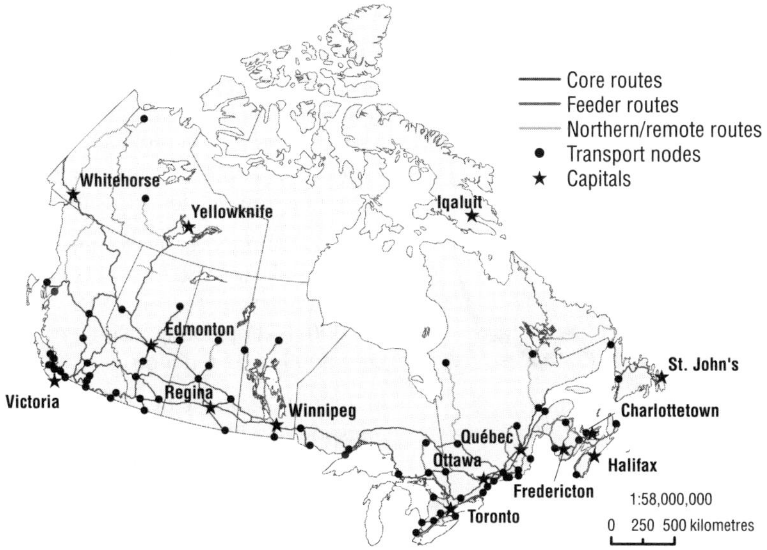

Source: Transport Canada.

Roads

Trucking generated $15.1 billion in 2006. While it continued to be the largest contributor to the transportation sector's GDP, trucking growth slowed in 2006 to 3%, following a 4% increase in 2005.

Canada's 3,700 for-hire trucking companies that posted annual earnings of at least $1 million improved their financial performance in 2006. Net operating revenues jumped 26% from 2005, to $1.3 billion.

Thanks to trade agreements like NAFTA, Canada's trade with the United States rose 191% from 1990 to 2005. For the for-hire trucking industry, this has meant an ever-increasing demand for freight movement across the border. On a tonne-kilometre basis, cross-border truck traffic grew five times faster than domestic traffic from 1990 to 2003.

Commuters driving personal vehicles continue to jam Canada's roads each weekday. Of 16 million people in the employed labour force, the great majority commute to work. However, growth in the number of workers driving to work was lower from 2001 to 2006 than from 1996 to 2001.

Chart 30.1
Net operating revenues and net profits of for-hire trucking companies

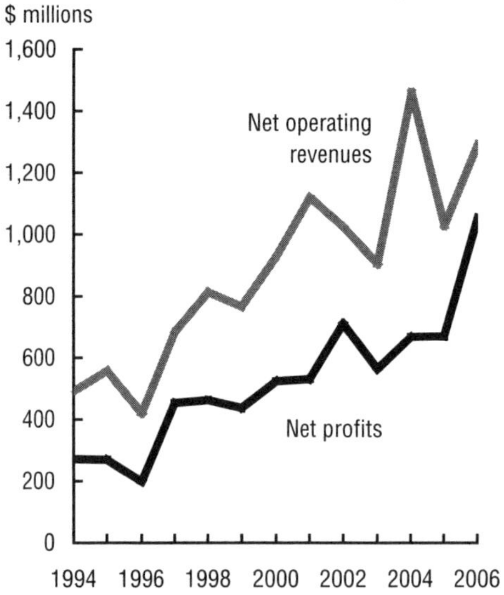

Source: Statistics Canada, CANSIM table 403-0003.

Table 30.a
GDP of the transportation industries, by mode of transport, 2006

	Share of transportation GDP	Growth from 2005
	%	
Total	**100**	**3.2**
Air	9	9.5
Rail	10	-0.3
Water	2	6.1
Truck	27	2.6
Transit and ground passenger	9	1.4
Pipeline	10	1.1
Scenic and sightseeing transportation and support activities	18	5.5
Postal services and couriers and messengers	11	1.8
Warehousing and storage	4	6.7

Source: Statistics Canada, CANSIM table 379-0027.

Railroads

The railway industry continued its strong performance in 2006. Among the factors contributing to the gain in operating revenues were a favourable economic climate, rising freight rates and higher fuel surcharges stemming from higher prices for crude oil.

Total operating revenues for the Canadian railway industry rose for an eighth consecutive year, reaching $10.4 billion in 2006. Net operating income rose 13% over 2005 to $2.6 billion.

In 2006, the volume of commodities transported within, into and out of Canada rose 1% over 2005, for a total of 282.8 million metric tonnes. Coal continued to be the main commodity by volume, followed by mixed loads or unidentified freight, then wheat. These three categories accounted for 28% of total tonnage in 2006.

Ports

Canadian ports handled 470.1 million metric tonnes of cargo in 2005, up 4% from the previous record set in 2004. Growth in the international sector was primarily responsible for the increase.

In 2005, 111 for-hire marine carriers earned $231 million in income, as revenues rose 10% over 2004, to $2.9 billion. Government marine carriers posted $828 million in revenues in 2005.

Domestic cargo remained stable in 2005. Gains occurred in shipments of logs and other wood; in stone, sand, gravel and crushed stone; in other metallic ores and concentrates; in gasoline and aviation turbine fuel; and in newsprint. However, these gains were offset by losses in iron ores and concentrates, fuel oils and coal.

Ports and marine terminals under the jurisdiction of 19 Canadian port authorities handled 53% of the total cargo, up slightly from their share in 2004. Activity at these port authorities increased 5.2% in 2005, a faster pace than the growth rate of 4.5% in 2004.

International container traffic at Canadian ports hit another high during 2005. Ports handled more than 3.8 million twenty-foot equivalents containing 31.9 million tonnes of cargo in 2005. However, the growth rate for both volume and tonnage of containerized cargo slipped from 2004.

Chart 30.2
Air traffic at Canadian airports

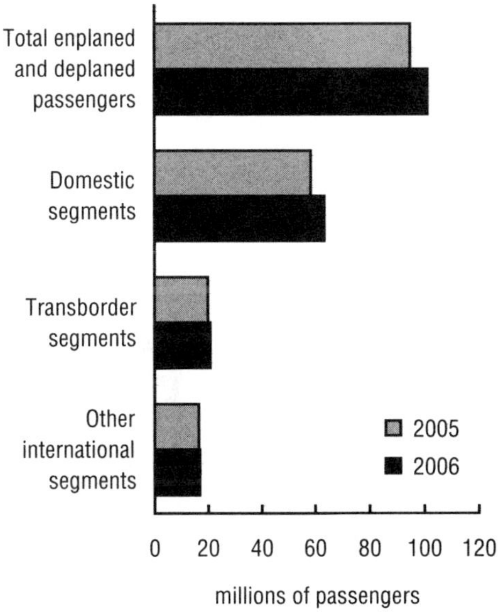

Source: Statistics Canada, Catalogue no. 51-203-XIE.

Air traffic

Following an 11% gain in 2005, the air transport industry's GDP grew 10% in 2006, and generated nearly $4.9 billion. This represents a five-year high.

In 2006, Canadian air carriers (Levels I to III) reported increase over 2005, to 3.8 million enplaned passengers, and passenger–kilometres rose by 11 billion (10%). These carriers also reported an increase of $1.3 billion (9%) in total operating revenues over 2005.

In 2006, air traffic at Canadian airports continued an upward trend begun in 2003, with the total number of enplaned/deplaned passengers (passengers either embarking and taking off, or landing and disembarking, from an airport in Canada) surpassing the 100-million mark for the first time. The number of passengers (101.0 million) increased 7% compared with 2005 (94.6 million).

The 42 Canadian airports with NAV CANADA air traffic control towers reported 4.9 million aircraft take-offs and landings in 2007, up 8% compared to 2006 (4.5 million). This marks the second consecutive annual increase in total aircraft movements.

Airlines are evolving

Gross domestic product in the air transportation industry rose 9.5% in 2006, 10.9% in 2005, and 9.4% in 2004, following three consecutive years of decline after the September 11, 2001 attacks. Industry employment followed roughly the same pattern.

The air transportation industry has been evolving in response to more than a decade of changes in its business environment. Legislation, including the signing of the Canada–U.S. Open Skies Agreement in 1995, moved it toward less regulated, more competitive operations. Likewise, the growth and popularity of low-cost carriers has changed the way airlines must compete in domestic and international markets.

While the number of commercial domestic flights in Canada fell slightly in 2005 from 2004, the number of seats available has been falling steadily. In 2005, airlines offered about 63.5 million seats in Canada, down sharply from 71.4 million in 1995. This decrease in seating capacity may contribute to upward pressure on airfares. In 2005, the average domestic and international airfare (all types) paid by passengers was $251, up 0.4% from $250 in 2004.

Part of the decline in seating capacity stems from changes made to aircraft fleets: smaller, more fuel-efficient planes are replacing big aircraft with large seating capacities. In 1996, large aircraft, such as Boeing 747 jumbo jets, accounted for 39% of the air fleet, medium-sized planes, 29%, and small planes, 32%. By 2005, jumbo jets accounted for only 4% of the fleet; medium-sized planes, such as the Airbus 320, jumped to 60%, and small aircraft, such as the Dash 8, rose to 36%. In 2005, for the first time in years, the proportion of medium-sized planes fell in favour of smaller planes.

Chart 30.3
Average air fares of Level I Canadian air carriers for scheduled services

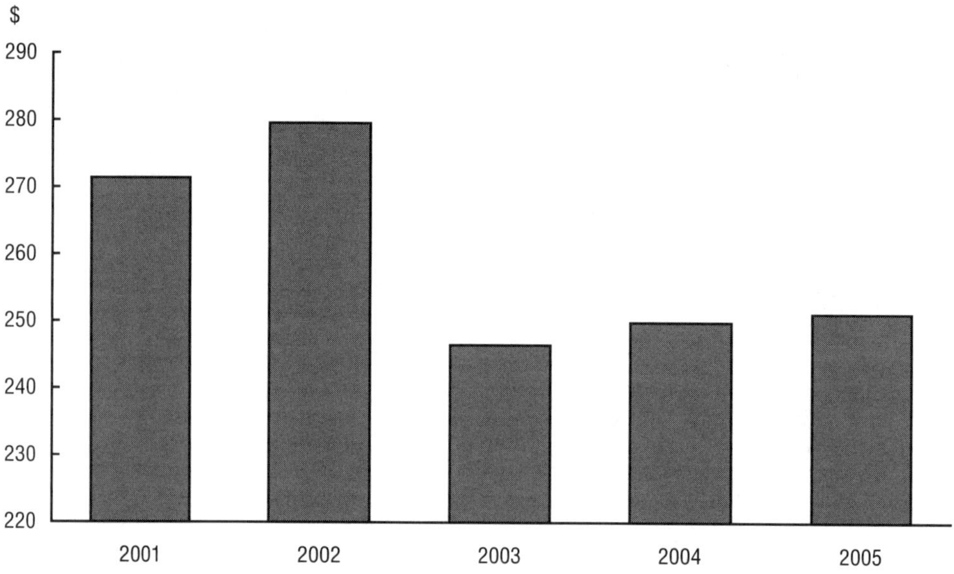

Source: Statistics Canada, Catalogue no. 51-004-XIE.

Public transit gaining riders

Public transit ridership for 2007 set a fifth consecutive all-time record, according to the Canadian Urban Transit Association. A total of 1.8 billion transit trips were taken across Canada last year, representing a 3% increase over 2006, and a 15% increase over the five-year period since 2002.

The 2006 Census enumerated 1,622,700 people who usually travelled to work on some form of public transportation, a 15% increase from 2001. Over the five years after 2001, the proportion that took public transit increased from 10.5% to 11.0%. In Canada's 33 census metropolitan areas (CMAs), this rate rose from 14.4% to 15.1%. In the same period, the proportion that drove to work declined from 73.8% to 72.3%.

Sustainable transit is gaining in popularity among workers living in the Toronto, Calgary, Vancouver, and Ottawa–Gatineau CMAs. More than 40% of commuters whose usual place of work is in Toronto, Vancouver or Montréal get to work either by public transit, or by walking or riding a bicycle.

In Ottawa–Gatineau, the percentage of those using public transportation rose to 19.4%, up from 18.5% in 2001; in Calgary it rose to 15.6% in 2006 from 13.2% in 2001. Toronto's percentage slipped from 22.4% in 2001 to 22.2% in 2006.

Public transportation appears to be making progress among young workers. From 2001 to 2006, the percentage aged 15 to 24 using public transportation in all CMAs was 35%, up from 34% in 2001. Among those aged 45 to 64, less than 18% used public transportation, a number that barely changed from 2001.

Chart 30.4
Employed labour force using public transit, by selected CMAs

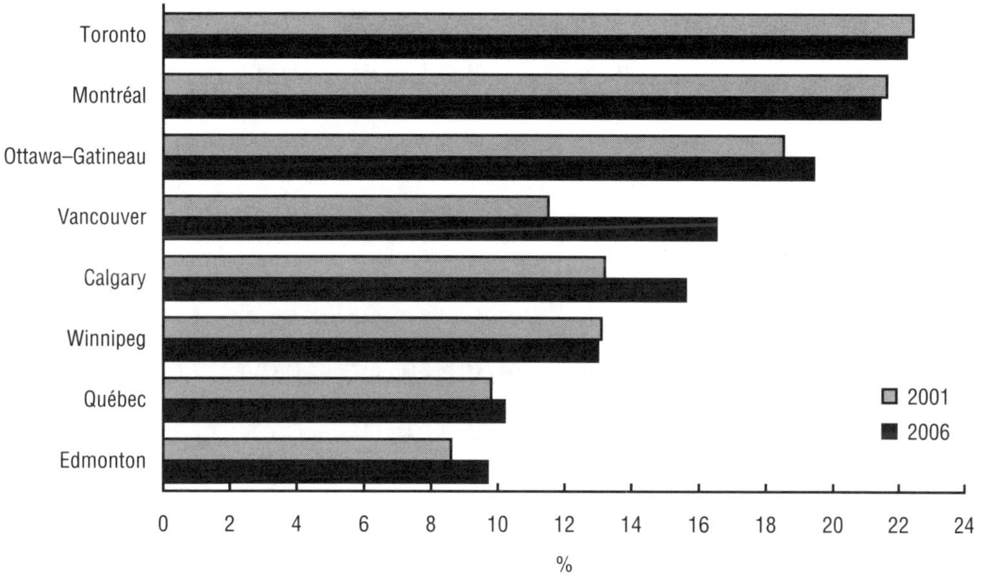

Source: Statistics Canada, Catalogue no. 97-561-XWE.

Table 30.1 Gross domestic product at basic prices for transportation and warehousing, by selected subsectors, 2001 to 2006

	2001	2002	2003	2004	2005	2006
	chained (2002) $ millions					
Transportation and warehousing	**50,176**	**50,066**	**50,270**	**51,960**	**53,802**	**55,501**
Air transportation	4,326	3,938	3,668	4,014	4,450	4,872
Rail transportation	4,994	5,074	5,151	5,463	5,634	5,615
Water transportation	1,135	1,151	1,123	1,186	1,207	1,281
Truck transportation	13,564	13,756	13,531	14,085	14,692	15,077
Transit and ground passenger transportation	4,683	4,987	4,885	5,051	5,122	5,192
Pipeline transportation	5,235	5,371	5,380	5,393	5,533	5,594
Postal service, couriers and messengers	5,774	5,556	5,834	5,877	5,968	6,075
Warehousing and storage	1,557	1,541	1,648	1,904	2,005	2,140

Notes: North American Industry Classification Sysytem (NAICS), 2002.
Certain subsectors are omited.
Source: Statistics Canada, CANSIM, table 379-0027.

Table 30.2 Operating statistics of Canadian railway carriers, 2001 to 2006

	2001	2002	2003	2004	2005	2006
	$ thousands					
Operating revenue	**8,155,559**	**8,213,346**	**8,307,268**	**8,861,767**	**9,821,994**	**10,405,395**
Freight revenue	7,222,552	7,256,434	7,354,925	7,879,379	8,759,069	9,351,672
Passenger revenue	268,504	287,394	255,776	265,192	282,881	294,529
All other operating revenue	664,503	669,518	696,567	717,194	780,044	759,193
Operating expenses	**6,594,028**	**6,621,037**	**6,713,296**	**6,951,895**	**7,506,354**	**7,793,955**
Ways and structures expenses	1,210,277	1,229,852	1,221,768	1,283,774	1,311,510	1,341,823
Equipment expenses	1,465,996	1,396,081	1,430,549	1,371,147	1,440,876	1,467,060
Rail operating expenses	2,796,495	2,718,701	2,776,794	2,929,148	3,216,111	3,388,501
General expenses	1,121,260	1,276,401	1,284,185	1,367,826	1,537,857	1,596,570
	thousands					
Transportation and other cost-generating sources						
Tonnes of freight transported	348,723	335,830	343,304	361,606	369,943	352,729
Tonne-kilometres of freight transported	323,210,721	317,806,584	318,263,125	338,897,938	352,139,700	352,373,981
Passengers transported	4,179	4,251	3,958	4,048	4,269	4,243
Passenger-kilometres of passengers transported	1,553,059	1,596,947	1,433,643	1,420,804	1,478,454	1,450,481
Litres of diesel oil consumed for all trains	1,982,053	1,969,741	2,007,813	2,097,070	2,130,224	2,120,107
	number					
Employees	39,538	37,282	36,312	35,591	34,995	34,137

Source: Statistics Canada, CANSIM tables 404-0004, 404-0005, 404-0013, 404-0016 and 404-0019.

Table 30.3 Shipping activities at Canadian ports, tonnage loaded and unloaded, 1994 to 2005

	Total	Domestic	International		
			Total	United States	Other
	thousands of tonnes				
Total handled					
1994	**351,316**	104,368	246,948	78,801	168,147
1995	**360,455**	100,740	259,715	85,198	174,518
1996	**357,513**	97,649	259,863	88,484	171,379
1997	**376,067**	93,418	282,650	94,313	188,337
1998	**376,032**	96,607	279,425	100,060	179,364
1999	**385,597**	104,398	281,199	101,983	179,216
2000	**402,783**	109,020	293,762	108,794	184,969
2001	**394,701**	107,842	286,859	107,955	178,904
2002	**408,141**	125,407	282,734	114,310	168,424
2003	**443,779**	137,079	306,700	123,366	183,335
2004	**452,328**	137,768	314,560	123,280	191,280
2005	**470,109**	139,163	330,946	128,664	202,282
Loaded					
1994	**222,222**	52,184	170,038	49,520	120,518
1995	**226,910**	50,370	176,540	49,939	126,601
1996	**223,096**	48,825	174,272	52,399	121,873
1997	**234,653**	46,709	187,945	56,891	131,054
1998	**227,346**	48,304	179,042	58,872	120,171
1999	**231,847**	52,199	179,648	59,727	119,921
2000	**242,351**	54,507	187,843	64,744	123,099
2001	**228,663**	53,939	174,724	62,038	112,685
2002	**237,051**	62,780	174,270	72,867	101,404
2003	**259,872**	68,485	191,387	81,180	110,207
2004	**264,999**	68,897	196,102	83,792	112,310
2005	**271,295**	69,540	201,756	85,750	116,006
Unloaded					
1994	**129,094**	52,184	76,910	29,282	47,629
1995	**133,546**	50,370	83,176	35,259	47,917
1996	**134,416**	48,825	85,592	36,085	49,506
1997	**141,414**	46,709	94,705	37,423	57,283
1998	**148,686**	48,304	100,382	41,189	59,194
1999	**153,750**	52,199	101,551	42,256	59,295
2000	**160,432**	54,513	105,919	44,050	61,869
2001	**166,038**	53,903	112,135	45,917	66,219
2002	**171,091**	62,626	108,464	41,444	67,020
2003	**183,908**	68,594	115,314	42,186	73,128
2004	**187,330**	68,871	118,458	39,488	78,971
2005	**198,814**	69,623	129,190	42,914	86,276

Source: Statistics Canada, Catalogue no. 54-205-XIE.

Table 30.4 Employment in transportation and warehousing, by selected subsectors, 1993 to 2007

	1993	1994	1995	1996	1997	1998	1999
	number						
Transportation and warehousing	**549,528**	**549,518**	**553,249**	**555,148**	**566,196**	**582,593**	**588,436**
Air transportation	45,184	45,461	48,399	49,823	55,414	60,367	62,400
Rail transportation	57,189	54,907	52,226	48,659	46,099	46,323	45,989
Water transportation	10,816	11,143	12,886	13,274	11,744	11,018	11,636
Truck transportation	133,101	137,754	141,304	145,125	155,044	156,256	156,362
Transit and ground passenger transportation	103,087	95,453	91,245	91,752	91,173	91,776	93,039
Pipeline transportation	5,483	5,310	5,086	4,842	4,943	4,694	4,653
Scenic and sightseeing transportation	1,735	1,791	1,931	1,872	1,786	1,780	1,903
Support activities for transportation	68,431	69,741	69,385	66,534	68,732	71,285	76,532
Couriers and messengers	34,904	36,070	36,815	37,047	38,160	39,215	38,501
Warehousing and storage	25,653	25,949	25,568	27,584	27,144	28,350	29,033

	2000	2001	2002	2003	2004	2005	2006	2007
	number							
Transportation and warehousing	**599,227**	**613,930**	**614,107**	**613,924**	**621,735**	**629,352**	**640,896**	**652,710**
Air transportation	62,751	62,349	57,121	59,742	60,380	60,926	62,118	64,367
Rail transportation	47,275	45,991	46,005	44,545	43,256	42,669	41,429	40,496
Water transportation	12,765	13,664	13,716	x	x	x	x	x
Truck transportation	157,250	164,293	167,331	165,689	170,660	175,197	176,826	177,841
Transit and ground passenger transportation	97,161	98,157	101,115	100,199	99,275	99,389	100,687	102,564
Pipeline transportation	4,949	4,989	5,012	x	x	x	x	x
Scenic and sightseeing transportation	2,051	2,855	2,879	x	x	x	x	x
Support activities for transportation	78,978	83,520	83,862	84,857	84,378	83,565	86,602	90,030
Couriers and messengers	38,271	39,766	39,978	40,549	41,561	43,034	44,103	45,294
Warehousing and storage	29,436	30,842	30,950	30,820	33,284	34,650	39,043	41,103

Notes: North American Industry Classification System (NAICS), 2002.
Certain subsectors are omited.

Source: Statistics Canada, CANSIM table 281-0024.

Table 30.5 Operating statistics of major Canadian airlines, 1997 to 2007

	1997	1998	1999	2000	2001	2002
	thousands					
Passengers transported	24,363	24,571	24,047	24,480	23,414	23,430
Passenger-kilometres	62,479,410	64,426,065	65,711,146	68,516,738	67,018,521	69,254,337
Kilograms of goods transported	449,828	431,150	451,801	407,876	361,834	355,493
Tonne-kilometres of goods transported	2,058,953	2,340,594	2,016,503	1,934,683	1,725,325	1,800,415
Hours flown	826	843	904	921	856	806
Litres of turbo fuel consumed	3,631,436	3,855,178	3,571,445	3,871,274	3,678,966	3,453,486

	2003	2004	2005	2006	2007
	thousands				
Passengers transported	20,042	28,159	32,091	33,439	35,568
Passenger-kilometres	59,508,960	76,122,855	83,909,440	88,323,198	93,363,940
Kilograms of goods transported	298,990	297,246	268,947	265,470	242,511
Tonne-kilometres of goods transported	1,419,988	1,478,716	1,378,548	1,425,103	1,301,260
Hours flown	703	926	981	1,010	1,078
Litres of turbo fuel consumed	2,999,282	3,660,671	3,855,953	3,980,077	4,137,528

Source: Statistics Canada, CANSIM table 401-0001.

Table 30.6 For-hire trucking, 1994 to 2004

	1994	1995	1996	1997	1998	1999
	thousands					
Tonnes of freight transported	195,587	210,941	228,974	223,313	233,931	269,285
Tonne-kilometres of freight transported	101,783,711	110,010,665	121,133,146	130,853,651	138,090,023	158,656,177
Shipments (units)	30,474	32,341	35,181	32,076	33,832	36,410

	2000	2001	2002	2003	2004[1]
	thousands				
Tonnes of freight transported	278,442	287,975	293,644	305,153	604,273
Tonne-kilometres of freight transported	164,981,978	170,936,593	177,215,621	184,963,662	225,608,043
Shipments (units)	35,561	36,917	38,492	40,259	65,884

1. The Trucking Commodity Origin and Destination Survey's scope expanded in 2004 to include local shipments of long-distance carriers and all shipments of local carriers.

Source: Statistics Canada, CANSIM table 403-0001 and Catalogue no. 53-222-XIE.

Table 30.7 Vehicle registrations, 2002 to 2007

	2002	2003	2004	2005	2006	2007
	number					
All vehicle registrations	**24,198,219**	**24,687,511**	**25,196,428**	**25,838,309**	**26,684,822**	**27,577,524**
Road motor vehicle registrations	18,617,413	18,883,584	19,156,055	19,515,295	20,065,171	20,593,251
Vehicles weighing less than 4,500 kilograms	17,543,659	17,768,773	17,989,919	18,275,275	18,738,941	19,198,960
Vehicles weighing from 4,500 kilograms to 14,999 kilograms	366,962	379,079	393,528	415,764	442,607	461,144
Vehicles weighing 15,000 kilograms or more	277,339	282,420	285,942	301,574	318,272	328,128
Buses	79,364	79,948	77,842	78,962	80,447	82,583
Motorcyles and mopeds	350,088	373,362	408,822	443,718	484,903	522,433
Trailers	4,161,491	4,315,996	4,513,641	4,722,563	4,961,184	5,231,114
Off-road, construction and farm vehicles	1,419,305	1,487,930	1,526,731	1,600,450	1,658,466	1,753,158

Source: Statistics Canada, CANSIM table 405-0004.

Table 30.8 Road motor vehicle fuel sales, 2002 to 2007

	2002	2003	2004	2005	2006	2007
	thousands of litres					
Net sales of gasoline	37,949,600	38,421,608	38,911,752	38,484,324	38,653,955	39,640,225
Gross sales of gasoline	39,205,669	39,797,315	40,146,013	39,845,934	39,918,335	40,854,912
Net sales of diesel oil	13,737,648	14,720,634	15,671,144	16,216,420	16,611,819	17,196,304
Net sales of liquefied petroleum gas[1]	323,935	313,019	358,459	324,286	325,747	316,239

Note: Gross is the total volume sold and net is the volume on which taxes were paid.

1. Data for British Columbia are not included.

Source: Statistics Canada, CANSIM table 405-0002.

Travel and tourism

31

Overview

Tourism is big business in Canada. In 2007 it accounted for $70.6 billion of spending in current dollars, a growth of 4% over the previous year, with most of that money coming from Canadians. Our spending on domestic travel in 2007 grew 7% from 2006, and accounted for 77% of the money spent in the sector.

But Canadians do not just like to travel within Canada; we enjoy visiting the United States, and in record numbers we also travel overseas. Indeed, for Canadian travellers, 2007 was record-breaking in a number of ways: it was the first time Canadians took more than 25 million overnight trips abroad, and our spending on those trips was the highest ever at $22.5 billion.

At the same time, Canada is an attractive destination for travellers from abroad, drawing more than 30 million visitors in 2007. That was three million fewer than in 2006 as our appeal to our major market, the United States, continued to decline. A strong Canadian dollar, border security, higher gasoline prices and a weakening U.S. economy were all part of the travel story.

Travel close to home increasing

When it comes to domestic travel, Canadians do most of their travelling within their home provinces. In 2006, 9 out of 10 domestic excursions were in-province: that was 188.9 million in-province visits and trips, compared with just 19.6 million between provinces. The majority of these, 119.2 million trips, were same-day visits. The remaining 87.2 million trips were for an average of three nights away from home, for a total of 265 million nights away. Slightly more than one-third of those nights were spent in commercial accommodation.

Chart 31.1
Domestic share of total tourism spending

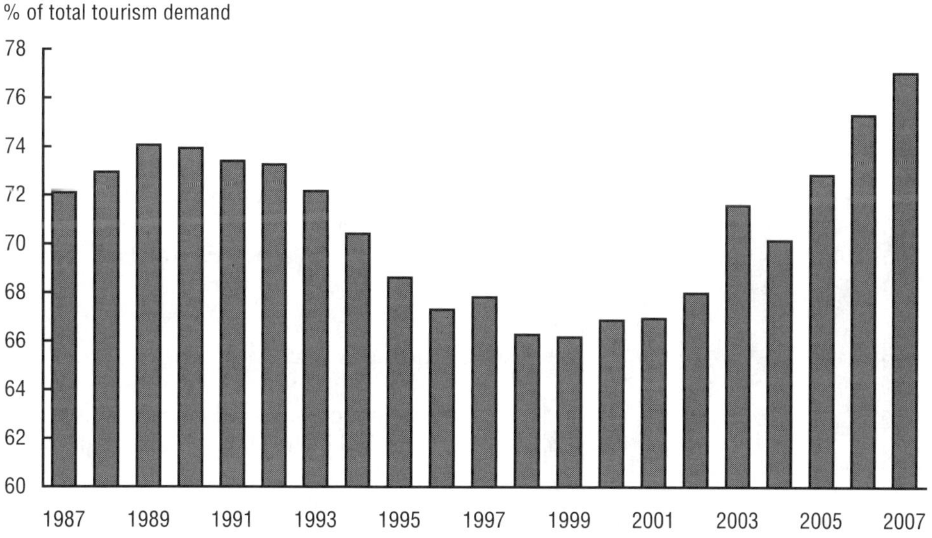

Source: Statistics Canada, CANSIM table 387-0001.

Whether visiting within their own province or in another, Canadians have two main reasons for their in-Canada travel: of the 206.4 million total domestic excursions in 2006, 182.6 million (88%) were either for pleasure or to visit friends and relatives.

Canadians enjoying higher loonie south of the border

Outside our own country, our number one destination is the United States. In 2007, Canadians made 42.6 million excursions there. More than half of that was same-day travel—24.2 million car visits, 3% more than in 2006.

But it was overnight travel that really heated up in 2007, rising 11% and, at 17.8 million trips, the highest level since 1992. In 2007, as the value of the Canadian loonie rose steadily against the American greenback—its value exceeded that of the U.S. dollar in September 2007 for the first time in 30 years—Canadians' spending in the United States rose to $11.5 billion, up 13% from 2006.

Chart 31.2
Same-day automobile travellers from United States to Canada

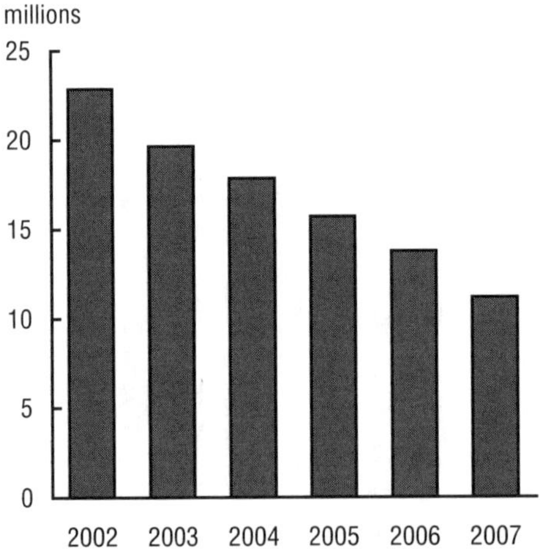

Source: Statistics Canada, CANSIM table 387-0004.

Table 31.a
Non-resident travellers entering Canada

	2003	2007
	thousands	
Total	**38,903**	**30,373**
From United States	35,509	25,695
By automobile	28,749	19,125
By plane	3,913	4,029
By train	114	130
By bus	1,293	941
By boat	874	1,001
By other methods	566	469
From other countries	3,393	4,679
By land	404	499
By air	2,907	4,037
By sea	82	143

Source: Statistics Canada, CANSIM table 427-0001.

Given its proximity to our most populous provinces—Ontario and Quebec—perhaps it is not surprising that New York State is Canadians' favourite overnight destination. In 2007, Canadians made three million overnight visits to the Empire State, 14% more than in 2006, and we spent $919 million, 20% more.

Given its winter appeal, Florida is Canadians' second most popular state to visit. Florida is also where we spend the most money. Canadians took 2.5 million overnight visits there in 2007 and spent $2.8 billion, an increase of 18% over 2006.

In percentage terms, though, it was North Dakota that received the largest gains in Canadian visitors and Canadian spending in 2007: a 26% increase in overnight visits and a 51% increase in expenditures during these visits. Most of that money was spent after the Canadian dollar achieved and exceeded parity with the U.S. dollar.

Canadians travelling more overseas

Canadians are also travelling more overseas, with a record high 7.4 million overnight trips in 2007. This was an increase of 10% over 2006 and the fifth consecutive annual rise. In 2007, travel increased to every overseas region except South America and Oceania.

Among the regions of the world, Europe attracted Canadians the most, drawing 4.2 million overnight visits in 2007, followed by the Caribbean, with more than 1.8 million overnight visits. But on an individual country basis, Mexico predominated for a second year in a row. Canadians' made more than one million visits to Mexico in 2007, up 21% from 2006. Canadians next favourite overseas destinations, in descending order, were the United Kingdom, France, Cuba and the Dominican Republic.

Growing numbers of overseas visitors

Just as we are travelling overseas more, growing numbers of overseas visitors are journeying to Canada. Travel from overseas nations to Canada rose for the fourth consecutive year in 2007, up 3% to 4.4 million overnight trips.

With 891,000 overnight trips, visitors from the United Kingdom remained Canada's most important overseas tourism market. The number of travellers from the United Kingdom rose 6% over 2006. Even more came from Australia: their 208,000 overnight trips in 2007 represented a 17% increase over the previous year. Overseas tourists contributed a total of $6.0 billion to Canada's economy in 2007, up 4% from 2006.

This increase in overseas travellers did not come close to compensating for the decline in U.S. visitors. Every year since 1999 has seen their numbers decline—down to 25.7 million in 2007. Americans' same-day car trips here dropped to 11.2 million in 2007, down 19% from 2006, while their overnight travel fell 4% to 13.4 million trips, the lowest level in a decade. The impact of these declines on spending was marked: Americans spent $7.8 billion in Canada in 2007, down 5% from 2006 and the lowest level since 1997.

Chart 31.3
Canada's international travel deficit

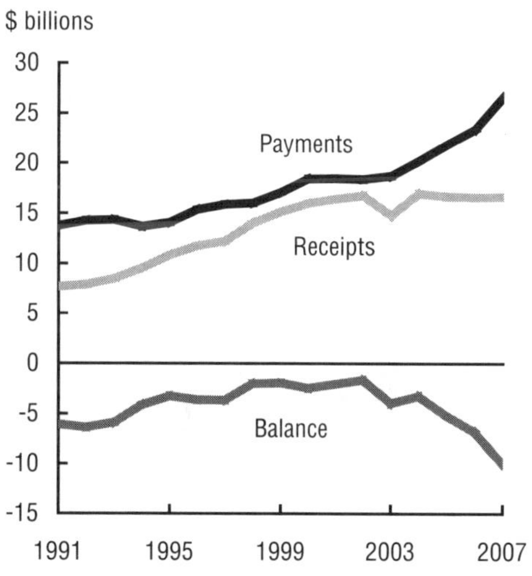

Source: Statistics Canada, CANSIM table 376-0001.

A record international travel deficit

The decline in numbers of foreign visitors to Canada, plus Canadians' increasing travel outside the country, added up to a record high international travel deficit. In 2007, the travel deficit (the difference between spending by Canadians abroad and spending by foreigners in Canada) hit $10.0 billion. While Canadians spent $26.9 billion outside the country, 15% more than in 2006, foreign spending in Canada edged up just 0.1% to $16.6 billion.

The previous record high deficit of $6.8 billion was posted in 2006. In 2002, the deficit was $1.7 billion.

The effect of the decline in American visitors and their spending is more telling: Canada's travel deficit with the United States climbed to $7.0 billion in 2007, $2.7 billion higher than in 2006. That broke the previous high from 1991 by almost $1.0 billion.

Where are travel and tourism jobs?

Occupations in travel and tourism range widely, from tour operator and pilot to chef and limousine driver, but the bulk are in food and beverage services. Food and beverage services—with 926,000 employees, or just over half of travel and tourism jobs in 2006 —is travel and tourism's largest employer.

Transportation; accommodation; recreation and entertainment; food and beverage services; and travel services make up the travel and tourism sector. Together, these industries employed 1.8 million people in 2006. That represents 11% of the Canadian economy's 16.8 million jobs that year.

From 2005 to 2006, the number of jobs in travel and tourism grew 2.1%, slightly faster than the 1.8% pace of job growth in the economy overall.

Jobs in food and beverage services were more likely to be part time: nearly half the employees worked fewer than 30 hours per week in 2006. They also paid the least, at an average hourly wage of $11.42 in 2006. Jobs in the air transportation industry paid the most, with an average hourly wage of $28.42.

Overall, the average hourly compensation in tourism-related industries was $17.95 in 2006, up 4% from $17.23 in 2005. This compensation level has been stable at about 70% of the national average from 1997 to 2006. Average hourly compensation includes gross wages plus contributions by employers to Employment Insurance, Canada/Quebec Pension Plans, company pensions plans, etc.

Just over one in five workers in travel and tourism was born outside Canada, while almost two in five are 15- to 24-years-old.

Travel services has the greatest share of female employees: 68% of staff were women in 2006. Conversely, 71% of transportation industry jobs were held by men.

Chart 31.4
Jobs in the tourism industry

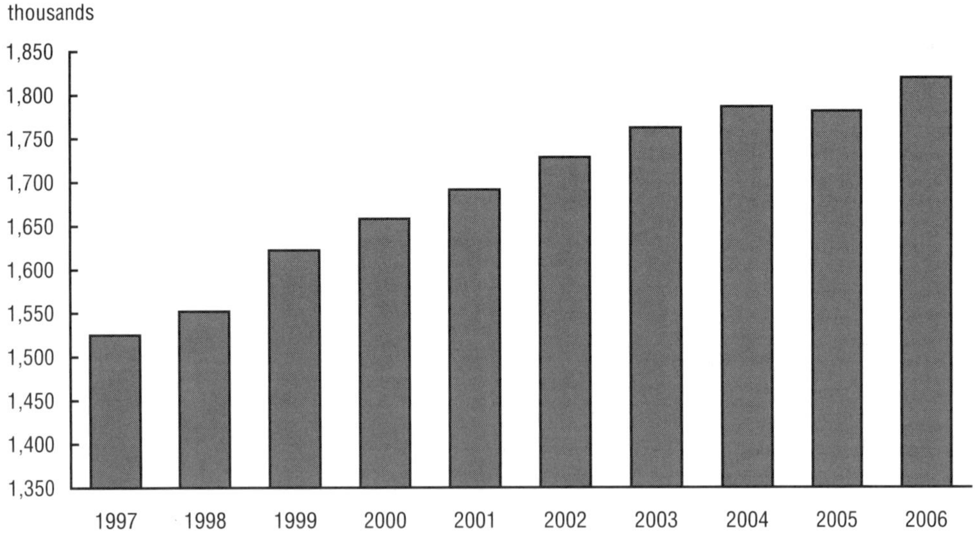

Source: Statistics Canada, Catalogue no. 13-604-MIE.

Government revenues from tourism

Governments at all levels (federal, provincial/territorial and municipal) raise tax revenues from the various activities of tourists. For instance, when a tourist pays for a hotel room, this generates a federal goods and services tax, a provincial sales tax, and a room tax for the various levels of government. In addition, income taxes are collected from the earnings of hotel employees and from the profits of the business enterprise itself.

In 2006, the tourism sector generated $19.4 billion in revenue, up 29% from $15.0 billion in 2000. This increase stemmed partly from the air travellers security charge introduced in 2002, as well as increased tax revenues from tourist purchases, such as alcohol and tobacco, vehicle fuel, and camping equipment.

Another important source of government revenues from tourism was tax on products. More than half the tax revenue attributable to tourism in 2006—or $10.3 billion—was collected this way. Income taxes on the earnings of workers in the tourism sector generated another $4.5 billion, or close to one-quarter of the total tax revenue from tourism.

Combined, Canadian and international tourists spent $66.8 billion in Canada in 2006. For every dollar, Canada's three levels of government collected 29.1 cents in 2006, up from 27.9 cents in 2000.

The federal government raised 13.6 cents, the provincial and territorial governments took in 13.9 cents, while municipal governments received 1.6 cents. Tourism accounted for 4% of government revenues in 2006—more than its 2% share of the gross domestic product.

Chart 31.5
Government revenues attributable to tourism

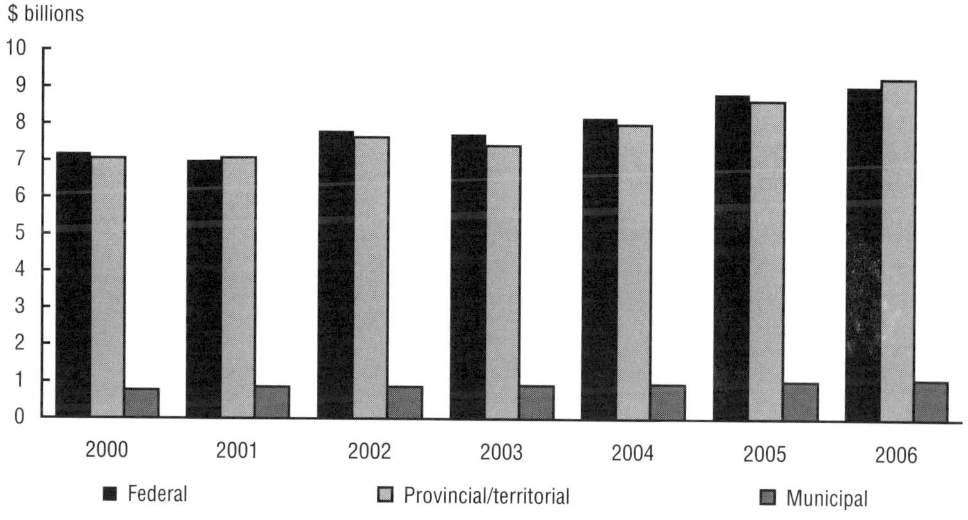

Source: Statistics Canada, Catalogue no. 13-604-MIE.

Table 31.1 Financial characteristics of the travel arrangement industry, 2001 to 2006

	2001	2002	2003	2004	2005	2006
	$ millions					
Operating revenue						
Accommodation services	12,165.4	12,780.2	12,314.6	13,197.8	14,193.0	15,201.1
Hotels, motor hotels and motels	10,755.4	11,291.0	10,902.6	11,492.3	12,344.8	13,083.2
Other accommodation industries	1,410.0	1,489.2	1,412.0	1,705.5	1,848.2	2,117.8
Travel agencies	1,518.3	1,542.1	1,480.0	1,501.1	1,592.3	1,668.7
Tour operators	5,738.1	5,735.4	6,105.8	6,288.0	6,971.7	7,266.6
Other travel arrangement and reservation services	218.4	216.5	229.5	240.7	264.7	279.0
Operating expenses						
Accommodation services	10,682.7	11,231.0	10,993.6	11,243.9	12,009.2	12,524.3
Hotels, motor hotels and motels	9,372.9	9,875.3	9,710.0	9,827.7	10,448.6	10,840.6
Other accommodation industries	1,309.8	1,355.8	1,283.5	1,416.3	1,560.6	1,683.7
Travel agencies	1,421.2	1,435.7	1,455.6	1,414.7	1,509.0	1,551.0
Tour operators	5,691.7	5,684.7	6,130.9	6,188.6	6,894.2	7,172.5
Other travel arrangement and reservation services	201.4	199.1	211.2	221.7	243.8	257.1
	%					
Operating profit margin						
Accommodation services	12.2	12.1	10.7	14.8	15.4	17.6
Hotels, motor hotels and motels	12.9	12.5	10.9	14.5	15.4	17.1
Other accommodation industries	7.1	9.0	9.1	17.0	15.6	20.5
Travel agencies	6.4	6.9	1.6	5.8	5.2	7.1
Tour operators	0.8	0.9	-0.4	1.6	1.1	1.3
Other travel arrangement and reservation services	8.0	8.0	8.0	7.9	7.9	7.8
	number					
Active establishments						
Accommodation services	16,330	16,407	16,355	15,576	16,293	F
Hotels, motor hotels and motels	9,015	8,814	8,624	7,989	8,495	F
Other accommodation industries	7,315	7,593	7,731	7,587	7,798	F
Travel agencies	5,341	5,362	5,364	4,997	4,785	4,738
Tour operators	1,147	1,207	1,237	1,238	1,238	1,152
Other travel arrangement and reservation services	281	282	294	306	338	332

Source: Statistics Canada, CANSIM tables 351-0002 and 351-0003.

Table 31.2 Canadians travelling in Canada, by province and territory of destination, 1999 to 2004

	1999	2000	2001	2002	2003	2004
	thousands					
Canada	**177,461**	**178,628**	**182,092**	**187,890**	**172,244**	**175,084**
Newfoundland and Labrador	3,975	3,955	3,902	3,784	3,236	3,107
Prince Edward Island	864	977	966	1,125	897	911
Nova Scotia	7,006	7,034	7,019	8,287	7,164	7,066
New Brunswick	5,376	4,794	5,344	6,075	5,613	5,038
Quebec	38,745	40,842	40,608	45,928	47,216	48,484
Ontario	63,282	65,220	67,160	70,257	62,168	65,290
Manitoba	6,895	6,542	6,621	6,265	5,938	6,009
Saskatchewan	9,043	8,222	8,139	8,029	7,413	7,451
Alberta	20,998	20,022	21,256	19,186	15,775	15,890
British Columbia	21,183	20,893	20,984	18,842	16,742	15,738
Yukon, Northwest Territories and Nunavut	F	F	92[E]	113[E]	83[E]	99[E]

Note: Trips of 80 kilometres or more.

Source: Statistics Canada, CANSIM table 426-0001.

Table 31.3 Canadians travelling in Canada, by selected census metropolitan areas of destination, 1999 to 2004

	1999	2000	2001	2002	2003	2004
	thousands					
St. John's	1,574	1,416	1,357	1,068	1,018	1,129
Halifax	2,786	2,905	2,999	3,513	2,769	2,870
Saint John	662	738	815	770	802	619
Saguenay	653	609	713	770	652	773
Québec	5,610	6,256	6,087	7,114	6,836	7,075
Sherbrooke	1,332	1,274	1,746	1,992	1,521	1,654
Trois-Rivières	1,151	1,188	985	1,293	1,434	1,512
Montréal	8,465	9,470	10,117	10,913	11,023	11,000
Ottawa–Gatineau	5,422	5,487	5,924	5,936	6,110	6,194
Toronto	13,752	14,708	14,144	13,894	12,706	13,738
Hamilton	1,968	1,712	2,308	1,966	1,675	1,766
St. Catharines–Niagara	3,010	4,110	4,056	3,949	3,806	4,157
Kitchener	1,858	2,618	2,371	2,833	2,031	2,337
London	3,647	3,124	3,107	3,478	3,282	3,341
Windsor	1,188	1,243	1,033	851	864	1,067
Greater Sudbury / Grand Sudbury	643	927[E]	1,164	1,002	965	1,005
Winnipeg	2,346	2,395	2,533	2,297	2,305	2,294
Regina	1,329	1,289	1,422	1,357	1,305	1,447
Saskatoon	2,321	1,991	1,980	1,951	1,888	1,854
Calgary	3,734	3,535	3,734	3,701	2,976	2,963
Edmonton	5,043	4,450	4,813	4,448	3,782	3,564
Vancouver	4,275	3,942	3,904	3,437	3,029	2,765
Victoria	1,776	1,800	1,630	1,801	1,568	1,599

Note: Trips of 80 kilometres or more.

Source: Statistics Canada, CANSIM table 426-0001.

Table 31.4 Expenditures by Canadians on trips in Canada, by province and territory of destination, 1999 to 2004

	1999	2000	2001	2002	2003	2004
	$ thousands					
Canada	**23,764,527**	**26,845,970**	**29,692,470**	**30,926,146**	**28,454,953**	**29,708,136**
Newfoundland and Labrador	629,831	745,069	795,488	812,691	791,499	722,995
Prince Edward Island	209,213	245,001	249,143	254,211	240,243	239,427
Nova Scotia	904,459	983,217	1,177,481	1,309,866	1,260,350	1,206,290
New Brunswick	748,223	798,979	856,011	970,911	842,605	812,595
Quebec	4,665,194	5,146,754	5,581,632	6,652,815	6,476,795	6,782,331
Ontario	7,483,373	9,241,261	10,497,261	10,246,161	9,541,466	10,154,235
Manitoba	871,953	865,858	1,033,426	905,212	919,443	967,300
Saskatchewan	942,592	1,024,053	1,151,025	1,112,872	1,076,599	1,120,068
Alberta	3,135,557	3,414,852	3,895,231	4,068,107	3,071,985	3,466,705
British Columbia	4,136,020	4,278,782	4,407,321	4,525,894	4,162,907	4,162,189
Yukon, Northwest Territories and Nunavut	F	F	F	67,405[E]	F	F

Note: Trips of 80 kilometres or more.

Source: Statistics Canada, CANSIM table 426-0001.

Table 31.5 Travel by Canadians to foreign countries, by selected destinations, 2001 and 2006

	2001			2006		
	Visits	Nights	Spending in country	Visits	Nights	Spending in country
	thousands		CAN$ millions	thousands		CAN$ millions
China	107	2,165	203	250	5,290	451
Cuba	348	3,026	312	638	5,295	579
Dominican Republic	251	2,371	229	536	4,644	508
France	481	5,938	585	645	8,263	872
Germany	251	2,579	215	334	3,035	291
Hong Kong	130	2,095	138	150	2,360	180
Italy	231	2,983	379	315	3,498	490
Mexico	689	7,003	691	841	9,177	894
Netherlands	146	1,403	103	239	1,967	194
Republic of Ireland	118	1,198	135	140	1,594	176
Spain	162	2,213	179	182	1,998	252
Switzerland	142	930	113	177	1,392	138
United Kingdom	673	8,881	807	778	9,628	942
United States	13,527	108,222	8,863	15,992	119,996	10,229

Note: Visits of one night or more.

Source: Statistics Canada, International Travel Survey.

Table 31.6 Travel by Canadians to the United States, by selected destinations, 2001 and 2006

	2001			2006		
	Visits	Nights	Spending in state	Visits	Nights	Spending in state
	thousands		CAN$ millions	thousands		CAN$ millions
California	910	8,015	858	1,037	9,152	874
Florida	1,887	37,370	2,300	2,098	37,816	2,372
Maine	644	2,241	155	746	2,477	200
Massachusetts	476	2,136	242	583	2,249	240
Michigan	1,133	2,729	215	1,323	3,348	273
Minnesota	496	1,491	142	614	1,477	174
Montana	382	1,321	87	513	1,671	127
Nevada	658	3,360	542	902	4,082	799
New York	2,200	6,337	605	2,596	7,240	769
Ohio	477	1,205	111	507	1,283	115
Pennsylvania	573	1,371	107	696	1,687	133
Vermont	577	1,620	96	642	1,846	131
Washington	1,538	4,728	281	1,775	5,161	363

Note: Visits of one night or more.
Source: Statistics Canada, International Travel Survey.

Table 31.7 Travel to Canada, by selected countries of origin, 2001 and 2006

	2001			2006		
	Visits	Nights	Spending in Canada	Visits	Nights	Spending in Canada
	thousands		CAN$ millions	thousands		CAN$ millions
Australia	158	2,464	244	178	2,238	278
China	82	2,781	163	139	4,007	257
France	357	5,254	436	361	5,705	464
Germany	330	5,281	454	298	4,594	407
Hong Kong	125	2,075	175	107	1,707	118
India	65	1.438	60	108	2,423	100
Israel	69	932	64	68	888	57
Italy	91	1,245	115	88	1,151	78
Japan	410	5,314	633	364	4,061	493
Mexico	148	1,693	187	202	4,004	274
Netherlands	114	1,737	132	118	1,728	142
South Korea	139	4,063	264	189	4,192	270
Switzerland	97	1,506	156	92	1,519	157
Taiwan	118	1,774	183	93	1,352	98
United Kingdom	826	10,092	1,026	842	10,598	1,148
United States	15,570	62,539	7,910	13,856	55,295	7,271

Note: Visits of one night or more.
Source: Statistics Canada, International Travel Survey.

Table 31.8 Travel to Canada from the United States, by selected states of origin, 2001 and 2006

	2001			2006		
	Visits	Nights	Spending in Canada	Visits	Nights	Spending in Canada
	thousands		CAN$ millions	thousands		CAN$ millions
California	1,051	5,530	817	986	5,116	750
Florida	375	2,676	337	381	2,376	306
Illinois	541	2,355	342	426	1,810	258
Maine	293	1,105	110	254	1,030	106
Massachusetts	738	2,757	378	599	2,161	273
Michigan	1,857	5,024	577	1,464	4,166	506
Minnesota	531	2,079	249	483	1,978	255
New Jersey	378	1,598	243	408	1,703	261
New York	1,967	6,751	711	1,714	5,588	640
Ohio	828	3,013	353	706	2,452	321
Pennsylvania	705	3,017	393	597	2,524	321
Texas	378	1,905	315	420	1,842	338
Washington	1,655	5,494	541	1,387	4,579	467
Wisconsin	364	1,878	217	298	1,436	181

Note: Visits of one night or more.

Source: Statistics Canada, International Travel Survey.

List of maps, charts and tables

Maps

Charts

Tables

Glossary

Aboriginal identity: People who identify with at least one Aboriginal group (i.e., North American Indian, Métis or Inuit), who are Treaty Indians, Registered Indians as defined by the *Indian Act*, or who are members of an Indian Band or First Nation.

Allophones: People whose mother tongue is neither English nor French.

Anglophones: People whose mother tongue is English.

Balance of international payments: A statistical statement that systematically summarizes, for a specific time period, the economic transactions of a country with the rest of the world.

Balance of payments (BOP): *See* Balance of international payments.

Blue-collar: Relating to manual or industrial labourers, usually paid wages rather than salary. *See also* White-collar.

Body Mass Index (BMI): Measure of an individual's weight in relation to his or her height. BMI is highly correlated with body fat and is widely used to indicate health risks. BMI is classified into six categories, each representing a different level of risk: 'Underweight' is less than 18.5 BMI; 'Normal weight' is from 18.5 to 24.9 BMI; 'Overweight' is from 25.0 to 29.9 BMI; 'Obese Class I' is from 30.0 to 34.9 BMI; 'Obese Class II' is from 35.0 to 39.9 BMI; and 'Obese Class III' is greater than or equal to 40.0 BMI.

Bovine spongiform encephalopathy (BSE): Fatal disease of cattle that affects the central nervous system. Also called 'mad cow disease,' it is attributed to the practice of feeding cattle a supplement made from either bovines already infected with BSE or from scrapie-infected sheep.

Building permit: Permit required in most jurisdictions for new construction, adding onto pre-existing structures and, in some cases, for major renovations.

Canada Pension Plan (CPP): Contributory, earnings-related social insurance program that provides a stable and dependable pension that can be build on for retirement. It also provides people and their dependants with basic financial protection in the event of disability or death.

CANSIM (Canadian Socio-economic Information Management System): Database that enables users to track trends in virtually every aspect of Canadian life. It contains over 26 million time series (observations for a subject at regular intervals).

Capital investment: Includes all expenditures on buildings, engineering construction and machinery and equipment.

Census: Survey that includes all units in a population (people, events, businesses, etc.).

Census agglomeration (CA): Area consisting of one or more neighbouring municipalities situated around a major urban core. A CA must have an urban core population of at least 10,000.

Census family: Married couple (with or without children of either or both spouses), couple living common-law (with or without children of either or both partners) or lone parent of any marital status, with at least one child living in the same dwelling. A couple may be of opposite or same sex. Children in a census family include grandchildren living with grandparent(s) with no parents present.

Census metropolitan area (CMA): Area consisting of one or more adjacent municipalities situated around a major urban core. A CMA must have a total population of at least 100,000, of which 50,000 or more live in the urban core. *See also* Small urban area *and* Rural area.

Census of Population: Survey conducted every five years to produce data on the population and dwelling counts for Canada, each province and territory, and smaller geographic units such as cities or districts within cities.

Central municipalities: Municipalities that are situated around an urban core. The urban core must have a population of at least 100,000. *See also* Peripheral municipalities.

Constant dollars: Dollars of a particular base year that are not adjusted (by inflation or deflation) to show changes in the purchasing power of the dollar.

Consumer Price Index (CPI): Measure of the percentage change over time in the average cost of a large basket of goods and services purchased by Canadians. The items contained in the basket are divided into eight broader categories: food, shelter, household operations and furnishings, clothing and footwear, transportation, recreation, education and reading, and alcoholic beverage and tobacco products. The quantity and quality of the items in the basket are held constant. As a result, changes in the cost of the basket are due to pure price movements and not to changes in its composition.

Core Index: A variant of the Consumer Price Index (CPI) that excludes eight of its most volatile components: fruit, vegetables, gasoline, fuel oil, natural gas, mortgage interest, intercity transportation, and tobacco products. These fluctuating components are found within the broader taxonomy of the consumer index, which includes food, shelter and transportation. The core index also excludes the effect of changes in indirect taxes on the remaining components. *See also* Consumer Price Index (CPI).

Core Public Administration (CPA): The group of federal public servants who work for the Treasury Board Secretariat of Canada.

Crude oil: Naturally occurring liquid mixture of hydrocarbons; liquid petroleum. The liquid hydrocarbons may be mixed with natural gas, carbon dioxide, saltwater, sulphur compounds and sand. Most of these substances are separated from the liquid hydrocarbons at processing facilities near the producing field.

Defined contribution plan: A retirement plan that provides a pension based on the accumulated contributions of the individual. That is, the employee and employer may contribute funds to the plan and upon retirement a pension can be drawn. The value of the pension is based on the total amount of contributions accumulated by the individual and the returns earned through investment. Total annual contributions are limited to 18% of earnings up to a maximum of $13,500.

Disturbance: Changes in forest structure or composition caused by natural events (e.g., fire, flood or wind, or mortality caused by insect or disease outbreaks) or human-caused events (e.g., forest harvesting).

Economic immigrant: Immigrants to Canada with the skills, education and work experience needed to make an immediate economic contribution to the economy.

Educators: All employees of the public school system who are required to have teaching certification as a condition of their employment. This includes teaching staff, principals, vice-principals, professional non-teaching staff (e.g., pedagogical consultants, guidance counsellors and special education teachers) and excludes substitute/supply teachers, temporary replacement teachers, teachers on leave, student assistants and teaching assistants.

Employed: People who, during the Labour Force Survey reference week, did any work at all at a job or business, that is, paid work in the context of an employer–employee relationship, or self-employment (also includes unpaid family work, which is defined as unpaid work contributing directly to the operation of a farm, business or professional practice owned and operated by a related member of the same household); or had a job, but were not at work due to factors such as own illness or disability, personal or family responsibilities, vacation, labour dispute or other reasons (excluding people on layoff, between casual jobs, and those with a job to start at a future date). *See also* Unemployed *and* Labour force.

Ethnic origin: Ethnic or cultural group(s) to which an individual's ancestors belong.

Exchange rate: Value of the Canadian dollar against the currencies of other countries.

Family-class immigrant: Immigrant sponsored by a person to whom they are related and who is already residing in Canada (e.g., spouse, conjugal partner, grandparent).

Farm Input Price Index (FIPI): Measures the annual price movement of specific farm inputs at the farm gate; that is, the annual price movement of the goods and services that comprise basic agricultural overhead costs. The specific farm inputs are building and fencing, machinery and motor vehicles, crop production, animal production, supplies and services, hired farm labour, property taxes, interest and farm rent.

Farm Product Price Index (FPPI): Measures the change through time in prices received for agricultural commodities at the first transaction point. These agricultural commodities include both crops and livestock and animal products including grains, oilseeds, specialty crops, fruit, vegetables, potatoes, cattle and calves, hogs, poultry, eggs and dairy products.

Fertility rate: Number of live births occurring in a given time period relative to the number of women of childbearing age.

Fine particulates: *See* Particulate.

Fossil fuel: Combustible substance derived from the decay of organic material over long periods of time and under high pressure (e.g., natural gas, oil, propane, coal).

Francophones: People whose mother tongue is French.

G8: Top eight industrialized countries in the world: Canada, France, Germany, Italy, Japan, Russia, the United Kingdom and the United States of America.

General government: Administrative part of governments. Excludes units such as schools and hospitals directly engaged in the delivery of services.

General Social Survey (GSS): Statistics Canada survey that gathers data on social trends to monitor changes in the living conditions and well-being of Canadians over time and to provide information on specific social issues of current or emerging interest.

Generation status: Indicates for how many generations a person and their family have been in Canada. It is derived from place of birth of respondent, the place of birth of the father and the place of birth of the mother. It only pertains to the population aged 15 years and older. People are defined as either 'first generation,' 'second generation' or 'third generation or more,' which are defined as follows. First generation refers to people born outside Canada. Second generation refers to people born in Canada with at least one parent born outside of Canada. Third generation and more refers to people who were born in Canada and whose parents were both born in Canada.

Goods-producing sector: Sector of the economy that is composed of agriculture, forestry, fishing and hunting; mining, oil and gas extraction; utilities (electric power, gas and water); construction; and manufacturing.

Greenhouse gases (GHGs): A group of gases that trap heat in the atmosphere by reflecting solar energy back toward the surface of the Earth. The most significant greenhouse gases produced by economic activities are carbon dioxide (CO_2), methane (CH_4), nitrous oxide (N_20) and chlorofluorocarbons (CFC).

Gross domestic product (GDP): Total unduplicated value of goods and services produced in the economic territory of a country or region during a given period. GDP can be measured in three ways: 1) as total income earned in current production; 2) as total final sales of current production; or 3) as total net values added in current production.

Heritage institutions: Institutions whose purpose is to acquire, preserve, study, interpret, and make accessible to the public, for its instruction and enjoyment, objects, specimens, documents, buildings and land areas of educational and cultural value, including artistic, scientific, historical, natural and technological material.

Home language: Language spoken most often at home.

Industrial Product Price Index (IPPI): Measures price changes for major commodities sold by Canadian manufacturers.

Inflation: Upward movement in the average level of prices or a persistent rise in the average price of goods and services; affects cost of living. The most widely used measure of inflation is the Consumer Price Index (CPI).

Information and communications technology (ICT): Any products or services provided by the telecommunications industry, including cellphones, personal computers, telephones and Internet and cable services.

Intellectual property: Form of creative endeavour that can be protected through a trademark, patent, copyright, industrial design or integrated circuit topography.

Internal migration: Movement within and between provinces and territories.

Kilowatt hour (kWh): Commercial unit of electric energy. One kWh is the amount of electricity consumed by 10 light bulbs of 100 watts burning for one hour.

Labour force: Civilian, non-institutional population aged 15 and older who, during the Labour Force Survey reference week, were employed or unemployed. *See* Employed *and* Unemployed.

Labour productivity: Real output per hours worked.

Large urban area: *See* Census metropolitan area (CMA).

Longitudinal survey: Type of survey or study over time of the same variable or the same group of respondents.

Machinery and Equipment Price Index (MEPI): Measures price changes for machinery and equipment purchases, relative to the gross annual accumulation of wealth as represented by the purchase of new machinery and the development and expansion of infrastructure.

Median: Value of the middle number of a series ranked in order of size.

Mother tongue: First language an individual learns at home and still understands.

Mountain pine beetle: Small insect that lives under the bark of pine trees.

Mortality rate: Number of deaths from all causes per 100,000 population.

Natural gas: Gaseous petroleum consisting primarily of methane with lesser amounts of (in order of abundance) ethane, propane, butane and pentane, and heavier hydrocarbons as well as non-energy components such as nitrogen, carbon dioxide, hydrogen sulphide and water.

Net census undercoverage: Difference between the number of people who should have been counted in a census but were not and the number of people who should not have been counted in a census or who were counted more than once.

New Housing Price Index (NHPI): Measures price changes for contractors' selling prices of new residential houses.

Non-contributory registered pension plan: A pension plan in which all required contributions are made by the employer.

Non-conventional oil: Crude oil that is extracted by non-conventional means. For example, Alberta's non-conventional crude oil (known as oil sands deposits) is too thick to flow in its natural state and requires special methods to bring it to the surface.

Non-ferrous: Metals or alloys free of iron (e.g., aluminium, cadmium, copper, lead, nickel, tin, uranium and zinc).

Not-for-profit organization: Organizations that are institutionally separate from governments, do not return any profits generated to their owners or directors, are independent and able to regulate their own activities, benefit to some degree from voluntary contributions of time or money, and are formally incorporated or registered under specific legislation with provincial/territorial or federal governments.

Noon spot rate: Foreign exchange rate between the U.S. dollar and the Canadian dollar based on the trading that takes place from 11:59 a.m. to 12:01 p.m. on any given day.

North American Industry Classification System (NAICS): Industry classification system developed to provide common definitions of the industrial structures of Canada, Mexico and the United States. Its hierarchical structure is composed of sectors (two-digit code), subsectors (three-digit code), industry groups (four-digit code), and industries (five-digit code).

Obese: *See* Body Mass Index (BMI).

Off-reserve: Aboriginal people not living on a reserve.

Organic compounds: Compounds based on carbon, usually containing hydrogen, with or without oxygen, nitrogen, or other elements.

Organisation for Economic Co-operation and Development (OECD): A group of 30 member countries sharing a commitment to democratic government and the market economy. The OECD produces internationally agreed upon instruments, decisions and recommendations to promote rules of the game in areas where multilateral agreement is necessary for individual countries to make progress in a globalized economy.

Overweight: *See* Body Mass Index (BMI).

Participation rate: Represents the labour force expressed as a percentage of the population aged 15 years and older. The participation rate for a particular group (age, sex, etc.) is the labour force in that group expressed as a percentage of the population for that group.

Particulate: Anything that can be filtered from the air. Large particles, like road dust or pollen, can irritate the eyes, whereas smaller particles (often called 'fine particulates') from smoke and fumes can be inhaled.

Per capita: For each person or per person.

Peripheral municipality: Municipality that is part of a census metropolitan area and next to the municipality that contains the urban core of the census metropolitan area. *See also* Central municipalities.

Petajoule: A unit of energy equalling 1,015 joules. A joule is a unit of energy equal to the work done when a force of one newton acts through a distance of one metre.

Petroleum products: End result of the petroleum refining process. It includes fuels like gasoline, aviation fuel, diesel and heating oil; products such as solvents and lubricants; and raw materials for manufacturing petrochemicals.

Population density: Number of people per square kilometre.

Potash: General term for several types of potassium salts, of which the most important is potassium chloride, the mineral sylvite. Potash is a nutrient essential for plant growth and is a cornerstone of modern fertilizers.

Profit margin: The difference between the cost of buying or producing something and the price for which it is sold.

Public sector: Public administration at the federal, provincial or municipal levels of government, as well as Crown corporations, liquor control boards and other government institutions such as schools (including universities), hospitals and public libraries.

Raw Materials Price Index (RMPI): Measures price changes for the purchase of raw materials by Canadian industries. The term 'raw material' refers either to a commodity that is sold for the first time after being extracted from nature, or a substitutable recycled product (e.g., metal scrap).

Recession: Two consecutive quarterly declines in real gross domestic product.

Registered Pension Plan (RPP): Pension plans for employees sponsored by employers or unions and usually funded through contributions by both employees and employers. RPPs must satisfy certain conditions and be registered for the purposes of the federal *Income Tax Act*.

Registered Retirement Savings Plan (RRSP): Program that allows savings for retirement to grow tax free in a special savings plan registered by the Canada Revenue Agency. Contributions to RRSPs can be made up to December 31 of the year the contributor turns 69.

Rural area: Area of a country not falling into either the large urban or small urban categories. *See also* Census metropolitan area (CMA) *and* Small urban area.

Services-producing sector: Sector of the economy composed of the following: trade; transportation and warehousing; finance and insurance, real estate and renting and leasing, and management of companies and enterprises; professional, scientific and technical services; information and cultural industries; arts, entertainment and recreation; administrative and support services; waste management and remediation services; educational services; health care and social assistance; information, culture and recreation; accommodation and food services; public administration; and other.

Social assistance: Transfer payments (including refundable tax credits) to help individuals and families maintain an acceptable level of earnings.

Telework: Arrangement where an employee fulfils his or her regularly scheduled job responsibilities at a remote location that is not operated by the employer, usually the employee's own residence.

Time stress: Measure of sleep deprivation used in the General Social Survey.

Tourism: The activities of people travelling to and staying in places outside their usual environment for less than one consecutive year for leisure, business or other purposes.

Tourism industries: Industries that would cease to exist or would continue to exist only at significantly reduced levels of activity in the absence of tourism.

Tourism commodities: Commodities for which a significant part of their total demand comes from visitors.

Tourism demand: Spending by Canadian and non-resident visitors on domestically produced commodities. It is the sum of tourism domestic demand and tourism exports.

Tourism domestic demand: The spending in Canada by Canadian visitors on domestically produced commodities.

Tourism exports: Spending by foreign visitors on Canadian-produced tourism goods and services. It includes spending that may take place outside of Canada (e.g., the purchase of an airline ticket from a Canadian international carrier to travel to Canada).

Trade deficit: Negative trade balance occurring when a country imports more goods than it exports.

Trade surplus: Positive trade balance occurring when a country exports more goods than it imports.

Twenty-foot equivalent (TEU): Standard unit describing a ship's cargo carrying capacity or a shipping terminal's cargo handling capacity. A standard forty-foot (40x8x8 feet) container equals two TEUs (each 20x8x8).

Unemployed: People who, during the Labour Force Survey reference week, were on temporary layoff with an expectation of recall and were available for work; were without work, had actively looked and were available for work in the past four weeks; or had a new job to start within four weeks from the reference week, and were available for work. *See also* Employed *and* Labour force.

Unemployment rate: Number of unemployed people, during the Labour Force Survey reference week, expressed as a percentage of the labour force (unemployed plus employed). The unemployment rate for a particular group (age, sex, province, etc.) is the number of unemployed in that group expressed as a percentage of the labour force for that group.

Urban area: An urban area has a minimum population concentration of 1,000 persons and a population density of at least 400 persons per square kilometre, based on the current census population count. *See also* Census metropolitan area *and* Rural areas.

Urban core: Large urban area around which a census metropolitan area or a census agglomeration is delineated. The urban core must have a population (based on the previous census) of at least 50,000 in the case of a census metropolitan area, or at least 50,000 in the case of a census agglomeration.

Visible minority: People, other than Aboriginal peoples, who are non-Caucasian in race or non-white in colour.

Visitors: People travelling to and staying in places outside their usual environment for not more than one consecutive year for leisure, business or other purposes. They are referred to as either tourists (those who stay overnight or longer in the place visited), or same-day visitors. *See also* Tourism.

Volatile organic compound (VOC): Organic compound that has a high tendency to pass from the solid or liquid state to the vapour state under typical environmental conditions. Such compounds participate in a range of processes that lead to atmospheric pollution, including the formation of urban smog.

White-collar: Related to performing non-manual, especially clerical, administrative or professional, work. *See also* Blue-collar.

List of sources

All sources are from Statistics Canada except those noted as "Other."

Chapter 1 Aboriginal peoples

Aboriginal Peoples in Canada in 2006: Inuit, Métis and First Nations, 2006 Census. Occasional. 97-558-XWE
A Portrait of Seniors in Canada. Occasional. 89-519-XWE
The Canadian Labour Market at a Glance. Occasional. 71-222-XWE
Women in Canada: A Gender-based Statistical Report. Occasional. 89-503-XIE

Other

Health Canada

Chapter 2 Agriculture

Canada Food Stats. Semi-annual. 23F0001XBB
Cattle Statistics. Semi-annual. 23-012-XIE
Farm Product Price Index. Monthly. 21-007-XIE
Food Statistics. Semi-annual. 21-020-XIE
Net Farm Income—Agriculture Economic Statistics. Semi-annual. 21-010-XIE
VISTA on the Agri-food Industry and the Farm Community. Occasional. 21-004-XIE

Chapter 3 Business, consumer and property services

Canada's International Trade in Services. Annual. 67-203-XWE
Employment, Earnings and Hours. Monthly. 72-002-XIB
Financial and Taxation Statistics for Enterprises. Annual. 61-219-XIE
Gross Domestic Product by Industry. Monthly. 15-001-XIE
Provincial and Territorial Economic Accounts Review. Semi-annual. 13-016-XWE
Trends and Conditions in Census Metropolitan Areas. Occasional. 89-613-MIE

Chapter 4 Business performance and ownership

Analysis in Brief. Occasional. 11-621-MIE
The Canadian Economy in Transition. Occasional. 11-622-MIE
Corporations Returns Act. Annual. 61-220-XIE
Financial and Taxation Statistics for Enterprises. Annual. 61-219-XIE
Public Sector Statistics. Annual. 68-213-XIE
Quarterly Financial Statistics for Enterprises. Quarterly. 61-008-XIE

Chapter 5 Children and youth

Canadian Social Trends. Quarterly. 11-008-XIE
Children and Youth Research Paper Series. Occasional. 89-599-MIE
Education Indicators in Canada: Report of the Pan-Canadian Education Indicators Program. Occasional. 81-582-XIE
Health Indicators. Semi-annual. 82-221-XIE
Income and the Outcomes of Children. Occasional. 11F0019MIE2006281
Income in Canada. Annual. 75-202-XIE

Chapter 6 Construction

Building Permits. Monthly. 64-001-XIE
Capital Expenditure Price Statistics. Quarterly. 62-007-XIE
Private and Public Investment in Canada, Intentions. Annual. 61-205-XIE

Other

Canada Mortgage and Housing Corporation; Canadian Institute of Mortgage Brokers and Lenders; U.S. Census Bureau

Chapter 7 Crime and justice

Canadian Centre for Justice Statistics Profile Series. Occasional. 85F0033MWE
Family Violence in Canada: A Statistical Profile. Annual. 85-224-XIE
Juristat. Irregular. 85-002-XIE
Police Resources in Canada. Annual. 85-225-XIE

Chapter 8 Culture and leisure

Broadcasting and Telecommunications. Irregular. 56-001-XIE
Canadian Social Trends. Quarterly. 11-008-XIE
Culture, Tourism and the Centre for Education Statistics—Research Papers. Occasional. 81-595-MIE
Motion Picture Theatres: Data Tables. Annual. 87F0009XIE
Radio Listening: Data Tables. Annual. 87F0007XIE

Chapter 9 Economic accounts

Annual Demographic Estimates: Census Metropolitan Areas, Economic Regions and Census Divisions, Age and Sex. Annual. 91-214-XWE
Canadian Economic Accounts Quarterly Review. Quarterly. 13-010-XWE
Canadian Economic Observer. Monthly. 11-010-XWB
EnviroStats. Quarterly. 16-002-XWE

Gross Domestic Product by Industry. Monthly. 15-001-XIE
National Balance Sheet Accounts, Quarterly Estimates. Quarterly. 13-214-XWE
National Income and Expenditure Accounts, Quarterly Estimates. Quarterly. 13-001-XIB
Provincial and Territorial Economic Accounts Review. Semi-annual. 13-016-XIE
Provincial Economic Accounts, Annual Estimates—Tables and Analytical Document. Semi-annual. 13-213-PPB

Chapter 10 Education, training and learning

Analytical Studies Branch Research Paper Series. Occasional. 11F0019MIE
Culture, Tourism and the Centre for Education Statistics—Research Papers. Occasional. 81-595-MIE
Education Indicators in Canada Report of the Pan-Canadian Education Indicators Program. Occasional. 81-582-XIE
Education Matters: Insights on Education, Learning and Training in Canada. Bi-monthly. 81-004-XIE

Chapter 11 Energy

Analysis in Brief. Occasional. 11-621-MIE
Canadian Economic Observer. Monthly. 11-010-XWB
The Consumer Price Index. Monthly. 62-001-XIB
Electric Power Generation, Transmission and Distribution. Annual. 57-202-XWE
Energy Statistics Handbook. Quarterly. 57-601-XIE
EnviroStats. Quarterly. 16-002-XWE
Report on Energy Supply and Demand in Canada. Annual. 57-003-XWE

Other

Centre for Energy; Canadian Wind Energy Association; National Energy Board; Natural Resources Canada

Chapter 12 Environment

Canadian Economic Observer. Monthly. 11-010-XIB
Canadian Environmental Sustainability Indicators. Annual. 16-251-XIE
Canadian Environmental Sustainability Indicators, Highlights. Annual. 16-252-XIE
Environmental Protection Expenditures in the Business Sector. Biennial. 16F0006XWE
EnviroStats. Quarterly. 16-002-XWE
Human Activity and the Environment Annual Statistics. Annual. 16-201-XIE
Households and the Environment. Biennial. 11-526-XIE

Chapter 13 Ethnic diversity and immigration

Canadian Social Trends. Quarterly. 11-008-XWE
Ethnic Diversity Survey: Portrait of a Multicultural Society. Occasional. 89-593-XIE
The Immigrant Labour Force Analysis Series. Occasional. 71-606-XWE
Immigrants in Canada's Census Metropolitan Areas. Occasional. 89-613-MWE2004003
Longitudinal Survey of Immigrants to Canada: Process, Progress and Prospects. Irregular. 89-611-XWE
Population Projections of Visible Minority Groups, Canada, Provinces and Regions. Occasional. 91-541-XIE

Chapter 14 Families, households and housing

Canadian Social Trends. Quarterly. 11-008-XIE
Changes and Challenges for Residential Real Estate Lessors. Occasional. 63F0002XIE
Changing Conjugal Life in Canada. Occasional. 89-576-XIE
General Social Survey Cycle 20: Family Transitions Survey. Occasional. 89-625-XIE
Spending Patterns in Canada. Annual. 62-202-XIE

Chapter 15 Geography

Agriculture and Rural Working Paper Series. Occasional. 21-601-MIE
Canadian Social Trends. Quarterly. 11-008-XIE
Geography Working Paper Series. Occasional. 92F0138MIE
Human Activity and the Environment: Annual Statistics. Annual. 16-201-XWE
Rural and Small Town Canada Analysis Bulletin. Occasional. 21-006-XIE
Standard Geographical Classification. Occasional. 12-571-XWE

Other

Fisheries and Oceans Canada; Indian and Northern Affairs Canada; Natural Resources Canada

Chapter 16 Government

Analysis in Brief. Occasional. 11-621-MIE
Financial Management System (FMS). Irregular. 68F0023XWE
Insights on the Canadian Economy. Occasional. 11-624-MIE
Labour Force Historical Review. Annual. 71F0004XCB
Public Sector Statistics. Annual. 68-213-XIE

Chapter 17 Health

The 2006 Participation and Activity Limitation Survey: Disability in Canada. Occasional. 89-628-XWE
Access to Health Care Services in Canada. Irregular. 82-575-XIE
Deaths. Annual. 84F0211XWE
Health Indicators. Semi-annual. 82-221-XIE
Health Reports. Quarterly. 82-003-XIE
Health Reports—Supplement. Annual. 82-003-SIE
Healthy Today, Healthy Tomorrow? Findings from the National Population Health Survey. Occasional. 82-618-MWE
Mortality, Summary List of Causes. Annual. 84F0209XWE
Your Community, Your Health: Findings from the Canadian Community Health Survey (CCHS). Occasional. 82-621-XWE

Chapter 18 Income, pensions, spending and wealth

Canada's Retirement Income Programs. Irregular. 74-507-XCB
Canadian Economic Accounts Quarterly Review. Quarterly. 13-010-XWE
Household Expenditures Research Paper Series. Occasional. 62F0026MIE
Housing and Shelter Costs, 2006 Census. Occasional. 97-554-XIE2006001
Income in Canada. Annual. 75-202-XIE
Income Research Paper Series. Occasional. 75F0002MIE
Income Trends in Canada. Annual. 13F0022XIE
National Balance Sheet Accounts, Quarterly Estimates. Quarterly. 13-214-XWE
Pension and Wealth Research Paper Series. Occasional. 13F0026MIE
Perspectives on Labour and Income. Monthly. 75-001-XWE
Spending Patterns in Canada. Annual. 62-202-XWE

Chapter 19 Information and communications technology

Analysis in Brief. Occasional. 11-621-MWE
Analytical Paper Series—Service Industries Division. Occasional. 63F0002XWE
Broadcasting and Telecommunications. Irregular. 56-001-XIE
The Canadian Economy in Transition. Occasional. 11-622-MIE
Canadian Internet Use Survey—Public Use Microdata File. Biennial. 56M0003XCB
Connectedness Series. Occasional. 56F0004MIE
The Digital Divide in Canada. Occasional. 56F0009XIE
Innovation Analysis Bulletin. Irregular. 88-003-XIE
Spending Patterns in Canada. Annual. 62-202-XWE
Quarterly Telecommunications Statistics. Quarterly. 56-002-XIE

Chapter 20 International merchandise trade

Canadian Economic Observer. Monthly. 11-010-XWB
Canadian Trade Highlights. Occasional. 65-508-XWE
Canadian Trade Review. Occasional. 65-507-MWE
International Merchandise Trade Annual Review. Annual. 65-208-XWE

Chapter 21 Labour

Canadian Economic Observer. Monthly. 11-010-XWB
The Canadian Labour Market at a Glance. Irregular. 71-222-XWE
Canadian Social Trends. Quarterly. 11-008-XWE
Employment, Earnings and Hours. Monthly. 72-002-XWE
Labour Force Activity, 2006 Census. Occasional. 97-559-XIE
Labour Force Historical Review. Annual. 71F0004XCB
Labour Force Information. Monthly. 71-001-XWE
Perspectives on Labour and Income. Monthly. 75-001-XWE
Using Languages at Work in Canada, 2006 Census. Occasional. 97-555-XWE2006051

Chapter 22 Languages

Aboriginal Peoples, 2006 Census. Occasional. 97-558-XWE
Canadian Social Trends. Quarterly. 11-008-XWE
The Evolving Linguistic Portrait, 2006 Census. Occasional. 97-555-XWE2006001
Knowledge of Official Languages Among New Immigrants: How Important Is It in the Labour Market? Occasional. 89-624-XWE
Minorities Speak Up: Results of the Survey on the Vitality of Official-Language Minorities. Occasional. 91-548-XWE

Chapter 23 Manufacturing

Analysis in Brief. Occasional. 11-621-MIE
Canadian Economic Observer. Monthly. 11-010-XWB
The Canadian Productivity Review. Occasional. 15-206-XWE
Economic Analysis Research Paper Series. Occasional. 11F0027MIE
Gross Domestic Product by Industry. Monthly. 15-001-XIE
Innovation Analysis Bulletin. Semi-annual. 88-003-XWE
Update on Economic Analysis. Irregular. 11-623-XIE

Chapter 24 Population and demography

Age and Sex, 2006 Census. Occasional. 97-551-XWE2006001
Annual Demographic Estimates: Canada, Provinces and Territories. Annual. 91-215-XWE
Annual Demographic Statistics. Annual. 91-213-XIB
Births. Semi-annual. 84F0210XIE
Canadian Social Trends. Quarterly. 11-008-XIE
Population Projections for Canada, Provinces and Territories. Occasional. 91-520-XWE
Population and Dwelling Counts, 2006 Census. Occasional. 97-550-XWE

Chapter 25 Prices and price indexes

Capital Expenditure Price Statistics. Quarterly. 62-007-XIE
The Consumer Price Index. Monthly. 62-001-XWB
Farm Product Price Index. Monthly. 21-007-XWE
Industry Price Indexes. Monthly. 62-011-XWE

Other

Bank of Canada; Canadian Real Estate Association

Chapter 26 Retail and wholesale trade

Analysis in Brief. Occasional. 11-621-MIE
Canadian Economic Observer. Monthly. 11-010-XWB
The Canadian Labour Market at a Glance. Irregular. 71-222-XIE
Retail Trade. Monthly. 63-005-XIE
Wholesale Trade. Monthly. 63-008-XWE

Chapter 27 Science and technology

The Canadian Economy in Transition. Occasional. 11-622-MIE
Federal Scientific Activities. Annual. 88-204-XIE
Gross Domestic Expenditures on Research and Development in Canada and the Provinces. Annual. 88-221-XWE
Innovation Analysis Bulletin. Irregular. 88-003-XIE
Science, Innovation and Electronic Information Division Working Papers. Occasional. 88F0006XIE
Science Statistics. Irregular. 88-001-XIE

Other

Organisation for Economic Co-operation and Development

Chapter 28 Seniors

The 2006 Participation and Activity Limitation Survey: Disability in Canada. Occasional. 89-628-XWE
Analytical Studies Branch Research Paper Series. Occasional. 11F0019MIE
Health Indicators. Semi-annual. 82-221-XWE
Health Reports—Supplement. Annual. 82-003-XIE
Perspectives on Labour and Income. Monthly. 75-001-XWE
Population Projections for Canada, Provinces and Territories. Occasional. 91-520-XIE
A Portrait of Seniors in Canada. Occasional. 89-519-XWE

Chapter 29 Society and community

The 2006 Participation and Activity Limitation Survey: Disability in Canada. Occasional. 89-628-XWE
Canadian Social Trends. Quarterly. 11-008-XWE
General Social Survey Cycle 20: Family Transitions Survey. Occasional. 89-625-XWE
Juristat. Irregular. 85-002-XIE
Women in Canada: Work Chapter Updates. Annual. 89F0133XWE

Chapter 30 Transportation

An Analysis of the Transportation Industry in 2005. Occasional. 11-621-MWE
Aviation Service Bulletin. Irregular. 51-004-XIB
Human Activity and the Environment: Annual Statistics. Annual. 16-201-XWE
Rail in Canada. Annual. 52-216-XWE
Shipping in Canada. Annual. 54-205-XWE
Trucking in Canada. Annual. 53-222-XIE

Other

Transport Canada

Chapter 31 Travel and tourism

Canadian Travel Survey: Domestic Travel. Annual. 87-212-XIE
Income and Expenditure Accounts Technical Series. Occasional. 13-604-MIE
International Travel: Advance Information. Monthly. 66-001-PIE
National Tourism Indicators, Quarterly Estimates. Quarterly. 13-009-XIB
Travel-log. Quarterly. 87-003-XIE

Index

Note: Statistics for provinces and territories are mainly under 'Provincial/territorial statistics'; those for urban areas are mainly under 'Census metropolitan areas (CMAs)'. Page references in *italics* denote a chart or table. CMA stands for 'Census metropolitan area'; CPI, for 'Consumer Price Index'; GHG, for 'greenhouse gas'; and ICT, for 'Information and communication technology'.

A

F

G

H

I

P

R

S

T

U

V

W

Y